CW01509111

1 MONTH OF
FREE
READING

at

www.ForgottenBooks.com

By purchasing this book you are
eligible for one month membership to
ForgottenBooks.com, giving you
unlimited access to our entire
collection of over 1,000,000 titles via
our web site and mobile apps.

To claim your free month visit:
www.forgottenbooks.com/free1211119

ISBN 978-0-428-68414-3
PIBN 11211119

ANNUAL REPORT

OF THE

ATTORNEY-GENERAL

OF THE

STATE OF NEW YORK

For the Year Ending December 31, 1910

EDWARD R. O'MALLEY
ATTORNEY-GENERAL

/ 9 / C

TRANSMITTED TO THE LEGISLATURE JANUARY 13, 1911

ALBANY
J. B. LYON COMPANY, STATE PRINTERS
1911

ן | ף | וי

JUL 9 1931

STATE OF NEW YORK

No. 9.

IN SENATE

JANUARY 12, 1911.

Annual Report of the Attorney-General for the Year 1910.

STATE OF NEW YORK.

ATTORNEY-GENERAL'S OFFICE,

ALBANY, December 31, 1910.

To the Legislature of the State of New York:

Pursuant to the requirements of section 66 of the Executive Law, I beg to submit herewith the Annual Report of the Attorney-General for the year 1910.

Respectfully,

EDWARD R. O'MALLEY,

Attorney-General.

ATTORNEY–GENERAL'S OFFICE.

1910.

Edward R. O'Malley	Attorney-General.
Daniel E. Brong	First Deputy.
Edward H. Letchworth	Second Deputy.
George A. Fisher	Third Deputy.
Andrew E. Tuck	Deputy.
J. Samuel Fowler	Deputy.
James S. Kiley	Deputy.
Edwin L. Ford	Deputy.
Everett E. Risley	Deputy.
Irving G. Vann	Deputy.
Nathan B. Smith	Deputy.
Chester G. Wager	Deputy.
Arthur S. Hamlin	Deputy.
George P. Pudney	Deputy.
William S. MacDonald	Deputy.
Luther E. Ellison	Deputy.
William H. Foster	Deputy.
Edward A. Gifford	Deputy.
Franklin Kennedy	Deputy.
Charles M. Stern	Deputy.
Charles R. McSparren	Deputy.
Wilber W. Chambers	Deputy.
Michael H. Quirk	Assistant to Deputy.
Michael A. Ford	Private Secretary.
Martin Dehn	Special Deputy Attorney-General.
Edward H. Leggett	Land and Tax Clerk.
William H. Thomas	Hearing Stenographer.
Delane E. Farr	Title Searcher.
Patrick H. Clune	Title Searcher.
John D. Monroe	Title Searcher.
Clarence R. Cummings	Title Searcher.
M. Vincent Ryan	Investigator of Claims.
John Widmer	Confidential Messenger.
Edward M. Long	Confidential Clerk.

NEW YORK CITY BUREAU.

Ezra P. Prentice	Deputy.
(Resigned October 5, 1910.)	
Frederick Tanner	Deputy.
(Appointed October 10, 1910.)	
Amos H. Stephens	Deputy.
Jacob Frank	Deputy.
Robert P. Beyer	Deputy.
Clarence H. Fay	Deputy.

ERIE COUNTY DEPUTY.

Walter F. Hofheins	Prudential Building, Buffalo.

REPORT

To the Legislature:

Section 66 of the Executive Law requires me to report to the Legislature upon the administration of my department for the preceding year. This section specifies certain items to be included in such report. It has also been customary to include such other matters as may be necessary to render a complete summary of the work of the department and to make such recommendations for changes in the statutes or in the organization of the department as experience has shown to be advisable.

This report is divided into two parts. The first contains an outline of the more important things accomplished during the past year and makes certain recommendations. The second division includes all the details required by law to be stated, together with copies of such opinions rendered during the year as seem to be of general public interest.

ADMINISTRATIVE CHANGES.

The last year has shown a marked improvement in the efficiency of the department and in its ability to handle the ever-increasing legal work of the State. At the last session, the Legislature gave five additional deputies at the Albany office and two deputies in the New York City Bureau. With this increase in the regular force, better organization and a more prompt dispatch of the work has been possible, and has greatly reduced the necessity of employing special counsel.

CENTRALIZATION OF WORK.

A significant change in the department is that by which the Legal Department of the Forest, Fish and Game Commission was transferred to the Attorney-General and has become the Forest, Fish and Game Bureau in this office.

The Forest, Fish and Game Commissioner recently requested that the Legal Department of the Commission be transferred to the Attorney-General's office. I was glad to co-operate, and on October 10, 1910, designated one of my deputies as Deputy Attorney-General in charge of the Forest, Fish and Game Bureau of the Attorney-General's office.

At a later place in this report I shall speak more in detail of the work accomplished by this Bureau. I refer to it here simply as a concrete step taken during the past year toward the sound policy of concentrating all the legal business of the State under its constitutional law officer. Since the consolidation of the Legal Department of the Forest, Fish and Game Commission with this office, the Lunacy Commission has recommended that its legal work should likewise be conducted by the Attorney-General. Other State departments have requested that a deputy be assigned to them so that they may be brought in closer touch with their legal advisers. During a large part of the year, in accordance with this request, I had a deputy assigned to the Comptroller. For a portion of the time he occupied a desk in the office of the Comptroller, but largely owing to the crowded condition of that office, he subsequently returned though continuing his close relationship with the business of that department.

I am glad to report a general recognition of the soundness and advantages of a policy of concentrating all the administration of the legal work of the State under a single responsible head. In that way only can the maximum degree of efficiency with a minimum expenditure be realized.

LIBRARY.

At my request last year, the Legislature granted an additional employee to have charge of the library. In accordance therewith I appointed an employee of the State Library to this position. An inventory of the books in the Attorney-General's office at Albany and in the New York City Bureau was immediately taken. As a result, the number of books and extent of this library is known together with missing volumes, in order to make it complete. The actual securing of these books, however, I have deemed wise to leave to the next administration. It is my belief that the library should receive careful attention and that the recommendations of the librarian as to a judicious expenditure upon it should be carried into effect.

OFFICE ACCOMMODATION.

The congestion to which I referred in my last report has increased to an even greater degree during the past year. The outside offices rented a year ago for the Special Franchise Tax Bureau and the Barge Canal Title Bureau are still retained. The Attorney-General's offices were planned when the Attorney-General had only two deputies. Now there are twenty attached to the Albany office, and the inadequacy of the accommodation can be easily imagined. It has been necessary to have most of the deputies in the library. As a result, no deputy has an office to himself, although to secure the greatest degree of efficiency the men employed in the more important work should have separate offices.

SPECIAL FRANCHISE TAX BUREAU.

In my last report I outlined the administrative changes made in the Special Franchise Tax Bureau and pointed out the complete reorganization which I had found it necessary to make in that department. During the year 1909 I succeeded in securing a settlement of approximately one-quarter of a billion of dollars litigated assessed valuations. During the year of 1910 the amount of such valuations so settled has arisen to more than one and one-half billions, thus increasing the results on the first year's efforts in the second year six-fold.

The chief reason for these numerous settlements has been the vacation of references and transferring of proceedings for trial to extraordinary terms of court. Various corporations as soon as they learned that these terms were to be convened in New York City endeavored in many ways to defeat and delay my efforts. I was accordingly forced to prepare nearly three hundred affidavits and seek the assistance of the courts in having the places of trial changed and references vacated. Mr. Justice Chester granted the motions which I made at Special Term, and his orders were sustained by the Appellate Division. As a result, the corporations were brought face to face with the alternative of trial before a judge in court or a settlement. In New York city alone more than twenty million dollars of taxes have been paid into the treasury. Like results were obtained throughout the State and an equal amount of taxes was paid.

These taxes are local in their nature and belong to the locality where the special franchise is situated. The direct benefit of the payment of this forty millions of dollars of taxes must necessarily be to lessen the tax rate in each locality. In the past these local tax districts have not felt the full benefit of this law as the payment of these taxes was delayed by litigation.

No doubt litigation will arise in the future, but it is hoped that most of the taxes will be paid by reducing the amounts to the value of real estate in each locality.

A number of steam railroads are attempting to procure a construction of the statute exempting their occupancy of the public highways from its provisions. They were successful in securing a favorable decision upon this question from a referee to whom the cases had been referred under the administration of my predecessor. When his report came before the Supreme Court for confirmation it was held that steam railroads were subject to the tax. An appeal has been taken from this decision by the railroad companies to the Appellate Division, but has not yet come on for argument.

In connection with this mass of litigation, work almost without limit has devolved upon this department. It is difficult to convey an adequate conception of the daily routine necessary to care for the large number of proceedings constantly being instituted. The thousands of cases involve the keeping of records, the preparation of returns, the making out of various motion papers, negotiations for settlement, a careful scrutinizing of final orders for errors in form and rate equalization, and the notification of local authorities, all of which require vigilance and care. At times it has been necessary for me to utilize practically my entire office force on those matters. The decision of the Court of Appeals in the cases brought by the Lehigh Valley Railroad Company and Buffalo Gas Company to compel the filing of a further return by the State Board of Tax Commissioners has greatly increased the clerical and legal work in connection with these litigations. The court held that the general allegations which had been in use in substantially the same form for years were not sufficient and that the Board should set forth in detail in its return the particular facts upon which it based its conclusions, including the results by the application of the various methods of valuations to each particular case.

Every proceeding in the entire State has received the direct attention of my department. My personal attention has been constantly given to these matters and every settlement throughout the State has been effected virtually through efforts started and carried through at Albany.

Certain amendments to the statutes would, in my judgment, strengthen the administration of this law. One of the chief reasons for delay in the payment of these taxes as the law now exists is the fact that the courts must be invoked if the assessments are to be equalized to the proportionate valuation at which other real estate in the same locality is assessed upon the same rolls. An amendment should be adopted empowering the State Board of Tax Commissioners to fix their final valuations upon this equalized basis.

Another effective amendment would be to make the payment of the tax a condition precedent to the institution of certiorari proceedings for its review. This is the provision of the statute in reference to proceedings to review the assessment of corporate franchise taxes under section 180–190 of the Tax Law, and there would seem to be no good reason why some similar provision should not be incorporated in the Special Franchise Tax Law. This would remove the temptation to postpone the payment of taxes indefinitely by litigation and, at the same time would not prejudice the rights of the companies concerned.

I also suggest that occupation of a highway shall be made conclusive evidence of the existence of a special franchise for the purpose of this tax, in order that trespassers cannot set up their own wrongs as a successful defense to the assessment of this tax. This has been done by one company whose contention was sustained by the Court of Appeals. Another amendment which would meet a prevailing complaint is one requiring that localities which receive the taxes be necessary parties to these proceedings, so that their official local counsel could be given the burden of the defense of the assessments, under the supervision of this office and without the expense of specially designated attorneys.

There are now pending in this department 1,315 certiorari proceedings for the review of special franchise tax assessments. Of these, 750 are for the review of assessments made in the years 1899 to 1909, inclusive, and 565 are for assessments made during the year 1910. In addition to the 1910 cases now pending, writs were filed in 190 cases which have been settled. The work in connection with special franchise tax assessments is more particularly shown in detail by the schedule attached to this report.

BARGE CANAL TITLE BUREAU.

The work of this bureau has been satisfactory during the past year. I pointed out last year the importance of and difficulty attending this work in connection with the construction of the new Barge Canal, and the change which I had made of having the work of examining the titles done entirely by the department at Albany, instead of employing local attorneys throughout the State. I also referred to the fact that the State Civil Service Commission had classified these appointees in the competitive class, and that the later appointments of these examiners had been made from lists certified by the Commission.

Prior to January 1, 1909, 212 Barge Canal titles had been examined and certified. During the year 1909 200 titles were so examined. In the past year the number disposed of has again greatly increased, amounting to 377.

In the course of the year I had prepared and presented to your honorable body a bill to remedy certain pronounced defects in the Barge Canal Law. This was passed and became chapter 286 of the Laws of 1910. It provides methods for the payment of awards in cases of infancy, lunacy and other similar conditions not provided for in the original law. The Legislature made an appropriation to pay county clerks for searches covering lands appropriated by the State. Before this it had been assumed that section 84 of the Executive Law, formerly section 3290 of the Code of Civil Procedure, required county clerks to do this work without compensation. This placed a heavy burden on county clerks through whose counties the Barge Canal passed. The result was, frequent disputes arose with county clerks who insisted they were entitled to compensation for this work, and that it was impossible to perform this work without compensation with their present forces respectively. Before conceding this, however, I brought a test case in the courts for an interpretation of the law. It was held by the Special Term and affirmed by the Appellate Division, Third Department, that county clerks could not be compelled to make title searches on requisition of State officers without compensation. Acting under this decision and using the fund appropriated at the last session so far as possible, I have been able to secure much more prompt and efficient service in the way of securing searches.

Interest is payable on these awards from the date of the appropriation. Under the law the State cannot force the land owner to a settlement if the latter does not care to file a claim in the Court of Claims or to enter into an agreement with the special examiner and appraiser. Since six per cent. interest is running on the value of his property, the land owner is often willing to allow the matter to rest indefinitely. I suggest that to remedy this condition the statute be amended so as to make it possible for the State authorities to take the initiative in having the claims fixed.

DEPARTMENT OF THE COURT OF CLAIMS.

The Court of Claims department shows especially gratifying results for the past year. There were twelve terms held, lasting from two to six weeks each, at Albany, Utica, Syracuse, Rochester and Buffalo. There were seven hundred and twelve claims disposed of during the year, amounting in the aggregate to $7,582,-810.45. One hundred and eighty-five Barge Canal claims were tried, the amount claimed being $7,121,406.99. Four hundred and eighty-three claims were dismissed, amounting to $1,554,-018.13. The following were the most important Court of Claims cases argued during the past year:

Fulton Light, Heat and Power Company vs. The State.

In this case an appeal was taken to the Appellate Division both by the claimant and the State from a judgment of the Court of Claims in favor of the claimant for the sum of $356,019.13. The case was argued at the May term of the Appellate Division in 1910, and resulted in an unanimous affirmance of the judgment without opinion. The State appealed to the Court of Appeals, and the argument of the appeal was brought on by special order of the court on the 14th day of December, 1910. Upon the final determination of this case a great deal depends, for there are involved the questions of the State's sovereign title in the beds of navigable streams, the rights of riparian owners to the use of surplus water at canal dams, and their right to compensation for the taking away of such water at a valuation based upon the head created by those dams. Consequently, upon the decision of this case the sufficiency of the $101,000,000 bond issue for the Barge Canal improvement to pay all claims for property damages in a great measure depends.

Ontario Knitting Company vs. The State.

In this case a claim was filed against the State for the appropriation of a factory at Oswego. The damages were alleged to be $1,019,051.78. The claim was contested by the State on the ground that the appropriation was absolutely void. While the Barge Canal Act authorized the State Engineer and Surveyor in 1907 to appropriate such lands, structures and waters as in his judgment were necessary for the improvement, it was alleged that under the circumstances in this case he could have exercised no judgment, for it was conclusively proven that there was no necessity for the appropriation of this property. The Court of Claims sustained this contention and granted a judgment dismissing the claim.

Kinser Construction Company vs. The State.
Ferguson Contracting Company vs. The State.

These are the first cases in which the Court has been called upon to pass on Barge Canal contracts. The first was a claim for $370,525.41 for an alleged breach of contract by the State. Because of the discovery of a peculiar material at a distance of some fifteen feet beneath the surface of the ground on the site of Contract 27, it was found impossible to construct the work provided for under that contract according to the plans. The State decided to remove lock No. 7 to a point farther south and beyond the limits of the contract and to adjust the plans to such removal. An alteration order carrying this into effect was served upon the contractor, who thereupon elected to treat the order as a breach of the contract by the State, and refused to perform the work pursuant to the order and abandoned the contract. The Court of Claims held that the conditions found rendering it impossible to build the lock on the site originally contemplated worked a discharge of the contract on the ground of impossibility of performance. Judgment was therefore granted to the contractor for work actually performed and not paid for, and also for damages caused by certain delays of the State and for the cost of materials brought upon the site, all in the sum of $77,425.46, but denied to the claimant any profits upon work which was not performed and which was changed by the alteration order. From this judgment the claimant has appealed to the Appellate Division.

In the second case there was also involved an alteration order which made changes in the construction work by substituting for clay puddle in the bottom of the prism on Contract No. 2 at Waterford, concrete lining and by extending in this contract the retaining walls to take the place of certain pile docking. The alteration accomplished a small percentage of increase in the cost of the work to the State. The contractor in this case elected to treat this alteration order as a breach of the contract and not as an exercise of a power reserved to the State to change plans and specifications. The contractor abandoned the work and sued the State for $120,-375.36. In this case, however, the claim was based not upon prospective profits but upon damages for certain alleged unlawful acts of the State in the way of delays in furnishing plans and the interpretation of specifications. It is hoped that in this case the State may obtain a holding of the court giving a broad interpretation of the clause of the contract, which is in practically the same form as incorporated in all Barge Canal contracts and which gives the State the right to make changes in the plans and specifications, or additions to or deductions from the work, without invalidating the contract. Decision in this case has not yet been rendered.

HEARINGS.

During the year a number of hearings were held upon applications for permission to commence actions and to dissolve and annul corporations and to test title to office. A detailed schedule showing the number of these proceedings appears in the summary annexed to this report.

MISCELLANEOUS LITIGATED CASES.

Some of the more important litigated cases which have arisen during the past year are the following:

Semi-monthly Pay Law.

Eight steam railroad companies brought actions to test the constitutionality of the Labor Law requiring steam railroads to pay their employees twice a month. The State was successful in sustaining the validity of the law. As pointed out in my last report I had then been successful in the lower court and in the Appellate Division, both courts holding that the railroad companies were not entitled to enjoin the enforcement of this law and sustaining its validity. During the past year I personally argued these cases before the Court of Appeals. That court unanimously sustained the validity of the law. No appeal from this decision to the United States Supreme Court has as yet been taken.

Eight-hour Telegraphers' Law.

In my last report I pointed out that the Appellate Division had held that this statute was inoperative on the ground that although it was a valid exercise of the police power in the first instance, yet it had been superseded by the Federal Law placing a maximum of nine hours on such employment.

The State took the position that there was nothing inconsistent with the Federal Law and the State Act inasmuch as the Federal Law simply prohibited working more than nine hours a day while the State Law, prohibiting working more than eight hours, was only an additional regulation and in no sense in conflict with the former. The Appellate Division refused to take this view. The Court of Appeals has unanimously held that there was no conflict between the two statutes. The decision is an extremely important one in the ever-broadening domain of concurrent regulation by the State and the Federal government.

CRIMINAL ACTIONS. ·

Pursuant to designations of Hon. Charles E. Hughes, Governor of the State of New York, as provided by section 62 of the Executive Law, criminal prosecutions and investigations have been conducted by my department during the year 1910 as follows:

Indictment and Trial of Frederick Skene, Former State Engineer and Surveyor.

Charges were filed with me by William R. Hearst that there had been gross irregularities and that the State had been defrauded out of large sums of money in connection with the highway improvement work during the administration of Frederick Skene, former State Engineer and Surveyor. I carefully investigated the facts upon which this complaint was based, taking testimony of such witnesses as could be found and were willing to testify. After an exhaustive investigation of the matter I decided that it should be submitted to the Grand Jury and accordingly petitioned the Governor to call an extraordinary term of the Supreme Court in Albany county for this purpose.

Such term was called by the Governor for July 18. Seventeen indictments were found by the Grand Jury against Mr. Skene, in most of which contractors and subcontractors were jointly indicted with him. Mr. John B. Russell, one of the contractors indicted, who had formerly refused to make any statement concerning his connection with a certain contract which I believed had been raised, finally made a confession in which he admitted that the contract was raised as claimed and further stated that Mr. Skene was personally a party to the proceeding and suggested it and had demanded and received $8,000 out of $9,000 which represented the raise.

This indictment was brought on for trial before the court in September last. The facts showing the raising of the bid were so conclusively established that the defendant's counsel in opening his case admitted that the bid had been raised in the manner claimed. He also admitted that probably fifty per cent. of the contracts let during the Skene administration had been likewise raised. Unfortunately for the State, Mr. Russell could not be produced at the trial for the reason that he was at that time in a sanitarium

with a well developed case of paresis. He was subpoenæd by the
State but medical experts testified that it would be dangerous to
his health and mental condition for him to be produced at Albany
to testify. I then made application to examine him at the sanitarium, which application was denied by the court. Although the
facts as claimed by the State were shown by several witnesses, the
jury acquitted the defendant.

As the defense admitted the commission of the crime their contention implicates the contractors as much as did the position
taken by the State. I would suggest and recommend therefore,
that the indictments against the contractors be prosecuted. In
this way evidence might develop disclosing the real culprit or cul-
prits in these cases. I would also advise that civil action be
brought against the contractors and Mr. Skene to recover moneys
of the State lost through this fraud or negligence.

Queens County.

On the 22nd day of September, 1910, the Governor directed that
I conduct an investigation in the place and stead of the district
attorney of Queens county in reference to many charges growing
out of dealings and transactions of various officials of the county
and the misappropriation of county funds. I designated Mr.
Arthur C. Train, of New York city, to take charge of such investigation before the grand juries of the county and to prosecute any
indictments that were found therein, growing out of such charges.
There were about thirty-five indictments which had been previously found by the district attorney of the county prior to my
designation of Mr. Train, which were turned over to him for prosecution and during such investigation some ninety-five more indictments were found against various persons, also growing out of
such charges. The result of such investigations is more particularly shown in detail by the schedule attached to this report.

Schenectady County.

On the 26th day of April, 1910, the Governor directed that I
conduct an examination in the place and stead of the district
attorney of Schenectady county into the subject-matter of investigations made by the State Comptroller into the accounts of the

various departments of the county. I designated Mr. Virgil K. Kellogg, of Watertown, an experienced lawyer in criminal matters to conduct the investigations and prosecutions. I also deputized my third deputy, Mr. George A. Fisher, likewise an experienced lawyer in criminal matters, to assist him. A large number of indictments were found together, with a number of convictions for violation of the various provisions of the Penal and County Laws. The result of such investigation is more particularly shown in detail by the schedule attached to this report.

Dutchess County.

Pursuant to designations by Governor Hughes, I directed my third deputy, Mr. George A. Fisher, to take charge of all criminal proceedings growing out of the management of the Dutchess Insurance Company and Dutchess Fire Insurance Company.

Lewis H. Vail, President of the Dutchess Fire Insurance Company was indicted for forgery, third degree. He was tried and the jury disagreed. The indictment is still pending.

ELECTION CASES.

Monroe County.

Complaint was made to the Governor by certain citizens of the city of Rochester, county of Monroe, regarding alleged illegal practice in connection with the special congressional election held in April, 1910. The Governor designated the Attorney-General to investigate the same in place of the district attorney, to appear before the grand jury in Supreme Court and to prosecute any violations of law which such investigation might discover. I designated Elmer E. Charles, former district attorney of Wyoming county, as special deputy to conduct these matters and also assigned one of my deputies to assist. About eighteen indictments were found by the grand jury, but it was impossible to apprehend most of the accused. The grand jury also presented a report calling attention to a disregard of the Election Law by the inspectors of election, it being shown that in only one election district in the city of Rochester were the registers properly filled out. Altogether, 250 witnesses were examined, about one-half being in John Doe proceedings. Two cases were tried, one against John Slat-

tery and one against John Delige, in both of which the defendants
were acquitted. Much of the evidence relied upon by the prosecution in the Slattery case was excluded by the court. Three other
indictments against Slattery and one against Delige were dismissed
by the court on application following these trials. The others are
still pending.

Greater New York.

Under the provisions of the Executive Law violations of the
Election Laws within the Metropolitan Elections District are
prosecuted by the Attorney-General.

During the year 1910 the New York office of the Attorney-General investigated or prosecuted upwards of 500 cases of violations
of the Election Law. One hundred and fifty-eight indictments
were found against one hundred and thirty-eight persons, of which
forty-five indictments against sixty-one persons were for offenses
committed at or in connection with the primaries, and one hundred and thirteen indictments against seventy-seven persons were
for offenses committed at or in connection with registration and
election. There were forty-five convictions under these indictments, all of which were for offenses committed on registration or
election day. There were twelve acquittals, of which seven were
charges of offenses committed on primary day and five were of
charges for offenses committed on election day.

In addition to the above proceedings under indictment there
have been during the year 1910, five convictions and four acquittals in the Courts of Special Sessions and two convictions in
the City Court of Yonkers and there are seven cases now pending
in the Court of Special Sessions.

There have been forty-six cases presented to different Grand
Juries who refused to find indictments.

In addition to the above cases there were a number of old indictments pending on January 1, 1910, which were disposed of,
some of these indictments having been found as far back as the
year 1899. After the new calendar practice was inaugurated in
January, 1910, in the Court of General Sessions the majority of
these old indictments were placed upon the calendar and some disposition of them became necessary. Upon examination eighty-
three were dismissed upon the consent of the Attorney-General,

it appearing to his satisfaction that convictions could not be had because of the age of the indictments, the disappearance of the witnesses and kindred causes. Twenty-three demurrers to these old indictments were sustained. Seven cases were tried of which there were four convictions and three acquittals, one defendant was discharged on his own recognizance upon a report of a Commission in Lunacy who found at the time of the alleged offense the defendant was not mentally responsible and twenty cases are still pending making a total of 135 indictments found prior to January 1, 1910.   ·

I believe that the result of the investigations and prosecutions of cases involving municipal graft in the various counties mentioned will be of great value. They disclose a great laxity in the Lusiness methods in county officers together with a great deal of petty graft which should be stamped out and new business methods adopted for conducting the public business. I am thoroughly convinced that these prosecutions and investigations will result in a wholesome respect for the provisions of law, enacted for the transaction of public business.

CORPORATION TAX CASES.

A number of important cases involving questions under the corporation tax sections of the Tax Law have been argued during the past year.

In People ex rel. Matheson Lead Company against Kelsey, the Court of Appeals sustained the decision of the Appellate Division and held that a corporation engaged partly in manufacturing and partly in general business within this State was not entitled to entire exemption of the corporate tax, even though the amount of its capital employed in manufacture was greater than the amount of its issued capital stock.

In People ex rel. Waclark Realty Company against Gaus, the Court of Appeals reversed the determination of the Appellate Division and held that the Comptroller was justified in imposing the tax upon the corporation. The contention was that the corporation was not taxable because it was engaged only in holding the title to certain real estate which was being used for constructing a dwelling for Senator W. A. Clark, the owner of the corporation. The Court held that as the capital of the corporation was being employed for the very purpose for which the corporation was formed it was taxable.

In the three cases brought respectively by the Consolidated Gas Company, the Westchester Lighting Company and the Astoria Light, Heat and Power Company against the Comptroller to compel a reduction of the tax assessed by deducting from the gross earnings upon which it was based, an amount equivalent to their expenditures for coal and other raw material entering into the production of gas and electricity, the Appellate Division and the Court of Appeals both sustained my position and confirmed the assessments.

The New York Central Railroad Company brought a certiorari proceeding to reduce the tax assessed against it on the ground that it had been based upon the amount of stock issued by it at the close of the preceding year, whereas it was claimed that it should have been based on the average amount outstanding during that year. My position, that the amendment to the law in 1906, making this tax payable in advance, justified the Comptroller in basing the tax on the amount of stock with which the year for which the tax was levied began, was sustained by the Appellate Division. The decision of the Court of Appeals has not yet been reported.

In the New York Mail and Newspaper Transportation case, the Court of Appeals held by a vote of four to three that the Comptroller had assessed the tax erroneously. The question was whether a corporation paying no dividends should be assessed upon the par value of its stock as claimed by the Comptroller, or upon the actual value as claimed by the company.

THAW CASE.

Mary C. Thaw made application to the Supreme Court to have her son, Harry K. Thaw, transferred from the Matteawan State Hospital to some other State institution on the ground that the surroundings at Matteawan were not conducive to his welfare, and that he was being maltreated. Mr. Justice Tompkins appointed a referee to take evidence on the question. I appealed from this decision to the Appellate Division, Second Department, which reversed the order of Judge Tompkins, and held that the proceeding was proper, inasmuch as the statutes gave the State Commission in Lunacy the right to make such transfers, and that it should have been applied to in the first instance. An appeal on behalf of Mrs. Thaw was taken to the Court of Appeals and the proceeding is now pending there.

ACTIONS TO FORFEIT UNUSED FRANCHISES.

Two actions were started by me in December, 1909, to forfeit certain special franchises of street surface railroads in New York city upon the ground that the companies had either failed to construct tracks under their franchises or had failed to operate railroads over them. The first of these were brought against the Forty-second Street, Manhattanville and St. Nicholas Avenue Railway Company. The defendants answered the complaint, but after negotiations, settlement was reached by which judgment was entered, forfeiting all the franchises involved in the action.

The second action was brought against the Bleecker Street and Fulton Ferry Railroad Company, the Twenty-third Street Railway and the Metropolitan Street Railway Company. Here the defendants removed the case to the Federal Court, but on my application that court remanded it to the State court. A demurrer was filed by the Bleecker Street and Fulton Ferry Railroad Company on the ground that the State should have applied for permission to the court before bringing the action. The special term overruled the demurrer and the Appellate Division, First Department, sustained this action. The result is extremely important in that its establishes the power of the Attorney-General to compel the cancellation of abandoned special franchises without first securing the leave of court.

CIVIL SERVICE CASES.

A number of cases have been litigated for the State Civil Service Commission. The most important is that of People ex rel. Kelly v. Milliken, in which the rule of the Civil Service Commission, declining to recognize a transfer from the exempt to the competitive class of the Civil Service unless the applicant was eligible to original appointment from the competitive class at the time of transfer, was sustained.

PRIVATE BANKING ACT LITIGATION.

Chapter 448 of the Laws of 1910 requires all persons engaged in the business of private banking in cities of the first-class to secure licenses from the Comptroller and deposit security with him for the benefit of their customers. This act went into effect on September 1, 1910. Prior to that time an action was brought by certain private bankers in the Circuit Court of the United States against the Comptroller, the district attorney of New York county, the police commissioner of New York city, and the Attorney-General, to restrain us from enforcing the provisions of the act on the ground that it was unconstitutional.

Hon. Louis Marshall, of New York city, who had been a member of the Commission on Immigration appointed by your body to investigate the condition of the immigrants of this State, volunteered his services in defending the constitutionality of the law. As the statute was passed as a result of the recommendations of this committee, and largely through the information contained in their report, I was glad to secure his services on behalf of the State.

The United States Circuit Court held the statute constitutional. From this decision an appeal was taken to the United States Supreme Court, and argued there, but no decision has yet been announced. Pending this appeal other private bankers instituted an action in the State Supreme Court to enjoin the enforcement of the statutes. A special term decision in their favor was reversed by the Appellate Division, First Department.

ACTIONS TO RESTRAIN WASTE OF SARATOGA MINERAL SPRINGS.

By chapter 429 of the Laws of 1908, passed on the 21st day of May, 1908, it was made unlawful to deplete the natural mineral water springs of the State by boring, pumping or other artificial means. Several corporations had formed and were actually engaged in pumping large quantities of mineral water in the vicinity of Saratoga to the detriment and destruction, as it was claimed, of the natural mineral springs, and by extracting the carbonic acid gas therefrom, the waters going to waste.

Several actions were commenced during the term of my prede-

cessor for injunctions restraining the acts of the several corporations in so wasting the mineral waters. Four of these actions
were brought to trial at an extraordinary term of the Supreme
Court appointed by the Governor to be held at the city of Albany
on the 20th of September, 1909. The trials resulted in a judgment in each case for a permanent injunction. From these judgments the defendants appealed to the Appellate Division where
they were affirmed. Upon further appeals to the Court of Appeals
the judgments were reversed upon rulings at the trial as to the ad-
missibility of certain testimony and new trials were ordered, which
are now in progress.

By chapter 569 of the Laws of 1909, passed on the 29th day of
May, 1909, the Legislature created a board called " The Commissioners of the State Reservation at Saratoga," empowering it to
locate and condemn such lands as, in the judgment of the commissioners, were necessary to create a State reservation for the
purpose of preserving and restoring the world's famed natural
springs at Saratoga. The commissioners accordingly located and
condemned certain lands whereby the ownership thereof was transferred to the State, and thereupon actions were instituted by me
in the name of the State to enjoin the wasting of the waters and
to conserve the natural resources of the State, which actions are
now pending.

ACTIONS AGAINST BROOKLYN COOPERAGE COM-
PANY AND CORNELL UNIVERSITY.

Under the administration of one of my predecessors, an action
was started by the State to enjoin the Brooklyn Cooperage Company and Cornell University from carrying out a contract entered into between them for the denudation of the so-called college
forest in the forest preserve in the Adirondacks. This action was
based on the ground that the superintendent of the college of
forestry in Cornell had exceeded his powers in entering into such
a contract. Under the terms of the contract, the Brooklyn Cooperage Company had the right to compel the college to remove
virtually all the timber from this tract of land in fifteen years and
were required to pay the college in return therefor, less than it
cost the college to cut and deliver the timber.

The case had been tried before Mr. Justice Fitts before I assumed office. Owing to his death, it was necessary to retry the case and submit the issues to Mr. Justice Chester for determination. His decision sustained the position of the State holding the contract invalid, and directing a conveyance of the entire property from Cornell University to the State.

LEHIGH VALLEY RAILROAD COMPANY vs. THE CANAL BOARD.

In the construction of the Barge Canal, it is necessary in many cases to raise railroad bridges crossing the present canal and crossing rivers which are to be canalized in the improvement of the new canal. The statute is not clear as to whether the expense thus caused shall be borne by the State, the municipalities or railroad companies owning the bridges. An action was brought by the Lehigh Valley Railroad.Company against the Canal Board to determine this question. This action was tried before Mr. Justice Foote at Rochester. The particular bridge in question was the one crossing the Seneca river near Jack's Reefs. Testimony was introduced by the State to show the navigable character of this stream. The railroad urged that the Legislature, in the Barge Canal Act, indicated no intention to compel the railroads to bear the expense of altering their bridges. The judge decided in favor of the railroad company upon this ground, although making findings favorable to the State as to the navigability of the river. If, therefore, your honorable body intended or intends to have the expense of altering or raising these bridges borne by the railroad companies, such intention should be clearly expressed in an amendment to the act which will be unambiguous. The judgment in favor of the railroad company has been appealed from on behalf of the State.

PEOPLE ex rel. LESLIE SUTHERLAND, FORMER COUNTY CLERK OF WESTCHESTER COUNTY.

Under the administration of former State Comptroller Glynn, an examination of the accounts of the county clerk of Westchester county was conducted. As a result, it was claimed that Leslie Sutherland, a former county clerk, had received upwards of $60,000, to which he was not legally entitled. The report pointed out that these charges had been made by his predecessors and he had apparently acted in good faith. At Mr. Sutherland's request the Governor called upon me to institute an action to determine the legality of their payment. An action was brought and turned over to a referee, who decided in favor of the defendant on the sole ground that since the charges had been audited by the board of supervisors they could not be collaterally attacked in this action. An appeal has been taken from this decision of the referee.

SARANAC LAND AND TIMBER COMPANY vs. ROBERTS AS COMPTROLLER.

Most of the land owned by the State in the forest preserve was acquired at tax sales. In 1885 an act was passed to quiet the title derived from such sales and making the conveyance of the Comptroller conclusive evidence of the legality of the sale. At the same time an act was passed permitting the Comptroller to advertise for six months, a list of the lands owned by the State in the forest preserve and providing that he should thereupon be considered in possession of such land. He did this in 1894. In 1894 and 1895, the Saranac Land and Timber Company which had acquired the underlying title to a large part of Township 24 in Franklin county instituted two actions in the Federal Court and two actions in the State Court against James A. Roberts, the then comptroller, to eject him from possession. One of the actions in the Federal Court was tried and decided in favor of the State, the court holding that the curative act of 1885 rendered the State's title unimpeachable. This decision was sustained by the United States Supreme Court. Following this decision the plaintiff secured an order for a new trial under the Code of Civil Procedure upon payment of costs but never brought the case on for trial.

In 1904 the company moved one of its actions in the State Court to trial. A referee decided in favor of the company. This decision was sustained by the Appellate Division and the Court of Appeals, it being held that the curative act of 1885 had no effect against the State until such time as the Comptroller by advertising under the act in 1894 put himself in possession of the lands so as to give the original owner opportunity to litigate his claim of title in the courts.

In view of the fact that the State on the first trial of this case had relied almost entirely on the act of 1885 and had made scarcely any effort to attack the alleged title of the plaintiff, it seemed to me that a new trial should be had. Accordingly I secured an order permitting a new trial. The case was tried before the Hon. Richard L. Hand, the referee appointed by the Court. No decision has as yet been announced.

PEOPLE ex rel. PHILLIPS vs. RAYNES.

Section 190 of the Labor Law provides that no convict-made goods shall be sold without a license in this State. Section 193 provides that all convict-made goods shall be branded with the words " Convict Made." The latter section had been held unconstitutional. It was uncertain, however, whether the same reasoning rendered section 190 of the act invalid. A case was brought to determine this question. The Court of Appeals held that the decision holding section 193 unconstitutional, applied equally to section 190. The ground of the decision was that it interfered with interstate commerce. It would seem to follow that if this requirement is desirable, Federal legislation permitting the State to pass laws upon this subject would validate both these sections.

SANTA CLARA LUMBER COMPANY CASE.

The Appellate Division, Third Department, at the May, 1910, term, unanimously affirmed an order of the Special Term vacating and setting aside a judgment and the order and stipulation upon which such judgment was obtained in the case of People v. The Santa Clara Lumber Company.

The judgment thereby vacated was obtained in an action brought by DeWitt C. Middleton, as Forest, Fish and Game Commissioner, to recover the value of cedar trees alleged to have been cut by the defendant from lands of the State in the Forest Preserve. Immediately following the joinder of issue in the case a stipulation was entered into between Middleton and the defendant " settling and compromising " the said action and an order and judgment was entered thereon dismissing the complaint on the merits and confirming in the defendant the title to a large tract of land from which the trees had been taken and also granting to the defendant other timber and water rights of great value.

It was contended by Mr. Jackson, my predecessor, and myself that this judgment was obtained by fraud and was further in violation of the Constitution and statutes of the State.

ACTIONS TO DISSOLVE CORPORATIONS AND TO ANNUL CORPORATE CHARTERS.

During the past year several actions have been brought to dissolve corporations and to annul their charters under the provisions of sections 101 and 131, respectively. The greater part of these actions arose where the corporations proceeded against were exercising privileges or franchises not conferred upon them by law. All of these actions have been successfully finished except two brought during the month of December, which are now pending.

PROCEEDINGS INVOLVING POSSIBLE ESCHEATS.

In cases where persons die leaving no known heirs or next of kin, the State is interested either as the representative of unknown heirs and next of kin, or in case none such appear, to preserve the estate for the State to which it then escheats. Under the Code, although the provisions are not entirely clear, it is customary to cite the Attorney-General in such cases. It is of the utmost importance that the Attorney-General should be represented in these cases from the beginning, because of the unnecessary and extravagant manner in which such estates are frequently administered. In one estate, consisting of $1,300, money in bank, the expense of administration was $1,190. In another, consisting of $23,000, stocks and bonds, $5,000 was expended in administration. In still another of $2,300, $1,400 was so expended, and the administrator on the stand frankly testified that it was his object to expend as much as possible because he thought the State would get what was left anyway. It would, therefore, seem to be imperative that the provisions of the Code be amended, particularly those applicable to the city of New York, providing clearly that the citation in every such instance be served upon the Attorney-

General. In that way, both in cases of intestacy, and in cases in which instruments purporting to be wills of the deceased are offered, the interest of the State and the interest of unknown heirs and next of kin would be much more adequately protected.

CLAIMS TO WITHDRAW FUNDS FROM THE STATE TREASURY.

During the year various claims to withdraw funds on deposit with the State Treasurer have been made. Most of these arose from the claims of alleged unknown heirs and next of kin of persons who have died intestate. In many instances the proof of relationship offered is extremely inadequate. During the past year such claims, amounting in the aggregate to more than $30,000, have been opposed by me successfully, while approximately $6,000 has been paid out by the Comptroller under such claims that have been established.

APPLICATION OF WILLIAM S. REYNOLDS et al. TO REVIEW THE PRESENT APPORTIONMENT OF THE STATE INTO SENATORIAL AND ASSEMBLY DISTRICTS.

In the early part of November the Governor, the President of the Senate, the Speaker of the Assembly and the Attorney-General were served with papers in the above matter, which is an application to the Supreme Court for an order vacating the apportionment made by the Legislature of 1907 for the various senatorial and assembly districts in the State, and adjudging that the apportionment as made by the Constitution of 1894 was still in effect. The main question raised is the power of the Legislature to make such an apportionment at an extraordinary session even though the attempt to do so had been made at the regular session and had failed. This case has not yet been argued.

PEOPLE vs. FRANK GASS.

This action was brought against the former register of New York county to recover the amount of a mortgage tax which should have been collected by him. The Park Row Realty Company conveyed certain premises in New York City situate on

Park Row and Ann street to Lord Rothschild and others. The instrument making this conveyance was in form an absolute deed, but a consent of the stockholders of the Park Row Realty Company which was recorded contemporaneously with it, disclosed that it was intended as a mortgage in fact. No tax was paid at the time of recording this instrument. The State Board of Tax Commissioners advised the register of New York county not to permit a reconveyance of any of the property until the tax was paid. The statute provides that no discharge of a mortgage shall be recorded when the tax has not been paid. When the reconveyance of the property was tendered it was recorded by the register without requiring the payment of the tax.

Upon the matter being called to my attention papers were drawn in an action to compel the Rothschilds to pay the tax. Owing to the fact that all the Rothschilds are nonresidents of New York, and that no property of theirs could be found within the State, it was impossible to commence this action. Accordingly an action has been started against the register and his surety to recover the amount of the tax.

MILK INVESTIGATION.

During the year I caused an investigation into the cause for the advance in the price of canned milk from eight to nine cents per quart in the city of New York. Under date of April 25, 1910, I transmitted a report showing the result of that investigation to your honorable body which was ordered printed. This report contained a vast amount of valuable information for the milk producer and consumer.

AGRICULTURAL CASES.

During the year 1910 over 3,000 cases were prosecuted. Of this number 1,674 were referred during the year 1910 and the balance during prior years. Of the cases received at this office during the year 1910, 886 were for violations of that part of the law relating to dairy products, 300 were for the adulteration or misbranding of food and food products, 107 related to concentrated commercial feeding stuffs and commercial fertilizers, and the balance to diseases of domestic animals and other provisions

2

of the Agricultural Law. Nine hundred and seventy cases have been disposed of by trial, payment of penalty or discontinuance. Judgments have been rendered in favor of the State, which still remain uncollected, in 81 cases, against the State in 35 cases, and 28 defendants were prosecuted criminally, making a total of 1,114 cases disposed of during 1910. Of the cases on appeal, 7 judgments have been affirmed in the Appellate Division, 7 in the Appellate Term and 1 in the Onondaga County Court. Judgments were affirmed in favor of defendants in 3 cases in the Appellate Term and 3 in the Appellate Division. There has been recovered in fines, penalties and judgments during the year 1910 the sum of $52,676.70, which is the largest amount that has ever been recovered in any one year.

INSURANCE CASES.

During the past year I have conducted a number of proceedings on behalf of the Superintendent of Insurance, particularly under section 63 of the Insurance Law. Under this section the Superintendent of Insurance acting through the Attorney-General, was empowered to take possession and liquidate the affairs of insurance corporations which were insolvent or refused to obey the legal orders of the Department.

The most important case was that of the Peoples' Mutual Life Insurance Association and League of Syracuse. On December 21, 1909, at the request of the Superintendent of Insurance, I assigned one of my deputies to assist him in an investigation of certain officers. Later an order was obtained to show cause why the superintendent should not take possession of the association's property and conduct its business. The association had been conducting a business which required certificate holders to make monthly payments for a period of five years, when dividend was to be made of "not to exceed" an amount therein stated, which amount was approximately two dollars for every one dollar advanced by the certificate holder. The society grew rapidly but with the payments of the first dividends it began to decline. Instead of paying two dollars on every one dollar paid in, the dividends barely equalled the amounts paid in without interest. The court granted the application placing the Insurance Superintendent in possession and authorizing him to liquidate. In the meantime, I started eight actions in equity against the directors of the association to compel them to account for the moneys and property of the association in their hands or lost because of their misconduct. A settlement was finally effected under which the appeals were withdrawn, the equity actions discontinued, and payment made by the directors to the Superintendent of Insurance for the benefit of the certificate holders of the full amount moved to Canada and all the moneys received by them as individuals for the illegal sale of their positions, together with interest and the costs incurred by the State in attempting to obtain a return of the money from Canada.

CERTIFICATES OF INCORPORATION OF INSURANCE COMPANIES EXAMINED.

Pursuant to statute, eighty-two proposed certificates of incorporation of insurance companies have been examined. Of these seventy-three were approved and nine disapproved.

CERTIFICATES OF INCORPORATION UNDER THE MEMBERSHIP CORPORATION LAW EXAMINED.

Pursuant to request of the State Board of Charities, fifty proposed charters of incorporation under the Membership Corporation Law were examined. Of these, forty-four were approved and six disapproved.

ABOLITION OF TOLL BRIDGES.

Chapter 146 of the Laws of 1909 provides for the abolition of toll bridges. Under this act it is the duty of the board of supervisors to first pass a resolution that public interests demanded the abolition of the bridge. Thereupon the State Commission of Highways must investigate and determine whether the toll bridge was of sufficient public importance to be abolished and either approve or disapprove the resolution. If the Commission approves it is to certify its approval to the Attorney-General who thereupon must institute proceeding to acquire the title to the bridge and to appraise the damages. Upon the award being made, the Attorney-General is required to certify the same to the board of supervisors and they must determine whether or not they will acquire the bridge on the award. One-half the expense is to be borne by the State and one-half by the county. It is provided by section 266 that the State's portion of the expense shall be paid "out of any specific appropriation made to carry on the provisions of this article."

Under this statute there has been transmitted to this office, six resolutions approved by the Highway Commission for the condemnation of toll bridges. In two instances this office has conducted proceedings for the acquirement of title to the bridges and the franchises. The first of these involved the acquirement of the property of the Black Lake Bridge Company, which owned and operated a toll bridge in the county of St. Lawrence, across a portion of Black lake. On the petition of the chairman of the Highway Commission, and without opposition on the part of the bridge company, commissioners in condemnation were appointed by the Supreme Court. An award of $26,378.75 was made by the commissioners and this award, together with the expenses of the commissioners and of this Department in conducting the proceedings, were certified to the board of supervisors and to the State Comptroller. No action has been taken by the board of supervisors or by the State toward the payment of any portion of the award.

Proceedings were also taken by me, under this statute, to acquire title to the toll bridge at Riverside, crossing the Hudson river between the towns of Johnsburg and Chester in Warren county. The commission made an award of $12,800 to the owner of the bridge which was certified to the State Comptroller and board of supervisors. The total expense of taking the bridge was $13,365.59. The board of supervisors last November approved this award and the only thing that remains, as far as the State is concerned, is the payment of its one-half by the Comptroller.

In the Warren county proceeding on motion for a final order, a claim was made by the bridge company for costs and allowances. This was opposed by me and the court has just handed down a decision granting the costs but denying the claim of extra allowances. In determining this question the court held that confirmation of the award and final order should be obtained before the confirmation by the board of supervisors of the expense of taking the bridge.

Inasmuch as these questions are very important as a precedent for future proceedings an appeal should be taken.

There also have been certified to this office by the State Commission of Highways, the following bridges to be condemned:

The Mechanicville bridge across the Hudson river, connecting the town of Schaghticoke, Rensselaer county, and the village of Mechanicville, Saratoga county;

The Stillwater bridge across the Hudson river, connecting the town of Schaghticoke, Rensselaer county, with the village of Stillwater, Saratoga county;

The Scotia bridge across the Mohawk river, between the city of Schenectady and the town of Glenville; and

The Freeman bridge between the city of Schenectady and the town of Glenville.

The State has not paid its one-half of the expense of acquiring the Riverside bridge, in Warren county, because no specific appropriations have been made to carry out the provisions of the article. An item of $75,000 was placed by the Legislature in the appropriation bill this last year but was excised by the Governor before he signed the bill. I have therefore declined to proceed with the condemnation of the other bridges which have been certified and have notified the Commission of Highways by letter that I do not think I would be justified in taking any further steps in the condemnation of any more bridges until some fund was available out of which the State might pay its proper share of the expense and cost of their taking.

It is well known that there are many bridges of great value throughout the State, the condemnation of which may be called for under this statute. I do not feel that these proceedings should be brought and prosecuted to final judgment in advance of specific appropriation for the payment of the State's share. If it were the intention of your honorable body that the title to these bridges should be acquired and the appropriations for the payment thereof made afterwards the statute should so provide. Certainly judgments amounting to millions should not be permitted against the State without your honorable body knowing what the probable cost is to be.

EXAMINATION OF RECEIVERS' ACCOUNTS.

I employed three certified public accountants to examine the accounts of the various receivers of corporations against which actions had been brought by the people for dissolution.

The accountants have filed reports with me of all of these receiverships with the exception of the Home Mutual Building and Loan Association of Albany. No particular provision is made in the appropriation for this office for the payment of services of this character, and I would respectfully suggest that, in view of the fact that this duty is placed upon the Attorney-General, an appropriation should be made out of which services of this character could be paid without necessitating their payment from other funds.

FOREST, FISH AND GAME COMMISSION.

I have already referred to the change whereby the legal work of the Forest, Fish and Game Commission was transferred to this department. A detailed report of this Bureau annexed hereto shows the status of all cases pending. A reorganization has been instituted to bring it in harmony with the methods pursued in this office. The short time in which I have been in charge of the work made it impossible to accomplish much more than to prepare for future accomplishments. It is hoped that the work done, however, will make easier the task of dealing adequately and promptly with the matters of litigation which concern this branch of the State government.

Since I have had the supervision of the legal work in the Forest, Fish and Game Bureau, I have caused to be partly examined the titles to upwards of fifty pieces of land proposed to be purchased as part of the forest preserve. Defects appear in almost every title for which reason none of them have been completed and approved.

MONEYS COLLECTED.

During the year the Attorney-General collected $364,972.80 on various old claims held by the State. The most important of these was the claim of the State against the city of New York for moneys that had laid unclaimed in the hands of the city chamberlain.

This fund was the accumulation of money paid into the court for the benefit of various persons who never appeared to claim it. The laws of 1892 provided that the city chamberlain should turn over to the State such court funds as had accumulated in his office and for which no claim had been made in twenty years. As a result of the suit brought by the Attorney-General, the city chamberlain in November, turned over to the State $240,403.58.

The Attorney-General pressed two claims against the Federal government which resulted in the collection of $89,569.22. Of this, $40,072.48 was for compensation of officers and men enlisted in the Spanish-American War. The residue, amounting to $49,541.74, represented a reimbursement to the State for ordnance stores furnished the United States in the same war.

A claim against the city of Syracuse resulted in a compromise in which the city of Syracuse paid the State the sum of $35,000. This claim arose from judgments obtained against the State by the riparian owners on Skaneateles lake. In the early history of the Erie canal, the Skaneateles lake was made a feeder. Later, the city of Syracuse was authorized by statute to take water from the lake for the purpose of supplying the inhabitants of the city. The withdrawal of water from the lake resulted in many judgments against the State in favor of riparian owners, who had suffered because of lack of water. After many of these judgments had been obtained, the State sued the city of Syracuse to be reimbursed, on the ground that the damage to the riparian owners was not due to any action on the part of the State but rather to the act of the city of Syracuse for appropriating the water for distribution to its inhabitants. After the suit had been begun the claim was compromised as aforesaid.

LAND BUREAU.

The Attorney-General is *ex-officio* a member of the Commissioners of the Land Office and is also their legal adviser. As a member of that board, he takes part in its deliberations and aids in framing its policies. As its counsel, he passes upon the form and legality of many of the applications and petitions presented to the board for its action. He is also chairman of its standing committee upon the hearing of remonstrances to grants of land under water.

During the past year seventy-five applications presented to the board were referred to him for examination and report. Hearings were had on various contested applications, both at Albany and elsewhere throughout the State. Many of the matters so referred to him require careful investigation, not only among State archives but locally.

The Attorney-General is also required to examine the titles to all lands purchased by the State for its various institutions. During the year 1910, he has passed upon titles of sixty-one parcels of land thus acquired included in the following tracts:

Cayuga inlet, Ithaca.
Senate house, Kingston.
State Farm for Women, Kinderhook.
Eastern New York Reformatory, Napanoch.
Elmira Reformatory, Elmira.
Blauvelt rifle range, Rockland county.
Cypress Hill cemetery plot.
State fish hatchery, Columbia county.
New Harlem prison, Wingdale.
New boiler house property, Albany.
Mohansic State Hospital, Yorktown.
Letchworth Village, Rockland county.
State Agricultural School, Morrisville.

The following report of the standing committee of the land board, which was unanimously approved by the commissioners at a meeting of the land board, held December 15, is of such importance that the same is here offered in full for the information of the Legislature:

"*December* 1, 1910.

To the Commissioners of the Land Office:

Gentlemen.— The undersigned, who at a meeting of your honorable board held on March 30, 1910, were appointed a special committee " to consider the advisability of having prepared maps showing all lands now owned by the State, the transfer to the office of the Secretary of State of all conveyances to the State and all records of conveyances from the State now deposited in other State offices; the advisability of changing the policy of the State relative to granting lands under navigable waters; and asking the Legislature to make an appropriation to carry into effect the purposes of this resolution " have the honor to report:

We have made an investigation concerning the records of lands of the State and find that no land list of lands now owned by the State is kept except that in the Comptroller's office there is kept a list of all lands acquired by the State under tax sales and also of lands acquired by the State on the foreclosure of loan commissioner's mortgages, and also in the forest preserve counties a list of lands acquired by the Forest Preserve Board by purchase. There are on file in the State Comptroller's office two large safes containing abstracts of titles and deeds of various State lands including State hospitals, armory sites, and lands occupied by other State institutions, but no list has ever been prepared showing accurately the boundaries of the various parcels included in said deeds.

We find that the sale of State lands has from the earliest State history been in the hands of various State officers for disposal. One of the earliest laws conferred upon the commissioners of forfeitures the power to convey lands which the State had seized upon attainder for treason during the Revolutionary War. There are some memoranda of these sales in the State library and also in the county clerk's offices of Dutchess and Washington counties, and some individuals have recorded deeds from the commissioners of forfeitures in various other county clerks' offices. There are some scattering records as to these sales also in the State Comptroller's office but the commissioners did not preserve copies of the deeds executed by them.

Prior to 1818 the Attorney-General was authorized to convey lands which had been acquired by the State on the foreclosure of loan mortgages. No copies of such deeds were ever preserved in the Attorney-General's office. Under an act passed in 1795, the Surveyor-General was authorized to sell certain lands acquired by the State from the Oneida, Onondaga and Cayuga Indians and execute conveyances therefor and to take mortgages for part pay-

ment. The Surveyor-General did not preserve copies of these
deeds, although he did preserve a record of the sales of these lots
covering about 60,000 acres of land on both sides of Cayuga lake.
Under an act passed in 1815 the Surveyor-General was also authorized to sell about 1,000 acres of land in the village of Oneida
Castleton, Oneida county. No copies of the various deeds of the
Surveyor-General of these lands were preserved. At different
times during the subsequent history of the State various other State
officers and boards, including the Governor, the Superintendent of
Public Works, the State Comptroller and others were authorized
to convey State lands. No records whatever are kept in the Secretary of State's office, except possibly by way of memoranda of
sales other than sales made by the Commissioners of the Land
Office.

In the past, lands have been acquired by the State in the names
of various State hospitals and other institutions and deeds run
to the institutions and not to the people of the State, so that in
many instances, there is no record of these deeds in any State office
in Albany.

The canal appraiser's records and the records of the board and
Court of Claims also contain records of awards covering many
thousand acres of land acquired for the use of the canals and for
other purposes. The Forest Preserve Board has, in addition to purchases made by it direct, the power to condemn lands and in a
few instances it has exercised this right of eminent domain, no
record of which appears in any other State office than the Court
of Claims.

Your committee is unanimously of the opinion that there
should be one central office for the recording of all conveyances
to and from the State.

Regarding the advisability of changing the policy of the State
relative to the granting of lands under the navigable waters of
the State, we desire to call your attention to a letter addressed to
your honorable body by Governor Roosevelt under date of October
19, 1899, which reads as follows:

"It seems to me questionable policy to alienate the land of
the State. Would it not be better to lease it for a fixed term

of say 25 years with power of renewal, or what conditions are deemed best? I don't say definitely that this course is the right one to follow but I would like your Board to consider what is the proper policy to pursue."

We also call your attention to the fact that the minutes of the Land Board for the year 1899, at page 177, show that a committee was appointed to confer with the Governor to consider the policy of the board in reference to future applications for grants of land under water, and the Land Board minutes of that year, at page 195, show that Attorney-General Davies of said committee reported that he had communicated with the Attorneys-General of the states of Ohio, Connecticut, Maryland, Massachusetts and Rhode Island, also New Jersey, asking information with reference to forms of grants of land under water in use in their respectives states, and a summary of the letters appears in his report from which it would appear that in nearly all of these states no grants are made of land under water, but in some states leases are made, some for short periods and others in perpetuity with provision for revaluation every twenty years as is the case in New Jersey.

Our attention has been called to the fact that the city of New York has never been authorized by the Legislature to grant these lands under water. It merely has the power to lease the same.

Your committee is therefore of the opinion that this whole question should be referred to the Legislature, and that a request be made of said Legislature that suitable action be taken so that an investigation of the above subjects of consolidating the land records of the State and also to consider whether lands under water should be, in the future, granted at all or not, or whether some scheme of leasing lands would be advisable. It seems to your committee that it is an unwise thing for the Land Board to be monthly giving grants of land under water at a time when, in the Court of Claims, the State is being daily assessed with heavy damages for lands which it had supposed it owned under the public waters, for the construction of the Barge canal.

The State is also about to undertake the problem of water storage and other undertakings in which public lands will be constantly needed in the future. Protests are accumulating daily before the Land Board by townships and municipalities and citizens against the granting of any more public lands for any purposes to individuals.

Furthermore, it is impossible for the Land Board to act intelligently in granting lands with the present equipment for ascertaining what the facts are. We are obliged to rely upon the papers submitted by the applicant. The State Engineer has no means of making surveys to cover any of these grants. The only thing the Attorney-General is able to do is to certify that the application is in accordance with the rules of this board. The result is that the Land Board has in the past voted upon land grants without accurate knowledge of what the facts are, giving grants of lands that must of necessity in the future be of immense value to the State and the public, for a nominal consideration.

Your committee is of the opinion that, until the Legislature shall act in the matter, as suggested, and define the policy to be pursued by the State, in reference to public lands, and especially those under water belonging to the State no further grants should be made except to municipalities.

Respectfully submitted,

(Signed)   EDWARD R. O'MALLEY,
Attorney-General.

SAMUEL S. KOENIG,
Secretary of State.

FRANK M. WILLIAMS,
State Engineer and Surveyor."

OPINIONS.

During the year the number of opinions rendered to the State departments has been greater than in any previous year. This work is one requiring the most careful attention and is of far reaching importance in the administration of the State's affairs. There is a tendency on the part of departments to refer all unusual questions to the Attorney-General, although in fact the questions are often those of policy rather than of law. I do not believe it was intended the Attorney-General should assume the responsibility of administrative policies. His work should be strictly limited to the interpretation of the statutes or to legal advice.

RECOMMENDATIONS.

I, therefore, respectfully make the following recommendations:

1. The Tax Law should be amended so as to give the State Board of Tax Commissioners the power to equalize the special franchise assessments and not require a resort to the courts in every instance before this relief can be obtained. In this, I concur in the recommendation of the State Board of Tax Commissioners.

2. The Tax Law should be amended to provide that occupation of a highway shall be prima facie evidence of the existence of the special franchise, so that trespassers cannot set up their wrong as a successful defense to the assessments against them.

3. Sections 447, 1594 and 1627 of the Code of Civil Procedure, under which the people of the State are joined as parties defendant in actions affecting real property, should be amended so as to require the complaint to specify the reason why the people are joined and the facts upon which that reason is based.

4. Sections 2616 and 2663 of the Code of Civil Procedure regulating the proceedings upon petition on probate of a will and petitions for letters of administration should be amended so as to provide unequivocally for service of citations upon the Attorney-General where the decedent left no known heirs-at-law or next of kin. Now many surrogates interpret the statute providing " where the surrogate is unable to ascertain to his satisfaction where the decedent left heirs or next of kin " as having no application where they are able to ascertain that no heirs or next of kin were left.

5. Supplementary to the preceding recommendation, I advise that the other sections of the Code governing accounting by executors and administrators be amended so as to provide for notices to the Attorney-General in such cases where there is a possible escheat, and that the Attorney-General in similar cases be given the right to compel an accounting if none is made. These amendments are of great importance if a proper administration of these estates is to be secured and a proceeding subject to adequate supervision to protect the interests of unknown heirs and next of kin : or interests of the people of the State.

6. The Barge Canal Law should be amended so as to provide explicitly that the expense of altering railroad bridges crossing navigable waters of the State for the purpose of making them

conform to the Barge canal improvement shall be borne by the railroads and not by the State. Under the decisions of the courts such expense may properly be imposed upon these corporations, but it has been held by a trial court in one case that the language of the law as it exists at present does not require the expense to be so borne. In my opinion this amendment, which is fully justified under the law, would save the State many thousands of dollars which it would otherwise be compelled to expend if the decision of this court should be sustained.

In addition to the foregoing, I wish to call your attention to two general principles which I believe should be applied to the administration of this department.

During my administration I have been called upon by the Governor to conduct criminal prosecutions or investigations before grand juries or the courts in the counties of Oswego, Monroe, Queens, Schenectady and Dutchess. Without in any sense criticising the wisdom of these particular designations, I nevertheless feel that it is unwise as a general proposition for the Attorney-General to have to do with the ordinary administration of the criminal law and thus to displace the district attorneys of the State. Under our Constitution it is only in extraordinary cases that the Attorney-General is supposed to take charge of criminal prosecutions. In criminal proceedings I believe the principle of home rule should apply, and the various counties should have charge of the enforcement of the criminal law. The Attorney-General's office is not equipped for the conducting of criminal cases and such action necessarily involves employment of special counsel. No doubt cases will arise from time to time making it advisable for the Attorney-General to take charge of some prosecutions. In my opinion this should be only in extreme cases, and the law should be amended so as to make the counties pay the total expense, including special counsel fees.

It was my earnest ambition throughout my administration to minimize the expense of the State from the employment of local and special attorneys, but the frequency with which these criminal actions were undertaken by my department made necessary a greater resort to such outside assistance than would otherwise have been required.

Finally I wish to emphasize the wisdom of entrusting the Attorney-General with supervision over all the legal business of the State. I have already referred to the steps taken in this direction during the past two years which indicate a recognition of the sound purpose underlying this policy. As at present conducted, the legal interests of the State are under many separate and independent heads subject to no central control or supervision. The result is not only a lack of harmony in the interpretation of the statutes, of the administration of the laws, but also a condition which makes it impossible to regulate properly the expense of such legal services or even to know with any degree of accuracy how much the State is paying each year for such services. The Attorney-General is the constitutional law officer of the State, and it would seem clear that economy, efficiency and consistency in the administration of the State's law business would be promoted through entrusting to him the general control and supervision over that branch of the State's administration which the Constitution evidently contemplated he was to have.

I here want to acknowledge again the efficient work that has been done by the deputies and all the assistants during the past two years in this department.

SUMMARY OF THE BUSINESS OF THE OFFICE FOR THE YEAR 1910.

Money recovered for the State during the year..	$417,649.50
Penalties and costs in actions brought to enforce the provisions of the Agricultural Law....... $47,906.48	
Amount received in satisfaction of judgments in actions brought to enforce the provisions of the Agricultural Law 4,770.22	
Amount turned over to the State by the New York City Chamberlain 240,403.58	
Amount collected from the Federal government as war charges 89,569.22	

Amount collected from the city of
  Syracuse for damages to ripa-
  rian owners on Skaneateles lake. $35,000.00
                                    —————————— $417,649.50

Written opinions furnished during the year (ex-
  cluding communications, formal and in-
  formal)   329
Abstracts of title referred to the office for ex-
  amination   377
Abstracts of title approved by the office........   377
Number of violations of the Agricultural and
  Pure Food Laws, referred to this office by the
  Agricultural Department................   1,674
Number of persons indicted for violation of the
  Election Laws   151
Number of proceedings instituted to review the
  determination of the State Board of Tax Com-
  missioners   755
Applications to Land Board.................   75
Mortgage foreclosure suits to which the State
  was a party............................   218
Partition actions to which the State was a party.   39
Proceedings in Surrogates' Courts to which the
  State was a party......................   301
Certificates of incorporation examined........   132
Quo warranto proceedings and other similar
  actions begun   9
Applications for leave to commence actions pre-
  sented to the Attorney-General............   27
Hearings had upon such applications.........   24
Number of claims disposed of in the Court of
  Claims   712
Amount claimed $7,782,810.45
Number of claims dismissed with no award.....   483
Amount of dismissed claims................ $1,554,018.13
Number of claims disposed of in 1910 more than
  in 1909   296

Number of claims disposed of in excess of number filed.............................. 171
Number of cases argued in United States Supreme Court for the year 1910 (undecided).. 1
Number of cases argued in Court of Appeals.... 36
Decided in favor of the State................ 27
Number of cases argued in the Appellate Division..................................... 53
Decided in favor of the State................ 33
Undecided in Appellate Courts.............. 10
Voluntary dissolutions of corporations........ 91
Sequestration actions...................... 42
Bonds approved by the office................ 517
Bonds disapproved........................ 251
Applications in behalf of Superintendent of Insurance to conduct business.............. 9
Actions against State officials.............. 39
Applications to amend certificates or for change of name............................... 29
Miscellaneous actions...................... 117

Further items and particulars are set forth in the schedules herewith presented.

Respectfully submitted,

EDWARD R. O'MALLEY,

Attorney-General.

COURT OF CLAIMS DEPARTMENT.

Outline of cases pending on appeal in the Court of Appeals and in the Appellate Division from the Court of Claims, and judgments received from the Court of Claims.

552 claims filed amounting to................$6,142,207 65
438 of these were Barge Canal amounting to..... 5,281,416 88
712 claims tried and disposed of amounting to.... 7,582,810 45
187 Barge Canal claims tried:
    Amount claimed 7,121,406 99
    Amount of judgments received............ 276,339 21
521 judgments received (including Rochester
      Bridge cases amounting to $75,000):
    Amount claimed 2,467,738 44
    Amount of judgments received............ 286,441 74
389 of these were canal judgments:
    Amount claimed 75,299 24
    Amount of judgments received............ 13,678 57
116 of these were Barge Canal judgments:
    Amount claimed 2,306,409 91
    Amount of judgments received............ 276,339 21
 10 were other than canal:
    Amount claimed 38,178 66
    Amount of judgments received............ 20,200 50
 7 were personal injury:
    Amount claimed 92,933 00
    Amount of judgments received............ 2,800 00
483 claims dismissed amounting to............. 1,554,018 13

(This includes 304 Rochester Bridge cases amounting to $75,-000, and 144 claims arising from damages caused by overflow of Black river amounting to $348,038.64).

COURT OF CLAIMS DEPARTMENT — IN COURT OF APPEALS.

FULTON LIGHT, HEAT AND POWER COMPANY AND MILTON J. WARNER, APPELLANTS, *vs.* THE STATE OF NEW YORK, RESPONDENT.

The above claim was filed for the sum of $3,428,028.16 for the permanent appropriation of land, riparian rights and other damages in the city of Fulton, for the use of the Barge Canal under chapter 147, Laws of 1903. The claim was tried at a term of the Court of Claims in Albany on June 22, 1908. On November 15, 1909, a judgment was entered in favor of the claimants for the sum of $356,019.13. From this judgment both the State and claimants appealed to the Appellate Division. The judgment of the Court of Claims was unanimously affirmed. An appeal was taken from this order to the Court of Appeals. The appeal was argued December 14, 1910.

ALONZO BURKS, CLARA G. BURKS, ALONZO BURKS, ROSALIA INDA, VERONICA OLSZEWSKA, APPELLANTS, *vs.* THE STATE OF NEW YORK, RESPONDENT. (Five separate claims.)

The above claims were filed for personal injuries received while riding on the inclined railway at the Niagara State Reservation at Niagara Falls, caused by the breaking of a cable and safety device, on July 6, 1907. The claims were all tried at Buffalo in June, 1909, and judgments rendered by the Court of Claims against the State in each of the claims. From these judgments both the State and the claimants appealed to the Appellate Division. The judgments of the Court of Claims were unanimously affirmed. The State has appealed to the Court of Appeals.

GEORGE BURK ELY, APPELLANT, *vs.* THE STATE OF NEW YORK, RESPONDENT.

This claim was filed for the sum of $1,800 for damage to land and crops in Clay, Onondaga county, by reason of raising the dam at Phœnix, and raising the waters of the lakes and rivers. The case was tried at Syracuse, February 18, 1907, and a judgment of dismissal rendered. The claimant appealed to the Appellate Division, where the judgment of the Court of Claims was affirmed. From the decision of the Appellate Division claimant appealed to the Court of Appeals. The judgment of the lower court was unanimously affirmed.

COURT OF CLAIMS DEPARTMENT — IN APPELLATE DIVISION.

CHAMPLAIN STONE AND SAND COMPANY, APPELLANT, *vs.* THE STATE OF NEW YORK, RESPONDENT.

This is a claim filed for $224,412.57, for the appropriation of land at Fort Ann, Washington county, and loss of leasehold rights in the Rice stone quarry at that place, owing to the appropriation of land for Barge Canal purposes. The case was tried October 1, 1908, and the court rendered judgment for $1,000 for the land appropriated and dismissed the claim as to the leasehold interest. From this judgment the claimant appealed to the Appellate Division. That court unanimously affirmed the decision of the lower court. An appeal has been taken to the Court of Appeals.

FREDERICK S. FLOWER ET AL., APPELLANTS, *vs.* THE STATE OF NEW YORK, RESPONDENT.

This claim was filed for the sum of $3,478.93 for the recovery of transfer taxes erroneously paid to the State Comptroller in excess of amount due on transfer of shares of stock. The case was tried on May 12, 1909, and dismissed by the Court of Claims. Claimant appealed to the Appellate Division.

DAVID L. HOUGH, APPELLANT, *vs.* THE STATE OF NEW YORK, RESPONDENT.

This claim was filed for $2,775 for services rendered the State of New York under a contract entered into in the city of New York for employment of claimant as one of the expert witnesses for the State in the appraisal of the Consolidated Gas Company's plant. The claim was tried October 11, 1909, at Albany, and judgment rendered by the Court of Claims for $1,350. From this judgment an appeal was taken to the Appellate Division. The case has not been argued.

MARY E. BASCOM ET AL., APPELLANTS, *vs.* THE STATE OF NEW YORK, RESPONDENT.

This is a claim filed for the sum of $1,044.55 for permanent appropriation of 15/100 acres of land in the village of Whitehall for the purposes of the Barge Canal. The claim was tried at Albany, April 17, 1908, and a judgment for $90.67 rendered by the Court of Claims. Claimant has appealed to the Appellate Division. The appeal has not been argued.

ANN S. BAILEY AND ANOTHER, APPELLANTS, *vs.* THE STATE OF NEW YORK, RESPONDENT.

This claim was filed for the sum of $16,527.55 for permanent appropriation of 35 56/100 acres of land in the village of Kingsbury for the purposes of the Barge Canal, with riparian rights, damage to lands, trees, etc. The case was tried at Albany, January 12, 1909, and a judgment rendered by the Court of Claims for the sum of $3,137.46. From this judgment the claimant has appealed to the Appellate Division. The case has not been argued.

HORACE N. COWLES, APPELLANT, *vs.* THE STATE OF NEW YORK, RESPONDENT.

This claim is for the sum of $21,582.60 damages for leakage from the canal in the city of Rochester, when claimant was laying a sewer system for the city, causing delay, extra labor, etc. The claim was tried at Rochester, October 18, 1909, and a judgment rendered by the Court of Claims for $1,440.02. Claimant has appealed to the Appellate Division. The case has not been argued.

PATRICK B. DALEY AND ISABELLA DALEY, APPELLANTS, VS. THE STATE OF NEW YORK, RESPONDENT.

This claim was filed for $21,314.55 for permanent appropriation of 20 26/100 acres of land in Kingsbury for the Barge Canal purposes. The claim was tried at Albany, November 20, 1908, and a judgment rendered by the Court of Claims for $3,704.51. From this judgment claimant has appealed to the Appellate Division.

LINA O'BRYAN, AS ADMINISTRATRIX OF ORIAN O'BRYAN, APPELLANT, VS. THE STATE OF NEW YORK, RESPONDENT.

This claim was filed for the sum of $20,080 for damages for the death of Orian O'Bryan on May 13, 1909, caused, as is alleged, by the falling of a bridge known as Peeksport bridge over the old Chenango canal in the town of Eaton. The case was tried at Syracuse, February 10, 1910, and judgment of dismissal rendered by the Court of Claims. From this judgment claimant has appealed to the Appellate Division.

NEW ENGLAND BRICK COMPANY, APPELLANT, VS. THE STATE OF NEW YORK, RESPONDENT.

This claim was filed for the sum of $3,508 for damage to brick yard, loss of brick and material, damage to house and loss of rent in the town of Half Moon near Mechanicville, caused by the culvert which runs under the canal and through which the water of Hart Brook flows, to back up and damage claimant's property. The case was tried April, 1910, and a judgment of dismissal rendered by the Court of Claims. From this judgment an appeal has been taken to the Appellate Division.

HENRY MULLETT, APPELLANT, *vs.* THE STATE OF NEW YORK,
RESPONDENT.

This claim was filed for the sum of $19,095.50 for permanent
appropriation of 6.520 acres of land and buildings in Pendleton
for the purposes of the Barge Canal.   The claim was tried at
Buffalo, June 13, 1910, and a judgment of $4,375 rendered by
the Court of Claims.   From this judgment claimant has appealed
to the Appellate Division.

———

JOHN MULLETT, APPELLANT, *vs.* THE STATE OF NEW YORK,
RESPONDENT.

This claim was filed for the sum of $6,246 for permanent appro-
priation of 1.540 acres of land and buildings in the town of
Pendleton for the Barge Canal purposes.   The claim was tried
at Buffalo, June 13, 1910, and a judgment for $1,293.70 ren-
dered by the Court of Claims.   Claimant has appealed to the
Appellate Division.

———

KINSER CONSTRUCTION COMPANY, APPELLANT, *vs.* THE STATE
OF NEW YORK, RESPONDENT.

This claim was filed for the sum of $370,525.41 for damage
and loss arising from breach by the State of Barge Canal contract
No. 27, made November 23, 1906, Champlain Canal contract,
section 2, for excavating canal and protecting its sides, constructing locks Nos. 7 and 8 and junction lock, necessary spillways,
power plants and appertaining structures, concrete arch bridge,
structures, etc., between station 1046-16, the south end of contract 25 at Dunham's basin road and the Hudson river at Fort
Edward, station 1245, including alterations Nos. 1, 2, 3, 4 and 5,
made thereunder, and for damage suffered on account of stoppage
of work under said contract from December 24, 1908, to January
1, 1909.   The claim was tried at a session of the Court of Claims
held at Albany, April 21, 1910, and a judgment rendered November 9, 1910, for $77,425.46.   From this judgment the claimant
has appealed to the Appellate Division.

L. MINNIE JILLSON, APPELLANT, *vs.* THE STATE OF NEW YORK, RESPONDENT.

This claim was filed for the sum of $3,193.30 for permanent appropriation of 17 31/100 acres of land in the town of White-hall for Barge Canal purposes and for consequential damages arising from said appropriation. The claim was tried at Albany, October 18, 1908, and a judgment for $1,645.46 rendered. Claimant has appealed to the Appellate Division.

FREDERICK HILFINGER ET AL., APPELLANTS, *vs.* THE STATE OF NEW YORK, RESPONDENT.

This claim was filed for the sum of $10,000 for permanent appropriation of 1 42/100 acres of land in Fort Edward for the purposes of the Barge Canal. The claim was tried at Albany, April 18, 1910, and a judgment rendered by the Court of Claims for the sum of $3,073.30. Claimant has appealed to the Appellate Division.

MARY C. HUMPHREY, APPELLANT, *vs.* THE STATE OF NEW YORK, RESPONDENT.

This claim was filed for the sum of $22,943 for permanent appropriation of .2056 acres of land in North Tonawanda for Barge Canal purposes. The claim was tried at Albany, November 4, 1909, and a judgment of dismissal rendered. From this judgment claimant has appealed to the Appellate Division.

MARY M. WAITE ET AL., APPELLANTS, *vs.* THE STATE OF NEW YORK, RESPONDENT.

This claim for the sum of $8,782.55 was filed for permanent appropriation of 27 63/100 acres of land in the town of Fort Ann for the purposes of Barge Canal. The claim was tried at Albany, November 25, 1908, and a judgment for $3,040.82 rendered. Claimant has appealed to the Appellate Division.

HOMER SHAFFER ET AL., APPELLANTS, *vs.* THE STATE OF NEW YORK, RESPONDENT.

This claim was filed for the sum of $22,085.80 for permanent appropriation of 10 359/1000 acres of land, with buildings, in the city of Lockport, for Barge Canal purposes. The claim was tried at Buffalo, June 13, 1910, and a judgment for $6,629.74 rendered. From this judgment claimant has appealed to the Appellate Division.

ROBERT EARL, AS EXECUTOR OF ROBERT EARL, DECEASED, APPELLANT, *vs.* THE STATE OF NEW YORK, RESPONDENT.

This claim was filed to recover the sum of $27,000 for balance of salary of Robert Earl, late of the village of Herkimer, as Justice of the Court of Appeals. The claim was tried at Utica, March 15, 1909, and a judgment rendered by the Court of Claims for the sum of $2,845.48. From this judgment the claimant has appealed to the Appellate Division. The appeal was argued November 29, 1910, and the judgment of the Court of Claims affirmed December, 1910.

JANE B. JOHNSON, APPELLANT, *vs.* THE STATE OF NEW YORK, RESPONDENT.

This claim was filed for the sum of $2,357.55 for damages for a permanent appropriation of land in the town of Whitehall, for Barge Canal purposes. The claim was tried and a judgment rendered by the Court of Claims for the sum of $569.65. From this judgment the claimant has appealed to the Appellate Division. The appeal has not been argued.

ALBERT E. PERKINS ET AL., APPELLANTS, *vs.* THE STATE OF NEW YORK, RESPONDENT.

Two claims for the sum of $800 were filed by the above claimants, for damages to real estate and crops in the town of Sullivan, Madison county, by percolation from the Erie canal. The claims

were tried at Utica, March 15, 1909, and judgment of dismissal
rendered by the Court of Claims. From this judgment the claimants have appealed to the Appellate Division. The appeals have
not been argued.

ROBERT PARKER, APPELLANT, vs. THE STATE OF NEW YORK, RESPONDENT.

This claim was filed for the sum of $1,655 for damage to pasture
land and crops in the town of Kingsbury, Washington county,
caused by the overflow of the Champlain canal. The case was
tried at Albany in April, 1909, and a judgment of dismissal rendered by the Court of Claims. From this judgment the claimant
appealed to the Appellate Division, where the judgment of the
Court of Claims was unanimously affirmed.

TOWN OF WHITESTOWN, APPELLANT, vs. THE STATE OF NEW YORK, RESPONDENT.

This claim was filed for the sum of $8,745.52 for the destruc-
tion of an aqueduct bridge over Oriskany creek in the town of
Whitestown, caused by the alleged negligence of the State in allow-
.ing an ice gorge to form and damage the bridge. The claim was
tried at Utica, March, 1909, and a judgment of dismissal rendered.
From this judgment claimant has appealed to the Appellate Division. The case has not been argued.

HENRY M. TAFT, APPELLANT, vs. THE STATE OF NEW YORK, RESPONDENT.

The above claim was filed for the sum of $10,415, personal
injury alleged to have been sustained by the claimant while crossing the canal bridge in the village of Watervliet, on August 8,
1908. The claim was tried at Albany in April, 1909, and a judgment of dismissal entered. The claimant appealed to the Appellate
Division. The judgment of the Court of Claims was unanimously
affirmed.

FRANCES A. BROWN, APPELLANT, *vs.* THE STATE OF NEW YORK, RESPONDENT.

This claim was filed for the sum of $3,422.55 for the permanent appropriation of 9 29/100 acres of land in the town of Fort Ann, Washington county, for Barge Canal purposes, water privileges and damage to remainder of farm. The claim was tried at Albany, and judgment rendered November 15, 1909, for the sum of $603.85 damages, with interest in the sum of $96.62, making the total amount of said judgment $700.47. From this judgment claimant has appealed to the Appellate Division. The appeal has not been argued.

JOHN M. BUTLER AND ANOTHER, APPELLANTS, *vs.* THE STATE OF NEW YORK, RESPONDENT.

This claim was filed for $1,529.25, for the permanent appropriation of 32/100 acres of land in the town of Whitehall, Washington county, including water privileges and depreciation in value of remainder of said premises. The claim was tried at Albany and judgment rendered for the sum of $136 with interest, amounting in all to the sum of $159.84. From this judgment the claimant has appealed to the Appellate Division. The record on appeal has not been received.

FOR THE STATUS OF THE FOLLOWING CASES ON APPEAL SEE ATTORNEY-GENERAL'S REPORT 1908.

Edward R. Bartow, an Infant, by Guardian v. The State of New York.

Henry W. Matthews and Another v. The State of New York.

George H. Babcock v. The State of New York.

Long Island Railroad Company v. The State of New York.

Veronica Jaeschke v. The State of New York.

William G. Russell v. The State of New York.

A. Bleecker Banks v. The State of New York.

Mary May v. The State of New York.

Margaret Mulvihill v. The State of New York.

Annie M. Smith v. The State of New York.
Edward Lynch v. The State of New York.
William Fitzgerald v. The State of New York.
Harriet S. Fisher v. The State of New York.
Henry P. Burgard v. The State of New York.
W. Newton Bennington v. The State of New York.
Joseph Endries *et al* v. The State of New York.
Lucien H. Rowe v. The State of New York.
Abby J. Varney v. The State of New York.
Alfred A. Hunt v. The State of New York.
John Vogel v. The State of New York.
August Ruthenberg v. The State of New York.
Josephine A. Warner v. The State of New York.
Charles L. Briggs v. The State of New York.
John Harris v. The State of New York.
Alexander U. Mayer v. The State of New York.
Gertrude J. Harris as Executrix, etc. v. The State of New York.

COURT OF CLAIMS.

CANAL JUDGMENTS RECEIVED.

Albany Term, January 10, 1910:

		Amount claimed.	Awarded.
8063	Smith, Mortimer	$400 00	$125 00
8693	Abeel, Barney & Ano..	3,785 00	650 00
9127	Swatling, James H....	132 25	107 25
9167	Greene, Margaret E....	400 00	90 00
9168	Jones, Marvin A......	350 00	135 00
9479	Baird, Henry	885 00	140 00
9726	Burr, James S.......	168 00	140 00
9729	Pearse, Frank T......	80 00	25 00
9730	Ives, John H.........	120 00	29 00
9731	Lasher, George and another as administr's..	40 00	20 00
9733	Pearse, James C......	120 00	35 00
9734	Smith, William H.. ..	100 00	30 00

		Amount claimed.	Awarded.
9732	Lasher, George	$60 00	$20 00
9735	Hall, Roland	40 00	20 00
9747	Pender, Ellen	700 00	700 00

Syracuse Term, February 7, 1910:

6561	Barry, John & William.	300 00	Judgment for State
7533	Fuller, James K......	360 00	Judgment for State
8294	Fuller, James K......	720 00	Judgment for State
8017	Denman, Jesse F.....	600 00	Judgment for State
8905	Denman, Jesse F.....	600 00	Judgment for State
9199	Pickard, Henry	200 00	Judgment for State

Albany Term, April 18, 1910:

9669	Hayes, William D.....	$133 42	$133 42
9670	Eldridge, Adell L.....	133 42	133 42
9222	Bargy, Mary	125 00	55 00
9223	Boudry, William	310 00	120 00
9295	Sterling, Frank	240 00	80 00
9296	Johns, Ada	250 00	120 00
9385	Houck, John J. & Ano.	200 00	130 00
8276	Peck, Smith	200 00	20 00
8660	Jennings, Dwight P...	6,000 00	400 00
9197	Jones, Anna F........	200 00	175 00
9198	Peck, Smith	200 00	20 00
9202	McIntyre, Charles W...	300 00	20 00
9206	Fuller, James K......	600 00	80 00
9517	Houghtaling, Rachel E.	75 00	15 00
9518	Clifton, Lewis J......	360 00	75 00
9519	Graham, Charles F....	500 00	55 00
9635	Stolusky, Jacob & Ano.	631 25	90 00
8273	Deming, Hugh	105 00	20 00
8920	Needham, Arthur	300 00	50 00
8922	Pike, John M. & Ano..	500 00	100 00
8923	Deming, Hugh	75 00	20 00
8939	Fenton, Charles S.....	200 00	45 00
8267	Voorhees, James, et al..	5,156 91	2,636 91
9181	Curtin, James J......	1,600 00	90 00

		Amount claimed.	Awarded.
9428	Parrish, Frank	$150 00	$20 00
9211	Grimes, John	158 00	98 00

Buffalo Term, June 13, 1910:

8817	Pronoth, William	500 00	150 00
7272	Fenaughty, Margaret ..	825 00	400 00
9186	Pronoth, William......	450 00	75 00
9545	Vail, Helen M........	2,462 90	160 00
9571	Gerlach, Andrew W. and another	503 00	400 00
9588	Holtz, Lipman........	199 00	199 00
9678	Launan, James........	60 00	45 00
9705	Mullet, John..........	57 20	29 98
9707	Mullet, Henry........	244 40	135 23
9714	Lenhart, George and another	111 20	104 82
9771	Emens, Lilla Alice.....	262 00	100 00
9789	Van De Water, Cornelius	196 60	107 50
9791	Manley, Frank........	138 10	85 00
9792	Nellis, Carl H........	80 00	40 00
9794	Pettengill, Walter T. and another........	196 60	107 50
9795	Bauer, Christopher....	134 05	68 00
9938	Pronoth, William......	450 00	75 00

Syracuse Term, July 25, 1910:

8726	Buffalo, Rochester & Pittsburgh Railway Company	4,722 72	1,555 77
9496	Lynn, Thomas M......	514 10	350 00
9530	Cowles, Horace N.....	21,582 60	1,440 02
9587	Chism, Charles J......	187 75	193 94
9717	Seefried, Katherine, et al	131 43	105 40
9751	Stevens, Charles.......	1,004 50	114 50
9796	Lynn, Thomas M......	420 00	250 00

		Amount claimed.	Awarded.

Albany Term, September 26, 1910:

9592	Lent, George B......	$300 00	$119 68
9566	Hardy, William.......	1,510 00	330 00
9567	Worthing, Charles E...	65 00	65 00
9790	Allen, Claude H.......	197 64	110 00
9793	Nellis, Minnie E......	146 20	100 00
9950	Josephs, Jessie M.....	626 00	50 00

Rochester Term, October 17, 1910:

9649	New England Brick Co.	3,508 00 Judgment for State
9591	Lent, John H.........	1,650 00	$1,200 00
7937	Kline, Jay B.........	1,500 00 Judgment for State

ROCHESTER CANAL BRIDGE ASSESSMENT CASES.

5441	Schwab, Bernard......	$42 33 Judgment for State
5442	Schwab, Bernard, Ind. and as Exec........	88 79 Judgment for State
5448	Fuchs, Jacob........	14 52 Judgment for State
5449	Kubel, John.........	37 50 Judgment for State
5450	Lazier, Lewis B.......	37 50 Judgment for State
5458	Hanvey, Mary J., and another..........	101 96 Judgment for State
5459	Hanvey, Mary J., and others............	29 69 Judgment for State
5481	Hargather, Peter R....	28 81 Judgment for State
5482	Hargather, Lewis......	30 93 Judgment for State
5483	Knapp, John........	23 46 Judgment for State
5455	Pond, Mary E........	33 75 Judgment for State
5457	Newell, Frank G., and another..........	2,140 99 Judgment for State
5471	Whitney, James W., as Ex., etc...........	638 83 Judgment for State
5472	Parsons Malting Co., E. B..............	372 29 Judgment for State
5762	Parsons, Augusta B....	30 37 Judgment for State
5473	Searle, Harriet E., et al.	44 25 Judgment for State
5763	Reynolds, Leale C.....	18 76 Judgment for State

		Amount claimed.	Awarded
546S	Whalen, John L. as Ad.	$34 13	Judgment for Stat
5479	Chapin, Amelia W.....	106 47	Judgment for Stat.
5631	Meyerhoff, George E...	128 22	Judgment for State
5644	Normalie, Henry et al..	46 88	Judgment for State
5480	Hutchinson, H. M. S...	130 67	Judgment for State
5484	Warner, Andrew J.....	1,701 02	Judgment for State
5486	Alliance Bank........	41 74	Judgment for State
5496	Bellew, John.........	58 06	Judgment for State
5501	Bicknell, Dudley J. C..	126 11	Judgment for State
5505	Bowman, Catherine E..	30 64	Judgment for State
5506	Bradt, James.........	39 52	Judgment for State
5507	Brady, Gilbert........	1,520 65	Judgment for Sta'
5526	Casey, Ann..........	40 07	Judgment for State
5528	Plymouth Church.....	96 00	Judgment for State
5529	Clark, Daniel et another as Adm...........	474 29	Judgment for State
5532	Connell, James........	61 15	Judgment for State
5533	Conway, John as Ex...	73 39	Judgment for State
5535	Copeland & Durgan Co.	900 28	Judgment for State
5537	Cowley, Edward A....	53 28	Judgment for State
5545	Daus, Mathew........	119 50	Judgment for State
5548	Dougherty, Elizabeth...	73 50	Judgment for State
5551	Dransfield, Thomas....	100 39	Judgment for State
5552	Durand, F. L.........	38 44	Judgment for State
5562	Frank, Jacob.........	37 33	Judgment for State
5557	Ertel, John..........	57 15	Judgment for State
5564	Friederich, John J. L. and another	102 69	Judgment for State
5565	Garrison, John........	42 18	Judgment for State
5569	Gerling, Jacob........	115 64	Judgment for State
5576	Greenwood, John......	43 01	Judgment for State
5577	Grace, Jennie........	38 11	Judgment for State
5580	Hallowell, Mary H....	56 26	Judgment for State
5581	Hardwood Lumber Co..	1,587 07	Judgment for State
5582	Hart, James C........	102 69	Judgment for State
5585	Heddich, Henry.......	118 08	Judgment for State
5586	Herschel, Emeline.....	55 85	Judgment for State

		Amount claimed.	Awarded.
5592	Howard, John.......	$38 43	Judgment for State
5593	Howard, John E. and another..........	63 57	Judgment for State
5595	Sill Stove Works......	392 71	Judgment for State
5597	Huck, Albert.........	52 50	Judgment for State
5598	Huck, Elizabeth H....	52 50	Judgment for State
5605	Kannan, Catherine C...	39 13	Judgment for State
5609	Knobles, Joseph W....	30 12	Judgment for State
5610	Knobles, Joseph W. as Adm............	43 10	Judgment for State
5611	Konath, Gottlief and another.............	87 08	Judgment for State
5612	Kondolf, Mathias......	513 78	Judgment for State
5627	McCormick, Katherine C...............	46 06	Judgment for State
5629	McIntyre, Katherine...	109 45	Judgment for State
5633	Miller, Frederick......	90 30	Judgment for State
5634	Mogridge, John.......	241 26	Judgment for State
5640	Muhl, Christina.......	65 36	Judgment for State
5643	Normilee, Henry......	73 86	Judgment for State
5655	Peacock, John V. and another..........	593 20	Judgment for State
5658	Potter, Charles B.....	44 65	Judgment for State
5659	Powers, John C. and others............	57 15	Judgment for State
5660	Flower City Hotel Co..	57 86	Judgment for State
5661	Pridmore, Joseph O....	37 55	Judgment for State
5664	Rau, Gustavus........	79 33	Judgment for State
5667	Roche, Rosa M........	129 18	Judgment for State
5668	Rochester Gas & Electric Company..........	204 95	Judgment for State
5672	Rowley, Caroline R. and others...........	46 88	Judgment for State
5673	Rowley, Caroline R....	42 33	Judgment for State
5676	Ryan, Roger..........	46 88	Judgment for State
5678	Savage, Morris........	40 36	Judgment for State
5677	Sanderson, George T...	46 83	Judgment for State

		Amount claimed.	Awarded.
5714	Willis, Sarah L......	$67 87	Judgment for State
5715	Woodruff, Thomas.....	67 61	Judgment for State
5683	Sheridan, Ann........	223 46	Judgment for State
5693	St. Patrick's Church Society............	112 78	Judgment for State
5697	Swikehard, George B...	47 61	Judgment for State
5699	Nazareth Convent and Academy, The......	88 40	Judgment for State
5700	N. Y. C. & H. R. R. R. Co..............	2,883 63	Judgment for State
5704	Vahue, Ezra F. and another............	41 50	Judgment for State
5705	Van Ingen, John A....	152 77	Judgment for State
5706	Vogler, Fredricka.....	118 17	Judgment for State
5782	Fitzsimmons, Michael H...............	42 74	Judgment for State
5485	Allen, Nora A........	66 95	Judgment for State
5488	Attridge, Eliza and others...........	16 60	Judgment for State
5489	Auer, Anna B. as Ex..	35 76	Judgment for State
5499	Bennett, Cyrus R......	13 31	Judgment for State
5502	Blackwood, Henry D...	15 72	Judgment for State
5503	Blumingstock, Fredericka...........	22 36	Judgment for State
5504	Bour, Catherine......	30 00	Judgment for State
5521	Burns, Mary A. and another as Adm......	5 14	Judgment for State
5527	Chappel, James M. et al	45 15	Judgment for State
5534	Corey, E. T.........	9 85	Judgment for State
5536	Cochefer, Richard.....	9 86	Judgment for State
5541	Curtis, Josiah........	13 67	Judgment for State
5543	Daley, Mary.........	10 08	Judgment for State
5544	Damon, Edmund J. as Executor.........	5 09	Judgment for State
5555	Ely, Caroline L.......	106 03	Judgment for State
5561	Fox, Ada and another.	19 99	Judgment for State
5563	Fraser, Mary et another.	11 00	Judgment for State

		Amount claimed.	Awarded.
5570	Giles, Martin J......	$11 00	Judgment for State
5571	Gillette, Sarah C......	11 00	Judgment for State
5587	Heusler, John........	21 57	Judgment for State
5588	Hills, Isaac..........	85 50	Judgment for State
5589	Hingst, Richard A. as Adm...............	8 50	Judgment for State
5591	Hopwood, Sarah R....	8 29	Judgment for State
5594	Howe, Mary and another	5 44	Judgment for State
5599	Hulbert, Isabella......	16 31	Judgment for State
5601	Hyde, D. C..........	5 30	Judgment for State
5613	Larsen, Elias T.......	22 29	Judgment for State
5614	Larsen, Georgiana.....	21 43	Judgment for State
5619	Loomis, John B.......	21 98	Judgment for State
5618	Lick, Elizabeth.......	16 90	Judgment for State
5623	Marson, William H....	17 66	Judgment for State
5628	McCormick, Dennis....	12 25	Judgment for State
5630	Messenger, Mary A....	8 58	Judgment for State
5632	Miller, Anthony J.....	7 90	Judgment for State
5635	Monroe, County of....	66 00	Judgment for State
5636	Montgomery, James H. and others.........	39 04	Judgment for State
5638	Mosher, Caroline A....	10 39	Judgment for State
5639	Murphy, Mary........	11 36	Judgment for State
5650	Oliver, Peter and another	10 50	Judgment for State
5651	Kane, John O........	12 97	Judgment for State
5654	Patterson, Sophia.....	6 32	Judgment for State
5662	Purdy, Frederick E....	4 91	Judgment for State
5665	Ries, John G. and another	12 07	Judgment for State
5666	Riley, A. W. and another as Exrs.......	33 00	Judgment for State
5671	Rogers, P. H........	7 51	Judgment for State
5686	Smith, Ella P.......	11 77	Judgment for State
5687	Spaith, Kathrina......	5 13	Judgment for State
5688	Spencer, Sarah M. and another	8 26	Judgment for State

		Amount claimed.	Awarded.
5691	Stonewall, Matilda T..	$2 25	Judgment for State
5692	Storer, Charles.......	24 12	Judgment for State
5698	Taylor, Thomas B. as Adm...........	7 04	Judgment for State
5702	Tower, William J.....	9 83	Judgment for State
5765	O'Loughlin, Michael...	26 10	Judgment for State
5766	Fay, Maria L.........	13 00	Judgment for State
5767	Melvin, Edward A. and others.......	16 18	Judgment for State
5487	Anderson, Jessie E....	38 89	Judgment for State
5491	Avery, Jennie Frame as Adm...........	17 19	Judgment for State
5492	Ayres, Fred as Ex.....	7 10	Judgment for State
5493	Bassett, Margaret H. et al.............	112 31	Judgment for State
5494	Bauman, Mary A.....	83 75	Judgment for State
5498	Bernish, Elizabeth as Adm...........	7 73	Judgment for State
5500	Bernhardt, Adam......	59 68	Judgment for State
5508	Brayer, Elizabeth as Ex.	3 57	Judgment for State
5509	Brown, Esther J. as Ex..	14 57	Judgment for State
5510	Brown, Katherine as Adm...........	93 59	Judgment for State
5511	Brown, Mary A. as Adm	5 84	Judgment for State
5512	Brown, Mary as Ex...	23 96	Judgment for State
5513	Brown, Robert B. and another as Exrs.....	116 38	Judgment for State
5514	Brown, William C. as Ex.............	39 02	Judgment for State
5515	Bauer, William H. as Adm...........	127 55	Judgment for State
5516	Buckley, Mary E. as Adm...........	5 26	Judgment for State
5517	Buell, George C. as Ex.	35 91	Judgment for State
5518	Buff, Pauline as Ex....	9 48	Judgment for State
5519	Burnham, Caroline A..	27 07	Judgment for State
5520	Burkhard, John as Adm	8 98	Judgment for State

		Amount claimed.	Awarded.
5523	Campbell, John H. as Ex.	$215 35	Judgment for State
5524	Campbell, John H. as Ex.	18 10	Judgment for State
5525	Campbell, Mary.......	3 85	Judgment for State
5530	Kline, J. B. as Ex.....	114 75	Judgment for State
5531	Cone, Clara P. as Adm.	3 86	Judgment for State
5538	Crombie, Hannah as Ex.	5 00	Judgment for State
5539	Curtain, James F. and another	46 82	Judgment for State
5540	Curtain, Margaret M..	112 39	Judgment for State
5546	Derrick, Timothy as Adm.............	·11 00	Judgment for State
5553	Ehrstein, Catherine....	9 57	Judgment for State
5556	Emerson, Sarah L. as Adm.	304 59	Judgment for State
5558	Fagan, Susan as Ex...	6 39	Judgment for State
5559	Finley, Elizabeth as Ex.	7 61	Judgment for State
5560	Fisher, Jacobina as Adm	62 02	Judgment for State
5567	Gaylord, Mary E. and another as Ex.......	6 94	Judgment for State
5568	Geddes, Margaret B. as Adm.............	303 35	Judgment for State
5572	Glasser, Frank C. as Ex.	42 58	Judgment for State
5573	Glenn, Sarah A. and another as Ex........	135 46	Judgment for State
5574	Gomeginger, Edward as Adm.............	9 88	Judgment for State
5575	Goodman, Daniel as Ex.	9 48	Judgment for State
5578	Guibel, Barbara.......	31 26	Judgment for State
5579	Haines, Anna J. and another as Ex.........	9 89	Judgment for State
5583	Hanvey, Joseph A. and another	39 76	Judgment for State
5584	Heywood, Emily S. as Ex.	8 02	Judgment for State

		Amount claimed:	Awarded.
5590	Hoffman, George F. as Ex.	$14 23	Judgment for State
5596	Hubachuck, Helene as Ex.	15 91	Judgment for State
5600	Husband, Thomas II. as Ex.	10 07	Judgment for State
5602	Hyde, II. as Ex.	193 14	Judgment for State
5604	Judson, J. Lee as Adm.	90 70	Judgment for State
5606	Kane, James E. as Adm.	3 88	Judgment for State
5607	Keegan, Arthur as Ex.	13 56	Judgment for State
5608	Kelly, J. Miller as Ex.	42 00	Judgment for State
5615	Leary, Herbert and another as Ex.	518 30	Judgment for State
5616	Lee, Pauline B.	13 02	Judgment for State
5617	Lehman, Gertrude as Adm.	62 19	Judgment for State
5620	O'Loughlin, Ellen as Ex	15 69	Judgment for State
5621	Mackwood, Robert as Adm.	22 21	Judgment for State
5622	McMahon, Anna as Adm	49 68	Judgment for State
5624	Mathews, Mary E. as Adm.	93 78	Judgment for State
5626	McClellan, Amelia J. as Adm.	25 94	Judgment for State
5637	Montgomery, Thomas C. and another as Ex.	15 42	Judgment for State
5646	O'Connell, Mary A. as Adm.	39 75	Judgment for State
5647	O'Connor, Anna as Ex.	8 47	Judgment for State
5648	O'Hara, Thomas A. as Adm.	7 84	Judgment for State
5649	Oldfield, Nicholas as Ex.	7 37	Judgment for State
5652	O'Reilly, Miles F. as Ex	79 56	Judgment for State
5657	Pillow, Edward F. as Adm.	13 44	Judgment for State
5663	Ratcliffe, Bertha A. and another	70 91	Judgment for State

		Amount claimed.	Awarded.
5670	Koehler, Barbara as Ex.	$15 78	Judgment for State
5674	Rothfretz, Louisa as Ex.	5 07	Judgment for State
5675	Reef, John as Ex......	2 10	Judgment for State
5679	Shafer, Charles F. et al.	104 73	Judgment for State
5680	Schuey, John N......	17 82	Judgment for State
5682	Seward, William R....	5,817 59	Judgment for State
5684	Liener, Kathrine as Ex.	8 09	Judgment for State
5685	Slattery, Anna as Adm.	8 99	Judgment for State
5689	Stoeckline, Martin as Adm.............	26 03	Judgment for State
5690	Stone, Jennie F. as Adm	5 42	Judgment for State
5694	Strausser, Elizabeth as Ex..............	63 00	Judgment for State
5695	Stride, Elizabeth Cannon as Adm........	118 76	Judgment for State
5696	Sweatman, Charles as Ex..............	66 67	Judgment for State
5701	Toppel, Louisa B......	17 13	Judgment for State
5707	Wagner, Emma L. as Adm............	11 00	Judgment for State
5708	Wehn, Louis W. as Ex..	195 30	Judgment for State
5709	Wehn, Lewis W. as Ex..	26 23	Judgment for State
5711	Whalen, James and another as Ex........	25 08	Judgment for State
5712	White, Mary J. as Adm.	29 01	Judgment for State
5713	Williamson, Martin F. as Adm.	106 32	Judgment for State
5716	Zeerele, Peter W. and another as Ex......	71 47	Judgment for State
5717	Zimmer, John F. as Adm.............	14 67	Judgment for State
5764	Edilman, Lewis as Ex..	28 11	Judgment for State
5780	Barrow, Martin	21 59	Judgment for State
5781	McEneny, John H. as Ex.	92 36	Judgment for State
5490	Austin, A. Judson....	9 22	Judgment for State

		Amount claimed.	Awarded.
5495	Bellew, Esther C. and another	$53| 62	Judgment for State
5497	Bellew, John	33 06	Judgment for State
5549	Dransfield, Elizabeth B.	42 33	Judgment for State
5550	Dransfield Thomas, as Ex.	26 25	Judgment for State
5603	Immel, Joseph, and another.	87 60	Judgment for State
5522	Callister, William D. and another	214 35	Judgment for State
5547	Denny, Agnes	37 28	Judgment for State
5554	Elliott, William H.....	7 82	Judgment for State
5641	Muhl, Ada A.........	2,140 99	Judgment for State
5656	Peoples, James A. et al.	27 37	Judgment for State
5669	Rochester Trust & Safe Deposit Co.	2,140 99	Judgment for State
5681	Searle, Ella R........	2,140 99	Judgment for State
5703	Uffleman, George P....	66 73	Judgment for State
5710	Westcott, Mary J. et al.	26 72	Judgment for State
5718	Zimmer, Catherine	45 08	Judgment for State
5566	Gavin, Michael	22 44	Judgment for State
5653	Otis, E. S. and others..	336 51	Judgment for State
5721	Bechtold, Henry	9 70	Judgment for State
5722	Buch, George L. and another.	54 25	Judgment for State
5723	Casey, James W......	94 58	Judgment for State
5724	Chamberlain, Jane	88 43	Judgment for State
5725	Churchill, William W. as Ex.	50 21	Judgment for State
5726	Curtis, Eugene F. as Ex.	28 80	Judgment for State
5727	Eastman, Emily J....	18 66	Judgment for State
5728	Ernst, Philip	9 32	Judgment for State
5729	Frost, Henry C. as Ex.	33 75	Judgment for State
5730	Frost, Sarah as Ex....	46 88	Judgment for State
5731	Fuchs, Katherine	9 67	Judgment for State
5732	Goetzman, Elizabeth ..	22 30	Judgment for State

		Amount claimed.	Awarded.
5733	Golzman, Henry W. and another	$9 50	Judgment for State
5734	Gorsline, William H...	656 00	Judgment for State
5735	Hoag, John as Ex.....	43 02	Judgment for State
5736	Hannan, John W......	4,469 31	Judgment for State
5737	Hannan, Mary E......	4,469 31	Judgment for State
5738	Hess, Helen M.......	58 94	Judgment for State
5739	Hoff, Margaret	23 42	Judgment for State
5740	Hollister, George C. as Ex..............	28 25	Judgment for State
5741	Hollister, George C. and another...........	38 23	Judgment for State
5742	Jennings, Nancy B....	58 20	Judgment for State
5743	Keener, John as Ex....	371 67	Judgment for State
5744	Kreft, Ludwig	9 71	Judgment for State
5745	Lee, Pauline B.......	13 02	Judgment for State
5746	Matthews, Elizabeth G.	49 50	Judgment for State
5747	McAlpine, Susan P....	53 48	Judgment for State
5748	Oyman, Augusta	10 38	Judgment for State
5749	Perkins, Gilman N. as Ex..............	118 49	Judgment for State
5750	Post, Jacob K.......	33 50	Judgment for State
5751	Rochester, John H....	74 22	Judgment for State
5752	Sage, Edwin O.......	85 28	Judgment for State
5753	Willis, Harriet S. as Ex.	22 50	Judgment for State
5754	Sage, W. L. Ex.......	79 15	Judgment for State
5755	Smith, Anna, as Adm..	119 53	Judgment for State
5756	Snow, H. Emily A....	29 25	Judgment for State
5757	Wehle, Caspar	10 71	Judgment for State
5758	Wick, Christine	26 36	Judgment for State
5759	Woodward, Homer H..	6 89	Judgment for State
5760	Youle, Oliver A.......	8 77	Judgment for State
5761	Zipkie, John	17 53	Judgment for State
5768	Brewster, H. Austin...	55 59	Judgment for State
5778	Klem, Michael and another.	83 58	Judgment for State

		Amount claimed.	Awarded.

Syracuse Term, November 14, 1910:

8766	Pfeifer, Peter and another	$1,500 00	$250 00
9679	Huston, Louis E.	1,500 00	1,065 00
9972	Lockport Leather Board Co.	584 29	232 25

BLACK RIVER CLAIMS.

8420	Andre, Stephen	$625 00 Judgment for State
8421	Altmire, Nicholas	1,201 80 Judgment for State
8422	Blade, Charles A	798 00 Judgment for State
8423	Bintz, Nicholas C	1,078 00 Judgment for State
8424	Brown, Irving D.	1,580 00 Judgment for State
8425	Dean, William E	728 00 Judgment for State
8426	Brown, Lyman W. and another	2,567 00 Judgment for State
8427	Bliss, Albert J	4,894 00 Judgment for State
8428	Burrington, Alvin	10,831 00 Judgment for State
8429	Boshart, Albert C.	1,336 50 Judgment for State
8430	Burdick, George A	1,961 00 Judgment for State
8431	Beyer, Peter	646 50 Judgment for State
8432	Beck, Aaron L.	632 50 Judgment for State
8433	Back, Nicholas	869 40 Judgment for State
8434	Bachmann, Frederick E.	506 00 Judgment for State
8435	Bachman, William C.	1,268 00 Judgment for State
8436	Cummins, James W.	942 00 Judgment for State
8437	Cropsey, Edward J	2,251 00 Judgment for State
8438	Culbertson, Robert	211 00 Judgment for State
8439	Clark, Eugene S. et al.	1,240 00 Judgment for State
8440	Crouse, Edward L	222 50 Judgment for State
8441	Dawley, Clark D. and another	1,800 50 Judgment for State
8442	Ebersol, Joseph E	1,240 00 Judgment for State
8443	Ellis, Christian R	1,565 00 Judgment for State
8444	Farney, A. R.	1,317 00 Judgment for State
8445	Fenton, John B	1,175 00 Judgment for State
8446	Farney, Le Roy V	10,127 96 Judgment for State

		Amount claimed.	Awarded.
8447	Farney, Otto J.......	$843 00	Judgment for State
8448	Farney, Benjamin F...	491 50	Judgment for State
8449	Farrar, John E.......	3,186 00	Judgment for State
8450	Feisthamel, Pauline ..	625 00	Judgment for State
8451	Farney, Joseph S.....	2,811 24	Judgment for State
8452	Goetremont, Lena	754 00	Judgment for State
8453	Gazine, John L.......	731 92	Judgment for State
8454	Ganzel, Lewis	950 00	Judgment for State
8455	Hirschey, Joseph	4,430 00	Judgment for State
8456	Howard, John	3,830 00	Judgment for State
8457	Hirschey, John C.....	1,232 00	Judgment for State
8458	House, J. H. ,.......	5,550 00	Judgment for State
8459	Hanno, Christopher ...	334 00	Judgment for State
8460	Honer, John M.	630 00	Judgment for State
8461	Hirschey, William	4,514 00	Judgment for State
8462	Koster, Albert D.....	474 00	Judgment for State
8463	Klein, Claude	1,119 00	Judgment for State
8464	Linstruth, Henry and another	2,788 00	Judgment for State
8465	Lomber, George P.....	415 00	Judgment for State
8466	Loson, Joseph	986 00	Judgment for State
8467	Lomber, John	477 00	Judgment for State
8468	Lomber, Lewis	669 80	Judgment for State
8469	Merz, William	759 50	Judgment for State
8470	Myers, Maria A.	622 70	Judgment for State
8471	Meeker, Harriett C....	450 00	Judgment for State
8472	Monnatt, Francis	1,401 00	Judgment for State
8473	Meister, Morris	4,700 00	Judgment for State
8474	Melnitz, Charles	930 00	Judgment for State
8475	Miller, Anthony	655 50	Judgment for State
8476	Noftsier, Christopher C.	624 00	Judgment for State
8477	Otis, R. C.	857 85	Judgment for State
8478	Petzoldt, Amos F.....	353 50	Judgment for State
8479	Petrie, Edwin J......	311 00	Judgment for State
8480	Rogers, Henry F.....	1,264 00	Judgment for State
8481	Riffanacht, Joseph	346 50	Judgment for State
8482	Rogers, Louisa H.....	416 00	Judgment for State

		Amount claimed.		Awarded.
8483	Rogers, Fred	$1,445	00	Judgment for State
8484	Briggs, C. W.	704	00	Judgment for State
8485	Wilder, Seth	2,241	00	Judgment for State
8486	Riffanacht, John	6,250	00	Judgment for State
8487	Rohr, Christian M....	3,078	00	Judgment for State
8488	Rubar, Charles	625	00	Judgment for State
8489	Snyder, Charles W....	2,005	00	Judgment for State
8490	Schorge, John C......	508	00	Judgment for State
8491	Stiles, Francis D......	3,636	00	Judgment for State
8492	Studer, Eliza A......	3,790	00	Judgment for State
8493	Schantz, Christopher R.	7,029	12	Judgment for State
8494	Slaid, George T. Exec., etc.	1,202	00	Judgment for State
8495	Snyder, Henry B.....	1,729	00	Judgment for State
8496	Simpson, Emma L....	625	00	Judgment for State
8497	Shea, Martin	8,235	00	Judgment for State
8498	Singer, Fred	586	00	Judgment for State
8499	Tyner, Truman J.....	992	00	Judgment for State
8500	Townsend, Ingham D..	16,555	00	Judgment for State
8501	Talbot, Michael	2,387	00	Judgment for State
8502	Tisse, John U........	566	00	Judgment for State
8503	Thompson, John	2,852	00	Judgment for State
8504	Thompson, William ...	1,188	50	Judgment for State
8505	Tafel, Ferdinand	1,102	00	Judgment for State
8506	Virkler, Joshua J.....	2,181	00	Judgment for State
8507	Virkler, Michael B. Exec., etc.	4,348	50	Judgment for State
8508	Virkler, Sidney	1,170	00	Judgment for State
8509	Virkler, Michael B....	5,939	00	Judgment for State
8510	Virkler, Jesse H.	5,018	00	Judgment for State
8511	Van Amber, Melville W.	6,871	00	Judgment for State
8512	Wildrick, Joseph	1,122	50	Judgment for State
8513	Wagner, John	1,153	00	Judgment for State
8514	Wetmore, Henry	1,970	00	Judgment for State
8515	Walseman, Frederick W.	2,234	00	Judgment for State

		Amount claimed.	Awarded.
8516	Werner, Herman C. and another	$1,499 00	Judgment for State
8517	Wetmore, Charles E...	525 00	Judgment for State
8518	.Wagner, Charles N....	330 00	Judgment for State
8519	Walseman, William ...	7,487 00	Judgment for State
8520	Wetmore, Jacob	1,885 00	Judgment for State
8521	Zahn, Augusta	1,575 00	Judgment for State
8522	Zecher, William	734 00	Judgment for State
8526	Boshart, C. Fred et al..	8,750 00	Judgment for State
8542	Boshart, Frank E.....	1,302 00	Judgment for State
8543	Boshart, Frank E.....	1,939 50	Judgment for State
8544	Bassett, Charles M....	4,881 00	Judgment for State
8545	Boshart, C. Fred and another	2,100 00	Judgment for State
8546	Bostwick, Adele P. et al.	4,348 00	Judgment for State
8547	Boshart, Clara A......	2,190 00	Judgment for State
8548	Easton, Frederick S. Adm., etc.	1,254 00	Judgment for State
8549	Einbeck, Henry	4,548 00	Judgment for State
8550	Farrar, Harvey D.....	4,563 00	Judgment for State
8551	Hopel, Libbie	2,808 00	Judgment for State
8552	Heimhilger, Lydia	620 00	Judgment for State
8553	Jacques, Fred C......	1,039 94	Judgment for State
8554	Koster, Florence L. et al.	11,010 00	Judgment for State
8555	Linstruth, Philip	1,320 00	Judgment for State
8556	Melnitz, Carrie	968 00	Judgment for State
8557	Merz, Charles	2,818 00	Judgment for State
8558	Moselle, Elizabeth	961 00	Judgment for State
8559	McGowan, A. H.	758 00	Judgment for State
8560	Northman, Henry C. Ex..............	1,240 00	Judgment for State
8561	Ossont, Peter	668 00	Judgment for State
8562	Peckham, F. R.	2,046 00	Judgment for State
8563	Pridell, Wesley C.....	2,039 00	Judgment for State
8564	Pelton, Charles E.....	11,057 28	Judgment for State
8565	Rohr, Samuel	5,352 00	Judgment for State
8566	Studer, John	1,201 00	Judgment for State

		Amount claimed.	Awarded.
8567	Streiff, John	$919 00	Judgment for State
8568	Salmon, X. Wells	7,774 00	Judgment for State
8569	Schorge, Fred A......	499 00	Judgment for State
8570	Tyner, George	845 00	Judgment for State
8571	Virkler, Christian F...	6,771 00	Judgmentfor State
8572	Ver Schneider, Elizabeth	880 00	Judgment for State
8573	West, Emma H. and another	8,311 00	Judgment for State
8574	Williams, Abiah D....	5,377 50	Judgment for State
8575	Wetmore, Andrew J....	655 00	Judgment for State
8576	Beach, John L........	1,550 00	Judgment for State
8579	Lomber, Magdalena ...	308 00	Judgment for State
8580	Nye, B. Frank........	810 00	Judgment for State
8611	Lehman, Simon F.....	411 00	Judgment for State
8638	Genzel, John	5,605 00	Judgment for State
8639	Hanschen, Martin	650 00	Judgment for State
9211	Grimes, John	158 00	Judgment for State

BARGE CANAL JUDGMENTS RECEIVED.

9301	Brett, George B. et al..	$3,500 00	$2,325 70
8979	Ryan, John	4,938 95	594 58
9076	Greene, Margaret E. et al.	12,244 20	3,441 79
9175	Warehouse & Realty Co. and another	12,000 00	6,207 00
9401	Holman, Chauncey J...	4,032 65	2,475 46
8165	Murray, John	1,700 00	1,371 51
8289	Rice, George	625 00	385 70
8358	Lewis, Sarah A. et al...	395 00	273 92
8415	Tosh, Henry	1,538 45	231 96
8417	Sperry, Fanny M.	525 00	319 13
8418	Bennett, Lewis M.	1,864 49	1,507 75
8631	Peterson, Schuyler	1,228 16	547 69
8928	Carpenter, Frank F. and another	21,584 55	7,676 50
8933	Allen, Frank H. and another	4,437 55	1,780 50

		Amount claimed.	Awarded.
8950	Van Buren, Cora et al..	$2,054 55	$602 75
8964	Emery, Mary P. Ind. and as Ex. of Thos. Van Buren	2,190 20	949 60
8974	Taft, Henry C. and another	4,473 55	1,198 19
8996	Blaisdell, Walter P. and another	4,622 55	1,233 94
8997	Jackson, James H.....	1,073 55	801 25
9021	Maxwell, Robert	17,742 10	1,314 12
9050	Griffin, Amos K. and another	1,912 55	405 24
9058	Graham, William L....	7,752 55	2,655 30
9274	Bailey, Anna S. and another	16,527 55	3,137 46
9283	Bruen, John and another	3,884 55	1,095 28
8718	Smead, Aquilla	7,213 55	2,423 00
8801	Wheeler, Mary et al....	1,829 55	846 18
8929	Schocke, Henry	1,194 55	615 00
8954	Bascom, Mary E. et al..	1,044 55	90 67
8961	Peters, Roxanna L.....	6,829 55	1,571 48
9099	Wells, Beecher	4,587 50	350 00
9132	Daley, Patrick B. and another	21,314 55	3,704 51
9217	Waite, Mary M. et al..	8,782 55	3,040 82
9218	Needham, Arthur J. and another	5,979 55	3,082 97
9723	Wells, Beecher	8,000 00	350 00
8757	De Lora, Josephine ...	1,689 55	1,450 60
8767	De Lora, Josephine ...	4,269 55	2,538 55
8771	Bebo, Mary et al......	7,339 55	2,846 81
8832	Trumpfo, James and another	3,860 20	286 04
8872	La More, Peter, Jr....	1,479 55	725 30
8975	Simmons, Stephen A., Sr. and another.....	1,044 55	212 10
9347	Donnelly, Mary A.....	1,200 00	362 65

		Amount claimed.	Awarded.
9856	Campbell, Frank, Inc., Pers., by Guard.....	$1,250 00	$1,334 79
9100	Dickinson, Ashley	1,545 00	150 00
8249	Burchard, Mary W....	4,500 00	1,297 50
9136	Wright, Charles T. and another	35,700 00	15,977 70
9720	Groton Bridge Company	8,588 63	Judgment for State
9784	Moroney, Martin J....	3,004 50	Judgment for State
9044	Powell, Ida M.........	4,828 55	826 71
9101	Champlain Stone & Sand Co.	224,412 57	1,170 83
9113	Bartholomew, Alanson D. et al	3,793 95	2,080 05
9306	Flanigan, Alice	41,860 00	7,596 29
9336	Miller, Cora A........	1,541 95	1,086 83
9364	Hitchcock, Charles H. and another	523 95	Judgment for State
9540	Humphrey, Mary C...	22,943 00	Judgment for State
9541	Miller, John B. et al...	25,000 00	Judgment for State
9708	Mullet, John	6,246 00	1,293 70
9712	Lenhart, George and another	9,399 30	2,022 52
9716	Mullet, Henry	19,095 50	4,375 00
9719	Shaffer, Homer et al...	22,085 80	6,629 74
9888	Lureman, Charles	4,183 10	703 18
9891	Art, Adam as Exr., etc.	7,415 00	1,538 97
9978	Dornfeld, William	2,528 40	1,802 47
9979	Dornfeld, Albert and another as Exrs.....	2,111 50	1,189 53
9887	Lureman, Charles	136 50	77 91
9388	Davison, Robert D. and another	4,456 35	1,250 41
9030	Hunt, Purl D.........	3,046 13	2,805 30
9331	Beardsley, John W. and another	1,350 95	1,015 50

		Amount claimed.	Awarded.
9338	Telford, William H. and another	$2,418 35	$1,405 00
9389	Doran, Frank J	2,223 91	1,156 34
9419	Laraway, Jennie E. and another, by Guard., etc.	10,117 43	4,329 03
9432	Haas, Luella	1,801 62	789 83
9462	Gay, John et al........	9,818 47	5,286 88
9471	Stevens, George A.....	3,451 25	2,104 99
9546	Forness, Margaret	1,500 00	274 16
9552	Forness, Frank J. and another	700 00	164 50
9601	Smith, George U. and another	12,468 00	6,656 03
9659	Merritt, Lavina R.....	1,500 00	861 12
9710	Seefried, Katherine et al., by Guard.......	12,389 86	4,202 15
9769	McCabe, Margaret	1,000 00	676 00
9896	McFadden, William D.	780 00 Judgment for State	
9897	Fowler, Norman A....	735 00 Judgment for State	
10029	Claxton, John P.......	458 00	250 00
9923	Kenyon, Charles and another	1,000 00	221 40
9917	Kanandarque Club	500 00	371 70
9702	Scherf, Frank J. and another	13,074 00	3,858 94
9213	Pierce, Henry J.......	21,325 00	2,160 80
9715	Scherf, Frank J. and another	263 80	159 63
9311	Hilfinger, Alexander et al., by Guard........	10,000 00	3,098 30
9864	Gutberlet, Andrew C...	137 00	50 00
9780	Claus, Philip and another	7,722 80	2,940 62
8052	Van Valkenburgh, Emma P. as Ex..........	2,600 00	1,943 75

		Amount claimed.	Awarded.
8093	Blanchard, Kitty L. as Admx............	$2,500 00	$2,320 38
9308	Vincent, Hattie A......	1,742 25	517 36
9337	Plaisted, John	947 71	622 91
9475	McKinley, Charlotte ...	701 62	772 37
9489	Gay, William J. and another	712 16	455 67
9534	Hazard, Louisa F.....	2,337 50	295 53
9556	Blacklock, James S. and another	250 00	99 93
9657	Jagow, John	1,200 00	731 48
9765	Sahr, Martin and another	450 00	270 91
9749	Kinser Construction Co.	370,525 41	77,425 46
9755	Tindall, Mary A.......	3,804 84	1,931 58
9756	Munson, Thomas	3,110 80	1,658 32
9757	Westbrook, Ida	500 00	407 19
9761	Casey, Catherine	4,965 75	1,355 00
9953	Sherman, Billings, by Guard............	2,736 76	2,823 25
9434	Burns, Patrick F. et al.	4,255 00	3,161 17

Syracuse Term, November 14, 1910:

9429	Fitch, Willard R......	501 62	150 93
9498	Hathaway, Amandus and another	701 62	440 94
8965	Pratt, Harriet E. as Ex.	17,054 55	1,980 80
9506	Casler, Benj. P. and another	5,000 00	4,825 32
9911	Goff, Gertrude P., an Infant	1,500 00	1,339 20
9451	Rossow, George and another	8,755 00	916 12
9845	Ontario Knitting Company	1,019,051 78	Judgment for State
9863	Smith, Walter E. et al..	1,100 00	1,085 64
9210	Potter, Geo. S. as Ex. of Frances	45,985 00	4,538 65

OTHER THAN CANAL JUDGMENTS RECEIVED.

		Amount claimed.	Awarded.
9305	Dyer, John, Jr........	$2,160 00	$1,300 00
9450	Flower, Frederick S...	3,478 93	Judgment for State
8106	City of Auburn.......	3,102 70	Judgment for State
9589	Crookston Milling Co..	1,455 00	1,267 35
9496	Kirby, Gustavus T.....	2,900 00	2,900 00
9344	Hough, David L.......	2,775 00	1,350 00
9391	Carroll, Edward et al..	8,921 03	10,632 38
8998	Bonneville, Margaret et al.	6,000 00	2,760 77
9542	Logan, William J.	5,000 00	2,272 50

PERSONAL INJURY JUDGMENTS RECEIVED.

		Amount claimed.	Awarded.
9439	Post, Anthony	$20,000 00	$1,800 00
9650	O'Bryan, Lina as Admx.	20,080 00	Judgment for State
9463	Crane, Alexander S....	10,305 00	1,000 00

SPECIAL FRANCHISE TAX.

CERTIORARI PROCEEDINGS TO REVIEW THE ACTION OF THE STATE BOARD OF TAX COMMISSIONERS IN THE ASSESSMENT OF SPECIAL FRANCHISES, IN WHICH THE ATTORNEY-GENERAL APPEARS FOR THE STATE BOARD OF TAX COMMISSIONERS.

SPECIAL FRANCHISE TAX PROCEEDINGS FOR THE YEARS 1900-1909 INCLUSIVE SETTLED DURING 1910.

NEW YORK CITY.
CABLE, TELEGRAPH AND TELEPHONE.
COMMERCIAL CABLE COMPANY.
Boroughs of Manhattan and Brooklyn.

1900	$84,047
1901	104,000
1902	97,000
1903	97,000
1904	102,000
1905	102,000
1906	131,000
1907	200,000
1908	210,000
1909	210,000

CONSOLIDATED TELEGRAPH AND ELECTRIC SUBWAY COMPANY.
Boroughs of Manhattan and Bronx.

1903	$3,780,000
1904	4,543,000
1905	4,850,000
1906	5,125,000
1907	6,435,000
1908	6,435,000
1909	6,725,000

NEW ENGLAND TELEGRAPH COMPANY (SUCCESSOR TO COMMERCIAL TELEGRAPH AND TELEPHONE COMPANY).
Boroughs of Bronx, Brooklyn and Manhattan.

1900	$207,500
1901	231,500

Boroughs of Bronx, Brooklyn, Manhattan, Queens and Richmond.

1902	216,900
1903	220,900
1904	226,800

1905	$231,800
1906	231,800
1907	360,400
1908	360,400
1909	360,400

NEW YORK TELEPHONE COMPANY (SUCCESSOR TO NEW YORK
AND NEW JERSEY TELEPHONE COMPANY).
Boroughs of Brooklyn, Queens and Richmond.

1908	$9,500,000
1909	9,564,000

NEW YORK TELEPHONE COMPANY.
Boroughs of Bronx, Brooklyn, Manhattan, Queens and Richmond.

1908	$28,400,000
1909	29,750,000

WESTERN UNION TELEGRAPH COMPANY.
Boroughs of Bronx, Brooklyn, Manhattan, Queens and Richmond.

1907	$671,500
1908	820,000
1909	819,100

ELECTRIC LIGHT AND POWER.

AMSTERDAM ELECTRIC LIGHT, HEAT AND POWER COMPANY.
Borough of Brooklyn.

1908	$55,000
1909	75,000

BRUSH ELECTRIC ILLUMINATING COMPANY OF NEW YORK.
Borough of Manhattan.

1903	$324,000
1904	228,000
1905	300,000
1906	320,000
1907	300,000
1908	300,000
1909	300,000

EDISON ELECTRIC ILLUMINATING COMPANY OF BROOKLYN.
Borough of Brooklyn.

1906	$6,720,500
1907	10,000,000
1908	10,500,000
1909	11,500,000

KINGS COUNTY LIGHTING COMPANY.
Borough of Brooklyn.

1908	$930,000
1909	1,200,000

NEW YORK EDISON COMPANY.
Boroughs of Manhattan, Bronx and Brooklyn.

1904	$12,110,000
1905	17,835,000
1906	22,576,000
1907	33,315,000
1908	39,075,000
1909	39,015,000

UNITED ELECTRIC LIGHT AND POWER COMPANY.
Borough of Manhattan.

1904	$1,521,000
1905	2,653,000
1906	3,101,000
1907	4,925,000
1908	4,925,000
1909	2,000,000

WESTCHESTER LIGHTING COMPANY.
Borough of Bronx.

1907	$275,000
1908	275,000
1909	200,000

GAS.
BROOKLYN UNION GAS COMPANY.
Borough of Brooklyn.

1901	$8,360,140
1902	8,724,450

CENTRAL UNION GAS COMPANY.
Borough of Bronx.

1901	$1,081,270
1902	1,112,000
1903	1,211,000
1904	1,517,000
1905	· 1,900,000
1906	1,900,000
1907	2,080,000
1908	2,280,000
1909	1,600,000

CONSOLIDATED GAS COMPANY OF NEW YORK.
Borough of Manhattan.

1901	$13,990,000
1902	16,275,000
1903	17,985,000
1904	21,900,000
1905	27,300,000
1906	31,900,000
1907	33,640,000
1908	33,640,000
1909	20,001,000

FLATBUSH GAS COMPANY.
Borough of Brooklyn.

1906	$551,000
1907	875,000
1908	950,000
1909	600,000

JAMAICA GAS LIGHT COMPANY.
Borough of Queens.

1907	$150,000
1908	165,000
1909	185,000

NEW AMSTERDAM GAS COMPANY.
Boroughs of Manhattan and Queens.

1901	$4,127,500
1902	4,413,000
1903	4,505,000
1904	4,732,000
1905	6,090,000
1906	6,700,000
1907	8,150,000
1908	8,150,000
1909	6,500,000

NEWTOWN GAS COMPANY.
Borough of Queens.

1907	$625,000
1908	675,000
1909	600,000

NEW YORK AND RICHMOND GAS COMPANY.
Borough of Richmond.

1906	$285,000
1907	300,000
1908	325,000
1909	325,000

NORTHERN UNION GAS COMPANY.
Borough of Bronx.

1901	$461,000
1902	459,000
1903	485,000
1904	550,000
1905	1,050,000
1906	1,125,000
1907	1,150,000
1908	1,150,000
1909	1,000,000

QUEENSBORO GAS AND ELECTRIC COMPANY.
Borough of Queens.

1909	$300,000

RICHMOND HILL AND QUEENS COUNTY GAS LIGHT COMPANY.
Borough of Queens.

1907	$125,000
1908	135,000
1909	115,000

STANDARD GAS LIGHT COMPANY.
Boroughs of Manhattan and Bronx.

1902	$3,240,500
1903	3,261,000
1904	3,322,000
1905	4,667,000
1906	4,670,000
1907	5,980,000
1908	5,980,000
1909	3,100,000

WOODHAVEN GAS LIGHT COMPANY.
Borough of Queens.

1907	$145,000
1908	155,000
1909	155,000

MISCELLANEOUS.

AUTOMATIC FIRE ALARM COMPANY.
Borough of Manhattan.

1905	$18,000
1909	75,000

CONSOLIDATED FIRE ALARM COMPANY.
Boroughs of Manhattan and Brooklyn.

1909	$20,000
1909	15,000

EMPIRE CITY SUBWAY COMPANY, LIMITED.
Boroughs of Manhattan and Bronx.

1908	$8,750,000
1909	8,900,000

MISCELLANEOUS RAILWAYS.

BUSH TERMINAL RAILROAD COMPANY.

Borough of Brooklyn.

1907	$350,000
1908	350,000
1909	350,000

CITY ISLAND RAILROAD COMPANY.

Borough of Bronx.

1909	$25,000

EDENWALD STREET RAILWAY COMPANY.

Borough of Bronx.

1906	$10,000
1907	12,000
1908	11,000
1909	11,000

NEW YORK CITY INTERBOROUGH RAILROAD COMPANY.

Boroughs of Manhattan and Bronx.

1908	$600,600
1909	675,000

NEW YORK AND LONG ISLAND TRACTION COMPANY.

Borough of Queens.

1909	$197,500

NEW YORK AND QUEENS COUNTY RAILWAY COMPANY.

Borough of Queens.

1909	$2,275,000

NEW YORK, WESTCHESTER AND CONNECTICUT TRACTION COMPANY.

Borough of Bronx.

1902	$5,000
1903	5,000
1904	4,000
1905	4,000
1906	4,000
1907	5,000

1908	$4,400
1909	4,400

PELHAM PARK RAILROAD COMPANY.
Borough of Bronx.

1909	$10,000

TWENTY-EIGHTH AND TWENTY-NINTH STREETS CROSSTOWN RAILROAD COMPANY.
Borough of Manhattan.

1900 ......,........................	$350,473
1901	353,800
1902	390,600
1903	370,000
1904	350,000
1905	350,000
1906	325,000
1907	425,000
1908	374,000
1909	150,000

WALL AND CORTLANDT STREETS FERRIES RAILWAYS COMPANY.
Borough of Manhattan.

1901	$10,000
1904	10,000
1905	10,000
1906	10,000
1907	15,000

YONKERS RAILROAD COMPANY.
Borough of Bronx.

1905	$68,000
1906	70,000
1907	83,000
1909 (Sutherland, Receiver)	73,000

STREET RAILWAYS.
Brooklyn Rapid Transit.
BROOKLYN HEIGHTS RAILROAD COMPANY.
Borough of Brooklyn.

1906	$95,800
1907	115,000

BROOKLYN, QUEENS COUNTY AND SUBURBAN RAILWAY COMPANY.
Boroughs of Brooklyn and Queens.
1907	$3,370,000

BROOKLYN UNION ELEVATED RAILWAY COMPANY.
Boroughs of Brooklyn and Queens.
1906	$11,265,000
1907	18,360,000
1908	18,727,300

CONEY ISLAND AND GRAVESEND RAILWAY.
Borough of Brooklyn.
1905	$80,000
1906	80,200
1907	140,000
1908	120,000

NASSAU ELECTRIC RAILWAY COMPANY.
Borough of Brooklyn.
1905	$7,345,000
1906	7,348,000

OCEAN ELECTRIC RAILWAY COMPANY.
Borough of Queens.
1908	$90,700

Metropolitan System.

BLEECKER STREET AND FULTON FERRY RAILROAD COMPANY.
Borough of Manhattan.
1900	$323,815
1901	326,420
1902	390,440
1903	475,000
1904	590,000
1905	700,000
1906	650,000
1907	830,000
1908	730,000
1909	730,000

BROADWAY AND SEVENTH AVENUE RAILROAD COMPANY.
Borough of Manhattan.

1900	$6,319,400
1901	6,309,700
1902	6,359,000
1903	6,540,000
1904	6,540,000
1905	6,750,000
1906	6,800,000
1907	9,040,000
1908	7,955,000
1909	7,955,000

CENTRAL CROSSTOWN RAILWAY COMPANY.
Borough of Manhattan.

1900	$585,693
1901	591,765
1902	633,600
1903	534,000
1904	510,000
1905	575,000
1906	575,000
1907	750,000
1908	660,000
1909	660,000

CENTRAL PARK, NORTH AND EAST RIVER RAILROAD COMPANY.
Borough of Manhattan.

1900	$1,954,712
1901	1,809,900
1902	2,297,200
1903	2,625,000
1904	2,600,000
1905	2,800,000
1906	2,800,000
1907	3,650,000
1908	3,312,000
1909	2,750,000

CHRISTOPHER AND TENTH STREETS RAILROAD.
Borough of Manhattan.

1900	$762,927
1901	719,820
1902	774,650
1903	875,000
1904	975,000
1905	1,200,000
1906	1,200,000
1907	1,560,000
1908	1,373,000
1909	1,172,000

EIGHTH AVENUE RAILWAY COMPANY.
Borough of Manhattan.

1900	$3,968,252
1901	3,970,150
1902	4,429,600
1903	4,460,000
1904	4,467,000
1905	4,680,000
1906	4,700,000
1907	6,590,000
1908	5,799,000
1909	4,800,000

FORT GEORGE AND ELEVENTH AVENUE RAILROAD.
Borough of Manhattan.

1902	$50,000
1903	74,800
1904	74,000
1905	74,000
1906	75,000
1907	200,000
1908	317,000
1909	317,000

4

FORTY-SECOND STREET AND GRAND STREET RAILROAD COMPANY.

Borough of Manhattan.

1900	$650,613
1901	752,125
1902	782,100
1903	785,000
1904	820,000
1905	1,100,000
1906	1,100,000
1907	1,430,000
1908	1,258,000
1909	1,600,000

FORTY-SECOND STREET, MANHATTANVILLE AND ST. NICHOLAS AVENUE RAILWAY COMPANY.

Borough of Manhattan.

1900	$2,047,149
1901	2,420,150
1902	2,905,000
1903	3,020,000
1904	2,950,000
1905	2,950,000
1906	2,900,000
1907	4,780,000
1908	4,206,000
1909	4,206,000

FULTON STREET RAILROAD COMPANY.

Borough of Manhattan.

1900	$104,530
1901	101,240
1902	133,500
1903	133,000
1904	125,000
1905	125,000
1906	125,000
1907	147,000
1908	129,000

METROPOLITAN STREET RAILWAY COMPANY.
Borough of Manhattan.

1900	$18,377,911
1901	17,577,975
1902	16,110,000
1903	18,413,000
1904	18,480,000
1905	18,676,000
1906	18,803,000
1907	24,600,000
1908	20,258,000
1909	20,258,000

NEW YORK AND HARLEM RAILROAD COMPANY.
Boroughs of Manhattan and Bronx.

1900	$6,405,075
1901	7,580,470
1902	7,587,500
1903	7,590,000
1904	7,610,000
1905	8,090,000
1906	8,150,000
1907	10,617,000
1908	9,343,000
1909	9,343,000

NINTH AVENUE RAILROAD COMPANY.
Borough of Manhattan.

1900	$1,787,386
1901	1,502,265
1902	1,738,400
1903	2,300,000
1904	2,350,000
1905	2,850,000
1906	2,850,000
1907	3,700,000
1908	3,256,000
1909	2,800,000

SIXTH AVENUE RAILROAD COMPANY.
Borough of Manhattan.

1900	$3,917,260
1901	2,756,500
1902	3,770,400
1903	3,790,000
1904	3,750,000
1905	3,750,000
1906	3,750,000
1907	5,170,000
1908	4,550,000
1909	4,550,000

THIRTY-FOURTH STREET CROSSTOWN RAILWAY COMPANY.
Borough of Manhattan.

1900	$783,547
1901	785,122
1902	845,500
1903	897,000
1904	950,000
1905	1,040,000
1906	1,050,000
1907	1,370,000
1908	1,206,000
1909	1,206,000

TWENTY-THIRD STREET RAILWAY COMPANY.
Borough of Manhattan.

1900	$1,979,276
1901	1,697,300
1902	1,888,700
1903	1,905,000
1904	1,925,000
1905	2,375,000
1906	2,400,000
1907	3,170,000
1908	2,790,000
1909	2,790,000

Third Avenue System.
BRONX TRACTION COMPANY.
Borough of Bronx.

1905	$150,000
1906	150,000
1907	200,000
1909	176,000

DRY DOCK, EAST BROADWAY AND BATTERY RAILROAD COMPANY.
Borough of Manhattan.

1901	$1,375,405
1902	1,577,700
1903	1,525,000
1904	1,475,000
1905	1,500,000
1906	1,300,000
1907	2,165,000
1908	1,905,000
1909	1,400,000

KINGS BRIDGE RAILROAD COMPANY.
Borough of Manhattan.

1902	$101,000
1903	525,000
1904	580,000
1905	650,000
1906	650,000
1907	862,000
1908	759,000

SOUTHERN BOULEVARD RAILWAY COMPANY.
Borough of Bronx.

1900	$155,395
1901	157,345
1902	195,000
1903	215,000
1904	225,000
1905	235,000
1906	200,000
1907	223,000
1909	196,000

THIRD AVENUE RAILWAY COMPANY.
Borough of Manhattan.

1901	$10,525,605
1902	10,086,000
1903	10,310,000
1904	10,300,000
1905	10,300,000
1906	10,500,000
1907	11,320,000
1908	7,920,000
1909	7,920,000

UNION RAILWAY COMPANY OF NEW YORK.
Boroughs of Manhattan and Bronx.

1901	$1,776,830
1902	2,676,600
1903	2,680,500
1904	2,875,000
1905	3,761,000
1906	3,760,000
1907	4,780,000
1908	4,206,000
1909	4,206,000

WESTCHESTER ELECTRIC RAILROAD COMPANY.
Borough of Bronx.

1901	$114,750
1902	114,500
1903	116,000
1904	105,000
1905	125,000
1906	138,000
1907	138,000
1909	121,000

WATER.
CITIZENS' WATER SUPPLY COMPANY OF NEWTOWN.
Borough of Queens.

1908	$750,000
1909	750,000

Flatbush Water Works Company.
Borough of Brooklyn.

1903 .... $452,500

Jamaica Water Supply Company.
Borough of Queens.

1907 .... $800,000
1908   850,000
1909   490,000

Woodhaven Water Suppply Company.
Borough of Queens.

1907 .... $210,000

SECOND JUDICIAL DISTRICT.
(Outside New York City.)

Long Island Railroad Company.
Nassau County.

Towns:

1908.	Hempstead	$12,000
	North Hempstead	18,600
	Oyster Bay	5,900
1909.	Hempstead	16,100
	North Hempstead	19,300
	Oyster Bay	5,900

Suffolk County.

Towns:

1908.	Babylon	11,500
	Brookhaven	3,700
	Port Huntington	800
	Southampton	12,000
1909.	Babylon	11,500
	Brookhaven	4,100
	East Hampton	5,400
	Huntington	600
	South Hampton	6,900

NEW YORK AND NEW JERSEY TELEPHONE COMPANY.
Nassau County.

Towns:

1907.	Hempstead	$246,300
	North Hempstead	81,800
	Oyster Bay	89,600
1908.	Hempstead	287,000
	North Hempstead	82,000
	Oyster Bay	115,000
1909.	Hempstead	320,000

Suffolk County.

Towns:

1907.	Babylon	$37,000
	Huntington	29,100
	Islip	34,900
	Hampton	47,750
1908.	Babylon	39,000
	Huntington	40,000
	Islip	45,000
	Southold	20,600

QUEENSBOROUGH GAS AND ELECTRIC COMPANY.
Nassau County.

Towns:

1908.	Hempstead	$80,000
1909.	Hempstead	85,000

THIRD JUDICIAL DISTRICT.

AMERICAN TELEPHONE AND TELEGRAPH COMPANY.
Albany County.

City:

1909.	Albany	$12,750

Columbia County.

Towns:

1908.	Greenport	$9,300
	Stockport	8,100
	Stuyvesant	14,400

Rensselaer County.

Town:

1908.	North Greenbush	9,800

HUDSON RIVER TELEPHONE COMPANY.
Albany County.

Towns:

1909.	Bethlehem	$14,500
	Colonie	34,500
	Green Island	11,500

Cities:

1909.	Albany	310,700
	Watervliet	39,200

Greene County.

Town:

	Catskill	17,300

Rensselaer County.

Towns:

1909.	Hoosick	13,000
	Schodack	13,000

City:

1909.	Rensselaer	26,000

Ulster County.

Towns:

1909.	Saugerties	19,500
	Ulster	10,250

City:

1909.	Kingston	82,000

NEW ENGLAND TELEGRAPH COMPANY (SUCCESSOR TO COMMER-
CIAL CABLE AND TELEGRAPH COMPANY.)

Albany County.

City:

1900.	Albany	$8,950
1901.	Albany	8,600
1902.	Albany	8,600
1903.	Albany	8,600
1904.	Albany	8,600
1905.	Albany	8,600
1906.	Albany	8,600
1907.	Albany	8,850

Town:

1907.	Colonie	8,850

City:

1908.	Albany	25,000

Town:

1908.	Colonie	8,850

City:

1909.	Albany	25,000

Columbia County.

Towns:

1902.	Ghent	2,900
1907.	Chatham	4,825
	Ghent	4,500
1908.	Chatham	4,850

Ulster County.

Towns:

1907.	Esopus	4,000
	Saugerties	4,600
	Ulster	4,875

TROY UNION RAILROAD COMPANY.

Rensselaer County.

City:

1909.	Troy	$244,000

UNITED TRACTION COMPANY.

Albany County.

Towns:

1907.	Green Island	$72,000
1908.	Green Island	105,000
1909.	Green Island	105,000

FOURTH JUDICIAL DISTRICT.

AMERICAN TELEPHONE AND TELEGRAPH COMPANY.

. Fulton County.

Towns:

1908.	Ephratah........................	$10,650
	Johnstown......................	18,150
	Oppenheim.....................	14,450
	Perth...........................	20,150

Schenectady County.

Town:

1908.	Glenville	27,000

City:

1908.	Schenectady....................	6,900

CENTRAL NEW YORK TELEPHONE AND TELEGRAPH COMPANY.

St. Lawrence County.

Towns:

1908.	Canton	$16,400
	Gouverneur.....................	18,450
	Massena	18,600
	Potsdam........................	17,600

City:

1908.	Ogdensburg.....................	25,950

Towns:

1909.	Canton..........................	16,400
	Gouverneur.....................	17,000
	Massena	16,500
	Oswegatchie....................	10,000
	Potsdam	17,500

CLINTON TELEPHONE COMPANY.
Clinton County.

Town:

1908. Beekmantown $1,100

HUDSON RIVER TELEPHONE COMPANY.
Essex County.

Town:

1909. North Elba $13,900

Montgomery County.

City:

1909. Amsterdam   11,000

Saratoga County.

Towns:

1909. Ballston   15,000
       Halfmoon   16,000
       Milton   13,000
       Moreau   11,000
       Saratoga   13,500
       Saratoga Springs   50,000
       Stillwater   12,500
       Waterford   12,000

Warren County.

Town:

1909. Queensbury   11,500

Washington County.

Towns:

1909. Greenwich   11,000
       Kingsbury   18,000

LOZIER LIGHT AND POWER COMPANY.
Clinton County.

Town:

1908. Plattsburg $4,000

NEW ENGLAND TELEGRAPH COMPANY (SUCCESSOR TO COMMER-
CIAL CABLE AND TELEGRAPH COMPANY.)

Fulton County.

City:

1900.	Gloversville	$1,500
1901.	Gloversville	1,150
1902.	Gloversville	950
1903.	Gloversville	950
1904.	Gloversville	900

Franklin County.

Town:

1908.	Franklin	2,250

Montgomery County.

Towns:

1907.	Glen	5,600
	Florida	6,400
1908.	Glen	5,500
	Florida	6,400

Saratoga County.

Town:

1902.	Stillwater	1,100

Schenectady County.

City:

1901.	Schenectady	1,300
1907.	Schenectady	4,950
1908.	Schenectady	4,950

St. Lawrence County.

Towns:

1908.	Norfolk	3,550
	Oswegatchie	3,700

PLATTSBURG HEAT, LIGHT AND POWER COMPANY.

Clinton County.

Town and City:

1908.	Plattsburg	$35,600

FIFTH JUDICIAL DISTRICT.

AMERICAN TELEPHONE AND TELEGRAPH COMPANY.
Oneida County.

Towns:

1908. New Hartford $16,000

Vernon 11,300

City:

1908. Utica 7,550

Onondaga County.

Towns:

1908. Manlius........................, 10,400

Onondaga 29,100

CENTRAL NEW YORK TELEPHONE AND TELEGRAPH COMPANY.
Herkimer County.

Towns:

1908. German Flats $21,823

Herkimer 25,000

City:

1908. Little Falls 27,625

Towns:

1909. German Flats 26,000

Herkimer 20,000

City:

1909. Little Falls 25,000

Jefferson County.

Towns:

1907. Clayton 3,175

1908. Leray 14,000

Watertown...................... 10,000

City:

1908. Watertown 75,000

Town:

1909. Leray........................... 14,000

City:

1909. Watertown 75,000

Oneida County.

Towns:

1908.	Camden	$5,850
	Deerfield	10,550
	Forestport	5,475
	Marcy	6,350
	New Hartford	8,000
	Trenton	21,100
	Verona	9,300
	Whitestown	8,850
	Vernon	9,000

Cities:

1908.	Rome	36,250
	Utica	175,000

Towns:

1909.	Deerfield	10,550
	New Hartford	10,000
	Trenton	20,000
	Verona	11,000
	Whitestown	10,500

Cities:

1909.	Rome	36,000
	Utica	195,000

Onondaga County.

Towns:

1908.	Dewitt	17,000
	Geddes	19,500
	Lysander	6,000
	Manlius	15,600
	Onondaga	19,500
	Van Buren	11,775

City:

1908.	Syracuse	610,000

Towns:

1909.	Dewitt	22,500
	Geddes	20,000
	Lysander	15,000

Manlius	$15,000
Onondaga	20,500
Van Buren	11,000

City:
1909. Syracuse	610,000

EMPIRE STATE TELEGRAPH AND TELEPHONE COMPANY.
Oswego County.

Towns:
1908. Mexico	$12,000
Richland	15,000
Scriba	7,000

City:
1908. Fulton	9,400

Towns:
1909. Mexico.......................	13,500
Richland	17,000

INDEPENDENT TELEPHONE COMPANY OF SYRACUSE AND ONE.
Onondaga County.

City:
1908. Syracuse	215,000

NEW ENGLAND TELEGRAPH COMPANY.
Oneida County.

Towns:
1907. Verona	$6,650
1908. Verona	6,650

Onondaga County.

Towns:
1907. Lysander	6,500

Cities:
1907. Syracuse	8,825
1908. Syracuse	8,650

ONEONTA & MOHAWK VALLEY RAILROAD COMPANY.
Herkimer County.

Towns:
1907. German Flats	$8,800
Warren	1,600

PEOPLE'S SUBWAY COMPANY OF SYRACUSE.
Onondaga County.

City:
 1908. Syracuse $115,000

UTICA GAS AND ELECTRIC COMPANY.
Oneida County.

Cities:
 1908. Utica $675,000
 1909. Utica   700,000

SIXTH JUDICIAL DISTRICT.

AMERICAN TELEPHONE AND TELEGRAPH COMPANY.
Chemung County.

City:
 1908. Elmira $7,200

Madison County.

Town:
 1908. Lenox   8,000

CENTRAL NEW YORK TELEPHONE AND TELEGRAPH COMPANY.
Chenango County.

Towns:
 1908. Norwich $21,000
 1909. Norwich   18,250

Madison County.

Towns:
 1908. Lenox   15,250
 1909. Lenox   11,500
City:
 1909. Oneida   25,000

Otsego County.

Town:
 1908. Otsego   20,200

City:

1908. Oneonta $42,000

1909. Otsego   17,000

City:

1909. Oneonta   33,000

EMPIRE STATE TELEPHONE AND TELEGRAPH COMPANY.

Cortland County.

City:

1908. Cortland $35,760

Town:

1909. Homer   17,500

City:

1909. Cortland   35,000

NEW ENGLAND TELEGRAPH COMPANY.

Tompkins County.

City:

1900. Ithaca $400

NEW YORK AND PENNSYLVANIA TELEPHONE AND TELEGRAPH
COMPANY.

Tioga County.

Towns:

1908. Barton $8,500

       Dix   4,125

1909. Barton   10,000

       Owego   14,000

SEVENTH JUDICIAL DISTRICT.

AMERICAN TELEPHONE AND TELEGRAPH COMPANY.

Cayuga County.

Town:

1908. Sennett $14,800

Livingston County.

Town:

1908. York $11,200

Ontario County.

Towns:

1908. Farmington ....   ¡12,000
       Manchester   10,900
       Phelps   19,500
       Victor   9,900

EMPIRE STATE TELEPHONE AND TELEGRAPH COMPANY.

Ontario County.

Towns:

1908. East Bloomfield $10,425
       Naples   10,425
       Canandaigua   19,900
       Phelps   9,800
1909. Canandaigua   17,000
       East Bloomfield   10,000
       Naples   10,000
       Phelps   11,000

Seneca County.

Towns:

1908. Seneca Falls   20,500
1909. Seneca Falls   20,000
       Waterloo   11,000

Wayne County.

Towns:

1908. Lyons   15,000
       Palmyra   10,500
       Sodus   8,225
1909. Arcadia   11,500
       Lyons   15,000
       Palmyra   11,000

Yates County.

Towns: .
1908. Jerusalem   8,500
      Milo   11,325
1909. Jerusalem   10,000
      Milo   10,000

NEW ENGLAND TELEGRAPH COMPANY.
Cayuga County.
City:
1901. Auburn $1,460

Ontario County.
Town:
1908. Seneca   3,075

Seneca County.
Towns:
1902. Waterloo   2,100
1907. Waterloo   3,650

Steuben County.
Town:
1908. Caton   3,500

Wayne County.
Towns:
1902. Rose   2,500
      Walcott   3,000

Yates County.
Town:
1902. Milo   900

NEW YORK AND PENNSYLVANIA TELEPHONE AND TELEGRAPH
COMPANY.
Steuben County.
Town:
1909. Bath $15,000

EIGHTH JUDICIAL DISTRICT.

AMERICAN TELEPHONE AND TELEGRAPH COMPANY.

Chautauqua County.

City:
1908. Dunkirk $7,200

Erie County.

City:
1907. Buffalo   38,250

Towns:
1908. Alden   10,750
     Lancaster   12,400
     West Seneca   9,750

City:
1908. Buffalo   60,000
1909. Buffalo   60,000

Genesee County.

Towns:
1908. Darien   13,500
     Pavilion   12,150

BUFFALO, THOUSAND ISLANDS AND PORTLAND RAILROAD
COMPANY.

Niagara County.

City:
1909. Niagara Falls. $9,500

LEWISTON AND YOUNGSTOWN FRONTIER RAILROAD COMPANY.

Niagara County.

Town:
1907. Lewiston $90,000

NEW YORK AND PENNSYLVANIA TELEPHONE AND TELEGRAPH
COMPANY.

Allegany County.

Town:
1909. Wellsville $11,500

Cattaraugus County.

Town:
1909. Salamanca $10,500
City:
1909. Olean 20,000

Chautauqua County.

City:
1909. Dunkirk 17,000

NINTH JUDICIAL DISTRICT.

CONSOLIDATED WATER COMPANY OF SUBURBAN NEW YORK.
Westchester County.

Town:
1909. Mt. Pleasant..................... $60,000

HUDSON RIVER TELEPHONE COMPANY.
Dutchess County.

Towns:
1909. Fishkill 43,500
       Poughkeepsie 46,500
City:
1909. Poughkeepsie 60,000

Orange County.

Towns:
1909. Goshen 13,900
       Newburgh 22,000
City:
1909. Newburgh 61,000

INTERURBAN STREET RAILWAY COMPANY.
Westchester County.

City:
1903. Mt. Vernon $25,000

NEW ENGLAND TELEGRAPH COMPANY.
Orange County.

Town:
1907.	Wallkill	$7,225
1908.	Wallkill	7,150

Westchester County.

City:
1901.	Yonkers	10,500
1902.	Yonkers	12,000

Towns:
1902.	Greenburg	6,200
	Harrison	3,700
	Mamaroneck	2,800

City:
1903.	Yonkers	11,500
1904.	Yonkers	11,500
1905.	Yonkers	12,000
1906.	Yonkers	15,400

Towns:
1907.	Greenburg	8,700
	Harrison	4,375
	Scarsdale	4,200

Cities:
1907.	Mt. Vernon......................	900
	New Rochelle....................	2,150
	Yonkers	16,080

Town:
1908.	Greenburg	8,700

City:
1908.	Yonkers	16,080
1909.	Yonkers	16,100

NEW YORK CITY RAILWAY COMPANY.
Westchester County.

City:
1904.	Mt. Vernon	$25,000
1905.	Mt. Vernon.....................	25,000

1906. Mt. Vernon...................... $30,000
1907. Mt. Vernon...................... 40,000
1908. Mt. Vernon...................... 40,000

New York Interurban Water Company.
Westchester County.

Towns:
1909. Harrison....................... $42,000
      Mamaroneck.................... 89,000
      Rye........................... 8,000
      Eastchester................... 35,000
City:
1909. New Rochelle.................... 30,000

Orange County Lighting Company.
Orange County.

City:
1909. Middletown...................... $90,000

Tarrytown, White Plains and Mamaroneck Railroad Company.
Westchester County.

Towns:
1901. Greenburg...................... $40,000
      Harrison, Mamaroneck and Scarsdale.. 50,000
      White Plains.................... 35,000
Towns:
1902. Greenburg...................... 42,000
      Harrison and Mamaroneck.......... 36,000
      Scarsdale and White Plains........ 61,000
Towns:
1903. Greenburg...................... 66,000
      Harrison and Mamaroneck.......... 51,000
      Scarsdale and White Plains........ 82,000
Towns:
1904. Greenburg...................... 66,000
      Harrison....................... 16,000
      Mamaroneck.................... 35,000
      White Plains.................... 55,000

Towns:
1905. Harrison $16,000
      Mamaroneck.................... 35,000
      White Plains................... 65,000
Towns:
1906. Greenburg..................... 70,000
      Harrison....................... 16,000
      Mamaroneck.................... 3,500
      White Plains................... 65,000
Towns:
1907. Greenburg..................... 107,000
      Harrison....................... 22,000
      Mamaroneck.................... 53,800
      White Plains................... 106,500
Towns:
1908. Greenburg..................... 93,000
      Harrison....................... 22,000
      Mamaroneck.................... 48,000
      White Plains................... 107,000
Towns:
1909. Greenburg..................... 96,000
      Harrison....................... 12,000
      Mamaroneck.................... 48,000
      Scarsdale...................... 48,000
      White Plains................... 114,000

WESTCHESTER ELECTRIC RAILROAD COMPANY.
Westchester County.

City:
1900. Mt. Vernon.................... $165,100
Town:
1901. Pelham........................ 26,000
City:
1901. New Rochelle.................. 149,000
Town:
1902. Pelham........................ 26,000
Cities:
1902. Mt. Vernon.................... 190,000
      New Rochelle.................. 151,000

Town:
  1903. Eastchester $30,000
       Pelham   30,000
Cities:
  1903. Mt. Vernon.....................   205,000
       New Rochelle....................   153,000
Town:
  1904. Eastchester   77,000
       Pelham   30,000
Cities:
  1904. Mt. Vernon.....................   240,000
       New Rochelle....................   175,000
Towns:
  1905. Eastchester   77,000
       Pelham   30,000
Cities:
  1905. Mt. Vernon.....................   245,000
       New Rochelle....................   185,000
       Yonkers   33,000
Towns:
  1906. Eastchester   85,000
       Pelham   35,000
Cities:
  1906. Mt. Vernon.....................   301,000
       New Rochelle....................   190,000
       Yonkers   38,000
Towns:
  1907. Eastchester   90,000
       Pelham ..·.....................   45,000
Cities:
  1907. Mt. Vernon   301,000
       New Rochelle....................   210,000
       Yonkers   38,000
Towns:
  1908. Eastchester   80,000
       Pelham   47,000
Cities:
  1908. Mt. Vernon   321,000
       New Rochelle....................   210,000

Towns:

    1909. Eastchester $80,000

           Pelham 47,000

Cities:

    1909. Mt. Vernon 321,000

           New Rochelle................... 210,000

           Yonkers 38,000

WESTCHESTER LIGHTING COMPANY.
Westchester County.

Town:

    1909. Greenburg.. .... $350,000

City:

    1909. New Rochelle.................. 480,000

YONKERS ELECTRIC LIGHT AND POWER COMPANY.
Westchester County.

City:

    1904. Yonkers $104,000

    1905. Yonkers 115,000

    1906. Yonkers 161,200

    1907. Yonkers 220,470

    1908. Yonkers 225,400

    1909. Yonkers 200,000

YONKERS RAILROAD COMPANY.
Westchester County.

Town:

    1901. Greenburg $10,000

City:

    1901. Yonkers 395,000

Town:

    1902. Greenburg 15,000

City:

    1902. Yonkers 449,000

Town:

    1903. Greenburg 21,000

City:

    1903. Yonkers 488,000

Town:
     1904. Greenburg........................ $21,000
City:
     1904. Yonkers.........................   615,000
Town:
     1905. Greenburg   21,000
City:
     1905. Yonkers   740,000
Town:
     1906. Greenburg   22,000
City:
     1906. Yonkers   758,000
Town:
     1907. Greenburg   30,000
City:
     1907. Yonkers   800,000
Town:
     1908. Greenburg   30,000
City:
     1908. Yonkers   800,000
Town:
     1909. Greenburg   25,000
City:
     1909. Yonkers   500,000

1910 PROCEEDINGS SETTLED.

SECOND JUDICIAL DISTRICT.
(Outside New York City.)

AMITYVILLE ELECTIC LIGHT COMPANY.
Suffolk County.

Town:
     Babylon........................ $20,000

AMITYVILLE WATER WORKS COMPANY.
Suffolk County.

Town:
     Babylon........................ $35,000

BABYLON ELECTRIC LIGHT COMPANY.
Nassau County.

Town:

Oyster Bay. $6,500

Suffolk County.

Towns:

Babylon.   35,000

Islip.   4,000

Village:

Babylon.   23,000

GLEN COVE RAILROAD COMPANY.
Nassau County.

Town:

Oyster Bay. $35,000

GREAT SOUTH BAY WATER COMPANY.
Suffolk County.

Towns:

Brookhaven. $58,700

Islip.   85,000

HUNTINGTON RAILROAD COMPANY.
Nassau County.

Town:

Oyster Bay. $24,000

Suffolk County.

Towns:

Babylon   15,500

Huntington.   43,000

JAMAICA WATER SUPPLY COMPANY.
Nassau County.

Town:

Hempstead. $20,000

LONG ISLAND ELECTRIC RAILWAY COMPANY.

Nassau County.

Town:

Hempstead. $20,000

LONG ISLAND RAILROAD COMPANY.

Nassau County.

Towns:

Hempstead. $19,900

North Hempstead   19,300

Oyster Bay.   5,900

Suffolk County.

Towns:

Babylon.   11,500

Brookhaven.   4,100

Easthampton.   5,400

Huntington.   600

Southampton.   6,900

NASSAU COUNTY WATER COMPANY.

Nassau County.

Towns:

North Hempstead. $23,000

Oyster Bay.   37,300

NEW YORK AND LONG ISLAND TRACTION COMPANY.

Nassau County.

Towns:

Hempstead. $323,000

North Hempstead.   95,000

QUEENSBORO GAS AND ELECTRIC COMPANY.

Nassau County.

Town:

Hempstead. $85,000

SEA CLIFF WATER COMPANY.

Nassau County.

Town:

Oyster Bay. $20,000

SUFFOLK GAS AND ELECTRIC LIGHT COMPANY.
Suffolk County.

Town:

Islip.............................. $50,000

SUMPWAMUS WATER COMPANY.
Suffolk County.

Town:

Babylon......................... $31,000

THIRD JUDICIAL DISTRICT.

ALBANY HOME TELEPHONE COMPANY.
Albany County.

City:

Albany......................... $125,000

ALBANY SOUTHERN RAILROAD COMPANY.
Rensselaer County.

City:

Rensselaer..................... $215,000

AMERICAN TELEPHONE AND TELEGRAPH COMPANY.
Albany County.

City:

Albany......................... $12,750

CAPITOL RAILWAY COMPANY.
Albany County.

City:

Albany......................... $120,000

CITIZENS STANDARD TELEPHONE COMPANY.
Ulster County.

Towns:

Hurley......................... $1,000
Olive.......................... 1,750
Rosendale...................... 2,300

Shandaken $2,500
Ulster   1,100
Woodstock   1,550
City:
Kingston   27,000
Village:
Rosendale   2,300

COHOES GAS COMPANY.
Albany County.

City:
Cohoes $160,000

COHOES RAILWAY COMPANY.
Albany County.

City:
Cohoes $110,000
Town:
Colonie   20,000

COHOES-WATERFORD HOME TELEPHONE COMPANY.
Albany County.

City:
Cohoes $23,000

COMMERCIAL UNION TELEPHONE COMPANY.
Albany County.

City:
Watervliet ....   • $9,100
Village:
Green Island   2,100

Rensselaer County.

Towns:
Brunswick   4,650
Hoosick   1,300
Pittstown   4,000
Schaghticoke   11,000
Villages:
Schaghticoke   3,500
Valley Falls   2,000

INDEPENDENT UNION TELEPHONE COMPANY.
Albany County.

Towns:

Bethlehem	$2,150
Coeymans	1,500
Colonie	12,500

City:

Watervliet	1,500

Greene County.

Towns:

Athens	2,500
Catskill	4,200
Coxsackie	1,000

Village:

Athens	800

Ulster County.

Towns:

Esopus	3,300
Lloyd	3,900
Marlboro	1,600
Saugerties	2,500
Ulster	3,000

Villages:

Marlboro	800
Saugerties	400

KINGSTON GAS AND ELECTRIC COMPANY.
Ulster County.

City:

Kingston	$200,000

MURRAY ELECTRIC LIGHT AND POWER COMPANY.
Sullivan County.

Town:

Thompson	$17,000

5

NEWBURGH LIGHT, HEAT AND POWER COMPANY.
Ulster County.

Towns:

Lloyd	$1,400
Marlboro	15,000

NEW YORK TELEPHONE COMPANY.
Albany County.

City:

Albany	$320,000

RENSSELAER HOME TELEPHONE COMPANY.
Rensselaer County.

City:

Rensselaer	$13,000

SCHENECTADY RAILWAY COMPANY.
Albany County.

Town:

Colonie	$360,000

City:

Watervliet	85,000

UNITED TRACTION COMPANY.
Albany County.

Towns:

Colonie	$100,000
Green Island	105,000

Cities:

Albany	2,100,000
Cohoes	160,000
Watervliet	135,000

Rensselaer County.

City:

Rensselaer	116,000

WEST SHORE HOME TELEPHONE COMPANY.
Greene County.

Town:

Catskill $12,700

Village:

Catskill   1,300

FOURTH JUDICIAL DISTRICT.

ADIRONDACK HOME TELEPHONE COMPANY.
Franklin County.

Towns:

Bangor	$2,900
Belmont	2,750
Burke	1,400
Chateaugay	2,300
Dickinson	750
Malone	16,000
Moira	1,500

Village:

Malone   11,000

St. Lawrence County.

Towns:

Canton	7,200
Lawrence	1,600
Parishville	1,800
Potsdam	15,000
Stockholm	1,200

Villages:

Canton	4,000
Potsdam	9,000

CHASM POWER COMPANY.
Franklin County.

Towns:

Belmont	$1,200
Burke	1,700

Chateaugay	$12,000
Malone	500
Village:	
Chateaugay	8,400

CLINTON TELEPHONE COMPANY.
Clinton County.

Towns:	
Beckmantown	$1,500
Chazy	1,395
Peru	1,000
Plattsburg	3,200
Saranac	1,100
City:	
Plattsburg	15,000

COHOES GAS LIGHT COMPANY.
Saratoga County.

Town:	
Waterford	$8,000

COHOES-WATERFORD HOME TELEPHONE COMPANY.
Saratoga County.

Town:	
Waterford	$8,950
Village:	
Waterford	6,500

COMMERCIAL UNION TELEPHONE COMPANY.
Essex County.

Towns:	
Chesterfield	$1,650
Crown Point	2,000
Essex	800
Westport	1,300
Willsboro	1,600

Saratoga County.

Towns:

Half Moon	$4,150
Malta	4,300
Milton	4,000
Moreau	3,200
Northumberland	1,700
Saratoga Springs	21,500
Saratoga	4,500
Stillwater	3,500
Wilton	2,700

Villages:

Ballston Spa	3,500
Mechanicville	3,750
Mechanicville	1,300
Schuylerville	3,700

Warren County.

Towns:

Caldwell	3,500
Queensbury	2,500
Warrensburg	3,500

City:

Glens Falls	22,000

Villages:

Lake George	2,800
South Glens Falls	1,600

Washington County.

Towns:

Argyle	1,500
Cambridge	1,000
Fort Edward	3,000
Granville	1,500
Greenwich	6,000
Hartford	3,200
Kingsbury	9,000
Whitehall	1,200

Villages:

Argyle	400
Cambridge	500
Fort Edward	2,100
Greenwich	6,000
Hudson Falls	7,200

Consolidated Electric Company.
Saratoga County.

Towns:

Northumberland	$500
Saratoga	7,000

Washington County.

Towns:

Cambridge	4,000
Easton . . '.	3,500
Greenwich	11,000
Jackson	700
White Creek	3,500

Co-operant Telephone Company.
Washington County.

Towns:

Dresden	$1,200
Putnam	4,500
Whitehall	6,800

Village:

Whitehall	5,200

Edison Electric Light and Power Company.
Montgomery County.

City:

Amsterdam	$37,000

Edison General Electric Company.
Schenectady County.

Town:

Rotterdam	$4,000

City:
   Schenectady $12,000

FONDA, JOHNSTOWN AND GLOVERSVILLE RAILROAD COMPANY.
Fulton County.
Cities:
   Gloversville $91,000
   Johnstown   65,500

Montgomery County.
City:
   Amsterdam   103,700

GLENS FALLS GAS AND ELECTRIC COMPANY.
Warren County.
City:
   Glens Falls $65,000

HANNAWA FALLS WATER POWER COMPANY.
St. Lawrence County.
Town:
   Potsdam $1,900

HUDSON VALLEY RAILWAY COMPANY.
Saratoga County.
Towns:
   Greenfield $1,100
   Halfmoon   50,000
   Milton   13,000
   Moreau   21,000
   Saratoga   17,600
   Saratoga Springs   53,500
   Stillwater   62,000
   Waterford   21,000
Villages:
   Ballston Spa   10,000
   Mechanicville   39,000
   Saratoga Springs   40,000
   Schuylerville   12,500

Stillwater	$18,000
South Glens Falls.	20,000
Waterford	10,000

Warren County.

Towns:

Caldwell	15,000
Queensbury	15,000

Village:

Lake George	12,000

City:

Glens Falls	90,000

Washington County.

Towns:

Fort Edward	44,000
Greenwich	22,000
Kingsbury	45,000

Villages:

Hudson Falls	27,000
Fort Edward	26,000
Greenwich	14,000

INDEPENDENT UNION TELEPHONE COMPANY.

Montgomery County.

Towns:

Florida	$6,100
Glen	2,200
Minden	1,250
Mohawk	3,500
Palatine	4,000
St. Johnsville	1,200

City:

Amsterdam	1,200

Villages:

Fultonville	500
Fonda	600
St. Johnsville	200

Schenectady County.

Towns:

Glenville.....................	$7,600
Niskayuna	1,300

INTERSTATE TELEPHONE COMPANY.
Montgomery County.

Towns:

Minden	$1,200
St. Johnsville	700

Villages:

Fort Plain	800
St. Johnsville	700

GRANVILLE ELECTRIC AND GAS COMPANY.
Washington County.

Town:

Granville...................	$18,000

LOZIER LIGHT AND POWER COMPANY AND PLATTSBURG LIGHT, HEAT AND POWER COMPANY.
Clinton County.

City:

Plattsburg	$37,000

MASSENA ELECTRIC LIGHT AND POWER COMPANY.
St. Lawrence County.

Town:

Massena	$14,000

MOUNTAIN HOME TELEPHONE COMPANY.
Essex County.

Town:

St. Armond	$2,000

Village:

Bloomingdale...................	150

Franklin County.

Town:

Harrietstown	3,500

Village:

    Saranac Lake $3,500

NORTHERN POWER COMPANY.
St. Lawrence County.

Towns:

DeKalb.........................	$12,000
Gouverneur	10,000
Lisbon	7,700
Pierrepont	400
Potsdam	6,700

PAUL SMITH'S ELECTRIC LIGHT AND POWER COMPANY.
Clinton County.   •

Town:

    Black Brook $400

Franklin County.

Towns:

Franklin	600
Harrietstown	40,000

PLATTSBURG GAS AND ELECTRIC COMPANY.
Clinton County.

City:

    Plattsburg $37,000

POTSDAM ELECTRIC LIGHT AND POWER COMPANY.
St. Lawrence County.

Town:

    Potsdam $14,000

RUTLAND RAILROAD COMPANY.
Clinton County.

Town:

    Champlain $28,200

Franklin County.

Town:

    Malone   12,700

SCHENECTADY HOME TELEPHONE COMPANY.
Schenectady County.

City:

 Schenectady $85,000

SCHENECTADY RAILWAY COMPANY.
Saratoga County.

Town:

 Milton $37,000

Schenectady County.

Towns:

 Glenville   45,000
 Niskayuna   160,000
 Rotterdam   63,000

City:

 Schenectady   950,000

ST. LAWRENCE WATER COMPANY.
St. Lawrence County.

Town:

 Massena $35,000

SPRING BROOK WATER COMPANY.
Warren County.

Town:

 Queensbury $5,000

Washington County.

Towns:

 Fort Edward   2,000
 Kingsbury   58,000

UNITED GAS, ELECTRIC LIGHT AND FUEL COMPANY.
Saratoga County.

Town:

 Moreau $16,000

Washington County.

Towns:

 Fort Edward   24,000
 Kingsbury   20,000

UNITED TRACTION COMPANY.
Saratoga County.

Town:

Waterford $110,800

WATERFORD WATER WORKS COMPANY.
Saratoga County.

Town:

Waterford $20,000

FIFTH JUDICIAL DISTRICT.

AMERICAN TELEPHONE AND TELEGRAPH COMPANY.
Onondaga County.

City:

Syracuse $15,000

CONSOLIDATED WATER COMPANY OF UTICA.
Oneida County.

Towns:

Deerfield $39,000
New Hartford   37,000
Whitestown   65,000

City:

Utica   775,000

INDEPENDENT UNION TELEPHONE COMPANY.
Herkimer County.

Towns:

Danube $2,600
Herkimer   1,400
German Flats   1,300
Little Falls   1,200
Schuyler   3,200

Village:

Herkimer   650

INTERSTATE TELEPHONE COMPANY.
Herkimer County.

Towns:

Danube	$2,500
Fairfield	3,000
Little Falls	2,000
Manheim	4,000
Salisbury	1,200
Stark	1,400

City:

Little Falls	14,000

Village:

Dolgeville	2,800

ONEIDA RAILWAY COMPANY.
Oneida County.

City:

Oneida	$90,900

ROME GAS, ELECTRIC LIGHT AND POWER COMPANY.
Oneida County.

City:

Rome	$175,000

SYRACUSE LIGHTING COMPANY.
Onondaga County.

Towns:

DeWitt	$34,000
Geddes	27,000

City:

Syracuse	$2,200,000

SYRACUSE RAPID TRANSIT COMPANY.
Onondaga County.

Towns:

DeWitt	$98,000
Geddes	65,000
Manlius	5,000
Onondaga	85,000
Salina	40,000

City:

Syracuse	2,100,000

UTICA GAS AND ELECTRIC COMPANY.
Oneida County.

Towns:

Deerfield	$17,000
New Hartford	35,000

City:

Utica	47,000

Herkimer County.

Town:

German Flats	60,000

UTICA AND MOHAWK VALLEY RAILWAY COMPANY.
Herkimer County.

Towns:

Frankfort	$37,800
Herkimer	30,000

City:

Little Falls	50,000

Oneida County.

City:

Utica	950,000

WHITESBORO WATER WORKS COMPANY.
Oneida County.

Town of Whitestown and Village of Whitesboro	$4,000

SIXTH JUDICIAL DISTRICT.

ELMIRA AND SENECA LAKE TRACTION COMPANY.
Chemung County.

Towns:

Horseheads and Veteran............	$10,000

Schuyler County.

Towns:

Dix	15,500
Montour	18,000
Reading	500

ELMIRA WATER, LIGHT AND RAILROAD COMPANY.
Chemung County.

Towns:

Elmira	$31,080
Horseheads	45,140
Southport	592

City:

Elmira	1,058,850

HOMER AND CORTLAND GAS LIGHT COMPANY.
Cortland County.

Towns:

Cortlandville	$4,000
Homer	7,000

City:

Cortland	60,000

HOME TELEPHONE COMPANY OF AMENIA.
Otsego County.

Town:

Maryland	$1,000

City:

Oneonta	21,000

ITHACA ELECTRIC LIGHT AND POWER COMPANY.
Tompkins County.

City:

Ithaca	$150,000

ITHACA GAS LIGHT COMPANY.
Tompkins County.

City:

Ithaca	$110,000

NORWICH GAS AND ELECTRIC COMPANY.
Chenango County.

Town:

Norwich	$40,000

ONEONTA LIGHT AND POWER COMPANY.
Otsego County.

City:

Oneonta $40,000

OWEGO GAS LIGHT COMPANY.
Tioga County.

Town:

Owego $11,000

YORK STATE TELEPHONE COMPANY.
Broome County.

Towns:

Baxter	$2,000
Chenango	2,700
Lisle	800
Triangle	1,000
Vestal	100
Windsor	2,000

Chemung County.

Towns:

Big Flats	800
Erin	2,000
Horseheads	10,500
Southport	500
Van Etten	1,000
Veteran	250
Elmira	2,400

City:

Elmira   56,000

Tioga County.

Towns:

Candor	2,000
Spencer	2,800

SEVENTH JUDICIAL DISTRICT.

CANISTEO GAS COMPANY.
Steuben County.

Town:

Canisteo $26,000

GENEVA-SENECA ELECTRIC COMPANY.
Ontario County.

City:

Geneva $77,000

Seneca County.

Towns:

Waterloo 7,500
Seneca Falls 16,000

HORNELL GAS LIGHT COMPANY.
Steuben County.

City:

Hornell $120,000

INDEPENDENT UNION TELEPHONE COMPANY.
Livingston County.

Towns:

Avon $2,000
Caledonia 2,200
Lima 2,500

Villages:

Avon 750
Caledonia 250
Lima 500

Ontario County.

Towns:

Canandaigua 2,600
East Bloomfield 2,350
West Bloomfield 1,750

Village:

Canandaigua 650

Penn Yan Gas Light Company.
Yates County.
Town:

    Milo $10,000

Seneca County Home Telephone Company.
Seneca County.
Towns:

    Seneca Falls $15,000

    Waterloo   800

Villages:

    Seneca Falls   9,000

    Waterloo   6,500

Wayne County Gas and Electric Company.
Wayne County.
Town:

    Galen $16,000

Wayne County Gas and Electric Company (Lyons Gas Light Company).
Wayne County.
Town:

    Lyons $6,800

Wayne County Gas and Electric Company (New Gas Light and Fuel Company).
Wayne County.
Town:

    Arcadia $32,000

Wayne County Gas and Electric Company (Newark Gas Light and Fuel Company).
Wayne County.
Town:

    Arcadia $18,000

WAYNE COUNTY GAS AND ELECTRIC COMPANY (PALMYRA GAS AND ELECTRIC COMPANY).

Wayne County.

Town:

Palmyra $11,000

WAYNE COUNTY GAS AND ELECTRIC COMPANY (WAYNE COUNTY ELECTRIC COMPANY).

Wayne County.

Town:

Lyons $24,000

EIGHTH JUDICIAL DISTRICT.

AMERICAN TELEPHONE AND TELEGRAPH COMPANY.

Erie County.

City:

Buffalo $60,000

BUFFALO GENERAL ELECTRIC COMPANY.

Erie County.

City:

Buffalo $1,600,000

BATAVIA HOME TELEPHONE COMPANY.

Genesee County.

Town:

Batavia $11,000

Village:

Batavia   7,500

BUFFALO NATURAL GAS FUEL COMPANY.

Erie County.

City:

Buffalo $1,500,000

BUFFALO SOUTHERN RAILWAY COMPANY.
Erie County.

Towns:

East Hamburg	$48,000
West Seneca	80,000
Hamburg	30,400

City:

Lackawanna	15,200

CATARACT POWER AND CONDUIT COMPANY.
Erie County.

City:

Buffalo	$1,875,000

CENTRAL DOCK AND TERMINAL COMPANY.
Erie County.

City:

Buffalo	$14,600

DUNKIRK HOME TELEPHONE COMPANY.
Chautauqua County.

City:

Dunkirk	$13,000

INDEPENDENT UNION TELEPHONE COMPANY.
Chautauqua County.

Towns:

Hanover	$1,500
Portland	2,200
Ripley	1,800
Sheridan	2,100
Westfield	2,200

Village:

Silver Creek	500

Erie County.

Towns:

Amherst	1,500
Brant	1,100

Evans	$2,400
Hamburg	1,400
Tonawanda	1,800

City:

Tonawanda	1,300

Village:

Kenmore	900

Genesee County.

Towns:

Alabama	2,800
Batavia	2,300
LeRoy	2,700
Oakfield	1,800
Stafford	2,300

Villages:

Batavia	2,300
LeRoy	700
Oakfield	200

Orleans County.

Towns:

Ridgeway	8,500
Shelby	3,500

Villages:

Medina	5,500
Medina	2,000

Wyoming County.

Towns:

Covington	1,250
Middlebury	2,500

KEYSTONE GAS COMPANY.
Cattaraugus County.

City:

Olean	$155,000

NIAGARA COUNTY HOME TELEPHONE COMPANY.
Erie County.

City:

Tonawanda	$6,500

Niagara County.

Towns:

Lockport	$2,000
Newfane	1,000

Cities:

Lockport	20,000
Niagara Falls	40,000
North Tonawanda	15,000

NIAGARA LIGHT, HEAT AND POWER COMPANY.

Erié County.

Towns:

Amherst	$6,000
Tonawanda	9,000

City:

Tonawanda	45,000

Niagara County.

City:

North Tonawanda . . . . '	41,000

WYOMING COUNTY HOME TELEPHONE COMPANY.

Wyoming County.

Towns:

Orangeville	$1,000
Warsaw	3,250

Village:

Warsaw	2,000

NINTH JUDICIAL DISTRICT.

CONSOLIDATED WATER COMPANY.

Westchester County.

Towns:

Greenburg	$175,000
Scarsdale	13,000

CORNWALL TELEPHONE COMPANY.
Orange County.
Town:

Cornwall $6,000

DUTCHESS COUNTY TELEPHONE COMPANY OF POUGHKEEPSIE, N. Y.
Dutchess County.
City:

Poughkeepsie $32,000

HUDSON COUNTIES GAS AND ELECTRIC COMPANY.
Orange County.
Town:

Cornwall $14,000

NEWBURGH HOME TELEPHONE COMPANY.
Orange County.
City:

Newburgh $25,000

NEWBURGH LIGHT, HEAT AND POWER COMPANY.
Dutchess County.
City:

Poughkeepsie $1,400

Orange County.
Towns:

New Windsor   18,000

Newburgh   6,000

City:

Newburgh   160,000

NEW YORK INTER-URBAN WATER COMPANY.
Westchester County.
Town:

Mamaroneck   93,000

ORANGE COUNTY TRACTION COMPANY.
Orange County.

Towns:

    Montgomery $40,000

    Newburgh   47,000

City:

    Newburgh   110,000

ORANGE COUNTY LIGHTING COMPANY.
Orange County.

City:

    Middletown $100,000

PORT JERVIS LIGHT AND POWER COMPANY.
Orange County.

City:

    Port Jervis $30,000

PORT JERVIS TRACTION COMPANY.
Orange County.

City:

    Port Jervis $10,000

PORT JERVIS WATER WORKS COMPANY.
Orange County.

City:

    Port Jervis $90,000

POUGHKEEPSIE CITY AND WAPPINGER FALLS ELECTRIC RAILWAY COMPANY.
Dutchess County.

City:

    Poughkeepsie $135,000

Town:

    Poughkeepsie   75,000

ROCKLAND LIGHT AND POWER COMPANY.
Rockland County.

Towns:

    Clarkstown $32,000

    Haverstraw   28,000

Orangetown	$110,000
Ramapo	20,000
Stony Point	500

SUFFERN GAS COMPANY.
Rockland County.

Town:

| Ramapo | $10,000 |

SPECIAL FRANCHISE TAX PROCEEDINGS PENDING.
NEW YORK CITY.

ELECTRIC LIGHT AND POWER.

NEW YORK AND QUEENS ELECTRIC LIGHT AND POWER COMPANY.
Borough of Queens.

| 1907 | $300,000 |

GAS COMPANIES.

BROOKLYN UNION GAS COMPANY.
Borough of Brooklyn.

1906	$15,600,000
1907	17,200,000
1908	18,500,000
1909	16,300,000

NEW YORK AND QUEENS GAS COMPANY.
Borough of Queens.

| 1907 | $140,000 |

NEW YORK MUTUAL GAS LIGHT COMPANY.
Borough of Manhattan.

1900	$2,326,174
1901	2,300,000
1902	2,400,500
1903	2,580,000

1904	$2,831,500
1905	2,980,000
1906	3,975,000
1907	4,050,000
1908	4,000,000
1909	2,225,000

STANDARD GAS LIGHT COMPANY.
Boroughs of Manhattan and Bronx.

1900	$3,127,790

MISCELLANEOUS COMPANIES.

ABRAHAM & STRAUS.
Borough of Brooklyn.

1909	$18,000

ARBUCKLE BROTHERS.
Borough of Brooklyn.

1908	$7,200

Borough of Brooklyn.

1909	7,200

CHRISTINA, ARBUCKLE, TRUST
Borough of Brooklyn.

1908	$1,100

AUTOMATIC FIRE ALARM COMPANY.
Borough of Manhattan.

1907	$60,000

EMPIRE CITY SUBWAY COMPANY, LIMITED.
Boroughs of Manhattan and Bronx.

1907	$7,840,000

A. D. MATTHEWS & SONS.
Borough of Brooklyn.

1909	$10,000

JOHN B. MCDONALD.
Borough of Bronx.
1902	$5,000
1903	5,000
1904	12,500

NEW YORK MAIL AND NEWSPAPER TRANSPORTATION COMPANY.
Boroughs of Manhattan and Brooklyn.
1906	$90,000
1907	90,000

NEW YORK PNEUMATIC SERVICE COMPANY.
Borough of Manhattan.
1907	$150,000

TUBULAR DISPATCH COMPANY.
Borough of Manhattan.
1906	$140,000

PETER COOPER'S GLUE FACTORY.
Borough of Brooklyn.
1906	$500
1908	11,000
1909	6,000

STOCK QUOTATION TELEGRAPH COMPANY.
Borough of Manhattan.
1907	$160,000

MISCELLANEOUS RAILWAYS.

HUDSON AND MANHATTAN RAILROAD COMPANY.
Borough of Manhattan.
1908	$6,900,000
1909	8,000,000

LONG ISLAND RAILROAD COMPANY.
Borough of Queens.
1901	$80,000
1902	80,000

Boroughs of Brooklyn and Queens.
1903 .... $87,000

Borough of Brooklyn.
1904   30,000

Borough of Queens.
1906   30,000
1907   100,000

Boroughs of Brooklyn and Queens.
1908   1,143,400
1909   1,113,100

MANHATTAN RAILWAY COMPANY.
Boroughs of Manhattan and Bronx.
1906 .... $62,700,000

Borough of Manhattan.
1907   72,000,000

Borough of Bronx.
1907   2,900,000

Borough of Manhattan.
1908   75,000,000

Borough of Bronx.
1908   3,500,000

Borough of Manhattan.
1909   75,000,000

Borough of Bronx.
1909   3,500,000

NEW YORK AND LONG ISLAND RAILROAD COMPANY.
(E. P. Bryan et al. as Trustees.)
Borough of Manhattan.
1908 .... $3,175,000

Borough of Queens.
1908   1,675,000

Borough of Manhattan.

1909 .... $3,350,000

Borough of Queens.

1909 1,500,000

RAILROAD COMPANIES.

HARLEM RIVER AND PORTCHESTER RAILROAD.
Borough of Bronx.

1903 .... $22,000
1909 601,900

JAMAICA AND SOUTH SHORE RAILROAD COMPANY.
Borough of Queens.

1908 .... $1,000

NEW YORK CENTRAL AND HUDSON RIVER RAILROAD COMPANY (PARK AVENUE).
Borough of Manhattan.

1900 .... $10,192,000
1901 10,050,600
1902 10,050,000
1903 10,050,000
1904 10,009,000
1905 10,300,000
1906 11,200,000
1907 11,500,000
1908 12,299,400
1909 13,115,200

NEW YORK CENTRAL AND HUDSON RIVER RAILROAD COMPANY (ELEVENTH AVENUE).
Borough of Manhattan.

1906 .... $1,650,000
1907 2,400,000
1908 4,629,900
1909 4,572,000

Borough of Bronx.

1906	$125,000
1907	200,000
1908	786,300
1909	898,100

Richmond Lighting and Railroad Company.
Borough of Richmond.

1907	$500,000
1909	534,900

Staten Island Railway Company.
Borough of Richmond.

1908	$84,800
1909	84,700

Staten Island Midland Railroad Company.
Borough of Richmond.

1907	$160,000
1909	175,000

Staten Island Rapid Transit Railway.
Borough of Brooklyn.

1908	$270,000
1909	316,000

Williams Terminal Railway Company.
Borough of Brooklyn.

1907	$4,000

Yonkers Railroad Company.
(Leslie Sutherland, Receiver.)
Borough of Manhattan.

1909	$73,000

STREET RAILWAY COMPANIES.
Brooklyn Rapid Transit System.

Brooklyn City Railroad Company.
Borough of Brooklyn and Queens.

1901	$9,476,950
1902	11,109,000

1903	$12,502,000
1904	11,260,000
1905	13,980,000

BROOKLYN CITY RAILROAD COMPANY (BROOKLYN HEIGHTS RAILROAD, LESSOR).
Boroughs of Brooklyn and Queens.

| 1906 .... | $17,374,000 |
| 1907 .... | 21,710,000 |

Borough of Brooklyn.

| 1908 .... | 19,810,400 |

Borough of Queens.

| 1908 .... | 1,967,000 |

Borough of Brooklyn.

| 1909 .... | 18,180,000 |

Borough of Queens.

| 1909 .... | 1,891,000 |

BROOKLYN CITY AND NEWTOWN RAILROAD COMPANY.
Boroughs of Brooklyn and Queens.

1907	$3,000,000
1908	3,000,000
1909	2,515,000

BROOKLYN EASTERN DISTRICT TERMINAL.
Borough of Brooklyn.

| 1909 .... | $75,000 |

BROOKLYN HEIGHTS RAILROAD COMPANY.
Borough of Brooklyn.

| 1905 .... | $95,000 |
| 1909 .... | 75,000 |

BROOKLYN UNION ELEVATED RAILROAD COMPANY.
Borough of Brooklyn.

| 1905 .... | $6,050,000 |
| 1909 .... | 18,019,000 |

BROOKLYN, QUEENS COUNTY AND SUBURBAN RAILROAD COMPANY.

Boroughs of Brooklyn and Queens.

1901	$1,835,100
1902	1,480,000
1903	1,575,000
1904	1,355,000
1905	1,910,000
1906	2,316,000
1908	3,235,200

Borough of Brooklyn.

1909	2,997,500

Borough of Queens.

1909	235,300

CANARSIE RAILROAD COMPANY.

Borough of Brooklyn.

1908	$34,600
1909	31,200

CONEY ISLAND AND BROOKLYN RAILROAD COMPANY.

Borough of Brooklyn.

1901	$1,139,000
1907	1,700,000
1908	2,750,000
1909	2,543,000

CONEY ISLAND AND GRAVESEND RAILWAY COMPANY.

Borough of Brooklyn.

1902	$145,000
1903	105,000
1904	95,000
1909	120,000

NASSAU ELECTRIC RAILROAD COMPANY.

Borough of Brooklyn.

1907	$10,950,000
1908	14,328,000
1909	13,280,400

NEW YORK, BROOKLYN AND MANHATTAN BEACH RAILWAY.
Boroughs of Brooklyn and Queens.

1908	$509,400
1909	669,400

NEW YORK AND ROCKAWAY BEACH RAILWAY COMPANY.
Boroughs of Brook'yn and Queens.

1908	$288,800
1909	254,800

SEA BEACH RAILWAY COMPANY.
Borough of Brooklyn.

1909	$87,100

PROSPECT PARK AND CONEY ISLAND RAILWAY COMPANY — SOUTH BROOKLYN RAILWAY COMPANY, AS LESSEE.
Borough of Brooklyn.

1907	$20,000
1908	32,500
1909	273,000

Metropolitan System.
Nothing.

Second Avenue System.

SECOND AVENUE RAILWAY COMPANY.
Borough of Manhattan.

1901	$4,055,480
1902	4,417,700
1903	4,210,000
1904	4,210,000
1905	4,425,000
1906	4,425,000
1907	5,770,000
1908	5,780,000
1909	4,500,000

Third Avenue System.
Nothing.

WATER COMPANIES.

CRYSTAL WATER COMPANY OF EDGEWATER.

Borough of Richmond.

1901	$195,000
1902	125,000
1904	128,000

QUEENS COUNTY WATER COMPANY.

Borough of Queens.

1900	$179,564
1901	179,500
1902	176,500
1903	179,000
1904	190,000
1905	190,000
1906	216,000
1907	240,000
1908	300,000
1909	275,000

MONTAUK WATER COMPANY.

Borough of Queens.

1908	$5,270
1909	5,300

———

SECOND JUDICIAL DISTRICT — OUTSIDE NEW YORK CITY

HUNTINGTON RAILROAD COMPANY.

Suffolk County.

Town:

1900. Huntington	$17,500

NEW YORK TELEPHONE COMPANY.

Nassau County.

Towns:

1909. Hempstead	$320,000
North Hempstead	$100,000

NEW YORK AND NEW JERSEY TELEPHONE COMPANY.
Suffolk County.

Towns:
1908. South Hampton.................. $58,000

QUEENS COUNTY WATER COMPANY.
Nassau County.

Town:
1900. Hempstead..................... $65,000
1901. Hempstead..................... 65,000
1902. Hempstead..................... 67,000
1903. Hempstead..................... 72,000
1904. Hempstead..................... 92,000
1905. Hempstead..................... 95,500
1906. Hempstead..................... 110,000
1907. Hempstead..................... 160,000
1908. Hempstead..................... 180,000
1909. Hempstead..................... 180,000

THIRD JUDICIAL DISTRICT.

ALBANY AND HUDSON RAILROAD COMPANY.
Columbia County.

Town:
1907. Kinderhook.................... $8,500
City:
1908. Hudson....................... 80,000

Rensselaer County.

City:
1909. Rensselaer................... 40,000

AMERICAN TELEPHONE AND TELEGRAPH COMPANY.
Columbia County.

Town:
1908. Livingston................... $9,350

Rensselaer County.

City:
1907. Troy $28,950
1908. Troy   28,950

CATSKILL MOUNTAIN RAILWAY COMPANY.
Greene County.

Town:
1909. Catskill $18,000

COHOES RAILWAY COMPANY.
Albany County.

Town:
1906. Colonie $18,000
1907. Colonie   20,000
1908. Colonie   20,000

COMMERCIAL UNION TELEPHONE COMPANY.
Rensselaer County.

City:
1908. Troy $115,000
1909. Troy   115,000

DELAWARE AND HUDSON COMPANY.
Albany County.

City:
1908. Albany $203,500

Rensselaer County.

City:
1909. Troy $200,000

FITCHBURG RAILROAD COMPANY.
Rensselaer County.

Towns:
1908. Hoosick $13,500
       Pittstown   2,300
       Schaghticoke   4,900
City:
1908. Troy   31,400

GREEN ISLAND WATER SUPPLY COMPANY.
Albany County.

Town:

1907. Green Island...................... $14,000

HUDSON RIVER BRIDGE COMPANY.
Albany County.

City:

1907. Albany........................ $220,470

1908. Albany........................ 798,700

1909. Albany........................ 781,500

Rensselaer County.

City:

1908. Rensselaer...................... 480,000

1909. Rensselaer...................... 630,000

HUDSON RIVER TELEPHONE COMPANY.
Albany County.

City:

1909. Albany......................... $310,700

Rensselaer County.

City:

1907. Troy........................... 103,200

1908. Troy........................... 115,500

McCREARY AND POWERS (D. & H.).
Albany County.

City:

1903. Cohoes......................... $5,000

MUNICIPAL GAS COMPANY.
Albany County.

Cities:

1907. Albany......................... $1,500,000

Watervliet...................... 40,000

Cities:

1908. Albany......................... 1,050,000

Watervliet...................... 40,000

Towns:
  1909. Colonie $4,000
  1909. Green Island.....................   9,000
Cities:
  1909. Albany........................... 1,135,000
          Watervliet   50,000

NEW ENGLAND TELEGRAPH COMPANY.
Rensselaer County.

City:
  1907. Troy $4,550
  1908. Troy   4,500

NEW YORK CENTRAL AND HUDSON RIVER RAILROAD COMPANY.
Albany County.

Cities:
  1907. Albany.......................... $257,600
Town:
  1908. Coeymans   6,000
Cities:
  1908. Albany..........................   199,300
          Cohoes..........................   15,100
Town:
  1909. New Scotland   4,600
Cities:
  1909. Albany..........................   192,600
          Cohoes..........................   15,100

Columbia County.

City:
  1908. Hudson   26,300
  1909. Hudson   26,300

Greene County.

Town:
  1908. Catskill   65,600
  1909. Catskill   65,600

Rensselaer County.

Cities:

1908.	Rensselaer	$300,700
	Troy	54,100

Town:

1909.	Schodack	3,500

Cities:

1909.	Rensselaer	295,800
	Troy	54,100

Ulster County.

City:

1907.	Kingston	16,500
1908.	Kingston	65,900
1909.	Kingston	67,600

NEW YORK, ONTARIO AND WESTERN RAILWAY COMPANY.
Ulster County.

Town:

1908.	Wawarsing	$8,400
1909.	Wawarsing	8,400

TROY GAS COMPANY.
Rensselaer County.

City:

1907.	Troy	$640,500
1908.	Troy	775,000
1909.	Troy	640,500

TROY UNION RAILROAD COMPANY.
Rensselaer County.

City:

1901.	Troy	$60,000
1902.	Troy	60,000
1903.	Troy	60,000
1904.	Troy	60,000
1907.	Troy	125,000
1908.	Troy	244,000

UNITED TRACTION COMPANY.

Albany County.

Town:

1902.	Bethlehem	$3,000
1905.	Bethlehem	3,000
1906.	Bethlehem	4,000

Rensselaer County.

City:

1907.	Troy	1,300,000
1908.	Troy	1,400,000
1909.	Troy	1,400,000

WEST TROY GAS LIGHT COMPANY.

Albany County.

Town:

1900.	Green Island	$8,000

City:

1900.	Watervliet	25,000

FOURTH JUDICIAL DISTRICT.

DELAWARE AND HUDSON COMPANY.

Clinton County.

Town:

1908.	Blackbrook	$18,750

City:

1908.	Plattsburg	29,500

Saratoga County.

Town:

1908.	Saratoga Springs	79,400

Schenectady County.

City:

1908.	Schenectady	114,000

Washington County.

Towns:

1908.	Fort Edward	53,200
	Whitehall	38,900

EDISON ELECTRIC LIGHT AND POWER COMPANY OF AMSTERDAM.
Montgomery County.
City:
1906. Amsterdam $48,000

FITCHBURG RAILROAD COMPANY.
Saratoga County.
Towns:
1908. Half Moon..................... $5,800
Saratoga 9,700
Stillwater 3,200

Schenectady County.
Town:
1908. Glenville 7,500

FONDA, JOHNSTOWN AND GLOVERSVILLE RAILROAD COMPANY.
Montgomery County.
Town:
1907. Amsterdam $12,000

GLENS FALLS GAS AND ELECTRIC COMPANY.
Saratoga County.
Town:
1907. Moreau $1,000

Warren County.
Town:
1907. Queensbury 60,000

NEW YORK CENTRAL AND HUDSON RIVER RAILROAD COMPANY.
Franklin County.
Towns:
1908. Altamont $3,000
Malone 2,000

Montgomery County.
Town:
1901. Canajoharie $20,000
1904. Canajoharie 15,500
1906. Canajoharie 40,000

Towns:
1907.	Canajoharie	$62,000
	Minden	59,000
1908.	Canajoharie	70,000
	Minden	62,000
	Mohawk	20,500
	Palatine	3,800
	St. Johnsville....................	4,800

City:
1908.	Amsterdam	62,600

Towns:
1909.	Canajoharie	69,300
	Minden	62,000
	Mohawk	9,800

City:
1909.	Amsterdam	37,900

Schenectady County.

City:
1900.	Schenectady	141,600
1908.	Schenectady	326,100

Town:
1909.	Glenville	12,300

City:
1909.	Schenectady	318,500

St. Lawrence County.

Towns:
1908.	Canton	9,000
	Gouverneur	14,500
	Potsdam	6,700

City:
1908.	Ogdensburg	18,170

Towns:
1909.	Canton	8,400
	Gouverneur	12,500
	Potsdam	6,700

City:
1909.	Ogdensburg	18,470

SARATOGA AND SCHENECTADY RAILROAD COMPANY.
Saratoga County.

Town:

1908. Milton $24,200

FIFTH JUDICIAL DISTRICT.

DELAWARE, LACKAWANNA AND WESTERN RAILROAD COMPANY,
AND ONE.
Oneida County.

City:

1909. Utica $83,400

Onondaga County.

City:

1908. Syracuse 80,000
1909. Syracuse 29,300

Oswego County.

1908. Oswego 135,000
1909. Oswego 119,100

LITTLE FALLS AND DOLGEVILLE RAILROAD COMPANY.
Herkimer County.

City:

1908. Little Falls $2,600

NEW YORK CENTRAL AND HUDSON RIVER RAILROAD COMPANY.
Herkimer County.

Town:

1907. Herkimer $15,000

Towns:

1908. German Flats 51,400
     Herkimer 33,600

City:

1908. Little Falls 46,300

Towns:

1909. German Flats 44,400
     Herkimer 33,000

City:
 1909. Little Falls $64,100

Jefferson County.

City:
 1907. Watertown   12,000
Towns:
 1908. Adams   5,700
    Antwerp   2,900
    Brownville   4,700
    Champion   2,300
    Lyme   13,100
    Philadelphia   9,700
    Wilna   69,400
City:
 1908. Watertown   62,800
Towns:
 1909. Champion   20,400
    Clayton   10,600
    Lyme   16,100
    Philadelphia   9,800
    Wilna   50,400
City:
 1909. Watertown   63,500

Lewis County.

Town:
 1908. Diana   4,500
Town:
 1909. Lowville   7,900

Oneida County.

City:
 1907. Utica   35,000
Towns:
 1908. Camden   3,000
    Vernon   4,700
Cities:
 1908. Rome   29,300
    Utica   392,400

Towns:
  1909. Camden $3,200
          Remsen   4,500
Cities:
  1909. Rome   111,700
          Utica   227,900

Onondaga County.

Town:
  1906. Manlius   12,100
City:
  1906. Syracuse   977,225
  1907. Syracuse   990,000
Town:
  1908. Manlius   16,800
City:
          Syracuse   1,341,880
Towns:
  1909. DeWitt   5,700
          Manlius   17,300
City:
  1909. Syracuse   1,366,300

Oswego County.

Town:
  1900. Oswego   117,498
Cities:
  1907. Fulton   12,000
          Oswego   126,000
Town:
  1908. Mexico   3,100
Cities:
  1908. Fulton   14,700
          Oswego   169,200
Town:
  1909. Schroeppel   6,000
Cities:
  1909. Fulton   14,700
          Oswego   181,300

NEW YORK, ONTARIO AND WESTERN RAILWAY COMPANY.
Oneida County.
City:
1908. Utica $40,500
1909. Utica   71,800

Oswego County.
City:
1908. Oswego   51,600
Town:
1909. Constantia   5,800
City:
1909. Oswego   73,900

NEW YORK STATE REALTY AND TERMINAL COMPANY.
Jefferson County.
City:
1909. Watertown $2,200

SYRACUSE, BINGHAMTON AND NEW YORK RAILROAD COMPANY.
Onondaga County.
City:
1909. Syracuse $89,600

— — — —

SIXTH JUDICIAL DISTRICT.

ALBANY AND SUSQUEHANNA RAILROAD COMPANY.
Otsego County.
Town:
1908. Oneonta $41,700

DELAWARE, LACKAWANNA AND WESTERN RAILROAD COMPANY, AND ONE.
Tompkins County.
City:
1909. Ithaca $19,400

ELMIRA AND LAKE ONTARIO RAILROAD COMPANY.
Chemung County.
Town:
1908. Horseheads $7,500
1909. Horseheads   9,000

Schuyler County.

Towns:

1908.	Dix	$3,900
	Montour	1,200
	Reading	2,600
1909.	Dix	3,000
	Montour	1,200
	Reading	2,600

Elmira Water, Light and Railroad Company.
Chemung County.

City:

| 1904. | Elmira | $699,000 |

Erie Railroad Company.
Broome County.

Town:

| 1908. | Union | $19,300 |

City:

| 1908. | Binghamton | 77,500 |

Town:

| 1909. | Union | 17,200 |

City:

| 1909. | Binghamton | 96,400 |

Chemung County.

City:

| 1908. | Elmira | 61,200 |
| 1909. | Elmira | 61,200 |

Tioga County.

Towns:

1908.	Barton	9,300
	Owego	9,300
1909.	Barton	5,300
	Owego	9,900

Ithaca Telephone Company.
Tompkins County.

City:

| 1907. | Ithaca | $28,000 |

NEW YORK CENTRAL AND HUDSON RIVER RAILROAD COMPANY.
Madison County.

Town:
| 1908. Lennox | $58,900 |

City:
| 1908. Oneida | 29,600 |

Town:
| 1909. Lennox | 62,900 |

City:
| 1909. Oneida | 39,000 |

NEW YORK, LACKAWANNA AND WESTERN RAILROAD COMPANY.
Broome County.

City:
| 1908. Binghamton | $56,300 |
| 1909. Binghamton | 91,800 |

Chemung County.

City:
| 1908. Elmira | 48,400 |
| 1909. Elmira | 48,400 |

NEW YORK, ONTARIO AND WESTERN RAILROAD COMPANY.
Chenango County.

Town:
| 1908. Norwich | $10,200 |

Delaware County.

Towns:
1908. Hamden	15,000
Walton	14,100
1909. Hamden	12,000
Sidney	9,200
Walton	2,500

Madison County.

Town:
| 1908. Hamilton | 3,400 |

City:
| 1909. Oneida | 9,600 |

NEW YORK AND PENNSYLVANIA TELEPHONE AND TELEGRAPH
COMPANY.
Chemung County.
City:
1908. Elmira $88,500

NEW YORK TRANSIT COMPANY.
Broome County.
Towns:
1900. Fenton $1,620
       Maine   13,000

Chemung County.
Town:
1900. Horseheads   12,800

Chenango County.
Town:
1900. Big Flats   5,600

ONEIDA RAILWAY COMPANY.
Madison County.
City:
1909. Oneida $90,900

SYRACUSE, BINGHAMTON AND NEW YORK RAILROAD COMPANY.
Broome County.
City:
1908. Binghamton $11,700
1909. Binghamton   12,900

VALLEY RAILROAD COMPANY.
Broome County.
City:
1908. Binghamton $16,400
1909. Binghamton   16,600

SEVENTH JUDICIAL DISTRICT.

American Telephone and Telegraph Company.
Monroe County.

City:
1908. Rochester $12,000

Avon, Geneseo and Mt. Morris Railroad Company.
Livingston County.

Town:
1908. Avon $2,800
1909. Avon   3,100

Buffalo, Rochester and Pittsburg Railway Company.
Monroe County.

City:
1908. Rochester   44,900
1909. Rochester   46,900

Corning Telephone Company.
Steuben County.

City:
1909. Corning $23,000

Elmira and Lake Ontario Railroad Company.
Ontario County.

Town:
1908. Canandaigua $11,500
1909. Canandaigua   11,900

Wayne County.

Town:
1908. Arcadia $25,700
1909. Arcadia   22,000

Yates County.

Town:
1908. Milo $9,000
1909. Milo   8,000

ERIE RAILROAD COMPANY.
Livingston County.

Town:

1908.	Avon	$9,500
1909.	Avon	9,500

Steuben County.

Cities:

1908.	Corning	59,100
	Hornell	33,600
1909.	Corning	59,100
	Hornell	51,600

HORNELLSVILLE TELEPHONE COMPANY.
Steuben County.

City:

1907.	Hornell	$18,000
1908.	Hornell	18,600
1909.	Hornell	20,000

INTER-OCEAN TELEGRAPH AND TELEPHONE COMPANY.
Monroe County.

City:

1907.	Rochester	$5,000

NEW ENGLAND TELEGRAPH COMPANY.
Monroe County.

City:

1900.	Rochester	$10,000
1901.	Rochester	8,400
1902.	Rochester	8,450
1903.	Rochester	8,450
1904.	Rochester	8,450
1905.	Rochester	8,500
1906.	Rochester	9,000
1907.	Rochester	12,000
1908.	Rochester	12,000
1909.	Rochester	15,000

NEW YORK CENTRAL AND HUDSON RIVER RAILROAD COMPANY.

Cayuga County.

Town:
1908.	Brutus	$67,000

Towns:
1909.	Aurelius	4,400
	Brutus	67,000

City:
1909.	Auburn	22,300

Monroe County.

Towns:
1908.	Greece	13,700
	Perinton	17,000
	Pittsford	32,200
	Sweden	17,100

City:
1908.	Rochester	605,500

Towns:
1909.	Greece	13,200
	Perinton	18,100
	Pittsford	35,000
	Sweden	15,100

City:
1909.	Rochester	723,300

Ontario County.

Towns:
1908.	Manchester	8,800
	Phelps	8,100

City:
1908.	Geneva	27,227

Towns:
1909.	Canandaigua	50,700
	Manchester	5,200
	Phelps	8,400

City:
1909.	Geneva	25,000

Seneca County.

Towns:

1908.	Seneca Falls	$20,500
	Waterloo	11,600
1909.	Seneca Falls	21,900
	Waterloo	11,000

Steuben County.

City:

1907.	Corning	75,000
1908.	Corning	103,000
1909.	Corning	99,000

Wayne County.

Towns:

1908.	Arcadia	50,300
	Lyons	12,400
	Wolcott	12,100
1909.	Arcadia	51,800
	Lyons	13,600
	Wolcott	11,300

Yates County.

Town:

1909.	Torrey	7,600

NEW YORK TRANSIT COMPANY.
Steuben County.

Town:

1900.	Jasper	23,000

NIAGARA, LOCKPORT AND ONTARIO POWER COMPANY.
Ontario County.

Town:

1908.	Phelps	$100

ROCHESTER GAS AND ELECTRIC COMPANY.
Monroe County.

City:

1904.	Rochester	$2,305,000

ROCHESTER RAILWAY AND LIGHT COMPANY.
Monroe County.

City:
1905. Rochester $2,580,000

ROCHESTER, SYRACUSE AND EASTERN RAILROAD COMPANY.
Monroe County.

City:
1908. Rochester $5,900
1909. Rochester   7,100

ROCHESTER TELEPHONE COMPANY.
Monroe County .

City:
1901. Rochester $197,950
1902. Rochester   210,880
1903. Rochester   210,840
1904. Rochester   227,775
1905. Rochester   295,000
1906. Rochester   450,000

WESTERN NEW YORK AND PENNSYLVANIA RAILWAY COMPANY.
Livingston County.

Towns:
1908. Mt. Morris $4,700
      Nunda   4,600
1909. Mt. Morris   5,200
      Nunda   5,400

Monroe County.

City:
1908. Rochester $82,100
1909. Rochester   86,000

EIGHTH JUDICIAL DISTRICT.

BUFFALO CREEK RAILROAD COMPANY.
Erie County.

City:
1908. Buffalo $166,922
1909. Buffalo   186,600

BUFFALO GAS COMPANY.
Erie County.
City:
1907.	Buffalo	$2,150,000
1908.	Buffalo	2,200,000
1909.	Buffalo	2,000,000

BUFFALO AND LAKE ERIE TRACTION COMPANY.
Chautauqua County.
Towns:
1908.	Pomfret	$55,000
	Ripley	2,000
	Westfield	65,000

City:
1908.	Dunkirk	160,000

Towns:
1909.	Hanover	26,900
	Pomfret	65,000
	Portland	58,000
	Ripley	38,000
	Westfield	130,000

Erie County.
Towns:
1908.	Evans	18,250
	Hamburg	70,200
	West Seneca	150,000
1909.	Evans	18,250

City:
1909.	Lackawanna	150,000

BUFFALO AND SUSQUEHANNA RAILWAY COMPANY.
Erie County.
Towns:
1908.	Concord	$1,400
	Hamburg	5,800

City:
1908.	Buffalo	35,175
1909.	Buffalo	37,800

BUFFALO SOUTHERN RAILWAY COMPANY.
Erie County.

Towns:
1908.	East Hamburg	$5,500
	Hamburg	45,000
	West Seneca	60,000

DELAWARE, LACKAWANNA AND WESTERN RAILWAY COMPANY.
Erie County.

Towns:
1900.	Alden	$2,500
	Crossings	106,164

City:
1907.	Buffalo	135,000
1908.	Buffalo	789,255
1909.	Buffalo	1,004,000

DUNKIRK STREET RAILWAY COMPANY.
Chautauqua County.

City:
1908.	Dunkirk	$160,000

ERIE RAILROAD COMPANY.
Alleghany County.

Towns:
1908.	Friendship	$7,500
	Wellsville	12,500

Town:
1909.	Wellsville	5,800

Cattaraugus County.

Towns:
1908.	Little Valley	4,000
	Persia	7,700

City:
1908.	Olean	4,500

Town:
1909.	Persia	8,600

City:
1909.	Olean	6,200

Chautauqua County.

City:
1908.	Jamestown	61,400
1909.	Jamestown	32,300

Erie County.

City:
1907.	Buffalo	25,500

Town:
1908.	Lancaster	5,300

Cities:
1908.	Buffalo	404,395
	Tonawanda	27,800

Town:
1909.	Lancaster	5,300

Cities:
1909.	Buffalo	481,800
	Tonawanda	29,000

Genesee County.

Towns:
1908.	Batavia	15,500
1909.	Batavia	16,600

Niagara County.

Town:
1908.	Niagara	4,800

Cities:
1908.	Niagara Falls	52,600
	North Tonawanda	69,500

Town:
1909.	Niagara	4,400

Cities:
1909.	Niagara Falls	109,300
	North Tonawanda	66,500

Wyoming County.

Towns:
1908.	Attica	9,600
1909.	Attica	12,900

FEDERAL TELEPHONE AND TELEGRAPH COMPANY.
Erie County.

City:
1909. Buffalo $651,200

FREDONIA NATURAL GAS LIGHT COMPANY.
Chautauqua County.

Town:
1908. Pomfret $6,000

FRONTIER TELEPHONE COMPANY.
Erie County.

City:
1907. Buffalo $640,000
1908. Buffalo 651,200

GRAND TRUNK RAILWAY COMPANY OF CANADA.
Erie County.

City:
1908. Buffalo $30,360
1909. Buffalo 26,100

INTERNATIONAL BRIDGE COMPANY.
Erie County.

City:
1908. Buffalo $36,440
1909. Buffalo 42,300

INTERNATIONAL RAILWAY COMPANY.
Niagara County.

City:
1908. North Tonawanda $181,000

INTER-OCEAN TELEPHONE AND TELEGRAPH COMPANY.
Erie County.

Town:
1907. Aurora $11,300

Orleans County.

Town:
1907. Murray 7,000

LEHIGH VALLEY RAILWAY COMPANY.

Erie County.

City:

1908.	Buffalo	$303,570
1909.	Buffalo	336,600

NEW ENGLAND TELEGRAPH COMPANY.

Chautauqua County.

City:

1909.	Jamestown	$3,500

Erie County.

1907.	Buffalo	60,000
1908.	Buffalo	52,000
1909.	Buffalo	52,000

NEW YORK CENTRAL AND HUDSON RIVER RAILROAD COMPANY.

Erie County.

Cities:

1907.	Buffalo	$472,000
	Tonawanda	40,000
1908.	Buffalo	1,623,407
	Tonawanda	62,600

Towns:

1909.	Cheektowaga	5,000
	Lancaster	7,000

Cities:

1909.	Buffalo	1,939,900
	Tonawanda	56,600

Genesee County.

Town:

1908.	Batavia	62,900
1909.	Batavia	75,400

Niagara County.

City:

1900.	Lockport	40,100

Cities:

1907.	Lockport	70,000
	North Tonawanda	65,000

Towns:
| 1908. Lewiston | 19,900 |
| Niagara | 3,600 |

Cities:
1908. Lockport	222,000
Niagara Falls	119,600
North Tonawanda	216,500

Towns:
1909. Lewiston	17,300
Niagara	5,100
North Tonawanda	35,500

Cities:
1909. Lockport	225,800
Niagara Falls	129,100
North Tonawanda	100,600

Orleans County.

Towns:
1908. Albion	11,800
Ridgeway	15,600
1909. Albion	13,000
Ridgeway	19,800

NEW YORK CENTRAL AND NIAGARA RIVER RAILROAD COMPANY.
Erie County.

City:
| 1909. Tonawanda | $20,200 |

NEW YORK AND PENNSYLVANIA TELEPHONE AND TELEGRAPH
COMPANY.
Alleghany County.

Town:
| 1908. Wellsville | $9,500 |

NEW YORK TRANSIT COMPANY.
Alleghany County.

Town:
| 1900. Clarksville | $600 |

Cattaraugus County.

Town:
    1900. Franklinville $1,600

Chautauqua County.

Town:
    1900. Greenwood   42,500

NIAGARA GORGE RAILROAD COMPANY.
Niagara County.

Town:
    1907. Lewiston $34,000

NIAGARA FALLS HYDRAULIC POWER AND MANUFACTURING COMPANY.
Niagara County.

City:
    1908. Niagara Falls $185,400

NIAGARA, LOCKPORT AND ONTARIO POWER COMPANY.
Erie County.

Towns:
    1908. Cheektowaga $1,950
           Hamburg   1,500
           Lancaster   6,250
    1909. Hamburg   2,100
           Lancaster   6,250

Genesee County.

Town:
    1908. Batavia   200
Towns:
    1909. Elba   500
           Oakfield   450

NYPANO RAILROAD COMPANY.
Cattaraugus County.

Town:
    1908. Randolph $11,900
    1909. Randolph   11,100

PENNSYLVANIA GAS COMPANY.
Chautauqua County.

City:

1900.	Jamestown	$236,600
1901.	Jamestown	211,780
1902.	Jamestown	205,000
1903.	Jamestown	195,000
1904.	Jamestown	195,000
1905.	Jamestown	199,000

PEOPLES' GAS LIGHT AND COKE COMPANY.
Erie County.

City:

1907.	Buffalo	$65,000
1908.	Buffalo	65,000
1909.	Buffalo	65,000

REPUBLIC METALWARE COMPANY.
Erie County.

City:

1909.	Buffalo	$6,200

SOUTH BUFFALO RAILWAY COMPANY.
Erie County.

City:

1908.	Buffalo	$12,250
1909.	Buffalo	6,600

TERMINAL RAILWAY COMPANY OF BUFFALO.
Erie County.

Town:

1908.	Hamburg	$28,700

TONAWANDA POWER COMPANY.
Niagara County.

Town:

1906.	North Tonawanda	$60,000

UNITED NATURAL GAS COMPANY.
Cattaraugus County.

Towns:
1900.	Little Valley	$13,000
	Otto	13,000

Erie County.

Town:
1900.	Collins	21,500

WESTERN NEW YORK AND PENNSYLVANIA RAILWAY COMPANY.
Alleghany County.

Towns:
1908.	Belfast	$750
	Cuba	3,900

Cattaraugus County.

Towns:
1908.	Alleghany	1,300
	Franklinville	1,000
	North Olean	3,800
	Portville	2,900
	Salamanca	4,500

City:
1908.	Olean	53,900

Towns:
1909.	Alleghany	1,600
	Franklinville	1,000
	Portville	1,800
	Salamanca	4,900

City:
1909.	Olean	7,560

Chautauqua County.

Towns:
1908.	Mayville	16,600
	Portland	6,000
	Sherman	800
	Silver Creek	8,800

City:
  1909. Dunkirk $13,500

Erie County.

· Towns:
  1908. Angola   500
        Blaisdell   700
        East Aurora   3,000
        Farnham   4,000
        West Seneca   4,600
City:
  1908. Buffalo   192,285
Towns:
  1909. Blaisdell   700
        East Aurora   4,200
        Farnham   3,600
City:
  1909. Lackawanna   9,200
        Buffalo   279,900

Wyoming County.

Town:
  1908. Arcade   1,100
  1909. Arcade   700

NINTH JUDICIAL DISTRICT.

CENTRAL NEW ENGLAND RAILWAY COMPANY.
Dutchess County.

City:
  1909. Poughkeepsie $720,100

CONSOLIDATED WATER COMPANY OF SUBURBAN NEW YORK.
Westchester County.

Towns:
  1907. Greenburg $175,000
        Mt. Pleasant   67,000
  1908. Mt. Pleasant   60,000

Edenwald Street Railway Company.

Town: *Westchester County.*

1907.	Eastchester	$1,500
1908.	Eastchester	1,500

Erie Railroad Company.

Towns: *Orange County.*

1908.	Chester	$16,000
	Goshen	10,500
	Port Jervis	31,000

Cities:

1908.	Middletown	32,000
	Newburg	30,800
1909.	Chester	10,000
	Goshen	11,000
	Port Jervis	43,500
1909.	Middletown	37,100
	Newburgh	29,500

Town: *Rockland County.*

1908.	Ramapo	18,700
1909.	Ramapo	19,000

Goshen and Deckertown Railroad Company.

Town: *Orange County.*

1908.	Goshen	$1,400
1909.	Goshen	1,400

Larchmont Water Company.

Town: *Westchester County.*

1904.	Mamaroneck	$37,000
1905.	Mamaroneck	37,000
1906.	Mamaroneck	43,000
1907.	Mamaroneck	53,900
1908.	Mamaroneck	45,000
1909.	Mamaroneck	45,000

7

MIDDLETOWN, UNIONVILLE AND WATER GAP RAILROAD COMPANY.
Orange County.

City:
1908. Middletown..................... $5,500

MONTGOMERY AND ERIE RAILROAD COMPANY.
Orange County.

Town:
1908. Goshen......................... $3,900
1909. Goshen.........................   3,900

NEW ENGLAND TELEPHONE COMPANY.
Orange County.

Town:
1908. Bloomingrove................... $4,650 .

NEW JERSEY AND NEW YORK RAILROAD COMPANY.
Rockland County.

Towns:
1908. Haverstraw..................... $8,800
       Ramapo.........................   4,800
1909. Haverstraw.....................   8,800
       Ramapo......................... .   4,800

NEW YORK CENTRAL AND HUDSON RIVER RAILROAD COMPANY.
Dutchess County.

Towns:
1908. Fishkill....................... $14,900
       North East.....................   3,900
City:
1908. Poughkeepsie...................   67,200
Town:
1909. Fishkill.......................   14,900
City:
1909. Poughkeepsie...................   67,200

Orange County.

Town:
1908. Montgomery.....................   8,100

City:
1908.	Newburgh	$44,400

Towns:
1909.	Cornwall	9,800
	Montgomery	8,400

City:
1909.	Newburgh	44,400

Putnam County.

Town:
1908.	Southeast	24,000
1909.	Southeast	24,000

Rockland County.

Town:
1908.	Haverstraw	25,400
1909.	Haverstraw	22,800

Westchester County.

City:
1900.	Yonkers	142,000

Cities:
1907.	Mt. Vernon	18,600
	Yonkers	40,400

Towns:
1908.	Cortland	9,300
	Greenburg	15,000
	White Plains	8,000

Cities:
1908.	Mt. Vernon	12,700
	Yonkers	106,500

Towns:
1909.	Cortland	9,300
	Greenburg	21,200
	Mt. Pleasant	19,900
	Ossining	9,600
	White Plains	17,700

City:
1909.	Mt. Vernon	10,800

NEW YORK INTERURBAN WATER COMPANY.
Westchester County.
Town:
   1906. Rye............................ $12,500

NEW YORK, NEW HAVEN AND HARTFORD RAILROAD COMPANY.
Westchester County.
Town:
   1908. Rye............................ $305,700
   1909. Rye............................   258,500
City:
   1909. Mt. Vernon   113,700

NEW YORK, ONTARIO AND WESTERN RAILWAY COMPANY.
Orange County.
City:
   1909. Middletown $27,400

NEW YORK AND STAMFORD RAILWAY COMPANY.
Westchester County.
Towns:
   1908. Mamaroneck $85,000
          Rye...........................   200,000

NEW YORK TRANSIT COMPANY.
Orange County.
Town:
   1900. Deerpark $5,196

NEW YORK, WESTCHESTER AND CONNECTICUT TRACTION COMPANY.
Westchester County.
Cities:
   1902. Mt. Vernon $35,000
          New Rochelle   10,000
Town:
   1903. Eastchester   16,000
City:
   1903. New Rochelle   10,000

Towns:
1904.	Eastchester	$16,000
	Pelham	5,000

Cities:
1904.	Mt. Vernon	18,000
	New Rochelle	10,000

Towns:
1905.	Eastchester	15,000
	Pelham	5,000

Cities:
1905.	Mt. Vernon	18,000
	New Rochelle	10,000

Towns:
1906.	Eastchester	16,000
	Pelham	5,000

Cities:
1906.	Mt. Vernon	22,000
	New Rochelle	12,000

Towns:
1907.	Eastchester	20,000
	Pelham	8,000

Cities:
1907.	Mt. Vernon	35,000
	New Rochelle	20,000

Towns:
1908.	Eastchester	25,000
	Pelham	8,000

Cities:
1907.	Mt. Vernon	35,000
	New Rochelle	20,000

NORTHERN WESTCHESTER LIGHTING COMPANY.
Westchester County.

Towns:
1908.	Cortland	$4,000
	Mt. Pleasant	5,000
	Ossining	68,000

NYACK AND SOUTHERN RAILROAD COMPANY.
Rockland County.

Town:
1909. Orangetown $7,700

PEEKSKILL LIGHT AND RAILROAD COMPANY.
Westchester County.

Town:
1900. Cortland $47,250

POCANTICO RIVER WATER COMPANY (NOW CONSOLIDATED WATER COMPANY).
Westchester County.

Towns:
1901. Greenburg $54,000
      Mt. Pleasant 55,000

TARRYTOWN, WHITE PLAINS AND MAMARONECK RAILWAY COMPANY.
Westchester County.

Town:
1904. Scarsdale $27,000
Town:
1905. Scarsdale 30,000

ORANGE COUNTY LIGHTING COMPANY.
Orange County.

City:
1909. Middletown $90,000

WESTCHESTER ELECTRIC RAILROAD COMPANY.
Westchester County.

Town:
1904. Mamaroneck $30,000
City:
1901. Mt. Vernon 174.000

CABLE, TELEGRAPH AND TELEPHONE COMPANIES.

COMMERCIAL CABLE COMPANY.

Borough of Manhattan $430,000

CONSOLIDATED TELEGRAPH AND ELECTRIC SUBWAY COMPANY.

Borough of Bronx....................... $325,000
Borough of Manhattan.................. 7,000,000

MEXICAN TELEGRAPH COMPANY.

Borough of Brooklyn.................... $30,000
Borough of Manhattan................. 50,000

NEW YORK TELEPHONE COMPANY.

Borough of Bronx....................... $2,100,000
Borough of Brooklyn 8,000,000
Borough of Manhattan.................. 32,230,000
Borough of Queens..................... 1,200,000
Borough of Richmond 640,000

POSTAL TELEGRAPH AND CABLE COMPANY.

Borough of Manhattan.................. $360,400

WESTERN UNION TELEGRAPH COMPANY.

All boroughs $814,200

ELECTRIC LIGHT AND POWER.

AMSTERDAM ELECTRIC LIGHT, HEAT AND POWER COMPANY.

Boorugh of Brooklyn $75,000

BRUSH ELECTRIC ILLUMINATING COMPANY OF NEW YORK.

Borough of Manhattan.................. $300,000

EDISON ELECTRIC ILLUMINATING COMPANY OF BROOKLYN.
Borough of Brooklyn ....:.. $12,000,000

KINGS COUNTY LIGHTING COMPANY.
Borough of Brooklyn $1,300,000

NEW YORK EDISON COMPANY.
Borough of Bronx....................... $1,600,000
Borough of Brooklyn   28,000
Borough of Manhattan   36,500,000

RICHMOND LIGHT AND RAILROAD COMPANY.
Borough of Richmond $550,000

UNITED ELECTRIC LIGHT AND POWER COMPANY.
Borough of Manhattan $5,100,000

WESTCHESTER LIGHTING COMPANY.
Borough of Bronx....................... $250,000

GAS COMPANIES.
BROOKLYN UNION GAS COMPANY.
Borough of Brooklyn $16,500,000

CENTRAL UNION GAS COMPANY.
Borough of Bronx $1,750,000

CONSOLIDATED GAS COMPANY OF NEW YORK.
Borough of Manhattan $20,001,500

FLATBUSH GAS COMPANY.
Borough of Brooklyn $800,000

JAMAICA GAS LIGHT COMPANY.
Borough of Queens...................... $200,000

NEW AMSTERDAM GAS COMPANY.

Borough of Manhattan	$5,000,000
Borough of Queens	1,500,000

NEWTOWN GAS COMPANY.

Borough of Queens	$650,000

NEW YORK MUTUAL GAS LIGHT COMPANY.

Borough of Manhattan	$2,225,000

NEW YORK AND RICHMOND GAS COMPANY.

Borough of Richmond	$340,000

NORTHERN UNION GAS COMPANY.

Borough of Bronx	$1,100,000

QUEENSBOROUGH GAS AND ELECTRIC COMPANY.

Borough of Queens	$250,000

RICHMOND HILL AND QUEENS COUNTY GAS LIGHT COMPANY.

Borough of Queens	$125,000

THE STANDARD GAS LIGHT COMPANY OF THE CITY OF NEW YORK.

Borough of Bronx	$150,000
Borough of Manhattan	3,300,000

WOODHAVEN GAS LIGHT COMPANY.

Borough of Queens	$195,000

MISCELLANEOUS COMPANIES.

ABRAHAM & STRAUS, ET AL.

Borough of Brooklyn	$18,000

AMERICAN MANUFACTURING COMPANY.

Borough of Brooklyn	$9,000

Arbuckle Brothers.

Borough of Brooklyn $16,200

James Matthews, et al.

Borough of Brooklyn $10,000

Empire City Subway Company.

Borough of Bronx $1,335,000
Borough of Manhattan   7,857,000

New York Quotation Company.

Borough of Manhattan $175,000

MISCELLANEOUS RAILWAYS.

Bush Terminal Railroad Company.

Borough of Brooklyn $350,000

Central Park, North and East River Railroad Company.

Borough of Manhattan $2,750,000

East River Terminal Railroad.

Borough of Brooklyn $74,500

Edenwald Street Railway Company.

Borough of Manhattan $6,000

Harlem River and Portchester Railroad Company.

Borough of Bronx $646,000

Hudson and Manhattan Railway Company.

Borough of Manhattan $10,900,000

Interborough Rapid Transit Company.

Borough of Manhattan $183,500

Long Island Electric Railroad Company.

Borough of Queens $425,000

LONG ISLAND RAILROAD COMPANY.

Borough of Brooklyn	$14,100
Borough of Queens	1,093,600

MANHATTAN RAILWAY COMPANY.

Borough of Bronx	$3,500,000
Borough of Manhattan	75,012,500

NASSAU ELECTRIC RAILROAD COMPANY.

Borough of Brooklyn	$3,056,400

NEW YORK CENTRAL AND HUDSON RIVER RAILROAD COMPANY.

Borough of Manhattan (Park Avenue)	$13,115,200
Borough of Manhattan	134,500
Borough of Bronx	838,100

NEW YORK CITY INTERBOROUGH RAILWAY COMPANY.

Borough of Bronx	$675,000
Borough of Manhattan	75,000

TRUSTEES, NEW YORK AND LONG ISLAND RAILROAD COMPANY.

Borough of Manhattan	$4,451,500
Borough of Queens	1,000,000

NEW YORK AND LONG ISLAND TRACTION COMPANY.

Borough of Queens	$197,500

NEW YORK AND QUEENS COUNTY RAILWAY COMPANY.

Borough of Queens	$2,275,000

NEW YORK, WESTCHESTER AND CONNECTICUT TRACTION COMPANY.

Borough of Manhattan	$4,400

PROSPECT PARK AND CONEY ISLAND RAILROAD COMPANY (By SOUTH BROOKLYN RAILWAY COMPANY, LESSEE).

Borough of Brooklyn	$273,000

STATEN ISLAND MIDLAND RAILWAY COMPANY.
Borough of Richmond $200,000

STATEN ISLAND RAPID TRANSIT COMPANY.
Borough of Richmond $316,100

STATEN ISLAND RAILWAY.
Borough of Richmond $84,700

TWENTY-EIGHTH AND TWENTY-NINTH STREETS CROSSTOWN RAIL-
ROAD COMPANY.
Borough of Manhattan $150,000

LESLIE SUTHERLAND, PERMANENT RECEIVER OF THE YONKERS
RAILROAD COMPANY.
Borough of Bronx $73,000

STREET RAILWAYS.
Brooklyn Rapid Transit System.

BROOKLYN. CITY RAILROAD COMPANY (BY THE BROOKLYN
HEIGHTS RAILROAD COMPANY, LESSEE).
Borough of Brooklyn $18,180,000

BROOKLYN CITY RAILROAD COMPANY (BY THE BROOKLYN
HEIGHTS RAILROAD COMPANY, LESSEE).
Borough of Queens $1,891,000

BROOKLYN, QUEENS COUNTY AND SUBURBAN RAILROAD COMPANY.
Borough of Queens $188,300

BROOKLYN HEIGHTS RAILROAD COMPANY.
Borough of Brooklyn $75,000

BROOKLYN HEIGHTS RAILROAD COMPANY, LESSEE OF A CERTAIN
TRACK, ETC.
Borough of Brooklyn $6,000

BROOKLYN UNION ELEVATED RAILROAD COMPANY.

Borough of Brooklyn $19,619,000

BROOKLYN, QUEENS COUNTY AND SUBURBAN RAILROAD COMPANY.

Borough of Brooklyn $2,600,000

CANARSIE RAILROAD COMPANY.

Borough of Brooklyn . . . . : $35,200

CONEY ISLAND AND BROOKLYN RAILROAD COMPANY.

Borough of Brooklyn $4,036,000

CONEY ISLAND AND GRAVESEND RAILWAY COMPANY.

Borough of Brooklyn $160,000

NASSAU ELECTRIC RAILROAD COMPANY.

Borough of Brooklyn $10,230,000

NEW YORK, BROOKLYN AND MANHATTAN RAILWAY COMPANY.

Borough of Brooklyn $706,300
Borough of Queens   33,300

NEW YORK AND ROCKAWAY BEACH RAILWAY COMPANY.

Borough of Queens $237,800

SEA BEACH RAILWAY COMPANY.

Borough of Brooklyn $118,300

SOUTH BROOKLYN RAILWAY COMPANY.

Borough of Brooklyn $47,400

Metropolitan System.

BLEECKER STREET AND FULTON FERRY RAILROAD COMPANY.

Borough of Manhattan $730,000

BROADWAY AND SEVENTH AVENUE RAILROAD COMPANY.

Borough of Manhattan $7,955,000

CENTRAL CROSSTOWN RAILROAD COMPANY.

Borough of Manhattan $660,000

CHRISTOPHER AND TENTH STREET RAILROAD COMPANY.

Borough of Manhattan $1,172,000

EIGHTH AVENUE RAILROAD COMPANY.

Borough of Manhattan $4,800,000

FORT GEORGE AND ELEVENTH AVENUE RAILROAD COMPANY.

Borough of Manhattan $317,000

FORTY-SECOND STREET AND GRAND STREET FERRY RAILROAD COMPANY.

Borough of Manhattan $1,600,000

FORTY-SECOND STREET, MANHATTANVILLE AND ST. NICHOLAS RAILWAY COMPANY.

Borough of Manhattan $4,206,000

METROPOLITAN STREET RAILWAY COMPANY.

Borough of Manhattan $20,258,000

NINTH AVENUE RAILROAD COMPANY.

Borough of Manhattan $2,800,000

NEW YORK AND HARLEM RAILROAD COMPANY.

Borough of Bronx $80,000
Borough of Manhattan $9,263,000

SIXTH AVENUE RAILROAD COMPANY.

Borough of Manhattan $4,550,000

THIRTY-FOURTH STREET CROSSTOWN RAILWAY COMPANY.

Borough of Manhattan $1,206,000

TWENTY-THIRD STREET RAILWAY COMPANY.

Borough of Manhattan $2,790,000

Second Avenue System.

SECOND AVENUE RAILROAD COMPANY IN THE CITY OF NEW YORK.

Borough of Manhattan................... $4,500,000

Third Avenue System.

BRONX TRACTION COMPANY.

Borough of Bronx...................... $250,000

DRY DOCK, EAST BROADWAY AND BATTERY RAILROAD COMPANY.

Borough of Manhattan.................. $1,400,000

KINGSBRIDGE RAILWAY COMPANY.

Borough of Manhattan.................. $759,000

SOUTHERN BOULEVARD RAILROAD COMPANY.

Borough of Bronx...................... $196,000

THIRD AVENUE RAILROAD COMPANY.

Borough of Manhattan.................. $7,920,000

JAMES N. WALLACE, ADRIAN ISELIN AND HARRY BRONNER (REP-RESENTING THE THIRD AVENUE RAILROAD).

Borough of Manhattan.................. $7,920,000

UNION RAILWAY COMPANY OF NEW YORK CITY.

Borough of Bronx $4,200,000
Borough of Manhattan.................. $220,000

WESTCHESTER ELECTRIC RAILROAD COMPANY.

Borough of Bronx...................... $150,000

Water Companies.

CITIZENS WATER SUPPLY COMPANY OF NEWTOWN.

Borough of Queens..................... $800,000

JAMAICA WATER SUPPLY COMPANY.

Borough of Queens..................... $550,000

QUEENS COUNTY WATER COMPANY.

Borough of Queens $275,000

SECOND JUDICIAL DISTRICT.
(Outside New York City.)

AMITYVILLE ELECTRIC LIGHT COMPANY.
Nassau County.

Town:

Oyster Bay $1,500

CITIZENS' WATER SUPPLY COMPANY OF NEWTOWN.
Nassau County.

Town:

North Hempstead $73,000

NASSAU LIGHT AND POWER COMPANY.
Nassau County.

Towns:

Hempstead	$45,000
North Hempstead	150,000
Oyster Bay	100,000

NEW YORK TELEPHONE COMPANY.
Nassau County.

Towns:

Hempstead	$330,000
North Hempstead	110,000
Oyster Bay	136,000

Suffolk County.

Babylon	50,000
Brookhaven	63,000
Easthampton	17,000
Huntington	48,000
Islip	65,000
Riverhead	16,500
Shelter Island	4,000
Smithtown	21,000
Southampton	69,000
Southold	30,000

QUEENS COUNTY WATER COMPANY.
Nassau County.

Town:

Hempstead $190,000

THIRD JUDICIAL DISTRICT.

ALBANY SOUTHERN RAILROAD COMPANY.
Columbia County.

City:

Hudson $80,000

Rensselaer County.

City:

Rensselaer $215,000

BOSTON AND MAINE RAILROAD COMPANY.
Rensselaer County.

City:

Troy $217,500

CATSKILL MOUNTAIN RAILWAY COMPANY.
Greene County.

Town:

Catskill $18,000

COMMERCIAL UNION TELEPHONE COMPANY.
Rensselaer County.

City:

Troy $115,000

DELAWARE AND HUDSON COMPANY.
Albany County.

City:

Albany $215,200

Rensselaer County.

City:

Troy 217,500

DELAWARE AND HUDSON COMPANY (BRIDGE).
Rensselaer County.

City:

Troy $100,000

FITCHBURG RAILROAD COMPANY.
Rensselaer County.

Towns:

Hoosick $12,600
Pittstown 5,300
Schaghticoke 5,700

City:

Troy $31,400

HUDSON RIVER BRIDGE COMPANY.
Albany County.

City:

Albany 781,500

Rensselaer County.

City:

Rensselaer 285,000

KINGSTON CONSOLIDATED RAILWAY COMPANY.
Ulster County.

City:

Kingston $140,000

MUNICIPAL GAS COMPANY.
Albany County.

Towns:

Bethlehem $4,000
Colonie $7,000
Green Island 10,000

Cities:

Albany $1,665,000
Watervliet 50,000

NEW YORK CENTRAL AND HUDSON RIVER RAILROAD COMPANY.

Albany County.

Towns:

Coeymans	$6,000
Green Island	14,000
New Scotland	4,600

Cities:

Albany	$192,600
Cohoes	15,100

Columbia County.

City:

Hudson	26,300

Greene County.

Town:

Catskill	65,600

Rensselaer County.

Town:

Schodack	3,500

Cities:

Rensselaer	108,800
Troy	100,000

Ulster County.

City:

Kingston	67,600

NEW YORK CENTRAL AND HUDSON RIVER RAILROAD COMPANY (BOSTON AND ALBANY RAILROAD COMPANY.)

Columbia County.

City:

Hudson	$22,800

Rensselaer County.

City:

Rensselaer	84,500

NEW YORK, ONTARIO AND WESTERN RAILWAY COMPANY.
Ulster County.

Town:

Wawarsing	$7,000

NEW YORK TELEPHONE COMPANY.
Albany County.

Towns:

Bethlehem	$17,000
Colonie	40,000
Guilderland	3,400

Cities:

Cohoes	17,500
Watervliet	40,000

Columbia County.

Towns:

Chatham	3,000
Claverack	4,900
Copake	300
Germantown	2,600
Ghent	2,200
Greenport	5,300
Kinderhook	4,300
Livingston	3,500
Stockport	4,000
Stuyvesant	4,200

Greene County.

Towns:

Athens	5,900
Catskill	18,000
Coxsackie	4,000
Hunter	4,000

Rensselaer County.

Towns:

Brunswick	3,500
Hoosick	13,000

North Greenbush	$3,450
Prestenkill	1,200
Sand Lake	1,600
Schaghticoke	6,500
Schodack	13,000

Cities:

Rensselaer	26,000
Troy	128,000

Schenectady County.

Towns:

Glenville	25,000
Niskayuna	12,000
Rotterdam	8,500

Schoharie County.

Town:

Schoharie	1,049

Sullivan County.

Town:

Mamakating	4,000

Ulster County.

Towns:

Esopus	4,600
Lloyd	5,500
Marlboro	3,000
Marbletown	4,000
New Paltz	6,500
Olive	5,500
Rochester	3,000
Rosendale	5,300
Saugerties	19,500
Shawangunk	650
Ulster	10,250
Wawarsing	3,000

City:

Kingston	90,000

POSTAL TELEGRAPH–CABLE COMPANY.
Albany County.

City:

　　Albany . . . .　　$37,000

RENSSELAER WATER COMPANY.
Rensselaer County.

City:

　　Rensselaer . . . .　　$48,000

SCHENECTADY RAILWAY COMPANY.
Albany County.

City:

　　Albany . . . .　　$100,000

TROY GAS COMPANY.
Rensselaer County.

City:

　　Troy . . . .　　$1,050,000

TROY UNION RAILROAD COMPANY.
Rensselaer County.

City:

　　Troy . . . .　　$217,500

UNITED TRACTION COMPANY.
Rensselaer County.

City:

　　Troy . . . .　　$1,600,900

FOURTH JUDICIAL DISTRICT.

DELAWARE AND HUDSON COMPANY.
Clinton County.

Towns:

　　Black Brook . . . .　　$12,000
　　Champlain . . . .　　6,100

City:

　　Plattsburg . . . .　　16,000

Essex County.

Town:

Ticonderoga $8,300

Franklin County.

Town:

Harrietstown 7,200

Saratoga County.

Towns:

Halfmoon 14,500
Milton 24,400
Saratoga Springs 74,900
Waterford 13,300

Schenectady County.

City:

Schenectady 131,400

Warren County.

City:

Glens Falls 11,800

Washington County.

Towns:

Fort Edward 55,000
Whitehall 99,200

FITCHBURG RAILROAD COMPANY.
Saratoga County.

Towns:

Halfmoon $6,600
Saratoga 9,700
Saratoga Springs 6,800
Stillwater 2,300

FONDA, JOHNSTOWN AND GLOVERSVILLE RAILROAD COMPANY.
Montgomery County.

City:

Amsterdam $22,000

FULTON COUNTY GAS AND ELECTRIC COMPANY.
Fulton County.
Cities:

Gloversville	$240,000
Johnstown	100,000

NEW YORK CENTRAL AND HUDSON RIVER RAILROAD COMPANY (MOHAWK AND MALONE RAILWAY COMPANY, No. 1).
Franklin County.
Town:

Altamont	$3,900

NEW YORK CENTRAL AND HUDSON RIVER RAILROAD COMPANY (NEW YORK AND OTTAWA RAILWAY COMPANY, No. 2).
Town:

Altamont	$2,800

Montgomery County.
Towns:

Canajoharie	85,800
Minden	83,000
Mohawk	12,800
Palatine	7,000
St. Johnsville	28,000

City:

Amsterdam	38,100

Schenectady County.
Town:

Glenville	18,800

City:

Schenectady	319,700

St. Lawrence County.
Towns:

Canton	8,400
Gouverneur	8,600
Morristown	4,000
Potsdam	6,700

City:

Ogdensburg $19,600

NEW YORK TELEPHONE COMPANY.
Clinton County.

Towns:

Ausable	4,000
Black Brook	3,100
Champlain	4,500
Chazy	2,800
Clinton	4,200
Mooers	6,000
Peru	3,300
Plattsburg	10,000
Saranac	3,700

City:

Plattsburg   21,150

Essex County.

Towns:

Chesterfield	5,500
Elizabethtown	3,500
Jay	4,700
Keene	8,000
Moriah	5,000
North Elba	13,900
St. Armand	4,100
Ticonderoga	3,100
Westport	6,000
Willsboro	3,200

Franklin County.

Towns:

Altamont	6,500
Belmont	3,200
Bombay	3,800
Burke	2,600
Chateaugay	2,500
Constable	2,800

Duane	$2,350
Ft. Covington	4,000
Franklin	4,000
Harrietstown	18,000
Malone	15,000
Santa Clara	2,000
Westville	4,200

Montgomery County.

Town:
| Amsterdam | 12,000 |

City:
| Amsterdam | 52,000 |

Saratoga County.

Towns:
Ballston	15,000
Greenfield	6,500
Half Moon	16,000
Milton	13,000
Moreau	11,000
Saratoga	13,500
Saratoga Springs	50,000
Stillwater	10,000
Waterford	12,000
Wilton	3,400

Schenectady County.

Towns:
Glenville	25,000
Niskayuna	12,000
Rotterdam	8,500

City:
| Schenectady | 190,000 |

St. Lawrence County.

Towns:
Canton	18,000
Colton	2,000
DeKalb	8,500

DePuyster	$600
Edwards	4,350
Fine	4,200
Fowler	3,800
Gouverneur	18,500
Hopkinton	1,100
Lawrence	3,800
Lisbon	5,500
Louisville	6,000
Madrid	5,000
Massena	16,500
Morristown	3,300

City:

Ogdensburg	27,000

Warren County.

Towns:

Bolton	1,254
Caldwell	2,275
Queensbury	5,082

Washington County.

Towns:

Argyle	4,150
Easton	3,500
Fort Ann	2,100
Greenwich	11,000
Jackson	2,000
Kingsbury	18,000
Putnam	3,500
Whitehall	5,200

TUPPER LAKE WATER COMPANY.
Franklin County.

Town:

Altamont	32,000

FIFTH JUDICIAL DISTRICT.

DELAWARE, LACKAWANNA AND WESTERN RAILROAD COMPANY
AND ONE.
Oswego County.

City:

Oswego	$119,100

NEW YORK CENTRAL AND HUDSON RIVER RAILROAD COMPANY.
Herkimer County.

Towns:

Frankfort......................	$27,000
German Flats	44,400
Herkimer	33,000
Little Falls	64,100

Jefferson County.

Towns:

Champion	20,400
Clayton	10,600
Hounsfield	3,900
Lyme	37,900
Philadelphia	10,500
Wilna	50,400

City:

Watertown	99,200

Oneida County.

Towns:

Lowville	7,900
Remsen	5,400

Cities:

Rome	40,000
Utica	327,900

Onondaga County.

Towns:

DeWitt........................	5,000
Geddes	28,400
Manlius	5,300

City:

Syracuse	1,396,500

Oswego County.

Towns:

Albion	$4,000
Schroeppel	6,000

Cities:

Fulton	14,900
Oswego	180,800

NEW YORK, ONTARIO AND WESTERN RAILWAY COMPANY.

Oneida County.

Town :

Vienna	$4,000

City :

Utica	71,000

Oswego County.

Town :

Constantia	6,100

City :

Oswego	72,500

NEW YORK TELEPHONE COMPANY.

Jefferson County.

Towns :

Adams	$6,800
Alexandria	8,500
Antwerp	5,500
Brownville	4,200
Cape Vincent	4,700
Champion	5,500
Clayton	7,000
Ellisburg	6,800
Henderson	4,200
Hounsfield	7,500
LeRoy	14,300
Lorraine	3,500
Lyme	6,000
Pamelia	5,200
Philadelphia	3,700

Rodman	$3,100
Rutland	5,000
Theresa	4,000
Watertown	9,000
Wilna	1,700

City:

Watertown	75,000

Herkimer County.

Towns :

Danube	6,500
Fairfield	1,500
Frankfort	3,650
German Flats	27,500
Herkimer	20,000
Little Falls	5,000
Manheim	4,500
Russia	1,650
Schuyler	1,800
Stark	1,600
Warren	1,700
Winfield	2,000

City:

Little Falls	25,000

Lewis County.

Towns:

Denmark	4,750
Diana	2,650
Lowville	3,400
Leyden	4,500
New Bremen	200
West Turin	1,000

Oneida County.

Towns:

Annsville	1,400
Boonville	5,850
Camden	6,300

Deerfield	$13,600
Forestport	5,500
Kirkland	3,700
Lee	1,550
Marcy	6,350
Marshall	3,100
New Hartford	10,600
Paris	7,150
Remsen	3,500
Sangerfield	3,500
Trenton	18,500
Vernon	5,206
Verona	11,000
Vienna	1,500
Westmoreland	4,000
Whitestown	11,300

Cities:

Rome	36,000
Utica	185,000

Onondaga County.

Towns:

Camillus	4,500
Cicero	2,800
Clay	6,000
DeWitt	24,500
Elleridge	8,200
Fabius	9,900
Geddes	20,000
La Fayette	8,400
Lysander	15,650
Manlius	15,000
Marcellus	5,500
Onondaga	21,150
Pompey	2,300
Salina	8,000
Skaneateles	5,500
Tully	7,200
Van Buren	11,000

City:

Syracuse $610,000

Oswego County.

Towns:

Albion	4,500
Constantia	3,750
Granby	5,000
Hannibal	4,000
Hastings	6,000
Mexico	13,500
New Haven	7,000
Oswego	8,800
Parish	3,500
Richland	18,000
Sandy Creek	3,800
Schroeppel	2,300
Scriba	8,800
Volney	3,700

Cities:

Fulton	7,000
Oswego	55,000

ONONDAGA INDEPENDENT TELEPHONE COMPANY.

Onondaga County.

City:

Syracuse $205,000

OSWEGO AND SYRACUSE RAILROAD COMPANY AND ONE.

Onondaga County.

Towns:

Lysander	$23,000
Van Buren	25,000

City:

Syracuse   23,400

PEOPLES' SUBWAY COMPANY OF SYRACUSE.

Onondaga County.

City:

Syracuse $115,000

SYRACUSE, BINGHAMTON AND NEW YORK RAILROAD COMPANY.
Onondaga County.
City:

    Syracuse $111,400

SYRACUSE AND SUBURBAN RAILROAD COMPANY.
Onondaga County.
Towns:

    DeWitt $17,000

    Manlius   35,000

City:

    Syracuse   145,000

UTICA GAS AND ELECTRIC COMPANY.
Herkimer County.
Town:

    Frankfort $32,000

UTICA, CHENANGO AND SUSQUEHANNA VALLEY RAILWAY COMPANY.
Oneida County.
City:

    Utica $83,400

UTICA AND MOHAWK VALLEY RAILWAY COMPANY.
Herkimer County.
Town:

    German Flats $80,600

Oneida County.
Towns:

    Deerfield   18,000

    New Hartford   95,000

    Whitestown   150,000

City:

    Rome   60,000

CAYUGA AND SUSQUEHANNA RAILROAD COMPANY AND ONE.
Tioga County.
Towns:

    Candor $900

    Owego   10,600

8

SIXTH JUDICIAL DISTRICT.

DELAWARE AND HUDSON COMPANY.
Otsego County.

Town:

     Unadilla $10,300

City:

     Oneonta   53,000

DELAWARE, LACKAWANNA AND WESTERN RAILROAD COMPANY AND ONE.
Tompkins County.

City:

     Ithaca $19,400

ELMIRA AND LAKE ONTARIO RAILROAD COMPANY.
Chemung County.

Town:

     Horseheads $8,000

Schuyler County.

Towns:

     Dix   2,800
     Montour   1,200
     Reading   700

ELMIRA AND WILLIAMSPORT RAILROAD COMPANY.
Chemung County.

City:

     Elmira $10,800

ERIE RAILROAD COMPANY.
Broome County.

Town:

     Union $17,400

City:

     Binghamton   96,400

Chemung County.

City:

     Elmira   61,400

Tioga County.

Towns:

Barton $5,300

Owego   10,700

Federal Telephone and Telegraph Company.
Schuyler County.

Town:

Dix $6,700

New York Central and Hudson River Railroad Company.
Madison County.

Town:

Lenox $61,400

City:

Oneida   39,500

New York, Ontario and Western Railway Company.
Chenango County.

Town:

Norwich $6,600

Delaware County.

Towns:

Hamden   12,000

Sidney   9,200

Walton   10,800

City:

Middletown   27,400

New York Telephone Company.
Broome County.

Towns:

Chenango $2,200

Union   6,500

City:

Binghamton   95,000

Chemung County.

Towns:

Chemung	$4,500
Elmira	4,500
Horseheads	11,000
Veteran	3,000

City:

Elmira	100,000

Chenango County.

Towns:

Bainbridge	2,350
Greene	4,500
Guilford	4,700
New Berlin	3,800
North Norwich	6,000
Otselic	1,700
Oxford	7,000
Plymouth	4,700
Sherburne	3,000
Norwich	21,500

Cortland County.

Towns:

Cincinnatus	4,000
Cortlandville	8,800
Cuyler	1,350
Homer	17,500
Marathon	3,800
Preble	3,500
Scott	3,500
Solon	3,500
Truxton	2,300

City:

Cortland	35,000

Delaware County.

Towns:

Davenport	2,400
Meredith	3,000
Sidney	2,000

Madison County.

Towns:

Bronkfield	$2,800
Cazenovia	4,500
DeRuyter	1,200
Eaton	6,500
Hamilton	7,000
Lenox	11,500
Lincoln	1,650
Madison	2,500
Nelson	1,600
Smithfield	1,600
Stockbridge	2,300

City:

Oneida	25,000

Otsego County.

Towns:

Burlington	1,500
Edmeston	1,600
Hartwick	3,500
Middlefield	6,500
Milford	6,500
Otsego	18,000
Richfield	7,000
Springfield	3,000

City:

Oneonta	33,000

Schuyler County.

Towns:

Dix	3,800
Montour	5,000
Reading	2,400

Tioga County.

Towns:

Barton	10,000
Berkshire	1,000
Owego	14,000
Tioga	5,000

Tompkins County.

Towns:

Caroline	$3,250
Dryden	5,500
Groton	2,150
Ithaca	3,500
Lansing	1,500
Ulysses	2,550

City:

Ithaca	38,000

NEW YORK, LACKAWANNA AND WESTERN RAILWAY COMPANY.
Broome County.

Town:

Union	$28,400

City:

Binghamton	91,800

Chemung County.

City:

Elmira	48,400

SYRACUSE, BINGHAMTON AND NEW YORK RAILROAD COMPANY.
Broome County.

City:

Binghamton	$12,900

VALLEY RAILROAD COMPANY.
Broome County.

City:

Binghamton	$16,600

YORK STATE TELEPHONE COMPANY.
Broome County.

Towns:

Dickinson	$1,300
Kirkwood	1,800
Union	8,500

City:

Binghamton	70,000

Tioga County.

Town:

Owego   350

SEVENTH JUDICIAL DISTRICT.

AVON, GENESEO AND MT. MORRIS RAILROAD COMPANY.
Livingston County.

Town:

Avon $3,100

BUFFALO, ROCHESTER AND PITTSBURG RAILWAY COMPANY.
Monroe County.

City:

Rochester $47,500

CRYSTAL CITY GAS COMPANY OF CORNING, NEW YORK.
Steuben County.

City:

Corning $100,000

ELMIRA AND LAKE ONTARIO RAILROAD COMPANY.
Ontario County.

Town:

Canandaigua $11,100

Wayne County.

Town:

Arcadia   19,700

Yates County.

Town:

Milo   8,000

ERIE RAILROAD COMPANY.
Steuben County.

Cities:

Corning $59,100

Hornell   51,600

FEDERAL TELEPHONE AND TELEGRAPH COMPANY.
Livingston County.

Town:

Geneseo	$6,500

Monroe County.

Towns:

Greece	8,000
Henrietta	6,900
Mendon	5,100
Perinton	8,000
Rush	17,000
Wheatland	10,000

Ontario County.

Towns:

Farmington	5,200
Manchester	6,900

Steuben County.

Towns:

Bath	10,600
Canisteo	5,300
Corning	23,000

City:

Hornell	24,000

GENEVA TELEPHONE COMPANY.
Ontario County.

City:

Geneva	$16,000

LIVINGSTON COUNTY TELEPHONE COMPANY.
Livingston County.

Towns:

Avon	$5,500
Geneseo	9,000
Leicester	5,600
Mount Morris	6,500
North Dansville	6,850
Sparta	5,000

NEW ENGLAND TELEGRAPH COMPANY.
Monroe County.

City:

Rochester $15,000

NEW YORK CENTRAL AND HUDSON RIVER RAILROAD COMPANY.
Cayuga County.

Towns:

Aurelius $37,900

Brutus   67,200

City:

Auburn   20,300

Monroe County.

Towns:

Greece   13,200

Perinton   18,100

Pittsford   35,200

Sweden   21,000

City:

Rochester   709,400

Ontario County.

Towns:

Canandaigua   54,400

Manchester   5,200

Phelps   9,600

Wolcott   17,600

City:

Geneva   22,000

Seneca County.

Towns:

Seneca Falls   70,700

Waterloo   11,000

Steuben County.

City:

Corning   102,500

Wayne County.

Towns:

Arcadia	$55,400
Galen	11,000
Lyons	18,900

Yates County.

Towns:

Milo	5,200
Torrey	7,600

NEW YORK TELEPHONE COMPANY.
Cayuga County.

Towns:

Aurelius	6,500
Brutus	9,000
Cato	3,500
Conquest	2,300
Fleming	5,000
Ira	2,200
Ledyard	5,500
Moravia	6,500
Niles	4,750
Owasco	2,200
Scipio	5,500
Sempronius	6,500
Sennett	4,500
Springport	9,500
Summerhill	1,500

City:

Auburn	70,000

Livingston County.

Towns:

Avon	12,000
Caledonia	14,000
Conesus	4,000
Geneseo	13,000
Groveland	6,300

Leicester	$7,200
Lima	7,000
Livonia	14,000
Mt. Morris	17,000
North Dansville	10,000
Ossian	100
Springwater	8,000
Sparta	2,200
West Sparta	2,700
York	13,000

Towns :

Monroe County.

Brighton	6,700
Chili	14,000
Clarkson	4,000
Gates	9,000
Greece	22,000
Hamlin	3,100
Henrietta	17,000
Irondequoit	6,000
Mendon	16,200
Ogden	18,000
Parma	3,500
Penfield	9,000
Perinton	10,150
Pittsford	5,000
Riga	10,000
Rush	8,500
Sweden	13,500
Webster	18,000
Wheatland	13,000

City:

Rochester	685,000

Ontario County.

Towns:

Briston	5,500
Canadice	2,200

Canandaigua	$17,000
East Bloomfield	10,000
Farmington	5,000
Geneva	6,000
Gorham	4,000
Hopewell	5,520
Manchester	6,000
Naples	10,000
Phelps	12,000
Richmond	6,000
Seneca	8,500
South Bristol	2,500
Victor	9,500
West Bloomfield	6,500

City:

Geneva	8,000

Seneca County.

Towns:

Covert	6,500
Fayette	9,000
Junius	3,500
Lodi	3,000
Romulus	4,800
Seneca Falls	20,000
Ovid	5,000
Tyre	4,000
Varick	3,000
Waterloo	11,000

Steuben County.

Towns:

Addison	4,500
Bath	15,000
Canisteo	4,000
Cohocton	4,300
Erwin	5,000
Greenwood	2,500

Lindsley	$3,000
Urbana	2,300
Wayland	9,500
Woodhull	2,000

Cities:

Corning	28,000
Hornell	12,300

Towns:

Wayne County.

Arcadia	13,000 .
Butler	2,000
Galen	5,500
Huron	9,000
Lyons	12,000
Macedon	7,000
Marion	2,700
Ontario	3,100
Palmyra	11,500
Rose	4,000
Savannah	2,300
Sodus	9,500
Walworth	3,250
Williamson	4,000
Wolcott	4,700

Yates County.

Towns:

Benton	3,200
Jerusalem	10,000
Middlesex	2,300
Milo	11,500
Starkey	2,300

Niagara, Lockport and Ontario Power Company.

Cayuga County.

Town:

Brutus	$700

Monroe County.

Town:

Perinton $1,000

Wayne County.

Towns:

Arcadia   750
Galen   350
Lyons   500

PENN YAN TELEPHONE COMPANY.

Yates County.

Town:

Milo $8,000

ROCHESTER TELEPHONE COMPANY.

Monroe County.

City:

Rochester $470,000

WESTERN NEW YORK AND PENNSYLVANIA RAILWAY COMPANY.

Monroe County.

City:

Rochester $86,000

EIGHTH JUDICIAL DISTRICT.

BUFFALO CREEK RAILWAY COMPANY.

Erie County.

City:

Buffalo $135,700

BUFFALO GAS COMPANY.

Erie County.

City:

Buffalo $2,000,000

BUFFALO AND LACKAWANNA TRACTION COMPANY.
Erie County.
City:

Buffalo $177,000

BUFFALO AND LAKE ERIE TRACTION COMPANY.
Chautauqua County.
Towns:

Hanover	$26,900
Pomfret	105,000
Portland	75,000
Ripley	38,000
Westfield	130,000

City:

Dunkirk 160,000

Erie County.
Towns:

Evans	27,000
Hamburg	67,000
Lackawanna	150,000

DEAWARE, LACKAWANNA AND WESTERN RAILROAD COMPANY.
Erie County.
City:

Buffalo $949,800

DUNKIRK STREET RAILWAY COMPANY.
Chautauqua County.
City:

Dunkirk $140,000

ERIE RAILROAD COMPANY.
Alleghany County.
Town:

Wellsville $5,800

Cattaraugus County.

Town:
Persia	$8,800

City:
Olean	6,200

Chautauqua County.

Cities:
Jamestown	32,300

Erie County.

Town:
Lancaster	5,300
Buffalo	472,200

Genesee County.

Town:
Batavia	15,500

Niagara County.

Town:
Niagara	4,400

Cities:
Niagara Falls	109,300
North Tonawanda	66,300

Wyoming County.

Town:
Avon	9,500

Village:
Attica	11,700

FEDERAL TELEPHONE AND TELEGRAPH COMPANY.
Alleghany County.

Town:
Wellsville	$8,000

Cattaraugus County.

Town:
Persia	6,700

Chautauqua County.

Town:

Cherry Creek	$5,500

Erie County.

Towns:

Alden........................	7,750
Aurora.......................	9,000
Cheektowaga..................	7,000
Collins......................	9,000
Concord......................	8,200
Eden.........................	6,500
Hamburg......................	9,000
Lancaster....................	7,700
Newstead.....................	6,500
North Collins	7,500

Cities:

Buffalo......................	652,000
Lackawanna...................	5,000

Genesee County.

Towns:

Batavia......................	5,500
LeRoy........................	11,000
Pembroke.....................	5,500

Orleans County.

Town:

Murray.......................	8,700

GRAND TRUNK RAILWAY COMPANY.
Erie County.

City:

Buffalo......................	$22,500

HANOVER TELEPHONE COMPANY.
Chautauqua County.

Town:

Hanover......................	$5,000

INDEPENDENT UNION TELEPHONE COMPANY.
Niagara County.

Towns:

Hartland	$3,000
Lockport	650
Niagara Falls	1,700
Pendleton	1,850
Royalton	6,500
Wheatfield	4,500

Cities:

Lockport	2,000
Niagara Falls	2,200
North Tonawanda	4,000

Village:

Middleport	500
Le Salle	850
Middleport	3,500

INTERNATIONAL BRIDGE COMPANY.
Erie County.

City:

Buffalo	$44,200

JAMESTOWN, CHAUTAUQUA AND LAKE ERIE RAILWAY COMPANY.
Chautauqua County.

Town:

Westfield	$6,200

LEHIGH VALLEY RAILWAY COMPANY.
Erie County.

City:

Buffalo	$328,800

NEW ENGLAND TELEGRAPH COMPANY.
Erie County.

City:

Buffalo	$52,000

NEW YORK TELEPHONE COMPANY.
Alleghany County.

Towns:

Amity	$4,200
Friendship	2,900
Henry	2,500
Scio	3,500
Wellsville	12,500

Cattaraugus County.

Towns:

Allegany	5,500
Ashford	4,500
Carrollton	4,500
Cold Spring	2,300
Dayton	5,000
Fredonia	3,100
Hinsdale	4,200
Little Valley	3,200
Machias	2,500
New Albion	2,400
Olean	4,000
Otto	1,300
Persia	2,300
Perrysburg	3,000
Randolph	5,000
Salamanca	10,000

City:

Olean	20,000

Chautauqua County.

Busti	3,000
Chautauqua	5,000
Cherry Creek	2,000
Clymer	3,700
Ellery	5,000
Ellicott	8,500
Ellington	2,000

Gerry	$2,650
Hanover	3,000
Harmony	6,300
Pomfret	7,800
Portland	5,000
Sheridan	4,500
Westfield	3,500

Cities:

Dunkirk	17,000
Jamestown	57,000

Erie County.

Towns:

Alden	4,200
Amherst	16,500
Aurora	20,000
Cheektowaga	13,000
Clarence	14,000
Colden	2,550
Collins	4,400
Concord	15,000
East Hamburg	6,500
Elma	2,600
Evans	5,000
Hamburg	24,000
Holland	3,900
Lancaster	16,000
Marilla	1,200
Newstead	21,500
Sardinia	4,500
Tonawanda	11,000
Wales	7,900
West Seneca	6,900

Cities:

Buffalo	1,300,000
Tonawanda	18,000

Genesee County.

Towns:

Alabama	$7,000
Alexander	11,000
Batavia	50,000
Bergen	12,000
Bethany	5,000
Darien	8,500
Elba	9,800
Leroy	19,000
Oakfield	19,000
Pavilion	7,000

Niagara County.

Towns:

Cambria	7,900
Hartford	8,800
Lewiston	8,200
Lockport	15,500
Newfane	16,500
Niagara	9,500
Pendleton	4,500
Porter	5,800
Royalton	17,500
Somerset	9,750
Wilson	10,000
Wheatfield	12,000

Cities:

Niagara Falls	80,000
Lockport	50,000
North Tonawanda	31,000

Orleans County.

Towns:

Albion	26,000
Barre	11,000
Carlton	27,000
Clarendon	6,000
Gaines	13,000

Towns:

Kendall	$12,000
Murray	16,850
Ridgeway	35,700
Shelby	3,200
Yates	28,000

Wyoming County.

Arcade	5,700
Attica	10,000
Bennington	3,500
Covington	6,000
Eagle	5,500
Middlebury	7,200
Orangeville	8,300
Sheldon	8,500
Warsaw	21,000
Wethersfield	3,000

NEW YORK CENTRAL AND HUDSON RIVER RAILROAD COMPANY.

Erie County.

Towns:

Cheektowaga	$5,000
Newstead	4,600

Cities:

Buffalo	2,195,800
Tonawanda	56,600

Genesee County.

City:

Batavia	75,400

Niagara County.

Towns:

Lewiston	17,300
Niagara	5,100

Cities:

Lockport	236,500
Niagara Falls	134,700
North Tonawanda	100,600

Orleans County.

Towns:

Albion	$13,000
Ridgeway	19,800

NEW YORK CENTRAL AND NIAGARA RIVER RAILROAD COMPANY.
Erie County.

City:

Tonawanda	$20,200

Niagara County.

City:

Tonawanda	35,500

NIAGARA, LOCKPORT AND ONTARIO POWER COMPANY.
Erie County.

Town:

Hamburg	$2,100

Genesee County.

Towns:

Elba	500
Oakfield	450

NYPANO RAILROAD COMPANY.
Çattaraugus County.

Town: .

Randolph	$6,200

PEOPLES' GAS LIGHT AND COKE COMPANY.
Erie County.

City:

Buffalo	$65,000

REPUBLIC METAL-WARE COMPANY.
Erie County.

City:

Buffalo	$6,200

ROGERS-BROWN IRON COMPANY.
Erie County.

City:

    Buffalo $34,600

SALAMANCA GAS COMPANY.
Cattaraugus County.

Towns:

    Great Valley $5,000

    Salamanca   35,000

SALAMANCA TELEPHONE AND TELEGRAPH COMPANY.
Cattaraugus County.

Town:

    Salamanca $7,000

SOUTH BUFFALO RAILWAY COMPANY.
Erie County.

City:

    Buffalo $6,600

TERMINAL RAILWAY COMPANY OF BUFFALO.
Erie County.

Towns:

    Cheektowaga $3,000

    Hamburg   3,700

City:

    Lackawanna   7,100

UNITED NATURAL GAS COMPANY.
Cattaraugus County.

Towns:

    Little Valley $19,000

    Olean   3,100

    Salamanca   11,500

City:

    Olean   6,000

Erie County.

Towns:

Aurora	$27,000
Collins	33,000
East Hamburg	21,000
Eden	67,000
Elma	3,500
Hamburg	120,000
Lancaster	1,400
North Collins	13,000
West Seneca	37,000

City:

Lackawanna	39,000

WESTERN NEW YORK AND PENNSYLVANIA RAILWAY COMPANY.

Alleghany County.

Towns:

Genesee	$1,200
Wellsville	5,800

Cattaraugus County.

City:

Olean	$74,000

Chautauqua County.

City:

Dunkirk	14,000

Erie County.

Cities:

Buffalo	250,200
Lackawanna	30,600

NINTH JUDICIAL DISTRICT.

CONSOLIDATED WATER COMPANY OF SUBURBAN NEW YORK.

Westchester County.

Towns:

Mt. Pleasant	$50,000

ERIE RAILROAD COMPANY.
Orange County.

Towns:

Chester	$10,000
Goshen	11,000

Cities:

Middletown	37,100
Newburgh	29,500
Port Jervis	32,500

Rockland County.

Towns:

Orangetown	1,800
Ramapo	8,400

GOSHEN AND DECKERTOWN RAILROAD COMPANY.
Orange County.

Town:

Goshen	$1,400

JOHN JOHNSTON.

Westchester County.

City:

Mt. Vernon	$20,000

MONTGOMERY AND ERIE RAILROAD COMPANY.
Orange County.

Town:

Goshen	$3,900

NEW JERSEY AND NEW YORK RAILROAD COMPANY.
Rockland County.

Towns:

Haverstraw	$8,800
Ramapo	3,900

NEW YORK CENTRAL AND HUDSON RIVER RAILROAD COMPANY.

Dutchess County.

Town:

Fishkill	$12,500

City:

Poughkeepsie	$92,500

Orange County.

Towns:

Cornwall	$9,800
Montgomery	8,400
Newburgh	44,400

Rockland County.

Town:

Haverstraw	22,800

Westchester County.

Towns:

Cortland	9,300
Greenburg	17,100
Mt. Pleasant....................	19,900
Ossining	9,600
White Plains....................	11,900

Cities:

Mt. Vernon......................	10,800
Yonkers	95,800

NEW YORK INTERURBAN WATER COMPANY.
Westchester County.

Towns:

Eastchester	$35,000
Harrison	42,000
Pelham	23,000
Rye	18,000
Scarsdale	18,500

NEW YORK, ONTARIO AND WESTERN RAILWAY COMPANY.
Orange County.

City:

Port Jervis.....................	$4,300

NEW YORK TELEPHONE COMPANY.
Dutchess County.

Towns:

Amenia	$3,550
Fishkill	43,550

Towns:

Hyde Park......................	$5,000
Pawling........................	2,750
Pleasant Valley....................	3,200
Poughkeepsie.....................	16,500
Rhinebeck......................	3,650
Washington	6,500

Cities:

Poughkeepsie....................	60,000

Orange County.

Towns:.

Deer Park......................	4,400
Goshen	13,900
Greenville	4,000
Hamptonville....................	6,000
Montgomery.....................	10,000
Newburgh......................	22,000
Tuxedo........................	2,250
Wawayanda	8,000

Cities:

Newburgh......................	70,000
Port Jervis.....................	9,500

Putnam County.

Towns:

Carmel	3,000
Kent	900
Patterson	1,500
Phillipstown....................	6,500
Putnam Valley..................	1,200
Southeast	4,000

Rockland County.

Towns:

Clarkstown	48,000
Haverstraw	16,800
Orangetown	90,000
Ramapo........................	70,000
Stony Point.....................	2,500

Westchester County.

Towns:

Cortland	$50,800
Bedford	20,000
Eastchester	55,000
Greenburg	278,700
Harrison	28,000
Mamaroneck	120,000
Mt. Pleasant.	94,000
North Castle.	18,100
Ossining	75,000
Pelham	35,000
Rye	208,000
Scarsdale	50,000
White Plains.	120,750

Cities:

Mt. Vernon.	230,000
Yonkers	395,000

NEW YORK, WESTCHESTER AND CONNECTICUT TRACTION COMPANY.

Westchester County.

City:

Mt. Vernon.	$20,000

NORTHERN WESTCHESTER LIGHTING COMPANY.
Westchester County.

Towns:

Cortland	$13,000
Mt. Pleasant.	27,000
New Castle.	1,200
Ossining	130,000

NYACK AND SOUTHERN RAILROAD COMPANY.
Rockland County.

Town:

Orangetown	$5,900

PEEKSKILL LIGHTING AND RAILROAD COMPANY.
Westchester County.

Towns:

Cortland	$175,000
Yorktown	1,200

POSTAL TELEGRAPH-CABLE COMPANY.
Westchester County.

City:

Yonkers	$17,000

POUGHKEEPSIE LIGHT, HEAT AND POWER COMPANY.
Dutchess County.

City:

Poughkeepsie	$250,000

WESTCHESTER ELECTRIC RAILROAD COMPANY.
Westchester County.

Towns:

Eastchester	$90,000
Mamaroneck	1,200
Pelham	47,000

Cities:

Mt. Vernon	321,000
Yonkers	38,000

WESTCHESTER LIGHTING COMPANY.
Westchester County.

Towns:

Bedford	$12,000
Harrison	60,000
Pelham	180,000
Eastchester	80,000
Scarsdale	17,000
Rye	425,000
Greenburg	365,000
Mt. Pleasant	42,000
Mamaroneck	210,000
New Castle	28,000

Towns:

North Castle	$600
White Plains	220,000

Cities:

Mt. Vernon	680,000
Yonkers	785,000

Villages:

Greenburg	365,000
Portchester	217,900
Rye	125,700
White Plains	220,000

YONKERS ELECTRIC LIGHT AND POWER COMPANY.

Westchester County.

City:

1910. Yonkers	$200,000

TAX CASES.

The following proceedings are pending in the Appellate Division, Supreme Court, Third Department:

THE PEOPLE EX REL. AMERICAN GLUCOSE CO. v. JAMES A. ROBERTS, AS COMPTROLLER.

Proceeding to review the action of the Comptroller in assessing a franchise tax against the relator. Writ issued May 2, 1898, and return filed June 11, 1898.

THE PEOPLE EX REL. THE CITY OF NEW YORK v. ERASTUS C. KNIGHT, AS COMPTROLLER AND THEODORE P. GILMAN, AS DEPUTY COMPTROLLER.

This is a proceeding to review the action of the Comptroller in canceling certain tax sales. Writ issued April 25, 1901. Motion made to quash writ October 26, 1901, which motion was denied.

THE PEOPLE EX REL. CORNELL STEAMBOAT CO. v. OTTO KELSEY, AS COMPTROLLER.

Certiorari to review action of the Comptroller in assessing a franchise tax against the relator. Writ issued October 19, 1904, and return made November 18, 1904.

THE PEOPLE EX REL. EAST RIVER RAILROAD CO. *v.* NATHAN
L. MILLER, AS COMPTROLLER.

Proceeding to review the action of the Comptroller in assessing a franchise tax against the relator. Writ issued May 28, 1903,
and return made June 20, 1903.

THE PEOPLE EX REL. INTERBOROUGH RAPID TRANSIT CO. *v.*
OTTO KELSEY, AS COMPTROLLER OF THE STATE OF NEW YORK.

Proceeding to review the determination of the Comptroller in
assessing a franchise tax against the relator. Writ issued March
30, 1906. Return filed May 22, 1906.

THE PEOPLE EX REL NEW YORK AND HARLEM RAILROAD CO.
v. WILLIAM C. WILSON, AS ACTING COMPTROLLER OF THE STATE
OF NEW YORK.

Proceeding to review the determination of the Comptroller in
assessing a franchise tax against the relator. Writ issued October
9, 1906. Return made February 28, 1907.

PEOPLE EX REL. HEWITT REALTY CO. *v.* MARTIN H. GLYNN,
AS COMPTROLLER OF THE STATE OF NEW YORK.

Proceeding to review the determination of the Comptroller in
assessing a franchise tax against the relator. Writ issued July
25, 1908. Return made September 10, 1908.

PEOPLE EX REL. PORT MORRIS LAND AND IMPROVEMENT CO. *v.*
MARTIN H. GLYNN, AS COMPTROLLER OF THE STATE OF NEW
YORK.

Proceeding to review the determination of the Comptroller in
assessing a franchise tax against the relator. Writ issued July
23, 1908. Return made September 10, 1908.

PEOPLE EX REL. BUFFALO GENERAL ELECTRIC CO. *v.* CHARLES
H. GAUS, AS COMPTROLLER OF THE STATE OF NEW YORK.

Proceeding to review the determination of the Comptroller in
assessing a franchise tax against relator. Writ issued March 20,
1909. Return filed April 5, 1909.

PEOPLE EX REL. LAKE PLACID CO. v. CHARLES H. GAUS, AS COMPTROLLER OF THE STATE OF NEW YORK.

Proceeding to review the determination of the Comptroller in allowing a redemption from tax sale. Writ issued August 5, 1909. Return filed September 20, 1909.

PEOPLE EX REL. MANHATTAN REALTY COMPANY v. CLARK WILLIAMS, AS COMPTROLLER OF THE STATE OF NEW YORK.

Proceeding to review determination of the Comptroller in assessing a franchise tax against the relator. Return filed September 26, 1910.

PEOPLE EX REL. SEA BEACH RAILWAY COMPANY v. CLARK WILLIAMS, AS COMPTROLLER OF THE STATE OF NEW YORK.

Proceeding to review determination of Comptroller in assessing a franchise tax against the relator. Return filed August 23, 1910.

PEOPLE EX REL. SOUTH BROOKLYN RAILWAY COMPANY v. CLARK WILLIAMS, AS COMPTROLLER OF THE STATE OF NEW YORK.

Proceeding to review determination of Comptroller in assessing a franchise tax against the relator. Return filed August 23, 1910.

STATEMENT RECITING THE PRESENT STATUS OF ALL ACTIONS FOR THE DISSOLUTION OF CORPORATIONS BROUGHT BY THE ATTORNEY-GENERAL PRIOR TO JANUARY 1, 1911.

SUPREME COURT — ALBANY COUNTY.

THE PEOPLE OF THE STATE OF NEW YORK

vs.

BANK OF STATEN ISLAND.

Litigation in regard to the accounts of the former receiver is still pending and prevents the closing of this trust.

9

SUPREME COURT — ERIE COUNTY.

THE PEOPLE OF THE STATE OF NEW YORK

vs.

STATE BANK OF FORESTVILLE.

Dividends to the amount of 90 per cent. have been declared in this receivership, a dividend of 10 per cent. being declared during the past year. There is still some litigation pending.

SUPREME COURT — ALBANY COUNTY.

THE PEOPLE OF THE STATE OF NEW YORK

vs.

THE HOLLAND TRUST COMPANY.

All the assets of this receivership have been reduced to cash with the exception of one piece of property. The receiver has made an application for an intermediate accounting to be held in January, 1911, at which time a dividend of 40 per cent. to the stockholders will probably be declared.

SUPREME COURT — NEW YORK COUNTY.

THE PEOPLE OF THE STATE OF NEW YORK

vs.

THE NEW YORK BUILDING LOAN BANKING CO.

The receiver has made application to sell certain real estate, which application has not as yet been passed upon by the court. The receiver should be able to make his final accounting soon after the sale of this property.

SUPREME COURT — ERIE COUNTY.

THE PEOPLE OF THE STATE OF NEW YORK

vs.

THE GERMAN BANK.

There is still litigation in this receivership which prevents its closing.

SUPREME COURT — ALBANY COUNTY.

THE PEOPLE OF THE STATE OF NEW YORK

vs.

THE METROPOLITAN MUTUAL SAVINGS AND LOAN ASSOCIATION.

This action has been terminated and the receiver discharged.

SUPREME COURT — KINGS COUNTY.

THE PEOPLE OF THE STATE OF NEW YORK

vs.

GUARDIAN SAVINGS AND LOAN COMPANY.

SUPREME COURT — NEW YORK COUNTY.

THE PEOPLE OF THE STATE OF NEW YORK

vs.

THE TREASURY CORPORATION CO-OPERATIVE SAVINGS LOAN ASSOCIATION.

Newell Lyon was appointed receiver in each of these corporations. No assets have come into his hands. The receivership is kept alive for the purpose of discharging fraudulent mortgages, the receiver generously consenting to continue to act without compensation for his trouble.

SUPREME COURT — ALBANY COUNTY.

THE PEOPLE OF THE STATE OF NEW YORK

vs.

METROPOLITAN BANK.

The affairs of this defendant are involved with those of the German Bank and the ultimate success of this action is dependent upon the adjustment of the complications arising from the latter institution.

SUPREME COURT — ERIE COUNTY.

THE PEOPLE OF THE STATE OF NEW YORK

vs.

MANHATTAN REAL ESTATE AND LOAN COMPANY.

The inability to sell certain real estate has prevented the closing of this receivership.

SUPREME COURT — KINGS COUNTY.

THE PEOPLE OF THE STATE OF NEW YORK

vs.

UNITED FREEMAN'S LAND ASSOCIATION No. 2.

Litigation as to the title of certain real estate is still pending and prevents the termination of this trust.

SUPREME COURT — Albany County.

The People of the State of New York

vs.

Cooper Exchange Bank.

Litigation which has delayed the closing of this trust for some time has been terminated in favor of the receiver, who should be able to file his final account within the coming year.

SUPREME COURT — Albany County.

The People of the State of New York

vs.

Home Mutual Building and Loan Association.

The receiver is to have his final accounting in January, 1911, and has served notice to that effect.

SUPREME COURT — New York County.

The People of the State of New York

vs.

International Graphophone Company.

Sufficient money has been realized through the settlement of various actions to pay the creditors of this receivership in full. The validity of certain of the creditors' claims is now being ascertained before a referee.

SUPREME COURT — New York County.

The People of the State of New York

vs.

Oriental Bank.

The question as to the amount of the receiver's fees and the allowances of his attorney is still pending on appeal.

SUPREME COURT — New York County.

The People of the State of New York

vs.

Twenty-eighth and Twenty-ninth Streets Crosstown Railroad Company.

The receiver is still operating these properties pending the termination of foreclosure proceedings instituted by the Central Trust Company.

SUPREME COURT — Ulster County.

The People of the State of New York

vs.

The Brooklyn Bank in the City of New York.

The Appellate Division of the Third Department has handed down a decision reducing the fees of the receivers and their counsel who have appealed to the Court of Appeals, which appeal is still pending.

SUPREME COURT — Albany County.

THE PEOPLE OF THE STATE OF NEW YORK

vs.

EMPIRE TITLE GUARANTY COMPANY.

The receiver has had his final accounting and been discharged.

SUPREME COURT — Albany County.

THE PEOPLE OF THE STATE OF NEW YORK

vs.

METROPOLITAN SURETY Co.

The receiver has been occupied during the past year with the liquidation of the assets of this receivership and of the claims against it.

SUPREME COURT — Albany County.

THE PEOPLE OF THE STATE OF NEW YORK

vs.

THE CAPITAL CITY LOAN COMPANY.

Action was instituted at the request of the Superintendent of Banks to dissolve the above corporation. Action is at issue awaiting trial.

SUPREME COURT — ALBANY COUNTY.

THE PEOPLE OF THE STATE OF NEW YORK

vs.

THE HARBOR AND SUBURBAN BUILDING AND
     SAVINGS ASSOCIATION.

An action was commenced in December, 1910, to dissolve this
corporation. The defendant's time to answer has not yet expired.

SUPREME COURT — ALBANY COUNTY.

THE PEOPLE OF THE STATE OF NEW YORK

vs.

NINETEENTH WARD CO-OPERATIVE SAVINGS
     AND LOAN ASSOCIATION.

· An action was commenced in December, 1910, to dissolve this
corporation. The defendant's time to answer has not yet expired.

MISCELLANEOUS ACTIONS.

SUPREME COURT — DELAWARE COUNTY.

THE PEOPLE OF THE STATE OF NEW YORK

vs.

WILLIAM HIGBEE NICHOLS.

This action has been settled and discontinued.

SUPREME COURT — Albany County.

THE PEOPLE OF THE STATE OF NEW YORK

vs.

CAPITAL CITY LOAN COMPANY AND FIDELITY
AND DEPOSIT COMPANY OF MARYLAND.

This action was commenced to recover the penalty of a bond given by the defendants in the sum of $5,000. It is at issue and awaiting trial.

SUPREME COURT — County of Erie.

THE PEOPLE OF THE STATE OF NEW YORK

vs.

THE ERIE COUNTY LOAN COMPANY AND THE
ILLINOIS SURETY COMPANY.

This is an action brought to recover a penalty of a bond given by the defendants in the sum of $5,000 and has been settled and discontinued.

SUPREME COURT — Herkimer County.

AMERICAN FELT COMPANY

vs.

JOHN M. RICHARDS, AS SHERIFF.

Action to restrain sheriff in collecting franchise tax. An appeal from a judgment in favor of the defendant has been dismissed on the stipulation of the parties to the action.

VOLUNTARY DISSOLUTION PROCEEDINGS INSTITUTED DURING THE YEAR 1910.

Jan.   6. Supreme Court — Ontario County. Inland Lumber
        Co.

       13. Supreme Court — New York County. J. B. Hackett
        Co.

       15. Supreme Court — New York County. Mishkind-
        Feinberg Realty Co.

       15. Supreme Court — Erie County. Whissel Lumber Co.

       27. Supreme Court — Jefferson County. Ward Concrete
        Stone Co.

       29. Supreme Court — New York County. Collino Co.

Feb.   1. Supreme Court — New York County. MacCracken-
        Hauer-Terry Co.

        5. Supreme Court — Westchester County. Gleason
        Transportation Co.

        8. Supreme Court — New York County. Calumet Con-
        struction Co.

       14. Supreme Court — Oneida County. Cosmopolitan Co.
        of Utica.

       24. Supreme Court — Monroe County. Rochester Busi-
        ness Men's Club.

Mar.   2. Supreme Court — Orange County. West Newburgh
        Bottling Works.

        4. Supreme Court — Orange County. Lenox Gypsum
        Co.

        4. Supreme Court — Monroe County. Nonrust Tinware
        Co.

       12. Supreme Court — Monroe County. Moloney Bros.
        Co.

       23. Supreme Court — Erie County. Erie County Loan
        Co.

       24. Supreme Court — Kings County. New Machines and
        Folding Beds Manufacturing Co.

       26. Supreme Court — New York County. Fliegelman-
        Reiss Co.

       30. Supreme Court — Monroe County. Brockport Loan
        and Building Association.

April 1. Supreme Court — Monroe County. Seneca Club of Rochester, N. Y.

6. Supreme Court — Oneida County. Utica Art Association.

8. Supreme Court — New York County. Standard Cordage Co.

11. Supreme Court — New York County. Edward Rorke & Co.

12. Supreme Court — New York County. C. Poyet, Inc.

15. Supreme Court — Kings County. Nassau Belt Line Traction Co.

22. Supreme Court — New York County. Crown Brush Co.

May 4. Supreme Court — New York County. Cosmopolitan Fire Insurance Co. of New York.

4. Supreme Court — New York County. Aldine Club.

6. Supreme Court — Kings County. Peoples Real Estate Tontine.

7. Supreme Court — Kings County. Second Church of Christ, Scientist.

9. Supreme Court — Chautauqua County. Dunkirk Furniture Co.

9. Supreme Court — New York County. Louis Meyer & Co.

13. Supreme Court — New York County. Rissicol Co.

14. Supreme Court — Broome County. Haddock, Fowler & Co.

20. Supreme Court — New York County. Black Motor Car Co.

23. Supreme Court — New York County. Ability Cigar Manufacturing Co.

26. Supreme Court — New York County. British Colonial Society of New York.

26. Supreme Court — New York County. H-Calk Co.

30. Supreme Court — Chenango County. Oxford Valley Telephone Co.

June   1. Supreme Court — Orange County.   Association of
           Brick Manufacturers and Agents.

         2. Supreme Court — Rensselaer County.   The Gibbs-
           Marvin Co. of the City of Troy.

         3. Supreme Court — Westchester County.   Hastings
           Lumber Co.

         4. Supreme Court — New York County.   Fort George
           Street Railway Co.

         9. Supreme Court — New York County.   American
           Safe Deposit Co.

        10. Supreme Court — New York County.   Spaventa' Em-
           broidery Co.

        24. Supreme Court — New York County.   B. D. Luce
           & Co.

        25. Supreme Court — New York County.   Louis Meyer
           & Co.

        30. Supreme Court — New York County.   Golden School.

        30. Supreme Court — Onondaga County.   B. E. Odell Co.

July   2. Supreme Court — Kings County.   Long Island Con-
           struction Co.

        21. Supreme Court — New York County.   William F.
           Sheehan & Co.

        23. Supreme Court — Kings County.   Koenig Co., Inc.

Aug.   1. Supreme Court — Erie County.   Carnival Court Con-
           cessions Co.

         3. Supreme Court — Erie County.   Reliable Auto Truck
           Co.

         8. Supreme Court — New York County.   Yerkes Manu-
           facturing Co.

        18. Supreme Court — Erie County.   Charles C. Faust Co.

        22. Supreme Court — Chenango County.   Oxford Shirt
           Co.

        23. Supreme Court — New York County.   White, Allom
           & Co.

        31. Supreme Court — New York County.   Naughton Co.
           and Arthur McMullen.

Sept.   1. Supreme Court — New York County.   Andrews
            Marsh Manufacturing Co.

         8. Supreme Court — New York County.   Wiley-Harker
            Lumber Co.

         9. Supreme Court — New York County.   Berliant
            Realty Co.

        12. Supreme Court — Orange County.   Warwick Wood-
            lands Realty Co.

        13. Supreme Court — New York County.   Empire Bat-
            tery Co.

        17. Supreme Court — New York County.   Cloud-Marts
            Co.

        26. Supreme Court — Steuben County.   State Bank of
            Corning, N. Y.

        29. Supreme Court — Monroe County.   I. X. L. Fly
            Paper Co. of Rochester, N. Y.

Oct.   1. Supreme Court — New York County.   Murray-Hey-
            liger Catering Co.

         1. Supreme Court — Westchester County.   Old Mexico
            Mining and Milling Co.

         6. Supreme Court — Ulster County.   The New York
            Cement Co.

        24. Supreme Court — Tioga County.   Owego Theatre Co.

        25. Supreme Court — Wayne County.   Sherman Realty
            Co. of Newark.

        29. Supreme Court — Cattaraugus County.   Wright &
            Miller Co.

        29. Supreme Court — Cattaraugus County.   Tunesassa
            and Bradford Railroad Co.

        29. Supreme Court — New York County.   Heilman
            Lithographing Co.

        29. Supreme Court — Erie County.   Buffalo Gum Co.

        31. Supreme Court — Erie County.   Buffalo Gelatine Co.

Nov.   7. Supreme Court — Schuyler County.   Sagoyewatha
            Co.

         7. Supreme Court — New York County.   Neptune In-
            surance Co. of New York.

Nov.   10. Supreme Court — New York County.   George Ring-
        ler & Co.

        19. Supreme Court — Wayne County.   Kemper-Buck
  ,   Mfg. Co. of Newark.

        26. Supreme Court — Kings County.   W. C. Vosburgh
        Mfg. Co., Limited.

Dec.   1. Supreme Court — New York County.   Northern
        Building Savings and Loan Association.

        15. Supreme Court — Oneida County.   Rome Stamping
        Co.

        16. Supreme Court — Nassau County.   Nassau County
        Bank.

        16. Supreme Court — Onondaga County.   Delevan Ave-
        nue and Pine Hill Improvement Co.

        28. Supreme Court — New York County.   Association of
        Employing Bookbinders of New York.

        28. Supreme Court — Broome County.   Tioga Dairy Co.

        30. Supreme Court — New York County.   Virgil Prac-
        tice Clavier Company.

        30. Supreme Court — Rensselaer County.   Union Wheel
        and Mfg. Co.

        31. Supreme Court — Erie County.   Buffalo Subway
        Railroad Company.

SEQUESTRATION ACTIONS INSTITUTED DURING THE YEAR 1910.

Jan.   27. Supreme Court — Erie County.   George Andrews v.
        Buffalo Motor Car Co. and others.

        27. Supreme Court — Erie County.   Lawrence Wex v.
        Lancaster Glass Works.

Feb.   5. Supreme Court — New York County.   Percival H.
        Gregory v. Downing's Storage Warehouse Co.

         5. Supreme Court — New York County.   Henry Rump
        and ano. v. Van Rensselaer Realty Co.

        11. Supreme Court — Erie County.   John A. Murphy v.
        Moore & Muir Co. and others.

Feb. 11. Supreme Court — New York County. Chester M. Freeman, etc., v. Julius E. Mosheim and others and Film Import and Trading Co.

16. Supreme Court — New York County. James G. Farmer and Clara G. Farmer v. Keller-Farmer Co., et al.

24. Supreme Court — Jefferson County. J. Francis Ward v. Ward Concrete Stone Co., et al.

28. Supreme Court — Chautauqua County. Loren J. Lamphere v. Canadaway Fertilizer Co.

Mar. 10. Supreme Court — Kings County. Henry Mindlin, et al. v. Star Embroidery Works.

16. Supreme Court — New York County. Emanuel Weingreen v. Solomon Michelbacher, Abraham J. Michelbacher, Joseph Wolf and E. Weingreen Co.

21. Supreme Court — New York County. David R. Sowal v. T. B. Peddie & Co.

April 6. Supreme Court — Monroe County. William N. Hallock and ano. v. Rochester and Southern Construction Co.

6. Supreme Court — Monroe County. Anna Clark as Executrix, etc. v. Rochester and Southern Construction Co.

8. Supreme Court — Richmond County. Johanna C. Veimeister v. Stapleton Garage.

19. Supreme Court — Kings County. Caroline Brickelmaier and ano. v. H. A. Medoff Drug Co.

30. Supreme Court — New York County. Long Island Engineering and Contracting Co. v. Charles E. Hoff Co.

May 2. Supreme Court — New York County. Watson F. Fuqua v. Inter-State Contract Co.

2. Supreme Court — Kings County. Cohn Cut Stone Co. v. Alfred Realty Construction Co. and ano.

13. Supreme Court — New York County. Henry J. Washburn v. The Rainier Co.

17. Supreme Court — New York County. Frederick A. Steele v. Steele-Simon Co. and ano.

June 6. Supreme Court — New York County. Lewis M.
Isaacs, et al. v. Haines Realty Corporation.

6. Supreme Court — New York County. Corbin Cabinet
Lock Co. v. Horsfall Construction Co.

22. Supreme Court — New York County. Edward A.
Willard, etc. v. Sherman & Tait, Inc.

27. Supreme Court — New York County. Harold W.
Davis v. Traction Engineering Co.

30. Supreme Court — New York County. Luella N.
Vonhagen v. Canadian Consolidated Mines Co.,
Limited.

July 26. Supreme Court — New York County. Wright V.
Abbott v. Haines Realty Corporation, et al.

30. Supreme Court — Kings County. Empire House
Wrecking Co. v. Kaufman Construction Co.

Aug. 2. Supreme Court — New York County. Jacobs Co. v.
Metropolitan Mercantile and Realty Co.

18. Supreme Court — New York County. Justus N.
Williams v. Mt. Morris Storage Co., et al.

18. Supreme Court — Westchester County. Ira L. Beebe
& Co. v. Kenyon Robinson Paper Co.

25. Supreme Court — New York County. Antonio
Perez v. Banco Popular de Medellin and Liborio
Echavarria Velez as Receiver, etc.

26. Supreme Court — Kings County. John J. Ascher v.
Evananola Manufacturing Co.

Sept. 1. Supreme Court — New York County. Barbara
Hirsch v. Lenox Garage Co., et al.

5. Supreme Court — New York County. Frank Pel-
letiere v. Independent Booking Agency.

17. Supreme Court — Kings County. Baldinger & Kupferman Mfg. Co. v. Graham Holding Co.

Oct. 15. City Court of the City of New York. William W.
Tait as Receiver of Sherman & Tait, Inc. v. Richmond Sales Co.

Nov. 15. Supreme Court — Oneida County. Utica City National Bank v. George W. Head Co.

19. Supreme Court — New York County. Conrad Horel
v. Jay Weinberg & Co.

Dec.   13. Supreme Court — New York County. Charles Flach-
bart and others doing business as Chelsea Pattern
and Model Work v. Requa-Gibson Co.

17. Supreme Court — Kings County. Solomon Bernikow
and ano v. Brooklyn House Wrecking Co.

20. Supreme Court — Kings County. Harold D. Watson
and others v. Graceland Farm and Land Co.

FORECLOSURE ACTIONS INSTITUTED DURING THE YEAR 1910.

Jan.   3. County Court — Kings County. Greenpoint Savings
Bank v. Franziska Borucka, et al.

4. Supreme Court — Kings County. Caroline Hillman
v. Esther Roth, et al.

5. County Court — Kings County. Alexander E. Orr
v. Jacob Duberstein, et al.

5. County Court — Kings County. The Sisters of the
Community of St. John the Evangelist v. Charles
J. Ten Broeck, et al.

5. Supreme Court — Kings County. Williamsburgh
Savings Bank v. Ella K. Russell, et al.

7. Supreme Court — Kings County. Raymond J. Mc-
Breen v. Rosa Landes, et al.

15. Supreme Court — St. Lawrence County. Adam O.
Rutherford v. Franklin J. Fielding, et al.

18. Supreme Court — Kings County. Alice A. Bishop
v. Fanny Duberstein, et al.

18. Supreme Court — New York County. Francis J.
Kuerzi v. Carmine Altieri, et al.

18. Supreme Court — New York County. Joseph L.
Buttenweiser v. David Greenfest, et al.

21. Supreme Court — Schenectady County. David M.
Olmstead, Jr. v. John A. Williams, et al.

21. Supreme Court — New York County. Mercantile
Trust Co. and William Bolles Baldwin as trustees
etc. v. Margaret Curran, et al.

24. Supreme Court — New York County. Henry L.
Bantelman v. John J. Egan, et al.

Jan. 25. Supreme Court — Kings County. Andrew Schirr-
meister v. Louisa Sloper, et al.

27. County Court — Kings County. The Savings Bank
of Utica v. Charles W. Miller, Jr., et al.

27. Supreme Court — New York County. Lawyers
Mortgage Co. v. Deby Simon, et al. (Two actions,
Nos. 1 and 2.)

27. Supreme Court — New York County. Julia E.
Bambey v. Hyman Rubin, et al.

28. Supreme Court — New York County. Rosa Rothschild v. Rachel Lederer, et al.

29. County Court — Kings County. Isidor G. Hagen-
bacher v. Otto Leyer, et al.

Feb.   1. Supreme Court — New York County. Nevelson
Goldberg Realty Co. v. Philip Cohen, et al.

3. Supreme Court — New York County. Susan C.
Woodford v. Val Fink, et al.

11. Supreme Court — New York County. Carl Ernst v.
Abram Zuker, et al.

14. Supreme Court — Westchester County. George Werner v. Emil Wagner, et al.

15. Supreme Court — New York County. Adrian H.
Jackson v. Mary Altieri, et al.

16. Supreme Court — New York County. John A.
Schappert v. Anna Messer, et al.

18. Supreme Court — New York County. William H.
Buhrman and ano. v. Rachel Juster, et al.

21. Supreme Court — Kings County. Aaron Mendlovitz
v. Joseph Simon, et al.

21. Supreme Court — Kings County. Samuel Rotten-
berg v. Joseph Simon, et al.

22. Supreme Court — Kings County. Rosamond Roberts
v. Minnie Hicks, et al.

26. Supreme Court — New York County. Hans Reiss
and one v. Margaretha Werner, et al.

Mar.   2. Supreme Court - - Kings County. Lawyers Mortgage Co. v. Kunnie Hammond, et al.

5. County Court — Kings County. Henrietta Griggs v.
Charlotte Edwards, et al.

March　8. Supreme Court — New York County. William Ran-. kin v. John LaSpina, et al.

　　8. County Court — Kings County. Georgiana Margaret Fronde v. Ferdinand Leyer, et al.

　　8. County Court — Kings County. John McCann and Theo. Kauffeld as Trustees, etc. v. Ferdinand Leyer, et al.

　11. Supreme Court — New York County. Adolph Seelig v. Michael A. Scudi, et al.

　11. Supreme Court — New York County. Samuel J. Gutter v. Margaret Curran, et al.

　11. Supreme Court — Kings County. George M. Schinzel v. Gertrude Schunk, et al.

　11. Supreme Court — Kings County. Peoples Trust Co. v. Patrick Dempsey, et al.

　11. Supreme Court. Kings County. Emigrant Industrial Savings Bank v. Anton Fresher, et al.

　14. Supreme Court — New York County. State Bank v. Jacob Cohen, et al.

　14. Supreme Court — St. Lawrence County. Barney S. O'Neill v. Sadie L. Stearns, et al.

　15. Supreme Court — Kings County. Christopher H. Koster v. Dora Aronstan, et al.

　16. Supreme Court — New York County. Clare M. Knoedler v. Anna M. E. Luhrs, et al.

　19. Supreme Court — New York County. Max Fine v. Isaac Laitin, et al.

　22. Supreme Court — New York County. Josephine Chedsey v. Morris J. Feinberg, et al.

　25. Supreme Court — New York County. Isidore D. Morrison v. Max Levine, et al.

　26. Supreme Court — New York County. Julia Linck and ano. v. Ferruccio Vazzana, et al.

　31. Supreme Court — New York County. State Bank v. Eliseo Saggese, et al.

April　5. Supreme Court — Kings County. Lavinia Lally v. Ellen Jane Eagan, et al.

April   5. Supreme Court — New York County. Stephen Duncan Pringle v. Davis Levy, et al.

   6. Supreme Court — Westchester County. Louis Viala v. Elizabeth Remsen LeRoy Dale, et al.

   7. Supreme Court — Queens County. Marie S. Power v. " John Priggen," et al.

   8. Supreme Court — New York County. Bazena T. Downes v. Ann Graham, et al.

   8. Supreme Court — New York County. Bazena T. Downes v. William Mulligan, et al.

   9. Supreme Court — New York County. John Everling v. Isidore Scherer, et al.

   15. Supreme Court — New York County. Paul Tuckerman, etc. v. Thomas F. O'Reilly, et al.

   16. Supreme Court — New York County. An Association for the Relief of Respectable and Aged Indigent Females in the City of New York v. Thomas R. Brown, et al.

   19. Supreme Court — Albany County. Albany Exchange Savings Bank v. Sarah Cohen, et al.

   22. Supreme Court — Kings County. Carl Guttman and ano., etc. v. Catharina Brutt, et al.

   22. Supreme Court — Chemung County. Chemung Valley Mutual Loan Association v. Mary A. McCarthy, et al.

   23. Supreme Court — New York County. Antonio Plescia v. Cristoforo Zuccaro, et al.

   26. Supreme Court — New York County. William A. Cameron v. Nicola Roberti, et al.

   27. Supreme Court — New York County. Hollister Logan as Executor and ano., etc. v. Stephen C. Barnum, et al.

   28. Supreme Court — Nassau County. Henry M. Post, etc. v. Henry M. W. Eastman, et al.

   28. Supreme Court — New York County. VanNorden Trust Co. v. Alexander Axt, et al. (Three actions, Nos. 1, 2 and 3.)

April   30. Supreme Court — New York County. Charles S.
Albert v. Augusta Tonelli, et al.

May   3. Supreme Court — New York County. Sadie I. Car-
lew and Emma C. Linson v. Alpheus Greene, et al.

4. Supreme Court — New York County. Anna S.
Stemme, et al. v. Charles W. Bauschatt, et al.

6. Supreme Court — New York County. Frederick T.
Hoffman v. Oscar G. Borkstrom, et al.

7. Supreme Court — Nassau County. John A. Ruth v.
Maria G. Fania, et al.

10. Supreme Court — Suffolk County. George H. Couth
v. Philip Sugerman, et al.

12. Supreme Court — Kings County. Fred C. Robbins
v. Nazzarena Giambruno, et al.

12. Supreme Court — Livingston County. Patrick Deneff
v. Thomas O'Brien, et al.

13. Supreme Court — New York County. Frederick Loe-
loff v. Augusta Bischoff, et al.

13. County Court — Kings County. Albro J. Newton v.
George H. Peterson, et al.

14. Supreme Court — New York County. Bernard F.
Golden v. Moses Shapiro, et al.

14. Supreme Court — New York County. German
Society of the City of New York, etc. v. Harry
Gleich, et al.

14. Supreme Court — Kings County. Annie E. Pinkney
v. Clarendon Construction Co., et al.

24. Supreme Court — New York County. Elizabeth G.
Muldoon v. Mary E. Mulvehill, et al.

25. Supreme Court — New York County. Lucille Kurtz
v. Max Gold, et al.

25. Supreme Court — Kings County. John J. Curry and
ano. v. Louis Flaxman, et al.

26. Supreme Court — New York County. Catherine
Cash v. Morris Marx, et al.

June   1. Supreme Court — New York County. Margaret
Marx v. Oscar Englander, et al.

June 1. Supreme Court — Kings County. Peter Dalio and
         one v. Joseph F. Feely, et al.

      3. Supreme Court — New York County. William H.
         Sands, et al v. David Levy, et al.

      8. Supreme Court — Schuyler County. Havana Bridge
         Works v. Rochester Bridge and Construction Co.,
         et al.

      8. Supreme Court — Westchester County. Louis Viala
         v. Elizabeth Remsen LeRoy Dale, et al.

      9. Supreme Court — Kings County. Joseph Stewart,
         Jr. v. Mary C. Simpson, et al.

      9. Supreme Court — New York County. Flora Nord-
         linger v. Oakley Meyers, et al.

     10. Supreme Court — New York County. Amy Angell
         Collier Montague v. Mary E. Mulvihill, et al.

     14. Supreme Court — New York County. Henry B.
         Singer v. Moses Leonard Frazier, et al.

     15. County Court — Queens County. George E. Clay v.
         Helen Crum, et al.

     16. Supreme Court — New York County. State Realty
         'Co. v. Hyman Levin, et al.

     17. County Court — Kings County. John E. Andrus v.
         Herman O. Bohlen, et al.

     17. Supreme Court — New York County. German Sav-
         ings Bank in the City of New York v. Charles W.
         Bauschatt, et al.

     22. Supreme Court — Niagara County. Cuthbert W.
         Pound v. Ann Eliza Carpenter, et al.

     23. Supreme Court — New York County. Max Kahlert
         and one v. Louis Schulze, et al.

     23. Supreme Court — New York County. Charlton Dows
         Cooksey v. John C. Betjeman, et al.

     25. Supreme Court -- New York County. Louis Belland
         v. Mary Altieri, et al.

     25. Supreme Court — New York County. Rosa B. R.
         Heintz v. Thomas F. Tressel, et al.

     27. Supreme Court — Richmond County. Edgar K.
         Whitford v. Josephine Johnson, et al.

June 30. Supreme Court — New York County. Jennie L. Ruffin v. Abraham Hurwitz, et al.

July 8. Supreme Court — Kings County. Bertha C. Herrfeldt v. John Welch, et al.

11. Supreme Court — New York County. Rachel Newman v. Brown-Weiss Realties, et al.

11. Supreme Court — New York County. Paul J. Baumgarten v. Bedford Park Construction Co., et al.

11. Supreme Court — New York County. John H. Knoeppel v. Bedford Park Construction Co., et al.

13. Supreme Court — Niagara County. Jessie A. Shaw v. People of State of New York, et al.

15. Supreme Court — Kings County. Amsterdam Savings Bank and Lawyers Mortgage Co. v. George Eckstein, et al.

16. County Court — Kings County. Mary E. Lyons v. Margaret V. Stripp, et al.

19. Supreme Court — New York County. Metropolitan Savings Bank v. William W. Watkins, et al.

19. Supreme Court — Westchester County. American Savings Bank v. Rice Realty and Construction Co., et al.

20. Supreme Court — Kings County. Arthur Smith v. Marcie Dunn as Executor, etc. (Two actions, Nos. 1 and 2.)

20. Supreme Court — Kings County. Kings County Trust Co. as Executor, etc. v. Lotto Giadess Peitchmann, et al.

21. Supreme Court — New York County. Francis Hendricks and Harmon W. Hendricks as Executors, etc. v. Samuel Kutler, et al.

21. Supreme Court — New York County. Francis Hendricks and Harmon W. Hendricks as Executors, etc. v. Florence Morill, et al. (Two actions, Nos. 1 and 2.)

21. Supreme Court — New York County. John Miller v. Jasper H. Livingston, et al.

July   26. Supreme Court — New York County. Emma **F.**
Routey v. Florence E. Robinson, et al.

29. Supreme Court — New York County. Susan Van
Praag v. Mevon Realty Co., et al.

Aug   1. County Court — Rochland County. Jefferson G. You-
mans v. Thomas Blake, et al.

2. Supreme Court — New York County. Charles **G.**
Moller v. Samuel C. Baum, et al.

3. Supreme Court — Kings County. Home Title Insurance Co. of New York v. Louis Flaxman, et al.

5. Supreme Court — Kings County. William Dewar
and one v. John Kramer, et al.

6. Supreme Court — New York County. Susan Van
Praag v. 130th Street Corporation, et al.

13. Supreme Court — Kings County. Louis Best v.
Sheldon S. Baker, et al.

16. County Court — Queens County. William Welsh v.
George Kose, et al.

16. Supreme Court — New York County. Metropolitan
Life Insurance Co. v. Louis Meryash, et al.

16. County Court — Kings County. Margaret Paris v.
Ida Selinger, et al.

24. Supreme Court — New York County. Henry Ettel-
son v. Louis Meryash, et al.

24. Supreme Court — New York County. New York
Protestant Episcopal Public School v. Barnet
Miller, et al.

25. Supreme Court — New York County. Bank for Savings in the City of New York v. William I. Brown,
et al.

25. County Court — Kings County. Anders Gustafson v.
Abraham Brettschneider, et al.

29. Supreme Court — New York County. Julius **M.**
Lowenstein v. Harry L. Block, et al.

Sept.   1. Supreme Court — Kings County. Morris Dornbush
v. Jacob Vogelfonger, et al.

3. Supreme Court — New York County. Hugo E. Dis-
telhurst v. Pine Investing Co., et al.

Sept. 3. Supreme Court — New York County. Leon B. Lowenstein and others as Trustees v. Hyman Levin, et al.

7. Supreme Court — New York County. United States Realty and Improvement Co. v. Joseph Cohen, et al.

7. Supreme Court — Kings County. Gilbert M. Young v. Anna M. Thiele, et al.

9. Supreme Court — Kings County. Williamsburgh Savings Bank v. John H. Mahnken Co., et al.

9. Supreme Court — Kings County. E. Covert Hulst v. Louis Flaxman, et al.

10. Supreme Court — New York County. Susan Van Praag v. Hyman Levin, et al.

10. Supreme Court — New York County. Susan Van Praag v. Josephine Miller, et al.

17. Supreme Court — New York County. Germania Bank of the City of New York v. John M. Dempsey, et al.

23. Supreme Court — Kings County. Sarah J. Day v. Emma J. McMullen, et al.

24. Supreme Court — New York County. Gene Bruder v. Tillie Burkan, et al.

28. Supreme Court — Kings County. William M. Calder v. Abraham Goldsmith, et al.

29. Supreme Court — New York County. Frederick W. Kroehle v. Abraham Ravitch, et al.

Oct. 1. Supreme Court — New York County. Emily Schaeffler, et al. v. Bertha Scheibel, et al. (Two actions, Nos. 1 and 2.)

3. Supreme Court — New York County. Charles W. Endel v. Alfonso Barrata, et al.

15. Supreme Court — New York County. John T. Brook v. Harry L. Toplitz, et al.

18. Supreme Court — Westchester County. Adolph G. Hupfel v. Mary Ann Gibbon Kennedy, et al.

18. Supreme Court — Erie County. Mutual Life Insurance Co. of New York v. Orinda L. Atkinson, et al.

Oct.   19. Supreme Court — New York County. George Edward Lapp v. Betty Gluck, et al.

25. Supreme Court — New York County. John T. Brook v. E. Osborne Smith, et al.

28. Supreme Court — New York County. Eliza Jane Moore v. Maria L. Leach, individually and as Executrix, etc., et al.

Nov.   1. Supreme Court — Kings County. Isaac Leader v. Lena Bloomgarden, et al.

5. Supreme Court — New York County. William S. Mason, et al. v. Samuel Williams, et al.

10. Supreme Court — Queens County. Italian Savings Bank of the City of New York v. Mansueto D'Amico, et al.

10. Supreme Court — Kings County. Roslyn Savings Bank v. Max Sparago, et al.

10. Supreme Court — Kings County. Wilma P. Stern, et al. v. George Schlitz, et al.   .

10. Supreme Court — Kings County. Brooklyn Trust Co. as substituted trustee, etc. v. Hyman Bloomgarden, et al.

11. Supreme Court — New York County. Gertrude de Graffenrich, individually and as general guardian of Violet L. Hamilton v. Linda F. Butler, et al.

11. Supreme Court — New York County. Greenwich Savings Bank v. Lizzie Flig, et al.

15. Supreme Court — Queens County. North Side Bank of Brooklyn v. Olga Hettesheimer, et al.

17. Supreme Court — Kings County. Carl Gutmann and ano. etc. v. Catherine Brutt, et al.

17. Supreme Court — New York County. J. Van Vechten Olcott and ano., etc. v. Barnet Miller, et al.

18. Supreme Court — Kings County. George B. Ellis v. Robert Porterfield, et al.

18. Supreme Court — Oswego County. John A. Coble v. George W. Klock, et al. (Actions 1 and 2.)

19. Supreme Court — Kings County. William Ocker v. Julius L. Cohn, et al.

Nov.   19. Supreme Court — Kings County. Howard Dubois
        v. Bertha Strehl, et al.

        21. Supreme Court — New York County. Irene Marx
        v. Hyman Levin, et al.

        21. Supreme Court — New York County. Lawyers Mort-
        gage Co. v. William L. Brown, et al.

        22. Supreme Court — Kings County. Adolf Timm v.
        Annie P. Grissler, et al.

        24. Supreme Court — Kings County. Augusta E.
        Northrup v. John McCormack, et al.

        24. Supreme Court — Kings County. James Pirnie, etc.,
        v. John McCormack, et al.

        29. Supreme Court — Kings County. The Dime Savings
        Bank of Williamsburg v. John J. O'Donnell, etc.,
        et al.

        29. Supreme Court — New York County. John A.
        Aspinwall and another, etc., v. Max Landesman,
        et al.

        29. Supreme Court — New York County. Jonas Weil,
        et al. v. Charles M. Kaufmann, et al.

        30. Supreme Court — New York County. Wilson M.
        Powell, Jr., etc., v. Samuel Kadin, et al.

Dec.   13. Supreme Court — Kings County. Oscar Hahne v.
        John McCormack, et al. (Actions 1 and 2.)

        13. Supreme Court — New York County. Samuel Gold-
        sticker v. Louis Goldsticker, et al.

        13. Supreme Court — Kings County. Celia Weyant v.
        John McCormack, et al.

        13. Supreme Court — Kings County. Helen J. Tanner
        v. John McCormack, et al.

        13. Supreme Court — Kings County. The Putnam
        County Savings Bank v. John F. O'Neill, et al.

        13. Supreme Court — Kings County. Lancaster and
        Westchester Realty Co. v. Mary Stephany, et al.

        17. County Court — Queens County. John Nadvornik v.
        George Kose, et al.

        20. Supreme Court — Kings County. Mary S. Baker v.
        Lena Bloomgarden, et al.

Dec.   21. Supreme Court — Kings County. Daniel W. Mc-
        Williams, etc., v. Waverly Associates, et al.

        21. Supreme Court — Kings County. Knickerbocker
        Trust Co., etc., v. Waverly Associates, et al.

        23. Supreme Court — Kings County. Eltoma Realty
        Co. v. George K. Day, et al.

        24. Supreme Court — New York County. Fannie Korn
        v. Charles C. Dow, et al.

        24. Supreme Court — New York County. Philip Schu-
        lang v. Abram Perelman, et al.

        30. Supreme Court — New York County. Robert Marks
        Realty Co. v. Siegfried Loewenthal, et al.

PARTITION ACTIONS INSTITUTED DURING THE
YEAR 1910.

Feb.   9. Supreme Court — New York County. Mayhew W.
        Bronson v. New York Life Insurance and Trust
        Co., et al.

        16. Supreme Court — New York County. Dora D.
        Schiffer v. Amelia G. Friedman, et al.

Mar.   4. Supreme Court — Westchester County. The Martha
        Wilson Home of the City of Mount Vernon v. Caro-
        line Batten, et al.

        9. Supreme Court — Fulton County. Edward F. Tietz
        v. Theodore R. Haviland, et al.

        16. Supreme Court —— Westchester County. Gustav A.
        Mornhinweg v. William F. Mornhinweg, et al.

        23. Supreme Court — Nassau County. Jane A. Titus v.
        Mary Alice Burt, et al.

        31. Supreme Court — New York County. William Es-
        selborn v. Emile Esselborn, et al.

April   4. Supreme Court — New York County. William A.
        Brazier, et al. v. Thomas J. Brazier, et al.

        6. Supreme Court — New York County. Nellie G.
        Richards v. Esther Hartwell, et al.

        19. Supreme Court — New York County. Ida Regel v.
        Augusta Engelhardt, et al.

April 29. Supreme Court — Kings County. Emelia Brach v. John G. Kusch, et al.

May 21. Supreme Court — Queens County. John C. Ball v. Annie Ball, et al.

30. Supreme Court — St. Lawrence County. Mary A. Fay v. James J. Brennan, et al.

June 1. Supreme Court — New York County. Walter E. Houghton, etc., v. Clarissa Goodman, et al.

24. Supreme Court — Erie County. John T. Canavan, et al. v. Clara Canavan, et al.

July 8. Supreme Court — St. Lawrence County. Philip Collins v. James Collins, et al.

12. Supreme Court — New York County. Bartholomew Jacob and one v. Emma L. Elin, et al.

16. Supreme Court — Kings County. Henrietta McCue v. John Sklar, et al.

16. Supreme Court — Henrietta McCue v. Harry Baskind, et al.

16. Supreme Court — Queens County. Henrietta McCue v. Minnie A. Knauber, et al.

16. Supreme Court — Kings County. Henrietta McCue v. Philip Cohen, et al.

16. Supreme Court — Kings County. Henrietta McCue v. Charles M. Geoffroy, et al.

20. Supreme Court — Kings County. Lucy Gordon Chichester v. Caroline F. Gorham, et al.

Aug. 13. Supreme Court — New York County. Julia P. McSwegan v. Robert Gilchrist, et al.

17. Supreme Court — Kings County. Rose McLaughlin v. Henry McCann, et al.

29. Supreme Court — Fulton County. John G. Robinson v. Mary Dunlop, et al.

Sept. 3. Supreme Court — Kings County. Mary Muller v. Henry C. Schalter, et al.

10. Supreme Court — St. Lawrence County. Horace G. Douglass v. Mary Douglass, et al.

10. Supreme Court — Queens County. Lena Van Bussum v. Rosa Koch, et al.

Sept.   29. Supreme Court — Westchester County. Bernhard A. Schaeffel v. Augusta Hastings, et al.

Oct.   7. Supreme Court — New York County. William C. Diehl v. Andrew Diehl, et al.

       15. Supreme Court — Queens County. Rose A. K. Snyder v. Nellie K. Parezo, impleaded with others.

Nov.   11. Supreme Court — Kings County. Hyman Bloomgarden v. Lena Bloomgarden, etc., et al.

       15. Supreme Court — Kings County. Emily Hertz v. Bertha R. Thomas, et al.

       30. Supreme Court — Genesee County. John Bohl v. George Bohl, et al.

Dec.   1. Supreme Court — New York County. Cora Rausch, etc., v. Louise E. Rausch, et al.

       5. Supreme Court — New York County. William Cook v. Alice V. Cook, et al.

       17. Supreme Court — Westchester County. William C. Burling, etc., v. William Burling Cocks, et al.

       30. Supreme Court — Kings County. Stephen C. Baldwin v. Augusta M. Baldwin, et al.

APPLICATIONS FOR AUTHORITY TO AMEND CERTIFICATES OF INCORPORATION OR FOR CHANGE OF NAME.

Jan.   13. Supreme Court — New York County. Widowed Mothers' Fund Association. (Amend certificate.)

       27. Supreme Court — New York County. H. Rudnick & Co. (Change name.)

Feb.   16. Supreme Court — New York County. N. Y. & Ohio Buckle Co. (Change name.)

       19. Supreme Court — Niagara County. Morse Ice Cream Co. (Change name.)

Mar.   5. Supreme Court — New York County. Briquette Coal Co. (Change name.)

       22. Supreme Court — New York County. David Blackley Co. (Change name.)

May   4. Supreme Court — Albany County. Excelsior Implement Co. (Change name.)

16. Supreme Court — New York County. Derry & Wright. (Change name.)

June   7. Supreme Court — Ulster County. Red E Products Co. (Change Name.)

24. Supreme Court — New York County. Schenenga-Carver Co. (Change name.)

28. Supreme Court — New York County. Yorkville Dispensary & Hospital for Women and Children. (Change name.) ·

30. Supreme Court — Erie County. L. M. Ericsson Telephone Manufacturing Co. (Change name.)

30. Supreme Court — New York County. The Barnett Store. (Change name.)

July   6. Supreme Court — New York County. Mendelsohn-Herbert Co. (Change name.)

Aug.   17. Supreme Court — New York County. Heyman, Nast & Cohn Co. (Change name.)

25. Supreme Court — New York County. Spanish Products Import Co. (Amend certificate.)

Sept.   8. Supreme Court — Erie County. The Maxwell-Briscoe Buffalo Co. (Change name.)

15. Supreme Court — Chautauqua County. Jamestown Hollow Cement Stone Co. (Change name.)

15. Supreme Court — Montgomery County. Beech-nut Packing Co. (Amend certificate.)

Oct.   12. Supreme Court — New York County. Perley & Bro. (Change name.)

19. Supreme Court — New York County. Aldine Association. (Change name.)

19. Supreme Court — New York County. H. Blumenstock Co. (Change name.)

Nov.   7. Supreme Court — Onondaga County. The Kenyon Paper Co. (Change name.)

18. Supreme Court — New York County. Kamp Kohut Kobbossee. (Change name.)

Dec.   9. Supreme Court — New York County.   Davenport &
          Treacy Piano Co.   (Change name.)
      16. Supreme Court — New York County.   Norwalk Bros.
          (Amend certificate.)
      22. Supreme Court — Erie County.   Superior Motor
          Vehicle Co.   (Change name.)
      23. Supreme Court — New York County.   First Presby-
          terian Church in the Village of West Farms.
          (Change name.)
      30. Supreme Court — Orange County.   The Wardlow
          Cutlery Co.   (Change name.)

MISCELLANEOUS ACTIONS AND PROCEEDINGS BROUGHT DURING THE YEAR 1910.

Jan.   7. Supreme Court — Cortland County.   People ex rel.
          Charles D. Sanders v. William A. Stockwell.   (Quo
          warranto — City Chamberlain of Cortland.)
      11. Supreme Court — New York County.   Matter of the
          Application of Adolph Jacobs for payment from
          the State Treasury of the residue of the Personal
          Estate of Felicite Wilmshurst, deceased.
      13. Supreme Court — New York County.   Leo K. Steiner,
          et al v. Burghard Steiner, et al.   (Construction of
          will of Sigfried Steiner.)
      14. Supreme Court — New York County.   Matter of the
          Application of Rembrandt Realty Co. for an order
          directing the amendment of a certificate of payment
          of one-half of the capital stock and the filing of the
          certificate as amended nunc pro tunc.
      15. Supreme Court — Chemung County.   Matter of the
          Application of Samuel Eastman and others for an
          order requiring John H. Deister, Treasurer of the
          Democratic County Committee of Chemung County,
          to file a new, correct and amended statement of the
          receipts and disbursements of said Committee re-
          specting the General Election held November 2,
          1909.

Jan. 17. Supreme Court — Onondaga County. People v. Eugene E. DeBarr. (To recover $13,500 in connection with the People's Mutual Life Insurance Association and League.)

17. Supreme Court — Onondaga County. People v. Willard H. Peck. (To recover $31,500 in connection with the People's Mutual Life Insurance Association and League.)

17. Supreme Court — Onondaga County. People v. Iram G. Reed. (To recover $15,000 in connection with the People's Mutual Life Insurance Association and League.)

17. Supreme Court — Onondaga County. People v. E. Olin Kinne. (To recover $30,000 in connection with the People's Mutual Life Insurance Association and League.)

19. Supreme Court — St. Lawrence County. People ex rel. Republican & Journal Co. v. Abram H. Wiggins et al. (Ceriorari re designation of newspaper to publish session laws.)

19. County Court — Chenango County. Matter of the Application of Fritz Shofkom, an insolvent debtor, to be discharged from imprisonment.

19. County Court — Chenango County. Matter of the Application of O. J. Pittsley, an insolvent debtor, to be discharged from imprisonment.

20. Supreme Court — Orleans County. The People v. Albion Water Works Co. (Injunction to restrain defendant from ceasing to deliver water to Western House of Refuge for Women at Albion.)

22. Supreme Court — Onondaga County. People v. Jerry E. B. Santee. (To recover $5,000 in connection with People's Mutual Life Insurance Association and League.)

24. Supreme Court — Onondaga County. People v. Slayter Laycock. (To recover $5,000 in connection with People's Mutual Life Insurance Association and League.)

10

Jan. 24. Supreme Court — New York County. Matter of the Application of Olivia Eggleston Phelps Stokes, as Executrix, and Anson Phelps Stokes, as Executor, etc., of Caroline Phelps Stokes, deceased, for the instruction of this court as to their duties in the administration and distribution of this estate.

29. Supreme Court — New York County. People, etc., v. John Niederstein. (To recover moneys.)

Feb. 1. Supreme Court — Oneida County. Michael H. Powers as Administrator, etc., v. Jay Ragan et al. (Construction of will.)

3. Supreme Court — Herkimer County. Matter of the Judicial Settlement of the Accounts of William W. Kirley as Committee, etc., of Adaline F. Kirley, an incompetent person. (Accounting by Committee of an incompetent confined in a State Hospital.)

4. Supreme Court — Tompkins County. County of Tompkins v. First National Bank of Ithaca, et al. (To ascertain and determine amount due and unpaid on construction, etc., of Road 483.)

7. Supreme Court — Rensselaer County. Thomas M. A. Burke, Bishop, etc., v. Attorney-General of the State of New York et al. (Construction of Trust agreement and to change a beneficiary.)

7. Supreme Court — Onondaga County. People v. Charles F. Wayte. (To recover $10,000 in connection with People's Mutual Life Insurance Association and League.)

19. Supreme Court — Appellate Division, Second Department. People ex rel. New York Central & Hudson River Railroad Co. v. James Gourley, et al., as Assessors of the Village of Haverstraw. (Certiorari under Special Franchise Tax Law. State Board of Tax Commissioners was allowed to intervene.)

21. Supreme Court — Westchester County. Margaretha Marth v. People of the State of New York. (Admeasurement of dower.)

Feb. 26. Supreme Court — New York County. Film Import. & Trading Co. v. Julius E. Mosheim, Charles Freidenberg, Max Marks and Sol. Richmond. (To remove directors and for an accounting.)

Mar. 4. Supreme Court — New York County. Charles Marvin v. Theodore L. Mason, et al. Petition of Sarah E. Sylvester, et al. (Application to withdraw moneys from State Treasury.)

12. Supreme Court — Erie County. The People v. Erie County Loan Co. and Illinois Surety Co. (Action to recover penalties.)

12. Supreme Court — Albany County. The People v. Capitol City Loan Co. and Fidelity & Deposit Co. of Maryland. (Action to recover penalties.)

17. Supreme Court — Delaware County. Cyrus Mead v. Hattie Havens, et al. (Application in surplus money proceedings.)

18. Supreme Court — New York County. Matter of Application of Herman J. Kumberger Co. (To remove from record in New York County Clerk's Office an alleged duplicate original certificate of incorporation.)

21. Supreme Court — Chenango County. Matter of the Application of Adelbert Butler, an insolvent debtor, for discharge from imprisonment.

23. Supreme Court — Albany County. People v. Lincoln Spring Co. and others. (Injunction to restrain pumping from mineral springs at Saratoga.)

23. Supreme Court — Albany County. People v. Natural Carbonic Gas Co. and others. (Injunction to restrain pumping from mineral springs at Saratoga.)

23. Supreme Court — Albany County. People v. New York Carbonic Acid Gas Co. and others. (Injunction to restrain pumping from mineral springs at Saratoga.)

24. Supreme Court — Kings County. Matter of the Application of the Home Bank for an order declar-

March 24.   ing its business closed pursuant to the provisions of section 99 of the Banking Law.

       28. Justice's Court — Putnam County. Town of Philipstown. The People v. George Harris. (Criminal action for violation of section 1530 of the Penal Law.)

April   6. County Court — Fulton County. Matter of the Application of Carrie Beakle to determine and assess damages under the Highway Law of the State of New York.

       7. Supreme Court — Albany County. The People v. Capital City Loan Co. (Dissolution.)

       8. Supreme Court — Niagara County. Charles A. Criqui v. Charles E. Fraser & Co., et al. (Foreclosure of lien.)

      19. Supreme Court — Richmond County. The People v Midland Railroad Terminal Co. (Action to vacate letters-patent.)

      20. Supreme Court — Dutchess County. Lewis H. Vail and others as Trustees, etc., of the Dutchess Insurance Co., a domestic corporation whose corporate existence has terminated, v. Peter H. Troy, et al. (To ascertain and determine creditors of insurance company.)

      20. Supreme Court — Warren County. Matter of the Application of the People of the State of New York to acquire a toll bridge in the County of Warren.

      22. Supreme Court — New York County. Nicholas Faillace and others v. Wills & Marvin Co., et al. (Foreclosure of lien.)

      25. Supreme Court — Albany County. People ex rel. John Miller v. Herman V. Mynderse. (Quo warranto; Village President of Scotia.)

      28. Supreme Court — Rensselaer County. Michael H. Gaffney vs. Harrison Rockefeller and the People, etc. (Foreclosure of lien.)

May   2. Supreme Court — Westchester County.   William
          Flandrau and Jane, his wife, v. Peter Flandrau, et
          al.   (To withdraw money from State Treasury.)

      2. Supreme Court — Kings County.   Matter of the
          Application of William H. Hotchkiss as Superin-
          tendent of Insurance to take possession of the prop-
          erty and conduct the business of the Hudson Horse
          Insurance Co. of New York, etc.

      6. Supreme Court — Albany County.   Mary D.
          Stephens v. Bridget Casey, et al.   (To direct pay-
          ment from State Treasury.)

      6. Supreme Court — Niagara County.   William H.
          Upson v. United Engineering & Contracting Co.,
          et al.   (Foreclosure of lien.)

      9. Supreme Court — New York County.   Matter of the
          Application of Robert P. Beck to have a lost mort-
          gage discharged from record.

     11. Supreme Court — Rockland County.   The People v.
          Isaac Bell, et al.   (Condemnation of lands for
          Blauvelt Rifle Range.)

     11. Supreme Court — Albany County.   Hygienic Ice &
          Refrigerating Co. v. John Franey as Clerk of
          Albany County.   (To recover money paid defend-
          ant under Mortgage Tax Law.)

     17. Supreme Court — Albany County.   Matter of the
          Final Judicial Accounting of William H. Storrs,
          Committee of the Person and Estate of Mary Fitz-
          gerald, an incompetent person.

     24. United States Circuit Court — Northern District of
          New York.   United States of America v. James B.
          Baker, et al.   (Condemnation of lands in Jefferson
          County.)

June 6. Supreme Court — New York County.   People ex rel.
          Joseph P. Fallon v. John J. Dwyer.   (Quo war-
          ranto to test title to office of Justice of Municipal
          Court.)

      6. Supreme Court — New York County.   Matter of
          Application of Benjamin Schwartz and Bettie

June 6. Schwartz for the restoration of their child, Rose
          Schwartz, in the custody of the State Training
          School for Girls.

      8. Supreme Court — Albany County. The People, etc.,
          v. John Franey as Clerk of Albany County. (Man-
          damus to compel clerk to furnish searches free of
          charge.)

      9. Supreme Court — New York County. Matter of the
          Application of U. S. Fidelity & Guaranty Co. of
          Baltimore, Md., for its discharge from liability as
          surety on a certain bond heretofore given by Theo.
          W. Foster as principal, and the said surety company
          as surety to the People under the Penal Code.
          (Gold and silverware bond.)

      9. Supreme Court — New York County. People ex rel.
          Charlotte Hitchcock v. Robert B. Lamb, Superin-
          tendent of Matteawan State Hospital. (Habeas
          corpus.)

     14. Supreme Court — Kings County. Benjamin Croner
          v. John Sniffen, et al. (To register title to real
          property.)

     20. Supreme Court — Kings County. Irving T. Smith v.
          Marion S. I. Martin, et al. (To register title to
          real property.)

     22. Supreme Court — Suffolk County. Matter of the
          Application of Riverhead Bank for an order declar-
          ing the said bank dissolved and corporate existence
          terminated.

     22. Supreme Court — New York County. Angelica
          Wakelee v. Erwin Davis. (Application to with-
          draw moneys from State Treasurer.)

July 5. Supreme Court — New York County. Ruth Louisa
          Bailey v. Charles Mascart, et al., doing business
          as the New York Taxicab Co., Limited. (Action
          for injunction.)

      6. Supreme Court — Washington County. Whitehall
          Water Power Co., Limited, and Champlain Silk
          Mills v. Atlantic Gulf & Pacific Co. (Action for
          injunction and damages.)

July   11. County Court — Steuben County. Matter of the
Application of John Glynn for certain surplus
moneys paid into the county treasury of Steuben
County in the action of Catherine Glynn v. John
Glynn, et al. (Surplus money proceeding.)

13. Supreme Court — Erie County. Horatio Shumway
Lee and one v. Julia H. Swope, et al. (Action to
register title to real property.)

16. Supreme Court — Onondaga County.   Skaneateles
Railroad Co. and John McLaughlin and Charles H.
Platt v. Charles H. Quereau, et al. (Foreclosure
mechanics' lien.   Two actions.   Roads 292 and
293.)

20. Supreme Court — New York County.   James C.
Crawford and William E. Diller as administrators,
etc., v. City of New York and others. (Action to
recover an award.)

21. Supreme Court — Erie County.   Simon Paltrovitch
and Sophia, his wife, v. Israel Platt Pardee and
Robert S. Donaldson as executors of James H. Lee,
deceased, et al. (Action to register title to real
property.)

23. Supreme Court — Kings County.   In the Matter of
the Wilkier Unterstitzunges Verein. In the Matter of The Sredniker Benevolent Association.
(Action to consolidate.)

23. Supreme Court — Queens County.   Emil G. Sauermilch as trustee, etc., v. Emil G. Sauermilch, et al.
(Accounting by trustee.)

28. Supreme Court — Montgomery County.   John H.
Voorhees, et al., v. Roy W. Brown, et al. (Action
for accounting.)

29. Supreme Court — Suffolk County.   Milton Gray
Andres and Mary M., his wife, v. Henry S.
Wyckoff, et al. (Action to register title to real
property.)

30. Supreme Court — Rockland County.   Alberta Jane
Goodlove v. Nichols B. Cushing, et al. (To register title to real property.)

Aug.   2. Supreme Court — Onondaga County. Sylvia Newell
v. Rebecca Ackels, et al. (Application by various
defendants to withdraw monies from State Treasury.)

2. Supreme Court — New York County. Louis F.
Gautier v. People, et al. (Five actions to foreclose
transfer of tax lien.)

3. Supreme Court — Onondaga County. Joseph M.
Tallcott v. C. H. Quereau Co., et al. (Foreclosure
of lien.)

3. Supreme Court — Onondaga County. John L.
Schultz and Warren B. DeWitt v. C. H. Quereau
Co., et al. (Foreclosure of lien.)

3. Supreme Court — Onondaga County. Frank H. Lud-
ington v. C. H. Quereau Co., et al. (Foreclosure
of lien.)

8. Supreme Court — Wayne County. Harry W. Ruggles
v. Crowell-Sherman-Stalter Co., et al. (Foreclosure of lien.)

20. Supreme Court — First Judicial District. Matter of
Application of East River Gas Co. of Long Island
City to acquire by eminent domain easements and
right of way in certain real property in the City
and County of New York.

31. Supreme Court — Kings County. Matter of the Application of the Attorney-General for the appointment of a person to execute a charitable trust under
will of Nathaniel Smith, deceased.

Sept.   2. Supreme Court — Suffolk County. People ex rel.
Edward Heinrich, et al. v. George Augustine Kier-
nan. (Action to oust from office of trustee of Sag
Harbor.)

5. Supreme Court — Kings County. Hartje v. Michael
J. A. Rooney. (Garnishment of wages.)

7. Supreme Court — Madison County. The People v.
E. B. French as City Chamberlain of Oneida.
(Ejectment in re estate of Thomas J. Costello, de-
ceased.)

Sept. 9. Supreme Court — Kings County. Minnie Hoffer v. Josiah Riley, et al. (To register title to real property.)

9. Supreme Court — Columbia County. The People v. Edward W. Scoville as County Treasurer, et al. (Action in ejectment.)

13. Supreme Court — Kings County. * Abraham Lachmann and Another v. People of State of New York, et al. (To register title to real property.)

13. County Court — Oneida County. Matter of John William Nicholas Parodi, an alleged incompetent. (Application for appointment of commission.)

13. Supreme Court — New York County. Matter of the second intermediate judicial accounting of Sidney J. Cowen as committee of the person and estate of Mary Ann Dunn, an incompetent.

17. Supreme Court — Saratoga County. Saratoga Trap Rock Co. v. John Harigan, et al. (Foreclosure of lien.)

24. Supreme Court — Suffolk County. David B. Wiggins v. Matthew Jagger, et al. (To register title to real property.)

24. Supreme Court — Erie County. American Body Co. v. Frederick Ogden, et al. (To register title to real property.)

Oct. 5. Supreme Court — New York County. Gertrude D. Hawes v. United States Trust Co. of New York, et al. (To register title to real property.)

24. Supreme Court — New York County. Jane Armstrong, et al. v. Harlem Savings Bank, et al. (To register title to real property.)

24. Supreme Court — Niagara County. Village of Middleport v. Empire Engineering Corporation. (Injunction in re Barge Canal Contract No. 64.)

Nov. 9. Supreme Court — New York County. Matter of the petition of the receivers of J. D. & J. M. Cornell Co. for authority to sell the business as a going concern.

Nov.   9. Supreme Court — Kings County. Helen Littauer v. People of State of New York. (To register title to real property.)

16. Supreme Court — Dutchess County. Charles A. Stovel, who sues on behalf of himself and on behalf of all stockholders and creditors of Dutchess Insurance Co., etc., v. Louis H. Vail, et al. (Appointment of receiver.)

17. Supreme Court — New York County. People ex rel. John P. Butler v. Max S. Griffenhagen, register of the County of New York. (Action to compel recording of deed.)

10. Supreme Court — New York County. Matter of application of William S. Reynolds, et al., petitioning on behalf of themselves and others to review the present apportionment of the State into Senate and Assembly districts.

26. Supreme Court — Kings County. Sarah Kelley v. Jane A. Ackland, et al. (To register title to real property.

Dec.   3. Supreme Court — New York County. Matter of the Application of Michele Lalli for an order to cancel and discharge of record a lost mortgage.

6. Supreme Court — Westchester County. Matter of the Application of State of New York to acquire certain real estate in the town of Yorktown, Westchester County, for the New York State Training School for Boys.

7. Supreme Court — New York County. Henry Neugass v. Edward F. Maloney, et al. (Foreclosure of tax lien.)

7. Supreme Court — Fulton County. Frank Cuyler v. Sarah Huyler Bame, et al. (Action to construe will.)

7. Supreme Court — Albany County. People v. Mutual Savings Life Insurance Society. (Dissolution.)

9. Supreme Court — Erie County. General Crushed Stone Co. v. Joseph Dunfee, et al. (Foreclosure of lien.)

Dec.   9. Supreme Court — Albany County. People v. Frank
             Gass and The Empire State Surety Co. (Action
             to recover payment of mortgage tax.)

         14. Supreme Court — Orleans County. William P. Mer-
             rill v. J. Parfitt Thorne, et al. (Action to compel
             payment from State treasury.)

         22. Supreme Court — Westchester County. Matter of
             the Application of Sallie E. Stone as Executrix, for
             the appointment of a successor trustee in the disso-
             lution of the Croton Lake Improvement Co.

         22. Supreme Court — Albany County. People v. Harbor
             and Suburban Building and Savings Association.
             (Dissolution and forfeiture of corporate charter.)

         28. Supreme Court — New York County. Matter of the
             Application of Gaetano Zingales for the return of
             moneys deposited and cancellation of bond given
             pursuant to Subd. 5, Sec. 29-h, Art. 3-a, General
             Business Law, as amended.

         28. Supreme Court — Albany County. People v. Nine-
             teenth Ward Co-operative Savings and Loan Asso-
             ciation. (Dissolution of corporation.)

         31. Supreme Court — New York County. People v.
             Companions of the Forest of America. (Action to
             vacate charter.)

         31. Supreme Court — New York County. People v. The
             Broadway and Seventh Avenue Railroad Company,
             Metropolitan Street Railway Company, Adrian H.
             Joline and Douglas Robinson, as Receivers of the
             Metropolitan Street Railway Company, City of
             New York, and Guaranty Trust Company. (For-
             feiture of franchise.)

ACTIONS AND PROCEEDINGS INSTITUTED AGAINST STATE OFFICIALS DURING THE YEAR 1910.

Jan.   13. Supreme Court — Queens County. People ex rel.
             John L. Webb v. Charles F. Milliken, et al., con-
             stituting the State Civil Service Commission.
             (Mandamus.)

Jan. 14. Supreme Court — Fulton County. Matter of the Application of the Board of Supervisors of Fulton County for a writ of certiorari directed to Egburt E. Woodbury, et al., constituting the State Board of Tax Commissioners. (To review determination of defendants in reversing the determination of the county as to equalization among the towns.)

 25. Supreme Court — Albany County. People ex rel. Joseph Abel v. Charles F. Milliken, et al., constituting the State Civil Service Commission. (Mandamus to compel reinstatement of relator.)

Feb. 11. Supreme Court — Suffolk County. People ex rel. Everett M. Price v. George L. Chichester as Clerk of the Town of Brookhaven and others and Samuel S. Koenig as Secretary of State. (Mandamus to compel filing.)

 11. Supreme Court — Suffolk County. People ex rel. Everett M. Price v. Dayton Hedges as Supervisor of the Town of Brookhaven, and Samuel S. Koenig as Secretary of State. (Mandamus to compel filing.)

 23. Supreme Court — Albany County. People ex rel. E. I. du Pont de Nemours Powder Co. v. State Board of Tax Commissioners. (Proceeding under Mortgage Tax Law.)

 24. Supreme Court — Albany County. People ex rel. Buffalo & Lake Erie Traction Co. v. State Board of Tax Commissioners. (Proceeding under Mortgage Tax Law.)

Mar. 3. United States Circuit Court — Western District of New York. People's Mutual Life Insurance Association and League, et al. v. William H. Hotchkiss as Superintendent of Insurance, etc., et al. (Injunction.)

 5. Supreme Court — Albany County. People ex rel. United States Mortgage & Trust Co. as Trustee v. Egburt E. Woodbury, et al., constituting the State Board of Tax Commissioners. (Certiorari under Mortgage Tax Law.)

Mar. 7. Supreme Court — Albany County. Matter of Application of Charles A. Phillips for a writ of mandamus v. Charles F. Milliken, et al., constituting the State Civil Service Commission. (Mandamus.)

8. Supreme Court — New York County. Matter of Application of Frank W. Blair for a writ of mandamus v. Charles F. Milliken, et al., constituting the State Civil Service Commission, et al. (Mandamus.)

9. Supreme Court — Monroe County. National Bridge Works v. State of New York, et al. (Foreclosure of lien, Allen street lift bridge contract, Rochester.)

12. Supreme Court. People ex rel. Aaron J. Rosenthal v. Robert B. Lamb, Medical Superintendent of Matteawan State Hospital. (Habeas corpus.)

12. Supreme Court — Westchester County. Fowler & Sellars Co. v. Armory Commissioners, et al. (Foreclosure of lien.)

25. Supreme Court — Cayuga County. Lehigh Valley Railroad Co. v. Canal Board, et al. (Injunction action to test right of State to compel plaintiff to raise its bridge over the Erie Canal without compensation.)

April 18. Supreme Court — Albany County. People ex rel. Lord Construction Co. v. Frederick C. Stevens, Superintendent of Public Works and another. (Injunction to compel defendant to entertain relator's bid on Barge Canal Contract No. 90, etc.)

25. Supreme Court — Westchester County. Richard G. Hiler v. Jesse D. Frost. (Action for damages against warden of Sing Sing prison.)

27. Supreme Court — Westchester County. People ex rel. James H. Brennan v. Civil Service Commission of New Rochelle and State Civil Service Commission. (Mandamus in re placing of position of health officer of New Rochelle in competitive class.)

May 5. Supreme Court — Albany County. Matter of Application of John Slattery for a writ of mandamus v. Cornelius V. Collins as Superintendent of State Prisons of the State of New York. (Mandamus.)

May   13. Supreme Court — Albany County. People ex rel.
           Frank Vesely, Paul G. Fourman and George Cohn
           v. Samuel S. Koenig as Secretary of State. (Man-
           damus to compel filing of certificate of Vesely &
           Co.)

       24. Supreme Court — Albany County. People ex rel.
           John T. Kelly v. Charles F. Milliken, et al., con-
           stituting the State Civil Service Commission.
           (Mandamus to compel approval of transfer of re-
           lator.)   .

June   2. Supreme Court — Westchester County. People ex
           rel. New York Inter-Urban Water Co. v. State
           Water Supply Commission, et al. (Certiorari re
           approval plan of Board of Water Commissioners
           of White Plains.)

       30. Supreme Court — New York County. People ex rel.
           Manhattan-Hudson Realty Co. v. Clark Williams
           as State Comptroller. (Certiorari to review assess-
           ment of taxes.)   .

July   8. Supreme Court — Albany County. People ex rel.
           Adrian II. Joline and Douglas Robinson as Re-
           ceivers of Metropolitan Street Railway Co. v.
           Clark Williams as State Comptroller. (Certiorari
           to review assessment of taxes.)

       18. Supreme Court — Albany County. People ex rel.
           Sea Beach Railway Company v. Clark Williams as
           State Comptroller. (Certiorari to review assess-
           ment of taxes.)

       18. Supreme Court — Albany County. People ex rel.
           South Brooklyn Railway Co. v. Clark Williams as
           State Comptroller. (Certiorari to review assess-
           ment of taxes.)

       27. Supreme Court — New York County. Jacob W.
           Loch, et al. v. Edward R. O'Malley as Attorney-
           General. (Action for accounting by Trustee in re
           General Slocum disaster.)

       29. Supreme Court — Erie County. People ex rel. Har-
           rison Burdsall, et al. v. William Verbeck as Ad-

July   29. jutant-General. (Certiorari to review dishonorable discharge of petitioners.)

Aug.   9. United States Circuit Court — Southern District of New York. Morris Engel v. Edward R. O'Malley as Attorney-General and others. (Injunction to restrain enforcement of Chap. 348, Laws of 1910, in relation to private bankers.)

         16. Supreme Court — Albany County. Matter of Application of Fifth Avenue Coach Co. for a peremptory writ of mandamus v. Samuel S. Koenig as Secretary of State. (Mandamus to compel filing of certificate of incorporation.)

         19. Supreme Court — Albany County. People ex rel. Tony Barracato v. Samuel S. Koenig as Secretary of State. (Mandamus to compel filing of certificate of General Express Co.)

         19. United States Circuit Court for the Southern District of New York. Samuel Kohan and others similarly situated v. Edward R. O'Malley as Attorney-General, et al. (Injunction action under Chap. 348, Laws 1910, private bankers act.)

ept.   8. Supreme Court — New York County. James Lee v. Edward R. O'Malley as Attorney-General and others. (Injunction action under Chap. 348, Laws 1910, private bankers act.)

         22. Supreme Court — Albany County. Matter of the Application of the Cattaraugus Canning Co. for a peremptory writ of mandamus directed to Samuel S. Koenig as Secretary of State. (Mandamus to compel filing of certificate.)

Oct.   8. Supreme Court — Albany County. People ex rel. Mary B. Ripley as Executrix, etc., v. Clark Williams as Comptroller. (Mandamus to compel issuance of receipt for transfer taxes.)

Dec.   6. Supreme Court — Erie County. People ex rel. Charles H. Fleming v. Edward R. O'Malley, Attorney-General of the State of New York. (Mandamus to compel defendant to certify to Superin-

Dec.   6.   tendent of Insurance an original declaration and
             charter of the Buffalo Casualty Co.)

       10.   Supreme Court — Erie County.   People ex rel.
             Charles H. Fleming v. William H. Hotchkiss as
             Superintendent of Insurance.   (Mandamus to com-
             pel defendant to approve an original declaration
             and charter of the Buffalo Casualty Co.)

       12.   Supreme Court - - Franklin County.   Matter of the
             Application of the Town of Brighton for a per-
             emptory writ of mandamus v. Clark Williams as
             Comptroller, etc.   (Action to reduce assessment of
             State lands.)

       15   Supreme Court - - Ulster County.   Ellis B. Long v.
             Elisha M. Johnson, et al., constituting the Com-
             mission on New Prisons of the State of New York.
             (Injunction to restrain awarding of contract.)

APPLICATIONS MADE IN BEHALF OF THE SUPERIN-
TENDENT OF INSURANCE UNDER SECTION 63 OF
THE INSURANCE LAW FOR PERMISSION TO TAKE
POSSESSION OF THE PROPERTY, CONDUCT THE
BUSINESS AND LIQUIDATE THE FOLLOWING IN-
SURANCE COMPANIES.

July   16.   Supreme Court — Oneida County.   Empire State
             Fire Insurance Association of Utica, Oneida
             County, N. Y.

       16.   Supreme Court - - Oneida County.   Citizens Fire In-
             surance Association of Utica, Oneida County,
             N. Y.

Sept. 19.   Supreme Court - - New York County.   United States
             Grand Lodge of the Independent Order Sons of
             Benjamin.

       19.   Supreme Court — Chemung County.   Dukes and
             Duchesses of Edom.

Oct.   31.   Supreme Court — New York County.   Knights of
             St. John and Malta, Fraternal Beneficial Society.

Nov. 15. Supreme Court — New York County. International Fire Office.

15. Supreme Court — New York County. New York Insurance Association.

17. Supreme Court — Broome County. National Benevolent Legion.

23. Supreme Court — New York County. Cosmo Benevolent Aid Society.

CERTIFICATES OF INCORPORATION PASSED UPON FOR THE INSURANCE DEPARTMENT.

Woodmen of the World, Omaha, Neb.

German American Insurance Company of Pennsylvania.

Royal Insurance Company, Ltd., Liverpool, England.

Northwestern Fire and Marine Insurance Company.

St. Louis Fire Company.

Torrens Title Insurance Company.

National Surety Company.

Law Union and Crown Insurance Company.

Commerce Insurance Company of Albany.

Fidelity-Phoenix Fire Insurance Company of New York.

Merchants' Fire Assurance Corporation of New York.

Equitable Accident Company.

Humboldt Fire Insurance Company of Pittsburg, Pa.

Franklin Insurance Company of Washington, D. C.

Independent Order Sons of Jacob.

Independent Surety Company.

Central National Fire Insurance Company of Chicago, Ill.

Servian Montenegrian Alliance.

The Life and Casualty Company of New York.

Government Surety and Casualty Company.

Standard Fire Insurance Company of Hartford, Conn.

Workmen's Compensation Indemnity Corporation.

The Cosmo Benevolent Aid Society.

Benevolent Society of the United States for Propagation of Cremation.

Workmen's Benefit and Benevolent Association of the United States.

Junior Order Benefit Association.

The London Guarantee and Accident Company, Ltd.

Brotherhood of American Yeomen.

United States Fidelity and Guaranty Co.

Massachusetts Fire and Marine Insurance Company.

Maryland Casualty Company.

Aetna Insurance Company.

General Fire Assurance Company of Paris, France.

Philadelphia Casualty Company.

Order of Adelphi.

Michigan Millers' Mutual Fire Insurance Company.

Niagara Fire Insurance Company.

Citizens' Surety Company.

Old Colony Insurance Company of Boston, Mass.

Union Fire Insurance Company of Paris, France.

Pacific Coast Casualty Company of San Francisco, Cal.

Alliance Insurance Company of Philadelphia, Pa.

Merchants' Fire Insurance Company of Denver, Col.

Royal Indemnity Company.

Order Sons of Zion.

Union Phenix Espagnol Insurance Company.

Ukrainian Ruthenian Progressive Worker Haydamaka Organization of America.

Buffalo Casualty Company of Buffalo.

Fidelity and Deposit Company of Maryland.

. American and Foreign Marine Insurance Company of New York.

Swiss Reinsurance Company, Zurich, Switzerland.

Continental Insurance Company of New York.

Marine Insurance Company, Ltd., of London, Eng.

Empire City Fire Insurance Company.

National Slavonic Society of the United States of America.

Queens Insurance Company of America.

Nationale Fire Insurance Company of Paris, France.

Niagara Fire Insurance Company.

Springfield Fire and Marine Insurance Company.

Empire Fire Insurance Company of New York City.

New Amsterdam Fire Insurance Company of New York City.

Sovereign Fire Insurance Company.

Balkan National Insurance Company of Sofia, Bulgaria.

Order of Equity.

Insurance Company of America.

Independent Western Star Order.

Westchester Fire Insurance Company.

Co-operative Fire Insurance Company.

Rossia Insurance Company.

Commercial Union Assurance Company, Ltd., London, Eng.

Germantown and Clermont Co-operative Fire Insurance Company.

Royal Exchange Assurance of London, England.

International Order of the Knights and Ladies of Liberty.

Dryden and Groton Co-operative Fire Insurance Company.

Hebron Co-operative Fire Insurance Company.

Butternuts Town Co-operative Fire Insurance Company.

Pittstown Co-operative Fire Insurance Company.

Federal Insurance Company of Jersey City, N. J.

Commercial Travelers' Mutual Accident Association of America.

United States Fidelity and Guaranty Company.

CERTIFICATES OF INCORPORATION PASSED UPON FOR THE STATE BOARD OF CHARITIES.

Maternity Aid.

People's Pedicure Clinic.

The Eastern Swedish Methodist Episcopal Bethel Church Home for the Aged.

The Lisa Day Nursery of the City of New York.

Hebrew Ladies Day Nursery of Brownsville.

South Side Dispensary of East New York.

Beth Jacob Hospital and Dispensary.

The A. R. Stern Hospital.

Our Lady of Victory Infant Home.

The South Shore Hospital Association.
The Nursing Sisters of the Sick Poor.
Tuberculosis Preventorium for Children.
The Hungarian Hospital.
The Babies' Dairy.
The Hempstead Hospital Association.
New York Congregational Home for the Aged.
The Crippled Children's Guild of Buffalo.
The Open Door Home for the Aged.
Zion Hospital and Dispensary of Brooklyn.
Brooklyn Dental Infirmary.
Hope House.
Emanuel Hospital of Brooklyn.
St. Ann's Day Nursery in the City of New York.
Swedish Home for Aged People Association.
St. Agnes' Home for Crippled and Atypical Children.
The Home of the Holy Childhood.
Ladies' Aid Society for Relief of the Needy of Brownsville.
Lenox Hill Clinic and Dispensary.
Lafayette General Hospital.
Help for the Sick Poor Society of Brownsville.
Amsterdam Dispensary.
Clear Pool Camp.
The Stapleton Day Nursery.
Norwegian Children's Home Association.
Owego Home for the Aged.
The Hebrew Ladies' Dispensary of Williamsburg.
The Charity Wards of the Saratoga Cure and Infirmary.
National Association of Junior Republics.
Caledonian Hospital.
West Suffolk Hospital Association.
Foundation Society for Home for Incurables.
Hebrew Kindergarten and Day Nursery.
Oppenheimer Hospital.
Babies' Milk Dispensary of Buffalo.
West Suffolk Hospital Association.
Norwegian Christian Home for the Aged.
Riverside Sanitarium.

AGRICULTURAL LAW.

The total number of violations of the agricultural and pure food laws referred to this office by the Agricultural Department during 1910, has been. 1,674

Unfinished cases on January 1, 1910, referred during 1907-8-9 1,323

The State has been successful by settlement or judgment in 685

Cases discontinued by reason of insufficient evidence, death of defendant, judicial decisions, etc. 285

Judgments were rendered against the People in... 35

Number of cases in which judgments have been recovered in favor of the State and which remain uncollected 81

Number of cases on appeal 10

Criminal proceedings brought against defendants.. 28

Number of cases referred during 1910, still in the hands of designated attorneys for prosecution.... 1,027

Amount of penalties and costs recovered and turned over to State Treasurer $47,906 48

Amount received in satisfaction of judgments and turned over to State Treasurer 4,770 22

Total $52,676 70

Amount paid for services and disbursements in the prosecution of agricultural cases during the year 1910, some bills not having been submitted or audited for the year $11,134 99

IN THE FOLLOWING CASES JUDGMENTS HAVE BEEN RECOVERED IN FAVOR OF THE STATE, BUT REMAIN UNCOLLECTED.

Defendants and Violations.	Amount of judgment.
William Neuhardt, quarantine	$50 and costs
Victor Lunch, milk, 17328....................	60 00
McDermott Dairy Co., milk, 16964............	117 50
Frederick Genke, milk, 15419	127 70
E. B. May, bob veal, 10765–10767–10768–10771–10772–10775	517 71
E. B. May, bob veal, 6163–a1264–a1265–a1033 to a1040, inclusive	2,308 89
W. E. Bradbury, bob veal, 10700, 10699........	196 17
John Guyer, bob veal, 10287' 10288............	337 65
Mary Hawkins, milk, 13192	79 69
Mrs. E. C. Helwick, vinegar, 5308............	100 00
Samuel Calama, milk, 16752	$50 and costs
Michael O'Connor, milk, 16204...............	188 95
Adam Czajkowski, milk, 15486...............	127 70
Joseph Gorecki, bob veal, 6026	130 29
Fred J. Yaw, milk, 19035....................	79 03
Joseph Bischoff, milk, 16952.................	62 0
Thomas Konz, milk, 16784....................	109 5
Gustav Sceffler, milk, 17358.................	62 0
James H. Kinney, quarantine.................	127 8
H. Gontleman, milk, 16832..................	59 6
Matthews & Harrison, C. C. F. S., 2181........	243 9
W. H. Mowerson & Son, bob veal, 2271.........	62 0
Robert L. Weston, molasses, 1001..............	125 8
Mary Murray, milk, 14754....................	125 81
E. D. Fuller, bob veal, a1312.................	144 57
Edward Medole, milk, 15564.................	132 38
Joseph Jakubiak, milk, 15556...............	131 72
Kream's Lunch Room, milk, 17326............	62 00
M. E. Arnold, bob veal, 10745...............	203 50

Defendants and Violations.	Amount of judgment.
M. E. Arnold, bob veal, 171–177–180	$389 00
Joseph Billi, bob veal, 6002	86 22
Thos. Bingham, bob veal, 301–321 inc., 4251 to 4259, 4260–4277	2,657 09
Thos. Bingham, bob veal, 210–222–224	1,196 01
Thos. Bingham, bob veal, 83, 610, 622, 902	200 00
Thos. Bingham, bob veal, 68, 862, 876, 890	200 00
John Schneider, milk, 17357	57 41
William Decker, bob veal, 7134	239 67
William Weckerle, milk, 15430	234 92
McDermott Dairy Co., milk, 17362	118 00
C. H. Reeve, C. C. F. S., 2695	117 41
Edward Anderson (Anderson Bros.), milk, 16518.	129 62
Charles Langjahr, milk, 16824	63 00
Charles Stranos, milk, 16949	63 00
Orlando R. Stevens, milk, 17431, 17432	112 90
Morris Levy, milk, 17423	112 90
Mrs. Ernestine Neppert, milk, 16865	62 00
Samuel Cohn and Max Mandelberg, milk, 17402	65 40
B. R. Slaughter, milk, 10324	124 00
Paul F. Kaminski, milk, 15440–15495	227 22
Jacob Cohen, renovated butter, 10644	119 41
Frank Diclara, bob veal, 2113	57 00
Frank Diclara, bob veal, 2117	57 00
Frank Diclara, bob veal, 2116	57 00
Joseph Perniciara, bob veal, 2347	63 00
Joseph Perniciara, bob veal, 2355	63 00
Joseph Perniciara, bob veal, 2357	63 00
Joseph Perniciara, bob veal, 2118	63 00
John J. Sullivan, oleomargarine, 10223	59 65
Victor Lunch, milk, 17328	60 00
Hyman Cohen, cream, 17380	27 00
Lewis C. Langworthy, C. C. F. S., 1201	100 79
Martin Strzelzyk, oleomargarine, 204	127 22
William Kolpack, oleomargarine, 6506	128 42
Dr. A. Barradell, improper certificates	200 00
Chan Sew, oleomargarine, 7067	178 22

Defendants and Violations.	Amount of judgment.
Nicholas Rubach, milk, 15479	$127 22
W. Decker, bob veal, 7084	219 19
Frank Pickarski, milk 15498	183 22
Lorenz Winnicki, milk, 15567, 15560, 15437	368 22
Matloff and Kross, lard, 186	50.00 and costs
Dirk Schmidt, oleomargarine, 5730	63 00
Albert Clark and William Butterfield, milk, 7848	164 15
Charles R. Smith, bob veal, 10245, 10246	168 21
Dr. Arthur Barradell, certificates	386 40
Morris Klein, renovated butter, 10207	60 00
Wilson Bros., oleomargarine, 3774	221 51
Wilson Public Market Co., Inc., oleomargarine, 193; renovated butter, 194	280 12
Clover Farms, 6 unclean milk cans	372 00
Fred Bracy, bob veal, 10479	240 66
Peter H. Von Kampen, oleomargarine, 6383	115 00
Thos. Bingham & Co., bob veal, 3000A, 3001B, 3002C, 2065, 2497	799 33

IN THE FOLLOWING CASES THE PEOPLE WERE DEFEATED.

Defendants and violations:
Allen T. Walters, quarantine.
Plaza Lunch (Ike Papkin, Prop.), milk, 16984.
H. Jaffarian, vinegar, 3961.
Joseph Lewis, lard, 2895.
Geo. Tsitsera, milk, 15829.
J. J. Kelley, bob veal, 182–237–1295–1465–1600–6691–6783.
John Shields, quarantine.
Frederick Jaeger, milk, 17359.
Grant Demoney, quarantine.
Jacob Slaff, butter, 153.
Thomas Anderson, lard, 1949.
James L. Reynolds, C. F., 4708.

William J. Schintzious, oleomargarine.
Alexander Van Amberg, quarantine.
Michael Carline, oleomargarine, 10263.
Mrs. P. E. Denton, milk, 15850.
Michael F. Dowling, coffee, 10224.
M. J. Bullion, milk, 10285.
Thomas Bingham, bob veal, 2480–2481.
John Furbush, milk, 15119.
Peter Cooper's Glue Factory, C. F., 4712.
Thomas Bingham, bob veal, 2285.
W. H. Mowerson & Son, bob veal, 2264.
Nicolo Di Marco, olive oil, 10924.
Donato Maddoloni, olive oil, 10928.
Abner M. Yeager, oleomargarine, 190.
Bernard Wieting, oleomargarine, 10671.
Howard Butler, bob veal, 4336–37.
George Tsitsera, milk, 15829.
Joseph Sorrento, olive oil, 10203.
William Garden, Jr., oleomargarine, 201.
Theodore F. Scherer, oleomargarine, 3309.
Eugene Simoni & Co., olive oil, 10975.
Max Fernbach, vinegar, 10625.

JUDGMENTS RECOVERED BY THE DEFENDANTS AGAINST THE PEOPLE AND CERTIFICATES FOR COSTS SIGNED BY THE ATTORNEY-GENERAL.

H. Jaffarin, vinegar, 3961	$85 69
Harry C. Quackenbush, quarantine	49 26
James J. Kelly, bob veal, 182, 237, 1295, 1465, 1600, 6691, 6783	63 38
William Decker, bob veal, 7084-5-6	190 47
Grant Demoney, quarantine	89 35
Thomas Anderson, lard, 1949	26 25
Marshall, Wood & Riley Co., turpentine, 56030	59 80
Alexander Van Amberg, quarantine	20 63

Mohican Company, bob veal, 10712..........	$35 88
Abner M. Yeager, oleomargarine, 190..........	58 00
Allen B. Russ, quarantine....................	57 75
Allen B. Russ, quarantine....................	83 75
Mrs. Mary Craft, oleomargarine, 329..........	10 00
M. J. Bullion, milk, 10285...................	76 40
Howard Butler, bob veal, 4536–37.............	92 71
Howard Butler, bob veal, 4536–37.............	10 00
Robert C. Clark, oleomargarine, 10234.........	44 50
Alfred Tompkins, milk, 7850.................	34 29

STATEMENT OF PENALTIES AND COSTS COLLECTED DURING THE YEAR 1910.

Defendant.	Violation.	Penalty.	Costs.
Alexander Delmars	Milk 13028	$50 00	....
Paul B. Reynolds..........	Milk 16525	100 00	....
Ray Stone	Milk 16520	50 00	$25 00
James Cavanaugh	Milk 16505	50 00	25 00
Jacob Bolster	Milk 16504	50 00	25 00
Silas Austin	Milk 13536	50 00	25 00
John O'Connell	Milk 17318	50 00	....
John McAuliff	Milk 15347	50 00	25 00
Deeg & Gallwert...........	Milk 17347	50 00	10 00
M. Zurlo	Cheap Lard 5357.......	50 00	1 00
George A. Branch..........	Milk 15043	50 00	....
S. Woods	Bob Veal 7272	50 00	25 00
Leon Clark	Milk 14861	50 00	25 00
A. L. Davis' Son............	C. F. 5630	50 00	25 00
Ray S. Cook................	Milk 13173	50 00	....
American Grocery Co........	Lard Comp. 6382	50 00	....
International Milk Prod. Co..	Milk 17291	50 00	....
James F. Smith.............	Molasses 1030	50 00	25 00
Albert Hawkins ....;.......	Milk 14862	50 00	25 00
J. E. Knox.................	Milk 14802	50 00	25 00
John W. McManus..........	Bob Veal 6001	50 00	26 00
Stein & Wittlin.......... ..	C. C. F. S. 2567	50 00	....
L. Hendrickson	Bob Veal a1290-1-2....	50 00	25 00
E. Buckout & Co............	C. F. 5594	50 00	....
Emory J. Odell.............	Milk 14456	50 00	25 00
Sorrentino Bros. & Vollaro...	Olive Oil 10733	50 00	6 00
Delaware Valley Feed & Lumber Company	C. C. F. S. 2314	50 00	25 00

Defendant.	Violation.	Penalty.	Costs.
Fred W. White	Milk 18027	$50 00	....
Amos Phelix and Bernager P. Clark.	Milk 7845	50 00	....
Edward M. Waldron	Milk 15571	50 00	$25 00
Herbert Foster	Milk 18029	50 00	25 00
James Nolan	Milk 14880	50 00	25 00
Geo. M. Bettinger	Milk 14828	50 00	27 75
Herman Bitter	Milk 14827	50 00	25 00
Louis Csermak	Milk 16857	50 00	10 00
Dennis & Herring	Bob Veal 190–191–254– 5455	150 00	....
John Michaelis	Milk 16881–16880–16877.	30 00	....
John Weidland	Milk 19049	50 00	....
Mrs Nancy A. Johnson	Milk 19048	50 00	....
Frank Bosher	Bob Veal 10905–12–19–20	50 00	....
Geo. L. Munroe & Son	C. F. 5724	50 00	25 00
Rock City Mercantile Co.	Vinegar 4763	100 00	42 14
L. Mittenmaier & Sons	C. F. 5621–5622	200 00	25 00
Max Smith	Milk 16827	100 00	....
John Keenan	Milk 14819	50 00	25 00
Samuel Neill	Quarantine	....	19 40
George H. Walker	C. F. 5400	50 00	....
Jessa Hawkins	Milk 15627	50 00	....
Beakes Dairy Co.	Milk 16863–6–17346– 10539–40–41	600 00	45 00
L G. Palmer	Vinegar 4915–5104	50 00	....
H C. Behme	C. C. F. S. 2619	50 00	16 00
A. J. Van Siclen	C. C. F. S. 3051	50 00	....
A. J. Van Siclen & Sons	C. F. 5062	50 00	25 00
A. Varon	Cheap Lard 5358	50 00	1 00
Frank Dillistin	Milk 13538	50 00	....
Burr Sheeley	Milk 16317	50 00	5 00
John Bosch & Son	Milk 14249	50 00	....
W. Scott Gillispie	Lard 5715–1	50 00	....
Thomas E. Cooley	Cream 18406	50 00	....
Tony Del Bello	Bob Veal 6025	50 00	25 00
Berton J. Fryatt	Butter 10	50 00	....
Hamilton Dairy Co.	Milk 17242–3	200 00	15 00
Frank Ahrenfordt	Milk 16872	50 00	7 50
L. Marmar and Ike Feltman.	Milk 17271	50 00	3 00
Miller Bros.	Milk 13537	50 00	....
Irving Partridge	Unsanitary Bldg	50 00	25 00
Abraham Downs	Milk 13596	100 00	....
Frank L. Robinson	Milk 14452	50 00	25 00
George W. Wambold	C. F. 5822	50 00	....
James McGuirk, Sr.	Lard 5315	50 00	1 00
J. Lindenberg	Bob Veal 1380–1338– 1485	50 00	25 00

Defendant.	Violation.	Penalty.	Costs.
Levi F. Doty................	Milk 10252	$50 00	....
A. C. Bull..................	Bob Veal a1391–a1392–		
	a1385–a1386–a1390 ...	200 00	....
Seymour Lake	Milk 14825	50 00	$25
M. Feidelman	Milk 16834	50 00	7
Chiesa & Morino...........	Milk 16830	50 00	7
John H. Doscher...........	Milk 16874	50 00	7
Oliver J. Briggs...........	Milk 14069	50 00	15
Dean & Lee................	Bob Veal 475–483–487–		
	488–495	100 00	20
Thomas Bingham	Bob Veal 5452–53–54...	25 00	....
Falkenstein & Languth......	Milk 16869	50 00	7
Thomas Lacy	Bob Veal 10390–1–2 ...	100 00	25
George Tamblin	Milk 13649	50 00	...
Nichols & Webster..........	C. F. 5361	100 00	...
R. N. Gurley..............	Bob Veal 2489–3858....	100 00	25
Harvey Allen	Milk 13646	50 00	25
Mrs. A. W. Carley and Charles			
Furman...	Milk 14863	50 00	...
Isaac Weinbrat	Milk 16215	50 00	27
Mrs. Patrick O'Hara........	Milk 14497	50 00	...
Matthew Mondore	Milk 13535	50 00	...
W. W. Noxon...............	Milk 14476	50 00	...
Rebscher & Cosgrove........	Bob Veal 2448	50 00	...
John Michaelis	Milk 16881	10 00	...
Mutual Milk and Cream Co..	Milk 16871–16886–17367.	300 00	28 50
August Pflam	Milk 15654	50 00	....
Fred Schirmirling .....:...	Milk 16875	50 00	....
Henry Sodeur	Milk 16882	50 00	....
Peter Karsten	Milk 16887	100 00	9 50
George Laurer	Quarantine	50 00	3 00
Knickerbocker Mills	Baking Powder 4662....	50 00	7 00
Vaughan's Seed Store........	C. F. 5585	100 00	....
J. H. Cummins.............	Milk 4492	50 00	....
Andrew Maxwell	Milk 16434	50 00	....
J. Crowe	Bob Veal 3178........	50 00	27 57
R. B. Matthews............	Bob Veal 2485........	50 00	....
L. Horowitz	Milk 17275	50 00	10 00
George Ferrick	Cream 18410	50 00	....
Antonio Barcia	Bob Veal 2450–2462–		
	2447–2449–2456–2446..	100 00	9 50
The Mapes Formula and Peru-			
vian Guano Co............	C. F. 5233	50 00	7 00
Charles W. Tilley..........	Milk 15243	50 00	27 00
Seminole Condensed Milk Co..	Milk Special	2,500 00	41 00
Arthur Willard	Milk 13648	100 00	....
Max Miller	Butter 156	50 00	25 00
Charles F. Eismael.........	Milk 15341	50 00	....
Noel F. Duchene...........	Butter 308	50 00	....

Defendant.	Violation.	Penalty.	Costs.
Thomas Jenkins	2453–2417 (Bob Veal)	$50 00	....
Curtis & Cunningham	Bob Veal 2454	50 00	....
Crowe & Scullen	Bob Veal 3480–3483	50 00	....
William Crowe	Bob Veal 2458	50 00	....
Fred Zanker	Milk 13647	100 00	....
W. H. Shaut	Vinegar 4764	100 00	$25 00
Geo. Espenlaub	Bob Veal 9197 etc.	300 00	....
Edward M. Statler	Cream 15560	50 00	....
Malone Dairy Co	Milk 17602	100 00	9 50
Charles Levison	Milk 15340	50 00	....
Daniel H. Bloomer	Milk 16253	50 00	....
John H. Kamman Co	Oleo. 4111–4112–3760–3775	100 00	....
Joseph Stanley	Milk 14500	50 00	....
Nicholas Greico	Milk 13595	50 00	25 00
Thomas Parkhurst	Milk 13593	50 00	25 00
Owen J. Owens	Milk 10325	50 00	25 00
Henry Kavanagh	Milk 16783	50 00	7 00
Anna and Lizzie Rickers	Butter 157	50 00	25 00
Isaac LaLond	Imitation Butter 4786	50 00	....
N. LaValley	Imitation Butter 4785	50 00	....
Peter Henderson & Co	C. F. 5704	100 00	9 15
Betsey Fuller and Lewis F. Twitchell	Milk 18151	50 00	....
John Michaelis	Milk 16881	10 00	....
Geo. N. Smith	Bob Veal 2888–2711–2853–2854–3856	100 00	....
Frank Leopardi	Bob Veal 10428–9	50 00	....
Decatur A. Rand	Milk 16416	100 00	30 00
Geo. M. Metzger	Bob Veal a1889–90–91	50 00	....
J. H. J. Watkins	Milk 10323	50 00	....
A. E. Mickle	Cream 15249	50 00	....
Charles A. Bickal	Butter 12	50 00	....
Austen & Griffin	C. F. 5732–33	50 00	....
Wendell G. Hitchings	Unlicensed Milk Agt.	50 00	27 00
William Daley	Milk 14866	50 00	27 00
Daniel Eddy & Sons	C. F. 5670	50 00	....
Jerry C. Sullivan	Milk 19047	50 00	17 40
James Sliker	Milk 15339	50 00	....
Benjamin Lounsberry and Sherman Aumick	Milk 14882	50 00	....
Mrs. Chas. Thiel	Milk 16435	50 00	....
Pietro Ciliberti	Olive Oil 10315	50 00	....
Lucian A. Frink	Butter 3	50 00	....
R. F. Stevens Milk Co	Milk 16948	100 00	8 50
T. G. & G. Zahner	Milk 15845	50 00	....
John Telfer	Milk 16934	50 00	....
Herman Pugsley	Milk 15843	50 00	....
Melton Bros.	Milk 16818	50 00	....

Defendant.	Violation.	Penalty.	Costs.
Purdy Bros.	C. C. F. S. 2805	$100 00	....
Franz Von Rein............	Chopped Beef 831	50 00	$25 00
Charles J. Doyle............	Milk 14823	50 00	25 00
W. D. Britton..............	Turpentine 8X	100 00	....
George Decker	Milk 13696	100 00	....
Paul Papalia	Olive Oil 16647	50 00	....
Mike Miller	Milk 15338	50 00	25 00
William Hall and Isaac Johnson.	Cream 16656	50 00	....
Miller H. Akins	Milk 15568	50 00	25 00
Henry J. Crocoll...........	Hamburg Steak 297	50 00	....
Edward H. Eddy...........	Maple Syrup 2692	50 00	25 00
John Michaelis	Milk 16881	90 00	....
J. H. Meyers...............	Milk 15821	50 00	6 00
Edward P. Mook............	Milk 18452	50 00	....
H. Warnken	Milk 15822	50 00	....
Robert F. Dygert...........	Milk 15494	50 00	25 00
Pasquale Novello	Olive Oil 10907	50 00	....
Max Miller	Lard 155	50 00	25 00
Mrs. Ezra Wheeler.........	Milk 14881	50 00	27 00
Fred C. Roy...............	Milk 15331	50 00	....
Jerry Flynn	Milk 15350	50 00	....
Alfred McIntosh	Milk 13625	50 00	28 00
David McIntosh	Milk 13625a	50 00	28 00
M. H. Renken & Co.	Milk 17425–7	50 00	7 00
John Daneke	Milk 17416	50 00	7 00
Theodore Faller	Milk 17415	50 00	7 00
Burt Kohler and Frank Miller.	Bob Veal 10240–10431..	50 00	....
Frank J. Miller.............	Bob Veal A1758–9–60–1–2–3	50 00	....
John Orb	Milk 13650	50 00	....
Charles T. Germain........	Milk 16703	50 00	....
Pliny G. Link..............	Milk 16528	75 00	25 00
Schwertfeger Bros	Ren. Butter 1003	50 00	25 00
George O. Glendenning	Milk 16821	50 00	6 00
Albert L. Fields............	Milk 15240	50 00	25 00
Frank B. Smith.............	Milk 16304	50 00	....
Oscar E. Moore............	Milk 16152	50 00	....
Edward Richards	Milk 14480	50 00	....
The Mohican Co., Inc., Frank Munsey, Prop.	Hamburg Steak 197....	50 00	25 00
The Mohican Co.	Ren. Butter 2437... ...	50 00	25 00
Dell W. Braga..	Milk 16522	50 00	25 00
Samuel J. Witt.............	Milk 16316	50 00	25 00
John Michaelis	Milk 16881 ⎫		
George Kunz	Milk 16877 ⎬ Final		
William Fried	Milk 16880 ⎭ payment.	10 00	....
Orville P. Knowlton........	Milk 15237	50 00	25 00

Defendant.	Violation.	Penalty.	Costs
Patrick O'Toole	Milk 15773	$50 00	$25 00
Thomas Diamond	Olive Oil 159	50 00	25 00
F. E. Bliss	Milk 14829	50 00	25 00
Charles Slottka	Vinegar 843	50 00	....
John and Charles Williams	Quarantine	50 00	29 00
Paolo Manganelli	Olive Oil 10900	50 00	3 00
Orange County Millk Ass'n	Condensed Milk	750 00	....
William H. Boucks	Cream 16670	50 00	....
John Bosch's Sons	Milk 16950	100 00	8 50
J. F. Peplinski	Bob Veal-A 1286-7-8	125 00	50 00
D. B. Overheiser	Milk 14883	100 00	8 50
John Follett	Milk 15553	100 00	....
Parsons Bros.	Lard 5	50 00	....
Jacob C. Smith & Sons	Milk 16923-4-5-6-7	100 00	....
Arthur F. Tayner	Oleomargarine 4415	50 00	4 50
John Damian	Milk 18456	50 00	....
Frank Theel	Process Butter 200	50 00	26 84
J. & S. Abramson	Milk 14035	50 00	7 50
N. E. Wood & Co.	Oleomargarine	50 00	25 00
C. H. Brooks	Oleomargarine	50 00	25 00
Francesco and Mary Curto	Olive Oil 10195	50 00	....
A. Fiore & Co.	Olive Oil 10197-10908	100 00	....
Benni Spinosi	Olive Oil 10906	50 00	....
E. D. Paparavilopulo, Inc.	Olive Oil 10198	50 00	....
Peter Paledes	Oleomargaine 6248	50 00	....
James Lantry	Bob Veal 2430	50 00	....
Duane H. Shepard	Milk 15242	50 00	27 00
Aaron Scott	Milk 15247	50 00	27 00
Harley Shaver	Milk 14479	50 00	....
Albert C. Frame	Milk 10052	50 00	....
Charles Schiender	Milk 17401	50 00	7 00
Gustave Meyer	Milk 17414	50 00	7 00
Henry Rauch & Co.	Milk 17368-17371	50 00	7 00
Conried F. Barthel	Milk 17417	50 00	7 00
John Vagilakos	Milk 17419	50 00	7 00
John F. Steilen	Milk 16823	50 00	....
Passarelli Bros.	Olive Oil 10652	50 00	7 50
Lewis A. Boore	Oleomargarine 6505	50 00	....
Anderson E. Lathrop	Milk 15236	50 00	25 00
J. C. Meisenzahl	Cream 16666	50 00	....
L. E. Scott & Son	Oleomargarine	50 00	25 00
George Nobles	Hamburg Steak, 322	50 00	15 00
Daniel Ryan	Adulterated Cream 16705	50 00	10 00
Edwin L. Sorg	Milk 15345	50 00	....
Charles F. Schroeder	Ren. Butter 18	50 00	10 00
Otto Staub	Adulterated Cream 16653	50 00	10 00
Paul Mittenzweryg	Milk 16822	50 00	6 00
Geo. Wehmann	Milk 16811	50 00	6 00

Defendant.	Violation.	Penalty.	Costs.
Martin Bukolt	Process Butter 213	$50 00	$1 00
P. J. Hastings	Molasses 1048	50 00	25 00
Sebastian Sippel	Ren. Butter 29	50 00	25 00
M. L. Mowry, Prop. (New Stanwix Hotel)	Oleomargarine 6776	50 00	....
W. A. Dexter	Cream 15587	50 00	25 00
Leo Saunder	Milk 16944–16945		
William Nunley	Milk 16946		
Peter Dillenberger	Milk 16942	160 00	
Valerie Kovats	Milk 16943		
W. H. Van Tassel	Turpentine No. 9	100 00	
Frank Lang	Oleo. 180, 181, 182	50 00	....
Herbert L. Peck	Milk 15244	50 00	27 00
Hiram Knapp and John W. Cramer	Turpentine 82	100 00	....
Cook Milk and Cream Co.	Milk 16814, 15817, 15820	150 00	7 50
Sarah S. Lieberman	Oleo. 310, 312, 310	100 00	....
Mrs. Henrietta Martin, Mgr., Tioga Dairy Co	Milk 16781	50 00	7 50
Daniel W. Spry	C. F. 5179	50 00	....
Fred Youngs	Milk 15241	50 00	25 00
Jacob Bruck	Comp. Lard 10230	50 00	7 50
Amos Post	Vinegar 4102	100 00	....
Lester La Fever	Ren. Butter 195	....	28 64
John Metjen	Oleo. 6337	50 00	....
William S. Newton & Co	Oleo. 309	50 00	....
Henry Kane	Oleo. 10254-5–10262	150 00	....
Ernest Lignore	Oleo. 6330	50 00	....
Josephine E. Spencer	Oleo. 6343	50 00	....
Michael F. Dowling	Oleo. 6309	50 00	7 00
Nellie Hindley, or Charles S. Hindley	Milk 15562	50 00	1 00
Walter Kurzynski	Pure Food 3123	50 00	26 00
William Lennon	Milk 15429	50 00	1 00
A. L. Heath	Milk 14888	50 00	3 00
Samuel Jacobs	Lard Comp. 3028	50 00	25 00
A. Masheri	Olive Oil 141	50 00	25 00
Kaufman Bros.	Milk 16702	50 00	....
Herman Schentzgow	Hamburg Steak 331	50 00	15 00
Mrs. John Glatz	Hamburg Steak 532	50 00	10 00
Lorenzo Blaisdell	Oleo. 944	50 00	10 00
N. N. Adams	Milk 18048	50 00	....
Mrs. Mary Gile	Milk 15245	50 00	27 00
Normanskill Farm Dairy Co.	Cream 151, 152	200 00	....
William Palmer	Oleo. 208	50 00	25 00
McDermott Dairy Co	Milk 17258	50 00	56 85
Frank Moore	Bob Veal 7646, 7647	50 00	25 00
A. B. Cady	Vinegar 54	50 00	25 00

Defendant.	Violation.	Penalty.	Costs.
Phair's Restaurant	Milk 16807	$50 00	....
Charles Cowan	Oleo. 4414	50 00	$3 00
J. S. Kaske	Oleo. 4416, 4417	100 00	5 00
Spaulding Hardware Co., Inc.	Turpentine 346	100 00	....
August F. Strassburg	Turpentine 336	100 00	....
Abramson & Fishhandler	Milk Shipping Station	....	163 46
Neymour Curtis	Milk 15778	50 00	30 00
Charles H. Feeck	Milk 15780	50 00	30 00
J. H. Fitzgerald	Bob Veal 8397-8, 8415	50 00	....
Eugene Villere	Milk 13594	100 00	....
Daniel W. Collins	Adult. Butter 178	50 00	1 00
Joseph H. Joubert	Oleo. 6344	50 00	....
Fred Andrews (Friend & Anderson)	Bob veal 3532	50 00	....
Vern E. Hopper	Milk 14892	50 00	....
Leland S. Van Kleeck	Milk 16254	50 00	....
Fred Andrews (Friend & Anderson)	Bob Veal 3532	....	26 00
W. J. & G. H. Rogers	C. F. 3829	50 00	25 00
William M. Warre	Milk 16526	50 00	25 00
Samuel Miller	Bob Veal 1983	50 00	....
F. Lewandowski & Sons	Bob Veal a1938, etc	100 00	25 00
Lewis Cominskey	Bob veal a1503	50 00	....
Patterson, Thompson Co., Inc.	Turpentine	100 00	....
William G. Lawyer	Milk 15779	50 00	30 00
Ernest Harrsen	Lard 220	50 00	....
John Camp	Bob Veal a1401	50 00	....
Mohican Co.	Hamburg Steak 312	50 00	10 00
Edward Schepp	Milk 12893	50 00	26 00
Lloyd Adsit	Milk 12897	50 00	26 00
Geo. L. Hebert	Van. Extract 32	50 00	....
Elias & Simon Cohen	Milk 14401	50 00	....
William Benjamin	Milk 16745	50 00	....
M. F. Delehant Est.	Lard 196	50 00	....
Thos. Battaly	Olive Oil 135	50 00	....
Robert Sigler	Bob Veal a1365	50 00	....
Harvey B. Nottingham	Milk 14859	50 00	....
Henry B. Grover	Milk 15775	50 00	25 00
Faske Bros.	Bob Veal 8460	50 00	4 50
Harry Goldner	Olive Oil 10920	50 00	....
Ames-Burns Co.	C. C. F. S. 3059	50 00	....
Henry and John H. Miller	Milk 16423	50 00	....
George Dunheiser	Milk 16436	50 00	....
Matthew Book	Milk 16424	50 00	....
John Corbett Mitchell	Milk 16151	50 00	....
William Stanley and Oliver Stanley	Milk 15390	50 00	4 88
John H. Reiman	Turpentine 266	100 00	1 00

11

Defendant.	Violation.	Penalty.	Costs.
H. S. Chordavayne	Milk 17391	$50 00	....
John Lang	Bob Veal 10148	50 00	....
B. C. Williams	Bob Veal 10658	50 00	$25 00
Asa Reed	Oleo. 6800	50 00	....
Mrs. John Cooper	Bob Veal 9240	50 00	....
Eben Richards	Quarantine.	50 00	17 00
Augusta Johnson	Oleo. 3664–6503	50 00	....
Jacob W. Roth	C. F. 5789	50 00	10 00
De Graw & Lawrence	Bob Veal 3657, etc.	100 00	....
Elijah H. Cannon	Oleo. 3665	50 00	....
Isadore Putziger	Bob Veal 8412	50 00	4 50
Pincus Hornstein	Oleo. 10232	50 00	....
R. Blair	Quarantine.	50 00	30 00
Edward I. Clark	Milk 16320	50 00	....
Mrs. Helen Wagner	Oleo. 317–318	50 00	25 00
W. S. Kelly & Son	Vinegar 4073	100 00	....
H. Perkins & Son	Vinegar 5283	100 00	....
David Franklin	Milk 20152	100 00	....
Mary Demerly	Oleo. 315	50 00	1 00
Conklin & Strong	C. C. F. S. 2966	50 00	
James Burnes	Oleo. 943	50 00	10 00
Jacob Johnson, Jr.	Hamburg Steak 370	50 00	....
Jacob Ihrig	Pork Sausage 195	....	....
	Hamburg Steak 197	50 00	....
Sylvester Matthews	Milk 15782	50 00	....
Elbert St. John	Milk 16218	50 00	3 00
Cyrenus Hoppenstedt	Milk 16224	50 00	....
W. W. Watts	Lard 187	50 00	....
Ellsite Fertilizer Co.	C. F. 5198	50 00	....
Frank B. Payne	Bob Veal	200 00	....
Edna Waag	Oleo. 205	50 00	1 00
Charles Laphman	Milk 16441	50 00	....
Albertis Cropsey	Cream 103	50 00	....
Robert Attridge	Hamburg Steak 199	50 00	....
Elderfield, Hartshorn Hardware Co., Inc.	Turpentine 341–1	100 00	....
Webber Hardware Co.	Turpentine 347	100 00	....
Wm. Bidell	Hamburg Steak 290	50 00	....
George L. Schupp	Milk 18442	50 00	....
Lobdell & Sayers	Bob Veal 10662–10670	150 00	3 00
W. F. Wenz	Bob Veal 8427-28	100 00	2 00
C. N. Easton	Bob Veal 10608–10158	100 00	2 00
Anna Feiner and Ida Fisher.	Ren. But. 30	50 00	2 00
Stanislaus K. Krajua	Milk 15589	50 00	1 00
Orange Co. Milk Ass'n	Milk 15848	50 00	....
Peter Biauchi	Bob Veal 8383–8388 inc.	100 00	25 00
W. J. Bach	Bob Veal a1504–a1888	100 00	25 00
S. H. Grems	Lard 39	50 00	....

Defendant.	Violation.	Penalty.	Costs.
Albert D. Quackenbush	Hamburg Steak 349....	$50 00	....
Nic Carmorinos	Oleo. 10241	50 00	$7 50
Jacob Gottlieb	Oleo 6341	50 00	7 50
M. H. Renken & Co.	Milk 17439-40-41-42	100 00	....
J. Miller	Milk 14839	50 00	25 00
Abram Jerushewitz	Milk 16601	50 00	....
George W. Aldrich	Oleo. 7089-7090	50 00	....
Louis Bloch	Ren. Butter 186	50 00	....
George Stanley	Hamburg Steak 348....	50 00	....
John B. Herson	Milk 14877	50 00	....
F. R. Allen	No Certificate	50 00	....
Frank Hill	Oleo 319	50 00	....
Henry Moskey and Homer A. Hogmire	Milk 15665	50 00	....
O. W. Tucker	Bob Veal 2460	50 00	25 00
Chas. H. Schintzius	Bob Veal 6052-6053....	50 00	....
J. H. Norman	Oleo. 5303	100 00	....
George H. Davis	Improper Certificate	100 00	29 00
Mitchell Bros.	Milk 17287	50 00	8 00
Angelo De Capua	Milk 19039-19040	50 00	....
Ezra Blanchard	Milk 15771	50 00	25 00
Charles Haman	Adult. Butter 179	50 00	26 00
Nathaniel W. Read	C. F. 112	50 00	....
D. C. Williams	Bob Veal 10136	50 00	25 00
Daniel H. Grandin	C. C. F. S. 3052	50 00	....
John Ahlstrand	Hamburg Steak 559....	50 00	....
Abner A. Stone	Milk 15169	50 00	16 00
Webb Harrison and Arthur Munson	Milk Shipping Station..	800 00	....
C. Kinch	Bob Veal 10909-10906-10907 - 10861 - 10908-a10506.	100 00	....
Albert E. Quackenbush	Milk 18062	50 00	25 00
John C. Grant	Milk 16683	50 00	25 00
John Hopkins	Milk 18061	50 00	25 00
Frank Green	Milk 19060	50 00	....
William Hughes	Milk 18753	50 00	....
Franklin Bliss Co.	C. C. F. S. 3202	50 00	....
Joseph Eyerer & Son	Milk 18464	50 00	....
Labar & Lain	C. C. F. S. 2908	50 00	....
Blooming Grove Orange Co.	C. C. F. S. 3095	50 00	....
Warwick Grange Co-operative Ass'n	C. C. F. S. 3094	50 00	....
Chester Grange Co. (Inc.)	C. C. F. S. 3092	50 00	....
E. Wilkins	Bob Veal 7108 and 6 others.	50 00	....
D. H. Bentley	Lard 54	50 00	25 00
Leon A. Conner	Hamburg Steak 562....	50 00	....

Defendant.	Violation.	Penalty.	Costs.
William Van Valkenburgh....	Milk 19603	$50 00	....
F. W. Oliver Co., Inc.	Turpentine 342	100 00	....
Louis Philips	Oleo. 221	50 00	....
Lewis J. Chesner	Vinegar 4075	100 00	....
Godfrey Braatz	Milk 18501	50 00	....
Hanover Lunch	Milk 18906–7–8	150 00	$15 00
Wm. H. Mays	Milk 18913–14	200 00	15 00
Buffalo Fertilizer Co.	C. C. F. S. 222–521–732–· 733.	200 00	....
A. A. Grinnell Co.	C. C. F. S. 455........	50 00	....
W. F. Hamilton	C. C. F. S. 426	50 00	10 00
W. F. Hamilton	C. C. F. S. 429, 427....	100 00	....
W. T. Hartman	C. C. F. S. 196........	50 00	10 00
DeEsting J. Scanlon	C. C. F. S. 154	50 00	10 00
L. P. Butts	C. C. F. S. 845........	50 00	....
Merrit B. Rowley	Hamburg Steak 558.....	50 00	....
Louis Simons	Bob Veal 8744–8766–8768	50 00	3 00
Max Andursky	Bob Veal 10065–8765...	50 00	3 00
W. H. H. Scott & Co.	Oleo. 7150–7151–7167 ..	100 00	25 00
Albert Goodermote	Milk 18271	50 00	....
Cyphers Incubator Co.	C. C. F. S. 3006–3036–3037–3038–3039.	150 00	25 00
William Holch	Hamburg Steak 615....	50 00	25 00
William C. Streube	Cream 157	50 00	....
Samuel Tannenbaum	Oleo. 6308	50 00	....
Frank Artale	Olive Oil 10206........	50 00	....
Nella P. Moore	Oleo. 10261	50 00	7 00
Edward and Wm. M. Scrafford	Milk 19604	50 00	....
Herbert B. Rood	Cider Vin. 18..........	50 00	....
Albert P. Miller and Andrew Grochowiak	Hamburg Steak 296. ..	50 00	....
Metcalf Bros.	Cream 17158	50 00	....
Hyman Bros.	Cream 19171 – 17154 – 17157 – 17228 – 17222– 17224 – 17226 – 17227– 17228.	300 00	....
Estella Snell	Milk 18418	50 00	....
Randall D. Marshall	Milk 18502	50 00	25 00
Crick Bros.	Oleo. 3770	50 00	....
Christian H. Van Buren	C. F. 88	50 00	....
George U. Sully	Oleo. 7086.............	50 00	25 00
Harvith Drug Store	Spts. Turp. 444........	100 00	....
W. Everett Wolcott and Gilson C. Wolcott	Milk 15185	50 00	....
Mary L. Connelly	Oleo 313	50 00	26 00
Mary & Catherine Wells	Oleo. 315	50 00	26 00
Dee Kilbury	Milk 18154	50 00	....
Silas J. Speer	Oleo. 331	50 00	....

Defendant.	Violation.	Penalty.	Costs.
Robert S. Everland	Oleo. 6856	$50 00	....
George Hannahs	Milk 15182	50 00	....
Faxon, Williams & Faxon	Vanillin Comp. 226	50 60	....
Lewis B. Richards	C. C. F. S. 2939	50 00	$25 00
Paul Bechtel	Milk 17638	50 00	....
William Gress	Milk 16786	50 00	....
Hamilton Dairy Co.	Milk 16797	100 00	....
Henry J. Palmer	Bob Veal a1318, a1319	50 00	25 00
George J. Norwig	Oleo. 187, 314	50 00	26 00
Doughty & Myer	Milk 17479	100 00	....
Bedford Dairy Co.	Milk 17399	100 00	....
P. K. Heldman	Spts. Turp. 9	100 00	31 00
Frank Torregrossa & Bros.	Olive Oil 10962	50 00	7 50
William Schumann	Rasp. Syr. 167	50 00	....
Wellington E. Crippen	Milk 18068	50 00	25 00
Yansen, Rury & Co.	Bob Veal a1460	50 00	....
The Citizens' Produce Co.	C. F. 412	50 00	20 00
John J. Ashley	Milk 14597	50 00	....
M. A. Richard Estate	C. F. 476	50 00	....
Willis H. Horning	Cid. Vin. 429	50 00	....
John H. Schoeller	Milk 19513	50 00	2 00
Carl J. Reichenberg Bros.	Milk 19507	50 00	....
John Lauricella	Olive Oil 10187	50 00	....
Alexander Penny	Milk 15961	100 00	....
Edward B. Conklin	Milk 13539	50 00	25 00
Harry DeVaul	Milk 12895	50 00	26 00
W. H. Delmore	Molasses 75	50 00	27 50
General Flour & Feed Co.	C. C. F. S. 2072	50 00	26 00
J. L. Shultz & Co.	C. F. 4349	50 00	25 00
Fred Frenz	Milk 17482	50 00	....
T. O. Smith's Sons	Milk 19516	100 00	....
Lewis Perry	Milk 20010	50 00	....
W. F. Greinke	Cream 17165	50 00	10 00
William W. Bonehille	Cream 17159	50 00	10 00
J. C. Meisenzahl	Cream 17233	100 00	....
William E. Gillease	Vinegar 437	50 00	....
Louis Helmanowitch	Vinegar 4380	50 00	....
Charles Lauricella	Olive Oil 10135	50 00	....
J. C. Maloney	Milk 18056	50 00	....
Genesee Provision Co.	Lard 8	100 00	....
George A. March	Lard 11	50 00	....
W. H. Mays	Milk 17172-3-4	100 00	....
American Grocery Co.	Oleo. 3054	100 00	....
Charles C. Foltz	Vinegar 376	100 00	....
Jacob Yochum and Charles Rogers	Vinegar 374	100 00	....
Nic E. Egbert	Milk 17366	50 00	5 00
Matthew Peifer	Milk 20006	100 00	....

Defendant.	Violation.	Penalty.	Costs.
Charles H. Neyer	Oleo. 10104	$50 00	....
Mrs. Elizabeth Fisher	Oleo. 10408	50 00	....
Thomas P. Foley	Oleo. 6160	50 00	....
Crisafulli, Aria & Co	Olive Oil 10100	50 00	....
John Schroeder	Cider Vinegar 425	50 00	....
Abram Goldman	Milk 14490	50 00	....
Max Hodes	Milk 13530	50 00	....
R. E. & W. C. Bie	Cider Vinegar 14	100 00	....
Melvin M. Montgomery and			
W. S. Talcott	Vinegar 2	50 00	....
Walker Ice Cream Co	Cream 18103	50 00	....
D. H. Grandin	C. C. F. S. 3159–3161	100 00	....
Forest, Cross & Co.	Vinegar 22	50 00	....
William Tiss	Milk 4497	100 00	....
Michael Krainiak	Milk 15670	50 00	....
Vaughan's Seed Store	C. F. 812–813	200 00	$24 00
A. F. Namm	Oleo. 10209	50 00	....
Empire Provision & Beef Co.	Pork Sausage 629	50 00	25 00
Geo. M. Lewis & Co	C. F. 160	50 00	....
Chas. N. Codner	C. F. 233	50 00	10 00
Chas. Low	C. F. 741	50 00	10 00
Daniel McKeighan	Bob Veal 2151–31482	100 00	10 00
Owen McGarvey	Milk 16413	50 00	....
James Johnson	Milk 16427	50 00	....
James Dalton	Milk 15235	50 00	....
Henry A. Kamman	Hamburg Steak 293	50 00	25 00
W. H. Bowman	Vinegar 4825	100 00	....
S. A. Smith	C. F. 392	50 00	....
Ware & Wyatt	C. F. 255	50 00	....
Pearce & Coe	C. F. 442–443	100 00	....
Geo. F. Pigots	Bob Veal 4337 – 10967 – 10968 – 10969 – 10970 – 10973	6 00	....
John Burghardtt	Milk 16951	50 00	....
C. H. Reeve	C. C. F. S. 2695	....	17 41
John Freitag	Milk 17339–40	50 00	....
J. F. McCauley	Milk 17334	50 00	....
Fred Krill	Oleo. 942	50 00	....
Clinton Milling & Grain Co.	C. C. F. S. 3130	50 00	26 00
Thomas Strager	Milk 18430	50 00	....
Sisson & Smalley Co.	C. F. 259	100 00	....
John O. Cairetsee and Geo. P.			
Zurbeck	Turpentine 608	100 00	....
Patrick J. O'Connell	C. F. 518–519	100 00	....
Lewis H. Kohler	Lard 481	50 00	....
John Bosch's Sons	Milk 17397	50 00	....
American Grocery Co.	Vinegar 3968	100 00	....
Valentine Reig	Milk 15884	50 00	5 00

Defendant.	Violation.	Penalty.	Costs.
Joseph Pfeister	Milk 15885	$50 00	$15 00
Mutual Milk and Cream Co.	Milk 17621	100 00	7 50
Manning Bros.	Milk 17615	50 00	5 00
James C. Aikin	Evap. Apples A–19	50 00	....
Albert Nowak & Son	C. C. F. S. 3148, 2883, 3174.	150 00	....
John F. Campbell	Milk 15233	50 00	....
Harvey Rich	Milk 15234	50 00	....
Wm. D. Beveridge	C. C. F. S. 2510–11	50 00	....
E. J. Skiff	Cheap Lard 5347	50 00	....
Wm. M. Johnston	Milk 16425	50 00	....
John Torrens	Milk 16430	50 00	25 00
Model Dairy Milk & Cream Co.	Milk 17338	50 00	....
T. Gillice	Bob Veal 2695–2708	100 00	27 60
Crawford H. Pierce	Oleo. 322	50 00	1 50
Lobdell & Sayers	Hamburg Steak 490	50 00	14 50
Ferguson Bros.	Vinegar 4916	50 00	....
Thomas Cavenaugh	Milk 16540	50 00	....
Frank Green	Bob Veal 10438–10445	50 00	25 00
William Halstead	Milk 16535	50 00	25 00
Elnathan W. Hoyt	Milk 18066	100 00	30 00
Charles H. Ostrander	Milk 16418	50 00	30 00
Charles A. Klocke	Extr. Lemon 2451	50 00	....
John Baller	Hamburg Steak 756	50 00	25 00
Alfred J. Kendrick	Hamburg Steak 755	50 00	25 00
Clark White & Son	Unsanitary surroundings in manufacture of cheese (Prairie Queen Cheese Factory)	50 00	....
Clark White & Son	Unsanitary surroundings, etc., at West Branch No. 1 Factory	50 00	....
Jacob Stanicki	Milk A–101	50 00	....
Walrath Bros.	Vinegar 12	100 00	....
George W. Turner	Milk 15681	50 00	....
I. S. Dignult	Milk 19621	50 00	....
Edmund D. Stowell	Milk 18428	50 00	....
Bruce Rowe	Milk 14498	50 00	25 00
George Redlein	Milk 15477	50 00	25 00
Arnold Weppner's Sons	Hamburg Steak 201	50 00	25 00
John W. Salisbury	Turpentine 379	100 00	....
Fred Albrecht	Milk 14855	50 00	25 00
Adams & Hynes	Milk 19518	50 00	....
W. L. Kinne	Milk 17461	50 00	....
Fall River Restaurant	Milk 17478	50 00	7 00
Guiton & Co.	Oleo. 6108–9	....	10 00
Jacob Brenner	Hamburg Steak 782	50 00	....
Catherine and Fred Koerner	Milk 18450	50 00	....

Defendant.	Violation.	Penalty.	Costs.
Harris Robert	Oleo. 6315	$50 00	$7 50
Wm. J. Wheelock	C. C. F. S. 2875	50 00	....
Max Schwartz	Milk 15893	50 00	7 50
Wolf Sheinker & Son	Vanilla 10545	50 00	....
John Szczpanski	Milk 18504	50 00	25 00
Ulysses G. Hawley	Hamburg Steak 780....	50 00	....
Luigi Marino	Olive Oil 480..........	50 00	6 00
Michele Ajello	Olive Oil 10457........	50 00	6 00
Joseph Westermeyer	Milk 17443	50 00	....
Oscar Witter	C. F. 672..............	50 00	....
Rensselaer Stickles	Milk 16523	50 00	....
C. J. Dodge	Oleo.	50 00	25 00
Mrs. Mary Mullin	Milk 16536	50 00	25 00
William Britton	Milk 16531	50 00	....
Stanley M. Smith	Milk 10326	50 00	....
Sam Gile	Bob Veal A-1764.......	50 00	....
Michael Carlin	Oleo. 5273-5890	100 00	....

JUDGMENTS COLLECTED DURING THE YEAR 1910.

Defendant.	Violation.	Amount.
John L. McDermott........	Milk 15968	$62 00
Empire State Dairy Co.......	Milk 16917	82 00
Inter-City Car Ad. Co.......	Milk 16928	62 00
Denis McDermott	Milk 15818	87 00
George C. Kline.............	Cider Vinegar 3935	117 00
E. B. May..................	Bob Veal 10433-10515...........	311 25
E. B. May..	Bob Veal 10765-10767-10768-10771- 10772-10775-6546. Acct. Judg..	188 75
Louise Albrecht	Oleo. 3790	127 70
American Lunch Co.........	Milk 16970	109 50
Daniel O'Neil	Milk 16852	56 00
Mary Hawkins	Milk 13192	80 72
Fred's Restaurant	Milk 17264	85 00
Peter Murray	Bob Veal 7544-7548-7764........	161 11
Adam Czajkowski	Milk 15486. on account............	76 00
Frank W. Brown...........	Milk 13176	133 56
Mrs. E. C. Helwick....... ..	Vinegar 5309	100 00
Albert Miller	Mill: 16868	62 00
DeWitt Snyder	Bob Veal A-1643 to A-1651.... ..	209 00
Thomas Bingham	Bob Veal 5452-5453-5454. On acct.	25 00
Thomas Konz	Milk 16784	109 50
Bernard Friedgood	Vinegar 10617	120 17
McDermott Dairy Co........	Milk 17266	90 33
W. H. Mowerson...........	Bob Veal 4294. On acct..........	100 00

Defendant.	Violation.	Amount.
John Guyer	Bob Veal 10284–10288	$341 36
Gustav Sceffler	Milk 17358	62 00
E. D. Fuller	Bob Veal A–1310–2–3	·144 57
McDermott Dairy Co	Milk 16964. On acct	125 00
McDermott Dairy Co	Milk 16964. Balance	17 00
W. H. Mowerson	Bob Veal 4294. On account	50 00
Charles Straus	Milk 16949	63 09
Charles Langjabr	Milk 16824	63 00
Dr. S. L. Honeyford	Improper Certificate	116 00
Konrad Bantle	Oleo 10231	57 00
Orlando R. Stevens	Milk 17361	58 00
Jacob Cohen	Ren. Butter 10644. On acct	75 00
William B. Shannon	Milk 13104	197 63
Guiseppe Afeltra	Olive Oil 10417	64 65
Nicola Galgano & Sons	Olive Oil 10415	64 65
James Myers	Milk 15405	86 62
W. H. Mowerson	Bob Veal 4294	25 00
Hyman Cohen	Cream 17380	27 00
W. H. Mowerson	Bob Veal 4294. Balance in full	25 00
L. C. Langworthy	C. F. 1201. On account	50 00
William Vigars, Jr	Milk 14635	50 00
Paul E. Tuppack	Oleo. 5984	62 00
Morris Cantor	Cream 17379	62 00
C. R. Smith	Bob Veal 10245–10246	89 72
Kream's Lunch Room (Levine, Mgr.)	Milk 17326	62 00
C. R. Smith	Bob Veal 10245–10246. On acct	78 49
Morris Klein	Ren. But. 10207	60 00
Vincenco Trossello	Olive Oil 10973	60 00
F. E. Rosebrook & Co	Dried Milk 10192	62 00
Herman Sievers	Milk 16795	62 00
Natan Peshkin	Vinegar 10622. On account	75 00
Frank Hahn	Milk 17488	62 00
Nicholas Wiede	Milk 17633	62 00
William Kolpack	Oleo. 6506	130 95
Bailey Bros.	Vinegar 5151	112 38
Lewis Mehltritter	Unclean milk cans	186 00
Matloff & Kross	Lard 186. On account	50 00

CRIMINAL PROCEEDINGS.

Defendant.	Violation and Sentence.
Joseph Vignola	Quarantine. Pleaded guilty. Sentence suspended.
W. E. Noxon	Vinegar 4760. Pleaded guilty. Fined. Sentence suspended.

Defendant.	Violation and Sentence.
Francesca Malatesta	Quarantine. Pleaded guilty. Sentence suspended.
Horace A. Warner	Butter 13. Pleaded guilty. Sentence suspended.
Jacob B. Widener	Butter 14. Pleaded guilty. Sentence suspended.
Minst & Greb	Oleo. 7700. Greb arrested, tried, found guilty and fined $100, which he paid.
H. R. McCarney	Vinegar 5024. Defendant arrested, pleaded guilty, sentence suspended.
J. W. Nott	Turpentine 5605-Y. Defendant pleaded guilty; sentence suspended.
Fifth Avenue Dairy Lunch...	Oleo. 5996. Defendant found guilty; fined $100 or five days in jail; elected to serve sentence.
Herman Lieberman	Lard 154. Defendant pleaded guilty. Sentence suspended.
Earl Taylor	Milk 13636. Tried in Court of Special Sessions; convicted. Fined $50 and sentenced to 60 days in jail. Fine was paid and sentence suspended.
John Doe	Oleo. Defendant found guilty. Fined $50; paid.
Lester La Fever	Ren. Butter 195. Defendant pleaded guilty and fined $50, which was paid.
Charles Hess	Quarantine. Jury found him "Not guilty."
Edward Lunenbergh	Quarantine. Discharged by Justice of the Peace.
James Geagan...............	Quarantine. Pleaded guilty, fined $10, which was paid.
C. W. Sisson	Quarantine. Pleaded guilty, fined $10, which was paid.
Jos. McDonald	Quarantine. Pleaded guilty, fined $10, which was paid
Robt. Wilkins	Quarantine. Pleaded guilty, fined $10, which was paid.
Lawrence Zamellon	Quarantine. Pleaded guilty, fined $10, which was paid.
George McKnight	Quarantine. Pleaded guilty, fined $10, which was paid.
Clarence Taylor	Oleo. 299. Convicted, fined $100; paid.
Ettie Siegel	Lard 190. Defendant tried, found guilty and sentence suspended.
Abram Kasenetz	Un-sanitary condition of stable. Defendant pleaded guilty. Sentence suspended.
Wm. J. Tomlinson	Milk 18055. Defendant pleaded guilty. Sentence suspended.

Defendant.	Violation and Sentence.
Herman Kiesel	Unsanitary condition of building. Pleaded guilty. Sentence suspended.
George Banham	Milk 18059, Cream 74. Pleaded guilty. Sentence suspended.
Eugene Wilsey	Unsanitary condition of building. Pleaded guilty. Sentence suspended.

CASES ON APPEAL.

The following cases on appeal were disposed of during the year 1910:

APPELLATE DIVISION, SECOND DEPARTMENT.

People v. George Tsitsera, milk, 15829. Appealed by the plaintiff from a judgment in favor of defendant. Appellate Division reversed judgment and ordered new trial.

People v. Robert C. Clark, oleomargarine, 10234. Defendant appealed from decision of Special Term overruling demurrer. Appellate Division affirmed interlocutory judgment.

People v. Robert C. Clark, oleomargarine, 10234. Plaintiff appealed from decision of Special Term denying motion for injunction. Appellate Division affirmed order.

APPELLATE DIVISION, THIRD DEPARTMENT.

People v. Matthews & Harrison, C. C. F. S., 2181. Defendant appealed from judgment and order in favor of plaintiff. Judgment and order unanimously affirmed by Appellate Division.

People v. William Decker, bob veal, 7133. Plaintiff appealed from judgment in favor of defendant. Judgment affirmed by Appellate Division.

People v. Abramson & Fishhandler, milk shipping station. Defendants appealed from interlocutory judgment overruling demurrer. Appellate Division affirmed judgment.

People v. Joseph Lewis, lard, 2895. Plaintiff appealed from judgment in favor of defendant. Appellate Division reversed judgment and new trial granted.

APPELLATE DIVISION, FOURTH DEPARTMENT.

People v. Daniel B. Wooden, milk, 1330. Defendant appealed from judgment in favor of plaintiff. Judgment affirmed by Appellate Division.

People v. David Butler, milk, 11419. Defendant appealed from judgment in favor of defendant. Judgment affirmed by Appellate Division.

People v. Allen B. Russ, quarantine. Plaintiff appealed from judgment dismissing complaint. Judgment affirmed by Appellate Division.

APPELLATE TERM, NEW YORK COUNTY.

People v. C. H. Reeve, C. C. F. S., 2695. Defendant appealed from judgment in favor of plaintiff. Judgment affirmed.

People v. Pietro Santangelo, bob veal, 2693. Defendant appealed from judgment in favor of plaintiff. Judgment affirmed.

People v. McDermott Dairy Co., milk, 16964. Defendants appealed from judgment in favor of plaintiff. Judgment affirmed.

People v. Gennaro Adams, bob veal, 2306. Defendants appealed from judgment in favor of plaintiff. Judgment affirmed.

People v. Thomas Bingham & Co., bob veal, 510. Defendants appealed from judgment in favor of plaintiff. Judgment affirmed.

People v. McDermott Dairy Co., milk, 17258. Plaintiff appealed from judgment in favor of defendant. Appellate Term reversed judgment and sent case back for new trial.

People v. McDermott Dairy Co., milk, 17266. Defendants appealed from judgment in favor of plaintiff. Judgment affirmed by Appellate Term, without opinion.

People v. Nicolo DiMarco, olive oil, 10924. Plaintiff appealed from judgment in favor of defendant. Judgment affirmed.

People v. Donato Maddoloni, olive oil, 10928. Plaintiff appealed from judgment in favor of defendant. Judgment affirmed.

People v. Thomas Anderson, lard, 1949. Plaintiff appealed from judgment in favor of defendant. Judgment affirmed.

ONONDAGA COUNTY COURT.

People v. Allan T. Walters, quarantine. Opinion rendered reversing judgment for defendant and reversing order denying the motion for a new trial.

The following cases are pending in appellate courts:

COURT OF APPEALS.

People v. James Butler, vanilla extract, 1945. Appealed by defendant from reversal of judgment by Appellate Division, Second Department.

People v. Nelson E. Spencer, as Trustee, etc., et al., vinegar, 718. Appealed by defendant from judgment in favor of plaintiff which was affirmed by Appellate Division.

People v. Webster & Bailey, milk, 16048. Defendant appeals from judgment of Appellate Division affirming a judgment of the Albany County Court.

APPELLATE DIVISION, SECOND DEPARTMENT.

People v. James L. Reynolds, C. F., 4708. Appealed by plaintiff from judgment in favor of defendant.

People v. Peter H. Von Kampen, oleomargarine, 6383. Appealed by defendant from judgment in favor of plaintiff.

APPELLATE DIVISION, THIRD DEPARTMENT.

People v. William Decker, bob veal, 7134. Appealed by defendant from judgment in favor of plaintiff.

People v. John A. Shields, quarantine. Appealed by plaintiff from judgment for defendant.

APPELLATE DIVISION, FOURTH DEPARTMENT.

People v. Fred Bellinger, quarantine. Appealed by plaintiff from judgment in favor of defendant.

People v. William J. Schintzius, oleomargarine, 4106. Appealed by plaintiff from judgment in favor of defendant.

People v. Allan T. Walters, quarantine. Appealed by defendant from judgment and order of the Onondaga County Court reversing the judgment and order of the Municipal Court of the City of Syracuse.

CASES DISCONTINUED DURING THE YEAR 1910 AND
REASONS THEREFOR:

*Recommendation of Commissioner of Agriculture, Opinion of the
Attorney-General, Interpreting the Pure Food Law, Death of
Defendants, Statute of Limitations, or Insufficient Evidence
to Sustain Action.*

Defendants and violations:

C. E. Scheuber, bob veal, 127–128–129–141.

G. B. St. John, bob veal, 118–132–145.

S. P. Fields, bob veal, 2143.

Linus Johnson, bob veal, 102.

H. B. Winship, bob veal, a1356.

James Moore, oleomargarine, 10708.

Schinerer Bros., oleomargarine, 10706.

H. D. Thompson Hardware Company, turpentine X 5.

Jelliffe, Wright & Co., bob veal, 2263.

Jelliffe, Wright & Co., bob veal, 2127–2139–2141–2140–2128–
2138–2131–2129–2137–2130.

Leo Priest, quarantine.

Fred Berry, milk, 16373.

Andrew C. Schaefer, oleomargarine, 3031.

John Barry, quarantine.

Paul Nicodare, quarantine.

Barber Cons. Feed Co., C. C. F. S., 2230–2285–2286–2287–
2473–2472.

Dodd Bros., milk, 15375.

Pasquela Bollardi, oleomargarine, 6003.

Titus S. Darling, C. F., 5200.

E. H. Leighton, cheap lard, 5355.

William Harrens, oleomargarine, 5889.

Mrs. A. Bolte, milk, 16999.

Ira Davenport, vinegar, 735.

M. Lane, bob veal, 1182–1498–1736–1751–1898.

W. B. Culver, bob veal, 1366–1478.

G. Bemsen, bob veal, 1561.

P. McEnroe, bob veal, 230.

E. R. Chapman, bob veal, 1051–1255–1908.

George W. Utter, bob veal, 1548.

D. B. McElway, bob veal, 1253.

D. G. Enever, bob veal, 175–1012.

Geo. P. Tabor, bob veal, 1433–1553–1555.

W. H. Fitch, bob veal, 181.

Mr. Lane, bob veal, 1011.

J. F. Walther, bob veal, 1411–1918.

G. Errickson, bob veal, 1556.

E. Coons, bob veal, 1919–20.

W. F. McCord, bob veal, 1432.

E. B. Chapman, bob veal, 1941.

Frank Wooden, bob veal, 275.

E. L. Barrett, bob veal, 1948.

A. B. Culver, bob veal, 1342–1483–1739.

Harry M. Tabor, bob veal, 1436–1552.

J. B. Hammond, bob veal, 1437.

E. W. Brusie, bob veal, 1270.

F. J. McEnroe, bob veal, 1499.

D. B. McElway, bob veal, 1734–35–56–7–9–60–1765–62–1992–3–5.

S. R. Mills, bob veal, 1430–1977.

E. Vincent, bob veal, 1946–47.

M. Lane, bob veal, 1974.

Mrs. Frank Bouchy, bob veal, 1262–1424–1431.

W. M. Dakin, bob veal, 1984.

Foster Cook, bob veal, 1264.

H. V. D. Reed, bob veal, 1978–80.

Frank Wooden, bob veal, 1263–1986.

John T. Walker, bob veal, 1973.

E. C. Cowdaw, bob veal, 1950.

F. N. Wheeler, bob veal, 1982.

John Bensic, bob veal, 1981.

Frank Sutherland, bob veal, 1779.

S. Booth, bob veal, 1429.

C. J. Rockefeller, bob veal, 1746.

D. B. McElway, bob veal, 1265–6–7–8–9–1590–2–3–4–1416–8–1420–1–6–7–8–1778–1924–5–1979.

John Birch, bob veal, 244–5.

Charles Handlin, bob veal, 1286.

E. A. Hoag, bob veal, 1674.

E. Phelps, bob veal, 1619.

Leonard Davis, bob veal, 1826.

Geo. P. Tabor, bob veal, 1825.

P. Van Hovenburg, bob veal, 1287.

II. J. Bursch, bob veal, 1687.

Dakin, bob veal, 1330.

F. W. Dakin, bob veal, 1888.

Mrs. F. Boucha, bob veal, 1867.

Myron Lane, bob veal, 1855.

Wm. B. Cutler, bob veal, 1671.

J. L. Walther, bob veal, 2852-64.

J. P. Walther, bob veal, 2708.

II. S. Loeper, bob veal, 2855.

Elmer W. Swan, milk, 14826.

T. S. Williamson & Bro., bob veal, 2233-2231-2468.

Mrs. Mary Cassidy, quarantine.

William II. Hull, quarantine.

Frank Stehlby, powdered milk.

Mrs. J. Halpin, butter, 5318.

Max Leipersohn, milk, 16867.

Dr. F. E. Eusten, quarantine.

W. II. Mowerson & Son, bob veal, 2493-3103-4-5-3162.

William II. Hartley, C. F., 5155-56.

John W. Grinnell, C. F., 5352.

James M. Coake et al., milk, 15319.

F. S. Hodge, milk, 18030.

Chas. R. McCormack, quarantine.

Simon Woulfe, quarantine.

Mrs. Rosella Stoll, milk, 15618.

Mohican Company, bob veal, 10712.

Ragus Tea and Coffee Co., lemon flavor, 2435.

Jacob Engels, oleomargarine, 10716-17.

Harman Shornack, oleomargarine, 10720.

James G. Murray, cream, 16665.

Geo. Schrader, milk, 16938.

Geo. D. Campbell, cider vinegar, 4236.

Adam J. Menges, adulterated butter, 969.

Schrodt & Merges, vinegar, 6450.

F. II. Ebeling, Com. Fert., 4359.

Lucius J. Smith, milk, 16876.

Bowman & Glover, turpentine, 64.

John Barr, turpentine, 74.

James L. Bowman, turpentine, 5600.

Philip Welch, milk, 16816.

Erle Foster, milk, 16521.

John Guyer, bob veal, A1284-5.

W. Cassidy, vinegar, 3956.

Wm. E. Hookway, quarantine.

F. J. Oakley, bob veal, 2886.

George D. Swart, milk, 15246.

Simeon J. Campbell, cream, 16660.

Harry Cohen, bob veal, 10050.

Alexander Knapp, milk, 14806.

Fred St. John, cream, 15584-15586.

Liberman Dairy Co., milk, 17422.

Peter Murray, bob veal, 2344-66-7-8-2393-2396.

Addison P. Jones, short barrels, 3, 5, 7, 10, 11.

Santa Clate, quarantine.

George Broswick, quarantine.

D. R. Taylor, milk, 13636.

John Smith, milk, 14481.

Thomas H. Clough, essence of lemon, 169.

Jacob House & Son, vanilla soda flavor, 2452.

John O'Hara, milk, 14836.

Julia Weber, oleomargarine, 7069.

John Szydlowski, process butter, 198.

William A. Cleaver, oleomargarine, 7071.

John H. Steiler, milk, 15848.

Marshall, Wood & Riley Co., turpentine, 5030.

Sowles, Hardware Co., turpentine, 9920.

Abraham Loeb, oleomargarine, 3666.

Mrs. Susan Rider, oleomargarine, 310.

Nelson H. Baker, manager and superintendent, oleomargarine, 7074.

Harry Goldner, olive oil, 10915.

F. S. Cook, bob veal, 1112.

William S. Silvernail, bob veal, 1123.

Philip McEnroe, bob veal, 1113.

N. A. Kilmer, bob veal, 7446.

H. Barton, bob veal, 134.

F. Brown, bob veal, 135–150.

Norman A. Kilmer, bob veal, A-1354, A-1374, A-1351, A-1362, A-1359, A-1389.

Daniel Giallella, oleomargarine, 3663.

Harvey A. & Norman C. Young, oleomargarine, 206.

Margaret Gilooly, superintendent, etc., oleomargarine, 7072.

W. H. Hatmaker, oleomargarine, 751.

Jacob Haltzer, oleomargarine, 6342.

Nelson H. Baker as superintendent, etc., oleomargarine, 7087.

A. C. Jetter, milk, 17277.

J. D. Colman, C. F., 2177.

J. B. Reed & Son., C. F., 2179.

Sam Rosenbloom, quarantine.

Edward Vincent & John Struebling, turpentine, 76.

James D. Bashford, vinegar, 4023.

Warren Tripp, bob veal, 39, 140, 124.

Miller & Bush, jelly, 1213.

William Unterfinger, oleomargarine, 203.

Fred Conrad, oleomargarine, 2376.

Mary T. Cahill, oleomargarine, 4148.

William Davison, oleomargarine, 7066.

Jacob Friedman, bob veal, 8767.

V. Hope, cheap lard, 121.

Knapp-Cramer Hardware Co., turpentine, 76.

Laura Treat, oleomargarine, 210.

E. Brandin, oleomargarine, 195–196.

John Owens, vinegar, 5252.

Clark Sisum, bob veal, 10911–10913.

J. D. Nooning, vinegar, 5280.

Clarence Pettebone, quarantine.

Mrs. James Grant, molasses, 1076; pepper, 1078.

H. V. Rose, quarantine.

Lester Clapper, bob veal, 6453.

C. A. Chandler, C. C. F. S., 2725.

Albert P. Miller, hamburg steak, 296.

J. C. Solace & C. Chapman, cream, 51.

Richard E. Ellis, cream, 52.

Cyphers Incubator Co., C. C. F. S., 3101.

William Decker, bob veal, 7085–7086.

Fred J. Sauer, oleomargarine, 217.

Peter Cooper's Fertilizer, C. F., 46, 624, 655, 656.

Anton C. Goldman, oleomargarine, 7085.

Martin A. Brecheisen, vanilla, 613.

L. G. Palmer, vinegar, 5023.

Rich's Jersey Creamery Co., cream, 18202, 18203, 18205.

Rich's Jersey Creamery Co., cream, 725.

John Kendall, bob veal, a–1572–3–4.

George F. Hallaran, vanilla, 10182.

Irving P. Hallock, vanilla, 10383.

Louis Reichart, vanilla, 10382.

P. S. McDonough, milk, 19612.

Geo. E. Robinson, C. C. F. S., 2722.

L. G. Palmer, vinegar, 5016.

H. Perkins & Son, cider vinegar, 616.

Aldis Owen Hall, oleomargarine, 211–216.

Fred Erbach, turpentine, 270.

Winans Lunch Room, milk, 16449; cream, 159.

Mrs. Mary Cohen, quarantine.

Christopher Simeone, quarantine.

Max Robinson, quarantine.

Gersher H. Stone, quarantine.

Mrs. Rizie Sumburg, quarantine.

D. Tulloh, vinegar, 44.

Willis F. Lee, vinegar, 5255.

Patrick Gompol, bob veal, 3536.

Horseheads Creamery Co., cream, 15669.

W. M. Evans, condensed milk, 18869.

Alabama Lumber and Cooperage Co., short barrels.

F. S. Mead, short barrels.

W. D. Wescott, short barrels.

T. V. Putnam & S. E. Tichner, short barrels.

S. O. Berean, short barrels.

Philip Sharer, quarantine.

Catherine Heilman, Mother Superior, etc., oleomargarine, 7073.

John Grobe, Jr., bob veal, 6007-8-9-12-13-14-15-16.

Jelliffe, Wright & Co., bob veal, 3597, 3520, 3527.

Louis Helmanowitch, vinegar, 4370.

Stumpp & Walter Co., C. F., 818.

W. J. Mahar, vinegar, 4928.

J. F. Carpenter, vinegar, 26.

Eugene Empie, vinegar, 28-1055.

William A. Cornell, vinegar, 5015.

William Bach, quarantine.

J. T. D. Blackburn, quarantine.

William Bookheim, quarantine.

Mrs. H. Bronk, quarantine.

E. T. Buckley, quarantine.

H. E. Campbell, quarantine.

Arthur Cardell, quarantine.

Robert Conkey, quarantine.

——— Coomb, quarantine.

Mary DeWitt, quarantine.

Mrs. William Donnelly, quarantine.

Curtis X. Douglas, quarantine.

D. H. Doyle, quarantine.

Mrs. Clarence B. Flint, quarantine.

R. P. Flower, quarantine.

Cosimo Franze, quarantine.

F. T. Grattan, quarantine.

Henry Hamman, quarantine.

William Harlfinger, quarantine.

Ferdinand Hauser, quarantine.

Mrs. Thomas J. Hopkins, quarantine.

Mrs. Emily X. Huyck, quarantine.

John H. Joyce, quarantine.

Catherine Kapps, quarantine.

Mitchell Mack, quarantine.

John Maher, quarantine.

Mrs. Augustus Meske, quarantine.

J. R. Messer, quarantine.

Adolph Meyers, quarantine.

L. Nath, quarantine.

Daniel M. Nero, quarantine.
Thomas P. Dolan, quarantine.
James Patterson, quarantine.
Thomas J. Reilly, quarantine.
J. G. Rudolph, quarantine.
Mrs. John Savoy, quarantine.
Mrs. Frank Schumaker, quarantine.
Mrs. Shaw, quarantine.
William Smith, quarantine.
Jacob Sperber, quarantine.
C. M. Stuart, quarantine.
Sarah Swift, quarantine.
Edward Thayer, quarantine.
Charles Tietz, quarantine.
Mrs. Mary Towson, quarantine.
————— Walsh, quarantine.
Henry V. Planz, quarantine.
Peter Frick, quarantine.
Arthur S. Dolan, quarantine.
Mrs. M. Burmaster, quarantine.
Thomas Bohanan, oleomargarine, 5712.
Hugo Woerle & A. Fallinger, oleomargarine, 5720.
Mrs. Tilly Benson, oleomargarine, 5716.
Rose Miller, oleomargarine, 5704.
Schenectady Public Market, lard, 2891 I.
Manhattan Co., lard, 2831 I.
James C. Andrews, milk, 16026.
Rochester Fertilizer Co., Com. Fert., 4519-20-21.
Grant Card, bob veal, 1121.

REPORT OF NEW YORK CITY BUREAU.

December 1, 1910.

Hon. EDWARD R. O'MALLEY, *Attorney-General, Capitol, Albany, N. Y.:*

SIR.— We have the honor to present herewith our report of the work of the New York City Bureau of the office of the Attorney-General for the year 1910 to December 1, 1910.

From January 1, 1910, until his resignation on October 5, the New York City Bureau was in charge of Deputy Attorney-General Ezra P. Prentice. From October 10 to date the office has been in charge of Deputy Attorney-General Frederick C. Tanner.

The work in the office has continued to increase during the year and has required much overtime work on the part of the office force. The office has been kept open until after six o'clock except on Saturdays and at times has been continuously open until after ten in the evening.

The office has investigated and conducted the prosecution of election cases in New York, Kings, Queens, Richmond and Westchester Counties, and has advised the Superintendent of Elections in relation to matters arising within the Metropolitan Elections District. It has taken proceedings on behalf of the Superintendent of Insurance against delinquent insurance corporations in accordance with Chapter 300 of the Laws of 1909, and has appeared in the proceedings taken under the Land Title Registration Act passed in 1908. It has also advised and assisted the Comptroller in the proceedings taken by him in accordance with Section 70 of the General Business Law to revoke detectives' licenses, and to enforce the amendments to the Banking Laws passed in 1909. Hearings have been held in applications to the Attorney-General to commence actions in the name of the people for the dissolution of corporations, or against their officers or directors. The office has continued to prosecute agricultural cases on behalf of the Department of Agriculture, and has represented various State institutions in habeas corpus proceedings. It has examined proceedings in the Surrogates' Courts and cases in the Supreme Court in which there was a possible escheat to the State, and has appeared in the cases or proceedings when the interests of the State made it proper to do so. It has examined papers and appeared when necessary in various proceedings for the dissolution of corporations, and has also conducted the various miscellaneous cases described in this report.

All of these matters are described more fully under appropriate headings.

In addition to the cases referred to in this report, the New York office has frequently been called upon to attend to matters in cases which are in charge of the Albany office.

We wish to commend Mr. Henry R. Brown, who, from the 2d day of October, 1910, has rendered valuable and efficient service to the State without compensation, and has been of much service to this office in examining and advising on questions of law.

ELECTION CASES.

The election cases presented during the year 1910 are described in detail in a separate report. The investigation and prosecution of these cases required the time not only of the regular force but of Special Deputy Attorneys-General, extra process servers and stenographers. The office was represented by Special Deputy Attorneys-General on primary day, all days of registration and election day in the various Magistrates' Courts and the Courts of General and Special Sessions in New York city. The Special Deputies took part in the examination on these days of upwards of 260 cases in the various Magistrates' Courts. One hundred and fifty-eight indictments have been found against 138 persons by different grand juries, and 45 persons have been convicted upon these indictments. Ten persons have also been proceeded against on information in the Courts of Special Sessions, of whom three have been convicted. The greater number of indictments found in the autumn of 1910 have not been reached in the Court of General Sessions for trial. The new rules regulating the calendar procedure in that court does not give the prosecuting officer control of the calendar, as formerly he had, and such cases must be tried in their regular order.

During the investigation of these cases it became apparent that where several persons had committed a series of offenses against the Election Law, it was frequently impossible to secure convictions if indictments were separately found for each of the offenses.

because on the trial of any such indictment testimony was admissible only as to the particular offense named in the indictment and evidence relating to other and different concurrent acts or acts committed immediately prior or subsequent to that named in the indictment was excluded as well as evidence relating to the other persons who acted with the person named in the indictment.

Also many of the forms of indictments previously used in the prosecution of election cases were found to be faulty. Mr. Mason Trowbridge, formerly Assistant District Attorney of New York County, was therefore retained, because of his experience in the drafting of indictments, for the purpose of redrafting, in co-operation with this office, the forms of indictments to be used in the prosecution of election cases and of drafting indictments charging conspiracy under Section 773 of the Penal Law in relation to General Elections, and conspiracy under Section 580 of the Penal Law in regard to primary elections. The form of these indictments has been sustained in all cases.

In the investigation and trial of the election cases it was necessary to employ extra stenographers and an extra force of process servers. The deputy in charge of the New York office was obliged to advance the money to pay these employees and subsequently to send in a voucher for the amount so spent. It was frequently impossible to secure payment of these vouchers for one or two months after they had been forwarded to Albany, and the employees were also compelled to wait a considerable time before receiving their wages or repayment of the amounts advanced by them for their travelling expenses. The deputy in charge of the New York office was required at times to advance over $2,000 for this purpose. The impropriety and difficulty of conducting a public office in this manner is apparent and should be remedied.

HEARINGS.

Hearings have been held in the New York city office in the following applications to the Attorney-General to commence actions in the name of the people for the dissolution of corporations or against the officers or directors of corporations. These hearings have been conducted here for the convenience of counsel and witnesses residing in New York city. Witnesses have been examined and the arguments of counsel heard.

In the Matter of Ludwig & Company, application of John H. Ludwig to the Attorney-General to commence an action against Charles A. Ericsson, Lycus D. Perry, John J. Ryan, Henry C. Schoeppy, and Herbert B. Rumrill, directors of Ludwig and Company for the removal of said directors and to compel them to account for and pay over to Ludwig and Company the value of certain property. Decided, February 14, 1910.

In the Matter of the Application of William D. Tyndall to the Attorney-General to commence an action against Abram C. DeGraw, William H. Locke, Jr., and William G. Ross, officers of Pinelawn Cemetery.

In the Matter of the Application of the Daimler Motoren Gesellschaft, for the dissolution of the Daimler Manufacturing Company of New York, pursuant to section 101 of the General Corporation Law.

In the Matter of the Application of Maurice Solomon to have an action instituted by the Attorney-General to dissolve the Shole Hotel Company. Hearing commenced August 2d, adjourned from time to time, now set for December 14, 1910.

In all of the above matters the hearings have been completed or discontinued and the reports upon each one forwarded with the exception of the matter of the Daimler Motoren Gesellschaft in which the hearing has from time to time been adjourned pending a proposed settlement.

PROCEEDINGS AGAINST DELINQUENT INSURANCE CORPORATIONS.

By chapter 300 of the Laws of 1909 the Legislature provided that whenever any insurance corporation became insolvent or it was found, after an examination, to be in such condition that its further transaction of business would be hazardous to its policyholders, or to its creditors, or to the public, or whenever it had done or failed to do certain acts specified, the Superintendent of Insurance might, the Attorney-General representing him, apply to the Supreme Court or to any judge in the judicial district, in which the principal office of the corporation was located, for an order directing the insurance corporation to show cause why the Superintendent of Insurance should not take possession of its property and conduct its business. It was provided upon the re-

turn óf the order to show cause and after a full hearing that the
court should either deny the application, or direct the Superintendent of Insurance to take possession of the property and conduct the business of the corporation until, after a like hearing, it
was made to appear to the court that the ground for such an order
had been removed, and that the corporation could properly resume
the possession of its property and the conduct of its business.

It was also provided that on a like application and hearing the
court might order the liquidation of the business of such insurance
corporation to be conducted under the direction of the Superintendent of Insurance.

Under this law proceedings were commenced on behalf of the
Superintendent of Insurance against the following insurance companies in New York and Kings Counties; during the year 1909:

Garfield Assurance Fire Lloyds.

New York and New England Underwriters at Lloyds.

Western New York Relief Association.

National Fraternal Association.

Traders and Travelers Accident Company.

Horse Insurance Company of New York.

Grand Temple of Templars of Liberty of America.

Union Life Insurance Company.

United States Horse Insurance Company.

National Provident Union.

And during the year 1910 such proceedings were commenced
against the following insurance companies:

Hudson Horse Insurance Company.

Chapter General of America, Knights of St. John of Malta.

Cosmo Benevolent Aid Society.

International Fire Office of New York.

New York Insurance Association.

United States Grand Lodge of the Independent Order Sons of
Benjamin.

These proceedings were novel and there were no precedents for
them subsequent to 1909. Many questions as to procedure and as
to the validity of the law arose during the conduct of the cases
which have been undertaken with great care.

The following proceedings have been pending during the year:

Garfield Assurance Fire Lloyds: An appeal was taken to the Court of Appeals from the order of the Appellate Division sustaining the order of Special Term directing the Superintendent of Insurance to take possession of the property of the company. This appeal was withdrawn on August 1, 1910.

New York and New England Underwriters at Lloyds: An appeal from the order directing the Superintendent of Insurance to take possession of the property of the company was dismissed by the Appellate Division on June 7, 1910.

United States Horse Insurance Company: Motion for an order directing the Superintendent of Insurance to liquidate the company was granted October 31, 1910.

Hudson Horse Insurance Company: Proceedings were commenced on May 2, 1910, and the motion for an order directing the Superintendent of Insurance to liquidate the company was granted on August 10, 1910.

Chapter General of America, Knights of St. John and Malta: Proceedings were commenced on October 31, 1910. The motion for an order directing the Superintendent of Insurance to liquidate the society being consented to by its attorneys was granted on the same day.

Cosmo Benevolent Aid Society: Proceedings were commenced on November 26, 1910, and the motion for an order directing the Superintendent of Insurance to take possession of the property of the company was granted on November 30, 1910.

International Fire Office of New York: Proceedings were commenced on November 18, 1910, and the motion for an order directing the Superintendent of Insurance to take possession of the property was granted on November 30, 1910.

New York Insurance Association: Proceedings were commenced on November 18, 1910, and are still pending.

United States Grand Lodge of the Independent Order Sons of Benjamin: Proceedings were commenced on September 21st and are still pending.

PROCEEDINGS UNDER THE LAND TITLE REGISTRATION ACT.

During the year 1909 the following proceedings were commenced under the Land Title Registration Act which was passed in 1908, and which enacted for this State substantially what is popularly known as the Torrens System for registering land titles:

Marvin Realty Company v. Barre. (Application No. 3.)

Fourth Universalist Society v. Heaton.

Duffy v. Shirden.

Southard v. Fowler.

Jordan v. Dean.

Voorheis v. Voorheis.

The following proceedings were commenced during the year 1910:

Marvin Realty Co. v. Wm. Barre et al. (Application No. 5.)

Milton Gray Andres v. Wyckoff.

Jane Armstrong et al. v. Harlem Savings Bank et al.

Benjamin Croner v. John Sniffen et al.

Alberta Jane Goodlove v. Cushing et al.

Minnie Hofer v. Josiah Riley et al.

Gertrude D. Hawes v. U. S. Trust Co. et al.

Abraham Lachmann et al. v. The People etc. et al.

Helen Littauer v. The People etc. et al.

David B. Wiggins v. Matthew Yager et al.

Irving T. Smith v. Marion S. I. Martin.

During the year 1909 it was found from practice that the Land Title Registration Act required amendment. Deputy Prentice and Deputy Stephens prepared and had introduced in the Legislature of 1910 amendments correcting certain features of the law which had proven unsatisfactory. Bills embodying their suggestions introduced in the Assembly were referred to the Committee on General Laws. Mr. Prentice and Mr. Stephens appeared before the committee, argued in support of the amendments and filed briefs. The bill passed the Assembly and in the Senate was referred to the Committee on Judiciary before which Mr. Stephens appeared in support of the bill. The bill passed the Senate and Mr. Stephens appeared in its support before the Governor. The bill was signed by the Governor and became a law, constituting chapter 627 of the Laws of 1910.

The amendment of most importance to the State is that requiring that the complaint shall state at the beginning thereof what claim, if any, the State of New York makes to the property in question or what interest, if any, it has therein other than the general governmental interest or such as exists as to all land in private ownership.

Another important amendment makes the allegations and statements of the examiner's certificate of title and of his abstract and searches and the survey, prima facie and presumptive evidence of the facts so alleged and stated.

Under the proceedings for registration commenced during the year 1909, four titles have been registered. Under the proceedings commenced during the year 1910, seven titles have been registered.

PROCEEDINGS FOR THE REVOCATION OF DETECTIVES' LICENSES.

Chapter 515 of the Laws of 1910 provided for the licensing of private detectives by the Comptroller after an investigation as to the character, competency and integrity of the applicant for a license. It also provided that the license should be revocable at all times by the Comptroller for cause shown.

Under the provisions of this chapter the Comptroller commenced proceedings for the revocation of the licenses of the following persons:

Harry Gottesfeld.
Leo. P. Siegel.
David Klarer.
John F. McCullough.
Ralph C. Olivett.
John B. Kern.
Charles E. Hall.
Joseph S. Wiley.
William A. Moore.
Sidney Strauss.
Maurice S. Schuss.
Maurice Ashner.
John Poole.
Leo. J. Ostro.
William L. Soyer.
Isaac Silverman.

This office has attended to the preparation of the papers and advised the Comptroller in respect to these proceedings.

PROCEEDINGS TO ENFORCE THE BANKING LAW.

To Test the Constitutionality of Chapter 348, Laws 1910.

Engel v. O'Malley.

Lee v. O'Malley.

Kohan v. O'Malley.

Cases Against Bankers.

People v. Hyman Korn.

People v. Andrea Ribando.

People v. Cleto Sciandone.

People v. Branower & Son.

People v. G. Russo & Co.

People v. Paolo Pagan.

People v. W. A. D'Ascoli.

People v. Luigi De Maio.

People v. Simonelli Bros.

People v. Auerbach & Goldberg.

People v. R. V. Rovnianek & Co.

People v. DeChicchio & Luciana Bank.

People v. Vasic Stephanof.

People v. A. J. Newbauer.

People v. A. Growchowski & Co.

People v. Max Kobre.

People v. John Kovacs.

PROCEEDINGS IN THE SURROGATE'S COURTS.

Proceedings in the Surrogate's Courts in New York, Kings and Queens counties in regard to the following estates have been conducted by the New York city office:

Cases Pending From 1909.

Estate of Amelia Bedford.

Estate of Maria B. Blanco.

Estate of Dennis and Mary Buckley.

Estate of John Bolden.

Estate of Thomas Calvert.

Estate of Lillian H. Caldwell.

Estate of Louise H. Leclere.

Estate of Theresa Murphy.
Estate of Minnie C. Nugent.
Estate of Susan Neimeyer.
Estate of Mary A. Peterson.
Estate of Thomas F. Ross.
Estate of Mary A. Sewell.
Estate of Bridget Torphy.
Estate of John Wilson.

Cases in 1910.

Estate of Charles Bible.
Estate of Eliza Delmar.
Estate of Elizabeth Doherty.
Estate of Mary Halley.
Estate of Edith Hynes.
Estate of Bridget Hoolihan.
Estate of Hannah Broy.
Estate of Bridget O'Donaghue.
Estate of Felicite Wilmshurst.
Estate of Mary S. Robinson.
Estate of Julia Reilly.
Estate of Gesche Schnackenberg.
Estate of Elizabeth Smith.
Estate of Nathaniel H. Smith.
Estate of Caroline H. Schumacher.
Estate of Christopher Taacke.
Estate of John Wilson.
Estate of John D. Brez.
Estate of John Doyle.

Agricultural Cases.

The following agricultural cases have been conducted by this office:

Pending From 1909.

People v. Thomas Anderson.
People v. Thomas Bingham.
People v. Dennis & Herring.
People v. W. H. Mowerson.

1910 *Cases.*

People v. J. Michaelis.
People v. John Doe. (Oleomargarine, 10450.)
People v. John Doe. (Oleomargarine, 6038.)
People v. Richard Doe. (Oleomargarine, 7654.)
People v. Hart & Dowling.
People v. John Doe. (Oleomargarine, 6177.)
People v. Charles Hansen.
People v. Isaac Popkin.

All of the above cases have been disposed of with the exception of the cases against Thomas Bingham.

Opinions to State Superintendent of Elections.

This office has from time to time advised and rendered opinions to the State Superintendent of Elections in respect to questions arising within the metropolitan elections district and submitted by the superintendent, copies of which opinions are attached hereto.

MISCELLANEOUS CASES.

In addition to the election cases, the proceedings against delinquent insurance corporations, proceedings under the Land Title Registration Act, proceedings for the revocation of detectives' licenses, proceedings under the amendments to the Banking Law, the proceedings in the Surrogate's Courts and the agricultural cases, this office has conducted the following cases:

Escheat Cases and Proceedings to Withdraw Deposits. Pending

From 1909.

DeBoer v. Smith.
Hayes v. Harrison.
Horn v. Callahan.
Bruner v. Torrey.
Bassand v. Billot et al.
Van Slingerlandt v. Buckingham and others.

1910 *Cases.*

Daly v. Stewart.
Marvin v. Mason.

Hill v. Fiske.

Wakelee v. Davis.

Estate of Mary Ann Dunn.

Application of Harry Mintz for release of land escheated.

Application of Adolph Jacobs for payment of the residue of the personal estate of Felicite Wilmshurst.

John Haffen et al. v. George Muller.

Estate of Theresa Murphy.

Estate of Susan Neimeyer.

Application of John Engelke for payment of certain moneys deposited with city chamberlain.

Esselborn v. Esselborn.

Bloom v. McKnight.

Flandrau v. Flandrau.

Habeas Corpus Proceedings.

Re Application of Benjamin Schwartz and Betty Schwartz for the restoration of their child Rose; in custody of the State Training School for Girls.

People ex rel. Charlotte Hitchcock v. Superintendent of Matteawan State Hospital.

Proceedings for Collection of Corporation Tax.

Albert Palmer, bankrupt.

New York Car & Truck Company.

Central Trust Company v. Third Avenue Railroad Company.

Vanderbilt Realty Company.

Physioc Press.

Mutual Reserve Life Insurance Company.

Dissolution and Receivership Proceedings.

Westchester Electric R. R. Company.

Tarrytown, White Plains & Mamaroneck Ry. Co.

Yonkers Railroad Company.

International Graphophone Company.

New York Building Loan–Banking Company.

Film Import & Trading Company.

12

Brooklyn Ferry Company.

Knickerbocker Life Insurance Company.

National Gramophone Company.

Rembrandt Realty Company.

Rump v. Van Rensselaer Realty Company.

Yerkes Manufacturing Company.

Baldinger & Kupferman Mfg. Company v. Graham Holding
 Company.

Matter of B. D. Luce & Company.

Matter of Standard Cordage Company.

New Machine and Folding Beds Company.

Johnson v. Ridgeway Belt Conveyor Company.

Jeffrey v. Dininny.

Empire Life Insurance Company.

People v. Luna Park Company.

Marseille Hotel Company.

Strauss v. Casey Machine Company.

Farmer's Loan and Trust Company v. Mason.

New Weston Hotel Company.

New German Theatre Company.

Yale v. New York Investment and Improvement Company.

Cosmopolitan Fire Insurance Company.

Ringler Brewing Company.

J. E. Munch Company.

Wiley-Harker Lumber Company.

Wight-Easton-Townsend Company.

Von Hagen v. Consolidated Canadian Mines Co., Ltd.

Murray-Heyliger Catering Company.

Crystal Water Company.

Von Hagen v. Canadian Consolidated Mines.

Miscellaneous Cases. Pending From 1909.

People v. American Ice Company.

Application of the Co-Operative Law Company.

Matter of Peter F. Mulvey.

Pennsylvania Railroad, etc. v. McGrane and others.

People v. Welz.   ⎫

People v. Glaser.   ⎬ Re Kissena Park.

People v. Paris & MacDougall. ⎭

Postal Life Insurance Co. v. Hotchkiss.

Ries v. New York Waist Company.

1910 *Cases.*

Application of Howard R. Bayne for an order directing Secretary of State to file certificate of nomination.

Strauss v. Casey Machine & Supply Company.

Application of the city of New York for the transfer of certain moneys known as special fund, Surrogate's Court.

Application of Maxwell Stevenson and others for payment of certain moneys out of the general fund of the Supreme Court.

Application of Patrick E. Callahan, refiling of certificate of nomination.

Application of William F. Haggerty, refiling of certificate of nomination.

Application of East River Gas Company to acquire certain real property.

Application of United States Fidelity and Guaranty Company of Baltimore, Md., for cancellation of a certain bond.

People ex rel. Glynn v. Mercantile Safe Deposit Company.

Loch v. O'Malley.

New York City Water Front Company v. Morrell. (Lands under water.)

Slavin v. Polk and others composing Municipal Civil Service Commission.

Steiner v. Steiner.

Shirmeister v. Sloper.

Shrady v. Appley.

Investigation Manhattan State Hospital.

Zena Straight Company.

Davis v. Julius Mayer, etc.

People v. Loan Commissioners.

Re New Method Laundry Company.

People v. John Neiderstein.

Estate of John Neiderstein.

People v. Midland Terminal Railroad Company.

The deputies of this office from time to time appeared on applications for the dissolution of corporations in cases in which no

notice of the applications or copies of the papers have been served
upon the Attorney-General in accordance with section 312 of the
General Corporation Law. (Formerly section 8, of chapter 378,
Laws of 1883.)

Respectfully,

FREDERICK C. TANNER,

Deputy Attorney-General.

In charge of the New York City Bureau.

EZRA P. PRENTICE.

FOREST, FISH AND GAME BUREAU.

ALBANY, December 31, 1910.

Hon. EDWARD R. O'MALLEY, Attorney-General, Albany, N. Y.:

MY DEAR SIR.— I respectfully submit the following report of
the Forest, Fish and Game Bureau from October 10, 1910, to date.

On October 10, 1910, pursuant to arrangement between the
Attorney-General and the Forest, Fish and Game Commission, the
legal work of the Commission was taken over by the Attorney-
General and I was designated by him as deputy in charge of this
bureau and was also designated by the Forest, Fish and Game
Commission as its chief counsel therein.

A detailed report of the nature, amount and extent of the
litigated business of which there was a record in this bureau, at
the time of the above change, has been heretofore rendered to the
Attorney-General, a brief summary of which is as follows:

Title actions	63
Trespass actions	38
Actions for penalty and damages for fire	8
Actions for violations of Fish and Game Law	38
Actions for violation of top-lopping law	16

Of the foregoing actions, two were on appeal in the Court of
Appeals, seven in the Appellate Divisions, seven actions were
awaiting submission or decision after submission and there were
three actions of ejectment awaiting retrial.

The Attorney-General was immediately substituted as attorney of record in all of the actions thus pending and orders to that end were obtained, entered and served. The papers in thirty-seven actions then pending have beèn transmitted to counsel employed by the Forest, Fish and Game Commission in six of the counties in the Adirondack and Catskill regions for inquest or for the trial thereof at the earliest possible term of the courts therein.

The following disposition has been made of, and the following proceedings have been had in, the actions pending in this bureau on October 10, 1910:

SUPREME COURT — ULSTER COUNTY.

THE PEOPLE

vs.

HUDSON RIVER PULP MFG. CO.

Discontinued.
December 12, 1910.
Without costs.

SUPREME COURT — HAMILTON COUNTY.

THE PEOPLE

vs.

BROWNELL.

Settled.
December 8, 1910.
Defendant paid $15 balance.

SUPREME COURT — ESSEX COUNTY.

THE PEOPLE

vs.

SKIFF.

Settled.
December 12, 1910.
Defendant paid $75.

SUPREME COURT — ESSEX COUNTY.

THE PEOPLE *vs.* OSTRANDER.	Motion to amend answer. Granted December 5, 1910. Appealed to Appellate Division.

SUPREME COURT — ESSEX COUNTY.

THE PEOPLE *vs.* SANTA CLARA LUMBER CO.	Same as last above. $25 costs paid.

SUPREME COURT — ESSEX COUNTY.

THE PEOPLE *vs.* SANTA CLARA LUMBER CO.	Same as last above. $25 costs paid.

SUPREME COURT — HAMILTON COUNTY.

OLMSTEAD *vs.* ROBERTS, as Comptroller.	Finally submitted. December —, 1910. Decision reserved.

SUPREME COURT — SARATOGA COUNTY.

THE PEOPLE

vs.

THOMPSON and Others.

Settled as to Thompson.
November 29, 1910.
Defendant paid $100.

SUPREME COURT — ESSEX COUNTY.

THE PEOPLE

vs.

MOORE.

Settled.
November 21, 1910.
Defendant paid $25.

SUPREME COURT — GREENE COUNTY.

THE PEOPLE

vs.

DEDRICK.

Settled.
December 10, 1910.
Defendant paid $25.

SUPREME COURT — ESSEX COUNTY.

THE PEOPLE

vs.

ALANSON MOORE and Another.

Settled as to Moore.
October 15, 1910.
Defendant paid $25.

SUPREME COURT — FRANKLIN COUNTY.

THE PEOPLE

vs.

N. Y. C. & H. R. R.

Demurrer argued.
Sustained November 12, 1910.
Appealed to Appellate Division.

SUPREME COURT — HAMILTON COUNTY.

THE PEOPLE

vs.

N. Y. C. & H. R. R.

Motion for particulars.
Argued December 3, 1910.
Decision reserved.

SUPREME COURT — ALBANY COUNTY.

THE PEOPLE

vs.

ESPENLAUB.

Judgment for plaintiff.
November 30, 1910.
$300 and costs.

SUPREME COURT — RENSSELAER COUNTY.

THE PEOPLE

vs.

SHRUMP and TEAL.

Settled.
December 29, 1910.
Defendants paid $25.

SUPREME COURT — NEW YORK COUNTY.

THE PEOPLE

vs.

ROTHSCHILD.

Tried.
December 23, 1910.
Verdict for defendant.

SUPREME COURT — NEW YORK COUNTY.

THE PEOPLE

vs.

SEVENTH AVE. M. & P. CO.

Verdict for plaintiff.
December 23, 1910.
$1,560.

SUPREME COURT — NEW YORK COUNTY.

THE PEOPLE

vs.

ROCHFORD.

Verdict for plaintiff.
November 25, 1910.
$200.

SUPREME COURT — NEW YORK COUNTY.

THE PEOPLE

vs.

FLAT IRON RESTAURANT CO.

Verdict for plaintiff.
November 15, 1910.
$85.

SUPREME COURT — NEW YORK COUNTY.

THE PEOPLE

vs.

HEINEMANN and Another.

Demurrer for misjoinder.
Sustained November 17, 1910.
New actions ordered.

SUPREME COURT — NEW YORK COUNTY.

THE PEOPLE

vs.

TUCKER.

Tried.
December 15, 1910.
Verdict for defendant.

SUPREME COURT — NEW YORK COUNTY.

THE PEOPLE

vs.

GILLOTTA.

Verdict for plaintiff.
December 23, 1910.
$80.

SUPREME COURT — NEW YORK COUNTY.

THE PEOPLE

vs.

FISCHER.

Settled.
November 29, 1910.
Defendant paid $100.

SUPREME COURT — NEW YORK COUNTY.

THE PEOPLE	Defendant's default opened.
vs.	December 30, 1910.
ANDUJAR.	$30 costs paid.

In addition to matters in suit, above referred to, there were on file in this bureau on October 10, 1910, reports that had been filed for investigation and action as follows:

For trespass...................................... 84
For fire violations 21
For top-lopping violations 19

Since that date, there have been reported to this bureau for investigation and prosecution the following:

For trespass...................................... 46
For fire violations 11
For top-lopping violations 7

Pursuant to a new plan adopted by the Forest, Fish and Game Commission upon the recommendation of this bureau with regard to the report and prosecution of violations of the fish and game laws, such matters are now being transmitted to this bureau through the chief game protector, after such inquiry and with such report as he deems necessary, with orders from the Commission that actions should be begun thereon by this bureau in case settlement for the violations is not otherwise effected; and there have been filed in this bureau since such plan went into effect thirty-nine reports for violations of Fish and Game Law.

Some delay was occasioned in the work of handling the large number of reports of trespass and of violations of the top-lopping, fire and fish and game laws that had already been and were being filed in this bureau for investigation and prosecution, until a formal opinion could be secured from the Attorney-General whether, under the law, settlement by way of compromise could be made of the claims for penalties so reported (until after action had been actually begun thereon) for any less amount than the penalty prescribed by law.

An opinion was rendered to the Forest, Fish and Game Commission by the Attorney-General, under date of November 16, 1910, to the effect that the Commission was authorized in continuing to settle claims for penalties for less than the total amount of such penalties before an action was instituted; and thereupon a basis of the minimum terms upon which settlement might be made was fixed by the Commission and was communicated to this bureau — since which time diligent effort has been devoted to the adjustment of such claims by affording defendants opportunity to make settlement prior to the commencement of action.

There have been collected by or through this bureau, since October 10, 1910, and paid over to the Forest, Fish and Game Commission, the following sums for violations reported and in settlement of actions and for costs not otherwise included in settlements:

TRESPASS.

L. S. Hunt, Oct. 28, 1910....................	$50 00
George Gilbert, Nov. 21, 1910................	10 00
David Willsey, Nov. 29, 1910................	10 00
David Brownell, Dec. 8, 1910................	15 00
Smyrna Wood, Dec. 17, 1910.................	20 50
John Skiff, Dec. 12, 1910...................	75 00
Thomas K. Brown, Dec. 19, 1910.............	60 00
John R. Carnell, Dec. 19, 1910..............	11 70
Charles Rogers, Dec. 19, 1910...............	20 00
Orren Burdett, Dec. 20, 1910................	14 00
Charles Selkirk, Dec. 21, 1910..............	10 00
Orson Brown, Dec. 22, 1910.................	18 00
Lafayette Knowlton, Dec. 29, 1910...........	10 00
C. E. Cooper, Dec. 28, 1910.................	10 00
H. R. Beguelin, Dec. 28, 1910...............	30 00
Edwin Young, Jr., Dec. 28, 1910.............	43 38
Giles & Hess, Dec. 27, 1910.................	50 00
Earl W. Covey, Dec. 29, 1910................	112 00
Dan Ainsworth, Jr., Dec. 28, 1910...........	32 00

Eldred W. Harpp, Dec. 28, 1910.............. $25 00
John Dezalia, Dec. 28, 1910................. 84 00
Robert D. Eaton, Dec. 28, 1910.............. 20 00

Fire.

Charles Paine, Nov. 9, 1910................. $25 00
Garrett Thew, Oct. 27, 1910................. 10 00
Luzerne R. Baker, Nov. 22, 1910............. 25 00 .

Top-Lopping.

Alanson Moore, Oct. 15, 1910................ $25 00
Beardsley Lumber Co., Oct. 19, 1910.......... 25 00
Lee Lyman, Oct. 19, 1910................... 20 00
George Russell, Nov. 10, 1910............... 25 00
Griffin Lumber Co., Nov. 11, 1910........... 25 00
John Moore, Nov. 21, 1910.................. 25 00
Thompson and Others, Nov. 29, 1910.......... 100 00
Peter P. Dohl, Dec. 6, 1910................. 75 00
Finch, Pruyn & Co., Dec. 10, 1910........... 150 00
William Sammons, Dec. 10, 1910.............. 50 00
Walter Dedrick, Dec. 10, 1910............... 25 00

Fish and Game.

James W. Fleming, Nov. 7, 1910............. $25 00
Thomas Burke, Nov. 14, 1910................ 50 00
Geo. Reissert and Another, Nov. 22, 1910........ 25 00
Charles Kick, Nov. 22, 1910................ 50 00
Knapp & Van Nostrand, Nov. 28, 1910......... 250 00
George Fischer, Nov. 29, 1910............... 100 00
Otto Boseck, Nov. 30, 1910................. 165 85
George Vail, Dec. 1, 1910.................. 50 00
Thomas Burke, Dec. 5, 1910................ 25 00
William Bixby, Dec. 6, 1910................ 37 50
Samuel Bixby, Dec. 6, 1910................. 37 50
Jay Taylor, Dec. 6, 1910................... 25 00
Otto Boseck, Dec. 6, 1910.................. 8 30
Gifford and Another, Dec. 10, 1910........... 250 00

Sed. Smith, Dec. 22, 1910...................	$25 00
S. Zodies, Dec. 22, 1910....................	10 00
Joseph Wright, Dec. 22, 1910...............	10 00
Andrew Savaree, Dec. 22, 1910..............	25 00
Robt. M. Whitegiver, Dec. 27, 1910...........	100 75
Jesse Goodrich, Dec. 27, 1910...............	100 00
Shrump and Teal, Dec. 28, 1910.............	25 00
E. D. Bushnell, Dec. 30, 1910...............	10 00
Charles Kick, Dec. 30, 1910.................	25 00

COSTS.

Santa Clara Lumber Co., Dec. 10, 1910.........	$25 00
Santa Clara Lumber Co., Dec. 10, 1910.........	25 00
Antonio Andujar, Dec. 30, 1910..............	30 00

A summary of the foregoing collections, since October 10, 1910, is as follows:

For trespass............................	$730 58
For failure to lop tops.....................	545 00
For fires to clear land.....................	60 00
For fish and game violations.................	1,429 90
For miscellaneous costs	80 00
Total..............................	$2,844 48

There have been instituted, since October 10, 1910, upon the order of the Forest, Fish and Game Commission, eleven new actions as follows:

For trespass..............................	2
For failure to lop tops..........................	1
For refund and cancellation of deeds................	2
For fish and game violations.....................	1
For fire violations	5

Advice, counsel and opinions have been given to the Forest, Fish and Game Commission and to its officers and employees as occasion has required; and, in the routine work of the bureau, something over 800 letters have been written and sent out.

I desire to make acknowledgment of the valuable services of the counsel and of the office force assigned to this bureau by the Forest, Fish and Game Commission and also of the information and assistance that has been at all times afforded by and through the Commissioner and his officers.

All of which is respectfully submitted.

WILLIAM S. MacDONALD,

Deputy Attorney-General.

REPORT OF INVESTIGATION OF SCHENECTADY GRAFT CASES.

To the Hon. Edward R. O'Malley, *Attorney-General, Albany, N. Y.:*

Sir.— In accordance with your request I herewith submit the following report of my transactions in connection with the investigation of graft charges and prosecutions therefor in Schenectady County:

The investigation received its initiative from the Hon. Edward T. Perine, Deputy Comptroller of the State, under section 35 of the General Municipal Law, and was continued down until the 16th of May, 1910, at which time a special and extraordinary trial term of the Supreme Court with a grand jury was convened under the direction of the Governor, and of which I had charge under appointment from you as Deputy Attorney-General.

The grand jury reported the following indictments, which were disposed of as follows:

Section 1868 *Penal Law.*— Prohibiting a public officer authorized to make a contract in his official capacity, from becoming interested individually in such contract, and making violation thereof a misdemeanor.

The persons indicted were all supervisors of said county and individually interested in contracts with the county, as follows:

Thomas W. Winne. For the sale of coal to the county, to be used in the county alms house, by the firm of Winne & McKain, of which he was a member, under the name of his partner James B. McKain.

ISAAC L. WHITMYER. For the sale of groceries to the county, by the firm of Whitmyer & Rankin, of which he was a member, under the name of C. Rankin, Jr., his co-partner.

JOHN W. HUDSON. For the sale of hardware to the county under his own name.

JAMES G. HILDERBRANDT. For the sale of coal to the county under the name of P. Eggerley, his clerk.

AARON P. HUFFMIRE. For the employment of team on High Bridge and Crane street roads, under the name of H. Millard, a fictitious person.

Two indictments for different periods.

ANSON H. CADY. For the employment of his team on the Crane street road, under the names of his drivers, J. Adams and . M. Waggoner.

Two indictments for different periods.

WILLIAM W. DAVIS. For the sale of lumber to the county, by the Madden Lumber Company, of which he was manager and stockholder.

Demurrers were interposed to each of these indictments upon the ground that the statute became inoperative as to each of these defendants, for that a county purchasing agent existed in the county of Schenectady upon whom rested the duty and who was clothed with the exclusive authority of purchasing the articles enumerated for the county and who alone had the authority to make such purchases and audit the bills therefor.

The indictment against Winne having been moved, the court directed that a jury be impanelled and directed the jury to find a verdict of not guilty.

The remaining indictments, standing upon the same footing, upon the motion of the prosecution were each dismissed.

Section 1861 *Penal Law.*— Misdemeanor.

JOHN H. PETERS. For falsely certifying as notary public that William Clark appeared before him and verified a bill subsequently audited by the board of supervisors.

Pleaded guilty. Sentence suspended.

IRVING S. VEDDER. For falsely certifying as a notary public that Anderson Smith appeared before him and verified a bill of the Acme Building Company, subsequently audited by the board of supervisors.

This latter indictment was based upon the evidence of Smith before the grand jury that he had not appeared and verified the bill. Later, upon the trial of George F. Sauter, who was the real party in interest in the Acme Building Company, Smith testified that he did appear and verify the bill, the only evidence as to the violation of the statute by Vedder being the evidence of Smith, the indictment was upon my motion dismissed.

Section 1872 *Penal Law.*— Presenting false bill for audit. Felony.

MYRON JACOBSON. A supervisor of said county, for presenting to the board of supervisors for audit, claims in the name of Frank Mooney, which were false and fraudulent and which were subsequently audited by said board.

Two indictments for separate bills so presented. On the twenty-third of June Jacobson pleaded guilty to one of these indictments and upon such plea was fined $500, which fine was paid.

All other indictments against him were dismissed.

AARON P. HUFFMIRE, a supervisor of said county, for presenting to said board of supervisors for audit, a claim in the name of William Clark, which he knew was false and fraudulent.

Section 1863 *Penal Law.*— Taking part in the auditing of false bills. Felony.

AARON P. HUFFMIRE, a supervisor of said county, for taking part as such in the audit of bill presented in the name of John J. Huffmire, known by him to be false and fraudulent.

MYRON JACOBSON, a supervisor of said county, for taking part as such in the auditing of a bill presented under the name of Frank Mooney, known by him to be false and fraudulent.

Two indictments for separate bills.

Section 1864 *Penal Law.*— Obtaining proceeds of fraudulent audit or payment. Felony.

GEORGE A. PEPPER. For obtaining payment from the county of a false claim, represented by him to be for work of team of one A. Gulick, upon the High Bridge and Crane Street roads.

Two indictments for different offenses.

CHARLES N. VAN DENBERGE. For aiding and conniving in the audit of false claim of William J. Palmer by wrongfully reporting time during which workmen were employed on building.

Section 580 *Penal Law.*— Conspiracy. Misdemeanor.

MYRON JACOBSON and WILLIAM II. DUNLEAVY. For conspiracy in securing the audit of a false claim presented in the name of Frank Mooney.

Indictment dismissed.

Section 21 of the County Law.— Prohibiting the auditing of a bill not itemized and verified.   Made a misdemeanor by section 29 of the Penal Law.

EDWARD H. ROBINSON, MYRON JACOBSON, ANSON H. CADY and WILLIAM W. DAVIS, Supervisors of said county, for participating in the audit of a bill, approved by said Robinson, Jacobson and Cady as members of the committee on miscellaneous audits of said board, which bill was presented in the name of William H. Winne, and allowed by said board and subsequently paid, and which contained false items of merchandise purchased by said Winne from a corporation known as the Davis Lumber Company, of which said Davis was president, and said Davis being chairman of said board of supervisors.

Dismissed by court on motion of defendant.

EDWARD II. ROBINSON, MYRON JACOBSON and ANSON H. CADY. For participating in the auditing of a bill approved by them as members of the committee on miscellaneous audits, which bill was presented in the name of Anson II. Cady for committee expenses, and which was not itemized.

Indictment dismissed.

(Not to be distinguished from last above.)

EDWARD II. ROBINSON, MYRON JACOBSON and ANSON II. CADY. For participating in the auditing of a bill approved by them as members of the committee on miscellaneous audits, which bill was presented in the name of C. W. Myers, and which was not itemized.

Indictment dismissed.

(Same as last above.)

ANSON H. CADY, a supervisor of said county, for participating in an audit of a bill made in the name of Lester Lasher & Company, of which said Cady was a member, and which bill he knew had not been verified.

On the twenty-second of June Cady pleaded guilty to this indictment and was fined $100, which was paid.

Section 887 *Penal Law.*— Forgery in the second degree. Felony.

CHARLES N. VAN DENBERGE. Forging the name of William M. Clark to a verification of an alleged claim against the county of Schenectady, said claim and verification being an instrument or writing purporting to be the act of said Clark, by which a pecuniary demand was created against said county.

Said Van Denberge was tried upon said indictment at said term of court, the trial beginning on the sixteenth of June and being concluded on the seventeenth of June; said Van Denberge being convicted.

Grand larceny, first degree.

MERRITT HAMMOND. Sheriff. Money obtained from the county upon false charges included in his bill as sheriff for board furnished the prisoners in the county jail of said county during the months of November and December, 1905.

The witness upon whose evidence conviction was expected to be had having died, and Hammond having restored money taken from the county to the extent of $10,000, the indictment was dismissed.

Grand larceny, second degree.

PHILIP MULDERICK. For money obtained from the county for false and fraudulent bill for plumbing works done upon the county jail.

On the twenty-second of June at said term of court, defendant pleaded guilty and sentence was suspended.

WILLIAM J. PALMER. For obtaining money from the county of Schenectady upon false and fraudulent bill for painting done upon the county courthouse in said county.

Pleaded guilty.

AARON P. HUFFMIRE. Supervisor. For obtaining money from said county by a false bill presented in the name of William H. Huffmire.

The accused was tried under said indictment at said term of court, the trial lasting two days, and was convicted. Upon such conviction he was fined $1,000, which was paid.

All other indictments against him were dismissed.

GEORGE F. SAUTER. For obtaining money from the county by false and fraudulent bills for mason work and repairs done upon the court house and jail in said county, under and in the name of the Acme Building Company.

Defendant tried, trial occupying two days; convicted. Fined $1,000, which was paid.

Three other indictments for like offenses, to which demurrers were interposed and sustained.

GEORGE F. SAUTER. For fraudulently presenting false bill for audit.

July 15th defendant pleaded guilty to this indictment and on September 23rd was fined $1,000, which was paid.

All other indictments against him were dismissed.

GEORGE A. PEPPER. For obtaining money from the county by false and fraudulent bill presented for work reported to have been done on the Crane street road by the team of one A. Gulick.

Convicted of petit larceny and fined $500.

GEORGE A. PEPPER. For obtaining from the county money by the aid of false and fraudulent bill presented for work reported to have been done on the High Bridge road in said county by the team of one A. Gulick.

On June 23rd defendant pleaded guilty to petit larceny. On September 23rd he was fined $500, which was paid.

All other indictments against him were dismissed.

Perjury.

FRED ROLFE. For testifying falsely on the examination before the Comptroller.

Indictment dismissed.

The work at Schenectady seems to have been very beneficial in its results. However, to thoroughly protect the public and especially the various municipal officers of the State, section 1868 should be by amendment so extended as to prohibit all transactions between such officers and their several municipalities which relate to matters which are subject to review, ratification or approval by them in their official capacity.

VIRGIL K. KELLOGG,

Deputy Attorney-General.

Dated, December 23, 1910.

REPORT OF INVESTIGATION OF QUEENS COUNTY GRAFT CASES.

December 27, 1910.

Hon. Edward R. O'Malley, *Attorney-General of the State of New York, Albany, New York:*

Dear Sir.— Having been duly deputized by you, in accordance with the requirement of His Excellency, Charles E. Hughes, Governor of the State of New York, dated September 22, 1910, pursuant to the provisions of section 62 of the Executive Law, I forthwith, pursuant to your instructions, beg to make a report of the results of my investigation conducted in Queens County.

On the morning of October 4, 1910, I attended the October Term of the Supreme Court of Queens County, held in the County Court House, Long Island City, and was present when Mr. Justice Kapper charged the grand jury in relation to their duties with respect to investigating the alleged condition of political graft existing in that county. I immediately filed a certified copy of the Governor's requirement, your designation, and my oath of office with the County Clerk, and commenced the examination of witnesses before the grand jury and the general work of investigation.

Organization.

At the outset I found myself much hampered owing to the fact that there seemed to be no funds available for my use in employing legal assistants, stenographers or detectives. The county authorities took the position that where the State intervened the State should bear the burden of necessary expenditures. I was fortunate enough, however, through the co-operation of the Comptroller of the city of New York, shortly to overcome this difficulty, and through the courtesy of the County Judge and of the District Attorney of Queens, to secure two suites of offices in the County

Court House at Long Island City. I was equally fortunate in obtaining the services, as my assistants, of several lawyers with whom I had previously been associated in the District Attorney's office of New York County; and my staff during the past ten weeks has at times numbered four lawyers, six stenographers and two confidential investigators. The average number of persons directly engaged upon the work has been ten. In this connection I might say that every phase of the work has been done by my own men. The thirty-five indictments found by the local District Attorney, and filed by preceding grand juries, were many of them redrafted and the evidence resubmitted; and everything connected with the investigation, from the subpoenaing of witnesses to the drafting of the bail bonds, has been performed independently of the county authorities.

INDICTMENTS PREVIOUSLY FOUND.

The following is a list of the various defendants indicted by the May (1910) Grand Jury, which indictments were transmitted to me by the District Attorney:

Name of Defendant.	Crime.	Total Number of Indictments.	Indictment Numbers.		
Burke, Cornelius J.....	Grand larceny, 2nd degree..	1	2849		
Cragen, John M.......	Grand larceny, 2nd degree..		2801	2802	2803
	Forgery, 2nd degree........	4	2790		
Geronimo, Maurice M..	Grand larceny, 2nd degree..	1	2826		
Goldner, Matthew J....	Grand larceny, 2nd degree..	1	2839		
Gresser, Lawrence......	Auditing false claims.......	1	2852 [*Dismissed*]		
Jordan, Cornelius J....	Petit larceny.......	4	2737	2739	2741
[*Convicted*, Dec. 15,			2742		
1910]	Grand larceny, 2nd degree..	10	2738	2740	2743
			2819	2820	2821
			2822	2823	2824
			2825		
Kreuscher, Robert......	Grand larceny, 2nd degree..	2	2850	2851	
Leahy, Patrick E......	Grand larceny, 1st degree...	4	2858	2859	2860
			2861		
	Grand larceny, 2nd degree..	1	2862		
Phillips, John M......	Presenting false claim......	1	2808		
	Grand larceny, 1st degree..	4	2853	2854	2855
			2856		
	Grand larceny, 2nd degree..	1	2857		

Total   35

During the past ten weeks my assistants and I have interviewed
and examined preliminarily some 500 or 600 witnesses, have in-
terrogated of these about 200 before the Grand Jury, and have
drafted 95 indictments, all of which have been duly found and
filed by the Grand Jury. The defendants in these indictments
include a former Superintendent of Highways, a former Superintendent of Sewers, a former Secretary to the Borough President,
the present Chief Engineer in the Bureau of Highways, the
present Chief Clerk in the Highway Department, a former Chief
Clerk in the Sewer Department, the City Architect, a former
under-Sheriff, the president of a prominent political club, and
several minor officials. The indictments also embrace several fore-
men and the so-called "tin-horse and cart" brigade; and would
include many others, officials and otherwise, were it not for the
Statute of Limitations.

Name of Defendant.	Crime.	Total Number of Indictments.	Indictment Numbers.		
Burke, Cornelius J.....	Violation § 774, Penal Code.	2	3249	3250	
Coco, Peter M.........	Violation § 439, Penal Code.	8	3210	3211	3212
			3213	3214	3215
			3216	3217	
Cragen, John M........	Forgery, 2nd degree	4	3185	3186	3187
			3188		
	Forgery, 3rd degree.	4	3189	3190	3191
			3192		
	Grand larceny, 2nd degree..	4	3243	3244	3245
			3246		
Cosgrove, James........	Petit larceny..............	3	3234	3231	3237
Cook, Robert..........	Petit larceny..............	2	3228	3241	
Broome, William.......	Petit larceny..............	2	3233	3234	
Dermody, James........	Petit larceny..............	4	3233	3223	3220
			3238		
Johnson, James H......	Conspiracy	1	3249		
Kreuscher, Robert......	Grand larceny, 2nd degree..	2	3199	3200	
Leahy, Patrick E......	Grand larceny, 1st degree...	4	3180	3181	3182
			3183		
	Grand larceny, 2nd degree..	1	3184		
Loughlin, Jr., Thos. F..	Petit larceny..............	3	3221	3230	3232
Morschauser, Daniel....	Petit larceny..............	4	3225	3226	3236
			3240		
Nelson, John B........	Grand larceny, 2nd degree..	4	3193	3204	3195
			3196		

Name of Defendant.	Crime.	Total Number of Indictments.	Indictment Numbers.		
Nowotny, Anton........Petit larceny...............		2	3227	3235	
Pagluicca, Felix........Petit larceny...............		2	3218	3239	
Phillips, John M.......Forgery, 2nd degree........		1	3201		
Grand larceny, 2nd degree and violation § 1872, Penal Code		1	3242		
Grand larceny, 1st degree...		4	3180 3183	3181	3182
Grand larceny, 2nd degree..		3	3184	3197	3198
Phillips, Joseph F......Grand larceny, 2nd degree..		2	3197	3198	
Ringe, Hermann........Conspiracy		1	3249		
Siegel, George.........Petit larceny...............		2	3247	3248	

Total	95

One of the most important results in the inquiry has been the indictment for perjury of Charles Bermel, the brother of former Borough President Joseph Bermel, who resigned subsequent to the Kissena Park investigation. The perjury in question was committed before the 1908 Grand Jury which was investigating Joseph Bermel's connection with the sale to the City of New York of Kissena Park and the likelihood of his having profited thereby, and related to the origin and identity of a certain sum of $20,000 which came into the possession of Charles Bermel subsequent to the sale in question, and which he now alleges that he in fact received from his brother Joseph.

Although the labor incident to the preliminary examination of these witnesses, their formal interrogation before the Grand Jury, the drafting of this large number of indictments, and the argument of the motions which have formed a part of the dilatory tactics pursued by defendants' counsel in every case, have rendered it practically impossible to dispose of these indictments by trial, there has been one conviction for petit larceny in the case of Cornelius J. Jordan, a clerk in the Department of Water, Gas and Electricity, resulting in the disposal of the fourteen indictments against him found last May by the present District Attorney, which were transmitted to me in conformity with the terms of the Governor's requirement.

This defendant was duly sentenced to six months in the Queens County Jail and to pay a fine of $250, and is now serving his sentence.

In pursuance of my general investigation into conditions existing in the local government of the Borough of Queens, I have made a careful study of the conditions existing in the office of the Borough President, with a view to determining how far he might himself be criminally responsible for such conditions.

As a result, John M. Cragen, a former secretary to President Gresser, is now under twelve indictments and awaiting trial.

I have also carefully investigated the topographical bureau, the bureau of sewers and the bureau of highways, with the result that many indictments have been found arising out of conditions discovered there.

I have also made a partial examination of the bureau of street cleaning and of the bureau of buildings, and the only department of the local government uninvestigated is that known as the department of public buildings and offices. I should recommend that the three departments last mentioned be made the subject of future investigation.

I am convinced that, for the sake of the Borough of Queens and for the community in general, the indictments which have been found by this and preceding grand juries should be vigorously prosecuted, to the end that as many of the persons indicted may be punished as possible. The borough has for the last twenty years been the subject of constant rumor and criticism, and the borough officials owe it to themselves to set these rumors definitely at rest by uniting in a common effort to see that those of their number who are unworthy should be cast out.

Respectfully submitted,

ARTHUR C. TRAIN,

Deputy Attorney-General.

OPINIONS OF THE ATTORNEY-GENERAL.

DECISIONS OF THE ATTORNEY-GENERAL IN APPLI-
CATIONS TO COMMENCE ACTIONS IN THE NAME
OF THE PEOPLE; ALSO SUCH OFFICIAL OPIN-
IONS RENDERED BY THE ATTORNEY-GENERAL
AS ARE DEEMED TO BE OF GENERAL PUBLIC IN-
TEREST, AND OPINIONS RENDERED IN MATTERS
BEFORE THE COMMISSIONERS OF THE LAND
OFFICE.

THE FOLLOWING APPLICATIONS FOR THE COM-
MENCEMENT OF CIVIL ACTIONS HAVE BEEN
PASSED UPON DURING THE YEAR 1910 AND THE
FINAL DISPOSITION IN EACH CASE IS INDI-
CATED.

Application of Fred Dussler to commence an action for the removal of Milton J. Blodgett from the office of president and director of the Buffalo Glass Company. Application denied.

Application of John Kreitner for the commencement of an action for the removal of certain officers of the Iroquois Brewing Company. Application denied.

Application of John J. Mullaney to commence an action for dissolution of the Ideal Opening Die Company. Application denied.

An application was made to commence an action to dissolve the Clinton Beckwith Engineering Company. Under section 102 of the General Corporation Law, I omitted to commence such an action for sixty days, as all necessary redress could be obtained by a creditor or stockholder, without involving the people therein.

Two applications were made by Louis L. Forman to commence an action in the nature of *quo warranto* to oust and exclude one Edward H. Bostwick from the office of City Judge of the city of Ithaca. The first application was withdrawn by the petitioner on February 7th and the second on the 25th of October and both proceedings were thus discontinued.

An application to commence an action to dissolve the Greenwich Insurance Company was denied March 23d, with leave to renew.

An application was made by Joseph Malcolm and others to commence an action against Edward E. Conrad and Max M. Hart to test their title to the positions of directors of the Malcolm Knitting Company, and the validity of their election to the offices of president and secretary and treasurer of said company, which was granted on the 23d day of February, 1910.

An application of Chester M. Freeman to commence an action against Julius E. Mosheim, Charles Freidenburg and Max Marks as officers of Film Import & Trading Company was granted on the 17th day of February, 1910.

An application was made by John J. Becker to begin an action for removal of Charles Wissman, Edward Greenwald and Alfred

Lust as officers, directors and managers of the Flat Iron Restaurant Company.

An application was made by Daniel H. Lewis, Olin H. Landreth and Andrew J. Provost to commence an action against Charles Sooysmith, Henry D. B. Parsons and Linsley R. Williams (Metropolitan Sewage Commission), to oust and remove them from their respective offices.

An application was made by John Miller to commence an action against Herman V. Mynderse to test his title to office of president of village of Scotia. Application granted.

In the matter of the application of Joseph P. Fallon v. John J. Dwyer, to test title to the office of Justice of Municipal Court, Eighth District, New York city. Application granted.

In the matter of the application for leave to institute action to oust and exclude Clarence Ames from office of trustee of village of Tivoli. Application granted.

In the matter of the application of Ellen Meaney for the dissolution of the Eagle Steam Laundry Company of Queens County. Application granted.

In the matter of charges preferred by A. D. Wales in behalf of Minnie M. Proctor to remove Walter F. Hofheins, Deputy Attorney-General. Application denied.

In the matter of the application of William D. Tindall v. Albion C. DeGraw et al., officers of Pine Lawn Cemetery. Application denied.

In the matter of the application of William A. Davidson to begin action against the Otsego & Herkimer Railway Company to test title of office of certain directors. Application denied with leave to renew on further facts.

An application was made by Louis N. S. Miller to bring an action against A. A. Gardenier to test his title to the office of supervisor of the town of Schodack. Application denied.

Application by Edward Heinrich for the removal of Augustus Kiernan from the office of trustee of Sag Harbor granted.

Application by William A. DeGroot to commence an action against James F. McLaughlin to test the title to the office of Justice of the Municipal Court in New York city, was granted.

An application was made by James W. McLaughlin to commence an action to test the title of Thomas F. Noonan and Thomas E. Murray to their respective offices of Justices of the Municipal Court for the Third District of the city of New York, Borough of Manhattan.

An application was made by John C. Schmidt for annulment of The International Automobile League. Denied.

An application was made by Bernard Moseman for the suspension of Isaac Levin as president of The Ellanan Adjustable Dress Form Company. Denied.

OPINIONS RENDERED THE GOVERNOR.

Prison Law — Section 214 — Indeterminate Sentence — Paroles.
Board of Parole has no authority to release on parole one George Sehm, sent to Auburn first on an indeterminate and again on a definite sentence.

(See opinion November 29, 1909, p. 819 Rep.)

STATE OF NEW YORK,

ATTORNEY-GENERAL'S OFFICE,

ALBANY, *January* 24, 1910.

To His Excellency, THE GOVERNOR, *Albany, N. Y.:*

Dear Sir.— I have the honor of acknowledging receipt of your esteemed favor of the 6th inst. in which you ask whether the Board of Parole had the power to release one George Sehm under the circumstances described in your letter, which are as follows:

It appears that Sehm was sentenced October 30, 1905, to Auburn prison for an indeterminate sentence of not less than one year and three months nor more than four years for the crime of assault in the second degree; that while he was out on bail upon a certificate of reasonable doubt he committed another felony for which he was convicted of the crime of grand larceny, first degree, and on March 6, 1906, sentenced therefor to Auburn prison for a definite term of two years and ten months; that the stay was vacated before the second sentence was imposed and on March 10, 1906, the sheriff took the prisoner to Auburn prison under both commitments; and that on November 11, 1907, after he had served one year and eight months, the Board of Parole purported to authorize the release of the prisoner and to order him discharged from the indeterminate sentence and the prison authorities then purported to confine him under the definite sentence of two years and ten months, which, with statutory commutation is now said to expire on January 31, 1910.

Under date of November 29, 1909, I rendered an opinion to Hon. C. V. Collins, Superintendent of State Prisons, in reply to a general question propounded by him in substance as follows: Whether the Board of Parole had the power in the case of a prisoner who is under confinement under two sentences, the first indeterminate and the second definite, to follow immediately upon the expiration of the first, to parole such a prisoner at the expiration of the minimum term of the first sentence in order that he may immediately begin the service of his second sentence, and in such opinion I stated that a prisoner confined under such conditions would not be entitled to a parole and discharge at the expiration of the minimum term of his first sentence in order to allow him to begin the service of his second sentence.

It is very apparent from a careful reading of section 214 of the Prison Law that the Board of Parole has the authority to parole such prisoners only as can " be allowed to go upon parole outside of said prison walls and inclosure upon such terms and conditions as said board shall prescribe." It is equally clear by section 2190 of the Penal Law that where a person is sentenced to two or more terms of imprisonment that his second or subsequent sentence shall commence at the termination of the first or other prior term or terms, and that his imprisonment must be continuous. I am unable to find any law whereby the Board of Parole are given authority to discharge a prisoner at the expiration of his first term to give him the benefit of a parole that he cannot be allowed to exercise, and in the absence of any statutory authority in such board I do not think it had the power to authorize the release of the prisoner Sehm, or to order him to be discharged from the indeterminate sentence as it purported to do on November 11, 1907. The power of the Board of Parole is wholly statutory, and it cannot be extended to include authority that is not definitely given or fairly implied by the statute under which it is acting.

If the prisoner referred to serves the two terms as one continuing term, and his behavior justifies it, his sentence can be

commuted as provided by article IX of the Prison Law, which
will very materially shorten his confinement, but I am of the
opinion that the Board of Parole had no power or authority to
shorten it by parole as it purported to do by the action taken on
November 11, 1907.

Yours truly,

EDWARD R. O'MALLEY,

Attorney-General.

Commission on State Farm for Women.

Appointment of Mrs. Charles L. Guy, as a member of the Commission, lawful, even though she had resigned from the
Women's Prison Association.

STATE OF NEW YORK,

Attorney-General's Office,

Albany, *June* 24, 1910.

IIon. Charles E. Hughes, *Governor, Albany, N. Y.:*

Dear Sir.— I have the honor to reply to your request for an
opinion concerning the appointment of a member of The Commission on State Farm for Women. Your communication states that
pursuant to the statute authorizing you to appoint two women as
members of this Commission, you appointed Mrs. Charles L. Guy,
who was at that time a member of the Women's Prison Association
of New York city. You state that she has resigned from that
association and is not now a member thereof; but the question
has arisen whether the severing of her relation with the Women's
Prison Association has of itself vacated her membership in The
Commission on State Farm for Women.

Chapter 467 of the Laws of 1908, which is an act to establish
a State farm for women, provides as follows:

> " The superintendent of prisons, the president of the state
> commission of prisons, a member of the state board of charities
> to be designated by the governor, and two women to be ap-
> pointed by the governor, one of whom shall be a member of

13

the Women's Prison Association of New York City, are hereby constituted a commission to be known as ' The Commission on State Farm for Women.' "

A member of this Commission is a State officer and not a local one. The duties imposed upon the Commission and the powers invested in it are to be exercised in behalf of all the people of the State. The intent of the statute was to secure a Commission, so far as possible, qualified with a knowledge of matters pertaining to prison affairs, and to secure these qualifications it is provided that one of the women appointees should be a member of the Women's Prison Association of New York city. By making the Superintendent of Prisons and the President of the State Commission of Prisons and a member of the State Board of Charities members of this Commission, it was sought to secure a Commission qualified for this work. If the Women's Prison Association of New York city were to pass out of existence, it could not be argued that that fact would vacate the membership of Mrs. Guy upon The Commission on State Farm for Women. In my judgment, the intent of the statute is complied with if the appointee has the specified requirements at the time the appointment is made. It is my opinion, therefore, that Mrs. Guy is still a lawful member of The Commission on State Farm for Women.

Yours respectfully,
EDWARD R. O'MALLEY,
Attorney-General.

Penal Law — Sections 43, 1140a, 1530, 1710.
Exhibition in the State of New York of moving pictures of the Jeffries–Johnson prize fight, held at Reno, Nevada, whether a violation of statute.

STATE OF NEW YORK,
ATTORNEY-GENERAL'S OFFICE,
ALBANY, August 22, 1910.

Hon. CHARLES E. HUGHES, <i>Governor, Albany, N. Y.:</i>

Dear Sir.— As requested by you in your communication of the 3d inst., I have examined the question whether the exhibition in this State of moving pictures of the Jeffries–Johnson prize fight recently held at Reno, Nevada, violates the Penal Law. As a result of this investigation, it is my opinion that except in unusual circumstances it does not.

The only provisions which it could be claimed were violated by this exhibition are sections 1530, 1140a and 43 of the Penal Law. The first of these sections defines a public nuisance as a crime against the order and economy of the State, which consists in unlawfully committing an act which "annoys, injures or endangers the comfort, repose, health or safety of any considerable number of persons," or "offends public decency." Section 1140a of the Penal Law makes it a misdemeanor to advertise, present or participate in any "indecent, immoral or impure exhibition, show or entertainment, which would tend to the corruption of the morals of youth or others." Section 43 of the Penal Law provides penalties for acts offending against public decency, not specifically prohibited by other sections of the law, by making it a misdemeanor to commit any act which "seriously disturbs or endangers the public peace or health or which openly outrages public decency."

There are no crimes in this State except those defined by statute (§ 22 Penal Law). Unless the statute expressly and clearly prohibits certain acts the doing thereof will not be held to be prohibited under the rules of construction applicable to penal statutes. In other words, by a fair interpretation of the terms of the statute it must be clear that the act or acts were intended to be prohibited. I am of the opinion that the exhibitions to which you call my attention do not offend public decency in the sense in which those words were used in section 1530 and section 43 of the Penal Law above mentioned. It is also my opinion that they do not constitute an immoral exhibition or show "which would tend to corruption of the morals of youth or others" as those words are used in section 1140a of the Penal Law. It would follow from this, therefore, that the mere giving of these exhibitions does not in itself constitute a violation of the Penal Law.

If, however, such exhibitions, as a matter of fact, tended to arouse race prejudice or to instigate any considerable number of persons to deeds of violence, they would, of course, become public nuisances as endangering the comfort, repose and safety of the community and would be violative of section 1530 of the Penal Law.

I have not overlooked the public policy of this State as declared in section 1710 of the Penal Law, prohibiting the holding of prize fights within the State, nor those decisions in several other states in which it is held that the giving of a prize fight could be enjoined on the ground that it is a public nuisance. But in my opinion, there is a difference in the effect upon spectators of an actual prize fight and of the mere visual representation of such a contest.

Respectfully yours,

EDWARD R. O'MALLEY,

Attorney-General.

Barge Canal.

Abandonment of Troy Dam, as proposed, would constitute permanent abandonment to the United States, and would be unconstitutional, since it is part of the canal system of the State. It might be destroyed by the Superintendent of Public Works with the consent of the Canal Board.

(See Opinion, July 14, 1910.)

STATE OF NEW YORK,

ATTORNEY-GENERAL'S OFFICE,

ALBANY, *August* 23, 1910.

Honorable CHARLES E. HUGHES, *Governor, Albany, N. Y.:*

Dear Sir.— I beg to acknowledge receipt of your communication of August 15, 1910, accompanied by copy letter to the Secretary of War from W. H. Bixby, Chief of Engineers U. S. A., House Document No. 719, 61st Congress, Second Session, and copy letter to you from Hon. Frederick C. Stevens, Superintendent of Public Works, asking my opinion with respect to the authority to abandon State dam and lock as proposed, and if such authority exists, by whom, and the manner in which it can properly be exercised.

1. I have noted carefully the suggestions and recommendations contained in the letter to the Secretary of War and in the House document as to the conditions, limitations and restrictions upon which the undertaking of the proposed work by the United States government may depend, and I am of the opinion that the State of New York may not constitutionally abandon the said dam and lock, " as proposed," as that would contemplate a consequent permanent abandonment and surrender to the Federal government and the subsequent maintenance and operation by it of what is now a part of the canal system of the State of New York.

2. I am of the opinion, however, that the State may *destroy* and ·thereby in effect abandon the existing State dam and lock, acting through its State Superintendent of Public Works (with the approval of the canal board) in the exercise of his incidental powers of supervision over the canals.

The provisions of the leases of water rights and privileges at the State dam, to which reference is made in the various papers accompanying your letter, are fully set forth in the House document at page 18 and reference thereto shows that, in addition to the right to resume control or limit the use of the water for the use of any State canal, there is also saved and reserved to the State the right, without making compensation to the lessees or any other persons claiming under them, wholly to abandon or *destroy* the work, by the construction of which the surplus water has been created, whenever in the opinion of the Canal Commissioners the occupation and use of said work shall cease to be *advantageous* to the State. The parties of the first part to the lease in question were the Canal Commissioners, whose powers and duties under article V, section 3 of the Constitution have been imposed on the Superintendent of Public Works, and under article III, section 15, subdivision 10, of the Canal Law, the Canal Board is given authority to act with reference to the leasing or disposal of surplus water.

Treating the proposition as one not for the abandonment, in the sense of relinquishment of control, of any part of the canal or its management, but rather in the nature of a resumption of control of the water, it would seem that, under reservation of the leases, the Superintendent of Public Works (with the approval of the Canal Board), if he is of the opinion that it will be advantageous to the State, may at any time provide for the destruction of the dam in question and the consequent extinguishment of all water power rights and privileges. A fuller discussion of this matter will be found in my opinion of July 14, 1910, referred to in the letter to you from the Superintendent of Public Works.

Very respectfully,

EDWARD R. O'MALLEY,

Attorney-General.

Forest, Fish and Game Law — Sections 98, 240.

Interpretation of statute prohibiting importation and sale of certain birds and plumage after July 1, 1911.

STATE OF NEW YORK,

ATTORNEY-GENERAL'S OFFICE,

ALBANY, *October* 18, 1910.

Hon. HORACE WHITE, *Governor, Albany, N. Y.:*

Dear Sir.— I beg to acknowledge receipt of your communication of October 10, 1910, enclosing a letter to you under date of October 5, 1910, from the Acting Secretary of State of the United States, transmitting copy of a letter under date of September 27, 1910, from the French Ambassador, and requesting my opinion as to the interpretation of the law of the State of New York prohibiting the importation into and sale of certain birds on and after July 1, 1911. I assume that the law referred to is found in section 98 and subdivision 18 of section 240 of the Forest, Fish and Game Law of the State of New York as amended in 1910. Section 98 of that law reads as follows:

"Section 98. CERTAIN WILD BIRDS PROTECTED.—Wild birds other than the English sparrow, crow, hawk, crow-blackbird, snow-owl, great horned owl and kingfisher, shall not be taken or possessed at any time, dead or alive, except under the authority of a certificate issued under this chapter. No part of the plumage, skin or body of any bird protected by this section *or of any birds coming from without the state whether be-*

*longing to the same or a different species from that native to
the state of New York, provided such birds belong to the same
family as those protected by this chapter* shall be sold or had
in possession for sale. The provision of this section shall not
apply to game birds for which an open season is provided in
this chapter; excepting that quail, English pheasants and
Hungarian partridges shall not be taken at any time in Richmond county prior to the year nineteen hundred and fourteen."

Subdivision 18 of section 240 of the law reads as follows:

" Section 240. DEFINITION.— 18. *Plumage includes any
part of the feathers, head, wings or tail of any bird, and
wherever the word occurs in this chapter reference is had
equally to plumage of birds coming from without the state as
to that obtained within the state, but it shall not be construed
to apply to the feathers of birds of paradise, ostriches, domestic fowl or domestic pigeons.*"

The italicised provisions of the sections quoted are to take effect
on the first day of July, 1911.

The French Ambassador, in the letter above referred to, says:

" It seems that the law gives a list of the birds that may be
imported and another naming those whose importation is prohibited. Now there exists a large number of birds which do
not appear on either list. According to the usual principles
of law, prohibitions being of a limitative character, the merchants concerned hold that birds that are not specified may,
doubtless, be freely imported into the United States as heretofore. They would be glad, however, to be so assured in
order to avoid any difficulty."

As will appear from an examination of the sections above
quoted, the law does not give any list of the birds which may be
imported or whose importation is prohibited. The question has
been raised whether the plumage, skin or body of a bird desired
to be imported belonged to a species native to the State of New
York and protected by the Forest, Fish and Game Law, or if not
belonging to a species native to the State of New York, whether it

belonged to the same family as one of the birds protected by the law. This is a question primarily to be determined by an ornithologist. I am advised that in June, 1910, the Forest, Fish and Game Commissioner of the State of New York employed the services of Mr. DeW. Miller of New York City, an ornithologist of high repute, to compile a list of birds which belong to the same species as those native to the State of New York and protected by such law and also a list of birds not belonging to the same species but which belong to the same families. Another list was likewise compiled giving the names of birds not belonging to the same species as those native to the State of New York and protected by the law and not belonging to the same families as those protected by the law.

These are the lists to which the French Ambassador doubtless refers as containing the names of birds, the importation of whose plumage is prohibited by the law, and of those, the importation of whose plumage is not prohibited, but such lists seem to be no more than the interpretation by the Forest, Fish and Game Commissioner as to the application of the law in question to the specific birds named in the several lists.

If there are birds whose names are not contained in either of the lists, it would still be a question for the ornithologist to decide in which list they should properly be included.

I have obtained from the Forest, Fish and Game Commissioner a copy of the lists in question which I take pleasure in transmitting to you with this opinion.

Respectfully yours,

EDWARD R. O'MALLEY,

Attorney-General.

LIST OF BIRDS THE IMPORTATION OF WHOSE PLUMAGE IS PROHIBITED.

Small owls (commonly called screech owls).
Yellow finches (commonly called gold finch).
Green merles (glossy starling).
Yellow heron.
Booby.
Snow birds (bunting).

Hawk.
White foot eagle.
Marabout.
Ferde Lauce.
Condor.
Magpies.
Tourterelle des Bois.
Owls Russie.
Albinos (white tern).
Green merle (starling).
Marabout (stork).
Merle (starling).
Brown heron.
Grey heron.
Alouottes (skylark).
Green ibis.
Red ibis.
Pelican.
Eagle.
Gros bouvreuil (haw finch).
Jasouer queue jaune (wax wing).
Petit hirondelle Formosa (swift).
Pinson des Ardonnes (brambling).
Bruants (bunting).
Grives royal (thrush).
Chardonnerets (gold finch).
Blue manakin.
Grives marron (thrush).
Black tanager.
Dark pigeon.
Garnet dull tanager.
Red tanager.
Blue jays.
Hirondelle Formosa (swift).
Etourneaux (starling).
Bergonnettes marron (bunting).
Grisselle (tern).
Tourterelle Collier Espagne (turtle dove).

Monatos (starling).
Pios Crieches Indes (shrike).
Petit Hirondelle de Cheminee (swallow).
Pies bleues (blue jay).
Petit bouvreuils (bull finch).
Starlings.
Pincon male chaffinch.
Pigeons (bronze Malacca).
Night heron.
Figuier brown head tanager.
Garnet tanager.
Veddiers (green finch).
Eveques (starling).
Dominoes (sooty tern).
Petit martin pecheur.
Eagle.
Miroir ruffe (stork).
Pelican.

LIST OF BIRDS THE IMPORTATION OF WHOSE PLUMAGE IS NOT PROHIBITED.

Senegal rolliers (commonly called rollers).
Guepiers.
Large red parrots.
Satyr (a species of pheasant).
Japanese green pheasant.
Goura (commonly called crown pigeon).
Harphang (commonly called snowy owl).
Velvet bird.
Six filet (paradise bird).
Pilet (species of duck).
Duck.
Partridge.
Tetras lvre (European black cock).
Grouse (partridge tail).
Aras (commonly called macaw).
Outarde (commonly called bustard).
Forest pigeon.

Faisanes (European pheasant).
Japanese brown pheasant.
Impeyan.
Guinea fowl.
Rhea (South American ostrich).
Touroucon.
Peacock.
Tetras.
Plover tail.
Partridge wing.
Junglecock.
Hawk.
Calfats gris (European sparrow).
Blue guepier (honey creeper).
Red head manakin.
Male loriet.
Snipes (marsh sandpiper).
Ignicolores (weaver bird).
Calfats brun (weaver bird).
Yellow head manakin.
Ring neck plover.
Touracco rouge (plantain bird).
Breves-pitta.
Red head blue body manakin.
Small ring neck plover.
Dark snipes (green sandpiper).
Rolliers senegal (rollers).
Green parrots.
Choucas (jackdaw).
Snipe (green plover).
Figuier (black head honey creeper).
Becassine a poix (painted snipe).
Calfat Isabelle (weaver bird).
Parrots ailes stricees.
Touracco vertes (plaintain eater).
Grives, grises, hypsipetes.
Golden oriole.
Chicken feathers of all kinds.

English pheasant plumage of all kinds.
Chinese golden pheasant.
Chinese silver pheasant.
Turkeys of all kinds.
Goose plumage of all kinds.
Swan plumage of all kinds.
Grouse plumage of all kinds.
Woodcock.
Rooster tails of all kinds.
East India fruit pigeon.
Numidic (crossoptilon pheasant).

State Institutions — State Hospitals.

Failure of member of board of managers to attend regular meetings of the board. When the " six months " begins to run.

(Section 42, Insanity Law.)

STATE OF NEW YORK,

ATTORNEY-GENERAL'S OFFICE,

ALBANY, *November* 4, 1910.

Hon. HORACE WHITE, *Governor, Albany, N. Y.:*

Dear Sir.—I have your letter of the 27th ultimo stating that one of the managers of the Binghamton State Hospital has attended no regular meeting of the board of managers since March 29, 1910, and asking whether this constitutes a failure for six months to attend the regular meetings of the board within the meaning of section 42 of the Insanity Law.

This section provides in part as follows:

"If any manager fails for a period of six months to attend the regular meetings of the board of which he is a member, the secretary of the board shall notify the governor of such absence, with any explanation thereof which may be submitted by such manager, and unless the governor shall, within thirty days thereafter, notify the secretary that he has excused such manager for such absence, the office of such manager shall thereupon be deemed to be vacant; and if any manager fails for one year to attend such regular meetings, his office shall become vacant."

It appears from your letter that the next regular meeting of the board after March 29 was April 29, and that the last regular meeting was held on October 11.

It is my opinion that the period of six months specified in this section does not begin to run until there has been a failure to attend a regular meeting. The manager should not be regarded as in default until he has actually committed a default. It therefore follows that the six months period did not commence to run until the failure to attend the meeting of April 29, and that it was not completed until October 29.

Very respectfully yours,
EDWARD R. O'MALLEY,
Attorney-General.

Election Law — Sections 292, 293 — Tie Votes.
Failure of city of Watervliet to elect alderman for fifth ward at election held November 8, 1910. Right of Governor to issue proclamation for special election, present alderman holding over until successor is elected.

STATE OF NEW YORK,

ATTORNEY-GENERAL'S OFFICE,

ALBANY, *November* 29, 1910.

Hon. HORACE WHITE, *Governor of the State of New York, Executive Chamber, Albany, N. Y.:*

Dear Sir.— I beg to acknowledge the receipt of a certain resolution adopted by the common council of the city of Watervliet and of a communication from John Francy, county clerk of the county of Albany, both relating to the failure to elect an alderman in the fifth ward of the city of Watervliet, at the election held therein on the 8th day of November, 1910, which have been forwarded by you to my department for advice regarding the same.

It appears from the resolution of the common council and statement of the county clerk that at the general election held on the 8th day of November, 1910, in the fifth ward of the city of Watervliet, Albany county, one Isaac G. Braman was a candidate upon the Republican ticket for the position of alderman in and for said ward, and that James J. Callahan was a candidate upon the Democratic and Independence League tickets for the same position, and that each candidate received 211 votes, thus making a tie vote as between the two candidates. John Breen also received seven votes and Edwin Beyer received three for the same office, but inasmuch as no candidate received a plurality of all the votes cast, there was a failure to elect anyone to the office.

It is provided by section 292 of the Election Law in part, as follows:

> "Upon the failure to elect to any office, except that of governor or lieutenant-governor, at a general or special election, at which such office is authorized to be filled, or upon the death or disqualification of a person elected to office before the commencement of his official term, or upon the occurrence of a vacancy in any elective office which can not be filled by appointment for a period extending to or beyond the next general election at which a person may be elected thereto, the governor may in his discretion make proclamation of a special election to fill such office, specifying the district or county in which the election is to be held and the day thereof, which shall not be less than twenty nor more than forty days from the date of the proclamation."

The above covers every office except Governor and Lieutenant-Governor, unless special provision is otherwise made, and I fail to find any conflicting provision in the charter of the city of Watervliet, and therefore the section above quoted applies to conditions now existing in the fifth ward of such city.

By section 293 of the Election Law it is made the duty of the Secretary of State, upon the filing in his office of a proclamation for a special election, to transmit to the county clerk of the county in which it is to be held, a notice of the office to be voted for at such special election, and the election then proceeds according to the Election Law.

The failure to elect does not work a vacancy in the office and the present incumbent will continue to hold over and exercise the functions thereof until a successor is elected and qualified.

People ex rel. Kehoe v. Fitchie, 76 Hun, 81.

The Governor's right to issue a proclamation under section 292 of the Election Law is strictly within his discretion and may or may not be exercised as he may decide, but until it is exercised and a new election is had and a successor is elected, the present alderman will have authority to act and hold the office.

Yours truly,

EDWARD R. O'MALLEY,

Attorney-General.

Forest, Fish and Game Commission.

Investigation of affairs of. Disclosure of communications from attorneys in connection with negotiations with Forest Purchasing Board. Whether such correspondence is privileged under section 835, Code of Civil Procedure.

STATE OF NEW YORK,

ATTORNEY-GENERAL'S OFFICE,

ALBANY, *April* 5, 1910.

Hon. H. LEROY AUSTIN, *Special Commissioner, Executive Chamber, Albany, N. Y.:*

My Dear Sir.— I acknowledge your letter of the 28th ult., asking my opinion regarding the following question which has arisen in connection with your investigation of the management and affairs of the Forest, Fish and Game Commission and the Forest Purchasing Board.

You state that a firm of New York attorneys lately represented a party who owned a large tract of land in the Adirondack Park and on behalf of their client conducted negotiations with the Forest Purchasing Board for the purchase of such lands by the State. They had considerable correspondence in reference to the matter with State officials and also with a third party who was likewise negotiating for the purchase of these lands and did sub-

sequently purchase them and sell them to the State. You desire
to inspect the correspondence which passed between these attorneys and the State and between them and the third party, but the
attorneys raise the claim that the correspondence is privileged
under section 835 of the Code of Civil Procedure. You ask my
opinion, therefore, as to whether they have the right to assert
privilege as to the following classes of communications:

1. Letters from the attorneys to State officials.

2. Letters received by the attorneys from State officials.

3. Letters from the attorneys to the third party, not their
client.

4. Letters received by the attorneys from the third party.

§ 835 of the Code of Civil Procedure provides as follows:

"§ 835. Attorneys and counselors not to disclose communications.— An attorney or counselor-at-law shall not be
allowed to disclose a communication made by his client to
him, or his advice given thereon, in the course of his pro-
fessional employment nor shall any clerk, stenographer or
other person employed by such attorney or counselor be
allowed to disclose any such communication or advice given
thereon."

It is clear, on examination, that there is nothing contained in
this section which makes privileged any communications had
between the attorneys and any person other than their client. I
therefore advise you that none of the correspondence referred to
above is entitled to be regarded as privileged under this section
of the Code.

Very truly yours,

EDWARD R. O'MALLEY,

Attorney-General.

OPINIONS RENDERED THE LIEUTENANT-GOVERNOR.

State Fair Commission — State Finance Law — Section 37.

Sale of team of horses by State Fair Commission and right to reinvest the money for another team legal under provisions of article 13, section 249, chapter 9, Laws 1909, creating Commission. Section 37 Finance Law not applying to said Commission.

STATE OF NEW YORK,

ATTORNEY-GENERAL'S OFFICE,

ALBANY, *May* 10, 1910.

Hon. HORACE WHITE, *Lieutenant-Governor, Albany, N. Y.:*

Dear Sir.— Replying to yours of the 6th inst., inclosing a letter from A. E. Brown, treasurer, addressed to you, in which he states that he has in his possession a check for $325 in payment of a pair of horses sold by Commissioner Perren, said horses being the property of the State Fair, and asking what disposition he shall make of said check, and your letter wherein you state " I am informed that Mr. Perren believes the Commission has a right to expend this money for the purposes of the State Fair. It is very desirable that it be expended for a new team of horses. My information is that the horses that were sold were unfit for the use of the Commission. It is also necessary to procure new horses suitable for this work," and asking whether or not it would be lawful to expend this money as above indicated. I beg to state as follows:

Section 37 of the State Finance Law provides:

" Every state officer, employee, board, department or commission receiving money for or on behalf of the State from fees, penalties, costs, fines, sales of property, or otherwise, . . . shall on the fifth day of each month pay to the state treasurer all such money received during the preceding month . . . This section shall be deemed to supersede any other provision of this chapter or of any other general or special law inconsistent therewith."

This would seem to be conclusive were it not for the provisions of article 13 of chapter 9 of the Laws of 1909, which creates the State Fair Commission and defines their powers and duties, and particularly section 294 which provides:

" The commission shall receive all moneys payable to the state on account of said fair, and make all disbursements therefrom and also from any appropriation made for that purpose by the legislature as may be needed, from time to time, in carrying on the work of the commission. The provisions of section thirty-seven of the state finance law requiring that money received for or on behalf of the state shall be paid monthly into the state treasury shall not apply to the state fair commission, and such commission may pay from the race and other entry fees, gate admissions and other receipts of such fair such expenses as shall be necessary for the proper conduct of the fair and the purposes of the commission. On or before the first day of January of each year the commission shall pay to the state treasurer any balance remaining in their hands received in connection with the state fair, and at the same time file with the comptroller an itemized verified report showing all receipts and disbursements for state fair purposes since the last report, together with the vouchers therefor approved by said commission."

It is therefore obvious that the Legislature intended to and did exempt the State Fair Commission from the provisions of section 37 of the State Finance Law. The money in question is money received from the sale of a team of horses which had become unfit for the use of the Commission.

I am therefore of the opinion that the reinvestment of this money for another team is legal and proper in view of the statute, which provides that moneys received by the Commission are not to be paid to the State Treasurer as provided by section 37 of the State Finance Law but are to go into the hands of the Commission, and which authorizes the Commission to pay out of such moneys " such expenses as shall be necessary for the proper conduct of the fair and the purposes of the Commission."

Very truly yours,

EDWARD R. O'MALLEY,

Attorney-General.

OPINIONS RENDERED THE SECRETARY OF STATE.

Stock Corporation Law — Section 62 — Reduction of Capital.
Language of statute "reduced capital" implies capital stock exclusively, not corporate assets.
(See opinion January 16, 1895, p. 64, Report; June 27, 1895, p. 173, Report; letter August 23, 1905, L. B. 88, p. 750; February 12, 1906, L. B. 92, p. 132.)

STATE OF NEW YORK,

Attorney-General's Office,

Albany, *January* 10, 1910.

Hon. Samuel S. Koenig, *Secretary of State, Albany, N. Y.:*

Dear Sir.— Replying to the request for an opinion regarding the construction of section 62 of the Stock Corporation Law, embodied in the letter of 6th inst., from your deputy, Mr. Fennell, I beg to advise that I have given the matter careful attention and that my opinion is as follows:

Section 62 of the Stock Corporation Law provides in part as follows:

"Increase or reduction of capital stock. Any domestic corporation may increase or reduce its capital stock in the manner herein provided, but not above the maximum or below the minimum, if any, prescribed by general law governing corporations formed for similar purposes. If increased, the holders of the additional stock issued shall be subject to the same liabilities with respect thereto as are provided by law in relation to the original capital; if reduced, the amount of its debts and liabilities shall not exceed the amount of its reduced capital, unless an insurance corporation, in which case the amount of its debts and liabilities shall not exceed the amount of its reduced capital and other assets. The owner of any stock shall not be relieved from any liability existing prior to the reduction of the capital stock of any stock corporation. If a banking corporation, whether the capital be increased or reduced, its assets shall at least be equal to its debts and liabilities and the capital stock, as increased or reduced."

The question which you ask is whether, in the provision that " if reduced, the amount of its debts and liabilities shall not exceed the amount of its reduced capital," the words " reduced capital " refer to capital stock or the entire corporate assets.

It is true that in many instances the word " capital " is used to represent entire corporate assets, but it is, in my opinion, clear from a perusal of the language of the entire section that the word as here used refers exclusively to capital stock. Wherever the contrary meaning is intended you will observe that the statute uses the expression " reduced capital and other assets " or similar language.

I therefore advise you that under the provision of this section no company can reduce its capital stock to such an extent that the capital stock so reduced is less than the amount of its debts and liabilities.

Very truly yours,
EDWARD R. O'MALLEY,
Attorney-General.

Stck Corporation Law — Section 51.

Milton Drug Company, proposal to incorporate under Business Corporations Law. Clause in certificate providing that shares of stock can not be transferable without consent in writing of board of directors, is invalid and against public policy. (Fisher v. Bush, 35 Hun, 641.)

STATE OF NEW YORK,

ATTORNEY-GENERAL'S OFFICE,

ALBANY, *February* 7, 1910.

Hon. SAMUEL S. KOENIG, *Secretary of State, Albany, N. Y.:*

Dear Sir.— I acknowledge your letter of the 15th ultimo enclosing proposed certificate of incorporation of the Milton Drug Company which proposes to incorporate under the Business Corporation Law, and asking my opinion as to the legality of one of the provisions of this certificate. The clause in question is as follows:

> "The shares of stock of this corporation shall not under any conditions be transferable without the consent in writing of a majority of the board of directors and the granting of such consent shall rest wholly within the personal discretion of said board of directors."

I have carefully examined the question as to the legality of this provision, and, in my opinion, it cannot be sustained. I find no specific provision of law authorizing it to be inserted in the certificate of incorporation. On the contrary, section 51 of the Stock Corporation Law providing that transfers of stock by stockholders indebted to the corporation may be prohibited by the directors under certain circumstances, implies, in my judgment, that the directors cannot have general power to prevent the transfer of stock in the hands of stockholders.

It might be claimed that the provision was valid as a term of a contract between the stockholders, entered into at the time the stock was acquired. It is frequently held that the provisions of the certificate of incorporation become part of the agreement under which the stockholder holds his stock. Upon this theory, for instance, the courts have recently decided that a provision limiting the right of common stockholders to vote in the management of the corporation is valid and binding as a contractual agreement.

> People ex rel. Brown v. Koenig, 133 App. Div. 756.

It is my opinion, however, that even if this clause is regarded as part of a contract, it is still invalid under the decisions in this State, as being against public policy. It was held in the case of Fisher v. Bush, 35 Hun, 641, that an agreement between stockholders not to sell their stock in a certain corporation without the concurrent consent of all signers of the instrument was void as in restraint of trade and against public policy. This decision has frequently been recognized and applied.

> Brown v. Britton, 41 App. Div. 57.
> Hey v. Dolphin, 92 Hun, 237.
> Kennon v. Sullivan County Club, 26 App. Div. 213.

It is therefore my opinion that under the principle of these decisions the clause in question is invalid as in restraint of trade and against public policy even if it could be regarded as a part of the contractual agreement consented to by the stockholders. I therefore advise you that the proposed certificate should not be filed in your office.

Very truly yours,

EDWARD R. O'MALLEY,

Attorney-General.

Corporations — Voting Power of Stockholders.

Empire Forwarding Company. Secretary of State may file certificate of incorporation containing provisions that stockholders may be entitled to one vote irrespective of the number of shares they own. (Cons. Gen. Corp. Law, sections 10, 23.) (See opinion, February 13, 1908; letter, March 12, 1909, L. B. 101, p. 812; letter, May 14, 1909, L. B. 104, p. 401; letter, June 21, 1909, L. B. 105, p. 938; letter, July 22, 1909, L. B. 107, p. 260; opinion, August 26, 1909, p. 323, Report; opinion August 31, 1909, p. 325, Report.)

STATE OF NEW YORK,

Attorney-General's Office,

Albany, *March* 21, 1910.

Hon. Samuel S. Koenig, *Secretary of State, Albany, N. Y.:*

Dear Sir.— Your letter of February 25 received, enclosing proposed certificate of incorporation of the Empire Forwarding Company. You ask an opinion from this office as to whether the certificate is entitled, under the law, to be filed in your office, containing a provision to the effect that " stockholders shall be entitled to one vote in the corporation, irrespective of the number of shares held therein by any one stockholder."

The provisions of law bearing on this question are found in the Consolidated General Corporation Law, comprising subdivision 2 of section 10, which reads as follows:

"The certificate of incorporation of any corporation may contain any provision for the regulation of the business and the conduct of the affairs of the corporation, and any limitation upon its powers, or upon the powers of its directors and stockholders, which does not exempt them from the performance of any obligation or the performance of any duty imposed by law."

They are also found in section 23 of the same law, which provides:

"Unless otherwise provided in the certificate of incorporation, every stockholder of record of a stock corporation shall be entitled at every meeting of the corporation to one vote for every share of stock standing in his name on the books of the corporation."

The recent decision of the Appellate Division, First Department, in People ex rel. Browne v. Koenig, holds in substance that stockholders may agree amongst themselves as to the manner in which the voting privilege of the stock may be exercised, and that such agreement, being merely a part of the contract assented to by every purchaser of stock, is not unlawful. Such a restriction on the right of voting is not regarded in the same light as a restriction upon the right of transfer of the stock, which, as I recently advised you, is held to be contrary to public policy.

Under the principle established by this decision, therefore, I must advise you that there is no objection to the filing of the certificate of incorporation here in question, and that the provision therein contained to the effect that the stockholders shall be entitled to one vote irrespective of the number of shares which they own, is legal. This, of course, would not in any way affect the specific provisions of law requiring the consent of stockholders owning a certain number of shares of stock for accomplishing various provisions.

Very respectfully yours,
EDWARD R. O'MALLEY,
Attorney-General.

General Corporation Law — Section 7 — Amended Certificates.
Proposed amended certificates of incorporation of Neil, Ward &
Company adding letter " e " to name of Ward, is not a change
of name of the corporation.

(See opinion, June 16, 1910.)

STATE OF NEW YORK,

ATTORNEY-GENERAL'S OFFICE,

ALBANY, *May* 18, 1910.

Hon. SAMUEL S. KOENIG, *Secretary of State, Albany, N. Y.:*

Dear Sir.— I acknowledge receipt of your favor of the 8th
ultimo enclosing a proposed amended certificate of incorporation
of Neil, Ward & Company for the purpose of adding the letter
" e " to the name of " Ward " in the corporate title.

It appears from the papers submitted to me by you that on the
10th day of March, 1910, there was filed in your office a certificate
of incorporation of Neil, Ward & Company. After said certificate
was filed, recorded and indexed in your office it was discovered by
the incorporators that the word " Ward " in the corporate name
should have been spelled " Warde," and they ask to file the
amended certificate enclosed in your letter. You ask my opinion
whether they are entitled to do so.

Section 7 of the General Corporation Law provides:

" If in the original or amended certificate of incorporation
of any corporation, or if in a supplemental certificate of any
corporation any informality exists or if any such certificate
contain any matter not authorized by law to be stated therein,
or if the proof or acknowledgment thereof shall be defective,
the corporators or directors of the corporation may make and
file an amended certificate correcting such informality or
defect . . ."

I am of the opinion that this is not a change in the name of the
corporation, but is such an informality as may be corrected by
filing an amended certificate, as provided in the statute quoted.

Yours very truly,

EDWARD R. O'MALLEY,

Attorney-General.

Executive Law — Section 82 *— Publication Session Laws.*
Secretary of State should provide for publication of amendment
to Education Law (chapter 140, Laws 1910) in same manner
as other session laws.

STATE OF NEW YORK,

ATTORNEY-GENERAL'S OFFICE,

ALBANY, *May* 20, 1910.

Hon. SAMUEL S. KOENIG, *Secretary of State, Albany, N. Y.:*

Dear Sir.— I acknowledge your letter without date, received on
the 19th inst., in which you ask for my opinion as to whether
chapter 140, Laws of 1910, entitled " An act to amend the Education Law generally," must be published in two newspapers in each
county of the State as provided by section 48 of the Legislative
Law, and also be published in the State paper at Albany as provided by section 82 of the Executive Law.

I note that the Education Law was originally enacted as chapter
21, Laws of 1909, and that it was then printed and distributed
pursuant to the provisions of chapter 87, Laws of 1909. This
latter chapter made a special exemption from the requirements
of the Legislative Law and the Executive Law that session laws be
printed in the newspapers, in reference to the Consolidated Laws
passed at the session of 1909, and provides first that 10,000 copies
of such Consolidated Laws should be printed and distributed by
the Secretary of State as therein provided, and then contains the
following provision:

> " Section 3. The printing, publication and distribution of
> such consolidated laws and such acts amending the code of
> civil procedure and the code of criminal procedure shall be in
> lieu of the publication provided for in section seventy-three
> of the executive law and in sections forty-eight and forty-nine
> of the legislative law, and such consolidated laws and acts
> amending the code of civil procedure and the code of criminal
> procedure shall not be published in any newspaper at the
> expense of the state."

It is obvious from an examination of this statute that it applies only to the Consolidated Laws as enacted at the session of 1909 and which were to be printed and distributed as herein provided. It can have no application to a general amendment to a Consolidated Law passed at a subsequent session, for the printing and distributing of which in pamphlet form there is no provision. I must therefore advise you that chapter 140, Laws of 1910, stands on precisely the same footing as any other session law and must be published in the same way as such other session laws.

Very truly yours,
EDWARD R. O'MALLEY,
Attorney-General.

General Corporation Law — Section 7 — Amended Certificates.
Certificates changing name of corporation from " Boehm & Mack " to " Boehm & Mack Co." may not be filed except by application to court.

(See opinion May 18, 1910.)

STATE OF NEW YORK,

Attorney-General's Office,

Albany, June 16, 1910.

Hon. Samuel S. Koenig, *Secretary of State, Albany, N. Y.:*

Dear Sir.— I acknowledge receipt of your favor of the 3rd inst. asking for my opinion as to whether an amended certificate changing the name of a corporation is entitled to be filed under the following state of facts:

On May 22, 1910, a certificate of incorporation was filed in your office pursuant to section 2 of the Business Corporations Law in which it was stated that the name of the corporation was to be " Boehm & Mack." This certificate has been filed, recorded and indexed in your office, and now the incorporators want to file an amended certificate changing the name of the corporation to " Boehm & Mack Co."

Section 7 of the General Corporation Law provides:

"If in the original or amended certificate of incorporation of any corporation, or if in a supplemental certificate of any corporation any informality exists or if any such certificate contain any matter not authorized by law to be stated therein, or if the proof or acknowledgment thereof shall be defective, the corporators or directors of the corporation may make and file an amended certificate correcting such informality or defect . . ."

In my opinion to you on May 18, 1910, in the Neil, Ward & Company matter, I held that adding an " e " to the word " Ward " was not a change of the name of the corporation. The defect there was obviously a stenographic error and by adding the letter " e " merely corrected an apparent misspelling of a proper name. Under the peculiar circumstances there, the incorporators were clearly entitled to correct the defect by an amended certificate, it being, in my opinion, an informality within the meaning of said section 7 quoted.

Here, however, we have an attempt to change the name of the corporation by an amended certificate which cannot be permitted except on application to the court, as provided in sections 60–65 of the General Corporation Law.

Yours very truly,

EDWARD R. O'MALLEY,

Attorney-General.

Highway Law — Article 11, *Section* 282 — *Motor Vehicles — Chauffeurs.*

Minor under eighteen years of age may not operate motor vehicle upon public highway even though he be the owner of such vehicle.

STATE OF NEW YORK,

ATTORNEY-GENERAL'S OFFICE,

ALBANY, *July* 22, 1910.

Hon. SAMUEL S. KOENIG, *Secretary of State, Albany, N. Y.:*

Dear Sir.— Your letter of the 14th instant requesting my opinion as to whether or not a person under eighteen years of age, who is the owner of a motor vehicle, may operate or drive the same upon the public highways under the restrictions stated in subdivision 2 of section 282 of article 11 of the Highway Law, is received.

I think the question submitted should be answered in the negative. One of the objects in the enactment of the additional article of the Highway Law, being chapter 374 of the laws of 1910, was to provide revenue for the maintenance and repair of the improved roads of the State under the direction of the State Commission of Highways; also another purpose was to furnish additional means for the identification of the owner or driver of such vehicles. It is evident, however, that another object of the statute was to require the exercise of greater care in the operation of motor vehicles and to protect the public from accidents due oftentimes to the operation of such vehicles by careless, incompetent and inexperienced drivers. It is a well known fact that serious accidents occur almost daily, which are due to the negligence, incompetency and inexperience of the operators of motor vehicles. The provision of this statute as to the examination of chauffeurs not only as to their competency but also to their character, and the adoption of new regulations as to the operation of such vehicles, show that one of the purposes of this legislation was to safeguard the public as above stated. The legislative judgment is clearly expressed, that a person should be at least eighteen years of age before he has judgment, discretion and experience sufficient to qualify him to operate a motor vehicle upon the public highways. Such intent and judgment are farther shown by the provision that no person shall receive a license as a chauffeur unless he is eighteen years of age or upwards, and that a person under that age shall not be permitted to operate such a vehicle unless accompanied by a duly licensed chauffeur or the owner of the vehicle being operated. If a minor who is under eighteen years of age, although he is the owner of such a vehicle, may operate or drive the same upon the public highways unattended or without the presence of a person of discretion, or a person who can control the movements of such a vehicle, then one of the beneficent purposes of the statute will be circumvented or defeated.

While it may be contended that a minor under eighteen years of age, who is the owner of a motor vehicle and has received a certificate of registration, should be allowed to operate the same as an adult, yet the restriction imposed by said subdivision 2 appears to be a reasonable regulation under the police power of the State. Infants may hold title to property, yet under the principles of the common law and by statutory enactments they are not permitted to dispose of and use their property in many respects as are adults. Furthermore, statutes enacted under the police power of the State for the preservation of the public safety, etc., are not to be construed as strictly as other penal statutes. The phrase "or the owner of the motor vehicle operated" as used in said paragraph contemplates, in my opinion, an adult owner or an owner who is over eighteen years of age and who can control the operations of such a vehicle. If a person under eighteen years of age owns and also operates or drives a motor vehicle, then he cannot be accompanied by the owner of the same vehicle. In other words, he cannot be a companion to himself or be accompanied by any person so as to comply with the restrictions imposed by said subdivision.

While more explicit language might have been used in framing this paragraph, a reasonable construction should be given to it, as the intent of such provision is plain.

Yours respectfully,

EDWARD R. O'MALLEY,

Attorney-General.

Corporations — Voting Rights of Stockholders.

Two ways in which voting rights may be differentiated: First by provision in original charter: Second, by provision defining rights of preferred stockholders; whether amended certificate of incorporation may be accepted by Secretary of State.

STATE OF NEW YORK,

ATTORNEY-GENERAL'S OFFICE,

ALBANY, *August* 1, 1910.

Hon. SAMUEL S. KOENIG, *Secretary of State, Albany, N. Y.:*

My Dear Sir.— I acknowledge your letter of the 27th ultimo in which you ask my opinion regarding certain matters relative to the changing of voting rights of the stockholders of a corporation. In this connection you call my attention to the fact that there are apparently only two ways in which the voting rights of the holders of different classes of stock may be differentiated. The first of these is by provision in the original certificate of incorporation which therefore becomes an agreement entered into with the unanimous consent of the incorporators and subsequent stockholders. The second way is by a provision defining the rights of preferred stockholders in a certificate of classification of stock filed pursuant to section 61 of the Stock Corporation Law as part of an amended certificate. This may be done with the consent of two-thirds of the stockholders given at a meeting. You also call my attention to the fact that under section 18 of the Stock Corporation Law, an amendment of the certificate of incorporation may be made with a vote of only three-fifths of the stockholders.

In view of the foregoing considerations, you ask my opinion as to whether you should accept an amended certificate of incorporation under either of the following conditions:

"First. Where the purpose of the amendment is to change, alter or redefine voting rights, and it is shown that only the vote required by § 18 of the Stock Corporation Law, has been obtained, to wit, that of a majority of the directors of the stockholders."

"Second. Where the purpose of the amendment is as above, but it is shown that all of the stockholders have voted in favor of the resolution to amend."

Under previous opinions rendered by me, it has been pointed out that under the decision in People ex rel. Browne v. Koenig, 133 A. D., 756, the validity of the classification of stock which provided that preferred stockholders should have no voting power in certain contingencies was sustained on the ground that it was an agreement contained in the original certificate and acquiesced in by all the stockholders. This reasoning would clearly have no application where any of the stockholders failed to give their consent. I therefore advise you that in my judgment, under the first statement of facts above set forth, you are not authorized to file the amended certificate of incorporation, but that under the second state of facts you are authorized, since in the latter case, all the stockholders having consented, the situation is the same in effect as if the provision were contained in the original certificate of incorporation.

Very truly yours,
EDWARD R. O'MALLEY,
Attorney-General.

Education Law (Amended) — (Chapter 607, L. 1910) — School Directors.

Notice of election should contain name, same as other town officers elected at general election. When elected in odd numbered year their names should be printed on same ballots as the names of candidates for other officers voted for at the general election. When elected in even numbered years in towns holding town meetings at time of general election, their names should appear on _separate_ ballots with other town officers. When election is held at any other time, names on _separate_ ballots.

(See opinion October 4, 1910).

STATE OF NEW YORK,
ATTORNEY-GENERAL'S OFFICE,
ALBANY, August 1, 1910.

Hon. SAMUEL S. KOENIG, _Secretary of State, Albany, N. Y.:_

Dear Sir.— I acknowledge the receipt of a letter addressed to you by M. D. Watkins, county clerk of Tioga county, and referred by you to me, in which he wishes to be informed, in substance, if

under chapter 607, Laws of 1910, the school directors therein
mentioned are to be voted for at the general election of 1910, and
if so, do you include them in your notice of election, or is he to
include them in his additional notice.

I also have a letter from Albert II. Overacker, county clerk of
Tompkins county, in which he asks whether the names of such
directors should be on the general election ticket, and in which
he says you referred him to this office for an answer.

In this opinion to you I will answer both letters and the several
questions therein asked.

Chapter 607, Laws of 1910, amends article 14 of chapter 27,
Laws of 1909. Section 382 of the amended article provides, in
part:

> " Two school directors shall be elected for each town at
> the general election held in the year 1910. One of such
> directors shall be elected to serve until January 1, 1913, and
> the other shall be elected to serve until January 1, 1916. A
> director shall be elected at the general election in 1912, and
> every fifth year thereafter and one shall be elected in 1915
> and every fifth year thereafter. The term of office of the
> directors elected in 1912 and thereafter shall commence on
> the first day of January following their election and continue
> for five years."

By this provision, two directors are to be elected at the general
election held in the year 1910, and thereafter school directors are
to be elected at a general election at the times therein mentioned.

You will note that the last sentence of the section provides:

> " Such directors shall be elected in the same manner that
> town officers are elected at town meetings held at the time
> of a general election, and the provisions of the election law
> relating to the nomination and election of such town officers
> shall apply to the nomination and election of such directors."

Paragraph 2 of section 293 of the Election Law provides that
each county clerk shall, upon receipt of a notice of election from
the Secretary of State provided for in the first paragraph of the
same section, publish it and shall also publish as a part of such
notice, a list of all town officers who may lawfully be voted for
at such election by the voters of such county or any part thereof.

School directors are town officers, and as hereinbefore stated, are to be voted for at a general election. Therefore it would be the duty of the county clerk to publish a notice of their election in the same manner as he is required to publish the notice of election of the town officers to be voted for at the general election as provided for by the Election Law referred to.

The ballot upon which the names of such directors should appear is prescribed in the last paragraph of section 341 of the Election Law, when read in connection with the provision above quoted. Such paragraph provides, as far as material to the question:

"In towns in which town meetings are held at the time of the general election in an odd numbered year, the names of the candidates for town offices shall be printed on the same ballots as the names of candidates for other offices voted for in such towns at such general elections. In towns in which town meetings are held on general election day, in an even numbered year, the names of candidates for town officers shall be printed on separate ballots; such ballots and sample ballots for town officers shall be provided by the town clerk in like manner and in the same form as at a town meeting held at any other time * * *."

In complying with section 382 aforesaid wherein it provides that such directors shall be elected in the same manner, etc., as town officers elected at town meetings held at the time of the general election, and having in mind the law providing the manner of election of such officers above referred to, the conclusion would be that when school directors of a town are to be elected in an odd numbered year, their names should be printed on the same ballots as the names of candidates for other offices voted for in such town at the general election of that year. When they are to be elected in an even numbered year in towns holding their town meetings at the time of the general election, their names are to be printed with other town officers to be voted for upon a separate ballot, and in towns holding their town meetings at any other time

14

than at the time of the general election, their names are to be printed upon a separate ballot; such ballots to be provided by the town clerk as provided in said section 341.

Yours very truly,

EDWARD R. O'MALLEY,

Attorney-General.

Motor Vehicle Law — Section 281 — Chauffeurs' Licenses.
Utility Car Company (motor cycles), not required to furnish licensed chauffeurs for their machines.

STATE OF NEW YORK,

ATTORNEY-GENERAL'S OFFICE,

ALBANY, *August* 4, 1910.

Hon. SAMUEL S. KOENIG, *Secretary of State, Albany, N. Y.:*

Dear Sir.— I beg to acknowledge your favor of August 3d with the accompanying letter from House, Grossman & Vorhaus, asking for an opinion in regard to the Callan Law as it affects the Utility Car Company.

Section 281 of the law in question provides that the term " motor vehicle " as used therein, except where otherwise expressly provided, shall include all vehicles, etc., except " motor bicycles, motor cycles," etc.

The description of the vehicle contained in the letter above referred to would indicate that the machines come fairly within the term " motor cycle " as that term is generally understood and defined in the later dictionaries. I find nothing in the law wherein it seems to be otherwise expressly provided and I am of the opinion that the operation of such machines is not within the provisions of the Motor Vehicle Law so as to require for their operation a duly licensed chauffeur.

Respectfully yours,

EDWARD R. O'MALLEY,

Attorney-General.

, . Corporations.

Gragnano Company, formed for purposes of receiving for safe keeping moneys and other property. Secretary of State should not file certificate of incorporation under the Business Corporations Law; it is properly within the provisions of the Banking Law.

(See sections 66, 300, Banking Law).

STATE OF NEW YORK,

ATTORNEY-GENERAL'S OFFICE,

ALBANY, *September* 1, 1910.

Hon. SAMUEL S. KOENIG, *Secretary of State, Albany, N. Y.:*

Dear Sir.— I acknowledge your letter of the 30th ultimo in which you enclose certificate of incorporation of the Gragnano Company which has been presented to your office for filing under the Business Corporations Law, and request my opinion as to whether or not you may properly file the same.

Among the objects of the corporation is the following:

"(d) To receive from customers for safe-keeping only, moneys, or other property, said moneys not being subject to be drawn upon by check or draft, but solely on demand, and not subject to the payment of interest thereon. The business of the corporation shall not be conducted as a banking business in any respect whatsoever."

Section 2 of the Business Corporations Law provides that a company may be incorporated "for any lawful business purpose or purposes other than a moneyed corporation, or a corporation provided for by the banking, the insurance, the railroad or the Transportation Corporation Law, * * *."

Section 22 of the General Corporation Law provides:

"No corporation except a corporation formed under or subject to the banking laws, shall by any implication or construction be deemed to possess the power of carrying on the business of discounting bills, notes or other evidences of debt,

of receiving deposits, or buying and selling bills of exchange,
or shall issue bills, notes or other evidences of debt for cir-
culation as money."

It is my opinion that under the foregoing provisions of law
you would not be authorized in filing the proposed certificate.
The fact that it is stated that the business of the corporation is
not to be conducted as a banking business can have no bearing
upon the situation, as the very purpose specified, namely, receiving
moneys or other property for safe-keeping, is included in the provisions of the Banking Law.

See Banking Law, §§ 66 and 300.

Very truly yours,

EDWARD R. O'MALLEY,

Attorney-General.

Highway Law — Section 285 — Motor Vehicles.
' Exemptions and privileges " granted to nonresidents operating
their machines on a public highway.
(See opinion August 16, 1910).

STATE OF NEW YORK,

ATTORNEY-GENERAL'S OFFICE,

ALBANY, *September 2, 1910.*

Hon. SAMUEL S. KOENIG, *Secretary of State, Albany, N. Y.:*

Dear Sir.— I have your request for my opinion as to whether
owners of automobiles, residing in states which permit residents
of this State to use their roads for a limited period of time without
registration of payment of a fee, are entitled to the benefits of
section 285 of the Highway Law, chapter 374, Laws of 1910.
This section provides that the requirements of the law as to
registration and the display of registration numbers shall not
apply to a motor vehicle owned by a nonresident of this State.
This exemption, however, is subject to the following proviso:

" The provisions of this section, however, shall be operative
as to a motor vehicle owned by a nonresident of this state
only to the extent that under the laws of the foreign country,

state, territory or federal district of his residence like exemptions and privileges are granted to motor vehicles duly registered under the laws of and owned by residents of this state."

As I advised you in my opinion of August 16, 1910, the words "like exemptions and privileges" in the above proviso can refer only to the exemption from registration and display of registration numbers, since these are the only exemptions granted by our law. It would follow, therefore, that if any State or country grants such exemption from registration to residents of this State, its residents are entitled to exemption in this State "to the extent" that the like exemption is granted by that State or country to our residents. In other words, if under the laws of another State, residents of this State are entitled to exemptions from registration for ten days in every year, the same privilege to the same extent should be accorded residents of that State under our law.

There is nothing in this opinion which in any way conflicts with my opinion to you under date of August 16, 1910. In that case you asked me whether residents of states which granted temporary licenses to nonresidents were entitled to exemption under our law, and I was compelled to hold that they were not. Such provision does not constitute in any sense an exemption from registration, and there is no machinery provided by our law for the granting of temporary licenses.

Very truly yours,

EDWARD R. O'MALLEY,

Attorney-General.

Election Law — Section 541 — Corrupt Practices Act.
General opinion on various amendments to the statute.

STATE OF NEW YORK,

ATTORNEY-GENERAL'S OFFICE,

ALBANY, *September 24, 1910.*

Hon. SAMUEL S. KOENIG, *Secretary of State, Albany, N. Y.:*

Dear Sir.— Concerning the questions asked of you as to the applicability of the recent amendments to the so-called Corrupt

Practices Act, I have the honor to render you the following
opinion:

The questions are:

First: Do delegates elected at primary elections as delegates
to party conventions come within this act, and if so are they required to file election expenses?

Second: Do members of a party committee, namely a ward or
town committee, elected at primary elections come within this
law, and are they required to file statements of their expenses?

Third: Under the definition of a convention do members of
the general committee of a party chosen by the ward or town committee come within this act? And are they required to file a
statement of their account?

Fourth: Do delegates who are chosen by a convention as representatives to another convention come within this act, and are they
required to file a statement of their expenses? As an example,
do delegates to the State convention elected from the Assembly
District Convention come within this act?

By the enactment of chapters 429, 430, 438 and 439 of the
Laws of 1910, it was sought to make applicable to elections at
primaries and party conventions the provisions of the Corrupt
Practices Act, which formerly had been applicable only to general
elections.

The questions above submitted necessitate the determination of
how that purpose has been actually accomplished by the wording
of the statute with reference to delegates and committeemen.

Section 541 of the Election Law, as amended by chapter 429
of the Laws of 1910, reads as follows:

"Section 541. Statement of campaign payments not made
through political committee. Any person, including a candidate, who to promote the success or defeat of a political
party, or to aid or influence the election or defeat of a candidate or candidates for public office; or to aid or influence
the election or defeat of a candidate for nomination at a
primary election or convention, including all proceedings prior
to such primary election, or of a candidate for any office
whether public or not to be voted for at a primary election,
or to aid, influence or prevent the nomination of a candidate

by petition under the provisions of the primary election law, directly or indirectly, himself or through another person, shall give, pay, expend or contribute, or shall promise to give, pay, expend or contribute, any money or other valuable thing except to the chairman, treasurer or a member of a political committee, or to an agent duly authorized thereto in writing by such committee, or to a candidate or an agent of such candidate authorized by the candidate thereto in writing, or except for personal expenses as hereinafter provided, shall file the statement required by section five hundred and forty-six, and shall be subject to all the duties by this chapter required of a political committee or the treasurer thereof."

The positions of delegate and committeeman if covered by this section are covered by the following words:

"Any person, including a candidate, who * * * to aid or influence the election or defeat * * * of a candidate for any office whether public or not to be voted for at a primary election, * * * etc."

By the use of the words "any office whether public or not," it is my opinion it was not intended to apply to all positions for which persons are chosen or selected at the primaries. A delegate in the ordinary and common understanding of the word is not an officer. He is chosen to represent a certain portion of his party in a gathering termed a convention. It is true that he is clothed with certain powers and charged with the performance of certain duties and might be considered under some definitions of the term "officer" made by lexicographers, but the application of the Election Law must be determined by the interpretation placed upon the word "delegate" by the Legislature in the enactment of the law. An examination of this statute discloses that a distinction has always been made between the position of delegate and officers of the party. In section 2 of the Election Law under the article containing general provisions for primaries is found the following:

"As used in articles two and three, a convention is an assemblage of delegates representing a political party or independent body duly convened for the purpose of nominating candidates for public office, electing delegates to other conventions, electing *officers* for party or independent organizations, etc."

Under section 4, subdivision 2 is found the following:

"Candidates and delegates and officers of the organization or committee shall be chosen by ballot."

Under section 49 is found the following:

"* * * such notice shall specify * * * the conventions, committees and offices for which delegates, members or candidates, as the case may be, will be voted for thereat. * * *."

In my opinion the above provisions show that the Legislature did not consider a delegate, whether chosen at a primary election, at a convention or by a committee, to be an officer. It must follow, therefore, that the requirements of section 541 do not apply to delegates.

As to members of ward or town committees or other party committees, elected at primary elections, I am of the opinion that persons so chosen are officers within the meaning of the law and are in that respect distinguished from delegates. In this I am fortified by the following provisions of the Election Law.

"Section 64. * * * The times when committees elected at primary elections shall take *office* shall be determined by the rules and regulations of the respective parties, * * *. * * * Members of committees in villages shall be apportioned and shall hold *office* as shall be provided in the rules and regulations of parties. * * *."

I am therefore of the opinion that delegates, whether chosen at primary elections or party conventions, are not required as such delegates to file the statement provided for in section 541. If the Legislature had intended to apply the law to delegates, it could have used the word "delegate" as distinguished from "officer" in the act and thus have made clear its meaning. If it is desirable to include delegates, it is an easy matter to have an amendment made to the law at the next session of the Legislature.

I am also of the opinion that members of committees whether chosen at primaries, committees or conventions, are within the meaning of section 541 and are required to file a statement of such expenses not excepted under that provision whether such expenses are incurred for their own selection as such committeemen or for the selection of candidates for public office.

Yours very truly,
EDWARD R. O'MALLEY,
Attorney-General.

Public Lands Law — Section 84 — State Forest Preserve.
Discovery of mines upon. Whether the Secretary of State shall file notices of.

STATE OF NEW YORK,

ATTORNEY-GENERAL'S OFFICE,

ALBANY, November 3, 1910.

Hon. SAMUEL S. KOENIG, *Secretary of State, Albany, N. Y.:*

Dear Sir.— I beg to acknowledge receipt of your communication of October 22, 1910, together with the accompanying letter to you from the Forest, Fish and Game Commission, wherein you ask my opinion as to whether you shall accept notices of discovery of mines upon lands which belong to the State and are located within the forest preserve.

In reply I beg to say that article 7 of chapter 46 of the Consolidated Laws, known as the Public Lands Law, provides for the working of mines, the private property therein, the notice of discovery and the bounty to the discoverer, and, further, provides at section 84 that nothing in the act shall

> " Be construed to give any person a right to enter upon or break up the lands of any other person or of the state or to work any mines in such lands unless the written consent of the owner thereof or of the commissioners of the land office, when the lands belong to the state, shall be previously obtained. Permission to erect buildings for working mines upon

state lands *within the forest preserve* may be given by the forest commission and elsewhere by the commissioners of the land office when such lands are entirely denuded of timber or when such commission or commissioners are satisfied that the erection or occupation of such buildings will not be detrimental to the interests of the state. Nothing in this article shall authorize any person working a mine upon state lands to cut or destroy any timber whatever except such trees as it may be actually necessary to remove in order to uncover or make a road to such mine   *   *   *."

The act in terms seems to give to the discoverer the right to assert his claim of discovery of a mine upon state lands, even when such lands are within the forest preserve, by filing with the Secretary of State the notice provided by statute. The right to enter upon the lands of the forest preserve to work such mines, however, can only be given, under the statute, by the authorities and under the circumstances therein mentioned. It may well be believed that, when such permission is sought, the question whether it may be legally given in view of the provisions of article 7, section 7 of the State Constitution will prove a bar to the granting of any such permission, but that question is not up for consideration here. It is sufficient to say that the statute seems to permit the filing of a notice of discovery of a mine upon State lands within the forest preserve, and, in my opinion the Secretary of State has no discretion to refuse to file a notice of discovery simply upon the ground that the mine is located upon such lands.

Respectfully yours,

EDWARD R. O'MALLEY,

Attorney-General.

Highway Law — Section 282 — Subdivision 8 — Article 2 — Motor Vehicles.

Manufacturer or dealer in motor vehicles duly registered may upon purchase of car operate such car under regular dealer's license, provided it be the style and type described in dealer's registration, and is purchased for resale, and notice of such transfer is made under section 8.

STATE OF NEW YORK,
ATTORNEY-GENERAL'S OFFICE,
ALBANY, *December* 1, 1910.

Hon. THOMAS F. FENNELL, *Deputy Secretary of State, Albany, N. Y.:*

Dear Sir.— I have the honor to reply herewith to your communication in reference to the interpretation of subdivision 8, section 282, article 2, of the Highway Law. The question presented is:

May a duly registered manufacturer or dealer, upon the purchase of a registered car, properly operate the same under regular dealer's license without further complying with the provisions of subdivision 8, above mentioned?

Subdivision 8 provides that upon the sale or transfer of a motor vehicle registered in accordance with the statute, the vendor shall immediately give notice of such sale with the name and residence of the vendee to the Secretary of State. Section 284 of the act provides that every person, firm, association or corporation manufacturing or dealing in motor vehicles may, instead of registering each vehicle, make a verified application for a general distinctive number for all vehicles owned or controlled by such manufacturer or dealer, which application must contain a brief description of each style or type of vehicle dealt in.

The first provision evidently is for the purpose of keeping a definite record of the name of the owner of each registered vehicle. The second provision gives a privilege to dealers to register all their vehicles under one number. In case a dealer or manufacturer purchases a duly registered vehicle, I see no reason why the spirit and also the letter of the law is not complied with if he thereafter operates that car under his dealer's number, provided the car is one of the style or type described in the application for the dealer's

registration, and provided also the car is purchased for resale or
for the same purpose as those usually operated under dealer's or
manufacturer's registration. In order to carry out the intent of
the act, however, so that a complete register may be maintained
of each separate vehicle, it is obvious that notice of the sale or
transfer to the dealer should be given as provided in subdivision 8.
With this qualification, therefore, my answer to your question is
in the affirmative.

The papers submitted to me are herewith returned.

Yours respectfully,

EDWARD R. O'MALLEY,

Attorney-General.

OPINIONS RENDERED THE STATE COMPTROLLER.

County Law.

Compensation of Supervisors, county of Greene, under chapter
263, Laws of 1903, a special act applicable to that county.
Amendment by chapter 414, Laws of 1908 recognizes the act
as still in existence.

STATE OF NEW YORK,

ATTORNEY-GENERAL'S OFFICE,

ALBANY, *January* 6, 1910.

Hon. CLARK WILLIAMS, *State Comptroller, Albany, N. Y.:*

Dear Sir.— Replying to the request from your Deputy Comptroller, Mr. Perine, under date of the 28th ultimo, as to whether
chapter 263, Laws of 1903, has been repealed by subsequent amendments to the County Law, I beg to advise as follows:

The County Law originally provided in section 23 (chapter 686,
Laws of 1892) for the compensation of supervisors, but excepted
certain counties therein named. The county of Greene was not
so excepted. Chapter 263, Laws of 1903, is a special local act
applicable only to the county of Greene, which fixes the compensation of supervisors in that county. Subsequent to the enactment
of this law, section 23 of the County Law referred to above, was
amended by chapter 20, Laws of 1905, and chapter 482, Laws
of 1907, both being amendments in respect to the county of

Niagara. It was amended by chapter 438, Laws of 1908, in respect to the counties of Schenectady and Steuben. Chapter 414, Laws of 1908, amended the special act in reference to Greene county, referred to above, as found in chapter 263, Laws of 1903, in respect to the compensation of the clerk of the board of supervisors.

Under these circumstances, it is my opinion that the act of 1903 making the office of supervisor in the county of Greene a salaried office, has not been repealed by subsequent amendments. It is well settled that a special and local statute providing for a particular case or locality is not repealed or modified by a subsequent statute, general in its terms, unless the intent to repeal or alter the prior act is manifest although the language of the general act would but for the special law include the latter.

> People ex rel. Leary v. Knox, 166 N. Y. 444.
> Clinton v. Knell, 125 App. Div. 157.

It is apparent that chapter 263, Laws of 1903, is a special and local statute relating only to the county of Greene and applicable to that county alone. Therefore, within the rule laid down in the above cases and many others, the Legislature is not presumed to have intended to repeal it by any of the foregoing amendments unless such intention is manifest. There is no specific repeal of the special act in any of these enactments. Moreover, by amending the special statute by chapter 414, Laws of 1908, the Legislature has expressly recognized its existence as amended. The enacting clause of this amendment is significant in that it enacts that

> " Section two of chapter two hundred and sixty-three of the laws of nineteen hundred and three entitled ' An act to make the office of supervisor of Greene County a salaried office, and to fix the compensation of the clerk of the board of supervisors,' "

is amended as therein provided. The amendment itself, although of a different section of the act than that affecting the salary of the supervisors, thus clearly recognizes that the entire act is still in existence. Yours respectfully,

EDWARD R. O'MALLEY,
Attorney-General.

Racing Associations.

Entrance fee of trotting or race meetings should constitute a part of gross receipts. Interest received on deposit of such receipts should be treated as an investment receipt rather than a part of the gross receipts.

STATE OF NEW YORK,

ATTORNEY-GENERAL'S OFFICE,

ALBANY, *January* 6, 1910.

Hon. CLARK WILLIAMS, *State Comptroller, Albany, N. Y.:*

Dear Sir.— I have your letter of the 3d inst., in which you ask my opinion, first, as to whether entrance moneys of trotting or running race meetings constitute gross receipts within the meaning of section 12, chapter 380, Laws of 1896; and, second, whether interest received by associations conducting such meetings, on their deposits, constitute a part of such gross receipts.

I have given these questions my attention. Chapter 380, Laws of 1896, is now embodied in the Membership Corporation Law, and section 292 of that law provides the following tax:

"Annual tax on gross receipts. A tax of five per centum upon the gross receipts of every corporation, person or persons from every trotting or running race meeting or meetings held within the state of New York, either under the provisions of this article or otherwise, shall be paid by any person or persons, firm or association or corporation holding such races, * * *."

It is my opinion that entrance fees constitute a part of the gross receipts received from the trotting or running race meeting at which they are charged, and that they therefore fall within the contemplation of the statute. In this regard, I agree with the ruling made by one of my predecessors, to which you refer, and with the uniform practice of your department, as stated by you.

In the second place, it is my opinion that interest received on deposits is not to be regarded as a receipt from a trotting or running race meeting. It is rather a receipt from an investment made by the person or corporation and as such does not come within the scope of this section. In this respect also I agree with the conclusion reached by your department.

Yours respectfully,

EDWARD R. O'MALLEY,

Attorney-General.

Canal Law (Consolidated) — Sections 61, 64.

Bonds of Division and Resident Engineers in sum of $40,000 legal and binding.

STATE OF NEW YORK,

ATTORNEY-GENERAL'S OFFICE,

ALBANY, *January* 17, 1910.

Hon. CLARK WILLIAMS, *State Comptroller, Albany, N. Y.:*

Dear Sir.— I beg to acknowledge your letter of January 12th, asking my opinion as to whether a bond given by a division and resident engineer in the sum of $40,000 would be legal and binding upon him and his sureties.

Section 61 of the Consolidated Canal Law provides that " division and resident engineers before entering upon the duties of their offices must execute an official undertaking in a sum not exceeding $20,000, to be fixed by the Comptroller."

Section 64 of the same law provides for advances of money to be made to the division and resident engineers for the purpose of meeting expenses of the engineer's department upon his division, and further provides that " advances unaccounted for to a division engineer shall, at no time, exceed $40,000."

You state that there are certain periods when advances to division engineers up to the sum of $40,000 are imperative. According to the provisions of section 61 you would not be authorized to require a division engineer to furnish a bond to exceed $20,000, but if a resident engineer and his surety should voluntarily execute and deliver a bond in the sum of $40,000 in my opinion it would be legal and binding upon them. The fact that the bond

was not required by law to be given would not be any defense
to the surety.

In the case of Museo v. United Surety Company, 196 N. Y.
359, which was an action to recover upon the bond of a steamship ticket agent given pursuant to the requirements of the General Business Law and in which the surety attempted to defend
upon the ground that the law requiring the giving of the bond was
unconstitutional, the court, while holding the law constitutional,
held that even if the law were unconstitutional this would not be
a defense for the surety.

In the analagous case of a resident engineer the same principle
would apply. If a resident engineer gave a bond in the sum of
$40,000, the fact that such a bond was not required by law would
not be any defense in an action brought to recover upon the bond.

Yours respectfully,

EDWARD R. O'MALLEY,

Attorney-General.

----

*General Business Law — Section 74, Article 7 — Private
Detectives.*

Badges worn by private detectives shall be issued by the State
Comptroller. Wear or display of other than such badge or
device, as provided by section 74, constitutes a misdemeanor,
and shall cause revocation of license.

(See opinion September 20, 1909).

STATE OF NEW YORK,

ATTORNEY-GENERAL'S OFFICE,

ALBANY, *January 18, 1910.*

Hon. CLARK WILLIAMS, *State Comptroller, Albany, N. Y.:*

Dear Sir.— Referring to my opinion to your predecessor under
date of September 20, in reference to the law requiring detectives
to be licensed, which had particular reference to the case of Lynn
P. Stoughton, my attention is now specifically called to a badge
which it is said was issued by Mr. Stoughton to one of his em-

ployes, and upon which there is represented the coat of arms of the State and the words " Stoughton's Detective " in large letters, above which appears the word " Sergeant " and also a number. I am informed also that badges of like design have been issued to his employes generally.

Section 74 of article 7 of the General Business Law provides, in relation to certificates and badges issued to and worn by private detectives under its provisions, that the Comptroller shall issue to a licensee a badge of such design as he may provide and such licensee is not permitted to part with the custody thereof. The section further provides that any person

> " Who shall wear or display any license, certificate, shield or badge purporting to authorize the holder or wearer thereof to act as a private detective unless the same shall have been duly issued pursuant to the provisions of this article, shall be guilty of a misdemeanor. Failure to comply with the provisions of this section shall be sufficient cause for revocation of such license."

The badge in question certainly purports to inform the world that its wearer has authority to act as a detective and is such. The intent is plainly expressed. This badge was not issued pursuant to the provisions of article 7 and it is a violation of law to wear the same. The issue of such badges by a duly licensed detective to his employes seems adequate cause for the revocation of his license under section 74.

Yours respectfully,

EDWARD R. O'MALLEY,

Attorney-General.

County Clerk — Ulster County.

Deputies and assistants in office of. Board of Supervisors no
authority to appropriate money by levying assessments on
taxable property to pay the salaries of deputies and assistants
in the office of the County Clerk. Chapter 103, Laws 1906,
provides for salary of County Clerk and four assistants, additional assistants to serve without expense to county.

STATE OF NEW YORK,

ATTORNEY-GENERAL'S OFFICE,

ALBANY, *February* 4, 1910.

Hon. CLARK WILLIAMS, *State Comptroller, Albany, N. Y.:*

Dear Sir.— I have your inquiry of January 12th in reference
to the legality of a resolution adopted by the Board of Supervisors
of Ulster county raising by levy and assessment upon the taxable
property of the county the sum of $600, to be disbursed for the
services of an attendant or attendants in the county clerk's office
of that county.

From the correspondence attached to your letter it appears that
the county treasurer has raised the question of whether or not he
can legally make this disbursement.

The office of county clerk of Ulster county is a salaried office,
having been made so by chapter 103 of the Laws of 1906. This
act specifies the salary of the county clerk and of four assistants,
to hold office at the pleasure of the clerk, and in section 8 provides that " the salaries and compensation of the said county clerk
and of his assistants shall be paid monthly by the county treasurer
upon the certificate of the county clerk showing the amount due
to each and for what due. Nothing herein contained shall prohibit said county clerk from appointing such special deputy clerks
or additional assistants as he may deem wise, but such special
deputy clerks or additional assistants shall serve without expense
to the county of Ulster."

In my judgment the foregoing provisions of law prohibit the
Board of Supervisors from appropriating money to pay deputies
or assistants in the office of the county clerk in addition to those

specially provided for in the act and any payment of county moneys for assistants in the office of the county clerk, in addition to these specified, would be illegal.

Yours respectfully,

EDWARD R. O'MALLEY,

Attorney-General.

Detectives — Licenses — Corporations.

Underwriters Protective Association, conducting business along the lines of " special investigations," supplying information as to " whereabouts of individuals," " character of prospective tenants," " resources of delinquent debtors," etc., should procure license under section 70. General Business Law.

(See opinion April 21, 1909, p. 350; July 30, 1909, p. 586 Rep.; September 20, 1909, p. 374 Rep.; January 18, 1910; February 4, 1910; February 10, 1910).

STATE OF NEW YORK,

ATTORNEY-GENERAL'S OFFICE,

ALBANY, February 4, 1910.

Hon. CLARK WILLIAMS, State Comptroller, Albany, N. Y.:

Dear Sir.— I am in receipt of your letter of the 2nd inst., with the following inclosures, viz: a letter from C. J. Hine, President of Underwriters Protective Association, and a pamphlet of such association evidently used for advertising purposes. You ask that I give an opinion whether it is necessary for this association to procure a detective license in order to legally transact the business now carried on by it.

Section 70 of the General Business Law provides:

> " No person nor partnership shall engage in the business of private detective for hire or reward, or advertise such business to be that of detective or as conducting a detective agency, without having first obtained a license so to do, as hereinafter provided, from the comptroller of the State of New York, and no person, partnership or corporation shall

engage in the business for hire or reward of furnishing or
supplying information as to the personal character of any
person or firm, or as to the character or kind of business and
occupation of any person, firm or corporation, or own or conduct a bureau or agency for the above mentioned purposes
except as to the financial rating of persons, firms or corporations, without having first obtained a license so to do as
hereinafter provided, from the Comptroller of the State of
New York."

The information before me as to the exact nature and form of
the business carried on by the Underwriter's Protective Association is very meagre. For instance, the letter of Mr. Hine states:
" We furnish information to fire and burglary companies under a
special confidential contract," and no further statement is made
relating to the nature of the information or the contents of the
contract. It is unnecessary to state that an opinion cannot be
predicated upon such a statement. The letter also states that the
association reports on fire losses throughout the United States and
furnishes fire insurance companies with " trade information on
business firms." What the nature of these reports is and what
the " trade information on business firms " consists of is not
shown in the papers before me.

The advertising pamphlet, however, recites the lines of information supplied to clients by the association under the following
headings: " Whereabouts of individuals," " resources of delinquent debtors " and " character of prospective tenants." The
pamphlet also states, " besides our reporting department, we hold
ourselves ready to make special investigations along any of the
above, *or other lines,* that may be required."

The question to be determined in this case is, does furnishing
such information bring the association within the provisions of
section 70.

Discovery of the " whereabouts of individuals " would certainly seem to be one of the usual and ordinary branches of a
private detective's business.

Furnishing information as to the " character of prospective
tenants " appears also to be a prohibited business unless a license
is procured. The information furnished by the association, as

far as the papers disclose, seems to go to the personal character
of the prospective tenant. This is further evidenced by the statement under the heading, "character of prospective tenants" as
follows: " This is the only concern in the country which can
give the property owner reliable information as to whether such
prospective tenant would affect the insurance on the building, or
of other tenants."

" Special investigations along any of the above *or other lines,*
that may be required," which the association holds itself out as
ready to make, also without further explanation seems to be an
advertisement to conduct investigations along lines open only to
licensees under such act.

I would therefore answer that from the information before me,
it would seem that the association is conducting business such as a
licensee only under section 70 of the General Business Law may
lawfully conduct.

Yours very truly,

EDWARD R. O'MALLEY,

Attorney-General.

Detectives — Licenses — Corporations.

International Detective Bureau of New York city. Employment
of detectives duly licensed, not sufficient where corporation
itself is carrying on a detective agency. Under section 70
of the General Business Law, it should procure a license.

(See opinions April 21, 1909; September 20, 1909; January 18,
1910; February 4, 1910; February 10, 1910).

STATE OF NEW YORK,

Attorney-General's Office,

Albany, *February* 4, 1910.

Hon. Clark Williams, *State Comptroller, Albany, N. Y.:*

Dear Sir.— I am in receipt of your letter of the 2nd inst., in
which you state that the International Detective Bureau of New
York city has not been licensed pursuant to law and has made no

application to be licensed; that it is a corporation organized to carry on and is now conducting the business of a detective bureau or detective agency; that said corporation claims through its attorney that whatever detective work is done through it is done by private detectives who themselves are duly licensed. You ask my opinion as to whether or not this corporation should apply for and receive a license pursuant to chapter 529 of the Laws of 1909.

If this corporation is actually carrying on any business as a detective or as a detective agency without a license, it is in violation of law, notwithstanding the fact that individuals employed by it are duly licensed detectives.

Section 70 of the General Business Law provides as to what persons and corporations must be licensed under the chapter referred to, and seems clearly to include such a corporation.

Section 71 provides:

" Any person, partnership or corporation, intending to conduct the business of detective or detective agency, and any person, partnership or corporation intending to conduct the business of furnishing or supplying information as to the personal character of any person or firm, or as to the character or kind of the business and occupation of any person, firm or corporation, *or intending to own or manage a bureau or agency for the above mentioned purposes,* except as to the financial rating of persons, firms or corporations, shall present to the comptroller of the State of New York, and file in his office a written application duly signed and verified, as follows * * *."

The license fee and bond required from a corporation is also larger than required from an individual. This provision might also be nullified if a corporation could do without a license by employing a duly licensed individual.

It is plain that the employment of a licensee under this act does not release the employer corporation, conducting a bureau or agency, from the necessity of procuring a license. .

.   Yours very truly,

EDWARD R. O'MALLEY,

Attorney-General.

Tax Law — Stock Transfer Tax.

Certificate of Great Northern Ore properties, representing beneficial interest only under terms of a trust agreement, are not
shares or certificates of stock, and such transfers or deliveries
are not taxable.

(See opinions June 8, 1909, p. 361, Report.)

STATE OF NEW YORK,

Attorney-General's Office,

Albany, *February* 8, 1910.

Hon. Clark Williams, *State Comptroller, Albany, N. Y.:*

Dear Sir.— On June 8, 1909, I wrote your predecessor an opinion in which I advised that from the facts then before me, the
shares of beneficial interest in the Great Northern Ore properties,
to which he called my attention, were not taxable under the Stock
Transfer Law.   On June 16, 1909, I supplemented this opinion
with the advice that unless the facts upon which my first opinion
was based were actually true, the opinion, of course, would not
represent the law, and I advised that the truth of these facts
should be established before you should permit transfers of these
certificates to occur without the payment of the tax.

Following the rendering of these two opinions, your predecessor
asked me to investigate the documents upon which these trustees'
certificates rested, and give my final opinion as to their taxability.
I endeavored to do this at once but have only just succeeded in
obtaining access to these papers.   From a careful examination of
these various documents, I am enabled to say definitely that the
facts assumed as the basis for my first opinion are the actual facts
in connection with these certificates, and that, therefore, transfers
of them are not subject to tax.

It appears that these certificates represent a beneficial interest
in certain properties transferred to certain individuals in trust,
under the terms of a trust agreement bearing date December 7,
1906.   This agreement was executed by the Lake Superior Company, Limited, party of the first part, and Louis W. Hill, James

N. Hill, Walter J. Hill and Edward T. Nichols, parties of the second part. By the terms of this agreement, the Lake Superior Company, Limited, transfers to the individuals named, certain shares of stock in various mining companies in trust, to hold them for the benefit of certificate holders. It is provided that certificates shall issue to the stockholders of the Great Northern Railway Company as they appeared upon the books of that company on December 6, 1906, in proportion to the number of shares of stock held by each in that company. It is further provided that the trustees, after paying the taxes and other expenses of the trust, " shall, from time to time, and at least once in every year, distribute and pay such portion of the net income or proceeds of the property held by them as such trustees, as they may deem proper to be so distributed, among and to " these certificate holders. It is further provided that the trustees may have full power to sell or exchange the property so conveyed to them and to reinvest the proceeds of such sale " in other property," and that in case of such reinvestment the property so acquired shall come under the terms of this trust. At the termination of the trust, which is to last for a period of twenty years after the death of the survivor of a large number of enumerated persons, it is provided that the trustees shall divide the property still remaining in their hands between the then certificate holders.

I have carefully examined this agreement and it is clear, in my judgment, that the certificates representing beneficial interests under this trust cannot in any sense be regarded as shares of stock. The holders of them have no interest in the management, profits or ultimate assets of any corporation. They are simply the cestui qui trustent under the trust. Their annual income rests wholly in the discretion of the trustees. Their right is simply to share in the profits of the investments made or continued by such trustees and under the agreement it would be possible for the trustees to exchange the shares of stock originally conveyed to them for any other kind of property.

The tax by the statute is imposed only upon sales, deliveries or transfers of " *shares or certificates of stock,* in any domestic or foreign association, company or corporation." These trustees' certificates of beneficial interest not being in any sense shares or certificates of stock, do not come within the scope of this tax. Under well settled principles, any doubt must be resolved in favor of the taxpayer, and I therefore advise you that transfers of such certificates are not taxable under this act.

Yours respectfully,

EDWARD R. O'MALLEY,

Attorney-General.

Tax Law — Stock Transfer Tax.

1. Reorganization of Western Maryland Company. (See opinion January 18, 1910.)
2. Procedure to recover amount of excess tax paid under 1906 Law, before declared unconstitutional, either by legislation or recourse to the Court of Claims.
3. Whether transfer of stock from executors under a will to themselves as trustees, is taxable.
4. Questions as to obsolete stamps. (See opinion June 8, 1909.) Stamps erroneously affixed, refund form, etc. (See opinion March 11, 1910.)

STATE OF NEW YORK,

ATTORNEY-GENERAL'S OFFICE,

ALBANY, *February* 8, 1910.

Hon. CLARK WILLIAMS, *State Comptroller, Albany, N. Y.:*

Dear Sir.— Referring to your letter of the 19th ultimo in which you ask my opinion on various questions regarding the stock transfer tax, I beg to say that I have given the matters therein contained very careful consideration.

The first question which you ask is in reference to the Western Maryland Railroad Company reorganization. This was covered in my opinion to your department under date of January 18, 1910.

The second question which you ask is as to the proper method of procedure on the part of certain individual brokers (members of the New York stock exchange) who paid excess taxes under the law of 1906 prior to its being declared unconstitutional in the

Court of Appeals in People ex rel. Farrington v. Mensching, 187 N. Y. 8.

As I have already advised you orally in a case of this character the procedure rests largely in your own discretion. If in your judgment the facts are established showing the validity of this claim and its amount, there would be no objection to your asking the Legislature to appropriate an amount sufficient to meet the same. On the other hand, if in your judgment the facts were not sufficient, or if you did not desire to pass upon the sufficiency of the evidence, you could very properly leave the claimants to present the matter to the Court of Claims. If no notice of intention to file such a claim has been given, as required by law, a special act of the Legislature would be necessary authorizing the Court of Claims to hear these claims.

Your third question is whether the transfer of stock from the executors under a will to themselves as trustees is taxable.

It is my opinion that as the executors are distinct persons in the eyes of the law from trustees, a real transfer within the meaning of the act takes place upon such a change of title even if the tax is not to be imposed on every physical transfer irrespective of change of ownership. This would, of course, be clearer if under the will the beneficial ownership were different in the two cases. However, it is my opinion that the transfer of legal title alone is sufficient to bring the transaction within the law.

Your fourth question is as to the proper course for you to pursue under my opinion to your predecessor of June 8, 1909, in reference to the retirement of stamps of the obsolete issue. You state that several brokerage houses are known to have on hand stamps of the old issue and insist upon using these in the payment of the transfer tax and that your office has no authority to refund, redeem or substitute new stamps for these worthless ones.

The question as to what course should be pursued is really one of policy. In my opinion, as I advised in the communication above referred to, these obsolete stamps are not now in compliance with the law. It would therefore seem that the matter is similar to that arising from the excess payment under the 1906 law. If in your judgment the administration of the act could be facilitated by a specific appropriation to you, giving you the authority to redeem these old stamps and appropriating the same therefor, you are, of course, at liberty to make such request from the Legislature. If, on the other hand, you think it wiser to have the Court of Claims pass upon these matters, that body would have jurisdiction either with or without a special enabling act, in accordance with the facts in each particular case. Finally, I can see no objection to a ruling by you, if you see fit, permitting these stamps to be used for a limited time.   The whole question, however, rests entirely in your discretion.

Your fifth question calls my attention to the fact that the statute provides that you may, upon satisfactory proof that stamps have been erroneously affixed and canceled in payment of the tax upon a transfer to the loss of an innocent person, refund the amount thereof from appropriations made for necessary expenses under this article, providing the tax justly due was paid upon such transfer. You call my attention to a few claims now pending in your office which apparently come within these facts. If in your judgment they do fall within this description, then on such amounts you are authorized to make a refund and charge it to your appropriations for necessary expenses, as above provided.

Your sixth question regarding claims for refund for stamps placed upon original issues of stock prior to the decision of the Court of Appeals holding that such issues were not taxable, is governed by the same principles as question number two and what I have said there applies equally, in my judgment, here.

Your seventh question regarding the taxability of beneficial certificates of Great Northern Ore properties has already been answered by me under a separate opinion.

I should be glad to take these matters up with you in further detail if at any time you so desire.

Yours respectfully,
EDWARD R. O'MALLEY,
Attorney-General.

Tax Law — Stock Transfer Tax.

Where a transfer of stock is made and title passed prior to the enactment of Stock Transfer Law, but transferred on books of corporation subsequently, this evidence of such transfer is not taxable.

(See opinion May 27, 1905, p. 430, Report; July 1, 1907, p. 298, Report; December 1, 1909, p. 383, Report.

STATE OF NEW YORK,

ATTORNEY-GENERAL'S OFFICE,

ALBANY, *February* 8, 1910.

Hon. CLARK WILLIAMS, *State Comptroller. Albany, N. Y.:*

Dear Sir.— Referring to your letter of the 3d inst., in which you enclose a question as to the applicability of the stock transfer tax to a purchase of stock made prior to the time when the Stock Transfer Law was enacted, it appears that the actual title to the stock in question passed before the act went into effect but that the transfer on the books of the corporation is to be made now. You ask whether this transfer on the books of the corporation is subject to the tax.

It is my opinion that the law was aimed to tax only the actual transaction — not the evidence of such transaction. If the transfer in ownership occurred before the act went into effect, the subsequent evidence of such transfer or consummation of it by issuing new stock would not be taxable.

Very truly yours,

EDWARD R. O'MALLEY,

Attorney-General.

Banks as Depositories of State Funds — Chapter 245, Laws, 1897.
Charge for publishing statement of balances not governed by
section 3317, Code of Civil Procedure. (Mack v. City of
Buffalo, 32 Misc. 330.)
(See letter March 24, 1909, L. B. 102, p. 349; July 22, 1909,
L. B. 107, p. 264.)

STATE OF NEW YORK,

ATTORNEY-GENERAL'S OFFICE,

ALBANY, *February* 10, 1910.

Hon. CLARK WILLIAMS, *State Comptroller, Albany, N. Y.:*

Dear Sir.— I have your letter of the 9th inst., in which you
ask my opinion as to whether in causing to be published a detailed
statement of the balances in the several banks designated as depositories of State funds, under chapter 245, Laws of 1897, the
charge for such publication is governed by section 3317 of the
Code of Civil Procedure.

In this regard I would say that I think the question is answered
by my letter to your predecessor under date of July 22, 1909, in
which I handed him a copy of a letter which I had previously
written to the State Engineer and Surveyor, calling attention to
the decision in Mack v. City of Buffalo, 32 Misc. 330, holding that
this section of the Code does not apply to any notices except those
relating to civil actions and proceedings under the Code, unless
otherwise specifically prescribed by law. In harmony with these
previous communications, therefore, I advise you that the publication in question is not governed by section 3317 of the Code of
Civil Procedure.

, Yours respectfully,

EDWARD R. O'MALLEY,

Attorney-General.

Detectives — Licenses — Sheriffs and Constables.

Person duly appointed and elected to official duty may not conduct
a private detective business under name of " Neef's Detective
Bureau " outside his regular duties, without a license under
chapter 529, Laws 1909.

(See opinion April 21, 1909, p. 350, Report; July 30, 1909, p.
586, Report; September 20, 1909, p. 374, Report; January
18, 1910; February 4, 1910; February 17, 1910.)

STATE OF NEW YORK,

ATTORNEY-GENERAL'S OFFICE,

ALBANY, *February* 10, 1910.

Hon. CLARK WILLIAMS, *State Comptroller, Albany, N. Y.:*

Dear Sir.— I am in receipt of your favor of the 8th instant in
which you ask my opinion as to whether or not the fact that a person is a duly appointed deputy sheriff and a duly elected town
constable would authorize him to conduct a business as an individual or in the name of " Neef's Detective Bureau," and advertise
for work as a detective without having first obtained the license
required by chapter 529 of the Laws of 1909. I have also the
brief submitted by counsel for Neef, contending that a license is
not required to permit a person holding such an office to engage
in the business of private detective.

The provision of law relied upon by Neef in support of his contention is contained in section 75 of the act, which in part reads:

" Nothing in this article shall apply * * * to any detective or officer belonging to the police force of the state, or
any county, city, town or village thereof, appointed or elected
by due authority of law, or to any person in the employ of
any police force or police department of the state, or of any
county, city, town or village thereof."

The effect of this provision, in my judgment, and the only intention in the minds of the Legislature in so enacting, was to
specifically exempt such officers in the performance of their duties
as such, from the provision of law requiring a license. They are

given direct statutory authority to perform any detective work and to supply information as to the character of persons and corporations in the line of their official duties without procuring a license. However, I do not think it was intended to give to such persons the right to conduct a private detective business separate from their official duties and to advertise as such and to engage in the private business of supplying the information mentioned in section 70 for which a license is required, without first obtaining such a license. If it meant anything further than to relieve such officers in the performance of their official duties from the requirements of the act, as the counsel for Neef contends it did, then it would confer upon certain citizens (namely, those who are officers of the police force of the State or of any county, city, town or village thereof) rights and privileges which are not conferred upon other citizens of the State.

The first section of the first article of the Constitution of the State provides:

> "No member of this state shall be disfranchised or deprived of any of the rights or privileges secured to any citizen thereof, unless by the law of the land, or the judgment of his peers."

It is well settled that the words "law of the land" do not mean a statute passed by the Legislature for the purposes of working the wrong, but that it must be ascertained judicially that the person deprived thereof has forfeited his rights and privileges. It is also a well settled rule of statutory construction that where two constructions of an act are possible one of which rendered the act constitutional and the other unconstitutional, the constitutional construction must prevail.

I am, therefore, of the opinion that where such an officer engages in the business of private detective outside of his official duties, he must, to keep within the law, procure a license.

Yours very truly,

EDWARD R. O'MALLEY,

Attorney-General.

State Institutions — State Charities Law — Section 55.

New York State Training School for Girls at Hudson. Contract
  for building sewage disposal plant. Lowest bid for contract
  being in excess of the appropriation made for such work, and
  an unexpended balance remaining from the appropriation for
  cottages and a trunk conduit, etc., such balance may lawfully
  be used for sewage plant.

STATE OF NEW YORK,

Attorney-General's Office,

Albany, *February* 26, 1910.

Hon. Clark Williams, *State Comptroller, Albany, N. Y.:*

Dear Sir.— I have the honor to acknowledge receipt of your
communication of February 16, 1910, enclosing a letter from the
State Architect. It appears that by chapter 466, Laws of 1908,
chapter 461, Laws of 1909, and chapter 433, Laws of 1909, there
have been appropriated $3,070.48 for building a sewage disposal
plant for the New York State Training School for Girls at Hudson.
The lowest bid for the contract for this work is $4,200, which is
$1,192.52 in excess of the aggregate of the appropriations made
for this purpose. To meet this deficiency it is proposed to use the
unexpended balance of $1,088.45 of an appropriation made by
chapter 466, Laws of 1908, amounting to $44,872.72 for two cot-
tages at the Training School for Girls at Hudson; and also it is
proposed to use an unexpended balance from an appropriation
made by chapter 461, Laws of 1909, amounting to $5,500 for a
trunk conduit to connect the boiler house at the same institution.

You request my opinion as to whether the unexpended balances
of the appropriations for the two cottages and for the trunk conduit at this institution can lawfully be applied to make up this
difference between the appropriation for the sewage disposal plant
and the amount of the lowest bid.

My answer to this question is in the affirmative. Section 55 of
the State Charities Law, as amended by chapter 149 of the Laws
of 1909, provides as follows:

  " If an appropriation be made for the erection, alteration,
  repairs or improvement of buildings or plant at a state insti-

tution reporting to the fiscal supervisor, in an appropriation act specifying two or more objects for which the appropriation . shall be applied, and any one of such objects shall have been accomplished for a less sum than the amount specified in the act, the unexpended balance shall be applicable to the completion of any other work .specified in the act, if after due advertisement no bids shall have been received within the amount specifically appropriated therefor."

The New York State Training School for Girls at Hudson is an institution reporting to the Fiscal Supervisor. Chapter 466, Laws of 1908, is an appropriation act for the erection or improvement of buildings or plant specifying two or more objects, viz., for two cottages, $44,872.72, and for sewage disposal plan, $870.48. Chapter 461, Laws of 1909, is also an appropriation act for the erection or improvement of buildings of plant specifying two or more objects, viz., for trunk conduit, $5,500, and for sewage disposal plant, $1,200. Upon the statement of the State Architect it appears that the object of building the two cottages has been accomplished for a less sum than the amounts appropriated, and the object of building the trunk conduit has also been accomplished for a less sum than the amount appropriated. As the appropriations for these two purposes were each specified in an act which also included an appropriation for the building of the sewage disposal, the unexpended balances from the appropriations for the cottages and for the trunk conduit come within the provisions of section 49, as above quoted, and are therefore applicable for use for the sewage disposal, for which, after due advertisement, no bids have been received within the amount specifically appropriated therefor.

Yours respectfully,

EDWARD R. O'MALLEY,

Attorney-General.

15

Saratoga Springs State Reservation — Chapter 569, Laws 1909.
As to constitutionality of act and provisions for acquisition of
private property for public use, compensation for, etc.

STATE OF NEW YORK,

ATTORNEY-GENERAL'S OFFICE,

ALBANY, *March* 4, 1910.

To the Honorable, THE STATE COMPTROLLER, *Albany. N. Y.:*

Dear Sir.— Your letter of February 11th was duly received, in
which you ask for my opinion as to the constitutionality of chapter 569 of the Laws of 1909, and put certain other questions involving the interpretation of this act and the powers of the commission.
You ask the following questions:

1. Do the provisions of this act come within the prohibition of
section 6 of article 1 of the Constitution of the State of New York,
which provides that private property shall not be taken for public
use without just compensation?   Two elements are involved:
(a) Is the acquisition of the property authorized by this act for a
public use?   (b) Is just compensation provided?

(a) The title of this chapter is as follows:

> " An act to authorize the selection, location and appropriation of certain lands in the town of Saratoga Springs, for a
> state reservation, and to preserve the natural mineral springs
> therein located, and making an appropriation therefor, and
> authorizing an issue of bonds to pay such appropriation."

The act further says, after providing for a commission to carry
out its terms:

> Section 2. " It shall be the duty of said board, and it shall
> have power, from time to time, to select and locate such lands
> in the town of Saratoga Springs, in the county of Saratoga,
> and any rights, easements, or interest upon or in any lands in
> said town, as it shall deem proper and necessary to be taken
> for the purpose of preserving the natural mineral springs in
> said town of Saratoga Springs, and of restoring said springs
> to their former natural condition, and for that purpose, to

acquire any rights, easements or interest in any property, the whole of which it shall not acquire, for the purpose of protecting the springs or mineral water rights upon any lands it shall acquire." * * *

Section 4. " From and after the acquisition of any piece of land by the board, as hereinbefore provided, the same shall be kept, and remain, and be known, as a part of the state reservation at Saratoga Springs, for the purposes of restoring, and forever preserving, the mineral springs and wells and mineral water, and the natural carbonic acid gas on, and in, and under said lands, and the rights, easements and interest acquired in, or upon, or over, lands, the fee of which shall not be acquired by such board, shall be held for the restoration, and perpetual preservation, of the mineral springs and wells, the mineral water and natural carbonic acid gas on, in or under the lands thus acquired. No part of such lands, rights, easements or interest thus acquired, shall be sold without the express direction of the legislature."

Section 5. " Said board shall have the care, custody and control of said reservation, and of all the mineral springs, wells, mineral water and natural carbonic acid gas thereon, therein, or thereunder, and of all the rights, easements, and interests acquired by it; it may prescribe and publish and enforce all proper regulations for the maintenance and care and protection of said properties, and may grant concessions and leases of any portion of the same upon terms to be fixed by it, and may limit and prescribe the terms upon which any excess of mineral water not used on said premises shall be sold and the labels to be attached thereto, or may, itself, sell such excess of water, and any violation of any regulation of said commission may be punished as a misdemeanor;" * * *

The purpose of this act is to acquire and preserve certain remarkable mineral springs. This is as far as the language of the act clearly states. A reasonable interpretation of the object of the act is that in addition to the mere preservation of these springs the public should have the right to enjoy and use the same. The

words, if any, which limit this interpretation are those contained
in section 5 " and may grant concessions and leases of any portion
of the same upon terms to be fixed by it." This expression may
reasonably be limited to the use of excess water, especially in
view of the language which follows and confines the sales by the
commission to the water not used on the premises. The public
in my opinion is entitled to free access to the premises and the
right to drink the water of the springs without charge. The act
should if possible be construed so as to be constitutional rather
than unconstitutional. Construing the act in the above manner
the use is public.

(b) The answer to the second element of this question, as to
whether just compensation is provided, requires the answer of your
inquiry as to whether the bonds authorized by this act could be
issued under article 7, section 2, of the Constitution.

> Article 7, Section 2. " The state may, to meet casual de-
> ficits or failures in revenues, or for expenses not provided for,
> contract debts; but such debts, direct or contingent, singly or
> in the aggregate, shall not at any time exceed one million of
> dollars; and the moneys arising from the loans creating such
> debts shall be applied to the purpose for which they were ob-
> tained or to repay the debt so contracted, and to no other pur-
> pose whatever."

Section 6 of the act in question reads:

> Section 6. " The sum of six hundred thousand dollars
> ($600,000), or so much thereof as may be needed, is hereby
> appropriated for the purchase of such lands, rights, easements
> and interest by said board, and the payment of any judgments
> that may be recovered therefor in the court of claims as here-
> inbefore provided. The state comptroller, upon the written
> request of such board, is hereby authorized and directed to
> borrow not more than six hundred thousand dollars for the
> purposes specified in this act, and to issue bonds or certifi-
> cates of the state therefor payable within ten years from their
> date, bearing interest at a rate not exceeding five per centum
> per annum, and which shall not be sold at less than par. The
> sum hereby appropriated shall be payable on the order of

such board, and upon the written approval of the governor, by
the treasurer on the warrant of the comptroller, only out of
the moneys realized from the sale of such bonds or certificates."

Article 7, section 2, of the Constitution is the only provision in
the Constitution under which these bonds could be issued, if at all.
The Legislature has at least twice previous to this occasion authorized the issue of bonds under similar circumstances.   The first
instance was for the payment of land appropriated for the reservation at Niagara Falls, when the sum of $1,000,000 was directed to
be raised in this manner. (Laws of 1885, chapter 182.)   Chapter
220 of the Laws of 1897, creating the Forest Preserve Board and
authorizing the acquisition of land in Adirondack Park, made use
of this method of raising $400,000 out of an appropriation of
$1,000,000.   The constitutionality of this statute was sustained by
the Court of Appeals in People v. Adirondack Railway Co., 160
N. Y. 225, but the constitutionality of issuing bonds in this manner was not directly passed upon.   In view of the fact that the
constitutional convention in 1894 did not change this provision of
the Constitution after the Legislature had authorized a similar
issue of bonds, it would seem that such an issue was recognized as
proper, provided, of course, that the bonds authorized, together
with all other bonds issued under section 2 of article 7 of the State
Constitution, do not exceed $1,000,000.   The issue of bonds being
legal, the credit of the State had been pledged for the payment of
the lands taken and just compensation has been assured, which is
a sufficient compliance with the provisions of the Constitution.
The fact that only $600,000 has been provided to carry out the
purpose of this act, conceding a much larger sum is necessary, does
not render compensation for the rights to be acquired uncertain,
but limits the power of the board as to the amount of property
they can acquire without further appropriation.   The same situation existed in the case of the appropriation for the acquisition of
lands in Adirondack Park.

2. You also ask whether you have any discretion in borrowing
or paying over this money upon the order of the commission.

Section 6 of the act provides that the State Comptroller, upon
the written request of such board, is hereby authorized and di-

rected to borrow not more than $600,000 for the purposes specified in this act and to issue bonds therefor. I am of the opinion that it is your duty to borrow the sums requested by the commission, not, however, exceeding $600,000. The payment of orders of the commission requires the exercise of some discretion upon your part. The orders for the payment of money in this case have not been presented to the Governor for his approval. In my opinion they should be so presented by the board rather than by the Comptroller. When approved by the Governor a warrant should be drawn for their payment, if the provisions of section 12 and section 36 of the State Finance Law have been complied with.

3. You ask further as to whether the death of Mr. Trask and the resignation of Mr. Shepard would have any effect upon the validity of requests and orders made before the occurrence of these events, but submitted to you after.

I am of the opinion that the validity of these requests and orders is not affected by the above events.

Yours truly,

EDWARD R. O'MALLEY,

Attorney-General.

General Business Law — Section 75 (Amended Chapter 529, Laws 1909) — Licenses — Fees.

State Comptroller may expend $3,500 annually out of moneys received from license fees, in the employment of agents, witness fees, etc., until the expiration of two years from passage of act.

(State Constitution, Article III, Section 21.)

ATTORNEY-GENERAL'S OFFICE,

STATE OF NEW YORK,

ALBANY, *March* 11, 1910.

Hon. CLARK WILLIAMS, *State Comptroller, Albany, N. Y.:*

Dear Sir.— I have your letter of the 9th instant, in which you call my attention to section 75 of the General Business Law, as amended by chapter 529 of the Laws of 1909, which provides that you may expend annually out of the moneys received as license fees under that article, not to exceed $3,500, in the employment of an agent or agents, the payment of witness fees and of other proper expenses.

You ask my opinion whether this article confers power upon you to make payments, not exceeding $3,500 annually, for the purposes named therein from such fees received, and pay the surplus into the State treasury, if such payments in all other respects are paid in compliance with the provisions of law with regard to the audit and payment of accounts in general by the Comptroller.

I have carefully examined the statute, and in my opinion it is sufficient authority for you to make such payment.

The Constitution provides, in article III, section 21:

"No money shall ever be paid out of the treasury of this state, or any of its funds, or any of the funds under its management, except in pursuance of an appropriation by law; nor unless such payment be made within two years next after the passage of such appropriation act; * * * * "

The enactment of the above section by chapter 529, Laws of 1909, was an appropriation of this amount out of the license fees received by you. It would therefore permit you to use such an amount annually for two years after the passage of such act.

I therefore advise you that, until the expiration of such two years, you are authorized under this act to expend this amount annually, as outlined in your letter.

Yours very truly,

EDWARD R. O'MALLEY,

Attorney-General.

Tax Law — Stock Transfers.

Stock transferred from firm of Cuyler, Morgan & Co. to its successors, Graham, Vaughan & Co., merely a transfer in beneficial ownership, and as such is not subject to tax.

(See opinion February 8, 1910.)

STATE OF NEW YORK,

Attorney-General's Office,

Albany, *March* 11, 1910.

Hon. Clark Williams, *State Comptroller, Albany, N. Y.:*

Dear Sir.— Referring to your letter of the 9th instant, in which you ask my opinion as to the taxability of the transfer of stock from the firm of Cuyler, Morgan & Company to the successors of interest of that firm, the beneficial ownership of the stock being in the same customers, I beg to advise as follows:

It appears from your letter and enclosure that the present copartnership of Cuyler, Morgan & Company expires by limitation on April 30th, and will go into liquidation at that time, and that the new firm of Graham, Vaughan & Company has been formed to occupy the same offices. It also appears that a great many of the clients of the former firm have requested the new firm to take over securities belonging to them which at present stand in the name of the former firm.

The question is asked whether, if any of these securities are presented for transfer at the offices of the various companies with the following endorsement placed upon them, they will be taxable, to wit:

"I hereby certify that this change of name does not involve a sale, nor any change of ownership."

You ask my opinion upon this question:

(1) When there is a change of name of a firm without any change of interest.

(2) When there is a change of name with a new partner admitted; and,

(3) When there is a change of name with a partner retired.

It appears to me that in all three of these instances the change is merely in the name or the personality of the holder of the legal title. The actual beneficial owner in every case remains the same. It is, therefore, my opinion that such transactions fall within the general rule already laid down by your department, with my approval, to the effect that the substitution of one trustee in place of another and the transfer of stock to his name from the name of his predecessor does not constitute such a transfer as is subject to the stock transfer tax, so long as the beneficial ownership remains identical.

I, therefore, advise you that in none of the cases mentioned in your letter is the transaction subject to a transfer tax.

Very respectfully yours,

EDWARD R. O'MALLEY,

Attorney-General.

State Institutions — Contracts.

Construction of New York State Agricultural School, St. Lawrence University. Contract with Clemence Construction Company, which it failed to complete. Filing of mechanic's lien, etc. State not liable to lienors for amount of retained percentage under judgment in action to foreclose mechanic's lien.

(See letter February 20, 1909, L. B. 100, p. 902; letter April 28, 1909, L. B. 103, p. 758.)

STATE OF NEW YORK,

ATTORNEY-GENERAL'S OFFICE,

ALBANY, *March* 14, 1910.

Hon. CLARK WILLIAMS, *State Comptroller, Albany, N. Y.*:

Dear Sir.— I have your letter of the 23d ult., asking my opinion in reference to the judgment in the matter of Tappen & Merritt against the Clemence Construction Company et al., filed in your office November 27, 1908.

It appears that this is a judgment in an action brought to foreclose a mechanic's lien. It appears from the judgment that the State entered into a contract with the Clemence Construction Company for the construction of the New York State School of Agriculture at St. Lawrence University for the sum of $75,471; that the said company performed and furnished materials in the construction of said building amounting to $42,961.19; that it was paid by the State of New York, on account of such work, $34,438.18; that there was owing and presently due and payable to the company on account of said contract the sum of $2,078.86; and that there was unpaid by the State the further sum of $6,444.15 earned under said contract " which will become due from the State of New York when said public improvement * * * is completed and accepted."

The judgment further recites " that said sums of money so due and to become due said Clemence Construction Company from the State of New York are subject to the payment " of costs and " to the liens hereinafter mentioned and shall be paid out as hereinafter specified by the Comptroller of the State of New York and treasurer of St. Lawrence University, pursuant to said chapter 682, Laws of 1906." Then follows in the judgment an enumeration of the various liens filed against the improvement, aggregating $10,477.20, which are directed to be paid in their order from the aforesaid sum.

It appears that the Clemence Construction Company failed to complete the contract and that the State secured its completion by another contractor. In the statement which is annexed to your letter it appears that the cost of this completion was $48,798.09. This sum, however, includes the entire $10,477.20, the amount of all the liens specified in said judgment. The actual cost of the completion of the contract, exclusive of this item, is $38,320.89. Adding this amount to the $34,438.18 paid the Clemence Construction Company on the original contract and to the $2,078.86 paid lienors as hereinafter set forth, and it appears that the State actually paid for the completion of the building $74,837.93. The net amount of the original contract was $73,338.50, showing that the excess cost of the work over the amount of this contract was $1,499.43.

You ask in your letter that I state the amount which you are to exact from the bonding company upon this contract, and you state that your department "has assumed that it was responsible for the total amount of the judgment."

It is clear, in the first place, that the bonding company is liable for the excess cost of the work over the net amount of the original contract which is above set forth. This includes, as has been seen, the amount of the liens already paid by you under advice from this department, amounting to $2,078.86, being so much of the liens as could be paid from the amount presently due the contractor at the time of the suspension of work, as found by the aforesaid judgment. It is also clear that the company is liable for the loss sustained by the State by failure to complete the contract, which is stated by you to be $1,170.

It is equally clear, under all the authorities, that the State is not liable to the various lienors for the aggregate amounts of the liens which they filed and that therefore it has no claim for such an amount against the bonding company. The assumption of your department that it was responsible to the total amount of these liens is erroneous. Under the Mechanic's Lien Law in this State the rights of lienors are derived merely by subrogation through the rights of the contractor and the owner of the property is never liable to lienors in an amount beyond that due to the contractor. In no event, therefore, is the State liable to these lienors for the full amount of $10,477.20.

The only remaining question is as to the liability of the State and its corresponding right against the bonding company for the item of $6,444.15 specified in the above judgment. This item represents the percentages retained by the State from the amounts earned by the Clemence Construction Company under the terms of the contract. The contract provides in part as follows:

> "The party of the first part hereby agrees to make payments as follows: Eighty-five per cent. of the value of the material and work incorporated in the building, as certified by the State Architect, monthly, as the work progresses, and the balance upon the satisfactory completion of the contract, when so certified by the State Architect, but the last pay-

ment on this contract shall not be made until all charges for extra work and allowances for omissions have been rendered, agreed to and certified by the State Architect, nor until the party of the second part has furnished satisfactory evidence that there are no outstanding liens or claims for materials furnished or labor performed on the said work."

The sum of $6,444.15 represents the 15 per cent. retained under this provision. The judgment recites that this sum will become due on the completion and acceptance of the work and that it is subject to the payment of the liens therein set forth. In fact, however, the cost of completing the work exceeded both the unearned portion of the contract price and the amount of these retained percentages. The total contract price was $73,338.50. The amount paid the Clemence Construction Company was $34,438.18; the amount due them was $2,078.86, and the amount of the retained percentages was $6,444.15, a total of $42,961.19. This left as the unearned part of the contract price $30,377.31 available for completing the contract. It has already been shown that it cost $38,320.89 to complete this work, leaving an excess over this amount available of $7,943.58. This excess cost of completing the work, therefore, over the amount of the contract price unearned by the contractor was greater by $1,499.43 than the amount of the retained percentages.

In other words, said sum of $6,444.15 was necessarily consumed by the State in completing this contract and it never became due to the Clemence Construction Company because of the cost of such completion. The question of law, therefore, which is presented is two-fold: first, whether retained percentages earned by the contractor but held back by the State under the terms of the contract are subject to the payment of mechanic's liens when the contractor abandons the work and when it costs the State the full amount of such retained percentages in addition to the contract price to complete it; and, second, if such percentages are not subject to those liens, whether in the present case the judgment which has been entered and to which the State is a party, compels such payment by the State.

I have carefully considered both of these questions. It is my opinion that under the law of this State, percentages retained by the State under such a contract are not subject to mechanics' liens when the cost of completing the contract exceeds the contract price by an amount equal to or greater than such percentages. Section 3418 of the Code of Civil Procedure, in defining a judgment in an action to foreclose a lien on account of a public improvement, provides as follows:

> "If, in an action to enforce a lien on account of a public improvement, the court finds that the lien is establshed, it shall render judgment directing the state or the municipal corporation to pay over to the lienors entitled thereto for work done or material furnished for such public improvement, and in such order of priority as the court may determine, to the extent of the sums found due the lienors from the contractors, so much of the funds or money which may be due from the state or municipal corporation to the contractor, as will satisfy such liens, with interest and costs, not exceeding the amount due to the contractor."

It is apparent from this that the test as to whether or not the State must pay the liens is whether or not an amount equivalent to them is due from it to the contractor. The law is clearly expressed in the leading case of Van Clief v. Van Vechten, 130 N. Y. 571, in which Judge Vann points out that the only sums to which the liens attach are those due to the contractor pursuant to the terms of the contract. (See also Doughty v. Devlin, 1 E. D. Smith, 625.)

It seems, under the decisions in this State, that the retention of a percentage of the payments to be made to the contractor by the State or city is for the benefit and security of the State or city, and not for the benefit of the contractor or material men or laborers. In other words, that where, as here, the State is compelled to pay out more than the amount so retained, for the completion of the work abandoned by the contractor, the percentages never become due to the contractor. That being so, it would seem to follow that the mechanic's liens would never attach to such percentages because they would never represent a sum due by the State to the contractor. The lienors being subrogated to the rights of the contractor, can have no greater claim against the State than possessed by him. This seems to be the view taken by the authorities.

> Weisemair v. City of Syracuse, 57 Hun, 48.
> McChesney v. City of Syracuse, 75 Hun, 503.
> Lawrence v. Dawson, 34 App. Div. 211.
> Jones v. Savage, 24 Misc. 158.
> Harley v. Mapes Company, 33 Misc. 626, 632.
> Herrman v. City of New York, 130 App. Div. 531-535.

Under the foregoing decisions and for the reasons which I have already expressed, it is my opinion that apart from the entry of the aforesaid judgment the State would not be liable to the lienors in this case in an amount represented by the retained percentages.

The remaining question is whether the entry of the judgment in the form in which it was entered will compel the State to recognize these liens to the extent of such percentages. The judgment does not, in my opinion, expressly direct the Comptroller to pay this sum towards the satisfaction of these various liens until it becomes due to the Clemence Construction Company. It is recited in the judgment that there was on February 5, 1908, unpaid by the State to the Clemence Construction Company this sum of $6,444.15 " earned by said Clemence Construction Company under said contract which will become due from the State of New York when said public improvement, which is being erected pursuant to chapter 682 of the Laws of 1906, is completed and accepted by the State of New York; that said sums of money so due and to become due said Clemence Construction Company from the State of New York are subject * * * to the liens hereinafter mentioned and shall be paid out as hereinafter specified by the Comptroller of the State of New York and Treasurer of St. Lawrence University pursuant to said chapter 682 of the Laws of 1906." It, however, in directing the payment of the liens, specifically directs that they shall be paid " out of said funds *or so much thereof properly* applicable thereto." (Fol. 11.) Moreover, in speaking of the deficiency judgments which are to be entered, it recites that judgment shall be had against the Construction Company " for the amount of any deficiency remaining unpaid after applying all moneys properly applicable thereto." (Fol. 15.) These expressions are repeated all through the judgment.

It is my opinion, therefore, that the true intent of the judgment is to direct the payment of the amount of these retained percentages towards the satisfaction of these liens only when the same become due to the Clemence Construction Company. This construction should certainly be given, if possible, because otherwise the judgment would be erroneous. That being so, in view of the fact that they have never become due, there would be no requirement that they be applied towards the satisfaction of these liens.

I therefore advise you that the State is not liable for the amount of these retained percentages to the lienors under this judgment, and that, accordingly, no claim for such amount could be sustained against the surety on the contract. The claim against that company should exclude only the excess cost of completing the contract above the contract price (which includes the $2,078.86 paid lienors) and the damage to the State from delay. If the foregoing figures are correct, the total amount of this claim is $2,669.43.

Very respectfully yours,

EDWARD R. O'MALLEY,

Attorney-General.

Detectives — Licenses.

Person employed solely by one corporation for information of a "personal character" regarding employees of such corporation, comes under provisions of statute requiring license, and must take out such license.

(See opinion April 21, p. 350, Rep.; July 30, 1909; September 20, 1909, p. 374, Rep.; January 18, February 4, 1910.)

STATE OF NEW YORK,

Attorney-General's Office,

Albany, *March* 17, 1910.

Hon. Clark Williams, *State Comptroller, Albany, N. Y.:*

Dear Sir.— I am in receipt of your letter of the 25th ultimo, in which you ask my opinion as to whether it is necessary for a person to secure a detective license if he be employed solely by one corporation for the purpose of keeping the president of that corporation informed in regard to its various employees.

Referring to the statute under which licenses are required, it is provided that " no person or partnership shall engage in the business of private detective for hire or reward   * * *   without having first obtained a license so to do," and again, " no person or partnership or corporation shall engage in the business for hire or reward, of furnishing or supplying information as to the personal character of any person or firm, or as to the character or kind of the business and occupation of any person, firm or corporation,   * * *   except as to the financial rating of persons, firms or corporations, without having first obtained a license so to do."

I take it for granted that the information furnished is " information as to the personal character " of persons and that your inquiry is directed solely to the question of whether a person supplying such information to a single employer instead of to any and all persons who may employ him is included within the act.

In State v. Tolman, 106 La. 662, which was a case brought for a penalty for carrying on the business of a money lender without a license, the court said:

> " The legal proposition announced by defendant, that as long as a party lends only his *own money* he cannot be charged for a license as for carrying on the business of a money lender, is entirely too broad."

And after stating that while an occasional loan of one's surplus means would not be the carrying on of the business of lending money, and then after referring to the extensive nature of the business done by the defendant, the opinion adds:

> " The constant daily repetition by the same person of the same kind of acts, each act bringing with it a money return, is certainly the carrying on by him of business in that particular line."

And the court held that a person who loaned money only for himself and who made that his daily business must, to lawfully engage therein, procure a license.

It would seem to me that while the Legislature probably did not have in mind such a case as that to which you refer, yet that the language employed by it covers such a case.

I cannot see how it can be consistently claimed that a person who is employed and who gives his time and energy to the business of ascertaining and supplying information as to the character of persons, and who is employed by a single person, is not engaged in such business as much as though he were employed by many persons.

Yours very truly,
EDWARD R. O'MALLEY,
Attorney-General.

Mortgages.

Method of foreclosure where mortgages are held by County Treasurer in the court and trust fund where involuntary bankruptcy proceedings are pending against the mortgagor. Petition may be made to bankruptcy court and if granted action may be maintained to foreclose lien as though no bankruptcy proceedings had been instituted.

STATE OF NEW YORK,

ATTORNEY-GENERAL'S OFFICE,

Albany, March 25, 1910.

Hon. Clark Williams, *State Comptroller, Albany, N. Y.:*

Dear Sir.— Your communication of the 1st inst., received, inquiring as to the method of procedure in foreclosing a mortgage held by a County Treasurer in the court and trust fund on default of the payment of interest where involuntary bankruptcy proceedings are pending against the mortgagor, the value of the mortgaged property being greatly in excess of the amount of the lien.

It seems to be well settled that where an action has been brought in a State court, founded upon a claim from which a discharge by the bankruptcy court would not operate as a release, such suit should not be restrained in the bankruptcy proceeding.

Bardes v. Hawarden, 178 U. S. 533.
Carling v. Seymour Lumber Co., 113 Fed. Rep. 482.
In re Neiman, 109 Fed. 111.

From the principle enunciated in these decisions, it would seem to me that under the facts which you set forth the bankruptcy court would, on petition, grant permission to join the trustee in bankruptcy as a defendant in such a mortgage foreclosure proceeding instituted in the state court. That seems to be the holding made In Re E. A. Porter & Bro., 6 Am. Br. Rep. 259, and I therefore advise you that such an application should be made, and that when it is granted an action to foreclose the lien may be maintained in the same manner as if no bankruptcy proceedings had been instituted.

Very truly yours,
EDWARD R. O'MALLEY,
Attorney-General.

Tax Law — Section 270 — Stock Transfers.

Where corporation affords stockholders opportunity to subscribe for stock to be paid for by instalments, and receipts are given therefor, such receipts to be exchanged for certificates of stock when final payment is made, such exchange is a transfer and as such is taxable.

STATE OF NEW YORK,

ATTORNEY-GENERAL'S OFFICE,

ALBANY, <i>March</i> 29, 1910.</div>

Hon. CLARK WILLIAMS, <i>State Comptroller, Albany, N. Y.:</i>

Dear Sir.— I acknowledge the letter under date of the 21st inst., from your Mr. Alford, requesting my opinion upon the taxability of the following transaction, under section 270 of the Tax Law:

It appears that a corporation has offered to its stockholders the privilege of subscribing for a proportionate amount of stock of the new corporation; that this stock is to be paid for in two instalments and upon the payment of the first instalment, negotiable receipts are to be issued; upon the payment of the final instalment the receipts are to be surrendered and the new stock is to be issued to the registered owner of the receipt or his assignee. It also appears that subscribers or assignees of these receipts receive dividends only after they have exchanged their receipts for certificates of stock, so that the receipts themselves do not carry dividends. It is provided, however, that the receipts may be transferred after payment of the first or second instalment. The question is whether such transfer of these receipts is within the terms of section 270 of the Tax Law.

Section 270 of the Taw Law (or, to be exact, ch. 241, L. of 1905) provides that all sales, transfers, etc., " of shares or certificates of stock " in any corporation shall be subject to the tax therein provided.

It is clear, in my opinion, that the receipts mentioned in your letter come within the provisions of this law. They represent stock or an interest in stock just as much as though the stock itself were issued before it was fully paid, and any contrary holding would afford an easy method of evading the payment of this tax.

I therefore advise you that all sales and transfers of these receipts are subject to the stock transfer tax.

Very truly yours,

EDWARD R. O'MALLEY,

Attorney-General.

Tax Law — Section 187 — Town and County Co-operative Insurance.

Church Insurance Association, of Rochester, N. Y., an association of the Methodist Episcopal Church, owning property to be insured and formed under a special act (chap. 134, Laws 1891), not a town and county co-operative association, and therefore not exempt from taxation.

STATE OF NEW YORK,

ATTORNEY-GENERAL'S OFFICE,

ALBANY, *March* 29, 1910.

Hon. CLARK WILLIAMS, *State Comptroller, Albany, N. Y.:*

Dear Sir.— Referring to your letter of the 2d inst., enclosing letters from the secretary of the Church Insurance Association of Rochester, N. Y., with the request that I advise you whether or not, in my opinion, this corporation falls within the exemption extended to town and county co-operative insurance companies by section 187 of the Tax Law, I beg to advise as follows:

It appears that this corporation was organized by special act of the Legislature, found in chapter 134, Laws of 1891. Section 1 of this act provides that a large number of enumerated Methodist Episcopal churches in the State of New York " which collectively own property of the value of four hundred thousand dollars, which they desire to have insured, and such other religious societies, and such pastors of religious societies as shall from time to time associate themselves with them in the manner hereinafter provided, are hereby made a body corporate by the name of the Church Insurance Association, for the purpose of co-operative insurance against loss or damage by fire or lightning in the several counties in the State of New York."

Section 187 of the Tax Law, which imposes a franchise tax upon insurance corporations, contains this provision :

" This section does not apply to a fraternal beneficiary society, order or association, a corporation for the insurance of domestic animals, a town or county co-operative insurance corporation,   *   *   *   ."

The question presented is whether the Church Insurance Association, incorporated by the above act, comes within the terms of this exemption.

It is claimed by the Association·that it is a town or county co-operative insurance association within the meaning of the statute, because it is incorporated for the purpose of co-operative insurance " in the several counties in the State of New York," and in support of this claim the association points out that in the report of the State Insurance Department on town and county co-operative insurance associations, issued December 23, 1909, it was classed as a town and county co-operative insurance association.

On the other hand, it appears from the correspondence submitted by your department, that this association has paid a franchise tax for many years past without objection, and that it was only when the report of the Superintendent of Insurance above mentioned was published that the question was raised by the association. I have been informed by the Superintendent of Insurance that his action in treating this association in said report was not evidence of an intention on the part of the department to classify it as a town and county co-operative fire insurance association, but was " on account of the fact that it appeared that a certain volume of its business was reinsured in town and county co-operative associations and that associations of such character made use of it." The Superintendent of Insurance also states:

"It appeared at that time that the association occupied what might be classed as a middle ground between the regular fire companies and the town and county co-operative associations, and this being so, it was decided to carry its financial statement in the special report referred to."

It is a well settled principle of law that exemptions from taxation must be strictly construed. It is my opinion, from a careful examination of the statutes, that the meaning of the words " town or county co-operative insurance corporations "used in section 187 of the Tax Law, refers only to such associations organized under Article IX of the Insurance Law. The provisions of that act seem to contain the only statutory recognition of so-called town and county co-operative insurance corporations, and the powers and duties of such corporations are carefully limited and defined therein. The Church Insurance Association, on the other hand, does not resemble in any way such corporations except that it is a co-operative insurance company and that it is authorized to do business " in the several counties in the State." There is no limitation whatever on the number of counties in which it can do business, as in the case of ordinary county co-operative insurance corporations, and the general provisions regulating it are entirely different from those contained in Article IX of the Insurance Law. Inasmuch as the corporation is not anywhere termed a town or county co-operative insurance corporation, and inasmuch as corporations organized under this section of the Insurance Law are termed such corporations, it is my opinion that the use of such designation in the Tax Law must be taken to refer only to corporations organized under this article of the Insurance Law.

I therefore agree with the ruling made by your department, that the association is not exempt from the tax imposed by section 187 of the Tax Law.

Very truly yours,

EDWARD R. O'MALLEY,

Attorney-General.

———

Counties — Rensselaer.

Examination by State Comptroller of accounts of Rensselaer County, regarding expenditures of County Clerk, compensation and fees of, etc. Office of Sheriff, appointment of deputies, fees, etc. Audit by Board of Supervisors of bills for advertising notices in newspapers. Salary of clerk, etc. Whether action of such officials is authorized.

(See opinion March 11, 1909, p. 344 Rep.).

STATE OF NEW YORK,

ATTORNEY-GENERAL'S OFFICE,

ALBANY, *April* 11, 1910.

Hon. CLARK WILLIAMS, *State Comptroller, Albany, N. Y.:*

Dear Sir.— I acknowledge your letter of the 6th inst., transmitting to me copy of the report made by your department of the accounts of the county of Rensselaer, together with your letter to the board of supervisors of such county and memoranda submitted by attorneys for the county clerk, the sheriff, and the board of supervisors, in opposition to the conclusions reached by your department and stated in such report and letter. You request that I give you my opinion relative to the several matters contained in the report and letter, which are covered by these memoranda.

The report of your examiners covers a wide field but my opinion is requested only upon those points controverted by the attorneys above mentioned. I will consider first the objections raised by the county clerk.

Your report states that bills of the county clerk aggregating $2,270.61 were audited by the board of supervisors without any warrant of law so far as you can discover. These bills are made up of fifteen items. Of these fifteen, all but two — the third and fourth — are claimed by the attorney for the county clerk to be proper.

At the outset I am confronted with the difficulty which also confronted your department — that these accounts do not specifically state or describe the items which they represent. It is not clear whether any of them represent disbursements actually incurred by the county clerk, or, if so, to what extent, nor is it possible in many instances to determine precisely what work the charge represents. In this opinion, therefore, I shall confine myself to determining whether or not from the facts before me I find legal justification for these charges.

It is well settled that the county clerk, both as county clerk and as clerk of the court, must perform all the duties required of him without fee or reward except as expressly provided by law. (Judiciary Law, § 252. Public Officers Law, § 67.) It is also clear that a board of supervisors cannot audit or allow a claim not authorized by statute. With these guiding principles, I will take up the various items claimed to be legal charges in the memorandum submitted on behalf of the county clerk.

" 6. Recording Supreme and County Court
Orders .... $845.00."

It is claimed for the county clerk that this is justified under
rule 7 of the general rules of practice of the Supreme Court
requiring clerks to keep (1) A book in which shall be entered the
title of all civil actions and special proceedings with entries under
each denoting papers filed, orders made, and the steps taken
therein; (2) A book in which shall be entered at large each bond
and undertaking filed; and (3) Such other books, properly indexed, as may be necessary to enter the minutes of the court,
docket judgments, enter orders, and other necessary matters. It
does not appear that the services (recording court orders) charged
for in this item were required by this rule, but even if they were,
no compensation therefor is provided.

It is also contended in reference to this item that the special
act contained in chapter 92 of the Laws of 1893 prescribing the
duties of the clerk of the county of Rensselaer and giving him a
salary as such clerk, does not prevent these charges.

Section 1 of this act provides in part as follows:

" The clerk of the county of Rensselaer shall receive as
compensation for his services as clerk of all courts of which
he is or shall be clerk an annual salary of two thousand
dollars."

Section 2 provides as follows:

" It shall be the duty of said clerk to perform all services
which he is or shall be required by law to perform as clerk of
such courts, and no compensation, payment or allowance, shall
be made to him or to any special deputy clerk for any services rendered at the sessions of said courts by such clerk,
or special deputy clerk, except the salary aforesaid, and said
salary shall be paid to the said clerk in the same manner
as the salaries of other county officers are paid."

The claim is made that inasmuch as under section 2 it is provided only that no compensation shall be made to the county clerk
or any special deputy clerk for services rendered " *at the sessions
of said courts* " except the salary provided by the first section,
there is no prohibition against additional compensation for services performed in connection with court work outside the actual

session of the court itself. The memorandum of the counsel treats this charge by implication as representing money expended by the county clerk in employing others to perform this work, and claims that under subdivision 9 of section 240 of the County Law the clerk is entitled to reimbursement therefor. This section provides that among county charges shall be

> "9. The moneys necessarily expended by any county officer in executing the duties of his office in cases in which no specific compensation for such services is provided by law, * .* *."

This provision of the statute was considered in Walsh v. Supervisors of Albany County, 20 App. Div. 489. It was pointed out that in order to justify a charge. under this section two things must be established: First, it must be shown that the moneys were *necessarily* expended; in other words, that the work could not have been done by the county clerk with his paid assistants so that outside assistance was necessary. Second, it must be shown that the services were of a nature for which prior to the enactment of the section he was entitled to make a charge; in other words, it was held that no services could be charged for as a disbursement, under this section, which but for the existence of this law the county clerk would have been compelled to perform without fee or reward. Neither of these facts is established by the papers before me and therefore I am unable to say that this item is a legal charge.

The opinion of a former county attorney to the board of supervisors is also relied upon to justify this charge. But in this opinion it was pointed out that the law was enacted to "change the manner of compensating the clerk of the courts of Rensselaer county, which before the passage of said act was made by allowing to such clerk certain fees for particular services which he rendered as such clerk during the sessions of court, such as swearing jurors, swearing witnesses, making day calendars, swearing grand jurors, filing papers, entering orders, etc." The conclusion of the opinion is that "the county clerk is entitled to the fees provided by law for any duties rendered by him *as county clerk* outside of the sessions of the courts." In other words, the conclusion would

seem to support the view of the Comptroller that the only fees
thereafter legally chargeable were those for work as county clerk —
not for work as clerk of the courts.

The second item is

> " 12.   Indexing, grantors, grantees, mortgagors,
>   mortgagees, etc..................... $247.23."

This charge is justified under section 316 of the Real Property
Law, which is in part as follows:

> " § 316.   Indexes.— Each recording officer must provide,
> at the expense of his county, proper books for making general
> indexes of instruments recorded in his office, and must form
> indexes therein, so as to afford correct and easy reference to
> the books of record in his office."

It is claimed that the words " at the expense of his county "
refer not only to the providing of the books but also to the making
of the indexes. In my judgment, this construction is not authorized. The intent of the statute is that the books shall be provided at the expense of the county and that the county clerk must
thereafter form indexes therein. Nor does it appear that the
amount represents disbursements which would be legal charges
under section 240 of the County Law, *supra*. I must therefore
advise you that under the facts before me I cannot say that this
charge is legal.

The next item is
> " 13.   Extending marginal indexes......... $263.51."

It is admitted that this represents part of the work directed by
the above law. It is claimed that it was undertaken at the instance of members of the bar of Rensselaer county and has made
the records of the county clerk's office particularly useful. My
attention is called to no provision of law authorizing the charge
and therefore what I have said about the preceding item applies
equally here.

The next item is

> " 9.   Criminal searches................... $16.50."

It is claimed on the memorandum that these charges represent searches for indictments made at the request of the district attorney to discover previous convictions of persons then under indictment, and it is pointed out that under the County Law the district attorney might, upon the order of a judge, have paid the county clerk directly for these searches and been reimbursed from the county treasury. If this claim is sound, of course the county has not been the loser by this transaction but this fact itself would not make this item a legal charge for the county clerk, as there is no provision of law authorizing such a charge to be made by him.

The next item is

"11. Keeping temporary loan book........ $10.00."

This is claimed to be justified by chapter 20, Laws of 1904, " as well as by a proper administration of public business." The statute referred to provides in part:

"The county clerk shall enter in a book, in his office, to be provided therefor at the expense of the county, the date of each such note, certificate of indebtedness or other county obligation, and the amount for which it was issued, the time when payable, and a general statement as to the resolution of the board of supervisors authorizing the issue thereof."

It is not stated that this charge represents the cost of the book and there is no provision for compensating the county clerk for the performance of the duties imposed upon him by this chapter. The presumption, therefore, is that they must be performed gratuitously.

The next item is

"10. Making court calendars, entering causes, indexing same, and civil and criminal. bond books .... $500."

This item is an extremely vague statement and does not conform to the provisions of the County Law requiring that all bills audited must be itemized. It is not claimed that the amount represents disbursements by the county clerk and my attention is called to no statute authorizing compensation to him and for his services in making up the calendars. In my judgment, this charge was not authorized.

People ex rel. Williams v. Supervisors, 15 How. Pr. 225.

The next item is

"1. Notice of court to judge, sheriff and
papers . . . . $18.00."

It is stated that this is made under section 1043 of the Code of
Civil Procedure. The provisions of this section are now found
in section 514 of the Judiciary Law. If this represents a disbursement made by him for publishing notices of court in the
newspapers, it is proper, but there is nothing before me indicating
that any such claim is made, nor is there any statute authorizing
compensation for his services in connection with this work.

The next item is

"2. Orders to publish same . . . . $14.00."

The same comment which I have made upon the last item applies
equally here.

The next item is

"5. Certificates to witnesses, jurors and court
attendants . . . . $177.72."

This is explained on the memorandum as representing certificates granted to the persons named so they could be paid by the
county treasurer, and the charge is justified under section 3304
of the Code of Civil Procedure, authorizing the county clerk to
charge "for a certificate other than a paper for the copying of
which he is entitled to a fee as a copy, twenty-five cents." In the
first place, it would seem clear that this work must be during the
sessions of court and therefore covered by the salary granted as
above. In the second place, this section of the code refers only
to the fees allowed the county clerk as county clerk, his fees as
clerk of the court being prescribed by section 3301, which contains no such provision. Finally, there is nothing to show that
any such charge was intended to be made payable by the county,
in any event.

The next item which is claimed to be proper is

"7. Preparing jury slips . . . . $104.28."

It is claimed that this is authorized under sections 1037 and
1038 of the Code of Civil Procedure. These provisions are now

found in sections 505 and 508 of the Judiciary Law. Section 505
prescribes that jury lists must be made out by the town board and
filed by these officers with the county clerk. Section 508 requires
the county clerk to make ballots containing separately the names
of the jurors. No compensation is provided for the performance
of this duty, and therefore it must be taken that he is compelled
to perform it without reward. In fact, it has been decided that
if he paid another for doing this work such payment could not be
recovered by him from the county as a matter of disbursement.

> Matter of Walsh v. Supervisors of Albany County, 20
> App. Div. 489.

This item, therefore, is clearly illegal.

    " 8.   Placing jury slips in envelopes........ $20.00."

This service was apparently gratuitous on the part of the clerk,
no provision of law being called to my attention imposing such
duty upon him. What has been said regarding the last item,
therefore, applies equally here.

    " 14.   Laundering towels................. $14.00."

It does not appear from the bill that this amount was to represent a disbursement. If it represented an actual expenditure
made by the clerk, it is, in my judgment, clearly a legal charge
against the county. On the other hand, if it was intended to
represent compensation to him and did not represent an actual
expenditure, it is as clearly illegal.

> See People ex rel. Caldwell v. Board of Supervisors, 45
> App. Div. 42, at page 52.

    " 15.   Furnishing sundry lists of officers.... $12.50."

It seems to be admitted that no provision of law requires the
clerk to furnish these lists, and no statute is cited as authority
for such compensation. Neither is it claimed that the amount
represents reimbursement. I cannot say, therefore, that this item
is a legal charge.

As to the charges made by the sheriff:

Your report criticizes in several particulars the conduct of the
office of the sheriff of this county and the charges made by him.

Three of these criticisms are claimed in the memorandum to be erroneous.

It appears that the sheriff appointed a special deputy sheriff in addition to the under-sheriff, three deputies and cook whom he is authorized to appoint by the special statute regulating his office (chapter 9, Laws of 1903, as amended by chapter 4, Laws of 1904). This special deputy was appointed to serve without salary. He was given a desk in the office of the sheriff and when papers requiring the performance of official duty for individuals were received, they were delivered to this deputy who took charge of the service of processes or collection of the execution and retained the fees therefor. It appears that the fees so retained amounted to $431.38 for the service of papers, $611.77 for poundage on execution, and $872.50 for county charges representing work performed for the county.

The special statute above referred to makes the office of sheriff of Rensselaer county a salaried office. It provides that the sheriff shall receive " as compensation for all of his services an annual salary of four thousand dollars per annum." It is next provided that it shall be his duty " to perform all the services which he is or shall be required or authorized by law to perform * * * for the county and for individuals, including his duties as officer of the courts and keeper of the jail, and no compensation, payment or allowance shall be made to him for his own use for any such services except the salary aforesaid." In section 3 of the act, it is provided that all fees " which such sheriff shall charge or receive, or which he shall legally be authorized, required or entitled to charge or receive, shall belong to the county of Rensselaer." By section 4 of the act, he is required to keep a book showing the services performed by him, his under-sheriff or deputies, and all fees received or chargeable by him pursuant to law; and by section 5, he is required to transmit monthly to the treasurer of the county a statement " of all moneys received by him for fees, perquisites and emoluments for all services rendered by him as aforesaid " and to pay over " the whole amount of the moneys so received by him for the benefit of said county." By a subsequent section of the act, it is made a misdemeanor for any officer named in the act to receive to his own use any fee, perquisite or emolument contrary to the provisions of that act.

The examination disclosed that the sheriff had transmitted for the period in question only $171.81 of fees to the treasurer; that the fees received by the special deputy as aforesaid were not turned over to the county but were retained by that deputy as compensation for his services.

To justify this charge it is claimed that the salary provided by the statute is to pay the sheriff only for *his* services; that the fees which are made the property of the county and required to be transmitted to the treasurer are only those for services " rendered by him as aforesaid; " and that fees paid this special deputy were not paid to the sheriff or for services performed by the sheriff.

The clear purpose of the act is to substitute the salaries therein specified for the fees which had previously been the source of remuneration of the sheriff and his deputies and to make these fees a county revenue. Fees paid to a deputy sheriff are paid to the sheriff and acts done by a deputy sheriff are the acts of the sheriff. The language of the statute, moreover, does not provide simply that the fees received by the sheriff shall be the property of the county, but also that the fees chargeable by him, which he is authorized or entitled to charge, shall belong to the county. The language of the act, therefore, makes it impossible for me to accede to the claim that the special deputy was authorized to receive these fees and retain them. They are the property of the county and when received by the deputy are received by the sheriff and must be turned over to the county.

The second claim is that the criticism contained in your report is improper in holding that the salaried deputies were improperly appointed by the sheriff to serve also as court attendants and receive compensation for such service in addition to the salaries. The special act already referred to by the same section granting the power to the sheriff to appoint his under-sheriff and deputies, provides: " The sheriff may appoint pursuant to law, not to exceed sixteen court attendants for any court at which a grand jury is not in attendance, and not to exceed eighteen for any court at which a grand jury is in attendance." Under this authorization the sheriff appointed his three salaried deputies to also serve as court attendants and they did so serve, as your report shows, for about one hundred days each during the year, receiving additional compensation therefor. It is urged that there is no legal objection to this course. The sheriff claimed that he was compelled to appoint the special deputy already referred to because he did not have sufficient assistants to perform the work of his department without such additional deputy. As pointed out in your report, the fact that the regular deputies served in the aggregate about three hundred days as court attendants would seem to show that but for their employment in such positions the appointment of the additional deputy might have been unnecessary. Even though, as appears from the statute, the duties of the three deputies are largely in connection with the jail, one being known as the jailor, one as the assistant jailor, and one as the night watchman, it does not follow that they could not have assisted the sheriff in the performance of these other duties which were actually performed by the special deputy.

Moreover, the same section of law which provides for their appointment and the appointment of the court attendants, contains this significant sentence:

"Said court attendants so appointed shall also when not actively engaged in the performance of their regular duties, perform such service under the direction of the sheriff as he may require."

This sentence clearly shows that the statute did not contemplate the appointment of the salaried deputies to the positions of court attendants. If they had not been so appointed, the services of three additional men during the terms of the courts might have been secured for the general work of the sheriff's office when they were not engaged in their duties as court attendants. Finally, it is my opinion that the positions of paid deputy on an annual salary and court attendant on a per diem salary are inconsistent and incompatible, and therefore, that the appointments, upon well settled principles of law, were improper. This conclusion is supported not only by the provisions of the law to which I have already referred and the facts showing the necessity for the employment of additional help in the office, but also by the fact that a deputy sheriff receiving an annual salary from the county must be presumed to be required to devote all of his time during regular office hours to the duties of his position.

The third question raised in connection with the sheriff's office is regarding certain bills audited to the deputy sheriff for the year 1907 for transporting criminals to the penitentiary and to the House of the Good Shepherd. For this service he charged a flat rate of $3 for each person so transported. It is claimed that this charge is sanctioned by ancient usage and also by section 3 of chapter 209, Laws of 1874. The latter statute is now found in the Prison Law and the Penal Law, section 1 being incorporated in section 320 of the Prison Law and sections 2 and 3 being found in section 2196 of the Penal Law. It appears from an examination of these sections that the first one provides that the board of supervisors in any county may contract with the board of supervisors in another county having a penitentiary for the custody of criminals of the former county in such penitentiary. The latter section provides that where this is done, the officers transporting the prisoners to such penitentiary shall be entitled to " such fees and expenses therefor as the several boards of supervisors of the several counties of this State shall prescribe and allow." In other words, it appears that this provision is not a general authority for the granting of fees in all cases for transporting criminals to prison, but is strictly limited to the case of a contract between two counties and the transportation of criminals from one county to the penitentiary of another county under such contract It does not appear from these charges whether or not such a contract exists in the case of the county of Rensselaer, or, if it does, whether any of the transportation herein contained consisted of carrying criminals to the penitentiary in another county. If it did, such charge would be legal. On the other hand, it affirmatively appears that some of the charges were not for these purposes, as they are stated to include the transportation of indigents to the House of Industry and other parties to the House of the Good Shepherd. The House of the Good Shepherd is located at Troy, Rensselaer county. (Chapter 603, Laws of 1902.) In so far as the charges were made for such services as these, they are illegal. For such services, the sheriff or his deputy is entitled only to reimbursement for actual expenses.

This covers all the points raised in the memorandum on behalf of the county clerk and the sheriff.

16

A memorandum is also submitted on behalf of the board of supervisors. This covers two questions. It first challenges the soundness of the report of your examiners in so far as the same criticised the audit of the bills of the Rensselaer County Eagle, the Rensselaer County Standard, and the Evening Standard Publishing Company by that board. It appears that these accounts were submitted in 1906 to the board of supervisors and that they were for advertising redemption notices of tax sales for the year 1906, amounting in each instance to $461.25. It further appears that these various items contained in the bills submitted by these newspapers were subtracted by the committee on printers accounts of the board of supervisors and that it was recommended that the bills be audited at the reduced amount. Such recommendation was subsequently adopted by the board. These bills were in later years again from time to time presented but generally marked " Not considered." Finally, in July, 1908, the same items thus rejected were allowed.

It is claimed by the county attorney that this allowance was proper. He points out that these newspapers were designated under chapter 512 of the Laws of 1892, which was a special act relating to Rensselaer county. Thereafter the Second Class Cities Law and the General Tax Law were passed (in 1898 and 1896 respectively) and there was doubt at the time these papers were designated for the publication of these notices as to whether the provisions of the two latter laws, general in their nature, had repealed by implication the provisions of the special act applying only to Rensselaer county. The general laws provided for the designation of different papers for the publication of these notices, it being admitted that these three papers were designated under the provisions of the special act. The learned county attorney points out that at the time these orders were given litigation was pending in the courts to determine this legal question. This litigation eventually resulted in the judgment of the Appellate Division and the Court of Appeals holding that the special act was repealed by implication by these two general acts.

Matter of Troy Press Company, 115 App. Div. 25; 187 N. Y. 279.

The latter decision was rendered in January, 1907.   It is claimed that these facts show that the original rejection by the board was not upon the merits and that the rule of law providing that a board of supervisors has no power to audit an account rejected by a former board, therefore, has no application.

It does not clearly appear that this rejection by the former board was not on the merits. The proceedings of record set forth in your report throw no light upon this. Evidently there was no rejection because of improper form or lack of proper itemization or verification, and under the circumstances, it is my judgment that there is such justification for the conclusion of your examiners that the rejection must be presumed to have been on the merits.

Even if this is not so, it seems to me that the same result must be reached. Under the decision of the Court of Appeals the designation of these newspapers to publish the notices was illegal as the law authorizing such designation had been repealed. It would therefore follow that the payment for such publication was also unauthorized and illegal.

The last point made by the county attorney is that your examiners erred in criticising the payment made by the board of supervisors of $625 to a clerk appointed by the finance committee. It appears that the duties performed by this clerk were duties imposed by the statute either upon the clerk of the board or the supervisors themselves. (See Article 3 of the Tax Law, §§ 50–63; § 50 of the County Law.)

It is urged that the employment of this clerk was ratified by the board of supervisors in approving and auditing his account, and that as an incidental power to their general powers they were authorized to make such expenditure. In view of the fact that the duties were imposed, however, upon other officers, it would seem that such expense was not justified. Moreover, under chapter 560 of the Laws of 1875, it is provided that it shall not be lawful for the board of supervisors of the county of Rensselaer to "pay for the services of any clerk or clerks of said board a greater amount in the aggregate than the sum of six hundred dollars in any one year," and although the amount of this salary has been raised, the act seems never to have been repealed. Finally, it is settled by authority that the board of supervisors has no right to create an office not already provided for by statute.

People ex rel. Masterson v. Gallup, 96 N. Y. 628.

For all these reasons, it is my opinion that the appointment and employment of this finance clerk did not come within the implied powers of the board, and that the payment of this amount was unauthorized.

It is but fair to say that it appears that in all the foregoing matters the county clerk, sheriff and board of supervisors acted in accordance with custom, and in some instances believed that they were acting under legal advice given to their predecessors. The county clerk stated to the examiners, as stated in your report, that he assumed and was advised by his office force that all the charges made by him were in conformity with an opinion which had been rendered prior to his incumbency of the office and also in conformity with the practices previously in vogue. There is no claim that any of these charges were made through improper motives or with any unlawful intent, and in holding that in my opinion many of the charges were improper and unauthorized I do not wish to be understood as in any way questioning the personal integrity or honesty of these officials.

It was stated on the memorandum in behalf of the county clerk that he had appeared before your representatives and given them all the information which he had and all the explanations which he could make concerning the propriety and legality of these items. The statements made by him to your examiners are contained in your report which was before his attorney when this memorandum was made. I therefore do not see that I could secure any further information from that official, and accordingly, although as I stated at the outset, the facts before me are meagre and inconclusive, I must base my opinion upon them.

Very truly yours,
EDWARD R. O'MALLEY,
Attorney-General.

*General Business Law — Article 7 — Detectives — Licenses —
Corporations.*

" International Detective Bureau " not entitled to do business as
a detective bureau without procuring license. Acts of Gerardo
Luisi, as director of such corporation, in engaging in the
business of detective as a corporation, instead of an individual, when his license was an individual license, in violation
of statute.

STATE OF NEW YORK,

ATTORNEY-GENERAL'S OFFICE,

. ALBANY, *April* 18, 1910.

Mr. FRANK WHITFIELD, *Detective Agent. State Comptroller's
Office, Albany, N. Y.:*

Dear Sir.— I am in receipt of your inquiry communicated to
me by Mr. Prentice under date of the 1st inst., as to whether
Gerardo Luisi, a duly licensed detective, who is doing business
under the title of the " International Detective Bureau " has
violated the provisions of article 7 of the General Business Law.

It appears that a corporation was formed in September last
under the name of the " International Detective Bureau;" that
Luisi was one of the incorporators and one of the directors named
in the certificate of incorporation, but it is stated that there are
no facts presented tending to show that the corporation ever did
any business.

It appears further that in January last Luisi filed a certificate
with the New York county clerk under the provisions of section
440 of the Penal Law, setting forth his true name and that he
was to conduct business under the name of the " International
Detective Bureau."

In these acts performed by him I can see no violation of the
statute in relation to private detectives unless he is carrying on
such business as a corporation instead of doing it as an individual.
His license runs to him individually and not to the corporation.

The cost of a license to an individual is less than to a corporation. If the corporation is not doing business and Luisi is in no way holding himself out as acting under or by virtue of the corporation but solely in his individual capacity, no violation of article 7 of the General Business Law has taken place.

But do the acts of Luisi show that he is merely carrying on business as an individual? A corporation is in existence, but recently created and of which Luisi was an incorporator, the name of which is the "International Detective Bureau." Soon after the creation of the corporation and while Luisi is a director thereof, business is commenced under the name of this corporation, namely, the "International Detective Bureau," with Luisi in charge.

It is true that shortly after the creation of the corporation Luisi filed a certificate in the county clerk's office setting forth that he was doing business under the assumed name of the "International Detective Bureau." He knew at that time that such name belonged to the corporation; that he was a director of said corporation and charged with the duty of protecting its interests and rights. As long as said corporation was in existence it was entitled to its corporate name and privileges. A director thereof had no right to appropriate either for his individual use. No other conclusion seems tenable to me than that Luisi is doing business in the name of the corporation created by him and that such corporation, the "International Detective Bureau," is not entitled to do business as a detective bureau until it has procured a license so to do.

Yours very truly,

EDWARD R. O'MALLEY,

Attorney-General.

Highways — Contracts — Liens.

Construction of the Lake Pleasant–Speculator Road No. 277, Hamilton county. Lien of New York State National Bank and assignment of interest of Robert Shafer, should be disregarded by the State Comptroller, and payments should be made to the Empire State Surety Company, according to certificates of the Highway Commission.

STATE OF NEW YORK,

Attorney-General's Office,

Albany, *April* 21, 1910.

Hon. Clark Williams, *State Comptroller, Albany, N. Y.:*

Dear Sir.— Answering your letter of April 15, in the matter of the contract dated April 12, 1906, entered into by the State Engineer and Surveyor with Robert Shafer, for the construction of the Lake Pleasant–Speculator Road, Hamilton county, known as Road No. 277, in which you ask for an opinion as to whether the lien filed by the New York State National Bank, on February 19, 1910, and the assignment by Robert Shafer to said bank, filed April 1, 1910, were effective and whether payment could be safely made under the situation, as set out in your letter to the Empire State Surety Company, I beg to state:

It appears from an examination of the original contract and the papers on file in your office, that the amount of the contract was $24,443.40, and that the Empire State Surety Company was bondsman on this contract to the amount of $12,220. That up to and including November 24, 1908, payments were made to said Robert Shafer aggregating $15,970.51. That on April 6, 1909, the State Commission of Highways (which had succeeded in highway matters to the position of the State Engineer and Surveyor), through its secretary, notified said Robert Shafer in writing, as provided by said contract, that if after ten days from that date he failed to provide men, labor, tools, etc., for the proper performance of his contract, that they would, as provided by said contract, complete the work in such manner as they deemed advisable. In accordance with the contract, a copy of this notice was served on the bondsmen, the Empire State Surety Company. That after the time stipulated, the bonding company, on June 5th, 1909, entered into a contract to complete the said original contract, No. 277, as fully and completely as if they had been the original contractor.

Between May 20, 1909, and December 21, 1909, certain liens were filed against said contract which have since either been discharged or died by limitation.

On September 10, 1909, the Highway Commission certified to the Comptroller that there was due the Empire State Surety Company, on account of said contract, a payment in the amount of $2,067.92, of which the county was to pay $1,000 and the State, $1,067.92. On November 11, 1909, the secretary of the Highway Commission, by direction of said Commission, notified the clerk of the Board of Supervisors and the County Superintendent of Highways of Hamilton County, of the intention of said Commission to accept said road, unless notice of protest was received as provided by law. On December 3, 1909, the road was finally accepted and the Highway Commission certified to the Comptroller a final certificate that the work had been completed and accepted and that there was due the Empire State Surety Company, $6,464.72, of which the county was to pay $3,653.82 and the State was to pay $2,810.90.

Section 12 of the Lien Law provides that

" At any time before the construction of a public improvement is completed and accepted by the State or by the municipal corporation, and within thirty days after such completion and acceptance, a person performing work for, or furnishing materials to, etc., may file a notice of lien with the head of the department or bureau having charge of such construction, and that the Comptroller of the State, or that the financial officer," etc.

It is, therefore, my opinion that the alleged lien of the New York State National Bank so filed on February 19, 1910, should be disregarded, as the time to file liens expired thirty days after December 3, 1909.

It is my opinion that the steps taken by the Highway Commission in notifying the contractor, Robert Shafer, that after ten days from April 6, 1909, if he still failed to provide men and proceed with the work that said Commission would complete said work, etc., a copy of which notice was served upon the bondsmen of Robert Shafer, and the agreement afterward entered into by said Commission with said bondsmen for the completion of the work, fully and effectively foreclosed all interest that the said Robert Shafer had in said contract and that his attempted assignment of his interest in said contract to said New York State National Bank, should be disregarded.

In view of the above, you are advised that the alleged lien of the New York State National Bank, filed on February 19, 1910, for $10,000 and the assignment, filed April 1, 1910, of the interest of Robert Shafer in said contract to said bank, should be disregarded and that you are justified in making payments to the Empire State Surety Company, stated above, as provided by the certificates of the Highway Commission.

Respectfully yours,

EDWARD R. O'MALLEY,

Attorney-General.

Tax Law — Sections 272, 276, 277 — Stock Transfers — Stamps.

1. When brokerage firm delivers a memorandum of sale of stock with *canceled* stamps affixed thereto by employees whose acts are unknown to them, such firm is liable for payment of the tax.

2. Transfer Agent of the United States Steel Corporation must require stamps to be affixed on all deliveries of stock. It is his duty to require tax to be paid before stock is delivered.

STATE OF NEW YORK,

ATTORNEY-GENERAL'S OFFICE,

ALBANY, *April* 27, 1910.

Hon. CLARK WILLIAMS, *State Comptroller, Albany, N. Y.:*

Dear Sir.— I acknowledge your letter of the 9th inst., in which you ask my opinion regarding the proper interpretation of certain sections of the Tax Law in reference to the Stock Transfer Act. You state that a large number of memoranda of sales of stock have affixed to them stamps which have been used and canceled prior to being so affixed. You also state that in most cases the members of the brokerage firms issuing these tickets or memoranda of sales are ignorant of these facts and that the transactions are usually the result of some action by an employee whose business it is to stamp the outgoing sales tickets; this employee substitutes a canceled stamp for the new one which is given him by the cashier in charge of the stamps, subsequently selling the uncanceled stamps.

You ask whether the brokerage firms in whose offices these transactions occur are in any way liable. You state that you have held that they are responsible for the payment of the tax in such cases but that they have questioned your ruling.

It is my opinion, from an examination of the statute, that they are liable for the payment of the tax. Section 272 provides as follows:

> "Any person or persons who shall make any sale or transfer without paying the tax by this article imposed or who shall in pursuance of any sale or agreement deliver any stock, or evidence of the sale of or agreement to sell any stock or bill or memorandum thereof, without having the stamps provided for in this article affixed thereto, shall be deemed guilty of a misdemeanor, and upon conviction thereof shall pay a fine of not less than five hundred nor more than one thousand dollars, or be imprisoned not more than six months, or by both such fine and imprisonment at the discretion of the court."

Section 276 provides that the Comptroller may examine the books kept as therein required, and then proceeds:

> "If from such examination the comptroller ascertains that the tax provided for in this article has not been paid he shall bring an action in his name as such comptroller in any court of competent jurisdiction for the recovery of such tax and for any penalty incurred by any person under the provisions of this article.

Section 277 provides as follows:

> "Any person who shall violate the provisions of this
> article shall in addition to the penalties herein provided for-
> feit to the people of the state a civil penalty of five hundred
> dollars for each violation. The state comptroller shall bring
> an action in his name as such comptroller in any court of
> competent jurisdiction for the recovery of any civil penalty
> and all moneys collected by him shall be paid into the state
> treasury."

It is my opinion that the broker or brokerage firms whose employees affix canceled stamps in payment of the tax, violate the
above provisions of the statute and are liable to the civil action
therein prescribed. It is probably true that they would not be
held criminally liable for the act of an employee, but civilly; acting through their employees, they have delivered a memorandum
of the sale of stock without having the stamps required by law
affixed thereto and such act on their part, although performed by
an agent, is sufficient, in my judgment, to render them liable for
the civil penalty prescribed by law.

The second question which you ask is in reference to the fact
that the transfer agent of the United States Steel Corporation does
not require of a transferee of stock of that corporation presenting a
certificate for transfer, that the same must be properly stamped or
accompanied by a memorandum of sale so stamped. You ask me
to advise you whether, under the statute, it is the duty of the
transfer agent to see that the stock transfer tax has been paid on
all stock so transferred.

It is my judgment that the foregoing sections of law clearly
make it the duty of a transfer agent to see that the tax is paid
before stock is delivered. A delivery of any stock without having
the stamps provided by the statute affixed, is distinctly made a
misdemeanor by section 272 above quoted. It would follow from
this that the transfer agent of the United States Steel Corporation
in deliberately neglecting to require the affixing of such stamps
is subjecting itself not only to a civil penalty, as above provided,
but also to prosecution for misdemeanor.

Very truly yours,
EDWARD R. O'MALLEY,
Attorney-General.

General Business Law — Sections 71, 73 — Detectives —
Licenses — Corporations.

Procedure where partnership having detective license is dissolved,
and members of such partnership desire to practice detective
business as individuals. Issue of separate licenses by Comptroller. No refund of copartnership license fee allowable
under section 73.

(See opinions April 21, July 30, S ptember 20, 1909, January 18,
February 4, April 16, May 7, 1910.)

STATE OF NEW YORK,

Attorney-General's Office,

Albany, *May* 4, 1910.

Hon. Clark Williams, *State Comptroller, Albany, N. Y.:*

Dear Sir.— I am in receipt of your letter of April 21st asking
my opinion as to the right of the members of a copartnership, to
which a copartnership detective license has been issued by your
office, to continue in the detective business as individuals after the
partnership has for all practical purposes been dissolved. You
also send a letter from A. P. Hallett stating that a detective license
was issued to a copartnership, composed of Frederick Wagner and
Jackman F. Stockdale; that subsequently they separated and discontinued the business at No. 320 Broadway where they were
authorized to conduct the same, and that each set up business for
himself independently of the other.

Manifestly the two cannot carry on in their separate individual
capacities the business of private detective under their partnership
license as that would produce a condition of two entirely separate
and unrelated agencies or business enterprises operating under one
license.

I think there is no doubt but that should a member of a partnership desire to retire therefrom, such an arrangement might be
effected, leaving the surviving partner in possession of the business
and the license and empowered to continue the business thereunder.

If such an agreement has been made in this case, or if the acts
of the parties have been such as to effect a withdrawal of one of the

members, leaving the other in possession of the business, such surviving partner may continue under the license and name of the partnership.

Mr. Hallett's letter states that the partnership discontinued the business at No. 320 Broadway and that one of the partners opened an office at 162 East Eighty-sixth street and the other at 445 Manhattan avenue. In this connection I call your attention to a part of section 73 of the General Business Law, which provides:

> " The license certificate shall specify the business address of the applicant to whom it is issued and the names and residences of the person or persons filing the statement required by section 71 upon which the license is issued and in the event of a change of any such address or residence the comptroller shall be duly notified in writing of such change within five days thereafter, and failure to give such notification shall be sufficient cause for the revocation of such license."

It is not stated whether or not this provision was complied with, nor is it possible to state which of the partners, if either, is entitled to carry on the business of the partnership under its license. That question is largely dependent upon the agreement, expressed or implied, between the parties themselves at the dissolution of the partnership, concerning the future conduct of its business. It is a question of fact as to what took place between them. This case illustrates the difficulty of arriving at a correct decision as to the legal rights of parties without a complete understanding of the facts derived from a full hearing of all parties interested.

Mr. Hallett also asks the following question: "Is there anything in the Detective Law to prohibit the State Comptroller from issuing separate licenses to these persons for the remainder of the term for which the copartnership was licensed upon their paying to the State Comptroller a proportionate part of the difference between the license fee of the copartnership and two individuals?"

I find no provision of law which would permit such an exchange of licenses. This would require the surrender of the partnership license and the issue of individual licenses to the members thereof.

Section 73 contains a provision that in the event of the revocation or surrender of a license no refund shall be made in respect to any license fee paid under the provisions thereof. The same section provides for the issue of licenses to indivduals, partnerships and corporations and the only provision for the issue of a license to an individual requires the payment of one hundred dollars as a license fee. This section would seem to forbid the exchange suggested in your inquiry.

Yours very truly,

EDWARD R. O'MALLEY,

Attorney-General.

Tax Law — Section 270 — Stock Transfers.

Transfer of preferred shares or certificates of stock of domestic corporation where payments have been made and credited but no certificates issued. Transfer of interest by subscribers to such preferred stock represents beneficial interest and is subject to tax. Computation upon such tax should be upon basis of exact amount paid on the stock which may be regarded as the face value.

(See opinion February 8, 1910.)

STATE OF NEW YORK,

ATTORNEY-GENERAL'S OFFICE,

ALBANY, *May 6, 1910.*

Hon. CLARK WILLIAMS, *State Comptroller, Albany, N. Y.:*

Dear Sir.— I acknowledge receipt of your letter of the 30th ult., signed by Mr. Alford, requesting my opinion as to the taxability of the following transaction under the Stock Transfer Tax Law:

It appears from the statement of facts in the letter enclosed in your communication, that a domestic corporation has authorized preferred and common stock; that the common stock has been issued in full and the preferred stock subscribed in full but only 10 per cent. has been paid in on each share of the latter class. The preferred stockholders have been accepted as such by the board of

directors but no preferred stock certificates have been issued. The
subscribers have been credited on the books of the company with
the payments made on account of their subscriptions. It is stated
that under the terms of the agreement, the subscribers or their
assigns are not entitled to receive certificates for stock until each
share has been paid in full.

The question is whether upon the assignment by all the subscribers to the preferred stock of their rights under these subscriptions to one man, by written assignment, such transaction is subject to taxation under the Stock Transfer Tax Law.

Section 270 of the Tax Law provides in part as follows:

> "There is hereby imposed * * * a tax * * *
> on all sales, or agreements to sell, or memoranda of sales, or
> deliveries, or transfers, of shares or certificates of stock, in
> any domestic or foreign association, company or corporation
> * * * whether made upon or shown by the books of the
> association, company or corporation, or by any assignment
> in blank, or by any delivery or by any paper or agreement
> or memorandum or other evidence of transfer or sale whether
> entitling the holder in any manner to the benefit of such stock,
> or to secure the future payment of money or the future trans-
> fer of any stock, * * * ."

It is my opinion that the transfer of the interest of the subscribers in the preferred stock above described is such a transfer
of a beneficial interest in that stock as comes within the provisions
of this statute. A beneficial interest in the shares of stock is transferred, amounting to the total payments previously made upon
that stock. Such transfer, in my judgment, is as much within the
purview of the statute as a transfer of trustees' certificates entitling
the holder to certain beneficial interests in stock in the hands of
a trustee. I therefore advise you that the transaction is subject
to a tax.

The second question presented is the basis upon which such tax
shall be computed. The statute provides that the tax shall be
imposed at the rate of two cents on each one hundred dollars *of
face value or fraction thereof.* Although in one sense the face
value of the stock in which an interest is being assigned is one

hundred dollars, in another sense this is not so for it probably
appears upon the face of the assignment that only ten dollars, or
whatever the amount may be, has been actually paid on such stock.
It would likewise seem to be inequitable to assess the tax upon a
transfer of stock upon which only ten dollars has been paid at the
same basis as if it were full paid. I therefore advise you that if
there is anything appearing on the face of the assignment or of
any certificate of the beneficial interest accompanying such assignment showing the exact amount paid in on the stock, such amount
may properly be regarded as the face value for the purpose of computing the tax.

Very truly yours,

EDWARD R. O'MALLEY,

Attorney-General.

---

*General Business Law — Sections 70, 75 — Detectives —
Licenses.*

Agreement between licensed private detectives and unlicensed
private detectives concerning work done in the name of the
licensed detective, and a share of profits therefrom. Whether
a violation of section 70.

(See opinions April 21, July 30, September 20, 1909, January 18,
February 4, April 16, May 4, 1910.

STATE OF NEW YORK,

ATTORNEY-GENERAL'S OFFICE,

ALBANY, *May* 7, 1910.

Hon. CLARK WILLIAMS, *State Comptroller, Albany, N. Y..*

Dear Sir.— I am in receipt of your letter of April 16, 1910, in
which you state the following case:

> " A, who is an unlicensed private detective, agrees with
> B, a licensed private detective, that any business which he
> (A) shall have confided to him shall be done in B's name and
> under the protection of his license and by B's operatives who

shall work under the direction of A, and that A and B shall divide the profits of that particular business."

You ask whether A violates section 70 of the General Business Law if he accepts work under these conditions.

As stated, all business provided for in this agreement between A and B is to be done in the name of B and therefore upon his responsibility. It further appears that such business shall be performed by B's operatives or employees, though under the direction of A.

Of course, if A is obtaining business from his clients or from the public in his own name and holding himself out as a private detective, or advertising as such, then a violation of section 70 has occurred. If, however, the business received by him has been in the name of B and carried on under the arrangement above set forth, it would seem that A might well claim that he was not carrying on the business of a private detective but rather that he was soliciting and performing services for and in the name of B.

Section 75 of the act in relation to private detectives contains the following provision:

> "Nothing in this article shall apply to employees of such duly licensed private detectives or detective agencies for whose good conduct in the business, however, the employers shall be responsible."

Yours very truly,
               EDWARD R. O'MALLEY,
                              Attorney-General.

Barge Canal — Bonds for Improvement.

Method of advertising notice of sale of $10,000,000 of bonds for
the improvement of the Erie, Oswego and Champlain canals,
and $1,000,000 for the improvement of the Cayuga and
Seneca canals. State Comptroller to use discretion in allotment of either class of bonds.

STATE OF NEW YORK,

ATTORNEY-GENERAL'S OFFICE,

ALBANY, *June* 6, 1910.

Hon. CLARK WILLIAMS, *State Comptroller, Albany, N. Y.:*

Dear Sir.— Replying to a letter of Hon. Edward T. Perine,
Deputy Comptroller, dated the 3d day of June, 1910, in which
this department is asked as to whether there are any legal objections to certain methods of advertising for the sale of barge canal
bonds, I beg to say that an examination of chapter 147 of the Laws
of 1903, chapter 66 of the Laws of 1910, chapter 391 of the Laws
of 1909 and chapter 139 of the Laws of 1910, discloses that whether
bonds are issued for the improvement of the Erie, Oswego and
Champlain canals or the Cayuga and Seneca canals, the statutory
instructions to the Comptroller for the conducting of the sales are
the same. It is stated by your deputy that it would seem desirable
to combine in one advertisement the notice of sale of $10,000,000
of bonds for the improvement of the Erie, Oswego and Champlain
canals and $1,000,000 of bonds for the improvement of the Cayuga
and Seneca canals, reserving to the Comptroller the discretion of
determining the allotment of bonds of either class. There seems
to be no statutory prohibition against this method of advertisement
and I am therefore of the opinion that there is no legal objection
to carrying out the suggestions outlined in the above mentioned
letter.

Very truly yours,

EDWARD R. O'MALLEY,

Attorney-General.

State Finance Law — Section 2a — State Officers and Employees — Salaries.

Amendment to law providing semi-monthly payment of salaries. Justices of the Supreme Court and Judges of the Court of Appeals defined in Public Officers Law, section 2, as State officers, are entitled to privileges under this act. Provision for payment by State Comptroller on the 1st and 16th days of months. He may also use discretion regarding necessary time for preparing checks, etc. Semi-monthly payment may be waived by any State officer or employee individually. (See opinion June 13, 1910).

STATE OF NEW YORK,

ATTORNEY-GENERAL'S OFFICE,

ALBANY, *June* 7, 1910.

Hon. CLARK WILLIAMS, *State Comptroller, Albany, N. Y.:*

Dear Sir.— I acknowledge your letter of the 2d inst., asking my opinion regarding certain questions which have arisen as to the proper interpretation of chapter 317, Laws of 1910. You inclose copy of proposed letter to be sent to heads of various departments in which you say that your department takes the view that payments can be made only upon the 1st and 16th days of each month or upon succeeding business days if those dates fall upon a holiday, and in which you request that payrolls be filed in your office at least three days before each of the dates named, in default of which payments will be held in abeyance until the next succeeding semi-monthly date for payment of salaries. In reference to this letter you ask the following questions:

" First. Could a similar letter be sent to all the Judges under the construction that they are officers of the State? "

" Second. Could payments to laborers or mechanics employed at the different institutions in the construction of buildings, or in making repairs thereto, and paid from special appropriations, be deferred for a period of substantially fifteen days, assuming that properly executed and audited vouchers would not be filed in this office until the first and sixteenth of each month, and probably later? "

"Third. Could this Department properly insist, as regards certain institutions which now make their payrolls up so that employees receive their salaries a full month later than the date to which salaries have accrued, that payrolls be rendered immediately at the dates of semi-monthly accruals of salaries?"

"Fourth. Could the drawing of semi-monthly checks and the delivery of such checks be waived, at the request of any department, institution or individual not wishing to be paid as often as twice each month?"

"Fifth. Could we construe this law as meaning that no salaries should be paid on any dates other than the first and sixteenth of any month, as in the case of advance payments of vacation money which we have been in the habit of advancing to individuals who will be absent from the service of the State at the time of their salaries accruing, or delayed payments such as might be necessary on account of the nonreceipt of payrolls or the physical impossibility of preparing and transmitting checks by the dates stipulated in this law?"

This law provides in part as follows:

> "The salaries of all officers of the State, and the wages of all employees thereof shall be due from and payable by the State twice each month, on the first and sixteenth days thereof, except where such days fall upon Sunday or a legal holiday when such payments shall be made upon the succeeding business day."

The purpose of this enactment is to provide that the salaries and wages of State officers and employees which have previously been paid monthly, should be paid semi-monthly. In the semi-monthly provisions found in the Labor Law it is distinctly stated that on the first of each month the employees shall be paid "the wages earned by them during the first half of the preceding month," and on the fifteenth, "the wages earned by them during the last half of the preceding calendar month." No such provisions are contained in this law. It therefore follows that if heretofore payments have been deferred for a month after the salary or wages have been earned, there is nothing to prevent this same practice being followed now. The only effect of the law is to require payments to be made semi-monthly.

The provisions of the law would not seem to be mandatory in the sense that failure to make payments on those days for good cause would necessarily constitute a violation of the law. If the employees or officers should refuse to accept payment on the dates specified or voluntarily waive it, you would not violate the law by failing to make payment under such circumstances. Likewise, if through the omission of some necessary precedent act such as the furnishing of payrolls, payment by you on that day would be practically impossible, your omission to do so could not be construed as a violation of the law.

In view of this and of the fact already mentioned, that the law does not prescribe for what period of service the respective payments shall be made, it is my opinion that you may properly make it a rule to pay only such wages and salaries as are represented by payrolls received by you at specified times before the dates prescribed, and that no payments will be made on intermediate dates.

In view of the foregoing discussion, the answers to your various questions are, in my opinion, as follows:

First. Justices of the Supreme Court and Judges of the Court of Appeals being included within the definition of State officers in section 2 of the Public Officers Law, are entitled to the same privileges under this act as other State officers.

Second and Fifth. In view of the fact that no period of the services for which payments are to be paid is prescribed by the law, it is proper for you to provide that payments shall be made on the first and sixteenth only for those services for which payrolls have been filed with you a certain number of days prior to such dates. The number of days prescribed must depend on the length of time necessary to prepare the checks after receiving the payroll, of which question, of course, you are the best judge. If such a rule is adopted, I am of the opinion that you may defer payment until the next succeeding date. Of course, notice of the adoption of the rule should be given to each department.

Third. As the law does not specify the period of service which each payment covers, I do not believe you are authorized to insist that institutions which now file payrolls in the month following the one in which the salaries or wages were earned, shall file their payrolls at the date of the semi-monthly accrual of such salaries. But if any such institutions desire payments to be made without such delay, they may do so by conforming to your rules and it would then be your duty to pay them as you pay other State departments.

Fourth. It is my opinion that the semi-monthly payment of salaries or wages may be waived by any State officer or employee. No waiver, however, could be made except by the individual entitled to receive the salary or wage.

All of which is respectfully submitted,

EDWARD R. O'MALLEY,

Attorney-General.

_____

Tax Law — Sections 182, 198 — Franchise Tax — Assessments — Corporations.

Filing application or affidavit with State Comptroller for the opening of an assessment on January 13 of succeeding year, when tax bill has been sent January 12 of preceding year, not legal. Section 198 provides that the application must be filed " within a year," etc., Sunday or holidays not excluded where term of years is prescribed.

STATE OF NEW YORK,

ATTORNEY-GENERAL'S OFFICE,

ALBANY, *June* 7, 1910.

Hon. CLARK WILLIAMS, *State Comptroller, Albany, N. Y.*:

Dear Sir.— Acknowledging your letter of the 3d inst., I beg to advise that in my opinion a corporation to which a bill for taxes provided by section 182 of the Tax Law was sent on January 12, of one year cannot have the assessment opened by an affidavit filed with your department on January 13 of the succeeding year.

Section 198 provides that such application must be filed " within one year from the time when such account shall be audited and stated." Under the decision of the Court of Appeals in Aultman v. Syme, 163 N. Y. 54, it was held that the provisions of section 27 of the Statutory Construction Law, to the effect " the day from which any specified number of days, weeks or months of time is

reckoned shall be excluded in making the reckoning " did not apply
to the computation of years.   The provisions of this section are
now found in section 20 of the General Construction Law without
change in this respect.   The same section provides:

"Sunday or a public holiday, other than a half holiday,
must be excluded from the reckoning if it is the last day of
any such period, or if it is the intervening day of any such
period of two days."

The words " such period " refer back to

"The number of days specified as a period from a certain
day within which or after or before which an act is authorized
or required to be done * * *."

Under the reasoning of the Court of Appeals in this case, therefore, the exclusion of Sunday or a public holiday would not be
permitted where the statute prescribes a period in terms of years
rather than of days.

It is therefore clear that the ruling made by your department
is correct, and that no application can be made on January 13 of
the succeeding year.   In fact, no application can be made on
January 12 even if the preceding day were Sunday or a holiday.

Very truly yours,

EDWARD R. O'MALLEY,

Attorney-General.

---

*United States Loan Commissioners — Counties of New York and
Cattaraugus.*

Provisions of chapter 201, Laws of 1910 take away from the Commissioners the power to make loans after April 29, 1910, and
require them to pay into the State treasury moneys belonging
to the United States Deposit Fund.

STATE OF NEW YORK,

ATTORNEY-GENERAL'S OFFICE,

ALBANY, *June* 30, 1910.

Hon. CLARK WILLIAMS, *State Comptroller, Albany, N. Y.:*

Dear Sir.— I acknowledge receipt of your favor of the 14th
inst., asking for my opinion as to the legality of the following

loans made by the United States Loan Commissioners of the United States deposit funds in the respective counties named:

On May 7, 1910, loan of $2,000 by Commissioners of Cattaraugus County.

On May 11, 1910, loan of $8,000 by Commissioners of New York County.

On May 11, 1910, loan of $5,000 by Commissioners of New York County.

On May 11, 1910, loan of $5,500 by Commissioners of New York County.

Chapter 201 of the Laws of 1910 provides:

" Section 81. INVESTMENTS.— The Comptroller shall invest and keep invested all moneys belonging to the common school, literature and United States deposit funds in the stocks and bonds of the United States and of this state, or for the payment of which the faith and credit of the United States or of this state are pledged, or in the judgments or awards of the court of claims of the state, or in the stocks or bonds of any county, town, city, village or school district of the state authorized to be issued by law." * * *

Section 2 provides:

" Section 2. Loan commissioners to pay into the state treasury all moneys now in their hands.— The loan commissioners of the several counties of the state of New York are hereby directed to pay into the state treasury, within thirty days after the passage of this act, all moneys in their hands belonging to the United States deposit fund."

This statute became a law April 29, 1910, so that the loan commissioners were required to pay into the State Treasury on or before May 28, 1910, all moneys in their hands belonging to said fund. The statute quoted took away from said commissioners the power to make loans after April 29, 1910, and as the loans in question were made subsequent to that date, they are illegal so far as the State is concerned.

The commissioners are bound to account as of April 29, 1910, for the moneys which came into their hands in one of two ways — (a) by paying over the money, or (b) producing mortgages given for loans made by them prior to April 29, 1910.

It is, therefore, my opinion that the thirty days provided by the statute having been spent, the commissioners should be called upon to pay into the State Treasury all moneys not loaned by them on or prior to said April 29, 1910, and no credit given them for any loans made after that date.

Yours very truly,

EDWARD R. O'MALLEY,

Attorney-General.

Agricultural Schools and Colleges — State School at Morrisville.

Act for establishment of State school (chapter 201, Laws 1908), authorizing Supervisors of Madison County to convey to State certain county buildings. Amendment in chapter 108, Laws of 1909, regarding appropriation therefor.

STATE OF NEW YORK,

ATTORNEY-GENERAL'S OFFICE,

ALBANY, *July* 14, 1910.

Hon. CLARK WILLIAMS, *State Comptroller, Albany, N. Y.:*

Dear Sir.— Your letter of recent date, submitting a question as to the duration of the life of the appropriation made under section 5 of chapter 201 of the Laws of 1908, as amended by chapter 108 of the Laws of 1909, was received.

In my opinion, while chapter 108 is denominated an amendatory act, it, for all practical purposes, superseded sections 5 and 6 of chapter 201. In other words, it was a re-enactment of said sections 5 and 6. The only change in the phraseology related to the time when the board of supervisors could convey the old site and county buildings to the State. A new appropriation of $20,000 was therefore made.

If it should be contended, however, that the appropriation under chapter 108 was not a new one, there can be no doubt but the Legislature intended to and did continue the appropriation provided for under chapter 201 and thereby reappropriated said sum, as section 5 of chapter 108 complied with all the requirements of section 23 of article 3 of the State Constitution since it distinctly specified the sum appropriated and the purposes to which it was to be applied.

In my opinion, therefore, the life of the appropriation made under chapter 201 has been prolonged and the money so appropriated is available at any time for the purposes mentioned in chapter 108, within the period of two years from its enactment.

Yours respectfully,

EDWARD R. O'MALLEY,

Attorney-General.

General Business Law — Chapter 348, Laws 1910 — Private Banking.

Application of act to private bankers acting as agent for express company. Exceptions in section 29-d apply to express and telegraph companies.

(See opinion July 26, 1910.)

STATE OF NEW YORK,

ATTORNEY-GENERAL'S OFFICE,

ALBANY, *July* 20, 1910.

Hon. CLARK WILLIAMS, *State Comptroller, Albany, N. Y.:*

Dear Sir.— I beg to reply herewith to a communication from your secretary requesting my opinion concerning the recent amendment of the General Business Law, chapter 348 of the Laws of 1910.

The statute referred to relates to the regulation of private banks and bankers and individuals and partnerships engaged directly or indirectly in the business of receiving deposits of money for safe keeping or for the purpose of transmission to another. The act requires those engaged in such business to procure a license from the Comptroller and to comply with certain other provisions, such as giving security for the honest conduct of such business.

The question submitted is whether or not the act applies to a private banker who has been appointed agent for an express company for the sole purpose of transmitting the funds of the express company.

An examination of the statute shows that section 29-d specifies several exceptions to which the provisions of the act shall not apply. Among these exceptions are express companies and telegraph companies receiving money for transmission.

If the business conducted by the person referred to consists solely of acting as agent for an express company, and if the business is conducted by him openly as the agent of the company, clearly the requirements of the statute do not apply. The purpose of the statute is to provide adequate security for those dealing with persons engaged in receiving money. If the money is received by the agent of an express company in the due course of his agency, the persons dealing with him have the security of the express company. If the transaction takes place between the depositor and the person doing business in his own name and on his own credit, the requirements of the statute should be fulfilled. Such a person must secure a license and otherwise conform to the provisions of the statute.

Very truly yours,

EDWARD R. O'MALLEY,

Attorney-General.

General Business Law — Chapter 348 — Laws 1910 — Licenses.
Licenses to corporations engaged in the business of receiving moneys for transmission in cities of the first class.

STATE OF NEW YORK,

ATTORNEY-GENERAL'S OFFICE,

ALBANY, *July 25*, 1910.

Hon. CLARK WILLIAMS, *State Comptroller, Albany, N. Y.:*

Dear Sir.— Your letter of recent date, requesting my opinion as to whether or not corporations which are engaged in the business of receiving money for transmission in cities of the first class are amenable to the provisions of chapter 348, Laws of 1910, was received.

I think the question submitted should be answered in the negative. By section 25, the applicants for the licenses provided in such statute are referred to as individuals or partnerships, and no provision is made for issuing licenses to corporations. Furthermore, individuals and partnerships are prohibited from carrying on such business without a license, and section 27 provides that penalties may be enforced upon individuals or partnerships and they are liable to criminal prosecution for violations of the law.

Yours respectfully,

EDWARD R. O'MALLEY,

Attorney-General.

General Business Law — Chapter 348, Laws 1910.

Surety under bond presented to the State Comptroller under exception 5, in section 29-d.

(See opinion July 20, 1910.)

STATE OF NEW YORK,

Attorney-General's Office,

Albany, *July* 26, 1910.

Hon. Clark Williams, *State Comptroller, Albany, N. Y.:*

Dear Sir.— Your letter of recent date in re chapter 348, Laws of 1910, and the suretyship which you may require if a bond should be presented under exception 5 in section 29-d, was received.

Section 25 makes it mandatory that the applicant and a surety company execute the bond which may be presented to the Comptroller for approval under such section. By analogy it would seem that the Comptroller has discretionary power to require that any bond presented under said exception 5 should be executed by the applicant and a surety company, as it devolves upon the Comptroller to approve of such bond as to its form and sufficiency.

Yours respectfully,

EDWARD R. O'MALLEY,

Attorney-General.

General Business Law — Chapter 348, Laws 1910 — Licenses.

Requiring of proof by State Comptroller when licensee desiring to retire from business should apply for return of securities.

STATE OF NEW YORK,

ATTORNEY-GENERAL'S OFFICE,

ALBANY, *July* 26, 1910.

Hon. CLARK WILLIAMS, *State Comptroller, Albany, N. Y.:*

Dear Sir.— Your letter of the 23d inst., requesting my opinion as to the conditions and proofs you should require when a licensee under chapter 348, Laws of 1910, desiring to retire from such business should apply for a return of securities deposited by him, was received.

In my opinion, the conditions and proofs provided for in the closing paragraph of section 26 in a case of revocation should be substantially followed. In other words, I think that in a matter of so much importance you would not be justified in returning such securities upon the *ex parte* application of the licensee in case of his alleged retirement from the business, but that he obtain an order of the court, upon due notice to you, and proof that the claims of all creditors have been satisfied.

Yours respectfully,

EDWARD R. O'MALLEY,

Attorney-General.

General Business Law — Chapter 348, Laws 1910.

Whether law applies to agents or representatives of corporations engaged in the business of selling money orders, letters of credit, tickets, etc.

STATE OF NEW YORK,

ATTORNEY-GENERAL'S OFFICE,

ALBANY, *July* 27, 1910.

Hon. CLARK WILLIAMS, *State Comptroller, Albany, N. Y.:*

Dear Sir.— In my opinion, the questions submitted in your letter of recent date, should be answered in the negative. These questions are as follows:

" First.— Whether druggists selling express companies' money orders and drafts are affected by this law."

" Second.— Whether steamship ticket agents selling drafts and money orders belonging to steamship companies for which they are agents only are affected by this law."

" Third.— Whether steamship ticket agents selling letters of credit, drafts, express orders and express and steamship companies' travelers' cheques which have been entrusted to them by banks and steamship companies and express companies for sale, are affected by this law."

The persons referred to in said questions are not engaged in the business of receiving deposits of money for safe keeping, or for the purpose of transmission to another, or for any other purpose contemplated in the provisions of this statute. The persons referred to are agents or representatives of other persons or corporations engaged in the business of selling money orders, drafts, letters of credit, tickets, etc. They issue such money orders, drafts, etc., to a purchaser and deliver the same for a consideration then paid.

The conditions prescribed for the bond of an applicant should be considered in the interpretation of the act. The conditions of such a bond are in substance that the licensee will hold the moneys so deposited in accordance with the terms of the deposit; for the repayment of such moneys; and that he will faithfully transmit any money which shall be delivered to him for transmission. It is further provided that in case of default or forfeiture of the bond, the money paid by the applicant or his surety shall constitute a trust fund for the benefit of the depositors of the licensee and of such persons as shall have delivered money to him for transmission. Furthermore, express companies are in the exempt class.

It is assumed, in giving this opinion, that such agents or representatives act strictly in accordance with their agency or the authority given in their commissions. For the above reasons, I think the questions should be answered in the negative.

Yours respectfully,

EDWARD R. O'MALLEY,

Attorney-General.

General Business Law — Chapter 348, Laws 1910.

Whether merchant comes under the provisions of above law, when
he allows employees to deposit their savings with him, he
paying them interest thereon.

STATE OF NEW YORK,

ATTORNEY-GENERAL'S OFFICE,

ALBANY, *July* 27, 1910.

Hon. CLARK WILLIAMS, *State Comptroller, Albany, N. Y.:*

Dear Sir.— Your letter of recent date in re chapter 348, Laws
of 1910, was received, submitting the following question: "A
merchant has been in the habit, in order to assist his employees,
to allow them to accumulate their savings with him, for which he
has been paying six per cent. interest. Will this party come under
the rulings of this law?"

I think the question submitted should be answered in the negative. The merchant referred to in the supposed case is not
engaged in the business of receiving deposits of money for safe
keeping or for the purpose of transmission to another or for any
purpose contemplated by the provisions of said chapter. A farmer,
merchant or lawyer who employs servants or clerks may ask for
an extension of time to pay their wages and in consideration of
such extensions he may promise to pay interest upon the earnings then due. He does not thereby receive deposits, but borrows
so much money. The employee does not deposit his wages or the
profits thereof. It seems to me that every person who borrows
money from his employee or any other person and gives his obligation or an oral promise to pay the amount thereof with or without
interest does not come within the provisions of said statute.

Yours respectfully,

EDWARD R. O'MALLEY,

Attorney-General.

Tax Law — Sections 150, 151 — *Sale of Land for Unpaid Taxes.*

County Treasurer should sell lands in same year as taxes are
reported as unpaid. Failure to do so does not prevent sale
taking place the subsequent year and conveying good title to
the purchaser.

STATE OF NEW YORK,

ATTORNEY-GENERAL'S OFFICE,

ALBANY, *August* 3, 1910.

Hon. CLARK WILLIAMS, *State Comptroller, Albany, N. Y.*:

Dear Sir.— I acknowledge your letter of the 19th ult., in which
you ask my opinion regarding the proper interpretation of sections
150 and 151 of the Tax Law, requiring the county treasurer to sell
lands for unpaid taxes. You state that you are unable to find any
authority authorizing him to sell lands except for the taxes for the
year preceding the year in which the sale is made, and ask, first,
whether the statute requires that he make the sale annually for
the taxes unpaid the preceding year, and, second, whether, if he
fails to do so, the titles conveyed by sales in subsequent years for
the unpaid taxes of years prior to the next preceding year are
valid.

In People ex rel. Carman v. Lewis, 102 A. D. 408, the court
affirmed an order directing a peremptory writ of mandamus to
issue to compel the county treasurer of Nassau county to advertise
and sell certain real estate in his county upon which taxes for the
years 1901, 1902 and 1903 remained unpaid. The order was
granted in 1904. In the course of the opinion the court said:

" So far as the order directs a sale it is proper. Sections
150 and 151 of the Tax Law provide that whenever a tax
charged on real estate situated in the county shall remain unpaid for six months from the first day of February, after the
same is levied, the county treasurer shall immediately thereafter proceed in the manner pointed out to sell such real
estate. Undoubtedly the county treasurer has a reasonable
time within which to act, and what is a reasonable time must

be determined by the circumstances of each case. But in respect to the taxes for the years in question, twenty-five, thirteen, and one month respectively had elapsed after the time fixed by the statute for the institution of proceedings to sell. And while we cannot say that a delay of one month is unreasonable, no explanation is presented to excuse a delay of thirteen and twenty-five months."

It is evident from the foregoing language that the court interpreted the sections in question as imposing a ministerial duty upon the county treasurer to make the sale as soon as reasonably possible. It is also apparent, however, that violation of this duty by unreasonable delay did not, in the opinion of the court, in any way invalidate the title which would be conveyed by a subsequent sale. Otherwise, the order directing the sale would scarcely have been granted if the sale would not convey valid title.

These conclusions fully sustain my own view of the law, which is to the effect that although the county treasurer should sell lands for unpaid taxes in the same year as they are reported to him as unpaid, nevertheless his failure to do so does not prevent the sale taking place in subsequent years and conveying a good title to the purchaser.

Very truly yours,

EDWARD R. O'MALLEY,

Attorney-General.

Liquor Tax Law — Section 7 — Special Agents — Excise Department.

Traveling expenses, per diem allowance, etc., whether Commissioner of Excise may pay, under appropriation act, chapter. 432, Laws of 1909.

STATE OF NEW YORK,

ATTORNEY-GENERAL'S OFFICE,

ALBANY, *August* 4, 1910.

Hon. CLARK WILLIAMS, *State Comptroller, Albany, N. Y.:*

Dear Sir.— Your communication of the 20th ult. received requesting my opinion as to whether under the appropriation act of

17

1909 (being chapter 432 of the laws of that year), the Commissioner of Excise, under section 7 of the Liquor Tax Law, can fix a per diem allowance for subsistence for the special agents in his department and thus supersede the provisions of the second section of the aforesaid appropriation law.

According to the letter of State Commissioner of Excise, Maynard N. Clement, to the auditor of his department on June 1, 1910, which you have enclosed herewith, it appears that the Commissioner of Excise determined, under section 7 of the Liquor Tax Law, to fix a per diem allowance in accordance with the terms of said section "for all agents and special detectives while on detail for duty away from their homes." Section 7 of the Liquor Tax Law clearly gives the Commissioner of Excise such power. It appears that the order of the Commissioner of Excise fixing the per diem allowance went into effect on June 1st last, and that the funds available for such traveling expenses were appropriated by the aforesaid appropriation act of 1909. That act appropriates $160,000 for "the expenses of special agents" in the State Department of Excise "including salaries of sixty special agents and salaries and expenses of special detectives and detective service."

Section 2 of this appropriation act, among other things, provides as follows:

> "* * * except as otherwise herein expressly provided, the appropriations made in this act for traveling expenses of officers or employees are for actual and necessary expenses only, in the performance of official duty and to be paid upon proper proof thereof, as required by section twelve of the state finance law, and no other or further or fixed allowance for expenses shall be granted or paid, anything in any other statute to the contrary notwithstanding."

Section 12 of the Finance Law requires that where traveling expenses are incurred an itemized verified voucher must be furnished of such expenses.

It is clear that the moneys appropriated by chapter 432 can only be expended in accordance with the limitations and restrictions which the Legislature has placed in that act. One of the provisions of the said act is that traveling expenses are only to be paid

" upon proper proof thereof " as required by section 12 of the State Finance Law, and it is further specifically and particularly provided that " *no fixed allowance* for expenses shall be granted or paid, anything in *any other* statute to the contrary notwithstanding."

While it is true that the terms of a special statute, as for instance section 7 of the Liquor Tax Law, will not be deemed to be repealed or abrogated by a general act except where the intention is very clear, yet, the sweeping character of the language quoted above from the appropriation act would seem to indicate that the Legislature intended that the money appropriated under such act should be paid only in accordance with its terms.

As stated in interview with yourself and me, the Commissioner of Excise says the asking of bills at hotels for subsistence oftentimes results in giving notice of the presence of the special agents in the community and thereby interferes with their work, which is largely of a detective nature. It was suggested in that interview that your department might accept the statements, if they were itemized, without voucher in cases where the Excise Department indicated it was desirable not to ask for hotel bills in their work. If this were done, it might obviate the objection which the Excise Department has to asking for hotel bills in all instances.

While the legal question is not entirely free from doubt, it is my opinion that the provisions of the appropriation act above quoted are controlling and that the traveling expenses of the aforesaid special agents can only be paid out of the funds appropriated by said act in accordance with the terms and restrictions.

Yours very truly,

EDWARD R. O'MALLEY,

Attorney-General.

State Comptroller — Employees.

Whether extra compensation may be paid clerks required to work outside of office hours preparing for tax sales.

(See opinions December 13, 1901, p. 313, Report; December 28, 1906, p. 491, Report; October 19, 1909, p. 589, Report.

STATE OF NEW YORK,

ATTORNEY-GENERAL'S OFFICE,

ALBANY, *August* 10, 1910.

Hon. CLARK WILLIAMS, *State Comptroller, Albany, N. Y.:*

Dear Sir.— I have the letter of the 6th inst., written by your secretary, in which my opinion is requested as to whether you can pay additional compensation to those of your clerks whom you require to work outside of regular office hours in preparing for the tax sale to be held by your department in December of this year.

Prior to 1906 it was customary to pay such additional compensation in your office. On December 29, 1906, however, Attorney-General Mayer rendered an opinion to the State Civil Service Commission in which he held that the provisions of section 4, chapter 521, Laws of 1901, prohibited such additional compensation. I find no provision of law which in any way modifies this opinion. The provision of the supply bill for the present year to which you call my attention, appropriating money for the preparing for and conducting of this sale has no connection with the method in which the money shall be spent.

Very truly yours,

EDWARD R. O'MALLEY,

Attorney-General.

Tax Law — Section 186, *Laws* 1910 — *Stock Transfers.*
Claims for erroneously paid transfer taxes under above law.

STATE OF NEW YORK,

ATTORNEY-GENERAL'S OFFICE,

ALBANY, *August* 16, 1910.

Hon..CLARK WILLIAMS, *State Comptroller, Albany, N. Y.:*

Dear Sir.— I have the honor to submit herewith my conclusions in reference to the documents presented to you which purport to be claims for erroneously paid stock transfer taxes under chapter 186 of the Laws of 1910.

This statute is as follows:

" § 280. Refund of tax erroneously paid. If any stamp or stamps shall have been erroneously affixed to any book, certificate of stock, or bill or memorandum of sale, the comptroller may, upon presentation of a claim for the amount of such stamp or stamps and upon the production of evidence satisfactory to him that such stamp or stamps was or were so erroneously affixed *so as to cause loss to the person or persons making such claim,* pay such amount, or such part thereof as he may allow, to such claimant out of any moneys appropriated for that purpose. Such claims shall be presented to the comptroller in writing, duly verified, and shall state the full name and address of the claimant, the date of such erroneous affixing, the face value of such stamp or stamps and shall describe the instrument to which the stamp or stamps were affixed and contain such evidence as may be available upon which the demand for such refund is based. * * * "

The copy of the alleged claim submitted to me appears to be made and verified by a broker. It does not contain the statement that the erroneous payment of the tax has caused the loss set out therein to fall upon the claimant, but it says that the taxes have been erroneously paid " so as to cause loss to the undersigned *and to the several customers* for whom said transactions were carried on by the undersigned as brokers, which customers afterward *reimbursed the undersigned* for the amount of the tax paid upon such transfer."

In my judgment, these claims do not meet the requirements of the statute, and I therefore advise you that they are not sufficient for your action either to allow or disallow the claim.

Very truly yours,

EDWARD R. O'MALLEY,

Attorney-General.

General Business Law — Chapter 348, Laws 1910 — Private Banks and Bankers — Licenses.

Validity of bonds and obligations for license or exemptions executed prior to September 1, 1910, and presented to State Comptroller for examination.

STATE OF NEW YORK,

ATTORNEY-GENERAL'S OFFICE,

ALBANY, *August* 23, 1910.

Hon. CLARK WILLIAMS, *State Comptroller, Albany, N. Y.:*

Dear Sir.— Your letter of recent date requesting my opinion as to the validity of bonds and obligations for a license or exemptions which may be executed prior to September 1, 1910, and presented to you for examination prior to such date, in re chapter 348, Laws of 1910, was received.

All contractual obligations, bonds, undertakings, deeds, mortgages and similar legal instruments do not become effective until they are delivered and accepted by the obligee, etc. Acceptance is an essential element of the delivery of such instruments. (See Ten Eyck v. Witbeck, 156 N. Y. 341, and the authorities cited.) Until such bonds and obligations which may be presented for examination under said statute are delivered, filed and approved or disapproved by you on and after September 1, they are not effective and neither principals nor sureties can raise the question of their validity because signed prior to the date aforesaid.

It appears from forms submitted, and should appear in all bonds presented before said day, either in the preamble or in the recital of the conditions, that the principal " is about to apply for a license " or that " he intends to engage in the business of receiving deposits," etc.

Very respectfully,

EDWARD R. O'MALLEY,

Attorney-General.

Tax Law — Stock Transfers.

Amalgamation of the United States Radiator Company. Four corporations turned over all stock to fifth in return for issuance of stock. These corporations directed new corporation to issue stock directly to a trustee. Trustee issued its certificates to the stockholders in the four original corporations. The issue of stock made by the new corporation *not* taxable. Trustees certificate to stockholders in the old corporation is taxable.

STATE OF NEW YORK,

ATTORNEY-GENERAL'S OFFICE,

ALBANY, August 26, 1910.

Hon. CLARK WILLIAMS, *State Comptroller, Albany, N. Y.:*

Dear Sir.— As requested by you in your favor of recent date I have carefully examined the papers submitted in reference to the amalgamation of the United States Radiator Company, with a view to answering the two questions asked with reference to the stock transfer tax.

It appears from the statement of facts that four corporations have turned over all their property to a fifth corporation in return for its issuance of stock. Having determined upon a pooling of the stock for five years, these corporations directed the new corporation to issue the stock directly to a trustee, which was accordingly done. Subsequently the trustee at the request of the several corporations, issued its certificates in the usual form direct to the stockholders in the four original corporations. The questions which are asked are (1) is the issue of stock made by the new corporation to the trustee taxable; and (2) is the issuance of trustee's certificates to the stockholders in the old corporations taxable?

In my opinion, the first question must be answered in the negative. The issue of stock to the trustee was clearly an original issue, and therefore not taxable under the decisions.

> People v. Duffy-McInerney Co., 122 A. D. 336; affirmed in Court of Appeals.

It is my opinion that the second question should be answered in the affirmative. The issuance of the trustee's certificates to the stockholders of the old corporation, in my judgment, constitutes such a transfer of beneficial interest as to fall within the statute. Whether or not the issuance of such certificates to the corporations themselves would have been taxable, the stockholders are separate legal entities and the issuance of the certificates directly to them constitutes a change in the beneficial ownership of the stock.

> Very truly yours,
> EDWARD R. O'MALLEY,
> *Attorney-General.*

General Business Law — Chapter 348, Laws 1910 — Private Banks and Bankers.

Firm of R. H. Macy & Company, and others if engaged in the business of receiving deposits after September 1, 1910, amenable to above statute.

STATE OF NEW YORK,

ATTORNEY-GENERAL'S OFFICE,

ALBANY, *September 2, 1910.*

Hon. CLARK WILLIAMS, *State Comptroller, Albany, N. Y.:*

Dear Sir.— In response to your request I have examined the letter and blank deposit slips or receipts for deposits issued by R. H. Macy & Company (a partnership), which were submitted to your department in relation to chapter 348, Laws of 1910.

In my opinion, if Macy & Company engage in the business of receiving deposits of money, as stated and indicated by said letter and blanks, after September 1, 1910, they will be amenable to the provisions of said statute. While they may not be engaged in the banking business as that term is used in the popular sense, yet one of the elements or factors in the banking business is "to receive deposits of money." (See § 2 of the Banking Law, chap. 10, L. of 1909, and chap. 2 of the Consolidated Laws.)

The deposits of money made by the customers are not payments of or upon an existing indebtedness of the customers. A deposit as defined in legal text books and by the courts is "money placed with a bank, banker or other person or corporation subject to order." While the receiving of such deposits of money may be a convenience for customers, yet such moneys are subject to the order of such customers. The relation of debtor and creditor is thereby created. If any portion of the deposit is not used in paying for subsequent purchases and charges against the same, it must be returned to the customer upon his order. I therefore think, upon the facts as stated and the papers submitted, that Macy & Company and other business houses who may be engaged in the business of receiving similar deposits of money after September 1 aforesaid will be amenable to the provisions of said statute.

Yours respectfully,
EDWARD R. O'MALLEY,
Attorney-General.

Code of Civil Procedure — Section 2747 — Estates and Legacies.

Checks received from estates for amount of legacies or distributive
 shares of estates where persons are unknown, should be collected at once, and paid into State treasury under section
 2747, and they do not, upon being paid into State treasury,
 become a part of the general fund of the State.

STATE OF NEW YORK.

ATTORNEY-GENERAL'S OFFICE,

ALBANY, *September* 3, 1910.

Hon. CLARK WILLIAMS, *State Comptroller, Albany, N. Y.:*

Dear Sir.— Your letter of August 25th stating that from time
to time checks for the amount of legacies or distributive shares
in estates where the persons entitled thereto are unknown are sent
to the State Treasurer, is received. You ask (1) whether the holding of these checks until the examination of the legal papers in
these matters is concluded might subject the State to loss in case
of the failure of the institution upon which they are drawn; (2)
whether a special account might be opened in some approved
depository until the funds should be permanently placed in the
State treasury or otherwise disposed of.

In reply to the same I beg to say, (1) that checks of this character should, in my opinion, be promptly collected and that delay
in collection might, under some circumstances, subject the State
to loss or at least to criticism; (2) that these checks are paid to
the State Treasurer in accordance with the provisions of section 2747 of the Code of Civil Procedure and do not upon being
paid into the treasury become a part of the general fund of the
State. This is concisely decided in the case of People ex rel. Evans
v. Alfred C. Chapin, as Comptroller, which holds that " money
paid to the State Treasurer, pursuant to section 2747 of the Code
of Civil Procedure, is not money of the State or money belonging
to any of its funds, or any of the funds under its management,
within the meaning of section 8, article 7 of the State Constitution (now section 21, article 3) and is not, therefore, subject to
the prohibition of that section."

By the provisions of section 2747 of the Code of Civil Procedure, money of this character is subject to the control of the surrogate or the Supreme Court, and I am therefore of opinion that there is no reason why such checks should not immediately be paid into the treasury of the State and the proceeds thereof kept in an account which will properly designate their status.

Yours very truly,

EDWARD R. O'MALLEY,

Attorney-General.

General Business Law — Chapter 348, Laws 1910 — Private Banks and Bankers.

Establishment of branch banks. Whether bank or banker should qualify for each branch under one bond.

STATE OF NEW YORK,

ATTORNEY-GENERAL'S OFFICE,

ALBANY, *September 6, 1910.*

Hon. CLARK WILLIAMS, *State Comptroller, Albany, N. Y.:*

Dear Sir.— I have your request for an opinion as to whether a private banker, authorized to do business under chapter 348 of the Laws of 1910, may transact that business in more than one place without taking out an additional license for each branch office. The statute provides that the license shall be posted and at all times conspicuously displayed " in the place of business for which it is issued." Section 35 of the General Construction Law provides as follows:

> " § 35. NUMBER, SINGULAR AND PLURAL.— Words in the singular number include the plural, and in the plural number include the singular."

Section 25 of the act in question provides that the license " shall not authorize the transaction of business at any place other than that described in the license certificate, except with the written approval of the comptroller." It is my opinion that this by implication per-

mits the transaction of business at other places with the written
approval of the Comptroller, and, taken in connection with the
clause from the same section previously quoted, that this written
approval may be endorsed on the original license.

That this is the equitable construction of the law admits of no
doubt. The licensee is required by section 26 to keep books of
account showing "all business transacted" and "all assets and
liabilities" and to make a statement to the Comptroller four times
a year setting forth "the amount of the assets and liabilities."
Likewise the application filed with the Comptroller upon which
the amount of the bond is determined is required to state "the
amount of the assets and liabilities of the applicant." It is clear,
therefore, that the bond given by any applicant will be based upon
his assets and liabilities as a whole irrespective of the number of
branch offices maintained by him. There would therefore seem
to be no practical reason for requiring this bond to be duplicated
in case the business is transacted in two places rather than one.

Very truly yours,

EDWARD R. O'MALLEY,

Attorney-General

General Business Law — Steamship Agencies — Licenses.

Whether Atlantic & Carribbean Steam Navigation Company shall
be required to take out a license.

STATE OF NEW YORK,

ATTORNEY-GENERAL'S OFFICE,

ALBANY, *September* 10, 1910.

Hon. CLARK WILLIAMS, *State Comptroller, Albany, N. Y.:*

Dear Sir.— I have your request for an opinion as to whether
the agents of the Atlantic & Carribbean Steam Navigation Company are required to take out licenses under the provisions of
chapter 349, Laws of 1910, before engaging in selling tickets.

Section 150 of the General Business Law, added by the above
chapter, provides in part as follows:

"LICENSES TO SELL TRANSPORTATION TICKETS OR ORDERS FOR TRANSPORTATION TO OR FROM FOREIGN COUNTRIES.— No person, firm or corporation, other than railroad companies or transatlantic steamship companies or agents of such railroad companies duly appointed in writing, shall hereafter engage in this state in the sale of steamship tickets for transportation to or from foreign countries, without having first procured a license to carry on such business from the comptroller."

The question presented by your inquiry, therefore, is whether or not the Atlantic & Carribbean Steam Navigation Company can be regarded as a transatlantic steamship company within the meaning of this provision. It appears from your letter that this company operates a line of steamships between New York and Venezuela, but that it does not operate any steamships to Europe or Africa. Strictly speaking the word transatlantic might be considered as referring only to the opposite side of the Atlantic ocean, and a transatlantic steamship company might be limited to one operating steamers between the eastern and western sides of the ocean. However, an examination of this statute seems to disclose that a broader meaning was intended to be given to the word than this, as it is apparently used interchangeably with the word "foreign." Moreover, if any other construction were placed upon it there would be grave reason for fearing that the act might be held unconstitutional, because of unreasonable discrimination. The general rule is that where more than one meaning is deducible from the language used, an act shall be given the meaning which will render it constitutional and valid.

In view of this rule, therefore, and the evident use of the word "transatlantic" as synonymous with the word "foreign" in the act, it is my opinion that the agents of the Atlantic & Carribbean Navigation Company if duly appointed in writing need not procure a license under the above statute before engaging in the sale of steamship tickets.

Very truly yours,

EDWARD R. O'MALLEY,

Attorney-General.

Tax Law — Stock Transfers.

Surrender of stock by Morton Trust Company and Fifth Avenue
Trust Company, to Guaranty Trust Company, of New York,
by reason of merger agreement, is not a taxable transfer.
(See Banking Law, sections 36, 37, 38, 39.)

STATE OF NEW YORK,

ATTORNEY-GENERAL'S OFFICE,

ALBANY, *September* 10, 1910.

Hon. CLARK WILLIAMS, *State Comptroller, Albany, N. Y.:*

Dear Sir.— I acknowledge your letter of the 9th inst. in which
you enclosed copy of the merger agreement between the Morton
Trust Company and the Fifth Avenue Trust Company into the
Guaranty Trust Company of New York.

I note that the shares of stock of the Morton Trust Company
and the Fifth Avenue Trust Company have been surrendered in
pursuance of this agreement and that the certificates of stock in
these two companies were all endorsed in blank and delivered to
the Guaranty Trust Company in exchange for stock of the Guaranty Trust Company as provided in this agreement.

I also note that the attorneys for the corporation hold such transfer is not taxable.

This merger was made under sections 36, 37, 38 and 39 of the
Banking Law. Section 37 of this law provides that after the
acceptance of the merger agreement by the stockholders

"It shall be lawful for said corporation into which the
others shall have been merged to require the return of the
original certificate of stock held by each stockholder in each
or either of the companies, and in lieu thereof to issue new
certificates for such number of shares of its own stock as
under the agreement of merger the said stockholder may be
entitled to receive."

The effect of this merger is to transfer all the property and rights
of each of the merging companies to the new corporation which is
substituted in their place.

It is my opinion that under these circumstances the surrender of stock in the merging corporations for cancellation by the merging corporation, in lieu of which stock in the merging corporation is issued, is not such a transfer as to be taxable under the statute. The law provides that new stock shall be " in lieu " of the original certificates and the transaction is merely the substitution of new evidence in place of old evidence of the interest held by the stockholders in the resulting corporation.   There is no change of ownership involved in the transaction.

Very truly yours,
EDWARD R. O'MALLEY,
Attorney-General.

Tax Law — Section 272 — Stock Transfers.

Transfer agent of the United Steel Corporation must require tax due on transfer to be paid before such transfer is made.

(See opinion April 27, 1910.)

STATE OF NEW YORK,

ATTORNEY-GENERAL'S OFFICE,

ALBANY, September 10, 1910.

Hon. CLARK WILLIAMS, *State Comptroller, Albany, N. Y.:*

Dear Sir.— Referring to my opinion of April 27, 1910, in which I held that it was the duty of the transfer agent of the United Steel Corporation making a transfer of stock upon the books of the corporation to see that any tax due upon such transfer was properly paid, and referring to the request of that company for a reconsideration of this ruling, I beg to advise that I have carefully considered the facts and arguments presented by their attorneys and that I still adhere to my original opinion.

It appears that the books upon which the transfers are noted are kept in the State of New Jersey, but that the old certificates are received and the new certificates delivered in the city of New York. When transfers are to be made the certificates are surrendered to this agent in New York, transmitted by it to New

Jersey and the actual transfer on the books there made. The new certificates are then transmitted to the office of the agent in New York city where they are delivered to the person entitled to receive them.

It is argued, first, that my original opinion was erroneous in that section 272 of the Tax Law can have no application to the act of the transfer agent, and second, that the method of transfer pursued in this case was such as to make the transaction take place outside the jurisdiction of this State and therefore not subject to this provision.

On reconsideration I see no reason to change my previous opinion as to the scope of section 272 of the Tax Law. This section provides in part that any person who shall " in pursuance of any sale or agreement deliver any stock * * * without having the stamps provided for in this article affixed thereto, shall be deemed guilty of a misdemeanor * * *."

It is argued that under the decisions holding that the transfer on the books of the corporation is not necessary to the transfer of title of the stock, it follows that the transfer agent cannot be regarded as delivering the stock in the sense intended by this statute. It is true that transfer on the books of the corporation is not an essential step to the transfer of title of the certificate. It is also true, however, that it is an essential prerequisite to the exercise of full ownership. If the transfer is in fact accomplished by means of such a transfer on the books, then the transfer agent in my judgment acts as the attorney for the transferor and must be regarded as included with him in the liability for the tax. Under such circumstances the transfer agent acting as such attorney becomes itself a party to the act of transfering, and if a tax is due and unpaid such agent is guilty under section 272 if it delivers the stock without requiring such payment. The ordinary stock certificate provides that shares are transferable only on the books of the corporation " by the registered holder in person or by attorney."

It is also my opinion that the method of accomplishing the transfer in this case is not such as to exempt the transfer agent from the operation of this law on the ground that the transfer itself takes place without the State. The delivery of the stock as a result of this transfer occurs in the city of New York. Until such delivery there is no violation of the law, and it is therefore my judgment that the transfer agent is within the jurisdiction of this State at the time the important act is performed.

Very truly yours,

EDWARD R. O'MALLEY,

Attorney-General.

Tax Law — Stock Transfers.

Where dissolution of the company is had, and transfer of stock is made through trustees to individual stockholders, it is not a taxable transfer.

STATE OF NEW YORK.

ATTORNEY-GENERAL'S OFFICE,

ALBANY, October 1, 1910.

Hon. CLARK WILLIAMS, <i>State Comptroller, Albany, N. Y.:</i>

Dear Sir.— Referring to your letter of the 30th ultimo enclosing letter from Messrs. Stedman & Stedman, attorneys, requesting your ruling upon the question there presented, I beg to advise as follows:

It appears that an old corporation transferred all its property to a new corporation formed for that purpose, and received in consideration for such transfer stock in the new corporation of the exact number of shares and at the same par value as the outstanding stock of the old corporation. Thereupon the old corporation was dissolved, and the directors, in dividing its property among its stockholders, propose to give to each stockholder the same number of shares of stock in the new corporation which he formerly held in the old. The question is whether such action on the part of the directors constitutes a transfer of the stock, subject to taxation under the stock transfer act.

It is well settled, under the decisions, that upon the dissolution of a corporation the directors act as trustees of its property, first, for the payment of its debts, and, second, for the division of the property among the stockholders. After dissolution, therefore, and payment of the creditors, the directors hold the shares of stock simply as trustees, the entire beneficial ownership being vested in the individual stockholders. It is therefore my opinion that the subsequent transfer from these stockholders, as trustees, to the stockholders, does not constitute a transfer within the meaning of the taxing statute. There is no change whatever in the beneficial ownership, the naked legal title alone being transferred.

Very truly yours,

EDWARD R. O'MALLEY,

Attorney-General.

Tax Law — Sections 197, 201.

Property of Liberty Driving Park Association purchased by Sullivan County National Bank, at sheriff's sale, may be sold to satisfy taxes.

STATE OF NEW YORK.

ATTORNEY-GENERAL'S OFFICE,

ALBANY, *October* 10, 1910.

Hon. CLARK WILLIAMS, *State Comptroller, Albany, N. Y.:*

Dear Sir.— I have your communication of September 2nd, together with letters referring to the Liberty Driving Park Association. The Sullivan County National Bank acquired this property May 28, 1910, by purchase at sheriff's sale. The taxes in question were levied during the years 1908 and 1909. Section 197 of the Tax Law declares the taxes a lien on the real and personal property of this corporation. A portion of the section reads as follows:

" Such taxes shall be a lien upon and bind all the real and personal property of the corporation, joint stock company or association liable to pay the same from the time when it is payable until the same is paid in full."

I must assume, in the absence of a review of the 1908 and 1909 taxes, that the same are valid. It is claimed by the Sullivan

County National Bank that the taxes ought not to be paid until a sheriff's deed is delivered after the period to redeem has expired, setting forth that if the taxes were paid and the property should be redeemed that the bank would be without a remedy. That is not so, as the taxes, as I have herein set forth, are a prior lien and if paid by the bank, the property could not be redeemed by any one unless the bank was reimbursed.

Section 197 of the Tax Law provides a penalty for failure to pay the taxes in the following language:

> "If such tax in any case is not paid within thirty days after the same became due, or if the report of such corporation is not made within the time required by this article, the corporation, association, joint stock company, person or partnership, liable to pay the taxes, shall pay into the state treasury in addition to the amount of such taxes a sum equal to five per centum thereof and one per centum additional for each month the tax remains unpaid, which sum shall be added to the tax and paid or collected therewith."

Section 201 of the Tax Law authorizes the Comptroller to collect the taxes where the same are not paid, in the following language:

> "The comptroller may issue a warrant under his hand and official seal directed to the sheriff of any county of the state commanding him to levy upon and sell the real and personal property of the person, partnership, company, association or corporation against which such account is stated, found within his county for the payment of the amount thereof with interest thereon and costs of executing the warrant, and to return such warrant to the comptroller and pay to the state treasurer the money collected by virtue thereof, by a time to be therein specified, not less than sixty days from the date of the warrant."

Under these sections the remedy is made clear. Whatever interest the Sullivan County National Bank acquired by reason of the purchase, at the sheriff's sale, may be sold under a warrant to satisfy the taxes in question.

Respectfully yours,

EDWARD R. O'MALLEY,

Attorney-General.

General Business Law — Chapter 348, Laws 1910 — Private Banks and Bankers.

Application of law to stock brokers receiving deposits on margins, etc.

(See opinion August 9, 1910.)

STATE OF NEW YORK.

ATTORNEY-GENERAL'S OFFICE,

ALBANY, *October* 18, 1910.

Hon. CLARK WILLIAMS, *State Comptroller, Albany, N. Y.:*

Dear Sir.— Request having been made to me by Messrs. Sullivan & Cromwell of New York City, for reconsideration of my opinion of August 9, 1910, to you, on the applicability of the Private Banking Act to stock brokers and on a certain ruling made by your department thereunder, and I having conferred with your secretary in reference to such request, I beg to submit my conclusions in regard to the same as follows:

My opinion dated August 9, 1910, holding that stock brokers were subject to this law where they carried an open account for their customers against which they can draw at any time, is, in my judgment, sound.

This general holding is attacked on the ground that the law applies only to persons " engaged in the business " of receiving deposits, and that a stock broker is not engaged in such *business,* but rather in the business of acting as agent or pledgee for his customer in the purchase and holding of stock.

Conceding the fact alleged, it by no means follows that a stock broker cannot also be engaged in the business of receiving deposits. It is admitted that the acceptance of money on open account is not a necessary part of the stock broking business. If, therefore, this is regularly and usually done by the stock broker, he is engaging in another line of business than that of purchasing and holding stocks. It may be that he is engaged in two kinds of business but it certainly cannot be said that he is not engaged in the business of receiving deposits when he regularly receives money to carry on an open account against which his customers may check.

Your ruling in reference to the placing of money with a broker on margins, although not covered by my opinion, seems sound. I understand you ruled on August 2, 1910, as follows:

> "A placing of money with a broker for the purpose of purchasing stocks on margins in the future, or for speculative purposes, is a deposit."

It is urged that this ruling is improper for the reason that money given a stock broker on margin is in fact and in law a part payment of the purchase price of the stock and therefore cannot be regarded as a deposit. There is much force in this suggestion. Your ruling, however, is apparently intended to apply only to deposits for the purpose of purchasing stocks on margins in the future and is not intended to apply to a deposit of money on margin accompanied with an order for immediate purchase of any stock. Under the authorities it is clear that money deposited as margin with directions to purchase certain stock must be regarded as part of the purchase price of that stock. The relation of debtor and creditor is not created between the stock broker and his customer as to such payment but title has been transferred absolutely to the stock broker. If the market value of the stock so purchased subsequently declines, the customer must increase his payment accordingly. If the value of the stock increases, the customer may withdraw so much of the margin as is in excess of 10 per cent. This last right would seem to indicate that the margin is in a sense a deposit, but in view of the holdings of the courts that it constitutes part of the payment for purchase price, the right to withdraw anything in excess of 10 per cent. would probably be regarded as a mere contract right and not as converting the original payment into a deposit.

The situation would seem to be very different, however, when the original payment to the stock broker is not accompanied with an order for the purchase of any definite stock. In such case it is clear that it cannot be regarded as part of the purchase price for there is as yet no purchase directed. So long as it remains in the hands of the stock broker for indefinite future use, merely to facilitate the transfer to him of margins when definite orders are given, it would seem that it must be regarded as a deposit of money rather than as a payment. Clearly, the customer would be entitled to withdraw it at any time prior to giving a definite order for purchase which would convert it into a margin in the strict sense of the word. If, therefore, a stock broker is engaged in the business of receiving such deposits of money as these in addition to or in connection with his business as a stock broker, he would seem to come within the prohibition of the Private Banking Act.

If your ruling was intended to do no more than this it would seem sound under the principles of my previous opinion. If, however, it is intended to apply to margins in the ordinary and strict use of the term where there is an actual present purchase of stock upon which the margin is paid, it would seem to be erroneous.

I am sending a copy of this opinion to Messrs. Sullivan & Cromwell.

Very truly yours,
EDWARD R. O'MALLEY,
Attorney-General.

State Finance Law — Section 121.

Detailed statement of items furnished the State of New York by merchants and others, must be accompanied by receipted bill, and furnished the State Comptroller before payment can be made by the State.

STATE OF NEW YORK.

ATTORNEY-GENERAL'S OFFICE,

ALBANY, *October* 31, 1910.

Hon. CLARK WILLIAMS, *State Comptroller, Albany, N. Y.:*

Dear Sir.— I am in receipt of your communication of the 28th inst. requesting my opinion as to whether or not merchants and others furnishing materials or services to the State must receipt their vouchers in advance of payment.

Section 12 of the State Finance Law makes provision for proofs required on audit by the Comptroller and requires, among other things, before the Comptroller shall draw his warrant for the payment of any sum that the person demanding the same present to

him a detailed statement thereof in items and "if for transportation, furniture, blank and other books purchased for the use of
offices, binding, blanks, printing, stationery, postage, cleaning and
other necessary and incidental expenses a bill duly receipted must
be attached to the statement."

It is my opinion that where payment is demanded for any of
the items specified above, then the voucher must be receipted in
advance. If, however, the bill relates to something not specified
in the above excerpt then its requirement that the bill duly receipted must be attached to the statement is not applicable. While
it may appear strange that the State should require a receipt before
payment is made, yet that is the requirement of the statute in
respect to the above items, and merchants and other persons must
be presumed to have knowledge of such legal requirements when
dealing with the State.

It may be wise to call your attention to the doubtful wisdom of
this requirement. A receipt is required doubtless in order to have
clear evidence of the fact that payment has been made. Where,
however, a receipt is required in advance of payment, then it is
clear that the receipt must lose most of its probative force. However, the terms of the statute must be complied with so long as it
is in force as the law of the State.

Very truly,
EDWARD R. O'MALLEY,
Attorney-General.

General Business Law — Chapter 348, Laws 1910 — Private
Banks and Bankers.
Publication of statement by Verrilli Bros. not illegal under section
27, Banking Law.
(See opinion September 17, 1910.)

STATE OF NEW YORK.
ATTORNEY-GENERAL'S OFFICE,
ALBANY, November 21, 1910.

Hon. CLARK WILLIAMS, *State Comptroller. Albany. N. Y.:*

Dear Sir.— Your letter of yesterday enclosing a clipping from
the newspaper *L'Araldo Italiano,* a newspaper published in the

city of New York, and requesting my opinion whether or not the advertisement of Verrilli Brothers as private bankers printed in such newspaper is a violation of section 27 of chapter 348 of the Laws of 1910, was received.

The advertisement translated into English is as follows:

"BANK OF VERRILLI BROTHERS.

Whoever has been for any length of time a member of the Italian colony knows the brothers Verrilli as well as he knows the Statue of Liberty. Two active, modest and thoroughly honest persons show how they have for many years been engaged in the banking business at 129 Mulberry and 193 Hester streets, New York. In whatever country we Italians of America are, the name of the Verrilli Bank is known and respected and this through its constantly correct dealings. There has been enacted a new law which aims to protect the interests of those who trust private banking houses. The Brothers Verrilli have been among the first to deposit with the State $10,000 in cash or reliable bonds. They also possess reliable property of considerable value in the city but they have preferred to deposit the cash, the fruit of their long, steady and honest labor. It is a safe bank and can be recommended."

That part of section 27 of the amended Banking Law which relates to unlawful publications and statements in relation to the private banking business is as follows:

" Who shall advertise or publish in any manner whatsoever, either orally or in writing, any statement intended to convey or actually conveying the idea or impression that such licensee is in any way under the supervision of this state or of any officer thereof or that this state or any officer thereof has passed in any way whatsoever upon the responsibility, solvency or qualifications of such licensee to engage in such business, or that this state or any officer thereof has examined any accounts of said licensee or has in any way certified that such licensee is in any way a fit person to carry on such business, shall be guilty of a misdemeanor."

I think the statements in such advertisement are not prohibited and are not unlawful under the provisions of such section. Construing all of the statements together, Verrilli Brothers only intended to convey the impression that they were reliable and honest bankers and that they had complied with the said Private Banking Law. Penal statutes or penal provisions in general statutes are to be construed strictly, and an interpretation in favor of innocence should be followed when alleged violations of such statutes are susceptible of two interpretations.

I assume in answering the questions submitted that Verrilli Brothers have been duly licensed to carry on the business of receiving deposits, etc., and that they are now complying with the provisions of such law.

Yours very truly,

EDWARD R. O'MALLEY,

Attorney-General.

Tax Law — Stock Transfers.

Taxability of transfer where transaction is made through power of substitution.

(See opinion December 19, 1910.)

STATE OF NEW YORK.

ATTORNEY-GENERAL'S OFFICE,

ALBANY, *December* 13, 1910.

Hon. CLARK WILLIAMS, *State Comptroller, Albany, N. Y.:*

Dear Sir.— Referring to your letter of the 8th inst., in which you ask my opinion as to the application of the Stock Transfer Tax Law to a transfer of certificates under a power of substitution, I beg to advise you as follows:

You state that many certificates of stock appear in the financial district endorsed in blank but conferring the power of transfer upon some party. The power of substitution as defined by you is the assigning of this power to transfer stock upon the books of the corporation and reads as follows:

> " We hereby irrevocably constitute and appoint ....
> .... our substitute to transfer the within named stock under the foregoing power of attorney, with like power of . substitution.
> New York ...., 19 .
> Witness:..........."

You state that in some instances as many as six of these powers appear upon a single certificate, and although the power in itself does not constitute a sale, yet where the name of the party to whom the stock is to be transferred is not filled in, a certificate may pass from one individual to another by this substitution of the power of transfer, in exactly the same manner as a certificate with the power of attorney on the back assigned in blank. As I understand it, you ask my opinion as to whether the passing of a certificate in this manner from one individual to another is subject to the stock transfer tax.

It is my judgment that if such a transaction in fact constitutes a transfer of the stock certificates, it is taxable. In other words, I see no reason why the method by which the transfer is consummated should have any bearing upon the taxability of the transfer itself. If each substitution of power of attorney represents in fact a transfer of the certificate from one owner to another, each such transfer would clearly come within the statute, although, as you say, the mere execution of the power of substitution in itself would not be taxable.

Very truly yours,

EDWARD R. O'MALLEY,

Attorney-General.

Prison Law — Sections 11, 12, 13 *— County Law — Section* 240.

Expenses of sheriffs in obeying orders of court in transporting convicts to State's Prison, should be audited by the Board of Supervisors.

STATE OF NEW YORK.

ATTORNEY-GENERAL'S OFFICE,

ALBANY, *December* 16, 1910.

Hon. CLARK WILLIAMS, *State Comptroller, Albany, N. Y.:*

Dear Sir.— I am in receipt of your communication of December 10th, 1910, wherein you ask whether or not the compensation of an assistant to the sheriff in transporting a convict to a State Prison is a proper charge against the county, and whether the board of supervisors of the county has authority to allow and audit such charges.

I note that you say that such assistant was employed by the sheriff pursuant to an order of the court in which the prisoner was convicted; that the order was granted to prevent possible escape of the convict who had been convicted of a serious crime and who was considered a dangerous person; that the sheriff paid such assistant for his services and transportation expenses and has presented the bill for the amount paid to the board of supervisors.

Sections 11, 12 and 13 of the Prison Law provide as follows:

"Section 11. DELIVERY OF COMMITMENT WITH PRISONER; PAYMENT OF FEES FOR TRANSPORTATION.—Whenever any convict shall be delivered to the agent and warden of any of said state prisons, in pursuance of such sentence, the officer so delivering such convict shall deliver to such agent and warden, the certified copy of the sentence received by such officer from the clerk of the court by which such convict shall have been sentenced, and such agent and warden shall deliver to such officer a certificate of the delivery of such convict, and the fees of such officer for transporting such convict shall be paid by the treasurer upon the warrant of the comptroller.

"Section 12.   FEES OF SHERIFF FOR TRANSPORT-
ING CONVICTS. — The compensation to sheriff for conveying one convict to a state prison from the county
prison, for each mile actually traveled, shall be
twenty cents; for conveying two convicts, for each
mile so traveled, thirty-five cents; for conveying
three convicts, for each mile so traveled, forty cents;
and for conveying four or more convicts, for each mile so
traveled, twelve cents each; with one dollar per day for the
maintenance of each convict while on the way to a state
prison but not exceeding one dollar for every thirty miles
of travel, in full of all charges and expenses in the premises."

"Section 13.   RENDERING ACCOUNTS ON DELIVERY OF
CONVICTS.— On the delivery of any such convicts to the
agent and warden of such prison, the sheriff or other person
having charge of the same, shall make and render to the
agent and warden of the prison, an account of the number of
days spent in coming, and the estimated time necessary in
returning home, the number of miles traveled, and of the
amount due therefor as prescribed by the preceding section;
which account shall then by him be certified under oath to
be correct, to which shall be added the certificate of the agent
and warden of such prison, setting forth the number of convicts so delivered, and the distance from such prison to the
place of their conviction."

The above sections govern the facts in this case unless the court
had power to make the order in question. The sheriff is an officer
of the court and it was his duty to obey its orders, and it having
appeared to the court that good and sufficient reasons existed that
necessitated the making of the order in question, the sheriff would
have been subject to great censure at least, if not to punishment
for contempt if he had neglected or refused to obey the order.

I believe that it was within the power of the court to make
the order in question and as the State was not obliged to pay the
expenses incurred under the provisions of the Prison Law above
quoted, one must turn to some other source or authority. The
board of supervisors can only audit such claims as are made a
county charge by statute.

Section 240 of the County Law defining what are county charges provides, among other things, as follows:

"Subdivision 9. The moneys necessarily expended by any county officer in executing the duties of his office in cases in which no specific compensation for such services is provided by law."

No specific compensation for the services of an assistant to a sheriff, in cases like the one submitted, is provided by law.

I am of the opinion that the above provision of the County Law is broad enough to cover this case; that it was the duty of the sheriff to obey the order of the court, and that the moneys expended by him in carrying out the order should be audited and paid him by the board of supervisors.

Yours very truly,

EDWARD R. O'MALLEY,

Attorney-General.

Tax Law — Stock Transfers.

Transfers of voting trust certificates are subject to stock transfer tax.

(See opinions May 27, 1905, p. 430, Rep.; July 1, 1907, p. 298, Rep.; December 1, 1909, p. 303, Rep.; opinion February 8, 1910, *withdrawn.*)

STATE OF NEW YORK.

ATTORNEY-GENERAL'S OFFICE,

ALBANY, *December* 19, 1910.

Hon. CLARK WILLIAMS, *State Comptroller, Albany, N. Y.:*

Dear Sir.—I acknowledge your letter of the 7th inst., enclosing copy of voting trust agreement, and requesting my opinion as to whether the transfers of voting trust certificates under such agreement from one holder to another are subject to the stock transfer **tax.**

It appears from this agreement that the voting trustees " shall possess, in respect of any and all such stock, and shall be entitled to exercise all rights of every name and nature, including the right to vote for every purpose and to consent to any corporate act " of said corporation. It also appears that the holders of the trustees' certificates are entitled to receive a certificate or certificates of stock of the number of shares therein specified but that no such stock certificates shall be due before October 1, 1915, nor until the expiration of such further period, if any, as shall elapse before the corporation in question shall have paid all of its six per cent. first lien notes issued under a certain deed of trust.

It is my opinion that notwithstanding the rights conveyed to the voting trustees, a transfer of the trust certificates still constitutes a transfer of the shares of stock within the meaning of the Stock Transfer Act. The holder of the certificate is the equitable owner of the shares of stock represented thereby. A transfer of the certificate transfers such ownership to the transferee. It entitles the holder to the receipt of dividends and to the ultimate delivery of the shares of stock themselves. There is, therefore, a substantial beneficial interest in the stock in the holders of such certificates prior to the delivery to them of the shares themselves, and there is also the equitable ownership of the shares which will become absolute after such delivery. It is therefore my opinion that transfers of such certificates are subject to the tax.

In the letter enclosed in your communication it is stated that the question has arisen in reference to a transfer of a certificate taking place outside of the State of New York between non-residents. Each certificate provides: " This certificate is transferable only on the books of the voting trustees by the registered holder, either in person or by attorney duly authorized, or surrender hereof; " and also " This certificate is not valid unless duly signed on behalf of the undersigned voting trustees by Central Trust Company of New York, their agent, and also registered by The Columbia Trust Company, as registrar." It is my judgment that if either or all of the above acts are performed within the State of New York, the transfer is taxable notwithstanding it may have originally occurred outside the State and between non-residents.

You had previously been advised by this department under my

opinion of February 8, 1910, that the transfer of the shares of stock from the stockholders to the voting trustees was taxable. In an examination of this question which I have made in preparing this opinion, I have come to the conclusion that my previous holding was erroneous. I understand from conference with the Chief Clerk of this bureau of your office that the taxes paid under my previous opinion have been inconsiderable, and that a withdrawal of it at this time will cause no practical difficulties.

I, therefore, advise you that the opinion of February 8, 1910, should be disregarded, and that hereafter all transfers of stock from stockholders to voting trustees should not be taxed.

Very truly yours,

EDWARD R. O'MALLEY,

Attorney-General.

Public Lands Law — Article 3.

Common School Fund. Real estate bonds held by the State for term of years, as investments, no payments having been received for a number of years. Whether said bonds are valid obligations, and if the State can enforce payment.

STATE OF NEW YORK.

ATTORNEY-GENERAL'S OFFICE,

ALBANY, *December* 20, 1910.

Hon. CLARK WILLIAMS, *State Comptroller, Albany, N. Y.:*

Dear Sir.— I acknowledge the receipt of a letter from Mr. Hudson, your former secretary, in the matter of certain bonds of long standing now held by the State, representing investments under the provisions of article 3 of the Public Lands Law.

The letter of Mr. Hudson, summarized, is as follows:

" Included in the investment of the Common School Fund are real estate bonds for lands and for loans showing a value upon the books of the Finance Bureau of $67,950.67. This amount represents investments originally made under the

provisions of article 3 of the Public Lands Law. All of these
bonds are of long standing and upon practically all of them
no payments of either principal or interest have been received
for a considerable number of years. If these bonds are now
valid obligations and liens upon lands supposed to be covered
by them, we would appreciate your advising whether the
State can enforce their payment, and if so the method of
procedure."

The question submitted cannot be answered fully without
further data or a fuller statement of facts as to payments, acknowl-
edgments of indebtedness, etc., by the original obligors, mortgagors,
certificate holders, vendees, their heirs or personal representatives
in the contracts of purchase.

Whether payments have been made on such obligations by the
obligors, mortgagors, vendees or certificate holders or their devisees
and owners of the equity in the land sold or whether acknowledg-
ments of the indebtedness have been made by the debtors and
persons liable to pay the same are all important and necessary
facts in determining the question whether as to any particular
bond or contract an action or proceeding may be maintained by
the State to enforce payment of the money unpaid on such
instruments.

Section 36 of the Public Lands Law, which is entitled, " Collection, forfeiture and cancellation of purchase money bonds," is as
follows:

> " The commissioners of the land office may direct the
> comptroller to sue upon any bond received by the state en-
> gineer on the sale of unappropriated state lands, if any pay-
> ment stipulated in such bond shall remain due one year, or
> they may direct the state engineer to resell the land for the
> payment of which such bond was given, and in case of such
> sale, all previous payments made on account of such land shall
> be forfeited to the people of the state, and the bonds may be
> delivered up and cancelled on the surrender of the certificate
> of sale."

As to methods of procedure concerning which you ask to be
advised, I suggest that you cause an examination to be made as

to all the bonds, contracts or mortgages, if any, particularly as to
the value of the premises, present ownership and occupation, also
whether any of the lands have been resold or whether the State has
released any portion of the lands or granted an extension of time
for payment, and upon the receipt of a report as to such facts and
any other facts which may affect the right to recover by the State,
this department can then advise the commissioners of the land
office in the premises and you can follow their directions as to the
commencement of actions or proceedings to enforce payment of
such bonds or the purchase-money liens or to recover possession of
the lands in question as the facts in each case may warrant.

Very truly yours,
EDWARD R. O'MALLEY,
Attorney-General.

Supervisors — Salaries — County of Rockland.

Act of 1910, chapter 279, providing that supervisors, county of
Rockland, shall receive annual salary of $400, applies to pres-
ent board of supervisors.

STATE OF NEW YORK.

ATTORNEY-GENERAL'S OFFICE,

ALBANY, December 31, 1910.

Hon. CLARK WILLIAMS, State Comptroller, Albany, N. Y.:

Dear Sir.— I beg to acknowledge the receipt of your favor of
November 30th, in which you say:

> " Chapter 279 of the Laws of 1910 provides that each su-
> pervisor of the county of Rockland shall receive an annual
> salary of $400.
> " Since the members of the present Board of Supervisors
> were elected prior to the passage of that law, will you please
> inform me as to whether or not in your opinion this law
> applies to the members of the present Board ? "

18

After due examination of the Constitution and statutes I find no law prohibiting its application to the members of the board of supervisors in office when the act was passed and went into effect. Therefore, in my opinion, it would apply to them.

Yours very truly,

EDWARD R. O'MALLEY,

Attorney-General.

OPINIONS RENDERED THE STATE TREASURER.

State Treasurer — State Comptroller.

No statute requiring either officer to procure a written receipt before paying out money by check.

STATE OF NEW YORK.

ATTORNEY-GENERAL'S OFFICE,

ALBANY, *June* 24, 1910.

Hon. THOMAS B. DUNN, *State Treasurer, Albany, N. Y.:*

Dear Sir.— I beg to acknowledge the receipt of your letter of June 16th, asking me if there is any statute which requires the State Treasurer to procure a receipt for moneys paid out of the treasury by him by check.

I have examined the statutes relating to the administration of the State Treasurer's and Comptroller's offices and have been unable to find any provision requiring either of these officers to procure a written receipt before paying out money by check. There is nothing in the law preventing your taking receipts, but if in the judgment of yourself and the Comptroller checks are sufficient vouchers for the payments that are made, you may in your discretion dispense with the additional receipts.

Yours very truly,

EDWARD R. O'MALLEY,

Attorney-General.

State Institutions — Western New York Institution, Rochester.

Appropriation bill providing for support of charitable institutions
for the deaf and dumb. Basis of $325 per capita, authorized
by Legislature of 1910, to be paid by counties:

STATE OF NEW YORK.

ATTORNEY-GENERAL'S OFFICE,

ALBANY, *July* 8, 1910.

Hon. THOMAS B. DUNN, *State Treasurer, Albany, N. Y.:*

Dear Sir.— I have the honor to acknowledge the receipt of your
favor of the 29th ultimo in which you ask to be advised as to the
interpretation of certain portions of the appropriation bill providing for the support of charitable and educational institutions for
the deaf and dumb.

It appears from your communication and the act in question
that there was appropriated and authorized to be paid for such
institutions the sum of $136,500 for the support of four hundred
and twenty pupils, and again the sum of $37,375 for the support
and instruction of one hundred and fifteen pupils at the Western
New York Institution in Rochester. These total amounts and
other amounts appropriated in this bill under the head of deaf and
dumb charitable and educational institutions give by actual computation the sum of $325 per pupil. Later under the same head-
ing the act reads that " the amount hereby appropriated for the
several institutions for the support and instruction of deaf mutes
is at the rate of $300 per capita."

Investigation of the circumstances under which these appropriations were made discloses that heretofore appropriations were made
on the basis of $300 per capita and the sentence above quoted was
taken from the previous appropriation bills and attached to the
appropriation authorized in this act. The clear intention of the
bill is gathered from the wording of the appropriations for the
various institutions and from conferences with the Speaker of the
House, the Assemblyman who introduced the bill and others. It
seems to me that the appropriation is available for the full amount
and that the subsequent declaration of the rate of $300 per pupil

is not binding. I am, therefore, of the opinion that State officials
are authorized to overlook the error in failing to correct the last
clause of this portion of the act and to authorize payments to be
made out of these appropriations at the rate of $325 per pupil.
This interpretation of the law is further strengthened by the fact
that there was passed by the Legislature of 1910 a bill authorizing
the counties to pay at the rate of $325 per capita for the care of
pupils in such institutions.

Yours very truly,

EDWARD R. O'MALLEY,

Attorney-General.

---

*Education Law — Section 59 — General Corporations Law —
Section 3.*

Educational corporation whose charter has been granted by Regents
of the University of the State of New York, authorizing
issuance of $100,000 of stock, in which holders thereof share
in surplus profits, is a stock corporation under section 3,
General Corporations Law, and is subject to tax under section
180 of the Tax Law.

STATE OF NEW YORK.

ATTORNEY-GENERAL'S OFFICE,

ALBANY, *November* 29, 1910.

Hon. THOMAS B. DUNN, *State Treasurer, Albany, N. Y.:*

Dear Sir.— I acknowledge receipt of your favor of November
16th, enclosing a letter from Clarke Breckinridge & Cafey, 32
Nassau St., New York City, asking for an opinion as to
whether an educational corporation to which the Regents of the
University of the State of New York, pursuant to section 59 of the
Education Law, have granted a charter, authorizing the issuance
of $100,000 of stock upon which, under certain circumstances,
dividends may be paid out of the surplus of the corporation, is
required by section 180 of the Tax Law, as amended by chapter

472 of the Laws of 1910, to pay the organization tax of one-twentieth of one per cent.

Section 180, above referred to in so far as material, reads as follows:

> " ORGANIZATION TAX.— Every stock corporation incorporated under any law in this state shall pay to the state treasurer a tax of one-twentieth of one per centum upon the amount of capital stock which the corporation is authorized to have, and a like tax upon any subsequent increase. Provided, that in no case shall such tax be less than five dollars. Such tax shall be due and payable upon the incorporation of such corporation or upon the increase of its capital stock."

Whether a stock corporation is subject to the tax imposed by this section would depend upon its being a stock corporation within the meaning of that term, as defined by law and as used in the section.

A stock corporation is defined by section 2 of the General Corporation Law as follows:

> "A ' Stock Corporation ' is a corporation having a capital stock divided into shares, and which is authorized by law to distribute to the holders thereof dividends or shares of the surplus profits of corporatioons. A corporation is not a stock corporation because of having issued certificates called certificates of stock, but which are in fact merely certificates of membership, and which is not authorized by law to distribute to its members any dividends or shares of profits arising from the operations of the corporation."

And section 3 provides:

> " The term ' non-stock corporation ' includes every corporation other than a stock corporation."

No exception is made by the statute regarding the formation of a corporation for any particular purpose or object. If it has capital stock divided into shares and is authorized by law to distribute to the holders thereof dividends or shares of its surplus profits then it is a stock corporation.

I am of the opinion that an institution or association incorporated pursuant to section 59 of the Education Law authorized to issue stock upon which may be distributed to the holders thereof dividends or shares of the surplus profits is a stock corporation, as that term is defined by section 3 of the General Corporation Law, and as used in section 180 of the Tax Law, and is subject to the tax imposed thereby.

Very truly yours,

EDWARD R. O'MALLEY,

Attorney-General.

OPINIONS RENDERED THE STATE ENGINEER AND SURVEYOR.

Barge Canal — Bridges — Railroads.

State should not construct bridges for Utica & Mohawk Valley Railroad Company over canal near Mohawk and Herkimer. Permit being revocable as to use and occupancy of bridge and railroad within ten rods of the Erie Canal, the Superintendent of Public Works may revoke permits of January 25, 1904, and August 10, 1905, and if railroad company is aggrieved, it may seek relief in the Court of Claims.

(Permit revoked January 22, 1910, by Superintendent of Public Works. See his letter same date.)

STATE OF NEW YORK.

ATTORNEY-GENERAL'S OFFICE,

ALBANY, January 15, 1910.

Hon. WILLIAM B. LANDRETH, *Special Deputy State Engineer,* *DeGraaf Bldg., Albany, N. Y.:*

Dear Sir.— I have your communication in reference to the two places where it will be necessary to construct bridges near the villages of Herkimer and Mohawk in order to carry the tracks of the

Utica & Mohawk Valley Railway Company over the new barge canal. The question which you submit is whether the State or the railroad company will be obliged to bear the expense of building these bridges.

Annexed to your communication was a map, which I return attached hereto, and which shows a line of railroad owned and operated by the Utica & Mohawk Valley Railway Company along the highway leading from Mohawk to Herkimer. The railroad line crosses the Erie canal upon a bridge built and owned by the railroad company. Permission to build this bridge was granted to the railroad on January 25, 1904, by Hon. Charles S. Boyd, who was then Superintendent of Public Works. This permit is in writing and states that the railroad may erect and maintain a bridge at its own cost and expense across the Erie canal at this point and that it may operate its line over the same. The permit was granted pursuant to section 35 of the Canal Law and is revocable both as to the use and occupancy of the bridge and also of the railroad line within ten rods of the Erie canal as the free and perfect use of the canal may require or as may be necessary for making any repairs, improvements or alterations in the same. Adjacent to this bridge the new channel of the barge canal extends westwardly at an acute angle with the channel of the Erie canal, the prism of the new canal intersecting the right of way of the railroad company at a point marked "A." All points of intersection of the new prism and the railroad's right of way are within ten rods of the blue line of the Erie canal. The construction of the new channel of the barge canal will necessitate the building of a bridge to carry the tracks of the railroad at this point.

From a point on the line of the West Shore Railroad near Mohawk the Utica & Mohawk Valley Railway Company operates a double track trolley line over a private right of way to the highway between Mohawk and Herkimer north of the Mohawk river. This route crosses the Mohawk river on a temporary bridge a short distance west of the said highway. A few rods south of this temporary bridge the railroad's right of way is intersected at nearly right angles by the prism of the new barge canal. This point is marked "B" on the map. The temporary bridge crossing the Mohawk, over which the railroad's tracks run immediately adjacent to the point "B," was built and is maintained pursuant to written permission granted to the railroad company by Hon. N. V. V. Franchot, former Superintendent of Public Works, on August 10, 1905. This permit contains the provision that the railroad company will " remove the temporary structure when so directed by the proper State authorities if the same shall be found to interfere with the Erie canal as improved pursuant to the provisions of chapter 147 of the Laws of 1903," and that " all work in connection with the temporary structure and the subsequent permanent structure will be done without prejudice to the State's rights as covered by chapter 147 of the Laws of 1903 and without prejudice to the State's interests."

In order that this railroad route continue to be operated it will be necessary to construct a bridge over the new barge canal at the point " B."

At the points " A " and " B " the railroad's right of way has been appropriated. The railroad is entitled to compensation for the value of the property taken. This property is of two kinds: tangible property, including the land and the tracks, poles and equipment, and intangible property, which consists of the right to maintain and operate a railroad at these points. If the State has a right to compel the discontinuance of the use of the tracks at " A " within ten rods of the canal, and also the right to compel the discontinuance of the use of the bridge at " B," then the right to maintain and operate these lines of road is of little or no value. If the contrary is true and the railroad owns a continuing right to operate its line along these routes, then the appropriation of a section of these routes would result in serious damage unless bridges were built so that the railroad would continue to operate these lines. The compensation would be measured by the fair cost of building and maintaining bridges, so that the right to operate these routes would not be impaired.

While I recognize the propriety of referring the questions here presented to this department, it appears that a decision of them would amount to determining the compensation due the railroad for the property appropriated. This is more properly a function of the Court of Claims.

It is the duty of the State officials to preserve as far as possible the State's rights and, therefore, I respectfully advise that the

Superintendent of Public Works forthwith revoke the right of the Utica & Mohawk Valley Railway Company to maintain and operate the bridges near the point "A" and the tracks within ten rods thereof, which was granted January 25, 1904, and also revoke the right to maintain and operate the bridge near the point " B," which was granted August 10, 1905.

In this way the canal officials, including the appraiser, will be in a position to protect fully all of the State's rights. If the railroad is aggrieved and contends that it is entitled to compensation equivalent to the cost of new bridges, its right will be preserved by the Court of Claims, but the State will have preserved any defense that it may have.

Therefore, without expressing any definite conclusion upon these two questions, but leaving them to be decided by the Court of Claims in case any controversy arises, I respectfully advise that you proceed upon the theory that the railroad company is liable for the cost of building and maintaining these bridges at the points above referred to.

Yours truly,

EDWARD R. O'MALLEY,

Attorney-General.

Barge Canal Law — Contracts.

Proposed alterations Contract No. 2-E, consisting of unfinished work on Contract No. 2, let to Ferguson Contracting Company, will not relieve said company from liability. Extra expense of State for such alteration adds further items for damages charged against contractors.

STATE OF NEW YORK.

ATTORNEY-GENERAL'S OFFICE,

ALBANY, March 18, 1910.

Hon. WILLIAM B. LANDRETH, Special Deputy State Engineer, Albany, N. Y.:

Dear Sir.— I beg to acknowledge the receipt of your letter of March 8, 1910, in reference to proposed alterations of Contract No. 2-E, which was let to Holler & Shepard.

It appears from your letter and from the records in connection with this contract that it embraces the unfinished work of former Contract No. 2, which was originally let to the Ferguson Contracting Company. On or about May 13, 1910, the State Engineer certified that Contract No. 2 was not being progressed in accordance with the terms thereof and for the best interests of the State, whereupon the Canal Board passed a resolution cancelling the contract and directing the State Engineer to prepare such estimates and data as were necessary to the placing of the work yet to be done under contract. This action of the State Engineer and the Canal Board was taken pursuant to the provision of the so-called Barge Canal Act, section 7 (chapter 147, Laws 1903, and amendments), and in accordance with a provision in the contract that " the contract may be cancelled and the work re-advertised and relet in the manner prescribed in chapter 147 of the Laws of 1903 * * * and in such case that any excess in the cost of completing the contract beyond the price which the same was originally awarded, shall be charged to and paid by the contractor."

The remaining unfinished work was relet to Holler & Shepard under Contract No. 2-E. It is now proposed to alter Contract No. 2-E in several particulars, which you state can be classed as of minor importance, and you ask my opinion as to whether or not by so doing the State would complicate its relations and its rights in respect to the Ferguson Contracting Company, or tend to relieve that company from liability for the excess in the cost of completing the work embraced in Contract No. 2.

I do not believe these alterations will affect the existing rights of the State in its relations with the Ferguson Contracting Company. Under a contract stipulating that in case of its amendment the contractor shall be charged with all extra expenses, he is liable for all expenses which would not have been incurred by the employer if the contract had been complied with. (Sutherland on Damages, 3rd ed., p. 2141, and cases cited.) Any extra expenses incurred by the State because of these alterations, which would not have been incurred if Contract No. 2 had been complied with and completed by the Ferguson Contracting Company, simply adds other items of damage chargeable to that company. Without entering into a discussion of the right of the State to recover such damages, it may be said that making such alterations would not relieve the Ferguson Contracting Company of any liability which it is now under.

Yours truly,

EDWARD R. O'MALLEY,

Attorney-General.

Lands Under Water.

Issue of letters-patent by State to Ames and Robinson for certain lands under waters of Lake Ontario in front of Oswego State Reservation, on condition that improvements, docks, wharves, etc., be constructed within ten years. Such improvements not having been made, title may be made to revest in the State by proceedings for revocation of such letters-patent.

STATE OF NEW YORK.

ATTORNEY-GENERAL'S OFFICE,

ALBANY, *April* 5, 1910.

Hon. FRANK M. WILLIAMS, *State Engineer and Surveyor, Albany, N. Y.:*

Dear Sir.— I have under consideration your favor of the 22nd ultimo asking for my opinion as to whether letters-patent ever issued to Ames and Robinson of certain lands lying under the water of Lake Ontario immediately in front of the State Reservation at Oswego.

An examination of the copy of the petition submitted with your letter, blue print and chapter 76 of the Laws of 1854 shows that the Commissioners of the Land Office were by that act authorized to make a patent to Cheney Ames and his associates of certain lands under water in the harbor of East Oswego, on the condition that certain improvements in the way of docks and wharves be constructed within ten years from the passage of the act. Section 1 of that act imposes this condition in the following terms:

> " * * * and any part of the land sold and conveyed under the provisions of this act, in front of which a pier or breakwater, exclusive of that of the United States, is not built within ten years from the passage of this act, shall revert to the people of the state."

Pursuant to that act the Commissioners of the Land Office issued a patent to Cheney Ames and Orville Robinson under date of July 19, 1854. The patent leaves blank the number of years within which the docks or wharves should be constructed. It is my opinion, however, that by making reference to the statute the patent impliedly contains this restriction, and as it appears that no docks or wharves have been constructed at any time, there is a violation of the condition and the State is entitled to be revested with complete ownership. The limitation thus imposed is in my opinion a condition subsequent. It follows that in order to revest the title to the patented lands in the State a proceeding should be brought for a revocation of these letters-patent pursuant to law.

From the facts presented it would seem to me that such a proceeding can be successfully maintained.

I herewith return the blue print submitted with your favor.

Yours respectfully,
EDWARD R. O'MALLEY,
Attorney-General.

Barge Canal — Bridges.

Construction of Barge canal necessitating the removal of bridge over Erie canal at Main street, Lockport, over which the tracks of the International Railway Company run, and erection of new bridge at such point. Ownership of bridge and steel trusses vests in the State and not the railroad company.

(Niagara Falls Suspension Bridge Co. v. Gardner, 29 U. C. Q. B. 194; Meason's Estate, 4 Watts [Pa.], 341.)

STATE OF NEW YORK.

ATTORNEY-GENERAL'S OFFICE,

ALBANY, *April* 20, 1910.

Hon. WILLIAM B. LANDRETH, *Special Deputy State Engineer, Lyon Block, Albany, N. Y.:*

Dear Sir.— I have the honor to reply herewith to your communication in reference to the bridge over the Erie canal at Main street, Lockport, N. Y. From your correspondence and the papers submitted to me it appears that in the year 1903 the International Railway Company made application to the Superintendent of Public Works for permission to lay and maintain railway track over this bridge and to operate upon it its cars. This application was granted upon the condition that the bridge be strengthened and adapted for such use by the railway company at its own cost and expense, all work in connection therewith to be done under the supervision of the Superintendent of Public Works. In carrying out this work the railway company removed certain steel trusses which were the property of the State and a part of the bridge, and replaced them with trusses of greater strength than those removed.

It also appears that in connection with the construction of the Barge canal it will be necessary to build at this point an entirely new bridge and that no part of the existing bridge can be utilized. The railway company claims that the existing trusses under its tracks belong to it and that it should be permitted to take possession of them after they are removed from the canal by the barge canal contractor. You request my opinion as to whether these trusses are the property of the company or of the State.

It seems clear to me that this bridge is real estate. It is a structure permanently affixed to the land. The abutments and the approaches, which are certainly real estate, are of no use without the bridge connecting them. It has been held by the courts that a suspension bridge across the Niagara river is land. (Niagara Falls Suspension Bridge Company v. Gardner, 29 U. C. Q. B. 194.) It has also been held that a toll bridge erected by two parties across a stream between their lands is real estate. (Meason's Estate, 4 Watts [Pa.] 341.) I do not find any expressions of opinion upon this precise question by the courts of this State, but I have no doubt that they would hold the same conclusion. The improvement of this property by the addition of heavier trusses, which are for all practical purposes permanently affixed to the property, vests in the State the ownership of these new trusses. In addition there is also to be considered the fact, as I am informed, that the railway company, when it made the improvement, secured possession of the old trusses which were removed. The written permission given to the railway company to improve and use this bridge contains no mention of the final disposition of these trusses in case the bridge should be taken down and it may be fairly presumed that it was the intention of the parties at the time the permission was given that the improvements should become and remain a part of the bridge itself and belong to the State.

On account of the foregoing considerations, therefore, I am of the opinion that this bridge and the whole of it, including the trusses in question, is the property of the State and may be disposed of to the best advantage of the State in connection with the contemplated improvement of the canal.

Yours truly,

EDWARD R. O'MALLEY,

Attorney-General.

Barge Canal — Contracts.

Arrangement with contractor on Contract No. 12, by alteration
order for deposit of material from Brewerton cut, in Oneida
river, at such price as State and contractor may agree.

, (See opinion March 23, 1909, p. 416, Report.)

STATE OF NEW YORK.

ATTORNEY-GENERAL'S OFFICE,

ALBANY, *June* 23, 1910.

Hon. FRANK M. WILLIAMS, *State Engineer and Surveyor, Albany,
N. Y.:*

Dear Sir.— In your favor of the 15th inst., you request my
opinion as to whether it is legal to arrange with the contractor on
Contract No. 12, for the depositing of material excavated from the
Brewerton cut, in certain pockets of the Oneida river rather than
in spoil bank as provided in the contract.

I respectfully call your attention to my opinion of March 23,
1909, to Special Deputy State Engineer William B. Landreth, in
which it was held that the State might, under the provisions of
this contract, alter the slopes by increasing the same, thereby causing further transportation of excavated material, without the payment of any extra compensation to the contractor, inasmuch as such
changes were within the contemplation of the parties when the
agreement was signed. The proposition that is now submitted to
me, however, involves the placing of excavated material in an
entirely different place and at an increased cost. If the State has
determined that this is advisable from the point of view of the
efficiency of the canal construction, in my opinion it is legal to
change, by an alteration order, the plans and specifications by
providing for the deposit of excavated material in the manner
described by you in your letter, and since this change must necessarily make a new item of work for which the original contract
contains no item price, the State may agree with the contractor
upon a fair price therefor.

Yours very truly, .

EDWARD R. O'MALLEY,

Attorney-General.

Canal Law — Chapter 350, Laws 1910 — Barge Canal Appropriations.

Agreement may be entered into between the Canal Board and the Superintendent of Public Works, and telephone and telegraph companies, providing that such corporations may have an easement over State canal lands for the erection of poles and wires, as part compensation for damages occasioned by Barge canal appropriation.

STATE OF NEW YORK.

ATTORNEY-GENERAL'S OFFICE,

ALBANY, *June* 23, 1910.

Hon. FRANK M. WILLIAMS, *State Engineer and Surveyor, Albany, N. Y.:*

Dear Sir.— I am in receipt of your favor of the 22d inst., in which you ask to be advised as to whether under the provisions of chapter 350, Laws of 1910, the Canal Board or the Superintendent of Public Works would be empowered to enter into an agreement with telephone or telegraph companies providing for an easement over State lands for the purpose of erecting poles as a part payment for the claims of such companies for damages by reason of appropriations for Barge canal purposes.

Chapter 350 of the Laws of 1910, is an amendment of subdivision 3 of section 15 of chapter 13 of the Laws of 1909, entitled the Canal Law. As amended, the portion of section 15 applicable to the matter under consideration reads as follows:

"Section 15. GENERAL POWERS.— The canal board may:

*   *   *   *   *   *   *   *

3. Determine whether any lands, taken for the purposes of the canals, may be sold or exchanged for other lands beneficially to the state, and in all cases of determination that any such lands may be so sold or exchanged, may sell the same, or may exchange the same for other lands required for the purposes of the canals, and in order to carry any such

sale or exchange into effect may authorize the superintendent of public works to execute and deliver to the purchaser, in the name of the people of the state, a quit-claim deed of such lands."

The statute above quoted clearly authorizes the Canal Board to provide for the sale or exchange of canal lands when such sale or exchange, within constitutional limits, may be beneficial to the State, the sale or exchange to be accomplished by the execution and delivery of a quit-claim deed thereof. It is my opinion that the statute means further that the Canal Board is thereby authorized to sell or exchange an easement in canal lands when such sale or exchange is for the best interests of the State. The term "lands" means, of course, real property with all its hereditaments and appurtenances, and while an ordinary application of this section would mean the conveyance of the fee of lands appropriated for canal purposes, it must also be considered to provide for the conveyance of some estate less than a fee, to wit, in this case, the conveyance of an easement.

1 am therefore of the opinion that the Canal Board may approve of settlements made with telegraph or telephone companies wherein it is provided that such companies shall, subject to such restrictions as are for the best interests of the canal construction and operation, receive as part consideration for the settlement of their claims for damages for appropriated lands, quit claim deed of an easement over canal lands for their poles and wires.

Yours very truly,

EDWARD R. O'MALLEY,

Attorney-General.

Barge Canal — Contracts — Alteration Orders.

Extra compensation to contractor on Contract No. 29 for additional
coffer-dams, pumping, bailing and drainage on alteration
order No. 1, being payment for the extra work of lengthening
and deepening four culverts. State may compensate contractor at a fair price.

STATE OF NEW YORK.

ATTORNEY-GENERAL'S OFFICE,

ALBANY, *June* 24, 1910.

Hon. FRANK M. WILLIAMS, *State Engineer and Surveyor, Albany,
N. Y.:*

Dear Sir.— I am in receipt of a letter dated the 14th inst. from
Special Deputy State Engineer William B. Landreth, asking for
my opinion as to whether the State can pay to the contractor on
barge canal contract No. 29 extra compensation for additional
coffer-dams, pumping, bailing and draining, necessitated by alteration No. 1 on that contract. On the 1st of April, 1910, I received
from the Secretary of the Canal Board a letter of the Maryland
Dredging and Contracting Company, the contractor on this contract, dated March 28, 1910, protesting against this alteration
order.

From an examination of that protest and your letter of April
26, 1910, with its enclosure, and the letter of the Special Deputy
above referred to, it appears that the alteration in question on this
contract increases the length and depth of four dive culverts, and
that this deepening and lengthening will increase the amount of
coffer-dams, pumping, bailing and draining required at these culverts over the amount required at the same place under the original
plans. Under this contract a lump sum was bid for all of the
coffer-dams, pumping, bailing and draining. By the provisions
of 18s of the special specifications it is provided that "if any
coffer-dams, pumping, bailing and draining is required for portions of the work other than those included in the above list, or if
any is required at any of these structures, etc., after the percentage
allotted for that portion of the contract has been estimated, it shall

be done by the contractor and the payment therefor shall be considered as included in the total lump sum bid for coffer-dams, pumping, bailing and draining."

I do not believe that this provision would require the contractor to furnish the extra coffer-dams, pumping, bailing and draining necessitated by the change of plans embodied in alteration order No. 1 without additional compensation, nor do I find any other provision in the contract or specifications which requires him so to do. This additional cost is rather pay for extra work than extra pay for the work in the original contract, for in reality the alteration order necessitates labor and materials under this head in addition to that covered by the lump sum bid.

I am therefore of the opinion that the State may agree with the contractor for the payment of such sum for this additional work as is fair compensation therefor.

I return you herewith alteration order No. 1 and suggest that in case an agreement is reached with the contractor on this question, the protest heretofore be withdrawn by it and the alteration order as a whole be accepted.

Yours very truly,

EDWARD R. O'MALLEY,

Attorney-General.

Barge Canal — Contracts.

Contract No. 43. Construction of additional junction lock at Rome where the Barge canal crosses the Erie canal. Alteration order may be issued in usual form.

STATE OF NEW YORK.

ATTORNEY-GENERAL'S OFFICE,

ALBANY, *September* 12, 1910.

Hon. FRANK M. WILLIAMS, *State Engineer and Surveyor, Albany, N. Y.:*

Dear Sir.— I beg to acknowledge receipt of a letter dated the 2nd instant signed by Hon. William B. Landreth, Special Deputy State Engineer, in which my opinion is asked as to whether a certain alteration can be made in contract No. 43.

It appears from the communication that the work provided for
under this contract entered into with the M. A. Talbott Company
of Baltimore, Md., includes the excavating of the canal prism, the
constructing of two guard gates, a junction lock and retention dam
at Rome, entrance and spillway for Nine Mile Creek, two highway
bridges, dive culverts and other incidental work from Oriskany
Road to Mud Creek just west of Rome. It now appears desirable
to add to the work an additional junction lock where the Barge
canal crosses the present Erie canal at Rome at a point within the
site of the contract as defined by the specification.

I am of the opinion that the lock may be constructed under this
contract by an alteration order in the usual form. Your attention
is called to paragraph 6 of the contract in which the power to issue
such an alteration order and the obligation of the contractor to
follow the terms thereof are set forth. I have been informed that
the contractor raises no objection to the issuance of the order and
agrees to execute the same, compensation for the work to be determined, of course, by the item prices set forth in the original contract. Under these circumstances there can, of course, be no question as to the legality of constructing the lock in this manner.

Yours very truly,

EDWARD R. O'MALLEY,

Attorney-General.

Canals — Bridges.

State Engineer may in construction of new lift bridge over the
Erie canal at Franklin street, city of Syracuse, include items
for signal device and for alteration of railroad tracks, etc.

STATE OF NEW YORK.

ATTORNEY-GENERAL'S OFFICE,

ALBANY, *September* 14, 1910.

Hon. FRANK M. WILLIAMS, *State Engineer and Surveyor, Albany,*
N. Y.:

Dear Sir.— Replying to your favor of the 12th inst., in which
you ask to be advised as to whether it is legal for you to include

in the plans and specifications for a new bridge across the present canal at Franklin street in the city of Syracuse, items for a signal device and for the alteration of the railroad tracks approaching the bridge and the track itself on the bridge, I beg to say that the construction of this bridge is authorized under chapter 527 of the Laws of 1910. There exists at the present time at Franklin street in the city of Syracuse an overhead foot bridge built and maintained by the State and a swing bridge used as a railroad bridge built by the railroad. I am advised that there was no highway at this point or roadway of any kind prior to the construction of the canal, or prior to the 20th day of April, 1839. It would seem, therefore, that under sections 121 and 126 of the Canal Law, there is no obligation upon the State for the construction of any bridge at this point other than that created by the special act above mentioned.

In this act provision is made for the contribution of $17,000 each by the city of Syracuse and the Rome, Watertown & Ogdensburg Railroad Company, or the New York Central & Hudson River Railroad company, as lessee of the Rome, Watertown & Ogdensburg Railroad Company. The act contains the following provision:

" * * * The Superintendent of Public Works is authorized to construct a lift or hoist bridge over the Erie Canal at Franklin Street in the City of Syracuse together with the necessary machinery for operating the same to replace the present overhead foot bridge and the swing bridge used as a railroad bridge at that point according to plans and specifications to be prepared by the State Engineer and Surveyor."

The determination of what constitutes the necessary machinery for operating the bridge is purely an engineering one. It would seem, therefore, that the State Engineer might legally include these matters if he determines that they are essential to the construction of the bridge. On the other hand, if he should deem them unnecessary or not within the meaning of the statute and should eliminate these items from the plans and specifications, it is my judgment that he may legally so do.

Yours very truly,

EDWARD R. O'MALLEY,

Attorney-General.

Barge Canal — Contracts.

State Engineer and Surveyor may issue alteration order on Contract No. 43, providing for the construction of a highway bridge at Mill street, made necessary by negotiations between the State and the New York Central Railroad and the Utica & Mohawk Valley Railroad.

STATE OF NEW YORK.

Attorney-General's Office,

Albany, *September* 24, 1910.

Hon. Frank M. Williams, *State Engineer and Surveyor, Albany. N. Y.:*

Dear Sir.— I have your favor of the 20th inst., in which you request my opinion as to whether it is legal for the State to include in an alteration order to Contract No. 43 the construction of a superstructure on a certain highway bridge.

It appears from your communication that at present Contract No. 43 does not contain any provisions for the construction of the superstructure for a highway bridge at Mill street, but only for the construction of abutments, and that it was originally intended to provide for this construction work in a separate contract, to be numbered 83. At the point where this bridge is to be constructed the channel of the new Barge canal crosses the highway at a point south of the crossing of this highway over the Mohawk river. At the present time there is a provision in the contract requiring the contractor to maintain traffic at this crossing and build temporary structures if necessary. It would be possible however for the contractor to postpone the work on the canal near the side of the bridge so as to reduce the cost of the maintenance of traffic to a low figure. It now appears necessary, because of negotiations and arrangements entered into by the State with the New York Central & Hudson River Railroad Company and the Utica & Mohawk Valley Railroad Company, to have this highway bridge constructed at the present time to the end that certain fills may be made where the new tracks of the Utica & Mohawk Valley Railroad will cross the channel of the Mohawk river. These fills will necessitate the cutting of the channel of the Barge canal in order to provide for the waters of the river. It follows that the construction of this highway bridge is deemed to be desirable at the present time.

The contractor is willing to accept an alteration order for the construction of this superstructure at contract prices for reinforced concrete, metal reinforcements and structural steel, and to accept your estimate of prices for creosoted lumber, wood block pavement and lattice railing, for which Contract No. 43 contains no item prices. If the work is constructed under an alteration order the bridge can be completed in from two to four months earlier than if it were constructed by a separate contract, and, as I am informed by your department, at a saving to the State.

It is my opinion that an alteration order may be issued pursuant to the provisions of paragraph 6 of Contract No. 43, providing payment for the work on the basis of item prices of the original bid so far as the same are applicable, and where there are no item prices applicable, by mutual agreement.

It is urged that because this particular piece of work was not in the original contract the State is not authorized in issuing this alteration order because there has been no advertisement as provided by the Barge Canal Act. I do not think that this contention is well founded. It must be borne in mind that this contract containing paragraph 6 is a part of the original advertisement, and so when a contractor bid upon the work to be done thereunder it must be deemed to have based that bid upon the powers of the State reserved in that contract, and since the power was reserved to make additions to the plans and specifications, increasing the quantities in the engineer's estimate, the power so to do was advertised, and in my opinion may be deemed an advertisement of this work.

Yours very truly,

EDWARD R. O'MALLEY,

Attorney-General.

Barge Canal — Contract.

Repair of culverts Contract No. 60, in widening and deepening prism of canal west of Rochester, done by direction of the Superintendent of Public Works, in order to preserve the structures, and the subsequent building of new, is emergency work, and the expense chargeable to Barge canal.

STATE OF NEW YORK.

Attorney-General's Office,

Albany, *October* 1, 1910.

Hon. Frank M. Williams, *State Engineer and Surveyor, Albany, N. Y.:*

Dear Sir.— Sometime ago you requested to be advised as to whether certain expenses incurred by the Superintendent of Public Works upon the canals are properly chargeable to Barge canal funds.

The first question involved the expense of the reconstruction of several culverts on contract 60, and the second the repairs to the Durhamville culvert. I am advised by the Superintendent of Public Works that the second question has been closed and that the expense has been charged by the Superintendent of Public Works to the maintenance and repair fund under his control.

As bearing upon the first question, the following facts appear in your communication. On contract 60 west of the city of Rochester the Barge canal follows closely the line of the present Erie canal. At various places beneath the old canal culverts existed. In the plans for the new channel the old prism was widened and deepened but the culverts were not rebuilt. It seems to have been considered sufficient to merely extend these culverts to meet the requirement necessitated by the increased width. In most cases the upper portions of the old culverts were strengthened by a casing of concrete or a blanket of clay puddle but no attempt was made to rebuild or strengthen the bottoms or floors of the structures. During the season of navigation of 1909 there were two successive breaks through the bottom of one of these culverts, caused by the operations of the contractor in rebuilding the canal, as a result of which the floor of the structure was subjected to increased water pressure.

The Superintendent of Public Works through the Western Division of his department caused repairs to be immediately made. The break was of such a nature that prompt action was necessary not only to preserve the canal structures from further damage but also to check the continuance of damage to surrounding property of private owners. The contract for this section of the improvement had not been completed. The contractor was still in possession of the site of this work. Subsequently it was determined to change the method of construction in respect to these culverts by building new structures instead of lengthening out the old ones.

I am of the opinion that such work is in the nature of emergency work necessarily incident to Barge canal construction and properly chargeable to the fund provided therefor. The funds provided for the use of the Superintendent of Public Works for repairs and maintenance were not in my opinion ever intended to be used for work so intimately connected with the Barge canal improvement as was the work under consideration.

I cannot close this opinion, however, without calling your attention to certain facts reported to the Superintendent of Public Works by distinguished engineers of the State and by the Superintendent of the Western Division in the Department of Public Works. An examination of these reports discloses that in the opinion of these gentlemen the work of the contractor in and about these old culverts was not performed in a workmanlike manner nor according to the plans and specifications. If this is so, and if the breaks in these culverts occurred by reason of the contractor's imperfect and improper workmanship then the expense of repairing the damage should be charged to him. This, of course, is a question of fact upon which I cannot pass but which I have taken the liberty of calling to your attention.

Very respectfully yours,

EDWARD R. O'MALLEY,

Attorney-General.

Barge Canal — Bridges — Highways.

Raising of highway bridge over Seneca river near Weedsport at
   expense of State.   Cost of maintenance to rest upon towns
   of Conquest and Mentz.

STATE OF NEW YORK.

Attorney-General's Office,

Albany, *November* 15, 1910.

Hon. Frank M. Williams, *State Engineer and Surveyor, Albany,
   N. Y.:*

Dear Sir.— Under date of October 31, 1910, Hon. William B.
Landreth, Special Deputy State Engineer, has requested my
opinion as to where the burden of the cost of maintenance will rest
after certain changes are made in a highway bridge over the Seneca
river near Weedsport.

It appears that under the provisions of contract 22 this bridge,
which is known as Free Bridge and is located four miles west of
Weedsport, is to be raised at the expense of the State. The changes
in the construction are such that the south span is elevated at both
ends nine feet while the north span is elevated at the south end
nine feet and at the north end nothing. The grade of this span
after the changes will be five per cent. The approach at the north
end of the bridge is unchanged while the approach at the south end
is increased to a five per cent. grade. It is claimed that travel over
the planking of the north span at a five per cent. grade will be
much more difficult than over a dirt road on the same grade, and
that the plank floor will wear out much more rapidly for that
reason, thus increasing the cost of maintenance.

This bridge was constructed and is maintained by the towns of
Conquest and Mentz.

The Superintendent of Highways of the county of Cayuga has
requested that both sides be raised to the same height.

The questions asked are whether, if the State places both spans
in a horizontal position so that the difficulty to travel and cost of
maintenance will not be increased over present conditions, future

repairs and maintenance will be a burden upon the State or the town by which the bridge was built, and whether, if only the south span is raised and the north span placed on a five per cent. grade, as shown on the plans, the cost of maintenance will be borne by the State or the town.

The Barge Canal Act contains no provision for the maintenance of bridges built pursuant to the improvement therein directed. The Canal Law, article 8, contains provisions concerning the maintenance of bridges at public expense, but such provisions apply only to road and street bridges over the canals in all places where such bridges were constructed prior to the 20th day of April, 1839. The present charge of maintaining this bridge rests upon the towns of Conquest and Mentz in which it is located because of the provisions of section 250 of the Highway Law, and while it is true that the Barge canal improvement is being carried along the thread of the stream of the Seneca river and necessitates the changes in this bridge above discussed and that such changes are made and to be made as the result of the directions of the Barge Canal Act, the Legislature does not seem to have relieved the towns of the maintenance of such structures after the changes so designated have been made. It must follow, therefore, that in both of the cases submitted in the above questions the cost of the maintenance of the bridge must rest upon the towns as heretofore until the Legislature has specifically relieved them of that liability.

Yours very truly,

EDWARD R. O'MALLEY,

Attorney-General.

Barge Canal — Highway Bridges.

Expense of highway bridge Three River Point to be charged as
in case of other highway bridges over navigable rivers in
course of canal improvement, to Barge canal fund.

STATE OF NEW YORK.

ATTORNEY-GENERAL'S OFFICE,

ALBANY, *December 30*, 1910.

Hon. FRANK M. WILLIAMS, *State Engineer and Surveyor, Albany,
N. Y.:*

Dear Sir.— Replying to your favors of the 5th and 21st inst.,
in which you ask to be advised as to whether a certain highway
bridge at Three River Point should be paid for from funds appropriated for Barge canal purposes, I beg to render you the following
opinion:

From affidavits of old residents in the vicinity of this bridge,
heretofore presented to this office, and from a report made to you
by Mr. Guy Moulton, Division Engineer for the Middle Division,
it appears that there exists at Three River Point a bridge called a
tow-path bridge crossing the Oneida river. The structure serves
as a cross-over bridge for animals towing boats in the Oswego
canal. It seems that prior to the construction of this bridge there
had existed at a point a short distance easterly from the location
of the structure a highway bridge connecting highways in the towns
of Schroeppel and Clay in the counties of Oswego and Onondaga.
In the improvement of the Oneida river, known as the Oneida river
improvement, this old bridge was destroyed by the State. One of
the affiants above mentioned stated that he purchased the materials
in the old bridge at the time of its destruction. The highways on
both the north and south sides of the river were diverted toward
the west so as to connect with the new tow-path bridge already mentioned. From that time to the present the highway traffic upon
those highways has passed the Oneida river by means of this tow-
path bridge.

Since in the Barge canal improvement, work upon which is being conducted at this point in the Oneida and Seneca rivers, no provision is made for a tow-path, it is not necessary to build or maintain a tow-path bridge at this point and there is, therefore, no obligation on the part of the State to rebuild this structure unless it is to be considered a public highway bridge. •

The Barge Canal Act contains the following clause:

> "New bridges shall be built over the canals to take the place of existing bridges wherever required or rendered necessary by the new location of the canals."

Under this provision of the statute the State is engaged in building or rebuilding highway bridges across the Oneida and Seneca rivers at points where the Barge canal improvement requires such changes. In the estimate of the probable cost of the canal improvement made in 1903, upon the basis of which the $101,000,000 bond issue was authorized, an item was included for the probable cost of the reconstruction of this among other bridges.

From the facts as set forth in evidence submitted to me and above referred to, I cannot see any reason for making any distinction between this bridge and other public highway bridges across navigable rivers in the pathway of the canal improvement.

I am, therefore, of the opinion that this bridge may be reconstructed in the usual way and that the expense thereof may be charged to the Barge canal fund.

Yours very truly,
EDWARD R. O'MALLEY,
Attorney-General.

OPINIONS RENDERED THE CANAL BOARD.

Barge Canal — Contracts.

Contract No. 64. Appropriation by State of lands in the village
of Middleport, Niagara county, adjoining the Blue Line of
the Erie canal, in order to provide facilities for public dockage
in village.

STATE OF NEW YORK.

ATTORNEY-GENERAL'S OFFICE,

ALBANY, *September* 12, 1910.

To the Honorable, The Canal Board, Albany, N. Y.:

Gentlemen.— Pursuant to a resolution of your honorable body,
passed on the 9th day of August, directing me to investigate the
question of the legality of the appropriation of certain lands
described in appropriation map No. 2533, contract 64, I took the
liberty of calling on the State Engineer for further facts with
reference to this question. From all the information before me it
appears that the property described in the appropriation lies in the
village of Middleport, in the county of Niagara, and immediately
adjoins the present blue line of the Erie canal on the north and
includes Vernon street on the west. At this point in the canal an
alteration in the original plans for the improvement was made so
as to change previously designated slope wall to a vertical wall
with a concrete facing and top. These changes were made to
provide facilities for public dock within the business center of the
village, and the point where the changes are being made is the only
available location for such a dock. It appears that without the
appropriation of additional lands it will be practically impossible
to make use of this dock. It is therefore proposed by the appropriation of the lands described in map No. 2533 to acquire sufficient lands to make this dock available for the free use of all the
public.

It is my opinion that the State may, pursuant to the provisions of section 4, chapter 147, of the Laws of 1903, as amended, appropriate the lands described in the above mentioned parcel map No. 2533 if such lands are necessary for the free and perfect use by the public of the dock structures.

I return herewith the tracing referred to.

Respectfully yours,

EDWARD R. O'MALLEY,

Attorney-General.

Barge Canal — Contract 14 — *Appropriation of Land.*

Crescent Ice Company must abide by contract made with Canal Appraiser regarding date from which interest shall run, in appropriation of lands described in maps 733, 975, 1323, 1324, 1325.

STATE OF NEW YORK.

ATTORNEY-GENERAL'S OFFICE,

ALBANY, *October* 13, 1910.

To the Honorable, The Canal Board, Albany, N. Y.:

Gentlemen.— Pursuant to a resolution of your honorable body passed on the 29th of September, 1910, I have made an examination of the petition of the Crescent Ice Company, in which the petitioner asks for the allowance of interest on a certain contract of settlement made by that company with the special examiner and appraiser for payment of lands described in maps Nos. 733, 975, 1323, 1324 and 1325, contract No. 14.   It appears that the petitioner desires interest upon the amount of settlement as agreed upon from the date of the service of the notices of appropriation instead of from the date of actual occupancy of the parcels, as certified by the State Engineer.   The contract in this case, dated the 21st day of December, 1909, and signed by the Crescent Ice Company and H. J. Donaldson, contains the usual clause with reference to payment of interest which reads as follows:

" * * * The said owner shall be entitled to receive from the State the sum of $36,000 with interest thereon from the date of actual occupancy by the State of the premises in question, the said date to be fixed and determined by the State Engineer and Surveyor and by him certified to the Comptroller and interest from the date aforesaid shall be certified by the Canal Board to the Comptroller for payment according to the terms and conditions of chapter 195 of the laws of 1908 and chapter 365 of the Laws of 1906."

The brief of counsel for the petitioner discusses at considerable length the question of the allowance of interest, arguing that the date of actual occupancy as used in the act and as the basis for the computation of interest is the same date as the date of the service of the notices of appropriation on the ground that the statute has made the date of the service of the notices of appropriation conclusive evidence of the entry upon and appropriation of the property by the State. However that may be, it is my opinion that the contract of settlement is conclusive upon the petitioner and that if it accepts the amount agreed upon as the fair value of the property it must abide by the further provision of the contract which fixes the date from which interest shall run as the date certified by the State Engineer and Surveyor to be the date of actual occupancy. It is alleged that the Ice Company supposed that the date of occupancy was the same as the date of the service of the notice of appropriation, but there is no charge of fraud or misrepresentation, and under these circumstances in my opinion the contract provisions should bind the parties. The same position was taken by this department in the matter of map No. 982, Hoy, Monroe county.

I return herewith the agreement made with this company by the special examiner and appraiser, brief submitted by Messrs. W. J. & W. C. Roach on behalf of the company, affidavit of Lawrence Shaughnessy, petition of Lawrence Shaughnessy and statement of Lawrence Shaughnessy.

Respectfully yours,

EDWARD R. O'MALLEY,

Attorney-General.

OPINIONS RENDERED THE COMMISSIONERS OF THE CANAL FUND.

State Finance Law — Sections 8, 62 — Canal Fund Deposits — Bonds.

Banking institutions designated by the State Treasurer and Comptroller as depositories of State moneys, may give one bond as security of deposits of both general and canal funds, to be filed with the State Treasurer.

STATE OF NEW YORK.

ATTORNEY-GENERAL'S OFFICE,

ALBANY, *January* 4, 1910.

To the Honorable, The Commissioners of the Canal Fund, Albany, N. Y.:

Sirs.— I beg to reply herewith to your request for my opinion as to whether or not under the existing law a banking institution which is a depository of both general funds and canal funds can give one bond to secure the deposits of both funds.

Security is required to be given for deposits of general funds by the provisions of section 8 of the Finance Law as follows:

" Banks designated for the deposit of State moneys under the provisions of this section shall before deposits are made severally execute and file with the treasurer a bond to the State in such form and with such sureties for such sum as may be prescribed and approved by the treasurer and comptroller, for the safe keeping and prompt payment of such moneys on legal demand therefor with interest at the rate agreed upon, or may in lieu of such surety bond deposit with the comptroller outstanding unmatured bonds issued by the State of New York * * *."

In the same manner security is required for deposits of canal funds. Section 62 of the Finance Law provides that the Com-

19

missioners of the Canal Fund may deposit the moneys belonging
to that fund in banking institutions and that they " may require
security for the deposit of such moneys by surety undertaking or a
deposit of bonds issued by the State of New York *in the same
manner as is provided by section eight of article two of this
chapter."*

Thus substantially the same requirements are made for security
for deposits of both the general fund and the canal fund. In case
any one banking institution happens to be designated by the treasurer and comptroller as a depository of general funds and also by
the Commissioners of the Canal Fund as a depository of canal
funds, there is, in my opinion, no legal objection to having that
banking institution give one bond to secure deposits of both funds.
Under the provisions of section 8 and 62 as quoted above, these
bonds should be filed with the treasurer.

I inclose herewith a typewritten form as requested for both the
surety bond and the assignment of State bonds.

Yours very truly,

EDWARD R. O'MALLEY,

Attorney-General.

OPINIONS RENDERED THE STATE ADJUTANT-GENERAL.

Poor Law (Consolidated) — Section 80.

Statute for relief of indigent soldiers, sailors or marines, applies
to " family " as living as one household, without regard to
ages.

STATE OF NEW YORK.

Attorney-General's Office,

Albany, *January* 22, 1910.

Hon. Nelson H. Henry, *Adjutant-General, Albany, N. Y.:*

Dear Sir.— I beg to acknowledge receipt of your favor of the
19th inst., with which you forwarded to me a letter from Tunis D.
Seaman, Chairman of Relief Committee of G. A. R. Post No. 82,

asking for my construction of section 80 of the Consolidated Poor Law so far as it applies to the support of "families" of indigent soldiers, sailors and marines.

Article 6 of the Poor Law reads in part as follows: "No poor or indigent soldier, sailor or marine who has served in the military or naval service of the United States, nor his family, nor the families of any who may be deceased, shall be sent to any alms-house, but shall be relieved and provided for at their homes in the city or town where they may reside, so far as practicable, provided such soldier, sailor or marine, or the families of those deceased, are, and have been residents of the State for one year." .The question is now asked if the term "families" as used in the above section will include children that have arrived at the age of twenty-one years, or is it of limited application, to only those children that are under sixteen years of age?

The word "family" as used in different statutes has been construed by several courts in various ways, but the current of authority construes it to mean "a collective body of persons who live in one home, under one head or manager," and adopting this construction the word "family" as used in section 80, *supra,* would include all the members of the family at the time the relief is furnished, whether they be under or over the age of twenty-one years. It might include a father or mother, or a crippled, sick or demented child of any age. I do not think it would include a child that had grown to manhood or womanhood and who had separated from the home and had formed other relations, or in any manner become disconnected with the family of the soldier, sailor or marine, nor would it include a parent who has a home of his or her own, separate and distinct from that of the veteran.

"A son or daughter of a parent, residing with the parent, does not cease to be a member of the family when he or she respectively arrives at the age of twenty-one or eighteen, from that fact alone. They must have ceased to reside with their parents in order to break the family relation."

Chicago & N. W. Ry. Co. v. Chisholm, 79 Ill. 584, 587.

The relation existing between such persons residing together as a family must be of a permanent and domestic character, not abiding together temporarily as strangers.

The purpose of the statute under consideration was to save the old soldier, sailor or marine, and his family, from the humiliation which would follow their becoming inmates of an almshouse and thus placed upon a level with a common pauper, and it is needless to say that in most instances the old soldier would feel the humiliation just as keenly to have his relatives and those associated with him closely by family ties taken to such almshouse, as if he were to go himself.

I am therefore of the opinion that the statute referred to was intended to apply to all the children or other relatives of the soldier, sailor or marine, who belong to his family as above indicated, without regard to their ages.

Yours truly,

EDWARD R. O'MALLEY,

Attorney-General.

Pensions — Naval Militia.

Authority of Adjutant General to consider claim of T. H. Froelich for pension for injury received while raising an anchor prior to a cruise of the " New Hampshire."

(Chapter 559, Laws 1893, section 129, repealed by chapter 212, Laws 1898, sections 162, 169.)

STATE OF NEW YORK.

ATTORNEY-GENERAL'S OFFICE,

ALBANY, *February* 19, 1910.

Hon. NELSON H. HENRY, *Adjutant-General, Albany, N. Y.:*

Dear Sir.— I beg to acknowledge receipt of your favor of January 28th, with enclosures, relating to the application of one T. H. Froelich for a pension for an injury incurred by him on August 19th, 1893, and my opinion is requested whether you can give consideration to such claim at this time.

It is disclosed by the papers forwarded to me that Mr. Froelich, was assisting in raising an anchor prior to a cruise of the New Hampshire, at the time above stated; the hook of the deck tackle parted and he received a compound fracture of the leg and was laid up in the hospital for several weeks, and has never recovered. Some spinal trouble developed after the injury and he is unable to do much work, and is almost totally incapacitated to earn a living.

The pension is claimed under section 129, chapter 559, of the Laws of 1893. This opinion is not intended to touch the merits of the application, but solely the question whether the Adjutant-General can give consideration to the claim at this time. It will be observed upon reference to the above-mentioned section that pensions are granted for injuries incurred in certain specified lines of duty, without limitation of time in which the application might be made.

By section 296 of the same act, all of the articles of that act, not incompatible with Article XV (Naval Militia) should apply to the naval militia as well as the National Guard; so it would seem that, unless the applicant is bound by some subsequent statute, his application can now be considered.

Section 162, chapter 212, of the Laws of 1898, reads as follows:

"162. PENSIONS.— Every member of the militia who shall be wounded or disabled while in the service of the State, in cases of riot, tumult, breach of the peace, resistance to process, invasion, insurrection, or imminent danger thereof, or whenever called upon in aid of the civil authorities, shall be taken care of and provided for at the expense of the State, and every such member who shall be wounded or disabled, or has been so disabled in the performance of any actual service of this State, *within ten years preceding the application for a pension under this act,* in case of riots, tumults, breach of the peace, resistance to process, invasion, insurrection or imminent danger thereof, or whenever called upon in aid of the civil authorities, or while engaged in any lawfully ordered parade, drill, encampment or inspection, shall upon proof of the facts, as hereinafter provided, be placed on the roll of invalid pensioners of the state, and shall receive, out of any moneys in the treasury of the state, not otherwise appropriated, upon the audit of the adjutant-general and approval of the governor, the like pension or reward that persons under similar circumstances receive from the United States; and in case of any

wound, injury or disease causing death, then the widow or
minor children of such member of the militia, shall receive
such pension or reward, from the time of receiving the injuries
on account of which such pension or reward is allowed."

Chapter 559 of the Laws of 1893 was repealed by Chapter 162
of the Laws of 1898, but section 169 thereof provides that the
repeal should not " affect any act done or offense committed, or
penalty, forfeiture or punishment incurred or accrued *prior to the
time when this act takes effect,* but the same may be enforced,
prosecuted and inflicted as fully as if such act had not been
repealed. * * * "

It thus appears that, if the applicant was entitled to a pension
under the law of 1893, the same was saved and reserved to him by
the act of 1898, and it will be noticed by the act of 1898 that the
ten year limitation was only intended to apply to acts done, offenses
committed, etc., which occurred or accrued after the passage of
that act.   The provisions of the act of 1898 were substantially
re-enacted in the Consolidated Military Law of 1909.

Section 31 of chapter 677 of the Laws of 1892 (Statutory Construction Law) reads in part as follows:

" The repeal of a statute or part thereof shall not affect or
impair any act, clause or right, accruing, accrued or acquired,
or liability, penalty, forfeiture or punishment incurred prior
to the time such repeal takes effect, but the same may be
asserted, enforced, prosecuted or inflicted, as fully, and to
the same extent as if such repeal had not been effected. * * ."

This provision was re-enacted and became section 93 of the Consolidated General Construction Law, passed in 1909.

It appears very clearly that, if the applicant became entitled, to
a pension under the act of 1893, it was reserved to him both by
the act of 1898 and by the Statutory Construction Law (now General Construction Law), and inasmuch as there was no ten year
limitation in the original act, his claim was not barred by the limitation contained in the act of 1898.

There is still another reason why I think the Adjutant-General
can consider this claim at this time.   It is a well settled rule in
this State that neither statutes nor their amendments have retro-

active force or effect unless the intention is clearly indicated in the act, and in order to make the ten year limitation found in the act of 1898 apply to this claim, it would be retroactive to that extent, for the claim, if any existed, had accrued some five years before the limitation was imposed, and there is nothing in the act that would indicate such an intention on the part of the Legislature. In fact, the act itself, by limiting it to " *pensions under this act* " seems to indicate that a contrary intention prevailed.

I am therefore of the opinion that the Adjutant-General can consider the application of Mr. Froelich at this time.

Yours very truly,
EDWARD R. O'MALLEY,
Attorney-General.

National Guard State of New York.

1. Power vested in the Governor as Commander-in-Chief of the State of New York, to order the State militia outside territorial limits for military maneuvers.

2. Power vested in the military tribunal of the State to inflict punishment for offenses committed by members of the State militia outside of State and while under orders of the Governor.

STATE OF NEW YORK.

ATTORNEY-GENERAL'S OFFICE,

ALBANY, *April* 13, 1910.

Hon. NELSON H. HENRY, *Adjutant General of the State of New York, Albany, N. Y.:*

Dear Sir.— I beg to submit my opinion requested by you in your communication of February 10, 1910, in relation to the following two questions:

First. As to the authority of the Governor to order the militia of the State outside its territorial limits for the purpose of taking part in military maneuvers for drill and instruction.

Second. As to the power of military tribunals of this State to inflict punishment for offenses committed by members of the organized militia outside the State when under orders of the Governor.

I will consider these questions in their order.

Article IV, section 4, of the State Constitution, provides:

> " The governor shall be commander in chief of the military and naval forces of the State."

Article XI, sections 1 to 6, contains provisions in relation to the State militia. Section 1 provides what citizens shall constitute the State milita, and by section 2 the Legislature may provide for such other persons as may make application to be enlisted; section 3 provides for the organization of the militia and its divisions into land and naval and active and reserve forces *by the Legislature,* and further provides that the Legislature make sufficient appropriation for its maintenance; sections 4, 5 and 6 relate to the appointment, election and removal of the military officers of the militia.

These are the provisions of the State Constitution in relation to the military forces of the State.

In considering these questions it is to be observed that there is involved not the powers of the Governor as the executive of the civil government of the State, but his powers as military commander over the organized military forces of the State. His relation to the organized military forces of the State as its commander-in-chief is somewhat different than his relation to the citizens of the State as their executive. The rules of law and construction applicable to his powers as executive may not be applicable to his powers as commander-in-Chief by reason of the inherent nature of his military office.

The Governor's powers as commander-in-chief are nowhere defined in the Constitution. He, therefore, must be held to have the powers incident and inherent in such military office with power to make such orders as will insure the best efficiency and discipline of the military forces under his command, limited, of course, by the other provisions of the Constitution as well as by our form of government.

This view of the implied powers of a commander-in-chief under our form of government is confirmed in Winthrop in his Military Law and Precedents, volume 1, second edition, in a very excellent treatment at pages 65 to 72. Speaking of the inherent power of the President without legislative enactment to order court martials, he says at page 69:

> " Upon the adoption of the constitution and the division of the powers of the government, the executive power, previously exercised by Congress, was transferred to the President, and with it the function of commander-in-chief. This function was not defined by the constitution. To it, therefore, were properly to be regarded as attached (with such modifications as the new form of the government required), the powers originally vested in Congress and delegated by it as above indicated to the commander-in-chief of its army, and which had been exercised by the latter up to this period. Among those powers was the authority, properly incident to chief command, of issuing to subordinates and the army at large such *orders* as a due consideration for military discipline might require," * * *.

The language of the court in People v. Ewen, 17 How. Pr. 375, is also very pertinent. In this case the legal right of the Governor, as commander-in-chief, to consolidate companies and regiments, was disputed. At page 377 the court said:

> " It may be plausibly contended that this is a right inherent in his command. Without it, could any military force be rendered efficient, particularly in a period of disturbance, riot or insurrection ? * * * If, then, at a period of actual service such an authority is necessary, why should it not be necessary at a period of public tranquility ? It is a common observation that the best way to avoid war is to be properly prepared for it. And is it not the best way to avoid internal disturbance to have the military force so prepared in discipline and organization, and in suitable combinations, as that it shall be able to act with the greatest possible efficiency and dispatch ? "

That the Legislature has passed certain acts in relation to the rendezvous of the State troops or in relation to camp service or the service of the naval militia can in no way nullify by implication the constitutional powers of the Governor as commander-in-chief.

The taking part in military maneuvers for drill and instruction by our military forces would undoubtedly be for the good and welfare of the service and increase its efficiency and discipline. Therefore, there being no constitutional inhibition, either express or implied, the Governor, as commander-in-chief, has the power to order the military forces under his command to take part in such maneuvers without the State, provided, of course, that permission of the sovereign authority of the foreign country has first been obtained.   .

In regard to the authority of the Governor to order the militia outside of the territorial limits of the State for the purpose of taking part in military maneuvers with the regular army of the United States, special considerations support the power of the Governor.

The Constitution of the United States by Article I, section 8, paragraph 16, provides:

> "The Congress shall have power: * * * to provide for organizing, arming and disciplining the militia and for governing such part of them as may be employed in the service of the United States; reserving to the states respectively the appointment of the officers and the authority of training the militia according to the discipline prescribed by Congress."

Under this section of the Constitution Congress passed a comprehensive act in relation to the militia, entitled "An Act to promote the efficiency of the militia and for other purposes." (Act of January 21, 1903, chapter 196, 32 Stat. L. 775.) By section 15 of that act it is provided:

> "That the Secretary of War is hereby authorized to provide for participation by any part of the organized militia of any State or Territory on the request of the governor thereof in the encampment, maneuvers, and field instruction of any part of the Regular Army at or near any military post or camp or lake or sea-coast defenses of the United States." * * *

There was a recognition of the provisions of the aforesaid act of Congress of 1903 by the Legislature of our State in the enactment of the Military Law, chapter 231, Laws 1908 (now chapter 41 of the Consolidated Laws). By this law the organization, armament and discipline of our organized militia were conformed to that prescribed for the regular and volunteer armies of the United States. This was done pursuant to section 3 of the aforesaid act of Congress.

Under this act of Congress, therefore, the Governor, in addition to his constitutional powers as commander-in-chief, has warrant for ordering the troops to participate in these maneuvers with the regular army where such participation is requested by him.

Your second question relates to the power of military tribunals of this State over the organized militia outside the State when under orders of the Governor.

Military tribunals are in their essential nature different from our civil or criminal courts created for the administration of justice in our civil government. They are in fact simply instrumentalities of the executive power provided by the Legislature for the Governor as commander-in-chief to aid him in properly commanding our military forces and enforcing discipline therein.

> Winthrop's Military Law, Vol. 1, second edition, pages 53 and 54.

Military tribunals have, therefore, as their basis the enforcement of discipline in a military organization. They are, as we have seen, an inherent power of the commander-in-chief. The principle of territoriality, therefore, applicable to civil courts cannot, in the nature of things, be applicable to military tribunals. Every member of a military organization lawfully in service under orders of his commander, whether within or without the borders of the State, must necessarily be subject to court martial in order that the integrity of the organization be maintained. This is amply confirmed by the regulations and usage of the United States army.

See the Military Laws of the United States prepared under the direction of the Honorable Elihu Root by Brigadier-General George B. Davis, Advocate General, United States Army. At page 686 appears this statement:

"The jurisdiction over persons in the military service covers all military offenses committed by them, whether within or beyond the territorial jurisdiction of the United States. Military offenses are not territorial. (Manual for Courts-Martial, p. 14.)

"The jurisdiction of courts-martial is non-territorial. In a case of an officer who exhibited himself in a drunken condition at a public ball in Mexico, held that his offense was cognizable by a court-martial of the United States, subsequently convened in Texas by the department commander. This for the reason that the military jurisdiction does not recognize territoriality as an essential element of military offenses, but extends to the same wherever committed, a principle which is amply confirmed by the comprehensive provision of the Sixty-fourth Article of War. See Dig. Opin. J. A. G. par. 169."

By section 13 of the Military Law of this State (chapter 41, Laws of 1909), it is provided that when the militia are on duty under orders of the Governor, "the articles of war governing the army of the United States, * * * and the regulations prescribed for the army and navy of the United States, so far as such regulations are consistent with this chapter and the regulations issued thereunder, shall be in force and regarded as a part of this chapter until said force shall duly be relieved from such duty." Also, section 256 of the same law provides that

"All matters relating to the organization, discipline and government of the National Guard and Naval Militia, not otherwise provided for in this chapter or in the general regulations, shall be decided by the custom and usage of the United States army and navy respectively."

It is, therefore, my opinion that the Governor has authority to order the militia of the State outside its territorial limits for the purpose of taking part in military maneuvers for drill and instruction, and that the military tribunals of the State have the power to inflict punishment for offenses committed by members of the organized militia outside the State when under orders of the Governor.

Respectfully,

EDWARD R. O'MALLEY,

Attorney-General.

Town Law — Section 336 — Burial of Soldiers.

Provision made for purchase of burial plots for soldiers, and annual care of such burial plots, applies only to soldiers' graves within such town plots, not to private burial plots.

STATE OF NEW YORK.

ATTORNEY-GENERAL'S OFFICE,

ALBANY, *April 23, 1910.*

Hon. NELSON H. HENRY, *Adjutant-General, Albany, N. Y.:*

Dear Sir.— In reply to your favor of April 18th, with which you forward to me a letter from Tunis D. Seaman, of Nyack, asking for an opinion relating to the purchase of soldiers' burial plots by town boards at the expense of the town, I beg to state, that section 336 of the Town Law provides a method by which burial plots in cemeteries "where no burial plots are now owned by soldiers' organizations" may be purchased for the burial of soldiers. It also provides for the annual care of such burial plots, not to exceed fifty cents for each soldier's grave therein; and the expenses incident to the purchase of such plots and the annual care of such graves are both chargeable against the town.

I think that a fair construction of this section leads to the conclusion that the annual care therein specified should only apply to the graves of such soldiers as are buried in soldiers' burial plots in cemeteries, and does not apply to soldiers' graves outside of soldiers' burial plots. If a soldier is interred upon a private plot with his family or elsewhere, such a plot would not be called a "soldiers' burial plot," within the meaning of the above-mentioned statute, and I do not think that a town board is compelled to pay

fifty cents annually for the care of such a grave, even if it is neglected or uncared for.

Yours truly,

EDWARD R. O'MALLEY,

Attorney-General.

---

*Soldiers, Sailors and Marines — Burial — Erection Headstones
Over Graves.*

Duty of supervisors of counties to provide for burial of soldiers
resident in such counties, dying without means to defray
expenses, and to erect suitable headstones at their graves.

(Poor Law, sec. 84.   See opinion August 26, 1909 p. 919. Rep.)

STATE OF NEW YORK.

ATTORNEY-GENERAL'S OFFICE,

ALBANY, *May* 4, 1910.

Hon. NELSON H. HENRY, *Adjutant-General, Albany, N. Y.:*

Dear Sir.— Your favor under date of April 22, 1910, with
letter from Charles M. Montgomery, was duly received, by which
inquiry is made as to liability of a county for the burial expenses
and headstones for soldiers, sailors and marines who die without
sufficient means to defray the same, but who have children with
sufficient means to pay for the same.

By section 84 of the Poor Law it is provided:

> " The board of supervisors of each of the counties shall
> designate some proper person or authority, other than that
> designated for the care of poor persons, or the custody of
> criminals, who shall cause to be interred the body of any
> honorably discharged soldier, sailor or marine * * *
> or the body of the wife or widow of any soldiier, sailor or
> marine, married to him previous to eighteen hundred and
> ninety, who shall die such widow, and who shall hereafter die
> without having sufficient means to defray his or her funeral
> expenses, but such expenses shall in no case exceed fifty dol-
> lars. If the deceased has relations or friends who desire to
> conduct the burial, *but are unable or unwilling* to pay the

charge therefor, such sum shall be paid by the county treasurer upon due proof of the claim, and of the death and burial of the soldier, sailor or marine, or of the wife or widow of such soldier, sailor or marine, to the person so conducting such burial * * * ."

Section 85 of the same law provides for the erection of a headstone at the grave of such a deceased soldier, sailor or marine whose grave is not marked by a suitable headstone and who died without leaving means to defray the expenses of such headstone, at an expense not to exceed $15 to be paid for by the county in which he shall die a resident. The provision in reference to a headstone does not apply to the wife or widow of a soldier, sailor or marine.

These sections are in harmony with many others of somewhat similar import that have been enacted by national and State legislatures as evidence of the public gratitude and appreciation for the services of such old soldiers, sailors or marines as have imperilled their lives in the defence of our country, and it was clearly intended by the Legislature of our State that the old veterans and their wives and widows should not be buried in the ordinary Potter's field or that their surviving friends and relatives should be humiliated by seeing them buried as common paupers. Provision is also elsewhere made for the support and maintenance of the old soldier, sailor or marine who is unable to support himself, in an entirely different way from that provided for the relief of the common poor; and it is equally clear that the Legislature did not intend to subject the family of the deceased soldier, sailor or marine to a wrangle over the expenses of his burial or headstone, as it is provided in section 84 that if he has relatives or friends who are *unable or unwilling* to pay the charge therefor, they shall have the right to conduct the last rites, and the expense shall be paid by the county treasurer to the person so conducting the same.

Article VIII of the Code of Criminal Procedure indicates the practice that must be pursued in reference to compelling the support of a poor person by the father, mother or children of such poor person, where such father, mother or children are of sufficient ability to do so, but no provision is made therein to compel either the father, mother or children of a poor person to pay for the burial expenses or headstone of any such pauper.

Soldiers' homes are provided for indigent soldiers, sailors or marines who have. no families or friends with whom they may be domiciled. (Section 83 of the Poor Law.)

It will be noted that by the provisions of sections 84 and 85 of the Poor Law that the expenses of burials of soldiers, sailors and marines and their wives and widows and the expenses of headstones for soldiers are to be paid by the county in which he had a residence at the time of his death, and I am unable to find that such expenses are directly chargeable to the town in which he lived at the time of his decease even in those counties where the distinction between town and county poor is still maintained.

I am, therefore, of the opinion that it is the duty of the boards of supervisors of the several counties of the State to provide for the burial of old soldiers and the erection of headstones at their graves, who are residents of their respective counties and die without leaving sufficient means to defray such expenses, and that such expenses are chargeable upon the counties, even if such soldier, sailor or marine has relatives or friends who desire to conduct the burial but are unwilling to pay such charges.

Yours very truly,

EDWARD R. O'MALLEY,

Attorney-General.

State Armories — Military Law — Section 182.

Changes in State Armory at Elmira regarding fire exits, etc.; whether a county charge. Power of Board of Supervisors concerning maintenance of armories. Construction of above law.

(See also County Law, section 12, subdivision 2).

STATE OF NEW YORK.

ATTORNEY-GENERAL'S OFFICE,

ALBANY, *May* 20, 1910.

Hon. NELSON H. HENRY, *Adjutant-General, Albany, N. Y.:* .

Dear Sir.— I acknowledge your letter of the 16th inst., in which you ask my opinion for the guidance of the service, upon the proper interpretation of section 182 of the Military Law.

It appears from the letters inclosed in your communication that on September 26, 1908, the officer in charge of the State Armory at Elmira certified to the necessity of changes in such armory to provide for proper fire exits, which certificate was approved by the Armory Commissioners and transmitted to the board of supervisors of Chemung county at their annual meeting in 1908. At that time it was referred to the military committee of such board but no action was taken until April 8 of this year when the clerk of the board was instructed to write to the Armory Commission for an estimate of the cost. The officer in charge of the armory states that the board had already plans and specifications from which they could have secured an estimate in a very short time, and that unless some action is taken at once to get this work under way at the same time with other work which the Armory Commission is now advertising, the military work of the Third Infantry will be seriously crippled next fall and some of this other work being done by the State will necessarily be torn out when the improvements are finally carried through.

It is also stated in these communications that the board of supervisors of Chemung county has in the years 1908 and 1909 cut the annual estimate for maintenance of this armory and claims the right to reduce such estimates.

You also inclose the opinion of the Judge Advocate in which he states that it is manifestly to the public interest that the board of supervisors should take prompt action upon this matter, and that, in his opinion, section 182 of the Military Law was inserted in 1908 for the express purpose of doing away with the revision of estimates by boards of supervisors after their approval by the brigade commander. It is at his suggestion that you request my opinion upon the proper construction of this law.

Section 182 of the Military Law provides in part as follows:

"§ 182. EXPENSES OF ERECTING, IMPROVING AND FURNISHING ARMORIES. The expenses of * * * altering * * * shall be a portion of the county charge of each county within the bounds of which is located any arsenal or armory occupied by the national guard, and shall be levied, collected and paid in the same manner as other county charges are levied, collected and paid.

" In case expenditure is required for * * * alteration, repair, * * * the necessity for such expenditure shall be certified to the armory commission by the officer having charge and control of the armory. If the armory commission shall approve such expenditure, it shall transmit such certificate approved by it to the board of supervisors of the county in which such armory is located. * * *

" The officer in charge and control of an armory shall on or before the first day of October in each year prepare and submit for approval to the commanding officer of the brigade to which his organization is attached * * * an itemized estimate in quadruplicate of the necessary expenditures to be made for the utensils, materials, means and supplies necessary and required for the next calendar year for the cleaning, care, proper keeping, maintenance and preservation of the armory * * *. Upon the approval of such estimate it shall be filed as follows: One copy with the adjutant-general of the state; one with the officer approving the same; one with the clerk of the board of supervisors of the county, and one at the armory. The board of supervisors shall levy and collect the moneys required, but shall have no authority to levy, collect or appropriate any money for the purposes provided in this section, until the certificates and estimate herein required are made and filed except as hereinafter provided. * * * "

It is thus evident that the expense of the alteration for providing proper fire exits is by the statute made a county charge, and that the board of supervisors is required to levy, collect and pay it in the same manner as other county charges upon receiving the certificate with the approval of the Armory Commission. It is likewise apparent that the annual estimate is also a county charge which shall be levied and collected by the board of supervisors upon receiving the estimate as provided by this section. It would follow from this, under well settled principles, that if the board unreasonably neglects to act upon these matters, it can be compelled by mandamus to do so.

Whether or not the board of supervisors has authority to revise the estimates for the annual expenditures is a more difficult question. The language of this statute would seem to be clear — that they " shall levy and collect the moneys required." At the same time, it is also provided that they shàll form a portion of the county charge of each county.

Section 12, subdivision 2, of the County Law provides in part:

" The board of supervisors shall * * * 2. Audit all accounts and charges against the county, and direct annually the raising of sums necessary to defray them in full."

It is held that where the amount of the charge is clearly fixed by the statute or by a valid contract, the board may be compelled to audit the charge at such amount. On the other hand, in the ordinary case it is given the right to pass judicially upon the charge, which would imply the power to reduce it if in the judgment of the board it was excessive. Its action, however, is always subject to review by the courts if contrary to the law or the evidence. In any event, therefore, if the estimates are unreasonably reduced, such reduction can be counteracted in a proper proceeding.

Very truly yours,

EDWARD R. O'MALLEY,

Attorney-General.

Military Law — Section 15.

Vacancies in Militia Council caused by expiration of term of service of brigadier-general, and promotion of General Verbeck to adjutant-general.

STATE OF NEW YORK.

ATTORNEY-GENERAL'S OFFICE,

ALBANY, *July* 19, 1910.

Mr. JOHN F. O'RYAN, *Captain First Battery, F. A. N. G. N. Y.,*
. *Adjutant-General's Office, Albany, N. Y.:*

Dear Sir.— Your communication of the 13th inst., received in regard to the filling of certain vacancies in the Militia Council, under section 15 of the Military Law, being chapter 417 of the Laws of 1909.

Section 15 provides in part as follows:

" There shall be for the state a militia council composed
of the major-general of the national guard, who shall be chief
of the council, the commanding officer of the naval militia,
the adjutant-general of the state, and six officers of the national
guard detailed by the governor and comprising one brigadier-
general commanding a brigade and five officers not below the
grade of captain, representing as equitably as practicable all
arms of the service. In the first instance one-third of the details shall be made for one year, one-third for two years and
one-third for three years * * *. In anticipation
of vacancies the militia council shall submit to the governor
the names of officers recommended for detail, these having
been selected by a committee of five officers of the active
militia appointed by the militia council and of which two may
be already serving as detailed members of the council.
* * *."

It appears that at present there are three vacancies in the council, two by expiration of term of service — that of General
Brigadier James H. Lloyd, who is brigadier-general on the council,
and that of Major Frederick A. Wells of the Twenty-third Infantry; and one vacancy created by the promotion of General William Verbeck to adjutant-general, leaving one year of his term of
service on the council unexpired. It further appears that a committee of the active militia, in accordance with the provisions of
section 15, selected the names of three officers to be detailed to fill
these vacancies. It also appears that pursuant to the statute the
committee has selected as one of these three officers a brigadier-
general but recommends him for the " short term," which I take to
mean the unexpired term.

You ask whether the brigadier-general selected by the committee can be detailed to fill any other vacancy than that caused
by the expiration of the term of the retiring Brigadier-General
Lloyd. You further ask whether or not the successor to General
Verbeck should be detailed for a full term of three years or for
the unexpired portion of General Verbeck's term of service.

I will answer the second question asked by you first in regard
to the unexpired term of General Verbeck. There remains a por-

tion of General Verbeck's term of service on the council still un-expired. Therefore, in my opinion, under section 15 the officer detailed to follow General Verbeck should be detailed for the un-expired portion of General Verbeck's term of service.

In reference to the other question asked by you in regard to the detail of a new brigadier-general, it is my opinion that the new brigadier-general detailed need not necessarily succeed the retiring brigadier-general. Section 15 simply requires the detail of six officers with the requirement only that one of them shall be a brigadier-general and the other five not below the grade of captain. So that so long as there is a brigadier-general on the council the terms of the statute are complied with and fulfilled.

Yours very truly,
EDWARD R. O'MALLEY,
Attorney-General.

Military Law — Section 16 — Subdivision 5 — Penal Law —
Section 1484.

Sale by adjutant-general at public auction of uniforms " unsuit-able for use of State " and mutilation of such uniforms before sale as to render impossible their further use as uniforms. Sale of obsolete uniforms on removal of buttons, straps, etc.

STATE OF NEW YORK.

ATTORNEY-GENERAL'S OFFICE,

ALBANY, November 28, 1910.

The Adjutant-General, State of New York, Albany, N. Y.:

Sir.— I am in receipt of your communication of the 16th inst., requesting my opinion as to the proper construction of subdivision 5 of section 16 of the Military Law (Laws of 1909, chapter 41) in relation to the mutilation of uniforms before being offered for sale. Subdivision 5 empowers the adjutant-general, under the direction of the governor, to sell at public auction military prop-erty of the State which, after proper inspection, " shall be found unsuitable for the use of the State," but it is further provided " all parts of uniforms before being offered for sale shall be so mutilated that they cannot be again used as uniforms." You desire to know " if a uniform or a part of a uniform which has become obsolete because of changes in the regulations of the State, should still be considered as a uniform within the meaning of this provision of law and are required to be mutilated accordingly, or whether having become obsolete they ceased because of that fact to be uniforms, and can properly be disposed of by the adjutant-general, as garments, on the removal of buttons, insignia of rank, or without further ' mutilation.' "

No doubt the provision in subdivision 5 in relation to mutilation of uniforms before being sold was to preserve to the National Guard the exclusive use of such uniforms and thus preserve the dignity and respect in which such uniforms should be held. Other statutory provisions have been enacted with the same purpose, namely, section 239 of the Military Law and section 1484 of the Penal Law. And it is my opinion that the provisions of subdivision 5 must be read in connection with these other provisions of law. Section 239 of the Military Law makes it a misdemeanor for any person to wear " any uniform or any device, strap, knot or insignia of any design or character used as a designation of grade, rank or office such as are by law or by general regulation, duly promulgated, *prescribed for the use of the active militia* or similar thereto * * *."

' Section 1484 of the Penal Law makes it a misdemeanor " for any person not a member of the National Guard, except members of organizations specially authorized to do so by the Military Law, who shall wear any uniform or designation of grade similar to those *in use* by the National Guard, issued or authorized under the provisions of said law."

It will be noted that the above provisions are aimed not at the wearing of obsolete uniforms but at the wearing of uniforms in use by the guard at the time the misdemeanor is committed. In my judgment the same interpretation must be given to the provisions of subdivision 5 in relation to the mutilation of uniforms. Where uniforms are sold which are prescribed for use by the guard at the time of sale, then they must be mutilated so " that they cannot be again used as uniforms." Where, however, the uniforms have become obsolete by duly promulgated regulations of the service and a new uniform not similar in appearance to those become obsolete has been prescribed for use by the guard, then in my judgment the obsolete uniforms can be disposed of by the adjutant-general as garments on the removal of buttons, straps, knots or insignia of rank without further mutilation.

Very respectfully,

EDWARD R. O'MALLEY,

Attorney-General.

Military Law — Sections 16, 243, 239, 142 — *State Finance Law — Section* 37.

Provisions of law relating to the rendering of account by Adjutant-General to the Governor, of sales, fines, etc. Section 37 of State Finance Law not intended to apply to the military organization of the State.

STATE OF NEW YORK.

ATTORNEY-GENERAL'S OFFICE,

ALBANY, *December* 12, 1910.

The Honorable Adjutant-General, State of New York, Albany, N. Y.:

Dear Sir.— I have your favor of November 30, 1910, in which you ask

> "whether the provisions of paragraph 5, section 16 of the Military Law as amended, which requires that the Adjutant General having disposed of obsolete or unserviceable property by sale ' shall from time to time render a just and true account of the sales made by him to the Governor, and shall expend the proceeds of the same in the purchase of other military or naval property as the Governor may direct;' the similar provision in paragraph 8 of section 16, the concluding sentence of section 239, the concluding sentence of section 142, and the further provision in section 142 relative to the disposition of fines collected from enlisted men, are in conflict with the Finance Law."

You also call my attention in your favor of December 2d to the provisions of section 243 of the Military Law which provides

" No section or provision of this chapter or any part thereof shall be deemed to be repealed, altered or amended by any statute passed by the legislature unless such statute explicitly refers to this chapter as the military law, or by its other titles as part of the general laws or annual legislation and explicitly repeals, alters or amends the same or some part thereof."

The State Finance Law was enacted prior to the enactment of the Military Law which was enacted in 1908, being chapter 231 of the Laws of 1908.

Section 37 of the State Finance Law, however, was amended in 1910 by chapter 440 of the laws of that year, by omitting the words " except the health officer of the port of New York." The last sentence of section 37 is as follows: " This section shall be deemed to supersede any other provision of this chapter or of any other general or State law inconsistent therewith."

The Military Law, being enacted after the State Finance Law, the provisions referred to by you are not affected by the State Finance Law except the Legislature in amending section 37 of the State Finance Law in 1910 intended that this section should apply to the Military Law as well as other acts. By section 243 of the Military Law the Legislature provided a specific method by which it should be repealed or amended. Inasmuch as this method was not followed in the amendment of section 37 of the State Finance Law, I am of opinion that the Legislature did not intend that that section should apply to the Military Law. A further reason for this opinion is that the military organization of the State is of a very different character from any other board or department. The Governor as commander-in-chief of the militia acts as a military official and not as a civil officer of the State, and it may well be that the Legislature, while desiring to limit the powers of the various civil officers of the State as to the disposition of money received by them did not wish to place this limitation upon the Military Department of the State.

Yours very truly,

EDWARD R. O'MALLEY,

Attorney-General.

State Armories — Military Law — Section 182.

Boards of supervisors under requirement of section 182 of the Military Law, to levy and pay money for the support, repair and maintenance of armories, have no authority to reduce the amount of the estimates certified to it by the State Board of Armory Commissioners.

(See opinion May 20, 1910.)

STATE OF NEW YORK.

Attorney-General's Office,

Albany, *December* 13, 1910.

Hon. William Verbeck, *Adjutant-General, Albany, N. Y.:*

Dear Sir.— I have your letter of the 9th inst., in which you call my attention to my opinion of May 20, 1910, and ask certain further questions for the guidance of the service as to the proper interpretation of section 182 of the Military Law.

The questions which you ask are, in substance, whether in either of the circumstances under which the board of supervisors is required by that section to levy and pay money for the support, repair and maintenance of armories, such board has the power to reduce the amounts which are certified to it by the Armory Commission or the officer in charge or control of the armory.

Section 182 of the Military Law provides that expenditure for erecting, repairing, altering or enlarging armories, etc., shall be certified to the Armory Commission by the officer having charge and control of the armory, and that, after such Commission shall approve the expenditure, it shall transmit such certificate, approved by it, to the board of supervisors. It is also provided that these expenses shall be a portion of the county charge and shall be levied, collected and paid in the same manner as other county charges.

The same section also provides that the officer in charge of an armory shall each year prepare and submit for approval to the commanding officer of his brigade, an itemized estimate of the necessary expenditures for the proper maintenance of the armory for the next year, and that upon approval of such estimate one copy shall be filed with the board of supervisors. It then provides:

" The board of supervisors shall levy and collect the moneys required." Your question is whether in either of these cases the board of supervisors has any right to modify the estimate so made or any authority to do other than levy and collect the moneys therein required.

It is my opinion that under the authorities, the board of supervisors has no authority to reduce the amounts of these estimates, and that it may be compelled by mandamus to raise the amounts therein specified.

> People ex rel. Bahm v. Board of Supervisors, 9 Hun, 440.
> People ex rel. Archambault v. Supervisors, 26 Hun, 395;
> 91 N. Y. 672.

In my opinion of May 20, 1910, I did not pass upon this question, and this opinion, therefore, may be regarded as supplementary to the former one.

> Very truly yours,
> EDWARD R. O'MALLEY,
> *Attorney-General.*

OPINIONS RENDERED THE STATE ARCHITECT.

State Architect — Contracts — State Buildings.

Clause in all contracts providing for liquidated damages may only be strictly enforced where actual damage has been sustained. State cannot recover for merely nominal damage.

(See opinion March 3, 1908, p. 483, Rep.)

STATE OF NEW YORK.

ATTORNEY-GENERAL'S OFFICE,

ALBANY, *January* 12, 1910.

Hon. FRANKLIN B. WARE, *State Architect, Albany, N. Y.:*

Dear Sir.— I have your letter of the 10th inst., in which you ask my opinion regarding the effect of the following clause which you state is contained in all contracts prepared by your office for the State of New York and contractors:

"It is understood and agreed that the party of the second part shall pay to the party of the first part, by way of liquidated and ascertained damages and not as a penalty, the sum of ten dollars for each and every day on which there is delay beyond the above named date for completion, to compensate the party of the first part for the loss sustained by reason of inability to enter into possession and on account of failure to complete the contract, and such sum or sums shall be deducted from any moneys which may be due or become due thereon. This provision shall not be taken to affect the rights with regard to this contract as set forth in the clause in the general conditions entitled: 'Delay'."

You ask my opinion as to whether, in order to exact the liquidated damages of ten dollars per day provided in such clause, it is necessary for the State to be able to show that there was some damage sustained by it.

The Court of Appeals has held in McCann v. City of Albany, 158 N. Y. 634, that where a contract for a municipal work requires the contractor to pay a certain sum per day as liquidated damages for each day the completion of the work is delayed beyond a specified date, the municipality will not be allowed to retain a substantial sum under the guise of liquidated damages for delay when in fact only nominal damages have been sustained.

Pursuant to this decision, former Attorney-General Jackson advised the Trustees of Public Buildings, under date of March 3, 1908, that in a similar case where the State had suffered no damage in fact, the liquidated damage clause could not be enforced.

It is my opinion that under this decision such advice was correct, and that in no similar case can the State recover liquidated damages where it has as a matter of fact sustained no damage. The burden, however, would probably be on the contractor to overcome the presumption of damage by proving that none actually resulted.

Very truly yours,

EDWARD R. O'MALLEY,
Attorney-General.

State Charities Law — Section 49 — State Finance Law — Section 35 — State Institutions — Contracts.

Contract between Erie Railroad Company and the New York State Industrial School at Industry, regarding certain changes in grade crossings, and additional tracks on property of school. Board of managers may not contract for such changes as will incur additional expense to State nor may they agree to save harmless the railroad company from losses and damage.

(See opinion March 9, 1910.)

STATE OF NEW YORK.

ATTORNEY-GENERAL'S OFFICE,

ALBANY, *February* 16, 1910.

Hon. FRANKLIN B. WARE, *State Architect, Albany, N. Y.:*

Dear Sir.— I have your letter of the 4th instant asking for my opinion as to the form of agreement between the Erie Railroad Company and the New York State Industrial School at Industry, N. Y., which you enclose, for improving the plant and property of said school by the elimination of a grade crossing of a private road on its property and the railroad of said company, and constructing at such point an overhead crossing.

By chapter 433 of the Laws of 1909 there was appropriated for this school, for under and over passes, $5,000, which appropriation was apparently expressly made for work contemplated by said contract.

The only authority in the board of managers to make a contract at all for improving the plant of said school is found in section 49 of the State Charities Law, and then the contract must have the approval of the Governor, the President of the State Board of Charities and the Fiscal Supervisor. This section further provides:

" All such contracts and special orders for the erection, alteration, repairs or improvements of buildings or plant of State institutions, reporting to the fiscal supervisor (and said school is one of them) shall contain a clause that the contract shall only be deemed executory to the extent of the moneys available, and no liability shall be incurred by the state beyond the moneys available for the purpose."

And along the same line, section 35 of the State Finance Law provides:

> "A state officer, employee, board, department or commission shall not contract indebtednes on behalf of the state, nor assume to bind the state, in an amount in excess of money appropriated or otherwise lawfully available."

The substance of the last mentioned statute is also in section 21 of Article III of the State Constitution in this language:

> "No money shall ever be paid out of the treasury of this state or any of the funds under its management, except in pursuance of an appropriation by law."

I am constrained, therefore, to disapprove the contract as to form, for it fails to contain any clause whatever as provided in the State Charities Law above quoted, that the "contract shall be deemed executory to the extent of money available."

Furthermore, the board of managers agrees, at its own expense, to make all the necessary changes in respect to said undergrade or overhead crossings, or either of them, which may be required, in connection with the construction and installation of any additional track or tracks by the railroad company on its right of way, which might incur an enormous expense to the State, and thereby be a violation of section 35 of the State Finance Law, already quoted.

The clause that the board of managers agrees to save harmless said railroad company from any losses, damages, suits, claims and demands which the company may directly or indirectly suffer, is a clause that might result in damages to the State, which would seem to be in conflict with the provisions of the Finance Law also.

For the reasons given, I do not feel that I can approve the contract in its present form.

Yours very truly,

EDWARD R. O'MALLEY,

Attorney-General.

State Institutions — Great Meadow Prison.

Bids for sewage disposal plant received by mail or messenger after
time limit stated in advertisement. Whether Superintendent
of Prisons may accept lowest bid received after such time
limit, and during the reading of the other bids.

(See opinion March 11, 1908, p. 303, Rep.)

STATE OF NEW YORK.

ATTORNEY-GENERAL'S OFFICE,

ALBANY, *April* 12, 1910.

Hon. FRANKLIN B. WARE, *State Architect, Albany, N. Y.:*

Dear Sir.— I have the honor to acknowledge receipt of your
favor of the 11th inst. enclosing copy of letter to you from the
Superintendent of Prisons, dated April 7, 1910, copy of your letter
to the Superintendent of the same date, letter of Welles-Boughton ·
& Co. to the Superintendent, dated April 5, 1910, printed notice of
advertisement and blue print tabulation of bids.

From your letter and enclosures it appears that the Superintendent of State Prisons advertised for bids for the construction
of a sewage disposal system for Great Meadow Prison. The notice
of advertisement stated that sealed proposals would be received at
the office of the Superintendent, Capitol, Albany, until twelve
o'clock noon on the 5th day of April, 1910. The bids were opened
at twelve-thirty p. m. of that day. During the reading of the first
bid, according to the Superintendent, and during the reading of the
fourth bid, according to one of the bidders, Welles-Boughton & Co.,
three additional bids were received, one from the Superintendent's
post office box and two by a messenger. These additional three bids
were opened and read with the others. Thereafter when it was
discovered that one of the three bids was the lowest, protest was
made by the Welles-Boughton Co. against the letting of the work
to any bidder whose proposal had not been received at or before
twelve o'clock noon of the 5th day of April, 1910. You desire my
opinion as to whether under these facts a contract can be let to the
lowest bidder even though that bid were received after the time
limit stated in the advertisement.

This work was advertised for under the provisions of chapter 459 of the Laws of 1909 and chapter 65 of the Laws of 1910, which authorizes the construction of the sewage system under the direction of the Superintendent of State Prisons by contract or by such other system or method as he may deem most expeditious and for the best interest of the State. The advertisement provided that any or all bids might be rejected. There seems to be no general provision of law which requires the advertising for bids or the letting of the work to the lowest bidder, and in the absence of such provision I do not think that the Superintendent of State Prisons is bound to accept only such bids as are received prior to the time fixed in the notice of advertisement. The method of publication was no doubt adopted for the purpose of obtaining the most satisfactory terms for the State. It does not appear that any injustice was done to any bidder or that the late bids were based in any way upon knowledge of those received prior to twelve o'clock on the day of opening.

It is, therefore, my opinion that the Superintendent may, as a strict legal proposition, accept the lowest bid even though it be one of those received after twelve o'clock noon on the 5th day of April, 1910. The receipt of additional bids after the opening of those received had begun, can, of course, be criticised as being unfair and if such a practice were indulged in extensively, it might mean the opening of a door for unfair, and possibly fraudulent practices and it might be that both safety and fairness in the future would require the adoption of a rule that no bids will be received after the bidding has been formally declared closed.

I return herewith the enclosure sent me with your favor of the 11th inst.

Yours very truly,

EDWARD R. O'MALLEY,

Attorney-General.

State Prisons.

Plans for buildings, residence of warden or keeper, farm building and buildings used in connection with prisons, but not used for inmates, need not be approved by the State Commission of Prisons.

STATE OF NEW YORK.

ATTORNEY-GENERAL'S OFFICE,

ALBANY, *August* 12, 1910.

Hon. FRANKLIN B. WARE, *State Architect, Albany, N. Y.:*

Dear Sir.— I beg to acknowledge the receipt of your favor of August 5th, in which you request an opinion as to the " necessity of having certain plans and specifications for buildings in connection with State prisons approved by the Prison Commission," reference being made to buildings *not* used for the accommodation of inmates of prisons, among which you enumerate the residence for the warden or principal keeper, barns and other farm buildings, ice house, keepers' quarters and employees' recreation buildings.

I am of the opinion that subdivision 3 of section 46 of the Prison Law, which provides that the State Commission of Prisons shall " aid in securing the erection of suitable buildings for the accommodation of the inmates of such institutions, and approve or reject plans for their construction or improvement," does not require approval by such Commission of the plans for the buildings you enumerate.

Respectfully yours,

EDWARD R. O'MALLEY,

Attorney-General.

State Institutions — State Hospitals.

Bids and proposals for construction of kitchen and dining room at Central Islip State Hospital. Right of State Architect and State Commission in Lunacy to allow lowest bid to be withdrawn under certain conditions.

STATE OF NEW YORK.

Attorney-General's Office,

Albany, *August* 24, 1910

Hon. Franklin B. Ware, *State Architect, Albany, N. Y.:*

Dear Sir.-- I beg to acknowledge receipt of your communication of August 17th, 1910, with enclosures, in the matter of the bids for kitchen and dining room building, etc., at the Central Islip State Hospital, in which you ask for an opinion —

(1). Whether you, as State Architect, or the State Commission in Lunacy have any right to allow the bid of the lowest bidder to be withdrawn and its certified check to be returned;

(2). Whether you are justified in recommending to the State Commissioner in Lunacy that the bid of the lowest bidder be rejected and its check returned and that of the next lowest bidder be accepted.

Strictly speaking, neither you, as State Architect, nor the State Commission in Lunacy has any right to allow the bid in question to be withdrawn and the certified check to be returned.

I note, however, what you say as to the financial condition of the company making the low bid, the attempted withdrawal of such bid, the time required by its bid for the completion of the work, the imperative necessity of the finishing of the buildings at the earliest possible moment and the general reservation of the right of the Commission in Lunacy to reject any and all bids. If you are satisfied that it will be for the best interests of the State, that the bid of the lowest bidder be rejected and the bid of the next to the lowest bidder be accepted, I see no objection to your so recommending to the State Commission in Lunacy.

If such recommendation be followed by the Lunacy Commission and it accepts the proposal of any other bidder than the lowest and awards the contract thereto, with the approval of the Governor

20

and the Comptroller, under section 65 of the Insanity Law, then the return of the certified check to the low bidder would follow.

Respectfully yours,

EDWARD R. O'MALLEY,

Attorney-General.

State Finance Law — Section 37.

Word " employee " in section 37, not intended to mean a contractor contracting for State work.

(Great Meadow Prison.)

STATE OF NEW YORK.

ATTORNEY-GENERAL'S OFFICE,

ALBANY, *December* 7, 1910.

Hon. FRANKLIN B. WARE, *State Architect, Albany, N. Y.:*

Dear Sir.— Referring to your letter of the 5th inst., in reference to the proper interpretation of section 37 of the State Finance Law, I beg to say that I have given the matter careful attention, and that in my opinion the word " employee " as used in that section does not include and was not intended to include an independent contractor with the State. The section is in part as follows:

" Every state officer, employee, board, department or commission receiving money for or on behalf of the state from * * * sales of property * * * shall on the fifth day of each month pay to the state treasurer all such money received during the preceding month * * * ."

In my judgment, the fact that the Hudson Valley Construction Company, the contractor in the case to which you call my attention, is performing the work on a percentage basis does not make that company an employee of the State. The work being governed entirely by contract and being performed by employees of the contractor, the company cannot be regarded as an employee of the State in the ordinary acceptation of the term.

Very truly yours,

EDWARD R. O'MALLEY,

Attorney-General.

OPINION RENDERED THE STATE BOARD OF ARMORY COMMISSIONERS.

State Armories — Bids and Proposals.

State Armory at Amsterdam. Where certified check of lowest bidder on repairs and improvements, is by oversight unequal to five per cent. of his bid, the Armory Commission may use its discretion in waiving irregularity and accepting such lowest bid. Statute does not require bid to be accompanied by check.

(Military Law, section 20).

STATE OF NEW YORK.

ATTORNEY-GENERAL'S OFFICE,

Albany, *January* 5, 1910.

Hon. F. A. McNeely, *Secretary, State Board of Armory Commissioners, Albany, N. Y.:*

Dear Sir.— I have your letter of the 3d inst., in which, by direction of the Armory Commission, you ask my opinion as to what action the Commission should take in regard to the bids made for repairs, improvements and betterments to the Amsterdam State Armory.

It appears from the inclosures contained in your letter that the specifications for this work provide:

" (Page 1). Each bid must be accompanied by a deposit of cash, or by a certified check equal in amount to five per cent. of the amount of the bid, as evidence of good faith, and to the effect that, if the proposal of the bidder should be accepted, the bidder will enter into a contract and furnish satisfactory bond of a regular surety or guarantee company authorized to transact business under the laws of the state of New York."

It is also provided on this same page of the specifications,

"Informal bids will not be considered."

It appears from the tabulation of bids that George Kinum of Schenectady, was the lowest bidder at $16,584, and that John Dyer, Jr., of Albany, was the next lowest bidder at $17,485. It also appears that the certified check accompanying the bid of George Kinum was not equal to five per cent. of his bid, as called for, and that John Dyer, Jr., the next lowest bidder protested the Kinum bid on the ground that it was informal. A letter embodying this protest, written by Mr. Dyer, is inclosed with your communication, as also a letter from Mr. Kinum under date of the 31st ult., in which he states that he has been informed that his certified check was insufficient and that he will present a certified check on January 3 to cover the necessary amount to make up the five per cent. He states that it was an oversight on his part in not putting in a check for the proper amount.

The statute under which these contracts are to be let provides as follows:

"Military Law, § 20. * * * When repairs are to be made, the expenditures for which will exceed five hundred dollars, the commission shall advertise for proposals, bids shall be received, and contracts regularly entered into."

You will observe that there is nothing in the statute requiring bids to be accompanied by a certified check. This provision is simply incorporated in the specifications by your Commission. It is, moreover, a provision intended simply for the protection of the State against irresponsible bidders. In view of the fact that a certified check was given although its amount was insufficient, it is my opinion that the failure to supply a check of the proper amount was simply an irregularity in connection with the bid. It appears to be clear, under the authorities, that such irregularities in matters intended for the protection of the State may be waived by the board empowered to enter into the contract, or may be treated by it as sufficient justification for a rejection of the bid.

McCord v. Lauterbach, 91 App. Div. 315, and cases cited.

I therefore advise you that the matter rests entirely in the discretion of the Commission, and that while the irregularity is such as to justify the rejection of the bid, it is still at liberty to enter into a contract with Mr. Kinum if it desires to do so, and waive the irregularity.

Yours respectfully,
• EDWARD R. O'MALLEY,
Attorney-General.

OPINIONS RENDERED THE STATE BOARD OF CHARITIES.

Tax Law — Section 4 — Subdivision 7.

Real property owned by Wiawaka Holiday House, a corporation formed under the Membership Corporations Law for the specific purpose of providing a summer boarding home for working girls, should be exempt from taxation.

STATE OF NEW YORK.

ATTORNEY-GENERAL'S OFFICE,

ALBANY, <i>February</i> 17, 1910.

Dr. ROBERT W. HEBBERD, <i>Secretary, State Board of Charities, Albany, N. Y.:</i>

Dear Sir.— Referring to your letter of the 10th inst., in which you inclose copy of certificate of incorporation of the Wiawaka Holiday House, organized under the Membership Corporations Law, and ask my opinion as to whether or not the real property owned by this corporation is subject to taxation, I beg to advise as follows:

It appears that this company was incorporated June 29, 1907, and that the objects for which it is formed are as follows:

" To provide, without profit, at cost price or less, board and lodging in the summer time for working girls and young women, having special reference to the maintenance of a house and grounds under the direction of the Board of Managers, at which girls and young women working for wages and salaries can, during the summer season, have board and lodging at prices affording no profit to the corporation or its Board of Managers."

I note that the corporation has received a small tract of land on Lake George and maintains in the three cottages located thereon a home for girls and young women who would otherwise have no opportunity for rest and recreation, and as an effort is made to prevent dependency, a small charge is made for board, but the reports show the actual expenditures in the maintenance of the institution are twice as much as the receipts from the board of inmates. I also note the churches and friendly societies in Troy, Albany and elsewhere are interested in the maintenance of the home and contribute to its support.

Under these circumstances, it is my opinion that the real property owned by the corporation and used exclusively for carrying out charitable or benevolent purposes, as set forth above, is exempt from taxation under section 4, subdivision 7 of the Tax Law, which provides in part as follows:

" The real property of a corporation * * * organized exclusively for * * * charitable, benevolent and * * * purposes, * * * and used exclusively for carrying out thereupon one or more of such purposes, and the personal property of such corporation shall be exempt from taxation."

Assuming that the statements which I have quoted above represent the facts, and that this corporation and its officers, members or employees receive no pecuniary profit from its operations, it is my opinion that it falls within the above provision and that its property is therefore exempt from taxation.

I return herewith the certificate which you inclosed.

Very truly yours,

EDWARD R. O'MALLEY,

Attorney-General.

State Charities Law — Section 10.

State Board 'of Charities has supervision over hospitals for the treatment of contagious diseases, and quarantine hospitals.

STATE OF NEW YORK.

ATTORNEY-GENERAL'S OFFICE,

ALBANY, *May* 2, 1910.

ROBERT W. HEBBERD, ESQ., *Secretary, State Board of Charities, Albany, N. Y.:*

Dear Sir.— Referring to your letter of April 20 in which you ask my opinion as to the scope of section 10 in defining the supervisory powers of the State Board of Charities, I beg to advise as follows:

You ask me whether the supervisory power of this board extends to public hospitals for the treatment of contagious diseases and hospitals established for quarantine purposes, which latter are established and maintained by the State. The section in question provides in part as follows:

"§ 10. VISITATION, INSPECTION AND SUPERVISION OF INSTITUTIONS. * * * all asylums, hospitals and institutions, whether state, county, municipal, incorporated or not incorporated, private or otherwise, except institutions for the custody, care and treatment of the insane, are subject to the visitation, inspection and supervision of the state board of charities, its members, officers and inspectors."

It is my opinion that this section is clearly broad enough to include the cases to which you refer.

Very truly yours,

EDWARD R. O'MALLEY,

Attorney-General.

State Charities Law — Sections 290, 291, 294 — Dispensaries.
Maintenance of " tuberculosis dispensaries " by local health boards
of municipalities where such dispensaries are supported by
public moneys or trust funds — not legal without license
from State Board of Charities.

STATE OF NEW YORK.

Attorney-General's Office,

Albany, *May* 6, 1910.

State Board of Charities, Albany, N. Y.:

Gentlemen.— I acknowledge the letter of April 20 from your
secretary, in which the following resolution adopted at the annual
meeting of your board was certified to me:

" Resolved, That the question of the right of maintenance
of tuberculosis dispensaries by towns or other municipalities,
without a license from the State Board of Charities, be submitted to the Attorney-General for his opinion."

Section 290 of the State Charities Law defines a dispensary as
follows:

" For the purposes of this article, a ' dispensary ' is declared
to be any person, corporation, institution, association or agent,
whose purpose it is, either independently or in connection with
any other purpose, to furnish, at any place or places, to persons nonresident therein, either gratuitously or for a compensation determined without reference to the value of the
thing furnished, medical or surgical advice or treatment,
medicine or apparatus, provided, however, that the moneys
used by and for the purposes of said dispensary shall be derived wholly or in part from trust funds, public moneys or
sources other than the individuals constituting said dispensary
and the persons actually engaged in the distribution of
charities of said dispensary."

It is stated in the letter of your secretary that certain so-called
" tuberculosis dispensaries " are being maintained by local health

boards in Cohoes, Rome, Oneida, New York City and other places, without licenses from your board to conduct such dispensaries, and the resolution in question was submitted to me for the purpose of determining whether or not such action is legal. I assume from your question that the dispensaries mentioned are supported in whole or in part from trust funds, public moneys or sources other than the individuals constituting said dispensaries. This being so, it is clear, in my judgment, that such dispensaries do come within the definition above quoted.

Section 291 of the same law provides in part as follows:

"A dispensary shall not enter upon the execution, or continue the prosecution of its purpose unless licensed by the state board of charities, as provided in this article."

Section 294 provides in part as follows:

"* * * nor * * * shall any person, corporation, institution, society, association, or agent thereof, except a duly licensed dispensary, display or cause to be displayed a sign or other thing which could directly or indirectly or by suggestion indicate the existence of the equivalent, in purpose and effect, of a dispensary."

A violation of any of the provisions of this article is made a misdemeanor. It seems to me, from a careful examination of the foregoing provisions of law, that the question certified to me must be answered by saying that no municipalities have the right to maintain tuberculosis dispensaries which come within the definition above quoted, without obtaining a license from your board, and that they are subject to your visitation and inspection and to the rules and regulations prescribed by the other sections of this same law.

Very truly yours,

EDWARD R. O'MALLEY,

Attorney-General.

State Charities Law — Sections 9, 13, 14 — Charitable Institu-
tions — Almshouses.

Power of State Board of Charities to investigate the administration
of charitable institutions, and issuance of orders for correction
of evils.

STATE OF NEW YORK.

ATTORNEY-GENERAL'S OFFICE,

ALBANY, *July* 7, 1910.

ROBERT W. HEBBERD, ESQ., *Secretary, State Board of Charities.*
Capitol, Albany, N. Y.:

Dear Sir.— I beg to acknowledge receipt of your communications dated June 27 and July 6, to which I reply herewith.

You call my attention to conditions existing in certain charitable
institutions throughout the State, and recite as examples that in
one almshouse the sick are not supplied with proper nurses; that in
another there is great overcrowding in the attic of the institution
which is used but not originally intended for dormitory purposes,
which use is occasioned by local poor law officers committing able
bodied inmates, some of whom at least should be sent to county
jails as vagrants; that elsewhere boards of supervisors have failed
to make provision for the erection of suitable buildings although
the necessity for such construction has frequently been brought to
their attention; and that in some institutions, necessary provisions
for fire protection have not been made. •

My attention is directed to sections 13 and 14 of the State Charities Law, which vest in the State Board of Charities certain powers
and impose upon it certain duties in reference to the investigation
and correction of evils existing in the administration of all institutions of a charitable, eleemosynary, reformatory or correctional
character or design, including reformatories (except those under
the supervision and subject to the inspection of the Prison Commission).

Section 13 provides that the board may direct an investigation
of the affairs of any such institution and empowers it to issue
compulsory processes for the attendance of witnesses and to admin-

ister oaths and to exercise the same powers in respect to such proceedings as belong to referees appointed by the Supreme Court. Section 14 is as follows:

" Section 14. ORDERS OF BOARD DIRECTED TO INSTITUTIONS. —If it shall appear, after such investigation, that inmates of the institution are cruelly, negligently or improperly treated, or inadequate provision is made for their sustenance, clothing, care, supervision or other condition necessary to their comfort and well being, said board may issue an order, in the name of the people, and under its official seal, directed to the proper officers or managers of such institution, requiring them to modify such treatment or apply such remedy, or both, as shall therein be specified; before such order is issued, it must be approved by a justice of the supreme court, after such notice as he may prescribe and an opportunity to be heard, and any person to whom such an order is directed who shall wilfully refuse to obey the same, shall, upon conviction, be adjudged guilty of a misdemeanor."

The specific question laid before me is whether or not section 14 is sufficiently broad to cover situations in institutions as above described.

The general powers and duties of the State Board of Charities are, in a large measure, of a directory and advisory character. Section 9 of the State Charities Law, which prescribes those general powers and duties, seems to indicate that the duties of the board consist mainly in aiding or advising in, or approving or disapproving of the organization or management of charitable institutions. But the exercise of such functions would undoubtedly be of little or no value without vesting in the board some means to exercise its influence and to enforce upon the management of these institutions such method of conducting them as in the judgment of the board seems fitting and proper. For this reason, evidently, the Legislature enacted section 14 which gives to the board a means of enforcing its orders. It will be noted that this statute is extremely broad, and states that after it has been established as a matter of fact by an investigation conducted in accordance with the provisions of section 13, that the inmates of institutions are not prop-

erly cared for and inadequate provision is made for their care and
sustenance, the board may make such specific orders as will correct
these conditions. If section 14 means anything, it is that the State
Board of Charities can issue orders to correct such conditions as
you state exist. My opinion, therefore, is that if it appears to the
board, after making proper investigation, that these facts exist as
above recited, such orders as are specified in section 14 may be
issued to correct the conditions.

Yours very respectfully,

EDWARD R. O'MALLEY,

Attorney-General.

OPINION RENDERED THE STATE BOARD OF EMBALMING EXAMINERS.

*State Board of Embalming Examiners — Licenses Undertakers
and Embalmers.*

Recent decision of Court of Appeals, January 4, 1910, holds that
chapter 572, Laws 1905, now section 295, Public Health Law,
is unconstitutional, in that it prevents licensing of undertaker,
unless he also be a licensed embalmer. State Board of Embalming Examiners should refuse further applications and
fees for such licenses after January 4, 1910.

STATE OF NEW YORK.

ATTORNEY-GENERAL'S OFFICE,

ALBANY, *January* 24, 1910.

WILLIAM J. PHILLIPS, ESQ., *Secretary, Board of Embalming
Examiners, Albany, N. Y.:*

Dear Sir.— By your favor of the 11th inst., I am asked to advise
what course your board should pursue in relation to receiving applications for undertakers' licenses in view of the late decision of
the Court of Appeals in the case of the People v. William A. Ringe,
and whether the applications and fees therefor should be returned

to the applicants, or whether the fees should be returned and the applications kept for future reference, and also whether your board should refuse to receive any further applications for undertakers' licenses as provided for in section 6a of chapter 572, Laws of 1905 (now section 295 of the Public Health Law).

The decision of the Court of Appeals in the case above referred to was rendered on the 4th day of January, 1910, and holds that section 6a, chapter 572, Laws of 1905, now section 295 of the Public Health Law, is unconstitutional upon the grounds that it prevents the licensing of an undertaker unless he is also a licensed embalmer, and also prevents the board from issuing a license to any person unless he shall have been employed as an assistant to a licensed undertaker continuously for a period of at least three years prior to the issuance thereof, and that the imposition of such conditions were unwarrantable interferences with the constitutional rights of the applicant, and by force of such decision that portion of such act which requires an undertaker to take out a license becomes absolutely null and void and is no longer of any force or validity, and as far as any future action is concerned it must be treated as if it had never been enacted.

The act being unconstitutional and void, all action or proceedings taken thereunder after the rendition of such decision was and is without authority and all applications and fees received by your board after January 4, 1910, should be returned to the applicant and you should in the future refuse to receive any further applications or fees for such a license.

Yours truly,
EDWARD R. O'MALLEY,
Attorney-General.

OPINIONS RENDERED THE STATE BOARD OF PHARMACY.

State Board of Pharmacy.

Appointment of new officers. Members of present board will hold
over and continue in office until the new board is appointed
and qualified to act. (Chapter 422, Laws 1910.)

STATE OF NEW YORK.

ATTORNEY-GENERAL'S OFFICE,

ALBANY, *July* 29, 1910.

State Board of Pharmacy, New York City:

Gentlemen.— I beg to acknowledge receipt of your favor of the
22d instant written by Steiner & Peterson, your attorneys, asking
for my opinion as to whether the members of your present board
will hold over and continue in office after August 1, 1910, and
until a new board is elected and qualified as provided by chapter
422 of the Laws of 1910.

I have given careful consideration to the above mentioned act
and I do not think it was the intention of the Legislature to abolish
the State Board of Pharmacy, but to change the number of the
members of the board and provide a different method for their
election, and to fix a definite and certain time for the expiration of
the terms of the members of the present board and the commencement of the terms of office of the incoming board, and unless the
office is abolished the members of the present board will hold over
and continue in office until a new board is appointed and qualified
as provided by the amendments specified in the above act. While
it is provided by section 231, as amended by chapter 422 of the
Laws of 1910 that the present " State Board of Pharmacy in office
when this section takes effect shall remain in office until August
first, nineteen hundred and ten," it does not say that the board shall
not continue to discharge its duties after that date if the new
board therein provided for is not appointed or qualified to act by

that time, nor does it abolish the board; so it follows that the present members will continue to hold over under the Public Officers Law until the new board is installed in office.

Yours very respectfully,

EDWARD R. O'MALLEY,

Attorney-General.

State Pharmacy Law — Section 241.

Newly appointed State Board of Pharmacy may act with same powers as old board, in all pending actions, civil or criminal.

STATE OF NEW YORK.

ATTORNEY-GENERAL'S OFFICE,

ALBANY, *October* 5, 1910.

To the Honorable, the State Board of Pharmacy, Albany, N. Y.:

Gentlemen.— I am in receipt of a communication from the secretary of your board, dated the 1st inst., in which he advises me of your desire for my opinion as to the meaning of section 241 of the Pharmacy Law, as amended, with reference to the prosecution of certain pending cases.

Section 241 reads as follows:

" This act shall not affect pending actions or proceedings, civil or criminal, brought by or against the state board of pharmacy, as the same was constituted prior to the taking effect of such act, but such actions or proceedings shall be prosecuted or defended to a final conclusion, in the same manner, by the state board of pharmacy constituted as herein provided, or by the officer having jurisdiction in respect thereto. The provisions of this act shall not be construed so as to affect or impair any act done, or right accruing, accrued or acquired, or any penalty, forfeiture, or punishment incurred prior to the time when this act or any part thereof takes effect, under or by virtue of the law amended by such act, but the same may be asserted, enforced, prosecuted or inflicted, as fully and to the same extent as if this amendatory act had not been passed."

By the use of the words " but such actions or proceedings shall oe prosecuted or defended to a final conclusion, in the same manner, by the State Board of Pharmacy constituted as herein provided, or by the officer having jurisdiction in respect thereto " it is apparent that the Legislature did not intend to disturb the prosecution of such cases by placing the same under any new head.

I am therefore of the opinion that the new Board of Pharmacy has the same powers with reference to such cases as the old Board had and that they may continue them under the same counsel if it appears to them to be best so to do. It does not follow, however, that the same counsel must be continued. I am of the opinion that if for any reason it should now be impossible or improper to continue the same counsel in these cases, others may in the discretion of the board be designated. The jurisdiction of the Attorney-General does not in my opinion extend to any pending proceedings.

Yours very truly,

EDWARD R. O'MALLEY,

Attorney-General.

Pharmacy Law — Section 234.

Term " licensed pharmacist " applies only to pharmacists licensed under the laws of the State of New York.

STATE OF NEW YORK.

Attorney-General's Office,

Albany, *November* 15, 1910.

To the Honorable, the State Board of Pharmacy, Albany, N. Y.:

Gentlemen.— Replying to your favor of the 12th ultimo, in which my opinion is requested as to whether the words " licensed pharmacist " used in section 234 of the Pharmacy Law, refers only to licentiates of the State of New York, I beg to say that an examination of the statute, chapter 422 of the Laws of 1910, being an amendment of article 11, chapter 49, of the Laws of 1909, provides in detail rules and regulations for the control of the practice of pharmacology in this State. Among other provisions are those which govern the issuance of licenses to pharmacists. All these provisions with reference to licensing pharmacists precede section 234, in which the words " licensed pharmacist " are used,

It seems to me to be clear from a reading of the whole statute that the intent of the Legislature in using these words was to refer to pharmacists licensed pursuant to the provisions of this law and none other. The State has the right to pass laws in the interest of the health of its citizens and to prescribe stringent rules and regulations to preserve their well being. This is the purpose of the Pharmacy Law and it is not to be presumed that it was passed with reference to any provisions of statute that may be applicable to pharmacists in other states.

I am clearly of the opinion that the words "licensed pharmacist" used in the section referred to mean only a pharmacist licensed under the laws of the State of New York.

Yours very truly,
EDWARD R. O'MALLEY,
Attorney-General.

OPINIONS RENDERED THE STATE BOARD OF TAX COMMISSIONERS.

Mortgage Tax Law — Section 260.

Recording officers should, upon leaving office, turn over to their successors all funds received on mortgages and held pending apportionment by State Board of Tax Commissioners, the incoming officers to give receipt therefor.

STATE OF NEW YORK.
ATTORNEY-GENERAL'S OFFICE,
ALBANY, January 6, 1910.

State Board of Tax Commissioners, Albany, N. Y.:

Gentlemen.— I have your letter of the 5th inst., in which you ask my opinion regarding the duty of a recording officer to turn over to his successor moneys received on mortgages pending determination and apportionment by your board.

I note that the statute requires that on the first day of each
. month the recording officer shall pay over to the county treasurer,
or the city chamberlain in Greater New York, all moneys on
account of taxes paid to him " except taxes paid upon a mortgage
which under the provisions of section 260 is to be apportioned by
the State Board of Tax Commissioners between several counties,
which taxes and money shall be paid over by him as provided by
the determination of said State Board of Tax Commissioners
within five days after the filing of said determination in his
office."

I also note that several funds are now being held pending
apportionment, and that you would like my opinion as to whether
the outgoing recording officer is required to turn such funds over
to his successor and the incoming officer required to accept them
and give his receipt therefor.

It is my opinion that this is the clear duty of both officers. The
taxes are held by them in their official capacity as an incident of
the business, and should therefore be turned over by the outgoing
officer and taken in charge by the incoming officer upon a change
of administration.

Yours respectfully,
EDWARD R. O'MALLEY,
Attorney-General.

Mortgage Tax Law — Section 256.

Indeterminate mortgages. Where such have been stamped and
accepted for record by recording clerk, without statement at
time of presentation for recording, or assurance that such
statement will be filed, the computation of tax should be upon
the *value* of the security.

STATE OF NEW YORK.

ATTORNEY-GENERAL'S OFFICE,

ALBANY, *January* 6, 1910.

State Board of Tax Commissioners, Albany, N. Y.:

Gentlemen.— I have your letter of the 5th inst., in which you
ask my opinion as to the proper interpretation of section 256 of

the Tax Law in reference to the computation of the amount taxable where indeterminate mortgages are recorded.

This section provides in part as follows:

> " MORTGAGES FOR INDEFINITE AMOUNTS OR FOR CONTRACT OBLIGATIONS.— If the principal indebtedness secured or which by any contingency may be secured by a mortgage is not determinable from the terms of the mortgage, * * * such mortgage shall be taxable * * * upon the value of the property covered by the mortgage, which shall be determined by the recording officer to whom such mortgage is presented for record, *unless at the time of presenting such mortgage for record the owner thereof shall file with the recording officer a sworn statement of the maximum amount secured or which under any contingency may be secured by the mortgage.*"

You state that you have been asked by several of the recording officers whether they have the right to accept " a sworn statement of the maximum amount secured " after the mortgage has been received and stamped for record, or whether the mortgage and statement must be simultaneously presented. As you point out, such a situation cannot arise if the recording officers perform their strict duty, as they are not authorized, under the law, to receive and stamp for record any mortgage until the tax has been paid. But, as you state, in many instances, through inadvertence or through the accommodation of the recording officer in assuming responsibility for the tax, mortgages are accepted for record, stamped, and have been actually recorded before the tax is paid.

You ask whether, if the required statement is not presented with such mortgage and the recording officer has made demands upon " the mortgagor or mortgagee to furnish him with proofs as to such facts as he deems necessary for the purpose of computing the value of the property covered by the mortgage," the owner can withdraw the mortgage and again present it for record with a sworn statement such as the statute prescribes. You further ask as follows:

" In other words, can the statute be construed so as to allow the recording officer to accept the statement for filing subsequent to the time the mortgage is received and accepted for record? Again, can he accept such statement in lieu of proof of the value of the property as the basis for the tax after the mortgage has been actually recorded? "

The question presented is the proper interpretation of the words " at the time of presenting such mortgage for record." It is clear that under this section a tax is imposed generally for mortgages for indeterminate amounts based upon the value of the security. The exception to this arises in case a statement is presented as therein provided. This, according to the statute, must be at the time of presenting the mortgage for record. It would seem to be clear, therefore, that this exception does not apply in case the mortgage has been actually stamped for record and accepted. After such time, the statement provided by the statute cannot be filed because the time of presenting the mortgage for record is past. On the other hand, the courts would certainly not take an unduly strict view of this language, and if the mortgage is taken by the clerk, and contemporaneously the question as to the basis for the tax is raised by the person presenting the mortgage, all forming part of one transaction, it would in all probability be held that the statement could be filed, notwithstanding the fact that the clerk might have stamped the instrument for record. This question is largely one of fact in each particular instance, but I believe that the principle to determine the decision in each case is that if the mortgage has been stamped and accepted for record without any contemporaneous understanding that a statement is to be filed, the tax must be computed upon the value of the security.

Very respectfully,

EDWARD R. O'MALLEY,

Attorney-General.

State Board of Tax Commissioners.

Where writ of certiorari has been procured for review of determination of State Board of Tax Commissioners, said Board have the power to amend such determination

(Matter of Application Supervisors Fulton County for writ of certiorari against State Board, etc).

STATE OF NEW YORK.

ATTORNEY-GENERAL'S OFFICE,

ALBANY, *January* 26, 1910.

State Board of Tax Commissioners, Albany, N. Y.:

Gentlemen.— Referring to your request for my opinion as to the power of your Board to amend your determination after a writ of certiorari has been procured for a review of the same, I beg to advise that I have carefully considered the question and, in my opinion, you possess this power.

It seems to be well settled that a court has the power to amend its judgment at any time, even after an appeal has been taken, until the decision of the Appellate Court upon such appeal.

See 23 Cyc., 862, Tit. "Judgments," and cases cited.

It is, of course, well settled that your Board, sitting as a board of equalization, acts in a judicial capacity, and it would therefore be my judgment that these decisions would apply. Further, upon an examination of the decisions in other States, I find that it is recognized that boards possessing similar functions to those exercised by your body, are held to have the right at all times to amend their own proceedings and determinations.

> See *Seymour National Bank v. Isaacs,* 68 N. E. Rep. 288 (Ind.).
> *Boyce v. Auditor General,* 90 Mich. 314.
> *Black v. McGonigle,* 103 Misc. 192.
> *State v. Central Pacific R. Co.,* 17 Nev. 259.
> See also Century Digest, Tit. "Taxation," § 871 and cases cited.

While these cases are not precisely in point, I find nothing to the contrary, and applying the principles which they establish in the light of the judicial nature of your Board, it is my opinion that you have the right to amend your determinations even after a writ of certiorari has been secured to review the same.

Yours respectfully,

EDWARD R. O'MALLEY,

Attorney-General.

Tax Law— Special Franchise Tax — Corporations.

Description of property, etc., prepared by State Board of Tax Commissioners for the purposes of assessment, is sufficient where owner of special franchise is able to identify it.

STATE OF NEW YORK.

ATTORNEY-GENERAL'S OFFICE,

ALBANY, *January* 26, 1910.

State Board of Tax Commissioners, Albany, N. Y.:

Gentlemen.— I return herewith the tentative descriptions which you prepared for special franchise of various classes of companies. I have examined these descriptions and also the decisions bearing upon the question of their sufficiency. It is my opinion that they are a sufficient description for use in making your assessments and for describing the property assessed upon the assessment roll.

It is a well settled principle of taxation that the description of property assessed must be sufficiently definite to enable the *owner* to identify it. A different principle seems to prevail where the property is sought to be sold under tax sales, and I therefore do not pass upon the sufficiency of these descriptions in case the special franchise were to be sold for nonpayment of taxes at a tax sale. There is not, however, anything to prevent a more definite and detailed description of the same property being employed in such cases than appears upon the assessment roll. It is my opinion that for the purposes of assessment these descriptions are

sufficient, since they enable the owner of the special franchises
to identify them and since any more particular description would
be, as a practical matter, almost impossible to set forth in the
majority of cases.

In this connection I call your attention to the following authorities bearing upon the proposition:

Wabash, etc., R. Co. v. People, 137 Ill. 181, 186.
People ex rel. Mohawk R. Co. v. Garmon, 34 Misc. 350,
352; 63 App. Div. 530.

Yours respectfully,

EDWARD R. O'MALLEY,

Attorney-General.

Mortgage Tax.

Trust deeds or mortgages given by the Larchmont Water Company, to the Farmers Loan & Trust Company, whether taxable under chapter 729, Laws of 1905, and entitled to be
recorded without taxation.

STATE OF NEW YORK.

ATTORNEY-GENERAL'S OFFICE,

ALBANY, *February* 17, 1910.

*To the Honorable, the State Board of Tax Commissioners,
Albany, N. Y.:*

Gentlemen.— I have your favor of the 27th ult. asking opinion
as to the taxability of two certain instruments under chapter 729
of the Laws of 1905, the first being given under the following
circumstances:

The Larchmont Water Company on the first day of June, 1898,
gave to the Farmers Loan & Trust Company a trust deed or mortgage to secure the issue of its bonds. This mortgage was recorded
in the office of the registrar of Westchester county on the 29th day
of June, 1898. The 8th article of said mortgage provided as
follows:

" 8th. The said Larchmont Water Company shall and will from time to time during the continuance of this trust and mortgage, make, execute and deliver all such further instruments and conveyances as may be necessary to vest in said trustee, or its successor or successors, the within described and all subsequently acquired property and rights of property to facilitate the execution of said trust."

On the 25th day of May, 1905, the Larchmont Water Company acquired by deed certain property, which deed was recorded in the office of the registrar of Westchester county on the 26th day of October, 1905. On December 15th, 1905, an instrument was executed by the Larchmont Water Company to the Farmers Loan & Trust Company, reciting the above facts and granting and releasing unto the said trust company the above mentioned lands acquired by the Larchmont Water Company, to have and to hold the same unto the said party of the second part, its successors and assigns forever, subject, however, to the terms of the aforesaid indenture of mortgage.

The provisions of chapter 729 of the Laws of 1905, under which, if any, this instrument could be taxed, are as follows:

" Section 291.   SITUS.— All debts and obligations for the payment of money, either presently or in the future, which shall at any time hereafter be secured in whole or in part by mortgage of real property situated within this state, together with the mortgages securing the same, shall be deemed by all courts, authorities and officers of this state to be property within this state, and subject to be seized and sold as provided in this article * * * ."

" Section 294.   LEVYING OF TAX.— Subject to the provisions of section two hundred and ninety-three, a regular annual tax is hereby imposed on each and every debt and obligation, and upon the mortgage securing the same, described in section two hundred ninety-one, except upon mortgages recorded prior to July first, nineteen hundred and five * * * which tax shall be equal to five mills on each dollar of the amount of the principal debt or obligation as the same shall be at nine o'clock ante meridian on the first day of July, nineteen hundred and six. * * * ."

The 8th article of the mortgage or deed of trust given by the Larchmont Water Company to the Farmers Loan & Trust Co. would operate as an equitable mortgage upon any after acquired property. This property having been acquired by the Larchmont Water Company on the 25th day of May, 1905, an equitable lien would have attached as of that date by virtue of the 8th provision of the deed of trust given by the Larchmont Water Company and a court of equity could have compelled the execution of a mortgage at that time. A mortgage actually executed and delivered later on would be considered as taking effect at that time on the principle that equity considers done that which ought to have been done. The debt was not increased nor was additional security given by the execution of this instrument. I am, therefore, of the opinion that the said instrument was not taxable under chapter 729 of the Laws of 1905.

The facts relative to the second instrument are as follows:

On the 20th day of April, 1903, William R. Bull and wife executed and delivered to Halsey Meade Smith a mortgage in the sum of $3,500 upon a certain piece of property, which mortgage was recorded in the office of the registrar of Westchester county on the 10th day of December, 1904, and on the same day William R. Bull assigned to said Smith as additional security a mortgage made by Minnie May Harris and Raymond Harris, her husband, to the said Bull to secure the payment of $3,500 together with the bond or obligation therein described, said mortgage being dated the 18th day of December, 1901, and recorded in the office of the register of Westchester county on the 13th day of January, 1902. This assignment was dated the 20th day of April, 1903, and was recorded in the registrar's office on the 10th day of December, 1904. Bull, after the assignment above mentioned, acquired the legal title to the premises upon which the Harris mortgage was given, and being desirous that the premises covered by the mortgage given by himself and wife to Halsey Meade Smith should be released from the lien of the mortgage, and the time of payment of the indebtedness extended to the 20th day of April, 1909, on the 2nd day of February, 1906, entered into an agreement with the said Halsey Meade Smith, whereby the said Smith released the piece of property first above described from the lien of the mortgage given by Bull and wife to the said Smith, and it was mutually agreed between Bull and Smith that the time when the principal sum of the indebtedness should become due and payable should be extended to and fixed at the 20th day of April, 1909, and that the said Bull should assume the payment of the principal and interest of the said Harris mortgage, and further assume on his part all the terms and conditions contained in the bond of obligation accompanying and referred to in the said Harris mortgage, and that the said bond or obligation accompanying the Harris mortgage and the Harris mortgage itself should be in all other respects ratified and confirmed and unchanged. This instrument was recorded in the office of the registrar of Westchester county on the 10th day of February, 1906. There are two features of this agreement (1) the discharge of the land covered, from the lien of the mortgage given by Bull and wife to Smith. This was not taxable. (2) The extension of the time of payment of the Harris bond and mortgage and the promise of Bull to assume the payment of the bond. The security of the Harris mortgage was not increased by this agreement, as it was fixed by its terms and conditions. Except for the extension of time the proposition is similar to the grantee in a deed assuming the payment of a mortgage. In view of the fact that neither the security or debt was increased, and that the only effect of the agreement was a personal promise to pay a debt at another time, I am of the opinion that this agreement was entitled to be recorded without taxation.

Yours very truly,

EDWARD R. O'MALLEY,

Attorney-General.

Tax Law — Sections 291, 294, 295 *(Chapter* 729, *Laws* 1905)—
Mortgage Tax Law.

Mortgage of real property situated within the State of New York.
Statement as to no money advanced at time of making
mortgage. Provisions in lease for quarterly payments in
advance, etc. Whether such mortgage was entitled to be
recorded in office of registrar, Westchester county, without
tax thereon.

(See opinion March 18, 1910; April 12, 1910.)

STATE OF NEW YORK.

ATTORNEY-GENERAL'S OFFICE,

ALBANY, *March* 4, 1910.

*To the Honorable, the State Board of Tax Commissioners,
Albany, N. Y.:*

Gentlemen.— Your favor of January 21st, 1910, is at hand.
In this you ask whether a mortgage dated May 17th, 1906, recorded in the officer of the registrar of Westchester county on the
19th day of May, 1906, for $10,000 and containing the following
statement, as required by section 295 of chapter 729 of the Laws
of 1905: ·

"There is no money advanced on this mortgage at the
time of the making thereof, as the bond secured hereby is
given as collateral security for the performance of the
covenants of a lease, and the maximum amount of principal
indebtedness or obligation which may be at any time under
any contingency outstanding so as to be secured by this
mortgage is $10,000."

was entitled to be recorded without the payment of any tax.

Since this letter you have furnished me with a copy of the lease
involved, which is dated the 23rd day of June, 1903, and provides
for the leasing of certain property from the 1st day of May, 1906,
at the yearly rental of $11,750, payable in equal quarterly pay-
ments in advance on the 1st days of May, August, November and
February in each year, the first payment to be made on the 1st

day of May, 1906. The provisions of this lease are the ones ordinarily found and there is no provision for the total amount of rent becoming due in case of default. Sections 291 and 294 of this law provide that all debts and obligations for the payment of money either presently or in the future, which shall at any time hereafter be secured, in whole or in part, by mortgage of real property situated within this State, together with the mortgages securing the same, shall be deemed property and subject to an annual tax of five mills upon each dollar of the amount of the principal obligation, as the same shall be at nine o'clock on the 1st day of July, 1906, and in each year thereafter, and shall be due and payable on the said first day of July.

The pertinent provisions of section 295, after providing that each mortgage shall contain a statement of the amount advanced at the time of the mortgage, and the maximum amount of the principal indebtedness, are as follows:

" No such mortgage not exempt under section two hundred and ninety-three nor the assignment thereof from an exempt owner to a nonexempt owner shall be accepted for record if tendered at any time after nine o'clock ante meridian of the first day of July in any year, and before the first day of the following July, unless there shall have been paid, or at the same time shall be paid, a tax at the rate of five mills per year on each and every dollar of the maximum amount aforesaid for the period between the date of the mortgage and the next succeeding first day of July, or if said mortgage by its terms falls due before the next succeeding first day of July, to the earlier due date of such mortgage. Where, however, only a portion or none of the principal of the indebtedness secured by a mortgage has been advanced at the time of its recording, the tax imposed by this section shall be computed only on the amount advanced on the mortgage at the time of recording; but in every such case an additional tax at the rate of five-tenths of one per centum per annum on each subsequent advance of principal on such mortgage from the date of such advance up to the first day of July next ensuing, or to the earlier satisfaction of said mortgage, shall be due and payable on the thirtieth day of July following, or at the earlier satisfaction of said mortgage, as the case may be. * * * ."

What is the meaning of the phrase " debt or obligation " for the payment of money, as used in this act? The word debt, in the light of the use of the word advanced in section 295, would seem to require that money should have actually been advanced and does not cover a case where there is merely a promise to pay money upon another person doing something upon his part. The word obligation originally meant a note or bond for the payment of money. This meaning has been departed from in many instances, but would, I think, apply, as it most aptly describes what the act construing it as a whole would seem to intend. (See Munzinger v. United Press Co., 52 App. Div. 338; Thorn v. Hall, 10 App. Div. 412.)

The tax is upon the debt or obligation and is not a tax for recording the mortgage. One purpose of this act was to relieve mortgages from taxation at the full rate by local authorities, and so to relieve real estate from a species of double taxation. This debt or obligation, if such it can be called, is what the owner of real estate is to receive for its use and I do not think that it should be subject to tax, except the intent of the Legislature is clear, and in this instance it is at least very doubtful. The facts are not plain as to one point, that is, whether the rent due on May 1, 1906, had been paid. If this rent was unpaid at the time of the execution of the mortgage, it would seem to be a debt within the purview of this act. The money not having been paid when due might be considered as advanced and under those circumstances I should consider that a tax should be paid before the mortgage could be recorded.

Yours truly,
EDWARD R. O'MALLEY,
Attorney-General.

Mortgage Tax Law — Section 263.

State Board of Tax Commissioners may compel recording officers to turn over to county treasurer or city chamberlain, all accrued interest on moneys received by them in payment of recording tax. The Tax Commissioners may also examine the *mortgage* accounts of the city chamberlain or county treasurer, to ascertain if recording officers have turned over such moneys. Power to examine the general conduct of such officers vests only in the Comptroller.

STATE OF NEW YORK.

ATTORNEY-GENERAL'S OFFICE,

ALBANY, *March* 10, 1910.

To the Honorable, the State Board of Tax Commissioners, Albany, N. Y.:

Gentlemen.— I have your letter of February 10 in which you ask whether the Board of Tax Commissioners has the jurisdiction to demand of the recording officer the payment to the county treasurer or city chamberlain of accrued interest on moneys received by him in payment of the recording tax on mortgages and deposited by him.

There is no question but that all interest that may have been earned on any moneys deposited by the recording officer should be paid over by him to the county treasurer or city chamberlain as the case may be.

You ask further as to the extent of the supervisory jurisdiction of the State Board of Tax Commissioners in regard to mortgage taxes and the accounts kept thereof by county treasurers and as to whether the Board has the power to cause an examination to be made of such accounts.

The provisions of the Mortgage Tax Law relating to the powers of your Board are as follows:

"Section 263. SUPERVISORY POWER OF STATE BOARD OF TAX COMMISSIONERS AND STATE COMPTROLLER.— The state board of tax commissioners shall have general supervisory power

over all recording officers in respect of the duties imposed by
this article and they may make such rules and regulations for
the government of recording officers in respect to the matters
provided for in this article as they may deem proper, provided that such rules and regulations shall not be inconsistent
with this or any other statute. The state comptroller shall
have general supervisory power over all county treasurers
and the chamberlain of the city of New York in respect to
the duties imposed upon them by this article, and may make
such rules and regulations, not inconsistent with this or any
other statute, for the government of said county treasurers
and chamberlain as he deems necessary and appropriate to
secure a due accounting for all taxes and moneys collected
or received pursuant to any provision of this article." * * *

Section 171 of article 8 of the Tax Law provides also that the
State Board of Tax Commissioners shall * * *

"Fourth. Take testimony and hear proofs, under oath,
with reference to any matter within the line of its official
duty. Any member of such board may be designated for that
purpose. And it may require from all state and municipal
officers such information as may be necessary for the proper
discharge of its duties."

"Eighth. Perform the other powers and duties conferred
upon it by law."

Construing these provisions together the State Board of Tax
Commissioners has the power to require any necessary informa
tion from all state and municipal officers, and also if necessary
to take testimony under oath with reference to any matter within
the line of its official duty.

The recording officer is bound to pay all moneys received by
him less his necessary expenses to the county treasurer or city
chamberlain. The State Board has supervisory power over all
recording officers in respect to the duties imposed by the Mortgage
Tax Law. If it is necessary to examine the accounts of the city
chamberlain or county treasurer to ascertain whether or not the
recording officer has paid over to him all moneys required by
statute to be paid, the State Board of Tax Commissioners would

have the right to do so, but its examination should be confined
to that particular object, as it would not have the power to make
a general examination of the conduct of the office of city chamberlain or county treasurer, which power is conferred upon the
Comptroller.

Yours very truly,

EDWARD .R. O'MALLEY,

Attorney-General.

---

*Tax Law — Sections 293, 295, 305 (Chapter 729, Laws 1905)—
Mortgage Tax.*

Mortgage made by Empire State Engineering Company to United
States Mortgage & Trust Company to secure bonds for
$250,000 a lien on real and personal property. State Board
of Tax Commissioners must determine the amount of lien
on such property, in order to ascertain exemption allowed at
time of recording.

(See opinion March 4, 1910; April 12, 1910.)

STATE OF NEW YORK.

ATTORNEY-GENERAL'S OFFICE,

ALBANY, *March* 18, 1910.

*To the Honorable, the State Board of Tax Commissioners.
Albany, N. Y.:*

Gentlemen.— I am in receipt of your favor of the 25th ult., together with enclosure, asking for my opinion as to whether in
making a determination at the present time under chapter 729 of
the Laws of 1905, the Board of Tax Commissioners must base
its determination on the actual conditions as they existed at the
time the mortgage was presented for record, or whether said Board
can take into consideration other facts accruing subsequently to
the time of offering the mortgage for record.

The facts therein are stated as follows:

On August 1st, 1905, a mortgage was recorded in the
Oneida county clerk's office, by the Empire State Engineer-

ing Company, Rome plant, to the United States Mortgage & Trust Company, to secure bonds in the aggregate amount of two hundred and fifty thousand dollars ($250,000). Appended to the mortgage is the statement at the end thereof and over the signature of the mortgager, " That the amount of the within mortgage at the time of the making thereof is two hundred and fifty thousand dollars ($250,000) and that the maximum amount of principal indebtedness or obligations, not including interest, taxes, assessments, water rates, insurance or other expenses made by the mortgagee to preserve the mortgage lien, which is or under any contin- gency may at any time be outstanding so as to be secured by the mortgages, is said two hundred and fifty thousand dollars ($250,000).

It also appears from other documentary evidence which you submitted with your letter, that said mortgage is a lien on both real and personal property, and that you have determined the value of the real and personal property upon which it is a lien to be $30,354 and $1,255 respectively.

You further state that it is now claimed by the United States Mortgage & Trust Co. that said statement at the end of the mortgage is untrue and that there was only $5,000 advanced instead of $250,000.

Section 295 of the Mortgage Tax Law of 1905 provides:

" Every mortgage made on or after said first day of July, nineteen hundred and five, shall contain at the end thereof, above the signature of the mortgagor, a statement of the amount advanced at that time on said mortgage and of the maximum amount of principal indebtedness or obligations, not including interest, taxes, assessments, water rates, insurance or other expenses made by the mortgagee to preserve the mortgage lien, which is or under any contingency may at any time be outstanding so as to be secured by the mortgage. When the mortgage shall have been delivered to and accepted by the mortgagee said statement shall thereafter at all times, and for all purposes, be binding and conclusive on both par-

21

ties to the mortgage, and all persons claiming or to claim through or under them or either of them."

The statement made at the time the mortgage was offered for record is therefore binding on the mortgagor and the mortgagee. Section 293 of the same law provides:

" When a mortgage is a lien upon both real and personal property such proportion thereof as the value of the personal property bears to the aggregate value of the real and personal property embraced therein shall also be exempt from the taxes imposed by this article."

Section 305 provides:

" Where the mortgage is a lien upon both real and personal property it shall be the duty of the state board of tax commissioners to determine the amount of property exempt under section two hundred ninety-three."

From this last section you will see that the only question which your board had the power to determine was the amount of the exemption allowed under said section 293 already quoted.

While chapter 729 of the Laws of 1905 has been repealed, still the tax which accrued to July 1st, 1906, is collectible (concluding clause of section 264 of the present Tax Law).

It is and it was your duty, therefore, to determine the amount of the real and personal property respectively upon which this mortgage was a lien so as to ascertain the exemption allowed by said section 293 as of the time when it was presented for record, and the tax computed accordingly.

Yours very truly,

EDWARD R. O'MALLEY,

Attorney-General.

Tax Law (Cons.) — Section 3 — Special Franchise Assessments.

Whether tangible property in connection with a special franchise
may be included in an assessment under section 3, even
though owned by another person or corporation under lease,
etc. (People ex rel. Met. St. Ry. v. St. Bd. Tax Com., 174
N. Y. 417; People ex rel. N. Y. & Harlem Railroad Co., 101
N. Y. 322.)

STATE OF NEW YORK.

ATTORNEY-GENERAL'S OFFICE,

ALBANY, *March* 30, 1910.

Hon. E. E. WOODBURY, *Chairman, State Board Tax Commis-*
sioners, Albany, N. Y.:

Dear Sir.— Your inquiry of the 23rd inst., whether an assessment of a special franchise should include the tangible property
used in connection with it, even though such tangible property be
owned by another person or corporation operating the franchise
under a lease or contract agreement, has not been directly determined by the courts.

Section 3 of the Consolidated Tax Law provides that,

"A special franchise shall be deemed to include the value
of the tangible property of a person, co-partnership, association or corporation situated in, upon, under or above any
street, highway, public place or public waters in connection
with the special franchise. *The tangible property so in-*
cluded shall be taxed as a part of the special franchise."

The Court of Appeals has recognized the inseparable character,
as set forth in the above provision of the Tax Law.

"The Legislature also brought in as an incidental part of
the system some tangible property which had been previously
assessed by local authority. No tangible property, however,
was affected except such as was situated in the public highways and was so incidental to and dependent upon the special
franchises as to have no substantial value unless used in con-

nection with them. The relation between the intangible right
to run cars in the streets and the tangible property in the
rails to run the cars on, is so intimate as to be inseparable in
any practicable *system of estimating values."* VANN, J.
People ex rel. Metropolitan Street Railway Company v. State
Board of Tax Commissioners, 174 N. Y. 417.

In an earlier case, the court in its opinion, said:

" *   *   * they (tracks,. etc.) are liable to assessment to
whosoever has that interest in the real estate which will protect the erection or affixing thereon of these structures, and
their possession." People ex rel. New York & Harlem Railroad Company v. State Board of Tax Commissioners, 101
N. Y. 322, 326.

Although the matter is not entirely clear, in view of this inseparable characteristic, and because the only interest in the real
estate protecting the erection of the tracks is the special franchise,
my conclusion is that the tangible property placed in the streets
by the lessee company should be assessed as part of the special
franchise.

Very truly yours,

EDWARD R. O'MALLEY,

Attorney-General.

Tax Law — Sections 290, 291, 294 (Chapter 729, Laws 1905, repealed by Tax Law of 1906) — Mortgage Tax.

Lease of real property for term of years grants to lessee right to possession of such property for the term demised, and a mortgage upon such leasehold creates a lien affecting title, and under section 253, Tax Law of 1906, is taxable. (People ex rel. Elias Brewing Co. v. Gass, 120 App. Div. 146, affirmed 190 N. Y. 565, concurring opinion Justice Ingraham.)

(See opinions March 4, March 18, May 10, 1910.)

STATE OF NEW YORK.

ATTORNEY-GENERAL'S OFFICE,

ALBANY, *April* 12, 1910.

To the Honorable, the State Board of Tax Commissioners, Albany, N. Y.:

Gentlemen.— I am in receipt of your favor of January 20, 1910, asking for my ruling as to whether there is a tax payable under the Mortgage Tax Law upon the following statement of facts:

A mortgage is given upon a lease of real property. The lease is for a term of two years with an optional privilege to the lessor of renewing at the end of the term for five years more. The mortgage specifies that it is a lien upon the lease for the term of "two years and any and all renewals and extensions thereof." Subsequently it is learned the lessor exercised his option at the end of the term of two years and extends the lease for five additional years, the mortgage still remaining in force.

In accordance with your oral communication of the 11th of February, 1910, I give my opinion upon the above statement of facts both as to the Mortgage Tax Law of 1905 and 1906.

UNDER THE TAX LAW OF 1905.

Section 294 of chapter 729 of the Laws of 1905 (now repealed) imposes an annual tax upon a mortgage securing a debt or obligation. The tax was five mills on each dollar.

Section 290 of the same law provides:

" The words real property and real estate as used in this article, shall be understood to include everything a conveyance or mortgage of which can be recorded as a conveyance or mortgage of real property under the laws of this state."

Section 290 of the Real Property Law defines the term " real property " to include tenements and hereditaments and chattels real, except a lease for a term not exceeding three years.

" * * * The term conveyance includes every written instrument, by which any estate or interest in real property is created, transferred, mortgaged or assigned or by which the title to any real property may be affected * * * except a will, a lease for a term not exceeding three years * * *."

Section 291 provides that

" A conveyance of real property within the state on being duly acknowledged by the person executing the same or proved as required by this chapter and such acknowledgment or proof duly certified when required by this chapter may be recorded in the office of the clerk of the county where such real property is situated, and such county clerk shall, upon the request of any party, on tender of the lawful fees therefor record the same in his said office."

A lease for two years is a chattel real, and being for less than three years was not entitled as a matter of right to be recorded and was good if not so recorded. The mortgage on this lease is not a conveyance within the meaning of section 290 of chapter 729 of the Laws of 1905.

It was the debt on which the tax was imposed and not the security, so that even if the right to a renewal was given for five years, it only enhanced the security while the debt remained the same.

An instrument such as you describe, if presented for recording prior to July 1, 1906, was, therefore, not taxable under the Mortgage Tax Law of 1905, and as no tax accrued on it prior to said date, and it having been already recorded, there will at no time be a tax payable upon it.

(See concluding clause of section 264, Tax Law; effect of repeal of chapter 729, Laws of 1905.)

UNDER THE TAX LAW OF 1906.

Section 253 of the Tax Law relating to tax on mortgages imposes a tax on every mortgage of real property recorded on and after July 1, 1906.

Section 250 of said act provides:

"The words real property and real estate as used in this article in addition to the definition thereof contained in section two of this chapter shall be understood to include everything a conveyance or mortgage of which can be recorded as a conveyance or mortgage of real property under the laws of the state. The words mortgage of real property as used in this article include every mortgage by which a lien is created over or imposed on real property or which affects the title to real property, notwithstanding that it may also be a lien on personal or other property or that personal or other property may form a part of the security for the debt or debts secured by such mortgage."

By said section 253 of the Tax Law it is the principal debt or obligation which is secured that is taxable. It makes no difference whether there might be under certain conditions additional security.

I believe in giving my opinion to your inquiry that I am bound by the decision in the case of People ex rel. Elias Brewing Company v. Gass, 120 App. Div. 146, affirmed in 190 N. Y. 565. In that case in a separate concurring opinion, written by Mr. Justice Ingraham and concurred in by Mr. Justice Laughlin, it was held that a lease of real property for a term of years grants to the lessee the right to possession of the property for the term demised and a mortgage upon such a lease creates a lien which affects the title to the real property within the definition of a "mortgage of real property" as used in section 253 of said Tax Law, and is taxable.

Following the reasoning in that case, a lease for two years being a lien upon the property demised affects the title to the real property and a mortgage upon such leasehold interest in real property creates a lien upon an interest in real property and a tax is, therefore, payable upon such mortgage.

Yours very truly,

EDWARD R. O'MALLEY,

Attorney-General.

Tax Law — Section 262.

Purchase of mortgage tax record book by recording clerk with the
approval of the State Board of Tax Commissioners. Failure
of clerk to pay publishers for book furnished on credit does
not make it the duty of the board to collect the debt.

STATE OF NEW YORK,

ATTORNEY-GENERAL'S OFFICE,

ALBANY, *May* 3, 1910.

To the Honorable, the State Board of Tax Commissioners.
Albany, N. Y.:

Gentlemen.— I have your communication of April 25, 1910,
asking my opinion in reference to the following facts:

The recording officer of a county in this state made application
to your board for authority to incur the expense of purchasing a
new mortgage tax record book, in accordance with section 262 of
the Tax Law, which provides that all necessary expenses of the
recording officer in connection with the collection of the mortgage
tax shall be first approved by your board and the amount thereof,
when approved, retained by the recording officer out of the moneys
coming into his hands. Approval of the items of expense at a sum
not to exceed $20 was given and this sum was retained by the
recording officer, although he has neglected and failed to pay the
publishers of the book.

The question presented is whether or not there is any duty
resting upon your board in the premises to arrange for the payment of this bill or to secure the amount from the recording officer
or his sureties.

So far as the people are concerned this account has been paid.
The money was deducted from the mortgage tax collections. No
action would lie either against the State or the county by the publishers to recover the price of the book. The statute contemplates
that the expenses will be paid by the recording officer, who may be
reimbursed for such expenses when approved by the Tax Commissioners. The law does not authorize the recording officer to create
a charge against his county or the State on account of mortgage

tax collections. Whoever deals with the recording officer in reference to such expenses is presumed to know the law and to carry on his transactions with the recording officer. There is no reason to believe that the publishers did not know the nature of the book they sold. In fact, they make a business of supplying books for the express purpose of recording mortgage taxes, and if they furnished such a book on credit, they must look to the recording officer for their pay. If the recording officer were unreliable, they were at liberty to demand payment on delivery. If they trusted him, there is no duty on your board to undertake to collect the debt.

Yours truly,

EDWARD R. O'MALLEY,

Attorney-General.

Tax Law — Section 250 — Mortgage Tax.

Chattel mortgage and assignment of a lease, whether taxable under section 250.

(See opinion April 12, 1910.)

STATE OF NEW YORK.

ATTORNEY-GENERAL'S OFFICE,

ALBANY, *May* 10, 1910.

To the Honorable, the State Board of Tax Commissioners, Albany, N. Y.:

Gentlemen.— I acknowledge receipt of your favor of March 7, 1910, enclosing to me copy of a chattel mortgage and an assignment of a lease, asking me for my opinion as to their taxability.

You also ask me for my opinion as to whether a mortgage on a lease running for three years or less is taxable under the Mortgage Tax Law. The latter question was answered in my opinion under date of April 12, 1910, to your board.

The facts as they appear from the copy of the mortgage and the assignment of the lease are as follows:

On February 16, 1910, one Edward Kelly being indebted to one Paul G. Wolff in the sum of $2,500, made and executed a chattel mortgage of certain personal property appertaining to a drug business to secure said indebtedness. On the same day Wolf made and executed to said Kelly an assignment of a certain lease dated March 8, 1904, made by one Robert B. Welton to said Wolf of a certain store in Brooklyn, New York, which lease was recorded in the registrar's office of the county of Kings. In the lease this clause appears:

> " This assignment is made subject to the provisions of a certain contract dated February 16, 1910, between the parties hereto and is not reassignable except on written consent of the party of the first part."

and I assume that this last mentioned clause in the assignment refers to the chattel mortgage already mentioned.

I am satisfied that the instrument designated as an assignment of a lease is in fact such and is in no sense a mortgage of the lease, and neither said mortgage nor the assignment of the lease come within the purview of section 250 of the Tax Law and are therefore not taxable.

Yours very truly,
EDWARD R. O'MALLEY,
Attorney-General.

Tax Law — Article XI — Mortgage Tax.

Assignment of real property lease as collateral security for debt, is a mortgage on a lease and is taxable on its recordation.

(See opinions March 4, March 18, April 12, 1910.)

STATE OF NEW YORK.

ATTORNEY-GENERAL'S OFFICE,

ALBANY, *May* 10, 1910.

To the Honorable, the State Board of Tax Commissioners. Albany, N. Y.:

Gentlemen.— I acknowledge receipt of your favor of March 16, 1910, asking me for my opinion upon the question of whether the recordation of an assignment of a real property lease as collateral security for debt is taxable under the provisions of article 11 of the Tax Law, and supplementing your letter you have submitted a copy of a form of assignment of such a lease.

Your question hinges on the point whether the assignment of a real property lease as collateral security for debt while styled an assignment is in fact a mortgage.

A mortgage is defined as an instrument intended by the parties at the time of making it to be security for the payment of money or the doing of some prescribed act.

> Thomas on Mortgages, page 11.
> Carr v. Carr, 52 N. Y. 251.

I have already advised you in an opinion dated April 12, 1910, that a mortgage on a lease for a term of years is taxable under the decision of the case of People ex rel. Elias Brewing Company v. Gass, 120 A. D. 147, affirmed in 180 N. Y. 565, on the theory that such a lease is real property within the purview of section 250 of the Mortgage Tax Law.

The form of the assignment of the lease submitted to me by you is, in my opinion, a mortgage on a lease, and is, therefore, taxable on its recordation on the same reasoning set forth in the case of People v. Gass, above cited.

> Yours very truly,
> EDWARD R. O'MALLEY,
> *Attorney-General.*

Tax Law -- Section 255 — Mortgages.

Supplemental mortgage filed in Erie county clerk's office for purpose of securing sum of $3,500 for which primary mortgage
was given and tax paid thereon; also of imposing a lien upon
real property not covered by primary mortgage; may be
recorded without payment of tax.

STATE OF NEW YORK.

ATTORNEY-GENERAL'S OFFICE,

ALBANY, May 20, 1910.

*To the Honorable, the State Board of Tax Commissioners,
Albany, N. Y.:*

Gentlemen.— I acknowledge receipt of your favor of the 12th
instant enclosing copy of an affidavit of John P. Abbott, verified
May 7, 1910, and filed in the Erie county clerk's office, and asking
for my opinion whether a mortgage is entitled to be recorded without the payment of a tax under the following circumstances:

On April 2, 1910, Theresa Steffan, as mortgagee, recorded a
mortgage in the Erie county clerk's office upon certain property
described therein, to secure the sum of $3,500 and paid to said
recording officer the tax upon said mortgage. Said mortgagee now
desires to file a supplemental mortgage for the purpose of imposing
the lien thereof upon a parcel of real property not covered by the
said primary mortgage and the purpose for making such supplemental mortgage is for the better securing the said sum of $3,500
for which the primary mortgage was given. There is no additional
amount of money advanced under the supplemental mortgage.
Pursuant to section 255 of the Tax Law said mortgagee, by her
attorney, filed an affidavit setting forth these facts and claiming
an exemption from any further mortgage tax because of the fact
that said supplemental mortgage was made only for the purpose of
better securing the principal indebtedness of $3,500.

Section 255 of the Tax Law, under which the exemption is
claimed, is as follows:

" If subsequent to the recording of a mortgage on which all
taxes, if any, accrued under this article have been paid, a

supplemental instrument or mortgage is recorded for the purpose of correcting or perfecting any recorded mortgage, or pursuant to some provision or covenant therein, or an additional mortgage is recorded imposing the lien thereof upon property not originally covered by or not described in such recorded primary mortgage for the purpose of securing the principal indebtedness which is or under any contingency may be secured by such recorded primary mortgage, such additional instrument or mortgage shall not be subject to taxation under this article, unless it creates or secures a new or further indebtedness or obligation other than the principal indebtedness or obligation secured by or which under any contingency may be secured by the recorded primary mortgage, in which case, a tax is imposed as provided by section two hundred and fifty-three of this chapter on such new or further indebtedness or obligation, and shall be paid to the proper recording officer at the time such instrument or additional mortgage is recorded. If at the time of recording such instrument, or additional mortgage any exemption is claimed under this section, there shall be filed with the recording officer and preserved in his office a statement under oath of the facts on which such claim for exemption is based. The determination of the recording officer upon the question of exemption shall be reviewable by the state board of tax commissioners."

Upon the facts stated above it is clear that said supplemental mortgage imposed the lien of $3,500 upon property not originally covered by the primary mortgage, and that the supplemental mortgage does not create or secure a new or further indebtedness other than the principal indebtedness of $3,500 secured in the primary mortgage. In such a case the statute says that the supplemental mortgage " shall not be subject to taxation under this article."

I am, therefore, of the opinion that the supplemental mortgage in question is entitled to be recorded without the payment of a tax.

Yours very truly,

EDWARD R. O'MALLEY,

Attorney-General.

Tax Law — Sections 258, 263 — Recording Deeds and Mortgages.

Where register of New York county has doubt as to deeds offered
for record, and running to the Illinois Surety Company, State
Board of Tax Commissioners may require him to demand
affidavit from the Surety Company that such deeds are not
mortgages, and he may refuse to record such without paymen·
of tax.

(See opinion December 6, 1910.)

STATE OF NEW YORK.

ATTORNEY-GENERAL'S OFFICE,

ALBANY, June 2, 1910.

State Board of Tax Commissioners, Albany. N. Y.:

Gentlemen.— I acknowledge your letter of June 1 in which you
ask my opinion as to the extent to which recording officers may go
in demanding information to show the true purpose of deeds,
absolute on their faces, which are offered for record and which
they have reasonable ground to believe are in fact mortgages. It
appears from your letter that the register of New York county
has received a number of similar deeds for record, which, on their
faces, appear absolute. All of these deeds run to the Illinois
Surety Company, and he has reason to believe that the property is
conveyed to said company for the purpose of indemnifying it
against loss by reason of its furnishing to the grantors surety
bonds. You ask whether the register is justified in refusing to
record such deeds without the payment of a tax where he is given
to believe that they are to operate as a mortgage, and whether he
has the right to demand from the Surety Company an affidavit to
the effect that these deeds are not in reality mortgages.

Section 258 of the Tax Law provides that no mortgage of real
property shall be recorded by any county clerk or register unless
there shall be paid the tax imposed by that article. Section 263
of the same law provides that the State Board of Tax Commissioners shall have general supervisory power over all recording
officers in respect of the duties imposed by that article, and that
they may make such rules and regulations for the government of

recording officers in respect to such matters as they may deem proper, provided such rules and regulations are not inconsistent with any statute.

. It is my opinion that under the foregoing provisions of law it is within the power of your board to provide that no recording officer, if he has reasonable grounds to believe that such instrument is in fact a mortgage, shall record an instrument which on its face is apparently an absolute deed, without the payment of the tax, unless he is furnished by the party offering the same for record with an affidavit setting forth that it is not a mortgage. If this were not so an easy method for evading the payment of this tax would be presented. All the information is in the possession of the party offering the deed for record, and the requirement of such an affidavit can cause only slight inconvenience if the instrument is in fact an absolute deed. On the other hand, if it is in fact a mortgage, it is only by such procedure as this that the recording officer can satisfactorily determine that fact.

Very truly yours,

EDWARD R. O'MALLEY,

Attorney-General.

Tax Law — Sections 50, 51, 52, 53, 175 *— Assessments.*

Equalization of assessments and correction of assessment rolls. Provision for review by appeal or certiorari where equalization is made by the Commissioners of Equalization. Act of said Commissioners considered the act of the Board of Supervisors and may be reviewed in the same manner as though made by the board itself.

STATE OF NEW YORK.

Attorney-General's Office,

Albany, *June* 8, 1910.

Hon. Egbert E. Woodbury, *Chairman, State Board of Tax Commissioners, Albany, N. Y.:*

Dear Sir.— I acknowledge your letter of the 23d ult., in which you ask my opinion as to whether or not there is any method for review of an equalization based upon the report of commissioners of equalization, either by appeal or certiorari.

I have given this matter careful attention and beg to advise you as follows:

Section 50 of the Tax Law provides that the board of supervisors of each county in the State shall equalize the assessments in the various tax districts in the county.

Section 51 provides for the appointment of commissioners of equalization to equalize the assessed value of real property among the several tax districts of the county. Section 52 prescribes their duties, and section 53 provides that they shall report each year to the board of supervisors the equalized valuations of real estate as made by them, which report shall be signed by a majority and filed with the clerk of the board of supervisors. The same section provides that the report " shall be binding and conclusive on such board of supervisors as an equalization of the assessments of real estate for such year." Section 175 of the same law provides for an appeal to the State Board of Tax Commissioners " from any act or decision of the board of supervisors, in the equalization of assessments and the correction of the assessment rolls."

There is no specific provision for an appeal or for review by certiorari in case of equalization made by the commissioners of equalization. However, it is my opinion that a fair interpretation of the law is one which will produce harmony in the method of reviewing equalization made in either of these two ways. Therefore, although the matter is not free from doubt, it is my opinion that the act of the commissioners of equalization becomes the act of the board of supervisors, although performed in the first instance through agents, and that such act may be reviewed under section 175 in the same manner as an equalization made originally by the board itself.

Very truly yours,

EDWARD R. O'MALLEY,

Attorney-General.

Tax Law — Sections 2, 43, 45 — Special Franchise Assessments.

Villages, school and highway districts, highway crossings, etc.
Decision in Haverstraw case does not apply to school or highway districts, but to special franchises comprising longitudinal occupancy of highways and streets as well as highway
crossings. (People ex rel. N. Y. C. & H. R. R. Co. v. Gourley et al.)

STATE OF NEW YORK.

ATTORNEY-GENERAL'S OFFICE,

ALBANY, *June* 9, 1910.

Hon. EGBERT E. WOODBURY, *Chairman, State Board of Tax Commissioners, Albany, N. Y.:*

Dear Sir.— I acknowledge your letter of the 25th ult., in which
you ask my opinion as to the effect of the decision of the Court of
Appeals in People ex rel. New York Central & Hudson River
Railroad Company v. Gourley et al., known as the Haverstraw
case, upon the work of your board. Your question resolves itself
into two parts:

First.— Does this decision apply to school and highway districts as well as to villages, requiring your board to make a separate
statement of valuation of the special franchise within each of these
districts as well as in each village?

Second.— Does it apply to special franchises comprised of
longitudinal occupations of the highways, or may it be limited in
its effect to special franchises comprised of highway crossings,
which alone were under consideration by the court in this case?

I have carefully examined the opinion with a view to answering these questions, and, in my judgment, it was not intended to
apply to school or highway districts. On the other hand, I am of
the opinion that its reasoning applies as strongly to cases involving
longitudinal occupancy of the streets as to those involving merely
highway crossings.

Very truly yours,
EDWARD R. O'MALLEY,
Attorney-General.

Motor Vehicle Law — Section 7.

Amendment to law (chapter 374, Laws 1910) exempting from taxation owners of automobiles, and providing registration fees in lieu of taxes. Such owners having assessment made against such automobiles may on grievance day eliminate the property so assessed, by correction of assessment roll.

STATE OF NEW YORK.

ATTORNEY-GENERAL'S OFFICE,

ALBANY, *June* 13, 1910.

Hon. EGBERT E. WOODBURY, *Chairman, State Board of Tax Commissioners, Albany, N. Y.:*

Dear Sir.— I have your letter of the 9th inst., in which you ask my opinion as to whether chapter 374, Laws of 1910, amending the law in reference to automobiles and imposing a State tax upon the same, exempts owners of automobiles taxed thereunder from personal property taxes imposed during the current year.

This act provides in part as follows:

"7. FEES IN LIEU OF TAXES.— The registration fees imposed by this article upon motor vehicles, other than those of manufacturers and dealers and those used solely for commercial purposes, shall be in lieu of all taxes, general or local, to which motor vehicles may be subject."

The act is to take effect August 1, 1910.

You state in your letter that the date of making assessment rolls is fixed as of the 1st day of July of the present year, or one month prior to the time when the motor vehicle act takes effect. At that time, a person owning such a vehicle will be liable to an assessment therefor as part of his personal property. The rolls, however, will remain open for correction and the hearing of grievances to the third Tuesday of August, 1910, when the assessors meet for the purpose of hearing such grievances and making such corrections. At that time this act will be in effect.

It is well settled that where an act of the Legislature containing an exemption of property from taxation takes effect between

the date of the preparation of the assessment roll and the date of
its final closing, the owner of such property is entitled to have
the assessment roll corrected by eliminating the property so
exempted.

> People ex rel. American Law Publishing Society v. Tax
> Commissioners, 142 N. Y. 348.
> Aetna Insurance Co. v. The Mayor, 153 N. Y. 331.
> Matter of American Fine Arts Society, 6 A. D. 496.

Your conclusion, therefore, that the owners of automobiles will
be entitled to exemption from taxation by having any assessment
made against such property on the assessment roll stricken from
the roll on grievance day, is in accordance with the well established authorities in this State.

> Very truly yours,
> EDWARD R. O'MALLEY,
> *Attorney-General.*

Mortgage Tax Law — Section 256.

Indeterminate mortgage, Westchester county. Maximum amount
secured under contingency. Mortgagor or mortgagee required to furnish recording officer with proof, for purpose of
computing value of property covered by mortgage.

STATE OF NEW YORK.

ATTORNEY-GENERAL'S OFFICE,

ALBANY, *July* 6, 1910.

*To the Honorable, the State Board of Tax Commissioners,
Albany, N. Y.:*

Gentlemen.— Your letter of May 20, 1910, enclosing copy of
mortgage recorded in Westchester county, asking my opinion as
to whether said mortgage "is an indeterminate mortgage or
whether the consideration, $1,000, is the maximum amount that
under any contingency may be secured," received and in reply will
say that the mortgage in question shows that it was given by
John A. Summers and wife of Brooklyn, N. Y., upon their real

property situate in Westchester county to the State Bank, a banking corporation organized under the laws of the State of New York, the consideration expressed therein being $1,000.

The mortgage provides for the payment thereof as follows: " Provided always, that if the said parties of the first part shall pay any and all indebtedness at any time due and owing by them or either of them, to the party of the second part on demand, then these presents shall become void, and the estate hereby granted shall cease, determine and be void. And the said parties of the first part covenant with the said party of the second part that the parties of the first part will pay the indebtedness as hereinbefore provided, and if default be made in the payment of any part thereof, the said party of the second part shall have power to sell the premises herein described according to law."

Section 256 of the Mortgage Tax Law provides:

" If the principal indebtedness secured or which by any contingency may be secured by a mortgage is not determinable from the terms of the mortgage, or if a mortgage is given to secure the performance by the mortgagor or any other person of a contract obligation other than the payment of a specific sum of money and the maximum amount secured or which by any contingency may be secured by the mortgage is not expressed therein, such mortgage shall be taxable under section two hundred and fifty-three of this chapter upon the value of the property covered by the mortgage, which shall be determined by the recording officer to whom such mortgage is presented for record, unless at the time of presenting such mortgage for record the owner thereof shall file with the recording officer a sworn statement of the maximum amount secured or which under any contingency may be secured by the mortgage. If such maximum amount is expressed in the mortgage or in a sworn statement filed as required by this section, such amount shall be the basis for assessing the tax imposed by this article. * * * If the maximum amount secured or which by any contingency may be secured by the mortgage is not expressed in the mortgage or in a sworn statement as authorized by this section, the recording officer at the time such mortgage is offered for record may require the mortgagor or mortgagee to furnish him with proofs as to such facts as he deems necessary for the purpose of computing the value of the property covered by the mortgage and such proofs shall be preserved in his office. * * * "

The amount of $1,000 expressed in said mortgage is simply a consideration. The consideration might have been $1.00 for the purposes of this mortgage. The power of sale is clearly given for the purpose of paying the debt, whether for $1,000 or more, and in my opinion is an indeterminate mortgage and unless at the time of presenting such mortgage for record the owner filed with the recording officer a sworn statement of the maximum amount secured or which under any contingency may be secured by the mortgage, the basis of the mortgage tax is the value of the property covered by the mortgage, which shall be determined by the recording officer to whom such mortgage is presented for record, and the mortgagor or mortgagee may be required to furnish the recording officer with proof as to such facts as he deems necessary for the purposes of computing the value of the property covered by the mortgage.

Very respectfully yours,

EDWARD R. O'MALLEY,

Attorney-General.

Tax Law — Sections 2, 3, 12.

A corporation having its entire capital invested in the capital stock of certain Pennsylvania corporations which are liable to assessment in the State of Pennsylvania, is exempt from taxation.

STATE OF NEW YORK.

ATTORNEY-GENERAL'S OFFICE,

ALBANY, *July* 26, 1910.

To the Honorable, the State Board of Tax Commissioners, Albany, N. Y.:

Gentlemen.— I am in receipt of your favor of the 11th inst. in which you enclose copy of a letter from Mr. Russell Wiggins, corporation counsel of the city of Middletown. You ask to is advised as to whether a corporation, of which the entire capita. is invested in the capital stock of Pennsylvania corporations which are liable to assessment and taxation in the State of Pennsylvania. is entitled to be exempt from personal taxation in local tax districts. If the capital stock of this corporation is taxable at all it is taxable under section 12 of the Tax Law, which provides as follows:

> "The capital stock of every company liable to taxation. except such part of it as shall have been excepted in the assessment roll or shall be exempt by law, together with its surplus profits or reserve funds exceeding ten per centum of its capital, after deducting the assessed value of its real estate, and all shares of stock in other corporations actually owned by such company which are taxable upon their capital stock under the laws of this state, shall be assessed at its actual value."

Personal property is defined in section 2. subdivision 5 of the Tax Law as follows:

> "The terms ' personal estate,' and ' personal property.' as used in this chapter, include chattels, money, things in action, debts due from solvent debtors, whether on account. contract, note, bond or mortgage; debts and obligations for the payment of money due or owing to persons residing within this state. however secured or wherever such securities shall be held; debts due by inhabitants of this state to persons not residing within the United States for the purchase of any real estate; public stocks, stocks in moneyed corporations. and such portion of the capital of incorporated companies. 'liable to taxation on their capital, as shall not be invested in real estate."

Section 3 of the Tax Law provides:

> "Section 3. PROPERTY LIABLE TO TAXATION.— All real property within this state, and all personal property situated or owned within this state, is taxable unless exempt from taxation by law."

Under the decisions of the courts of this State shares of stock in foreign corporations owned by a resident of this State are not taxable. It would seem that the Legislature did not intend to tax as a part of the capital of a corporation property which would not be taxable if in the hands of an individual.

I am, therefore, of the opinion that the capital of this corporation is not subject to taxation.

Yours very truly,
EDWARD R. O'MALLEY,
Attorney-General.

Tax Law — Section 7.

Assessment of personal property tax of certain rolling stock of the Pennsylvania Railroad Company, should be made in the tax district where the principal office or place of business is located.

STATE OF NEW YORK.

ALBANY, July 27, 1910.

ATTORNEY-GENERAL'S OFFICE,

State Board of Tax Commissioners, Albany, N. Y.:

Gentlemen.— I acknowledge your letter of recent date in which you ask my opinion as to whether certain steam engines, freight cars and passenger coaches owned by the Pennsylvania Railroad Company, a foreign corporation, are assessable in the city of Olean. I note you state that if the company is assessable for this property, it is under the provisions of section 7 of the Tax Law. This section provides as follows:

"§ 7. 1. Nonresidents of the state doing business in the state, either as principals or partners, shall be taxed on the capital invested in such business, as personal property, at the place where such business is carried on, to the same extent as if they were residents of the state.

2. The personal property of nonresidents of the state having an actual situs in the state, and not forming a part

of capital invested in business in the state, shall be assessed in the name of the owner thereof for the purpose of identification and taxed in the tax district where such property is situated, unless exempt by law. This subdivision shall not apply to money, or negotiable collateral securities, deposited by, or debts owing to, such nonresidents nor shall it be construed as in any manner modifying or changing the law imposing a tax on real estate mortgage securities."

It appears from the letter of the chairman of the assessors of the city of Olean, which you enclose, that the Pennsylvania Railroad Company has at all times an average of 25 engines stationed in the yard in Olean, and an average of from 500 to 800 freight cars and 50 passenger coaches, and that the assessors believe that this property should be assessed by them.

It is clear that the capital of the Pennsylvania Railroad Company invested in this rolling stock does form part of its capital invested in business in this State. It therefore cannot come within the second subdivision above quoted since that, by its terms, has no application to personal property forming part of capital so invested. The only question, therefore, is whether it is taxable under the first subdivision above quoted. The Pennsylvania Railroad Company, although a foreign corporation, is engaged in business in this State. It is also clear that the capital which it has converted into rolling stock is invested in such business. It would therefore seem to follow that under this subdivision it should be taxable for such rolling stock unless there is some principle of law which would prevent.

It is well settled that there is no constitutional objection to a tax upon the instrumentalities engaged in interstate or foreign commerce simply because they are so employed, and that if the tax is otherwise equitable and legal it will be sustained.

>   Pullman's Palace Car Company v. Pennsylvania, 141
>   U. S. 18.

It is also well settled in this State that foreign corporations doing business here are taxable on the amount of personal property invested in such business within this State which is found within the borders of the State at the date of the assessment.

People ex rel. Armstrong Cork Company v. Barker, 157 N. Y. 159.

People ex rel. Crane Company v. Feitner, 49 A. D. 108.

People ex rel. Sherwin-Williams Company v. Feitner, 60 A. D. 628.

People ex rel. Carey Mfg. Company v. Commissioners of Taxes, 39 Misc. 282.

Conversely, it is held that personal property owned by a domestic corporation situate outside the State is not taxable.

People ex rel. Orinoka Mills Company v. Barker, 84 A. D. 469.

People ex rel. Hyde & Sons v. O'Donnel, 116 A. D. 161; affirmed 188 N. Y. 557.

In the latter case it was held that raw material owned by a domestic corporation which was in process of manufacture in a foreign state is not taxable here as personal property although it is subsequently brought into this State. In this case, also, the court holds that the proper test is the situs of the property on the second Monday in January, the date of the assessment. These two decisions follow the earlier decision of the Court of Appeals to the same effect under the provisions of the old revised statutes.

· Hoyt v. Commissioners of Taxes, 23 N. Y. 224.

In all of the above cases it is recognized that the old doctrine that personal property follows the domicile of the owner has no application in matters of taxation. It is also recognized that although the personal property may not be permanently located within the State, nevertheless if its average amount is about the same, the tax may properly be levied upon its amount at the date of the assessment.

It is, therefore, my opinion that the Pennsylvania Railroad Company, though a foreign corporation, is taxable for the amount of its rolling stock which represents capital invested in business in this State as personal property.

The only remaining question is whether this rolling stock may be taxed by the assessors of the city of Olean. Section 11 of the Tax Law provides in part as follows:

" All the personal estate of every incorporated company liable to taxation on its capital shall be assessed in the tax district where the principal office or place for transacting the financial concerns of the company shall be, or if such company having no principal office, or place for transacting its financial concerns, then in the tax district where the operations of such company shall be carried on."

It is, therefore, my opinion that the personal property tax upon the rolling stock of the Pennsylvania Railroad Company in this State should be assessed against that company in the tax district where its principal office or place of business within this State is located.

Keystone Gas Company v. Assessors of Olean, 15 N. Y. St. Rep. 461.

Very respectfully yours,
EDWARD R. O'MALLEY,
Attorney-General.

Tax Law — Section 36.

Designation by board of assessors of the town clerk's office as a convenient place for the safe keeping of the assessment-roll, is a compliance with the statute.

STATE OF NEW YORK.

ATTORNEY-GENERAL'S OFFICE,

ALBANY, *July* 27, 1910.

To the Honorable, The State Board of Tax Commissioners. Albany, N. Y.:

Gentlemen.— I am in receipt of yours of the 19th inst. wherein you state that you desire my opinion upon the following question:

" Can the board of assessors designate one of their number to take the roll and at the same time specify the town clerk's office as the place where the roll can be examined, or must the roll be kept in the actual custody of the member of the board designated to retain it?"

Section 36 of the Tax Law provides as follows:

" The assessors shall complete the assessment roll on or before the first day of August and make out a copy thereof to be left with one of their number and forthwith cause a notice to be conspicuously posted in three or more public places in the tax district, stating that they have completed the assessment roll and that a copy thereof has been left with one of their number at a specified place where it may be seen and examined by any person until the third Tuesday of August next following.   *   *   *."

This section of the Tax Law requires that a copy of the assessment roll shall be left with one of the assessors at a specified place and leaves it to the board of assessors to designate the place where " it may be seen and examined."

I am therefore of the opinion that it was not the intent of this section of the statute to require the assessor to have the actual and physical possession of the roll but that the assessors were empowered in their discretion to designate a place which, in their judgment, would be most convenient and accessible where the roll might be seen and examined by any person, and if, in their discretion, they specify the town clerk's office this would be a compliance with the statute.

Yours very truly,
EDWARD R. O'MALLEY,
Attorney-General.

Tax Law - - Section 4 — Subdivision 7 — Fraternal Associations.

Real property of Greeley Lodge No. 69, Independent Order of
   Odd Fellows, New Castle, being used exclusively for purposes for which it was formed, exempt from taxation.

STATE OF NEW YORK.

ATTORNEY-GENERAL'S OFFICE.

ALBANY, *August* 23, 1910.

To the Honorable, The State Board of Tax Commissioners.
   Albany, N. Y.:

Gentlemen. — I am in receipt of your communication of August
12th in which you state:

> " The State Board of Tax Commissioners is in receipt of
> a communication from the counsel for the board of assessors
> for the town of New Castle concerning exemption of real
> property owned by Greeley Lodge No. 69, Independent Order
> of Odd Fellows, in that town. A copy of this letter is
> enclosed herewith and your opinion is asked if such property
> is exempt from taxation under the provisions of the Tax law."

I also received the enclosure, in which the facts relating to the
question referred to in your letter are stated as follows:

> "Greeley Lodge No. 69, I. O. O. F., was incorporated
> under the Benevolent Orders Corporation Law which gives
> it the power to purchase real estate and build thereon. This
> they have done and the building is a three-story building.
> The basement of the building is used by the lodge for its
> heating plant and storage; the first and second floors are
> leased for living apartments and the third floor is used as a
> meeting place for said lodge and also a meeting place for two
> other fraternal organizations. The income from said build-
> ing after the payment of interest and insurance amounts to
> not over $100 per year and this amount is placed in the
> lodge treasury for the relief, support and care of worthy and
> indigent members of the fraternity, their wives, widows or
> orphans. As this seems to comply fully with subdivision 7

of section 4 of chapter 62 of the Laws of 1909, I see no reason why this property should not be exempt. I might add that the second floor of this building is occupied by the janitor and the rent for the same is given in payment of his services."

If the property referred to is exempt from taxation, it is by reason of that part of subdivision 7 of section 4 of the Tax Law which provides:

" * * * and further provided that the real property of any fraternal corporation, association or body created to build and maintain a building or buildings for its meeting or meetings of the general assembly of its members, or subordinate bodies of such fraternity and for the accommodation of other fraternal bodies or associations, the entire net income of which real property is exclusively applied or to be used to build, furnish and maintain an asylum or asylums, a home or homes, a school or schools, for the free education or relief of the members of such fraternity, or for the relief, support and care of worthy and indigent members of the fraternity, their wives, widows or orphans, shall be exempt from taxation * * *."

This provision modifies the provision preceding it in the same section, which exempts from taxation only that portion of the real property of a corporation or association which is used exclusively for one or more of the purposes for which it was formed and subjects the remainder to taxation, by exempting the whole of such property of a fraternal corporation when the entire net income thereof is exclusively applied or to be used for one or more of the purposes therein mentioned.

I am of the opinion that the facts above stated are sufficient to bring the corporation in question within the provision of the law above quoted and that its property above referred to is exempt from taxation.

Respectfully yours,
EDWARD R. O'MALLEY,
Attorney-General.

Tax Law — Sections 14, 25 — Banking Law — Section 2.

Individual and private bankers, where to be assessed.

STATE OF NEW YORK.

ATTORNEY-GENERAL'S OFFICE,

ALBANY, *August* 25, 1910.

WILLIAM R. WEED, Esq., *Secretary, State Board of Tax Commissioners, Albany, N. Y.:*

Dear Sir.— I beg to acknowledge receipt of your letter of the 22d inst., reading as follows:

> "Does the term 'individual banker' as used in § 14 of the Tax Law, include every person excepting a private banking business so as to render such person liable to taxation upon the amount of capital invested in such business at the place where the business is located, or is the term 'individual banker' as used in that section confined to such individual bankers as have complied with and are conducting a banking business under the banking laws of the State? In other words, is a person conducting a private bank but who has not complied with the provisions of the banking law relating to individual bankers, and who claims that he is not operating under or subject thereto, liable to taxation under § 14 of the Tax Law upon the amount of capital invested in his banking business in the tax district where the place of such business is located?"

I think the words "individual banker" as used in sections 14 and 25 of the Tax Law mean an individual banker as defined by section 2 of the Banking Law, to wit:

> "The term 'individual banker' when used in this chapter means a person who has complied with the requirements of law and is authorized by the Banking Department to engage in the business of banking and is subject to the Banking Law and the supervision of the Superintendent of Banks."

In my opinion, the statutory definition of the term "individual banker" must be followed in applying section 14 of the Tax Law.

The term " individual banker " and " private banker " are sometimes used interchangeably as synonyms and some confusion has
arisen as to methods of taxation.   There is no statutory definition
of the terms " private bank " or " private bankers."   Chapter 409,
Laws of 1882, in which the terms " individual banker " and
" private banker " are used synonymously and denote an individual
banker, was repealed by the Banking Law of 1909, chapter 2 of
the Consolidated Laws.   The term " individual banker " has
acquired a distinct meaning in our statutes and reports.   It means
a person who has received authority from the Banking Department to engage in the business of banking and is thereby subject
to its supervision, burdens and privileges.   The term " individual
banker " is a coinage of the statute law, and the term " private
banker " is only applicable to persons who are doing business
without special privileges from the State.   (See Perkins v. Smith,
41 Hun, 47; 116 N. Y. 441.)   The terms, therefore, " private
banker " and " individual banker " should be distinguished in
applying the Tax Law as well as other statutes.   (See People v.
Doty, 80 N. Y. 225.)

The residence of an individual banker doing business under
the Banking Law is for the purpose of taxation of his banking
capital in the town or place specified as the location of his banking office.   In other words, the bank, banking business and capital
of an individual banker have a location, and such situs determines
the place where such property should be assessed or taxed without
regard to the legal residence of the banker or owner; but the property of private bankers as such follows the residence of the owner.
(See Miner v. Fredonia, 27 N. Y. 155.)

Yours respectfully,

EDWARD R. O'MALLEY,

Attorney-General.

Tax Law — Section 260 — Mortgage Tax.

State Board of Tax Commissioners may in making determination
and apportionment under mortgage executed by the American
Ice Company, consider leasehold interests as " tangible property," and determine such values.

STATE OF NEW YORK.

ATTORNEY-GENERAL'S OFFICE,

ALBANY, *September* 19, 1910.

State Board of Tax Commissioners, Albany, N. Y.:

Gentlemen.— I beg to acknowledge receipt of your favor of
August 30, 1910, relative to a pending determination and apportionment (pursuant to section 260 of the **Tax Law**) under a mortgage executed by the American Ice Company covering, among
other properties, various leasehold interests, in which you ask for
an opinion:

1. Whether the board shall consider such leaseholds as are included in said mortgage as being " tangible property."

2. If so, upon what basis should their values be determined and
what information and date should be required by your board to
make the determination.

A lease of real property grants to the lessee the right of possession of the property for the term demised and may be mortgaged. When such leases demise real property for a term exceeding three years they are included in the term " real property " as
used in article 9 of the Real Property Law relating to the recording of instruments affecting real estate.

It has been held by the courts of this State that such a lease
creates an interest in real property; that a mortgage upon such a
leasehold interest created thereby becomes an interest in tangible
which affects the title to real property within the definition of a
" mortgage of real property " and that a tax is thereupon imposed
upon recording such a mortgage. A leasehold interest is not
separable from the property to which it attaches any more than
an ownership in fee is separable from the land covered by it.
When the lease, therefore, is a lease of *tangible* real property, the

leasehold interest creates a lien upon an interest in real property property; and, in my opinion, in determining values and making an apportionment under section 260 of the Tax Law the State board may consider such leasehold interests as tangible property.

In fixing the values of such leasehold interests for the purposes of this act no inflexible rule can be laid down that will cover every case as to what shall be the basis of value or what information or data should be required. Each determination must, almost of necessity, turn upon particular facts and circumstances. It is to be borne in mind that it is the value of the *lease* that is to be ascertained; and in this connection the board may consider the amount and value of the land leased, the estate granted, its duration and many like circumstances which may have a bearing upon the question of value.

Very truly yours,

EDWARD R. O'MALLEY,

Attorney-General.

Tax Law — Section 4 — Subdivision 5 — Exemption Veterans.
Veteran entitled to exemption under statute on property purchased with pension money, even though renting portion of such property and occupying the other.
(See opinion February 20, 1908, p. 496 Rep.).

STATE OF NEW YORK.

ATTORNEY-GENERAL'S OFFICE,

ALBANY, *October* 17, 1910.

To the Honorable, The State Board of Tax Commissioners, Albany, N. Y.:

Gentlemen.— Your letter of August 20th was duly received, in which you ask for my opinion as to the exemption from taxation, if any, to be allowed upon real estate owned by veterans under the following circumstances:

(a) A veteran owns a house and lot assessed at $1,200 in the purchase of which pension money to the amount of $1,000 was expended, and rents one-half of the house and lives in the other half.

(b) A veteran owns a house and lot assessed at $2,000 in the purchase of which pension money to the amount of $1,400 was expended, and rents the whole house except two rooms which he reserves for his own use.

Section 4, subdivision 5 of the Tax Law provides as follows:

"All property exempt by law from execution, other than an exempt homestead. But real property purchased with the proceeds of a pension granted by the United States for military or naval services, and owned and occupied by the pensioner, or by his wife or widow, is subject to taxation as herein provided. Such property shall be assessed in the same manner as other real property in the tax districts. At the meeting of the assessors to hear the complaints concerning assessments, a verified application for the exemption of such real property from taxation may be presented to them by or on behalf of the owner thereof, which application must show the facts on which the exemption is claimed, including the amount of pension money used in or toward the purchase of such property. If the assessors are satisfied that the applicant is entitled to the exemption, and that the amount of pension money used in the purchase of such property equals or exceeds the assessed valuation thereof, they shall enter the word 'exempt' upon the assessment-roll opposite the description of such property. If the amount of such pension money used in the purchase of the property is less than the assessed valuation, they shall enter upon the assessment-roll the words 'exempt to the extent..........dollars' (naming the amount) and thereupon such real property, to the extent of the exemption entered by the assessors, shall be exempt from state, county and general municipal taxation, but shall be taxable for local school purposes, and for the construction and maintenance of streets and highways."

I am of opinion that this exemption cannot be apportioned according to the value of the portion of the premises occupied by the pensioner. The veteran is either entitled to the entire exemption or is entitled to none. Inasmuch as he is owner of the property and occupies a portion of the same, I am of opinion that upon proper application he is entitled to an exemption of $1,000 in the first instance and $1,400 in the second.

Yours very truly,

EDWARD R. O'MALLEY,

Attorney-General.

Tax Law — Section 15 — (Chapter 428, Laws 1904, Repealing Chapter 689, Laws 1900).

Published list of exempt property, city of Oneonta, may include only such as is situate within the city limits.

STATE OF NEW YORK.

ATTORNEY-GENERAL'S OFFICE,

ALBANY, *October* 21, 1910.

State Board of Tax Commissioners, Albany, N. Y.:

Gentlemen.— I acknowledge your letter of recent date in which you inclosed communication from the clerk of the board of supervisors of Otsego county, asking whether the list of exempt property to be published in the city paper of the city of Oneonta should include all of the exempt property in the county or only that situate in the city.

By chapter 689, Laws of 1900, a provision was, for the first time, made for the publication of lists of exempt property in the several cities of the State. The act was entitled "An act in relation to real property exempt by law from taxation, and providing for the publication of lists thereof annually by the several cities of the State." The act in question, among other things provides:

" *   *   * and the said assessors or other officers making such statement shall forthwith post a copy of such statement and verification in a conspicuous place in the office in which said assessment rolls are made, and cause a copy thereof to be published in the official paper or papers of said city at least once each week for three successive weeks. The expense of said publication shall be a city charge and shall be audited and paid in the same manner as charges for other city notices are audited and paid."

Chapter 438, Laws of 1904, added a new section (§ 15) to the Tax Law, substantially in its present form and repealed chapter 689, Laws of 1900, *supra.* The time of publication was afterward changed by amendment so that two publications were provided for with an interval between publications of three weeks. Section 15 was re-enacted in the present Tax Law, and provides, among other things, for the making out and transmission to clerks of boards of supervisors of lists or statements of exempt property, and further provides:

" Immediately upon the receipt of the completed reports by the various clerks of the boards of supervisors,   *   *   *, those officials shall prepare a tabulated statement of the returns received and shall post a copy thereof in a conspicuous place, and in all cities of the State cause a copy thereof to be published in the official paper or papers of said city twice with an interval between publications of three weeks. The expense of such publication shall be a city charge and shall be audited and paid in the same manner as charges for other city notices are audited and paid."

Section 15 was designed to make the provisions first above quoted apply to all towns as well as to cities, to which it had been theretofore restricted. In framing section 15 the wording of chapter 438, Laws of 1904 (which it repealed) was followed almost verbatim. The attempt to make the language of an existing statute cover, without material change of phraseology, the additional cases intended to be brought under its provisions, has led to a situation which it does not seem to me the law intended. Publication is not apparently deemed to be of importance to afford information as to the exempt list from towns outside of cities, else it would seem that there would have been a provision for publication in some county or village paper in counties where there is no city. If there is no city within the county mere posting is sufficient. Because there may be a city within the county does not, to my mind, afford a reason why publication of the entire exempt list of the county should be required in the papers of that city, or, if there should happen to be two or more cities, why the entire exemption list should be published in the papers of each city.

What I believe was intended is that the provision as to posting the exemption list in a conspicuous place satisfies the requirements of the law so far as the property outside of cities is concerned; and that, in addition thereto, in each city from which returns of exempt property are received, there shall be published in the official papers of such city a copy of the exempt list from such city as disclosed by said returns. My opinion is strengthened by reference to the sections above referred to wherein provision is made for the making of the expense of publication chargeable against the city, which it does not seem would have been made if the list is to be an entire list from the whole county.

I therefore advise you that the list of exempt property to be published in the city newspaper of the city of Oneonta need include only such exempt property as is situate within the limits of such city.

Very truly yours,
EDWARD R. O'MALLEY,
Attorney-General.

Tax Law — Section 2 — Subdivision 4 — Sections 43–49.
Assessment of highway bridge forming part of overhead crossing of railway.

STATE OF NEW YORK.

ATTORNEY-GENERAL'S OFFICE,

ALBANY, *October* 28, 1910.

To the Honorable, The State Board of Tax Commissioners, Albany, N. Y.:

Gentlemen.— I have the honor to acknowledge the receipt of your communications asking whether a bridge which is a part of an overhead crossing of a railway by a highway is assessable by the town assessors, and if so to what extent.

You state that this bridge is built as part of an overhead crossing of a railway by a highway and constructed in accordance with the provisions of sections 62 to 65 of the former Railroad Law, now sections 91 to 94 of the Railroad Law enacted by chapter 49 of the Consolidated Laws. You further state that upon each side of the bridge are graded approaches. You also submit a sketch of this crossing which shows that the right of way of the railroad is about 120 feet and that the railroad crosses the highway diagonally. It would further appear from the sketch that by reason of the angle at which the railroad crosses the highway the crossing is more than 250 feet in length. If this is so the crossing including the bridge should be assessed by your board as a special franchise. (Sections 43 to 49 of the Tax Law.) In case, however, the sketch is not accurate and the crossing is less than 250 feet in length the matter would come within the jurisdiction of the town assessors as section 2, subdivision 4 of the Tax Law provides:

" The term ' special franchise ' shall not be deemed to include the crossing of a street, highway or public place outside the limits of a city or incorporated village where such crossing is less than two hundred and fifty feet in length, unless such crossing be the continuation of an occupancy of another street, highway or public place."

Section 2, subdivision 3 of the Tax Law makes the portion of structure owned by the railroad company real estate and taxable.

By section 93 of the Railroad Law the bridge and its abutments are to be maintained and kept in repair by the railroad company, while the approaches and the highway upon the bridge are to be kept in repair by the municipality in which the same are situated.

For the purpose of taxation I think that it is immaterial whether the abutments of the bridge are situated wholly upon the railroad lands or partly upon the lands of the highway and also whether any portion of the approaches is situated upon the land of the railroad company.

I am of opinion that the bridge itself and its abutments exclusive of the highway crossing the same or the approaches should in case the crossing is less than 250 feet in length be assessed by the town assessors.

Very truly yours,

EDWARD R. O'MALLEY,

Attorney-General.

Tax Law — Sections 253, 257 — Mortgage Tax.

Liability of Bankers Loan and Investment Company on recording of certain mortgage in Westchester county.

STATE OF NEW YORK.

ATTORNEY-GENERAL'S OFFICE,

ALBANY, *November* 4, 1910.

To the Honorable, The State Board of Tax Commissioners, Albany, N. Y.:

Gentlemen.— In your letter of September 30, 1910, you request my opinion with respect to the amount of the tax for which Bankers Loan and Investment Company became liable on the recording of a certain mortgage, bearing date July 24, 1906, and recorded in Westchester county on July 30, 1906.

It appears from the copy of the mortgage annexed to your letter that the same was given to secure the payment of the sum of $2,100 and, on a contingency named therein, the further sum of $5,000, making in all the sum of $7,100.

Section 253 of the Tax Law provides:

> "A tax of fifty cents for each one hundred dollars and each remaining major fraction thereof of principal debt or obligation which is, or under any contingency may be secured at the date of the execution thereof or at any time thereafter by mortgage on real property situated within the state recorded on or after the first day of July, nineteen hundred and six, is hereby imposed on each such mortgage, and shall be collected and paid as provided in this article."

Under this section I am of the opinion that the tax should have been collected on the whole amount for which the mortgage was given as security, namely, $7,100.

It appears from the correspondence between the register of Westchester county and Bankers Loan and Investment Company, that the latter claims to have paid the tax on the full amount of $7,100. It is admitted on both sides that the company paid to the registrar $35.50 on July 30, 1906. The registrar claims that this sum was paid to cover the tax on two mortgages, one of which was a $5,000 mortgage to the Penn Mutual Life Insurance Company by John Sabolyk and the other of which was the mortgage here in question. The tax on the former amounted to $25 and the tax on the latter $35.50. If the check received from the Bankers Company was applied partly to pay the full tax on the former and the balance of $10.50 was paid on the tax on the latter and its receipt was so entered, an action may be maintained under section 266 of the Tax Law to recover the balance due from the Bankers Loan and Investment Company.

But if the registrar made a record of such receipt of $35.50 on account of the tax on the mortgage to the Bankers Company, no action can be maintained against that company, for section 257 of the Tax Law provides, among other things:

"It shall be the duty of such recording officer to indorse upon each mortgage a receipt for the amount of the tax so paid. Any mortgage so indorsed may thereupon or thereafter be recorded by any recording officer and the receipt for such tax indorsed upon each mortgage shall be recorded therewith. The record of such receipt shall be conclusive proof that the amount of tax stated therein has been paid upon such mortgage."

As the last sentence makes the record of the receipt conclusive evidence of the amount paid, I respectfully suggest that you provide me with a transcript of the record of the receipt before any proceeding is begun.

Very respectfully yours,

EDWARD R. O'MALLEY,

Attorney-General.

Tax Law — Article 11.

Method of affixing engraved stamps to bond signed by recording officer.

STATE OF NEW YORK.

ATTORNEY-GENERAL'S OFFICE,

ALBANY, *November* 15, 1910.

State Board of Tax Commissioners, Albany, N. Y.:

Gentlemen.— I beg to acknowledge your letter of even date, by Mr. Thompson, your mortgage tax clerk, asking my opinion as to whether the indorsement upon bonds required to be made by article 11 of the Tax Law, by a recording officer, of the payment of the tax as provided therein, may be in the form of engraved adhesive stamps affixed to the bond and signed by the recording officer.

In my judgment, such a method of indorsement is. perfectly legal and a full compliance with the requirements of the law.

I am returning the correspondence which you handed me with your letter.

Very truly yours,

EDWARD R. O'MALLEY,

Attorney-General.

Tax Law — Sections 258, 263.

When recording officers believe mortgages and deeds offered for record are a reconveyance of property conveyed as security or as a, release, and no tax has been paid on the original instrument, the State Board of Tax Commissioners may direct such officers to refuse to record such instrument.

(See opinion June 2, 1910).

STATE OF NEW YORK.

ATTORNEY-GENERAL'S OFFICE,

ALBANY, *December* 6, 1910.

State Board of Tax Commissioners, Albany, N. Y.:

Dear Sirs.— On June 2, 1910, I advised you that in my opinion a rule of your board directing recording officers not to record instruments presented for record, absolute on their face but which they had reasonable grounds to believe were intended as mortgages, without the filing of an affidavit stating that they are not mortgages, was valid. I now have your letter of the 30th ult., in which you ask whether this opinion would include a rule applying to similar instruments offered for record which the recording officers have reasonable grounds to believe are intended as a reconveyance of property conveyed as security or as a release of such property, where no tax was paid on the original instrument. I note that you say there is in possession of your board abundant evidence which would warrant the promulgation of such an additional rule.

In my judgment, the same reasons set forth in my previous opinion apply equally to the promulgation of such a rule as this, and make it a reasonable exercise of the supervisory powers of your board.

Very truly yours,

EDWARD R. O'MALLEY,

Attorney-General.

Regular Army United States — Retired Soldiers.

Property purchased with money received as a retired soldier, exempt to the same extent as that of a pensioner purchasing real estate with the proceeds of a pension.

STATE OF NEW YORK.

Attorney-General's Office,

Albany, *December 23, 1910.*

State Board of Tax Commissioners, Albany, N. Y.:

Gentlemen.— I am in receipt of your letter of October 31st, 1910, wherein you ask my opinion as to whether real property purchased with the money received by one Solomon Evans on account of pay as a retired soldier in the regular army of the United States is exempt from taxation.

By the act of Congress of March 2, 1907, chapter 2515, it was provided that an enlisted man, who had served thirty years or more, might be placed upon the retired list with a certain percentage of the pay and allowances of which he might then be in receipt.

The precise question under consideration seems to have been settled in People ex rel. Kenny v. Reilly, reported in 41 A. D., at page 378. The court in that case says:

> "Accepting the facts alleged in the petition as true, that the petitioners purchased the properties against which the assessments were made, and paid for them out of the bounty paid by the United States or from the pay which they received for services rendered to the government, are they as a matter of law entitled to exemption? No good reason occurs to us, nor has any such reason been suggested by counsel, why the bounty and pay of a soldier when invested in real property, should be wholly exempt from taxation while the pension of a disabled soldier, under the same circumstances, should be called upon to contribute to the local school expenses and those of the highways."

After discussing the opinion of the court in the case of Yates County National Bank v. Carpenter, 119 N. Y. 555, the court further stated:

> "The fact that the Legislature has had this section of the Code of Civil Procedure before it since the decision in the case of Yates County National Bank v. Carpenter (supra), and that it has made special provision for collecting local school and highway taxes upon property purchased by the use of pension money, making no reference to property paid for by the bounty and pay of soldiers, furnishes a strong presumption that the Legislature never intended to exempt such bounty and pay beyond the period of its use in the purchase of exempt property for the use and enjoyment of the soldier or those who were permitted to share it with him; and in the absence of direct language, there can be no justification for extending indefinitely the list of exempt property in this State."

It would, therefore, appear that if Mr. Evans could show that the pay received by him from the United States government as a soldier was invested in the real estate sought to be exempted from taxation, and that it was being occupied by himself or his wife, then in that case he would be entitled to the same exemption as a pensioner who had purchased real estate from the proceeds of a pension received from the United States government and that the same proceedings relating to the assessment rolls should apply in his case as are applicable in the case of pensioners. The exemption would inure to the benefit of the claimant and his wife only when the property was owned and occupied by him or her, but in any event such property is taxable for school and highway purposes.

My opinion is, therefore, that Mr. Evans' position is identically the same as that of a pensioner who has purchased real estate with the proceeds of a pension and the same course should be pursued by him and by the assessors of the town where the property is located.

Yours very truly,
EDWARD R. O'MALLEY,
Attorney-General.

Mortgage Tax Law — Sections 263, 264.

Taxing of bonds secured by corporate trust and mortgage. Authority of recording officers in matter of endorsements, etc., and of State Board of Tax Commissioners to make ruling for such officers to follow. Provisions relating to endorsements after tax is paid, and when it is paid only in part, etc.

STATE OF NEW YORK.

ATTORNEY-GENERAL'S OFFICE,

ALBANY, December 27, 1910.

Hon. E. E. WOODBURY, *Chairman, State Board of Tax Commissioners, Capitol, Albany, N. Y.:*

Dear Sir.— I have your letter of the 15th inst. in which you ask me several questions concerning the interpretation of the Mortgage Tax Law.

You call my attention to the fact that section 264 of this law expressly allows owners of bonds secured by corporate trust mortgages, recorded *prior* to July 1, 1906, and known as prior advance mortgages, or the mortgagor or mortgagee thereunder, to file a statement, pay the mortgage tax thereon, and have a statement of the payment of such tax endorsed upon the bonds by the recording officer.

You ask several questions which I shall take up in their order:

1. Can bonds secured by a corporate trust mortgage, covering property situated partly within and partly without the State, recorded *after* July 1, 1906 (therefore falling under the provisions of section 260 of the Tax Law), which have been taxed upon the basis of the relative value of the mortgaged property situated within this State, pursuant to section 260 of the Tax Law, be brought in by any one (by statement filed) and taxed, either upon the proportionate part untaxed or upon the full face value thereof, and thereupon have the endorsement of the payment of such tax made thereon by the recording officer?

It is my opinion that this question must be answered in the negative. These mortgages are not under section 264, and there is no provision for any endorsement of bonds secured by them. The tax having been paid there is no provision under which the bond can be again presented and an additional tax paid.

2. Does the statute confer any authority, mandatory or permissive, upon recording officers to make an endorsement of the payment of the mortgage tax upon any bonds which have been *wholly or partially taxed* in any case where such bonds are secured by mortgage recorded *after* July 1, 1906?

This question must be answered in the negative. The only provision in the statute concerning endorsement of payment is found in section 264, which applies only to mortgages recorded prior to July 1, 1906.

3. If not, has the State Board of Tax Commissioners the authority, under its supervisory powers over recording officers, to promulgate a rule or regulation requiring such recording officers to make an endorsement of taxes paid upon such bonds, when the tax has been paid in whole or in part, similar to that required to be made upon bonds secured by *prior advance mortgages* under section 264 of the Tax Law?

It is my opinion that this question must be answered in the negative. The commissioners are given general supervisory power, by section 263, over all recording officers in respect to the duties imposed by this article, and may make rules and regulations for the government of the recording officers in respect to the matters provided for in this article as they may deem proper, provided that they are not inconsistent with statute. No duty to furnish receipts or evidence of the payment of taxes to bond holders is imposed upon the recording officers, except in cases arising under section 264. The article does specifically provide what receipts shall be given by the recording officers. It is, therefore, my opinion that the proposed rule or regulation would impose additional duties upon the recording officers not contemplated by this article, and would be in a measure inconsistent with the provisions of this article.

4. In case of bonds secured by corporate trust mortgages brought in for taxation and endorsement under section 264, where the mortgage tax security consists of real property situated partly within and partly without the State, and where such bonds have been taxed only upon the proportionate part represented by the relative value of the security within the State, are such bonds to be taxed upon the full face value thereof, or only upon the basis of the proportionate part which has not been taxed?

There is no provision in the statute for apportioning the amount of taxes to be paid on single bonds presented under section 264. In the case supposed in your question since the bonds have been taxed only upon the proportionate part represented by the relative value of the security within the State, it is evident that they form part of the subsequent advancement on a prior advanced mortgage. In that case the holder of the bond is not given the right by the statute to present them for endorsement. That right is conferred in the case of subsequent advancement only upon the mortgagor, and it is stated that he " may, at the time of paying such tax," present the bond for endorsement. I am, therefore, of the opinion that such bonds cannot be presented for endorsement by their holders if the mortgagor has failed to exercise the right.

If the bonds represent prior advancements, however, then under the latter part of the amendment to section 264 the mortgagor could bring them in. In such case the tax would have to be paid on the full amount of the bond since there are no provisions for apportioning the indebtedness in relation to the amount of property within and without the State.

5. Again, can a person who may become the owner of bonds, secured by a corporate trust mortgage covering real property *wholly within the State,* which represents an advancement upon a *prior advance* mortgage, under section 264, and upon which the trust mortgagor or mortgagee has *paid* the tax, but *did not present such bonds for endorsement as permitted by that section,* afterwards present a statement, showing that such mortgagor or mortgagee has paid the tax thereon, and have such bonds endorsed by by the recording officer to the effect that the tax has been paid, without paying any further tax thereon; or must the tax again be paid, by him, on these bonds before he is entitled to have them so endorsed?

The answer to the above question appears from my comments on the fourth question. Section 264 provided for endorsement in two cases. For subsequent advancement the mortgagor is given the option at the time of paying the tax of presenting the bonds for such endorsement. As to payments of prior advancements, either the mortgagor or mortgagee or the holder of any bond may elect to pay the taxes and present the bond for such endorsement. In the case presented by you if the advancement upon which the tax was paid was a prior advancement, then in my opinion the holder of the bond could present the same for endorsement, since the right is conferred both upon him, and upon the mortgagor and mortgagee. If, however, the advance upon which the tax was paid represents a subsequent advancement then the bond holder would have no right to present the bond for endorsement since the mortgagor to whom alone that privilege is given has seen fit to waive it.

6. Sixth, and finally, is it your opinion that the endorsement of a bond upon which the tax has been paid only in part (which would be the case where the security is partly within and partly without the State and hence only proportionately taxable), in words as follows: "Statement filed and tax paid pursuant to Article Eleven of the Tax Law," is a compliance with the terms of the statute requiring such endorsement?

It is my opinion that the language quoted is a compliance with the terms of the statute. Whether the tax is paid on the entire face value of the debt or on only a proportionate part the statement is accurate. And in view of the varying proportion upon which the tax might be based if part of the property is outside of the State it would seem to be the only practicable endorsement.

Yours very truly,

EDWARD R. O'MALLEY,

Attorney-General.

OPINIONS RENDERED THE STATE CIVIL SERVICE COMMISSION.

Civil Service Law — Rule 5.

Sheriff, Kings and Queens counties, subordinate positions in office of, whether excluded from Civil Service. (Flaherty case 193 N. Y. 564.)

(See opinion January 13, 1911.)

STATE OF NEW YORK.

Attorney-General's Office,

Albany, *April* 1, 1910.

Hon. John C. Birdseye, *Secretary, State Civil Service Commission, Albany, N. Y.:*

Dear Sir.— I have the honor to acknowledge the receipt of your various communications concerning the subordinate positions in the offices of the sheriffs of Kings and Queens counties. These communications relate to the positions of assistant equity clerk and bookkeeper of jail in the office of the sheriff of Kings county, and auditor, entry clerk, law clerk, index clerk and messenger in the office of the sheriff of Queens county. You ask me to express my opinion as to whether these positions are excluded from the operation of the civil service rules, except those relating to the certification of payrolls, in accordance with the decision in the Flaherty case, reported in 193 N. Y. 564.

The Flaherty case was a proceeding brought by the sheriff of Kings county to compel the State Civil Service Commissioners to certify the payroll of certain subordinates in his department. Prior to the commencement of the proceeding the office of sheriff of Kings county had been made a salaried office by statute, and the civil service rules and regulations had been extended to apply to the appointees in question in that case. These rules, however, were disregarded by the sheriff and consequently the certification of the payrolls was withheld. The decision of the Court of Appeals was to the effect that subordinates and appointees of the sheriff of Kings county whose duties pertained to civil matters are " not subject to the Civil Service Law, but as under the statute to enable them to receive their salary it is necessary that the Civil Service Commission should certify their payroll, a mandamus should issue directing such certification." The decision was upon the ground that a sheriff is liable for the negligence or misconduct of his subordinates and that he alone is liable, not the culpable deputy or subordinate. The court said: " The question which lies at the threshold of this controversy is whether the deputies, assistant deputies and other appointees of the sheriff are, as far as they discharge the duties of the sheriff relating to civil process, in the service of the county or in the service of the sheriff personally. * * * Before the office in Kings county was made a salaried one, what I may term the civil business of the sheriff was plainly and exclusively his own. * * * Nor has the statute which makes the office of sheriff a salaried one changed the nature of the relation between the sheriff and his appointees." It appeared that the duties of some of the appointees in question in that case pertained partly to civil and partly to criminal matters. As to these the court held: " So long as there is no separation of the duties, we think those subordinates must also be held exempt from the civil service regulations."

The office of sheriff of Queens county is also a salaried office, having become so by chapter 502, Laws of 1909, so that the principles involved are the same as to the appointees of the sheriffs of both counties. Each sheriff is authorized by the statutes making their respective offices salaried ones to prescribe the duties of his subordinates. From the communications and papers submitted to me it appears that the duties of all of the positions in question pertain, in part at least, to civil matters. It therefore appears clear to me that the decision of the Flaherty case would apply to these positions in question in the office of the sheriff, not only of Kings county, but also of Queens county.

As a result of the decision in the Flaherty case the State Civil Service Commission adopted a rule which has been approved and now has the effect of a statute, as follows:

" No provision in these rules, except those relating to certification of payrolls, shall be held to apply to any employee or appointee of a sheriff whose duty relates exclusively or in part to the functions of the sheriff's office in civil matters."
(Amendment of July 22, 1909, to Rule 5).

This rule applies to the office of all sheriffs. It therefore follows that, not only by reason of the decision of the Flaherty case. but also in accordance with the .provision of Rule 5 of the Civil Service Commission, these positions are excluded from the operation of the Civil Service Rules, except those relating to the certification of payrolls.

Yours very respectfully,
EDWARD R. O'MALLEY,
Attorney-General.

County Law — Section 169.

Court clerk in office of county clerk, Nassau county, increase of salary. · Civil service rules relating to promotion not applicable.

STATE OF NEW YORK.

ATTORNEY-GENERAL'S OFFICE,

ALBANY, *April* 12, 1910.

Hon. JOHN C. BIRDSEYE, *Secretary, State Civil Service Commission, Albany, N. Y.:*

Dear Sir.— I am in receipt of your communication of March 8, 1910, with enclosures, in which you ask my opinion as to

whether or not the provisions of the Civil Service Law and Rules
are applicable to the proposed increase of salary of Samuel C.
Ransom, court clerk in the office of the county clerk of Nassau
county.

It appears from the enclosures that Mr. Ransom was originally
appointed in January, 1908, pursuant to section 169 of the
County Law. That section, presumably applicable to Nassau
county, provides among other things, that

> " The county clerk may, subject to the approval of the jus-
> tice of the supreme court residing within the judicial district
> of the appointee, from time to time, by an instrument in writ-
> ing, filed in his office, appoint, and at pleasure remove, one
> or more special deputy clerks to attend upon any or all of
> the terms or sittings of the court of which he is clerk."

And it further provides that

> " The salary of such special deputy clerks shall be fixed
> by a justice of the supreme court, residing in such county
> and when the salary shall be fixed, the ·same shall be paid
> from the court funds of said county or from an appropriation
> made therefor."

It appears from the approval in writing of the Supreme Court
judges, a copy of which is enclosed, that Mr. Ransom was appointed
special deputy county clerk to attend the sittings· of the Supreme
Court and County Court in Nassau county. It further appears
from the written appointment by the county clerk, which is
enclosed, that at the time the county clerk made the appointment,
the compensation of Mr. Ransom was fixed at the rate " of $1,200
per year, payable monthly." This was done by the board of supervisors, as appears in a later communication from the county clerk.
It also appears that on January 21, 1910, Judge Townsend Scudder of the Supreme Court, residing in the county of Nassau, made
an order fixing the salary of Mr. Ransom on and after the first
day of January, 1910, at the sum of $2,100 per annum. The
order of Judge Scudder, fixing the salary of Mr. Ransom at
$2,100, seems to be the first time that the salary of Mr. Ransom
was, pursuant to section 169 of the County Law, fixed " by a
justice of the Supreme Court residing in such county."

It would appear from the above that the salary of Mr. Ransom was never lawfully fixed, pursuant to section 169 of the County Law, until the order of Judge Scudder was made on January 21. 1910. His salary had been theretofore fixed at $1,200 by the board of supervisors. However, section 169 of the County Law requires that the salary of such special clerks be fixed by a justice of the Supreme Court residing in the county in which the special deputy clerks are appointed, and it is only when the salary is " so fixed " that it can be paid from the court funds of the county or from appropriations made for that purpose. Inasmuch, therefore, as the salary of Mr. Ransom was never lawfully fixed until Judge Scudder's order, the order of Judge Scudder is not an increase of Mr. Ransom's salary from $1,200, but it is an order fixing Mr. Ransom's salary in the first instance. It, therefore, follows that the Civil Service Law and the Rules relating to promotion are not applicable thereto.

Yours respectfully,

EDWARD R. O'MALLEY,

Attorney-General.

Bureau of Military Records — Adjutant General's Office.

Positions in Bureau of Records War of the Rebellion in the office of the Adjutant-General of the State of New York, are in the military, not the civil service.

(See opinions March 27, 1895, p. 111 Rep.; January 4, 1905. p. 365 Rep.)

STATE OF NEW YORK.

ATTORNEY-GENERAL'S OFFICE,

ALBANY, *December* 30, 1910.

Hon. JOHN C. BIRDSEYE, *Secretary, State Civil Service Commission, Albany, N. Y.:*

Dear Sir.— I beg leave to submit my opinion in relation to the following question submitted to me by your Commission some time ago: " Whether or not all positions in the Bureau of Records of the War of the Rebellion, Adjutant-General's office, are in the military or civil service."

The Civil Service Law of the State was enacted by the Legislature under section 9, article 5 of the State Constitution; that section of the Constitution authorized the Legislature to pass laws to secure " appointments and promotions in the *civil service* of the State, and of all the civil divisions thereof " according to merit and fitness, to be ascertained as far as practicable by examination.

In the revision of the Civil Service Law in chapter 370 of the Laws of 1899, the civil service for the first time was defined by statute, and this definition is to be found in section 2, subdivision 3 of the present Civil Service Law: " ' The civil service ' of the State of New York or any of its civil divisions or cities includes all offices and positions of trust or employment in the service of the State or of such civil division or city, *except such offices and positions in the militia and the military departments as are or may be created under the provisions of Article XI of the Constitution.*"

Without considering how far the Legislature may constitutionally place positions in the civil service of a military character, I will proceed to consider whether or not positions in the Bureau of Records of the War of the Rebellion are positions created under the aforesaid Article XI of the Constitution.

The Bureau of Records of the War of the Rebellion is authorized in the present Military Law (chapter 41, Laws of 1909), in section 19. By that section said bureau is to be established and maintained *as a part of the Adjutant-General's office;* and he is made custodian of all the books, relics, records, flags, etc., of the War of the Rebellion; and it is further provided that " the Legislature shall annually make suitable appropriations to enable the Adjutant General of the State to carry out the provisions of this section." This section 19 was derived from chapter 247 of the Laws of 1887. This act of 1887 was only an amplification of an existing bureau of records and statistics in the Adjutant General's office. In 1863 the Legislature passed " an act in relation to the Bureau of Military Statistics," which provided that an abstract of its work should accompany the annual report of the Adjutant-General (chapter 113). In 1865 the title of the bureau was changed to " The Bureau of Military Records " (chapter 690, Laws of 1865). In 1866 by chapter 665 of the laws of that year

the Bureau of Military Records was organized " as an additional
military staff department to be known and designated " The
Bureau of Military Statistics " and the Governor was authorized
to appoint a chief of the bureau " who should have the rank of
colonel and be commissioned as an officer of the general staff, and
who shall be subject to the general regulations for the government
of the same." In 1868 the supply bill contained a clause " The
Bureau of Military Statistics is hereby transferred and constituted a bureau in the department of the Adjutant-General."
(Chapter 717, Laws of 1868.)

It will therefore be observed that the Bureau of Military
Records and Statistics has always been treated as a part of the
military department of the State. Its military character is further
emphasized by the fact that the Governor in effecting the transfer
of the Bureau of Statistics under the aforesaid act of 1868, and
in establishing the Bureau of Records of the War of the Rebellion as a part of the Adjutant-General's office under the aforesaid
act of 1887 treated such bureaus not as a part of the civil government of which he is the executive, but as a part of the military
service, and as a commander-in-chief he issued military orders
to carry out the provisions of the statutes. (See G. O. 10, A. G.
O., April 30, 1868; G. O. 35, A. G. O., 1887.)

The establishment by the Legislature of the Bureau of Records
of the War of the Rebellion as a part of the Adjutant-General's
office was in accordance with established military usage. (See
Farrow's Military Encyclopedia, Title " Adjutant-General's
Department; " also Ingersoll's History of the War Department,
page 194.)

It will therefore be observed that the employees of the Bureau
of Records of the War of the Rebellion have to do with military
records and property in the custody of the Adjutant-General.
It will be further observed that the bureau has for many years
been treated by the Legislature as an appropriate part of its
department, and in carrying its enactment into effect the governors
of the State have looked upon the bureau as one subject to military
administration to be controlled by military orders. The Military
Law which relates solely to the military service of the State is the
only authority for the existence of the bureau and for the employ-

ment of the clerks who work in it whose employment is expressly reserved to the military officer, the Adjutant-General of the State. It will also be observed that the Adjutant-General's office exists not merely for the management from day to day of the military force, but is necessarily the office of record of that force for the preservation of everything relating thereto.

In my judgment therefore the employees of the Bureau of Records of the War of the Rebellion are members of a bureau which is essentially and necessarily military in its character.

The only question that remains is whether because of the clerical character of their duties the employees of such bureau may be said to be not created under article XI of the Constitution.

Attorney-General Hancock in an opinion to your department in 1895 held that the chief clerks as well as other clerks in the staff department of the national guard were in the military service and not in the civil service. (Report of Attorney-General 1895, page 111.) In 1897 in a proceeding arising in that year, the Court of Appeals in Bryant v. Palmer, 152 N. Y. 412, held that armorers and janitors of armories were in the military service and not the civil service. Following the definition of the civil service in the Civil Service Law of 1899 in an opinion of January 4, 1905 (see Attorney-General's report 1906, page 365), the Attorney-General held that employees in local armories appointed by military officers were in the military service and not the civil service. (See also opinions of the Attorney-General of the United States, 19, Op. Atty. G., 533, 27 Op. Atty. G. 468. Also In re Thomas, 23 Fed. Cas. 931; 7 Dec. Comp. Treasury, 715, 14 Id., 198. Also in re Flint, 12 Q. V. Div. 488.) Taking into consideration the above decisions I am of the opinion that the employees of the Bureau of Records of the War of the Rebellion are as much within the military service of the State as are the employees who care for the military equipments and public property stored in armories. Both classes of employees deal with military public property. The difference is only in kind. There is no substantial reason for saying that an employee who prepares an order issued by the Governor through the Adjutant-General is in the military service, but that the employee who keeps the files of such papers after they have been issued is not, nor is

there any substantial reason for saying that the records of current
business are military records, and the records of business that
have been completed are not.

I am therefore of the opinion that the positions in the Bureau
of the War of the Rebellion, Adjutant-General's office, are in the
military service and not in the civil service.

In view of this holding it is not necessary to consider the second
question submitted by you in relation to this matter.

Very respectfully yours,
EDWARD R. O'MALLEY,
Attorney-General.

OPINIONS RENDERED THE STATE COMMISSION IN LUNACY.

State Institutions — Craig Colony.

Superintendent of colony may institute proceeding to have inmate
of Craig Colony adjudged insane.   (See section 113 State
Charities Law. See section 82 Insanity Law.)

STATE OF NEW YORK.

ATTORNEY-GENERAL'S OFFICE,

ALBANY, May 19, 1910.

T. E. McGABB, ESQ., Secretary of State Commission in Lunacy,
Albany, N. Y.:

Dear Sir.— I am in receipt of your communication of the 28th
ult., and I beg to submit my opinion requested therein as to the
power of the superintendent of Craig Colony for Epileptics to
institute a proceeding to have adjudged insane and committed
to an insane asylum, an inmate of his institution.

It will be noted that the status of an inmate of an institution
such as the Craig Colony for Epileptics is different from the status
of an inmate of an insane asylum; in one he is a voluntary patient,
submitting himself to treatment in a charitable institution main-

tained by the State, and in the other he is an involuntary patient,
restrained of his liberty in the interests of the public welfare.

Section 113 of the State Charities Law (chapter 57, Laws of
1909) provides:

> " Should an epileptic become insane, such patient, if a
> state patient, shall be sent to the State hospital of the district
> of which he was a resident just prior to his admission to the
> Colony, *in the manner prescribed by law* * * *. Pri-
> vate patients, who may become insane, shall be committed,
> *as prescribed by law,* subject to the regulations of the State
> Commission in Lunacy, to such institution for the insane as
> may be designated by the relations, guardians or friends of
> such insane person, * * *. * * * and after any pa-
> tient shall, as aforesaid, be so certified to be insane, *as pre-
> scribed by law,* such patient shall come under the supervision
> of the State Commission in Lunacy."

An inmate of Craig Colony, therefore, can only be committed
as prescribed by law, and the provisions prescribed by law relating thereto are in the Insanity Law (chapter 32, Laws of 1909)
section 80 *et seq.;* and provide that the certificate of lunacy of
the medical examiners, on which the order of the court must be
based, must be accompanied by a verified petition. It is provided in section 82 who may apply for an order of commitment
and make such petition, to wit:

> " Any person with whom an alleged insane person may
> reside or at whose house he may be, or the father or mother,
> husband or wife, brother or sister or child of any such per-
> son and any overseer of the poor of the town and superin-
> tendent of the poor of the county in which any such person
> may be, may apply for such order by presenting a verified
> petition containing a statement of the facts upon which the
> allegation of insanity is based and because of which the appli-
> cation for the order is made."

It will be noted that neither the superintendent of Craig Colony
for Epileptics nor superintendents of State charitable institutions
in general are specifically included within the category of persons
who may apply for an order of commitment. However, in my

judgment the superintendent of Craig Colony is within the spirit of the language, " Any person with whom an alleged insane person may reside," contained in the above section. As we have seen, he is charged with the duty under the provisions of the State Charities Law to have an insane inmate of his institution committed to an institution for the insane. Inasmuch as the above sections of the Insanity Law are the only sections under which such inmate may be committed to an instituton for the insane. I am of the opinion that the superintendent may fairly be said to be a person with whom an insane inmate resides, and he, therefore, has the power to institute a proceeding under such sections.

It may be observed that the language of the section is not as clear as it might be and an amendment of the section to specifically cover such a case as is here presented might well be considered. It may also be well wherever possible to have the petition made by one of the persons specifically named in section 82 of the Insanity Law.

Yours very truly,

EDWARD R. O'MALLEY,

Attorney-General.

State Institutions — Kings Park State Hospital.

Power of board of managers to take and hear testimony concerning charges against officers or employees of institutions and to administer oaths. (See section 43 Insanity Law. See section 843 Code of Civil Procedure.)

STATE OF NEW YORK.

ATTORNEY-GENERAL'S OFFICE,

ALBANY, *May* 20, 1910.

T. E. McGARR, Esq., *Secretary of State Commission in Lunacy, Albany, N. Y.*:

Dear Sir.— Your communication of the 11th inst., received, requesting my opinion as to the power of the board of managers of Kings Park State Hospital to administer oaths in the course of investigations made by them in relation to charges preferred against officers or employees of that institution.

The powers of the board of managers of such an institution are set forth in section 43 of the Insanity Law, which provides in subdivision 7 as follows:

"Each board shall * * * investigate, hear and determine the truth of all charges made against the superintendent or other officer or employee of the hospital, issue subpoenas and take and hear testimony in respect to such charges. * * *"

Section 46 of the Insanity Law specifically makes the above section applicable to Kings Park State Hospital.

Section 843 of the Code of Civil Procedure provides:

"Where an officer, person, board or committee has been heretofore, or is hereafter authorized by law, *to take or hear testimony* * * * in relation to a matter, concerning which he or it has a duty to perform, the officer or person, or a member of the board or committee, may administer an oath for that purpose. * * *"

These provisions of law speak for themselves. By section 43 the board of managers is given the power to take and hear testimony concerning charges against any officer or employee. Having been so authorized under the above section 843 of the code, they have the power to administer oaths.

Yours very truly,

EDWARD R. O'MALLEY,

Attorney-General.

Insanity Law — Chapter 221 — Laws of 1903 — State Commission in Lunacy — Medical Inspector.

Appointment of successor and fixing salary, subject to approval by Governor and legislative appropriation. If no change in salary, successor may be appointed by Commission without the signature of the Governor. Commission has the right to appoint a successor to Dr. William L. Russell at a salary of $5,500 without the approval of the Governor, having understanding regarding future amount, providing such agreement is approved by Governor and action of Legislature.

STATE OF NEW YORK.

ATTORNEY-GENERAL'S OFFICE,

ALBANY, *August* 2, 1910.

State Commission in Lunacy, Albany, N. Y.:

Gentlemen.— In accordance with request of your president under date of the 27th ult., I take pleasure in rendering you herewith my opinion regarding the provisions of law governing your appointment of a successor to the former medical inspector.

By chapter 221, Laws of 1903, the Insanity Law was amended to create the office and prescribe the duties of a medical inspector to be attached to your commission. This act provided that the salary should be $3,500 per annum. Under this statute, Dr. William L. Russell was appointed medical inspector and he continued in the office from September 16, 1903, until June 1, 1910.

Chapter 490, Laws of 1905, amended the above provision so as to provide that the inspector should receive " an annual salary to be fixed by the commission subject to the approval in writing of the Governor and the action of the Legislature, not to exceed five thousand dollars, and all his actual and necessary traveling expenses." I note that under this act, on January 17, 1906, your commission fixed the salary of the medical inspector at $5,000, to date from October 1, 1906, but that the amount inserted in the annual appropriation bill signed by the Governor was only $4,500 for such salary. Accordingly, Dr. Russell received a salary of $4,500 from October 1, 1906, until October 1, 1909.

By chapter 157, Laws of 1909, the provision was further amended so as to read as follows:

> "Such inspector shall receive an annual salary to be fixed by the commission subject to the approval in writing by the Governor and the action of the Legislature, not to exceed $5,500, and all his actual and necessary traveling expenses."

I note that under this provision the commission subsequently fixed the salary at $5,500 and that this amount was inserted in the annual appropriation bill for 1909, passing the Legislature and being signed by the Governor.

It now appears from your letter that Dr. Russell resigned from this position June 1, 1910, and that on July 22, 1910, your commission appointed Dr. Robert E. Doran from the eligible list of the Civil Service Commission, as medical inspector, fixing his salary at $4,500 per annum, Dr. Doran to take office August 1, 1910. Under these circumstances you ask the following questions:

> "1. In view of the terms of the statute in section 4 of the Insanity Law is it necessary that this action of the commission in reducing the salary shall be approved in writing by the Governor and receive the action of the Legislature, before Dr. Doran can take office? The appropriation bill covering the salary list from October 1, 1910, for the next year thereafter contains the item of $5,500 for the annual salary of the Medical Inspector."

> "2. If there is no change made in the salary by our commission have we the power to appoint a new man in Dr. Russell's place without securing the Governor's approval?"

> "3. Would it be improper for us to appoint Dr. Doran at a salary of $5,500, without the approval of the Governor, and have an understanding with Dr. Doran that after the Legislature has passed an enabling act the commission will reduce his salary to $4,500 with the further understanding that it shall be increased from time to time until it reaches $5,500 as a maximum?"

It is my opinion that under the language of the 1909 amendment above quoted, your commission has full power to fix the salary to be paid the medical inspector, subject, first, to the written approval of the Governor, and, second, to action by the Legislature in making the necessary appropriation therefor. In other words,

I do not believe that the statute requires the Legislature to "approve" the salary so fixed, as is required in the case of the Governor, but simply that the salary is subject to legislative "action" in providing a sufficient appropriation. From this it would follow that your commission may fix the salary at $4,500 and that such action will be effective as soon as it is approved in writing by the Governor. The Legislature having already appropriated sufficient to pay the salary at the rate of $5,500 until October 1, 1911, no further "action" on its part is necessary for that period.

Answering your second question, it is my judgment that if no change is made in the salary by your commission you have the power to appoint a successor to Dr. Russell without the Governor's approval.

Answering your third question, there would, in my judgment, be nothing illegal in your commission appointing a successor to Dr. Russell at the present salary of $5,500 without the approval of the Governor, and at the same time having any understanding with him regarding its future amount which you care to make — provided, always, that such understanding is subject to the approval of the Governor and the action of the Legislature.

I trust that I have answered all the questions which you asked. If not, I shall be glad to give you any further assistance which you may desire.

Very truly yours,
EDWARD R. O'MALLEY,
Attorney-General.

State Institutions — State Hospitals.

Kings Park State Hospital.   Right of Lunacy Commission to enter into a contract for the lowest bid for work on dining room and kitchen, and appropriate the sum of $8,500 from the emergency fund of $250,000 to meet expense therefor.

STATE OF NEW YORK.

ATTORNEY-GENERAL'S OFFICE,

ALBANY, *September* 23, 1910.

Hon. ALBERT WARREN FERRIS, *President State Commission in Lunacy, Albany, N. Y.*:

Dear Sir.— I have the honor to acknowledge receipt of your favor of the 19th inst., in which you ask for my opinion as to the right of the Commission in Lunacy to allot the sum of $8,500 from the general appropriation of $250,000 made available by chapter 507 of the Laws of 1910, in order to make up the sum necessary to meet the low bid received for the construction of kitchen, dining rooms, etc., for which an appropriation of $118,700 was made by chapters 507 and 513 of the Laws of 1910.

From your favor and from a copy of a letter of the State Architect to Hon. Sheldon T. Viele, dated September 12, 1910, the following facts are disclosed:

By chapter 462 of the Laws of 1909, an appropriation of $300,000 was made for additional accommodations at the Kings Park State Hospital.   A contract for the construction of buildings was made pursuant to this act providing accommodation in the way of dormitories and day rooms, with the understanding that subsequently other buildings would be erected providing kitchens and dining rooms.

By chapters 507 and 513 of the Laws of 1910, the further sum of $118,700 was appropriated for the construction of these necessary buildings, including kitchen and dining room buildings, conduits, steam mains, etc.   This amount was the total estimated by the State Architect as sufficient for the erection of these buildings and their connection with the groups of patients' buildings at Kings Park.   The work was advertised for construction by contract and the lowest bid received was the sum of $131,419, which, with the bid of the Prison Department for certain material amounting to $2,270, made the total cost of the work $133,689, an amount in excess of the specific sum appropriated therefor by $14,989.

Since the receipt of the bids it appears that the State Architect has made a careful examination of the plans with a view to making deductions in order that the construction contemplated might be brought within the specific appropriation. The Architect states that it is impossible to reduce the size or change the location of these buildings in order to reduce the cost; neither can the style of architecture, which is not elaborate and which is non-fireproof, be altered because it is designed to conform to the buildings now under contract. It is stated that the cottages will be completed within a few weeks, but without the kitchen and dining room buildings and necessary connections the cottages cannot be used until a new appropriation is made by the Legislature and new bids advertised for, which would possibly result in contract prices in excess of the bids now received. The reasons given for the difference between the sum specifically appropriated and the lowest bid for the work are that the Architect figured probably too closely, and that between the date of his estimate and the date of the making of the bid the price of materials had advanced somewhat.

It also appears from your communication that the Kings Park institution is overcrowded, and in fact the same condition exists throughout the whole State, and that there should be relief at the earliest possible date. The situation, therefore, with which your Commission is faced is a serious one from which there is no present relief unless it can be found that there are other funds which may be legally deemed as having been made available for this work, so as to authorize the acceptance of the low bid and the letting of the contract to that bidder.

It seems that there are certain balances which are made available under section 65 of the Insanity Law amounting to $6,500. By chapter 507 of the Laws of 1910, entitled "An Act making appropriations for construction, additions and improvements at the state hospital for the insane," there was appropriated at the end of section 1 thereof, following a list of hospitals for which specific appropriations were made, " for miscellaneous repairs, improvements, emergencies or equipment, two hundred fifty thousand dollars ($250,000)."

It is my opinion that the facts set forth in your communication and that of the State Architect constitute an emergency within the meaning of this appropriation; that a contract may therefore, all other requirements having been complied with, be entered into with the lowest bidder above described, and that the amount necessary to complete, according to that contract price, the specific buildings, over and above the two sources mentioned in your communication,. may be considered available out of the emergency appropriation of $250,000.

This opinion is not to be considered in any way a precedent and is based solely upon the statement of facts presented in the above mentioned communications and upon the assumption drawn therefrom that by your inability to accept the bid and make the contract the interests of the insane of the State would suffer, and that delay until a specific appropriation could be made by the next Legislature would result in an increased cost of these same buildings, and upon the further assumption that it is not possible by change of design or of plans and specifications to so economize in the construction as to bring the cost within the specific estimate of $118,700.

Yours very truly,

EDWARD R. O'MALLEY,

Attorney-General.

23

OPINIONS RENDERED THE STATE COMMISSION OF HIGHWAYS.

Highway Law — Section 209 — County Roads — Boundaries.
County highway in town of Delhi, an old established road. Where
no record may be found as to width, boundaries, etc., the
town superintendent may remove obstructions, cause survey
to be made, removing fences and encroachments, and opening
up road to width of at least two rods according to statute.

STATE OF NEW YORK.

ATTORNEY-GENERAL'S OFFICE,

ALBANY, *March* 3, 1910.

Hon. S. PERCY HOOKER, *Chairman, State Highway Commission,*
Albany, N. Y.:

Dear Sir.— I have your favor of February 17th, 1910, with
which you forward a letter from Deputy Commissioner Lyon,
asking for my advice in the matter of the obstruction of a county
highway in the town of Delhi, and I note that the only question
that demands consideration in this matter relates to the power and
authority of the Commission and the local authorities to remove
or cause to be removed such obstructions where the boundaries of
the highway are not definitely established.

The highway in question has been used for many years as a
public highway and under section 209 of the Highway Law it
is the duty of the town superintendent to open it up to the width
of at least two rods, and to remove any obstructions within that
width, if there is no record whatever of the road.

All public roads which have been laid out by a commissioner
of highways are required to be at least three rods in width and
this has been the law since the passage of chapter 166, Laws of
1821, and became section 80, part I, chapter XVI of the First
Revised Statutes.

The road in question is a very old road and may have become a part of the old colonial system, as provided by chapter 131 of the Colonial Laws of 1703, and if so, it was four rods wide, and the description can probably be found either in the Ulster or Otsego county clerk's office, as the last section of the act last above referred to provided that the commissioners appointed thereunder were required to make return to the respective clerks of the counties of "a full and perfect report and description of ye manner and extent of every road they shall from time to time lay out and the clerk of every county is hereby required to record all and every such return and report * * *." The county of Delaware was originally carved out of the counties of Ulster and Otsego, in 1797.

If no proper definite boundaries can be found of the road in which the obstructions appear, it is the plain duty of the town superintendent, under subdivision 8 of section 47 of the Highway Law, to have the boundaries ascertained, described and entered of record in the town clerk's office of the town of Delhi.

It is possible that a full description of this road can be found somewhere, but if none can be discovered, the road has been used as a public highway for a great many years, and if it was never regularly laid out, it has long been dedicated to the public use and has been so used for a period far greater than twenty years, and the only doubt that can exist is about its width, and if no record can be found and no width established by any records, then resort will have to be made to extraneous facts, such as the location of fences, etc., to show that the encroachment or obstructions are within the bounds of the highway.

One of the photographs which you have sent me indicates very plainly that the logs are within the bounds of the highway as fenced.

Where a highway has been dedicated to the public for the prescribed period of twenty years or more, the town superintendent may cause the survey to be made thereof and remove fences or other encroachments within the limits of such highway, and the adjacent owner has not become vested with any rights within the bounds of the highway, as against the public, to defeat such a remedy.

James v. Sammis, 132 N. Y. 239, 248.

The failure of the town authorities to cause a public highway long in use to be opened to its full width, for thirty years, does not extinguish the rights of the public in the parts not opened.

> Walker v. Caywood, 31 N. Y. 51.

User for twenty years will make a road a highway with or without dedication.

> Town of Corning v. Head, 86 Hun, 12.
> Wiggins v. Tallmadge, 11 Barb. 457.
> Chapman v. Swan, 65 Barb. 210.

If a record can be found the road should be opened up to the width provided in such record, but if no record can be found, all encroachments and other obstructions should be removed to the width of at least two rods, as directed by section 209 of the Highway Law, and if it can be shown by record, by location of fences, or otherwise, that the road is more than two rods wide, all encroachments within the bounds that can be established should be removed.

Ample authority is found in sections 52 and 53 of the Highway Law to compel the removal of obstructions by the adjacent owner, and in the event of his failure, by the town superintendent of highways, and section 55 provides for the assessment of the costs against the owner.

> Yours very truly,
> EDWARD R. O'MALLEY,
> *Attorney-General.*

Highway Law — Article 5 — State Aid Apportionment.

Action of town board of West Seneca to transfer moneys from highway fund to general fund of town (city of Lackawanna being a part of West Seneca) in accordance with section 270 of the city charter, is unauthorized by law. The board of supervisors should guard such highway moneys and keep in a separate fund not to be used for town purposes.

STATE OF NEW YORK.

ATTORNEY-GENERAL'S OFFICE,

ALBANY, *March* 10, 1910.

Hon. S. PERCY HOOKER, *Chairman, State Highway Commission, Albany, N. Y.*:

Dear Sir.— In reply to your communication of February 8, 1910, regarding the action of the town board of the town of West Seneca, Erie county, in transferring from the highway fund the sum of $13,997.15 to the general fund of said town, would say that from the papers and data in relation to the matter submitted by you with your communication it appears that in the highway year commencing November 1, 1908, there was raised by tax the sum of $21,000; that the State appropriated $9,095 as " State aid " for the town of West Seneca, which money was received by Henry G. Lien, supervisor of said town; that this money which totaled $30,095, was for the repair and improvement of highways of the town; that thereafter the city of Lackawanna, theretofore a part of the town of West Seneca, was incorporated by chapter 574 of the Laws of 1909 and organized as a city on July 7, 1909, and the territory within the city limits ceased to be under the town government; that at the time of the organization of the city of Lackawanna there was unexpended of the highway money aforesaid the sum of $13,997.15, which sum on the 31st day of December, 1909, the town board of the town of West Seneca transferred by resolution to the general fund of the town.

On the 1st day of January, 1910, Christian L. Schudt became supervisor of the town of West Seneca, and as such made a demand upon Mr. Lien for said $13,997.15, which was refused, and that

Mr. Lien tendered Mr. Schudt the sum of $1 as the unexpended highway fund.

The provisions of the Highway Law, article 5, and the rules and regulations of the State Highway Commission provide a system for the receipt and disbursement of highway moneys, whereby they can be traced from their receipt to their application. The supervisor is to receive such moneys and keep them in a separate fund from all other moneys and is permitted to disburse them only upon the order of the town superintendent of highways, and such order must state the purpose for which the money is to be expended. The plain purpose of these provisions is to prevent such moneys from being diverted from the uses and purposes for which they are appropriated and raised.

There is no authority given by the Highway Law to divert the highway moneys of a town and those raised under the " State aid " to any other purpose than for the repair and improvement of highways. Mr. Lien concedes that this is so, but claims he was authorized to transfer the fund from the highway fund to the general fund by the resolution aforesaid, and by section 270 of the charter of the city of Lackawanna.

The section claimed to be applicable thereto is as follows:

"And all unexpended moneys belonging to the town of West Seneca remaining in the hands of the supervisor of said town, or any official of said town or any other person, shall be apportioned by said referee between the said city of Lackawanna and said town of West Seneca in the manner and on the basis as is herein provided."

This provision, in my opinion, does not abrogate the Highway Law relating to the application of such highway fund. This fund, if remaining in the highway fund of the town when apportioned, could be turned into the highway fund of the city and town respectively.

It would appear from the language of the section in the sentence following the part quoted that the Legislature intended to provide against any such diversion of this fund.

The words " to the credit of the proper fund of said city " would indicate that it was the intention when the funds were apportioned that they should be credited to the same funds of the city and town respectively to which they belonged originally in the town funds.

Any construction of this charter that it authorized this highway fund to be transferred to the general fund would work an injustice to the State and the taxpayers who provided it for the repair and improvement of highways. It would also be discriminating against other towns which received " State aid " and are required to use it for highway purposes.

In my opinion, the diversion of this highway fund in question from its use for highway purposes to the general fund of the town of West Seneca by the town board and supervisor, as aforesaid, cannot be sustained by law.

At the time the charter took effect the highway fund aforesaid was unexpended moneys belonging to the town of West Seneca which would have been used for the repair and improvement of highways if such use had not been deferred by the act incorporating the city of Lackawanna. The act provides that all " unexpended moneys belonging to the town remaining in the hands of the supervisor or other official of said town shall be apportioned between the city and town as therein provided." Therefore, this highway fund, being unexpended moneys belonging to such town, the act would require that it be apportioned between the city and town for highway purposes, in the manner and proportions as therein provided, according to their respective assessed valuations, and the State would not be entitled to recover the part thereof appropriated to the town as " State aid."

Yours very truly,

EDWARD R. O'MALLEY,

Attorney-General.

Highways — Contracts.

Construction of road No. 770, Westchester county. Refusal of
Deccico Contracting Company to proceed with the work, and
liability of company and surety. In awarding new contract
Highway Commission should call for proposals on the same
plans and conditions as with the Deccico Company, or in case
of revision or change of route of highway, a supplemental
contract should be made.

STATE OF NEW YORK.

ATTORNEY-GENERAL'S OFFICE,

ALBANY, *April* 23, 1910.

Hon. S. PERCY HOOKER, *Chairman, State Highway Commission,
Albany, N. Y.:*

Dear Sir.— By your favor of April 18, 1910, I am informed
that on the 20th day of November, 1908, a contract was executed
by the State Engineer and Surveyor with the Deccico Contracting
Company for the improvement of road No. 770, Westchester
county, upon what is known as an itemized proposal, and the
specifications attached to the contract being those then in use by
the State Engineer and Surveyor; that at the time of the execution
of the contract the Deccico Contracting Company gave a surety
company bond for the fulfillment of the contract; that the contractor failed and neglected to proceed with the work and the ten
days' notice required by the contract was served upon the contractor and the bonding company; that the contracting company
still refuses to proceed with the work and that the contract has
been declared forfeited and an advertisement inserted in a newspaper at the county seat of Westchester county, and the State
paper at Albany, calling for proposals for the improvement of
the road on May 6, 1910.

You also inform me that it is possible that your Commission
may be unable to relet the building of the road at the same price
for which the Deccico Contracting Company agreed to do the
work, and that the contractor and surety company will be liable for
the excess cost of the work if it does exceed the original contract

price and my advice is asked as to whether your Commission should call for proposals on the same form used by the State Engineer and Surveyor for road No. 770 or whether you may use the itemized proposal sheet now in use by your commission.

Upon examination and comparison of the two proposals I find them quite different in several particulars, and it also appears under the proposal used by the State Engineer and Surveyor at the time the original contract was made, the bid price was in each instance placed upon the unit of the work, and this amount multiplied by the whole number of acres, yards or feet as the case may be, which were actually worked out during the construction of the road, would give the amount to which the contractor would be entitled in the end for each particular kind of work, and the aggregate amount of all the different kinds of work would make up the sum total to which he was entitled upon the completion of the work. In the contract now in use a different system is adopted; while the unit of measure is still used and itemized proposals are called for, such itemized prices are only useful in the event of omitted or extra work to determine the value thereof upon the final adjustment of the contract.. A lump or gross sum is bidden and the contract is let for such lump sum and the contractor is paid, in the end the whole amount of such lump sum which is only varied by omitted or extra work.

If it ever becomes necessary to make a claim against the contractor and bonding company it will be important to show that the new contract was awarded upon substantially the same terms and conditions as the one which was defaulted and if a new proposal was substituted for the one which was used when the Deccico Contracting Company made its contract, it might be claimed that it was a waiver of the conditions of the old contract and consequently a waiver of all damages for its default. In any event I think it would be advisable to use the same proposals that were used when the original contract was made. I also note that revised plans have been adopted and a change in a part of the route has been made, so that as the matter now stands a different road with different plans and specifications is proposed to be advertised and let. I think the State's right of recovery would be very doubtful if a different route were adopted from that which

the Deccico Contracting Company agreed to build, and it would
be difficult to reach the true measure of damage with proposals
for a substituted road.   The new route may be longer or it may
be more difficult to build and might cost quite considerably more
than the one which the company contracted to build.   If litigation
is to follow it is quite important that every defense which can be
interposed should be provided against so far as possible, and I,
therefore, advise upon this branch of the subject that your commission should call for bids for the improvement of road No. 770
on the same plans which were in existence at the time the Deccico
Contracting Company made its contract, and if changes are made
either in route or plans they should be provided for by a supplemental contract.

Yours very truly,
EDWARD R. O'MALLEY,
Attorney-General.

Highway Law — Sections 20, 93, 94, 250 — Bridges.

Condemnation of bridge over Fox Creek near village of Schoharie,
by the State Highway Commission.   Necessity for construction of new bridge which would exceed $1,500.   Duty of
Commission where town refuses to adopt any provision for
rebuilding of said bridge.

STATE OF NEW YORK.

ATTORNEY-GENERAL'S OFFICE,

ALBANY, May 3, 1910.

Hon. S. PERCY HOOKER, Chairman, State Highway Commission,
Albany, N. Y.:

Dear Sir.— Your favor of April 13th was duly received, and it
appears therefrom that your commission on October 3d, 1909,
condemned a bridge over Fox Creek near Schoharie village as
unsafe for public travel; that plans and specifications were prepared for the erection of a new bridge, the estimate for which was
more than $1,500; that a proposition for the raising of the amount

was submitted to the voters of the town and was voted down; that
the bridge is unsafe and accidents are likely to occur; and I am
asked as to what procedure your Commission should adopt in
reference to this bridge as you state there are a number of others
throughout the State which have been condemned by the
Commission.

It is provided by section 250 of the Highway Law:

> " The towns of this State, except as otherwise herein pro-
> vided, shall be liable to pay the expenses for the construc-
> tion and repair of its public free bridges constructed over
> streams or other waters within their bounds * * *."

And while section 74 makes the town liable for all damages to
person or property sustained by reason of any defective bridge,
existing because of the neglect of any town superintendent of
such town, and assuming that the right of the public for injuries
sustained by defective bridges have been properly and sufficiently
safeguarded, such provisions do not relieve the traveling public
from the inconvenience incident to the condition that exists where
a condemned bridge is allowed to remain across a stream upon a
public thoroughfare over which the public cannot travel. It is
the scheme of our highway law that the roads and bridges shall at
all times, so far as practicable, be kept open in a safe and proper
condition for the accommodation and use of the traveling public.

Section 20 of the Highway Law provides that the State Commission shall examine any bridge reported to be unsafe and if
found to be unsafe for public use it shall condemn it and notify
the county or district superintendent, also the town superintendent
and supervisor of the town of that fact. It is then made the duty
of the county or district superintendent to prepare or approve
plans and specifications for the rebuilding or repair of such bridge,
and then follows this language:

> " The town shall provide for the construction or recon-
> struction of such bridge, as provided for by section 93 of this
> chapter."

Section 93 above referred to is broad enough to meet the situation if it were not for the limitation found in subdivision 4 of
section 94 of the Highway Law which reads as follows:

"Section 94. LIMITATIONS OF AMOUNTS TO BE RAISED.—
The amounts, to be raised by tax upon the vote of a town
board, as provided in this article, shall be subject to the following limitations: * * *

4. Not more than fifteen hundred dollars shall be levied
and collected in any one year in any town for the repair or
construction of any highway or bridge which has been
damaged or destroyed as provided in section ninety-three or
which has been condemned by the commission as provided
in this chapter, unless duly authorized by a vote of a town
meeting."

A bridge cannot be built or repaired unless the money is provided in some way for the work, and we thus find the whole underlying scheme of the Highway Law defeated if the vote of the
town is adverse to the proposition. The bridges that the towns
are bound to support span many rivers, streams and ravines where
fording or other means of crossing would be impossible, and if a
town refused its consent to the construction or repair of a bridge
which would cost more than $1,500, and the bridge has either been
washed away or become too dangerous for use, the road would
have to be abandoned, travel along it discontinued and the general
public inconvenienced until the taxpayers of the town could be
persuaded to vote the necessary appropriation.

I am unable to find any provision of the Highway Law that
just meets the present situation. Section 15, subdivision 3, gives
the State Highway Commission power and authority to "compel
compliance with laws, rules and regulations relating to such highways and bridges by highway officers and see that the same are
carried into full force and effect," but there is no authority conferred upon the commission to act in the event of the failure of
the electors of the town to vote the necessary appropriation. The
right to vote upon such a question as each individual voter should
decide certainly cannot be changed by mandamus. Such action
on the part of the people calls for the exercise of their judgment
and such exercise cannot be controlled by mandamus, and there is
no power or authority given to anybody to go ahead with the construction or repair of a bridge, no matter how dangerous it may
be, if it costs more than $1,500 and the voters of the town have

registered against it, so I am unable to find any way that the repair or rebuilding of such a bridge can be compelled by mandamus.

This is an important public matter and I think the courts would be inclined to take liberal views in regard to the questions involved, upon such an application, but it must be borne in mind that by common law the expense of building and maintaining bridges did not devolve upon the towns, but by a series of legislative enactments the duty was finally placed upon them and the courts (no matter how liberally inclined they might be) would hesitate to assume the right to compel a town to build a bridge at an expense exceeding $1,500 where the electors had voted against such a proposition under the present statute.

I have grave doubts about mandamus lying to compel a town to construct or repair a bridge at an expense of over $1,500 where the proposition has been voted down by the electors of the town, but I think an amendment could be made to section 170 of the Highway Law providing that in the event of an adverse vote by the town, that the whole subject should be submitted to the Supreme Court at Special Term, upon proper notice to the town board for it to show cause at a specified time and place why an order should not be made directing such board to raise the necessary amount to make the repairs upon the credit of the town. Provision could be made for the commencement of such a proceeding upon proper proof by the State Commission or by the county or district superintendent of the county or district in which the bridge is located. I think such an amendment could be worked out that would relieve the situation from further embarrassment and provide a method that would compel the construction or repair of an unsafe bridge.

Perhaps a better remedy could be adopted by a provision to the effect that if the town liable to repair or rebuild a bridge which has been destroyed or condemned by the commission, shall fail to make any provision for such rebuilding or repairs within sixty days after such destruction or condemnation, that all State aid will be withheld from the town so failing until the bridge or bridges have been fully repaired or rebuilt and placed in a safe condition.

If the bridge over Fox Creek referred to in your letter is upon one of the main thoroughfares in that vicinity and great necessity exists for its early restoration to a safe condition, action might be asked of the present Legislature for an amendment that will force a repair or rebuilding thereof.

Yours truly,
EDWARD R. O'MALLEY,
Attorney-General.

Highway Law — Sections 19, 104, 108.

Authority of State Highway Commission over method of keeping town accounts by town superintendents and supervisors, on blank forms prescribed by the commission. The commission may also require supervisors to keep highway funds in separate accounts, and compel compliance with the rules and regulations of the commission.

STATE OF NEW YORK.

ATTORNEY-GENERAL'S OFFICE,

ALBANY, <i>May</i> 4, 1910.

Hon. S. PERCY HOOKER, <i>Chairman, State Highway Commission, Albany, N. Y.:</i>

Dear Sir.— In reply to your favor of April 1, I beg to state that by section 108 of the Highway Law it is made the duty of your commission to

> "prescribe the method of keeping town accounts of moneys received and expended, as provided by this article, for highways, bridges, purchase, leasing, rental or hire and repair of machinery, tools and implements, the removal of obstructions caused by snow, and miscellaneous purposes, which shall be uniform, so far as practicable, throughout the state. * * * The town superintendent and supervisor shall keep their accounts in the method, and shall use the blanks and forms, prescribed by the commission."

By section 104 the supervisor is made the custodian of all moneys belonging to the town for highway purposes, which includes all moneys paid over as State aid, under section 101.

By section 19 of the Highway Law, your commission is given authority to examine the accounts and records of highway money, and all county and town officers are required to produce such records, accounts, etc., for examination by your commission at any time the same be demanded.

The rules and regulations made by your commission requiring the supervisors to keep the highway funds of the town in a separate account, are clearly within your authority and considered in the light of the several provisions of the statute above referred to, it is made your duty to formulate and provide the same, and it is clear that you can compel compliance with such rules and regulations in the event of a failure or refusal to comply therewith.

Yours truly,

EDWARD R. O'MALLEY,

Attorney-General.

Highway Law — Sections 46, 97, 137, 138 *— State Roads.*

Construction of road from Farmingdale to Huntington Harbor sixteen feet in width as determined upon by Highway Commission, but in certain parts not adequate for public travel. Authority of town, with consent of commission, to appropriate the $12,000 needed for the desired widening of road to twenty-eight feet, commission to impose certain conditions in such consent as will protect said roadway.

STATE OF NEW YORK.

ATTORNEY-GENERAL'S OFFICE,

ALBANY, *May* 7, 1910.

Hon. S. PERCY HOOKER, *Chairman, State Highway Commission, Albany, N. Y.:*

Dear Sir.— I beg to acknowledge receipt of your favor of April 27th, with which you forward a copy of letter of A. Hecksher.

I am advised by these communications that the State has improved a highway (a portion of which is still under construction) from Farmingdale, in the township of Huntington, to Huntington Harbor, and it is claimed that a portion of the sixteen feet wide roadway is much too narrow for the public travel over the portion from Huntington station to Main street, and that it is very desirous that such portion of the road bed should be widened to twenty-eight feet; that it will require an additional expenditure of about $12,000 to construct a roadway of the desired width, and that some doubt exists as to the authority of the town to appropriate the amount which will be necessary to do its share of the work.

I am also informed that your commission has adopted the policy to build only sixteen feet wide roadways in roads improved under your supervision.

Ample provision is made by sections 137 and 138 of the Highway Law for the construction through villages of roads of greater width than sixteen feet, and the additional cost of construction is charged upon and paid by the village.

There can be no doubt but that the town, with the consent of your commission, as provided by section 46 of the Highway Law, can make any improvement, upon either or both sides of the roadway along the whole or any portion of the road which is being constructed by your commission, as it may desire. It would be the duty of your commission to impose such conditions in your consent as would protect the roadway which you have built or are building from encroachment or injury by the widening thereof.

The town board cannot authorize the desired improvement without a vote of the electors of the town, as the amount required exceeds $1,500 (section 94, Highway Law) but ample provision is made by section 97 of the Highway Law for borrowing any amount which the voters of the town may see fit to appropriate for constructing or repairing the sides of the road, and if a proposition is submitted to the voters of the town as provided by the last above-named section, and the necessary amount is appropriated, it would appear that all further details would be arranged and the work taken up at an early date.

Yours truly,

EDWARD R. O'MALLEY,

Attorney-General.

Highway Law — Section 130, *Subdivision* 3 — *State Roads.*

Bids and proposals for construction of Road No. 770, submitted by C. F. Jordan & Co. and W. F. McCabe. Award of contract to C. F. Jordan Company even though contract was informal and contained slight error in estimate for guard rail. Highway Commission may waive such informality.

STATE OF NEW YORK.

ATTORNEY-GENERAL'S OFFICE,

ALBANY, *May* 10, 1910.

Hon. S. PERCY HOOKER, *Chairman, State Highway Commission, Albany, N. Y.:*

Dear Sir.— It appears by your favor of May 6th that in opening the bids for a contract to complete Road No. 770, the lowest bid received was from C. F. Jordan & Co., and amounted to $33,645, and the second lowest bid was made by W. F. McCabe, and amounted to $33,916, it thus appearing that the Jordan bid was $271 less than the McCabe bid. It also appears that the Jordan Company made a bid or proposal of 15 cents per lineal foot for the work of resetting a guard rail, and that in carrying out the gross amount, it was incorrectly stated at $52, when the total amount if the same had been correctly computed would have amounted to $52.50, a difference of fifty cents.

My attention is also called to pages 2 and 3 of your printed " information for proposers," in which it is stated that " all proposals will be deemed *informal* which do not contain prices set opposite to each and all of the several items exhibited in the form of proposal, or where the gross sum for which the work will be performed is not the correct sum of all the products of the quantity of such item by the item price," and on page 3 it is further stated that " award can be made only to the lowest responsible bidder for doing the work, whose proposal shall comply with all the provisions required to render it formal."

You also inform me that your commission, acting under the impression that the above quoted regulation required that each bid should be absolutely formal, announced that the bid of C. F.

Jordan & Company was informal and the contract would be awarded to W. F. McCabe, the next lowest bidder; that a protest has been entered by Mr. Nolan, attorney for Jordan & Company, against such award to Mr. McCabe; that the contract has not been formally awarded to either party, and that Mr. McCabe has been notified that it will not be awarded until my opinion is given as to the rights and duties of your commission.

There was no doubt a substantial compliance on the part of C. F. Jordan & Co. with your rules and regulations, in reference to proposals, and while there was a mistake made in the carrying out of the gross amount bid for the resetting of the guard rail, it is one that can be waived by the commission. A strict and liberal construction of the language above quoted would lead to the conclusion which was at first adopted by your commission, but when it is considered that it was merely a mistake and the informality is so slight, I am of the opinion that it may be waived and the contract awarded to C. F. Jordan & Co. I think any other view might be violative of subdivision 3 of section 130 of the Highway Law, which reads as follows:

> " The contract for the construction or improvement of such highway or section thereof shall be awarded to the lowest responsible bidder, except that no contract shall be awarded at a greater sum than the estimate made for the construction or improvement of such highway or section thereof in accordance with such plans and specifications. The lowest bid shall be deemed to be that which specifically states the lowest gross sum for which the entire work will be performed, including all the items specified in the estimate therefor."

The simple announcement that the bid would be awarded to W. F. McCabe did not make a contract and he could not hold the State for damages on account of such announcement. If the contract had actually been drawn and signed and the bond given, a different condition would exist. As it is, neither the State nor Mr. McCabe will be injured by the award of the contract to the Jordan Company.

Yours truly,

EDWARD R. O'MALLEY,

Attorney-General.

Highway Law — Sections 208, 94 — Highways — Towns — Bridges.

Opening and construction of new highway, bridge, etc., in town of Delaware, Sullivan county, where expense of bridge exceeds $1,500, cannot be done by either the town superintendent or town board without a vote of the town.

STATE OF NEW YORK.

Attorney-General's Office,

Albany, *June* 10, 1910.

Hon. S. Percy Hooker, *Chairman, State Highway Commission, Albany, N. Y.:*

Dear Sir.— In acknowledgment of your favor of May 18, with which you forwarded to me a letter from George H. Raum making inquiry in reference to the authority of a town board to direct the opening and construction of a new highway where the expense for a bridge will exceed $1,500, without a vote of the town, I beg to state that it appears by section 203 of the Highway Law that the damages to land owners and costs incident to the laying out of a new highway are not subject to the limitations of section 94, but such damages and costs are to be audited by the town board without limitations as to the amounts, placed in the town abstract, and levied and collected in the town in which the highway is situated, and paid over to the supervisor to be disbursed by him to the several persons entitled thereto, but I think a fair construction of section 94 leads to the conclusion that if the amount required for the construction of the road and bridges exceeds the sum of $1,500 it cannot be built until the amount is appropriated by a vote of the town.

Section 208 of the Highway Law provides that the final determination of the commissioner shall be filed and entered, and closes with this sentence:

"And every such decision shall be carried out by the town superintendent of the town, the same as if they had made an order to that effect."

But it was held in Matter of Midland v. Bowron, 193 N. Y. 180, that a commissioner of highways

> "Is given no power to expend town money except such as may be in his hands within the statutory limit of five hundred dollars, and he cannot create an indebtedness against his town for the actual opening of a road." (Page 183.)

And at pages 184 and 185 the court says:

> "The town board was as powerless in the premises as the commissioner. The statute limits and defines the powers and duties of town boards quite as strictly as those of highway commissions, and the acts of either in excess of statutory authority are equally void."

The very same language was used in the part of the section under consideration in that case that is found in section 208 (above quoted) of the present Highway Law except the present law uses the term "town superintendent" instead of "commissioner of highways."

Section 94 of the Highway Law reads in part as follows:

> "§ 94. LIMITATIONS OF AMOUNTS TO BE RAISED.— The amounts to be raised by tax upon the vote of a town board, as provided in this article, shall be subject to the following limitations:
>
> *   *   *   *   *   *   *   *   *
>
> 2. Not more than fifteen hundred dollars shall be levied and collected in any one year in any town for the repair and construction of a bridge unless duly authorized by a vote of a town meeting."

In the light of the foregoing opinion of the Court of Appeals and the phraseology of those portions of section 94 above referred to, I must advise you that neither the town superintendent nor the town board of the town of Delaware, Sullivan county, N. Y., have the authority to expend more than $1,500 for the construction of a new bridge upon a newly laid out highway without being authorized so to do by a vote at a town meeting.

Very truly yours,

EDWARD R. O'MALLEY,

Attorney-General.

Highway Law — Section 60 — Cattle Passes.

Where cattle passes exist under a license from the town it is not necessary for State to rebuild or renew said pass. If unsuited to improved highway, owner must make provision for reconstruction under section 60.

STATE OF NEW YORK.

ATTORNEY-GENERAL'S OFFICE,

ALBANY, *August* 16, 1910.

Hon. S. PERCY HOOKER, *Chairman, Department of Highways, Albany, N. Y.:*

Dear Sir.— I beg to acknowledge the receipt of your communication of August 4, 1910, with the accompanying letter to you from your Bureau of Plans and Surveys, in which you ask for an opinion as to the rights of the owners of cattle passes and the duties and obligations of your department in reference thereto.

The letter accompanying your request assumes the erection and maintenance of such crossings by towns, in certain cases, as a part of the consideration for the land taken for the highway, as to which no opinion is asked. Attention, however, is particularly directed to those cases where the owner, without such consideration, has obtained from the town superintendent or his predecessor a permit of some sort to construct a cattle pass at the owner's expense, or where a town superintendent has assumed the maintenance of such cattle pass when in reality he has no justification for doing so.

Section 60 of the Highway Law, headed "DRAINAGE, SEWER AND WATER PIPES, CATTLE PASSES OR OTHER CROSSINGS IN THE HIGHWAYS," provides that the town superintendent may, with the consent of the town board, upon the written application of any resident of his town or a corporation, grant permission for an overhead or underground crossing or to lay and maintain drainage, sewer and water pipes underground within the portion therein described of a town highway. If the highway is a State or county highway, such permission shall be granted with the consent of the county or district superintendent of the town board. This section

goes on to provide the conditions upon which such crossings may
be constructed and maintained and how the permission therefor
may be granted and revoked.

It is, of course, impossible to give an opinion that will cover
every case without knowing the precise facts involved; but, assuming, as I am bound to assume from the statement accompanying your request, that the erection and maintenance of such
cattle passes is by mere sufferance or by a license that is revocable,
it would seem that it is not necessary to make provision for the
renewal by you of such structures and that, in so far as they interfere with or are unsuited to the construction of improved highways under State aid, the owners must make provisions for their
reconstruction or repair, under section 60 of the Highway Law
above referred to, or must abandon them.

It would seem prudent, not only in fairness to the parties maintaining such structures, but also for the purpose of creating, so
far as may be, an estoppel, in case they should subsequently claim
to have been deprived of property rights, to serve a notice substantially as follows:

"To ....

It appearing that you are maintaining across the highway
proposed to be improved in front of and along your premises, a private cattle pass (or flume or other structure, as the
case may be) which will interfere with or be unsuited to the
proposed improved highway, and that such occupancy of the
highway by you is by mere sufferance or revocable license,

You are hereby notified that if you desire to maintain
such cattle pass (or flume, etc.) across the improved highway,
application for such permission and for the necessary reconstruction or repair of such structure by you must be made
under section 60 of the Highway Law; and that in default
thereof within .... days the same will be deemed to
be abandoned by you."

Very truly yours,

EDWARD R. O'MALLEY,

Attorney-General.

Highway Law — Section 101, *and Articles* V, VII — *State Roads.*

State aid to towns. Whether moneys contributed for, may be used in construction of new roads or for payment of damages to property owners by reason of such construction. Legislation on subject, amendments to law, etc.

STATE OF NEW YORK.

ATTORNEY-GENERAL'S OFFICE,

ALBANY, *October* 18, 1910.

Hon. S. PERCY HOOKER, *Chairman, State Highway Commission, Albany, N. Y.:*

Dear Sir.— I received your favor under date of July 14th, supplemented by one of August 3rd, in which I am asked several questions in relation to the construction of new roads or highways laid out under article VIII of the Highway Law, the most important of which is the inquiry, whether the money paid by the State to the several towns under the provisions of article V of the Highway Law and generally known and referred to as "State Aid" can be used for the purpose of building or constructing new roads.

I am also in receipt of a letter under date of September 28th, written by Mr. Buck, Assistant Deputy Commissioner, with your permission, in which reference is made to section 101 of the Highway Law, and further examination by my department is requested of the questions involved in your inquiries under dates of July 14th and August 3, 1910.

Inasmuch as the practice of giving State aid to towns is of recent origin, it will be useful, in arriving at a correct conclusion, to briefly trace the legislation upon that subject.

The first departure from the old labor system of working highways was enacted by section 53 of chapter 568 of the Laws of 1890, and it was therein provided that any town voting in favor of the money system could raise an amount by tax that would be equal to one-half the value of the commutation rates of the highway labor which was assessable under the labor system.

This act was amended by Chapter 412 of the Laws of 1893, by providing for the exemption of villages from taxation for certain highway purposes when any town should adopt the money sytem.

It was again amended by chapter 351 of the Laws of 1898, by providing that in such towns which had adopted the money system "the Comptroller should draw his warrant upon the State Treasurer in favor of the treasurer of the county in which such town is situated, for an amount equal to 25 per cent. of the amount so levied in each town * * * to be used by him (town commissioner of highways) for the *repair and permanent improvement of such highways therein.* * * *"

By chapter 156 of the Laws of 1902 the law was further amended for the same purpose by providing that the State aid should be allowed " for an amount equal to 50 per cent. of the amount so levied in each town," * * * to be used for the *repair and improvement of such highways therein.*

The same act was again amended by chapter 228 of the Laws of 1903, and by chapter 183 of the Laws of 1904; but the amendments are not material to the question under consideration. It was again amended by chapter 478 of the Laws of 1904, by limiting the amount of State aid that should be paid to any town, by providing that the State aid should not exceed in any one year, one-tenth of one per centum of the taxable property of such town, except in towns where the assessed valuation of the real and personal property was less than $1,000,000, but in all of the several amendatory acts it was provided that the State aid was to be used for the *repair and improvement of the highways of such town.*

It was found in 1905 that so many towns were taking advantage of the provisions of the several acts hereinbefore referred to, and so many county roads were being improved and constructed under the provisions of chapter 115 of the Laws of 1898, that a large amount was being drawn from the State treasury as State aid for the repair and improvement of the highways in the various towns of the State and for building and constructing roads now known as county roads, that it would be necessary to make provisions for meeting the large drafts being made upon the treasury; and out of the conditions that existed at that time was evolved the constitutional amendment of 1905 and the legislation that followed in the interests of good roads throughout the State.

After the adoption of the amendment to the Constitution above referred to, chapter 716 of the Laws of 1907 was passed, being "An Act to amend the Highway Law, in relation to State aid in towns under the money system," which provided in substance that all towns voting in favor of the money system could receive a certain amount of State aid, and that "the Comptroller shall draw his warrant upon the State Treasurer in favor of the treasurer of the county in which such town is situated, for an amount equal to the amount of tax so levied *for the repair of highways* in towns whose assessed value of real and personal property, * * *. The moneys collected under this section and received from the State, as provided by this section shall be paid out by the supervisor upon the written order of the commissioner or commissioners of highways *for the repair and permanent improvement of the highways of the town* * * *. The town board and the commissioner or commissioners of highways shall together constitute a board to determine under this section, the amount of moneys to be raised annually by tax *for the repair and maintenance of highways* * * *."

The "money system" so called had absolutely nothing to do with the building or construction of new highways, and as the legislation providing for the expenditure of State aid only applied to towns which had adopted or should adopt the money system in working the highways and was only granted to aid such towns in *the repair and improvement of highways,* it is clear that down to the enactment of chapter 330 of the Laws of 1908 (present Highway Law) none of the State aid money could be used or appropriated for the building or construction of new highways, laid out by statute in the various towns.

Article 5 of the Highway Law deals with the subject of State aid. Section 101 thereof provides in part as follows:

" There shall be paid by the State to the several towns, in the manner hereinafter provided, an amount based upon the amount of taxes levied therein *for the repair and improvement of highways, sluices, culverts and bridges having a span of less than five feet,* and to be determined as follows: (The balance of the section relates to the apportionment of the State aid in the several towns.)

Section 105 of the same law is entitled, " Expenditures for repair and improvement of highways," and the section reads in part as follows:

> " The moneys levied and collected for the repair and improvement of highways, including sluices, culverts and bridges having a span of less than five feet, and the moneys received from the state, as provided by section one hundred and one, shall be expended for the *repair and improvement* of such highways, sluices, culverts and bridges, at such places and in such manner as may be agreed upon by the town board and town superintendent.'

It will be noted that the present law uses the same language as the older statutes, allowing towns under the money system to have State aid, and it is needless to say that the money system related exclusively to the working and repair of highways, and had no relation whatever to the building of new roads, laid out by town authority. It was first granted to those towns which adopted the money system of working their highways, and has been continued for that purpose alone, and by the new highway law all towns are brought under the money system and State aid is given them to aid in the *repair and improvement* of their highways, and many hundred thousand dollars are expended annually by the State for that purpose, and if the Legislature had intended that such money could be used for building new highways, buying machinery, building bridges, removing obstructions or any other purpose than the repairs and maintenance of the roads, there would have been some language employed or intimation given that such was its intention, and a right to use it for building new roads would have been indicated in some way and not allowed to depend upon doubtful and ambiguous terms.

The only way that the statute can be construed to authorize the building of new roads with the moneys known as State aid, is by giving the word " improvement " a strained and unnatural construction, one which is unwarranted by the word itself, the manner in which it is used, the purposes for which it was called into use in the first instance, and the distinction made by the Legislature between " constructions of new highways " and " permanent improvement of existing highways " as shown in section 48 and other provisions of the Highway Law.

The subject has been up here in the Attorney-General's office in both 1904 and 1906, and on both occasions the same conclusion was reached that I have been forced to adopt.

Attorney-General's Report, 1904, page 308.
Attorney-General's Report, 1906, page 341.

It would be a bad precedent to hold that the State aid can be diverted for the purpose of building new town roads, for if it can be used for that it can be used for buying machinery, removing snow, building bridges or any other purpose which the town authorities might see fit to use it for, and thus defeat a very wise scheme of the statute and the intention of the Legislature, and instead of having good roads, kept in good repair, we would have no repairs, if there happened to be a new road or bridge to build in the town, and the State Highway Commission would be powerless to enforce its rules and regulations in reference to the maintenance of the town roads in the town, and the town superintendent would be unable to keep the highways in order for lack of funds.

It is claimed that the language used in section 48 justifies the contention that such money can be used for the building of new roads, and that part relied upon reads as follows:

> " When such work (building new roads) is completed pursuant to the terms of such contract, and the plans and specifications therefor are accepted by the district or county superintendent and town board, as being in accordance therewith, the cost of the work under the contract shall be paid out of moneys available therefor, in the same manner as other highway expenses."

It is evident that to use such moneys for building new roads would be in direct violation of the above quoted portion of section 48, for the moneys raised for the repair and improvement of highways, including the State aid, are never " available " for the construction of new town roads and cannot be legally diverted to any other use. The different funds are required to be kept separate by section 107 of the Highway Law, also by order of the

State Highway Commission, and a surplus in one fund is not available for use in other work.

I am, therefore, of the opinion that moneys known as " State aid " cannot be used for the building and construction of new town roads, or for the payment of damages awarded to land owners for the laying out of a new highway, or for any other purpose except the repair and improvement of the highways of the town.

In reply to that part of your inquiry as to how the town can procure the necessary money to build a highway " if it cannot be taken from the general fund for repair and improvement of highways," I beg to state that section 90 of the Highway Law requires the town superintendent to make estimates of the amounts that should be raised by tax in the town for the ensuing year, and by subdivision 4 thereof he could make an estimate and present it to the town board of the amount which he deems necessary should be raised for building a town highway that has been newly laid out. It is certainly a miscellaneous purpose not provided for in any other subdivision of that section. There is no limitation of the amount that can be raised for miscellaneous purposes except as it is controlled by the public necessities of the town. It is also a purpose that can only arise occasionally in any town and is not of annual recurrence like most of the other purposes mentioned in the act referred to.

The estimates above mentioned are then laid before the town board and if it approves, the several amounts are laid before the board of supervisors and raised in the same way as other highway taxes in the town, but if this method is not deemed expedient, and if any town board should not feel that it was authorized to raise the amount as above outlined, a proposition can be submitted as provided by section 97 of the Highway Law, to the voters of the town.

Yours very truly,

EDWARD R. O'MALLEY,

Attorney-General.

Highway Law — State and County Roads.

Not the intent of chapter 233, Laws 1910, to allow construction of county highways through cities, even to form a connecting link. City of Rensselaer may not have county road built through its streets.

STATE OF NEW YORK.

ATTORNEY-GENERAL'S OFFICE,

ALBANY, *October* 20, 1910.

Hon. S. PERCY HOOKER, *Chairman of State Highway Commission, Albany, N. Y.:*

Dear Sir.— After a careful examination of section 123 of the Highway Law, as amended by chapter 487, Laws of 1909, and section 137, as amended by chapter 233, Laws of 1910, I do not think it was the intention of the Legislature to allow the construction of a county highway through a city, even to form connecting link between other highways which have been or may be improved under article VI of the Highway Law.

The only provision I am able to find that could possibly be construed as authorizing the construction of a county highway in a city is found in section 123 of the Highway Law, amended by chapter 487, Laws of 1909, and upon a careful reading of the same, in connection with other provisions of the Highway Law, I am of the opinion that it was the intention of the Legislature that the words " unless it be necessary to complete the connection of such highway with a highway already improved or to be improved under this article," should apply only to a connecting link through a village, and does not apply to a connection to be made through a city, and in reply to your inquiry under date of October 5th, I therefore advise you that a county highway cannot be constructed through a street of the city of Rensselaer.

Yours truly,
EDWARD R. O'MALLEY,
Attorney-General.

Highway Law — Section 54.

Duty of abutting owners to cut weeds and brush and remove obstructions from highway.

STATE OF NEW YORK.

Attorney-General's Office,

Albany, *October* 25, 1910.

Hon. S. Percy Hooker, *Chairman, State Highway Commission, Albany, N. Y.:*

Dear Sir.— I beg to acknowledge receipt of your communication of September 8th, 1910, supplemented by your further communication of September 19th, 1910, relative to the construction of section 54 of the Highway Law.

My opinion is asked on the following questions:

1. Where a highway has been constructed entirely across one man's land, his title extending to the line fence and including the roadway, is the obligation to cut the weeds and brush upon both sides of the road upon him?

2. In case he refuses, or neglects to cut such weeds and the work is done by the town superintendent, will that portion of the assessment for cutting the weeds and brush on the farther side, lie against such owner?

3. Assuming that the title to the land on either side of the highway runs only to the highway fence and includes no portion of the highway, is there any question of the duty of the abutting owner to cut the weeds and brush?

The portion of section 54 of the Highway Law to which you direct my attention provides as follows:

> "It shall be the duty of the owner or occupant of lands situated along the highway to cut and remove the noxious weeds growing within the bounds of the highway, fronting such lands * * *. Unless otherwise directed by the commission it shall be the duty of such owner or occupant to cut and remove all briers and brush growing within the bounds of the highway, fronting such lands, * * * it

shall also be the duty of such owner or occupant to remove brush, shrubbery and other obstructions within the bounds of the highway, causing the drifting of snow upon said highway, * * *."

The section goes on to provide that if such owner or occupant fails to cut or remove such brush, weeds, etc., the town superintendent shall cause the same to be done and the expense thereby incurred shall be paid out of the moneys available therefor, and the amount thereof shall be charged against such owner or occupant.

Section 55 of the same law provides that the town superintendent shall assess the cost of cutting and removing weeds, etc., against the owner, occupant or company neglecting to perform the duty imposed by the section above referred to. The section specifies the notice to be given and the various steps to be followed in making such assessment and its presentation to the board of supervisors who are to cause the amount stated therein to be levied against such owner, occupant or company; and declares that any uncollected tax shall be a lien upon the land affected.

Section 54 as it now stands is the outgrowth of progressive amendment of former laws until it reached its present shape. The statute was, at one time, limited to a provision requiring the owner or occupant of lands abutting on a highway to cut all weeds, etc., *growing upon such lands* within the bounds of the highway. A section was subsequently added making it the duty of the *owner* of lands situated along a highway to cut the weeds, etc., along the sides of the highway fronting his lands. The law as declared by these sections was variously amended, from time to time. The words " growing upon such lands " were omitted and the provision was changed to require of owners and *occupants* of any lands situate along a highway to cut and remove all weeds, brush, etc., within the bounds of the highway fronting such lands.

Those sections were consolidated under section 54 of the Highway Law of 1908, since which time the law has been as it now appears in section 54 of the present Highway Law, referred to by you.

In order to keep the highways free from noxious weeds that may spread and from briers and brush that may interfere with the free use of the highway and from obstructions that may cause drifting snow, the State has exercised its police power by enacting that certain persons, for their own and the general good, shall be charged with the duty of cutting down and removing such weeds, brush, etc. The persons selected are those who, from the situation of the lands owned or occupied by them, have the power and ability to perform this work with the promptness and convenience which the benefit of the community requires. It is made the duty of the owner *or occupant* of lands situated along the highway to cut the weeds, etc., growing *within the bounds of the highway* fronting on such lands. By the statute it seems that the question of ownership of the fee of any part of the highway does not necessarily enter into the consideration. The duty is imposed upon him whose land lies along the highway, whether his title to such land includes the entire width of the highway or whether he owns to the center of the highway only or whether he runs only to the highway fence and has no fee in any part of the land included in the highway. Such duty is likewise laid upon the occupant of such lands equally with the owner. Moreover, the cutting and removing is not restricted to the weeds, brush, etc., on one side of the roadway, but extends to those growing within the bounds of the highway.

In view of the foregoing I answer your first and second questions above set forth in the affirmative and also give it as my opinion that, upon the assumption contained in your third question, the duty is likewise imposed upon the abutting owner to cut the weeds and brush.

The intelligent enforcement of the statute lies with the town superintendent as to whether, under the circumstances, he shall require any owner or occupant to cut and remove the weeds, brush, etc., on both sides of the highway.

Respectfully yours,

EDWARD R. O'MALLEY,

Attorney-General.

Highways.

Construction of storm sewer by State contractor under the tracks of the New York Central Railroad at Albany street, Herkimer. Additional expenditure of $7.80 by railroad company for alleged shoring or props not furnished by contractor, not a proper charge against the State.

STATE OF NEW YORK.

ATTORNEY-GENERAL'S OFFICE,

ALBANY, *November* 2, 1910.

Hon. ROBERT EARL, *State Highway Commission, Albany, N. Y.:*

Dear Sir.— I beg to acknowledge the receipt of your favor of the 11th instant. I am also in receipt of a letter from Alexander S. Lyman, general attorney for the N. Y. C. & H. R. R. Co., relating to the same subject, by which I am informed that last summer a contractor of the State, James W. Johnson, was given permission by the above company to construct a storm sewer under the tracks of the company in Albany street, Herkimer, which necessitated an expenditure of $7.80 on the part of the company to support its tracks, during the work for which they ask reimbursement, and I am requested to advise you whether the above amount is a proper charge against the State, or not.

I take it that it became necessary in the construction of the road in question to provide an outlet for water that accumulated upon or along the street in times of storm, and that the most practicable way to dispose of it was to carry it under the company's line, that permission was given by the company, and the sewer was accordingly constructed.

It appears that during the work the support provided by the contractor was not regarded as absolutely safe and sufficient by the company, and that it caused some additional timbers or props to be put into position for the purpose of strengthening its roadbed, and expended for that purpose the aforesaid sum of $7.80.

Under these conditions I think it very clear that under the principle laid down in the cases of Interborough R. T. Co. v. Gallagher, 44 Misc. 536, affirmed in 96 App. Div. 632; Brooklyn El.

24

R. R. Co. v. City of Brooklyn, 2 App. Div. 98, the New York Central & H. R. R. R. Co. must stand the additional expense made necessary by the work of putting in the storm sewer, and I therefore advise you that the State is not liable to the company for $7.80 referred to.

Yours truly,
EDWARD R. O'MALLEY,
Attorney-General.

Highway Law — State and County Roads.

Right of State Highway Commission to regulate the use of traction engines in hauling stone, etc., over the public highways, by restricting weight of loads.

(See opinion July 13, 1909, p. 654, Report.)

STATE OF NEW YORK.

Attorney-General's Office,

Albany, December 16, 1910.

Hon. S. Percy Hooker, *Chairman, State Highway Commission, Albany, N. Y.:*

Dear Sir.— In reply to your favor of August 18th relating to proposed rules and regulations restricting use of traction engines hauling heavy loads of stone over State and county highways, I beg to state that I think the rule submitted would be a discrimination against the use of the public highways by persons or parties desiring to use traction engines, as it absolutely prohibits them from traveling over the State and county roads with traction engines except to pass from one site of work to another, thereby depriving a certain class of the liberty which the Constitution guarantees to all persons, but as stated in a former opinion under date of July 13, 1909, I think you have the right to regulate the use of the road by limiting the weight of loads to be drawn over or upon the same.

Would not a notice similar to the following answer every purpose?

"Any person using a traction engine upon any state or county highway for the purpose of drawing heavy loads is hereby prohibited from carrying along or upon such roads any loads of greater weight than —— tons, upon a single cart, wagon, truck or other vehicle; and the tires of all such loaded vehicles shall be at least eight inches wide. All stone scattered along the route of such highways by persons using the same shall be cleaned up and removed by the person, firm or corporation under whose employment the same were scattered. All persons, firms, contractors or corporations using the State and county highways for hauling or drawing heavy loads along or over the same will be required to repair the same if it is injured by such use, and will be held liable for all damages which may be occasioned to such State or county highways by the use thereof for the purposes above specified."

I think the above or something along those lines would be only a reasonable regulation which the courts would uphold, and at the same time might be a sufficient remedy for the trouble complained of.

I would also suggest that in the future a provision or covenant be incorporated in your contracts to the effect that the contractor shall not draw any of the material over or along a State or county highway with a traction engine. Such a provision would probably be more salutary than the promulgation of any rule or regulation you may make, but it could only be made to apply to future contracts.

Yours truly,

EDWARD R. O'MALLEY,

Attorney-General.

*Highway Law — Chapter 247, Laws 1910 — State and County
Roads.*

Supplemental contracts. Effect of repeal of certain provisions of
Highway Law upon contracts for roads made previous to
such repeal, and also where such surveys and estimates were
made and resolution passed by board of supervisors, but contract not let until after said act became a law.

STATE OF NEW YORK.

ATTORNEY-GENERAL'S OFFICE,

ALBANY, *December* 19, 1910.

Hon. S. PERCY HOOKER, *Chairman, State Highway Commission,*
Albany, N. Y.:

Dear Sir.— I am in receipt of your favor of the 17th inst.,
asking for my opinion as to the effect which the amendment and
repeal of certain provisions of the Highway Law, made by chapter
247 of the Laws of 1910, will have upon supplemental contracts
relating to roads for the construction of which contracts have been
made previous to such repeal; and also what effect such act would
have upon the construction of roads where the initiatory steps had
been taken, surveys and estimates made, and the final resolution
passed by the boards of supervisors, but contract not let until after
the time when such act took effect. I have also received an inquiry
from the Comptroller under date of December 10th, asking for an
opinion as to the effect of such act on supplemental contracts
(which subject is involved in your first inquiry), and I will therefore answer both inquiries in this communication.

By chapter 717 of the Laws of 1907, it was provided that boards
of supervisors were authorized to adopt final resolutions approving
plans, specifications, etc., for construction of roads within their
counties, and to either appropriate and make immediately available the county's and town's shares of the expense of such road, or
it could request the State to advance the entire cost of the work
in the first instance, and charge the county and town annually each

year for a period of fifty years with such an amount as would at the end of that time repay the State the amount so advanced with interest.

The same provisions were substantially contained in chapter 33 of the Laws of 1908 (new Highway Law) and were re-enacted in the Consolidated Laws of 1909.

By the aforesaid chapter 247 of the Laws of 1910 several sections of the Highway Law were amended and some portions repealed and that part of the statute which provided for the payment of the entire expense of construction of county roads, by the State in the first instance and the charging back of the county's and town's share thereof upon such municipalities was repealed, and the boards are now required to appropriate and make immediately available the county's and town's share of the cost thereof. This act took effect May 6, 1910.

It now appears that in several instances contracts have been let for the construction of highways and the boards of supervisors availed themselves of the privilege given them by the statute to have the entire amount paid in the first instance by the State, and while the work was in process of construction it was deemed expedient to make some changes in the original contracts, and since May 6, 1910, supplemental contracts have been made in relation to some roads which in some instances involved an additional expenditure.

In all such cases the parties are not affected by the changes made by the enactment of the last aforesaid act, and the additional expenses caused by such supplemental contracts should be paid in the first instance by the State and charged back against the county and town as provided by the statute before such changes were made.

The statute as it stood before chapter 247 took effect, when acted upon by the board of supervisors before such change was made created contractual relations between the State and the counties and towns which could not be changed or impaired by subsequent enactment. The respective parties' rights became vested upon the execution of the original contract, and both parties had the right to rely upon the continuance of their contractual relations, not only in reference to such original contract but in reference to all sup-

plemental contracts relating to the same work and the same could
not be abrogated by later legislation.

> Cooley on Constitutional Limitations, p. 238.
> People ex rel. Fountain v. Supervisors of Westchester,
>   4 Barb. 64, cited with approval in Van Dyke v.
>   McQuade, 86 N. Y. 38, at 49.
> Close v. Patten, 2 Misc. 1.
> Benson v. The Mayor, etc., 10 Barb. 223.
> Louisiana v. Police, 111 U. S. 716.
> Edwards v. Kerzay, 96 U. S. 595.

In reference to those roads in which no contracts have been
awarded, prior to May 6, 1910, but where resolutions have been
passed by the board of supervisors, surveys and estimates made by
State Engineer or Highway Commission, and plans approved by
the board of supervisors, providing for the State to advance the
entire cost in the first instance, the law is not so clear. It is provided by section 128 of the Highway Law in part as follows:

> " When a board of supervisors has once adopted a resolution
> providing for the construction or improvement of a highway
> or a section thereof in accordance with such plans and speci-
> fications, no resolution thereafter adopted by such board shall
> rescind or amend such prior resolution either directly or indi-
> rectly, excepting under the advice and with the consent of the
> commission."

It is also specified by chapter 247 id., that where a final resolution has been previously adopted, providing for a payment in the
first instance of the entire expense of the construction of a road by
the State, that the board of supervisors may adopt a resolution
rescinding and changing the former resolution so as to provide for
the appropriation of the county's and town's shares, and make the
same immediately available, and then as a part of the same section
we find the following: " If such prior resolution shall not be so
rescinded it shall have the same force and effect which it had
prior to the amendment of this section."

I think it is clear from the sentence last above quoted, that the
Legislature intended that in all cases where the final resolution
had been adopted by the board requiring payment of the whole

amount by the State in the first instance that it should be carried through according to such resolution unless the board voted a change to the other plan, and such an intention would be in keeping with the case hereinbefore cited.

I am therefore of the opinion that all roads being constructed, or that may hereafter be constructed under a resolution adopted prior to May 6, 1910, providing that the whole expense shall in the first instance be paid by the State, will have to be carried through and payments made in that way, unless the resolution is changed as provided by chapter 247.

Yours truly,

EDWARD R. O'MALLEY,

Attorney-General.

OPINIONS RENDERED THE STATE COMMISSION ON NEW PRISONS.

Prison Law — Chapter 447, Laws 1909 —·Contracts — State Prisons.

Erection prison at Sing Sing. Appropriation by Legislature for $2,220,000, and making but $500,000 of such amount available, is constitutional even though the contract incurs expenditure exceeding the $500,000 — and supersedes section 35, State Finance Law. State Constitution, article III, section 21, forbids appropriations being made by the Legislature which are not available within two years after passage of act.

STATE OF NEW YORK.

ATTORNEY-GENERAL'S OFFICE,

ALBANY, *January* 24, 1910.

Hon. GEORGE McLAUGHLIN, *Secretary, Commission on New Prisons, Capitol, Albany, N. Y.:*

Dear Sir.— I have your letter of the 24th inst., in which you request my opinion on the following questions:

You state that by section 2 of chapter 447, Laws of 1909, your commission was authorized to let a contract for the erection and completion of a prison plant to take the place of Sing Sing, at a cost not exceeding $2,200,000, and made the sum of $500,000, of such amount available at once but made no appropriation for the additional expenditure authorized.

You ask two questions — first, whether, in my judgment, these provisions are in constitutional form, that is, whether or not the Legislature can authorize a contract incurring an expenditure exceeding the amount of the appropriation made available to meet the expenditure, and, second, whether the Legislature could appropriate the whole amount, making one-third available the first year after the act took effect, one-third the second year, and one-third the third year, or whether all of such appropriation must be made available within two years after the passage of the act.

I have carefully examined the act in question, and in my opinion the first question must be answered in the affirmative. The only provision preventing a contract being made in excess of the amount appropriated is found in section 35 of the State Finance Law. This, not being a constitutional requirement, may be superseded by the Legislature in any particular case. Section 2, chapter 447, Laws of 1909, specifically authorizes entering into such a contract and therefore, to that extent, supersedes the general provision of the Finance Law above referred to.

Upon the second point I must advise you that under the Constitution it would be impossible for the Legislature to appropriate the amount for this purpose, making the same available more than two years after the passage of the act. The Constitution provides, in article III, section 21:

" Appropriation bills.— § 21. No money shall ever be paid out of the treasury of this state, or any of its funds, or any of the funds under its management, except in pursuance of an appropriation by law; nor unless such payment be made within two years next after the passage of such appropriation act; * * *."

Under the foregoing provision it is clear, in my opinion, that no appropriation can be made by the Legislature which is not available within two years after the date of the passage of the act.

Yours respectfully,

EDWARD R. O'MALLEY,

Attorney-General.

State Prisons — Great Meadow Prison.

Appropriation of $738,000 by chapter 65, Laws of 1910. Plans by State Architect for construction of prison. Adoption by Commission on New Prisons of certain changes in plans increasing expense beyond amount appropriated. Where appropriation for work may be exhausted before completion such plans should be agreed upon as will bring the entire work within the appropriation, or the matter should be presented to the Legislature for further appropriation.

(See opinion December 13, 1910.)

STATE OF NEW YORK.

ATTORNEY-GENERAL'S OFFICE,

ALBANY, *June* 10, 1910.

GEORGE McLAUGHLIN, ESQ., *Secretary, Commission on New Prisons, Albany, N. Y.:*

Dear Sir.— I beg to acknowledge the receipt of your letter of May 26, 1910, asking my opinion concerning the appropriation for the Great Meadow prison.

Your communication refers to chapter 65 of the Laws of 1910, which appropriates $738,000 for buildings at this prison site. You call attention to the statute which appropriates this sum

" for completing, equipping and furnishing the buildings now in course of construction at the Great Meadow prison in accordance with the provisions of chapter four hundred and fifty-nine of the laws of nineteen hundred and nine, including the completion, equipment and furnishing of the north wing

and the cell house, to provide accommodations for not less
than six hundred prisoners; and for the construction and
equipment and furnishing of the cage, connecting corridors,
laundry and bath-house, mess hall, kitchen, bakery, storehouse, powerhouse and punishment prison, including heating,
lighting and plumbing of the same; and for a permanent
sewage disposal system."

This act also provides that the plans for the above structures
shall be prepared by the State Architect and be subject to the
approval of the Commission on New Prisons and also of the State
Commission of Prisons.

It appears from your letter and also from facts presented to me
by the State Architect that, since the appropriation act above
quoted was passed, some of the members of the Commission on
New Prisons have been considering the advisability of adopting
changes in the plans which will increase the cost of the work,
possibly beyond the amount appropriated. It seems that at the
time the sum of $738,000 was decided upon, these changes in con-
struction had not been contemplated either by the Legislature or
by the persons who had in charge the computation of the estimates
of the cost of the proposed work.

The question presented is this: Assuming these changes in the
plans will absorb the whole appropriation without finishing the
work, can it legally be begun and the appropriation exhausted
without bringing to a final completion all the work specified in
the act?

As to the construction of the north wing, it seems clear that the
Legislature intended that this particular part of the work should,
in any event, be constructed within the appropriation. Your
attention is called to the fact that the act uses the words " completing " and " completion " when speaking of the north wing and
of the buildings already in course of construction. It specifies
that the money is appropriated for the completion of the north
wing to provide for six hundred prisoners. Therefore, there
seems to be no doubt that the north wing must be fully completed,
equipped and furnished with the money appropriated by this act.

As to the remaining buildings and structures, the question is
not so readily answered. In many contingencies it is lawful and

proper to expend an appropriation on a public work without completing it. Unforeseen difficulties often arise involving additional expense. Conditions occur which are impossible to forecast and expenditures become necessary which cannot be previously estimated. On this account it probably cannot be said that it is unlawful to expend any of this money until such a time as it can be definitely determined that the work could be wholly finished within the appropriation.

But, when it is planned, at the outset, to begin the construction of a public work in such a manner as will exhaust the appropriation without completing the work, another question arises. In my judgment such a procedure would be contrary to the intent of the statute. This conclusion may not be altogether free from doubt, but it is strongly fortified by the principles of public policy. If doubt exists in the interpretation of a statute, that doubt may and should be resolved in favor of that interpretation which is supported by a wise and sound public policy, concerning which, in this instance, there can be no uncertainty.

Whatever might be held to be the technical effect of the statute, unquestionably the Legislature supposed, when it appropriated $738,000, that this sum was in fact sufficient to complete the buildings and structures specified in the act.

In view of the foregoing considerations my conclusion is that plans should be agreed upon, if possible, under which the whole work can be done within the appropriation. If such plans can not be agreed upon, then the difficulty should be presented to the Legislature, the members of which should be given to understand that the money they had voted for this work was inadequate for a proper construction of it. Then intelligent and definite action could be taken by the Legislature in the premises, and the officers charged with the duty of constructing this work could act accordingly.

Yours respectfully,

EDWARD R. O'MALLEY,

Attorney-General.

State Commission of Prisons.

Right of to inspect and approve plans for the erection of a building
as part of the New York City Reformatory, at Hart's Island.

STATE OF NEW YORK.

ATTORNEY-GENERAL'S OFFICE,

ALBANY, *August* 20, 1910.

GEORGE MCLAUGHLIN, Esq., *Secretary, State Commission of
Prisons, Albany, N. Y.:*

Dear Sir.— I have been requested by your commission to express
my opinion as to whether or not plans for the erection of a building as part of the New York City Reformatory at Hart's Island
may be lawfully adopted without the approval of your commission.

The Hart's Island institution is now known as the New York
City Reformatory of Misdemeanants, and to it the courts may
commit male persons between the ages of sixteen and thirty years,
convicted of crimes other than felonies. (Greater N. Y. Charter,
section 698.)

The Constitution says (article VIII, section 11) that the Legislature shall provide for a State Commission of Prisons which shall
visit and inspect all institutions used for the detention of sane
adults charged with or convicted of crime, or detained as witnesses
or debtors. Accordingly, the Legislature has enacted the Prison
Law, section 46 of which is as follows:

"Section 46. GENERAL POWERS AND DUTIES OF COMMIS-
SION.— The state commission of prisons shall visit and inspect
all institutions used for the detention of sane adults charged
with or convicted of crime, or detained as witnesses or debtors,
excepting such reformatories as are subject to the visitation
and inspection of the state board of charities; and shall:
1. Aid in securing the just, humane and economic administration of all institutions subject to its supervision. 2. Advise
the officers of such institutions or in control thereof in the performance of their official duties. 3. Aid in securing the erection of suitable buildings for the accommodation of the inmates of such institutions, *and approve or reject plans for
their construction or improvement.* * * * "

The Prison Law further invests the commission with powers of visitation, inspection and investigation, and, in section 48, provides that, after investigation if it appears that inadequate provision for the sustenance, clothing, care, supervision and other necessary conditions suitable for the well being of the inmates is not furnished, the commission " may apply for an order of the Supreme Court, directed to the proper superintendent, commissioner, agent and warden, manager, keeper or other officer of such institution or in control thereof, requiring him to modify such treatment or apply such remedy, or both, as shall therein be specified."

The reformatory in question is clearly an institution used, in part at least, for the detention of adult males charged with or convicted of crime, and is within the jurisdiction and under the supervision of the Commission of Prisons. The discretion vested in the commission to approve or reject plans must be exercised reasonably and properly. If so exercised, application may be made to the court to direct that such decision by the commission be heeded by those in charge of the institution.

It appears to be the intent of the law to provide an adequate and uniform supervision of the construction and maintenance of penal institutions. From the foregoing considerations and in view of the express provisions of the statute, I am of the opinion that the plans for the improvement of this institution are subject to the approval of the Prison Commission before they may be carried out.

I have carefully examined the opinion of the corporation counsel of New York city, in which he reaches a contrary conclusion, but although I recognize the force of his reasoning I am unable to agree with his conclusions. The decision of the Appellate Division, Third Department, in People v. Brannan, upon which he relies, held merely that Bellevue Hospital was not an almshouse, and therefore not subject to the jurisdiction of the State Board of Charities.

Respectfully yours,

EDWARD R. O'MALLEY,

Attorney-General.

State Prisons — Great Meadow Prison.

Construction of dormitory building. Authority of Commission on New Prisons to allot additional sum of $18,000 from the appropriation made by chapter 65, Laws of 1910, for payment for extra work. Provisions of supply bill and State Finance Law do not conflict.

(See opinion June 10, 1910.)

STATE OF NEW YORK.

ATTORNEY-GENERAL'S OFFICE,

ALBANY, *December* 13, 1910.

To the Honorable, Commission on New Prisons. Albany, N. Y.:

Gentlemen.— I am in receipt of your letter of December 3, 1910, wherein you state that on May 3, 1910, the dormitory building then in course of construction at Great Meadow Prison settled; that immediate action was necessary and was taken to shore up the building and to protect it from further settlement and damage, to repair the damage done by the settlement, to restore the wall to its proper position and place under it such extra foundations as were necessary to hold the wall in place; that this matter was reported to the Legislature and an item of $25,000 placed in the supply bill just before adjournment, for constructing extra foundations and repairing the dormitory building; that the State Architect reports to your commission that the time was too short to give a sufficient opportunity to make a survey of the damages and a correct estimate of the amount that would be required to repair the same * * * and that a subsequent examination of the underlying soil, made by an expert employed by him, showed that the conditions demanded more extensive renewals of the foundations than it was at first thought necessary; that the additional $25,000 became available June 18, 1910, and that at that time work had been done to repair this damage to the amount of $18,970; that the State Architect now estimates that the total cost of this work will amount to $43,772.05, and that the work is practically completed.

You ask the opinion of this office as to whether your commission
has authority to approve of the allotment of $18,000 from the
appropriation of $738,000, made by chapter 65 of the Laws of
1910, for the purpose of paying for this additional work, which
amount is needed over and above the $25,000 provided for in the
supply bill.

Chapter 65 of the Laws of 1910 provides:

"Section 1. The sum of seven hundred and thirty-eight
thousand dollars ($738,000), or so much thereof as may be
necessary, is hereby appropriated out of any moneys in the
treasury not otherwise appropriated, for completing, equipping and furnishing the buildings now in course of construction at the Great Meadow prison, in accordance with the provisions of chapter four hundred and fifty-nine of the laws of
nineteen hundred and nine, including the completion, equipment and furnishing of the north wing of the cell house, to
provide accommodation for not less than six hundred
prisoners;   *   *   *."

" § 2. Plans and specifications for the work herein provided for shall be prepared by the state architect, and shall be
subject to the approval of the commission on new prisons as
constituted by chapter six hundred and seventy of the laws of
nineteen hundred and six and the acts amendatory thereof.
Such plans and specifications shall also be subject to the
approval of the state commission of prisons, as now required
by law. The state architect shall also prepare all contracts
and shall supervise the work of construction, heating, lighting and plumbing authorized by this act, and shall see that
the materials furnished and the work performed are in
accordance with the plans and specifications, and that the
interests of the state are fully protected."

" § 3. Subject to the approval of the commission on new
prisons and the state architect, the superintendent of prisons
is hereby authorized to enter into contract or contracts for
the work herein provided, or to have the work done by such
other systems or methods as may be deemed most expeditious

and for the best interests of the state. All expenditures of money under the provisions of this act shall be made on the certificate of the state architect and approved by the superintendent of prisons prior to their audit by the comptroller."

The above chapter became a law April 1, 1910. I am informed by the State Architect that the dormitory building was one of the buildings specified in section 1 of the above law as a building " in course of construction," the walls having been completed and roof placed thereon; that it was the wall of this building that settled on May 3d; that the accident or damage to said building was not caused by the negligence of the contractor or officials having said work in charge or connected therewith. In fact, that the accident could not have been foreseen.

Referring to the question asked by you it would seem that it was intended by the Legislature that the buildings then (April 1st) in course of construction should be completed. The Legislature recognized that causes had arisen that necessitated the expenditure of an additional amount above that provided for by chapter 65 and that the State was liable for the extra work and approved of said work by inserting the following provision in the supply bill (chapter 513, Laws of 1910):

" For constructing extra foundations for and repairing the dormitory building at Great Meadow prison, the sum of twenty-five thousand dollars ($25,000), or so much thereof as may be necessary, to be expended subject to the same direction, approval and certification as the amount authorized to be expended by chapter sixty-five of the laws of nineteen hundred and ten."

At the time this last appropriation was made an indebtedness had been incurred to repair the damage caused by the settlement of the wall.

It was necessary to do all this work in order to complete the dormitory building, the completion of which was first required to be done by chapter 65.

The appropriation made by chapter 65 was first to be used for the completion and furnishing of the buildings under construction. By an opinion rendered by this office on June 10, 1910, your commission was so advised. The dormitory building could not be completed according to the certificate of the State Architect without the expenditure of $43,772.05. The building is now practically completed and there is more than sufficient on hand from the appropriation made by chapter 65 to pay therefor.

I am of the opinion that from the language of chapter 65, your commission is authorized to allot the sum of $18,000, being the amount needed according to the certificate of the State Architect, from the appropriation made by that chapter for the purpose of paying for this extra work; and that on the certificate of the State Architect and approval of the Superintendent of Prisons, that amount may be audited and ordered paid to the parties who perform the work.

It was the duty of your commission to see that this dormitory building was completed according to the provisions of said chapter 65 and within the appropriation made therefor, and as there are sufficient funds on hand from said appropriation to pay for the completion of said building, it is the duty of the officials having charge of the work to pay the parties who perform the work.

The provisions of the State Finance Law and of the supply bill above quoted do not appear to conflict with or forbid such action.

Yours very truly,

EDWARD R. O'MALLEY,

Attorney-General.

OPINIONS RENDERED THE STATE COMMISSIONER OF AGRICULTURE.

Agricultural Law — Section 310 — State and County Fairs.
Apportionment of moneys by Commissioner of Agriculture to agricultural fairs, permitting " ring throwing at knives or canes." Such games being tests of skill do not come within prohibition of above section.

(See opinion August 5, 1908, p. 341, Report.)

STATE OF NEW YORK.

ATTORNEY-GENERAL'S OFFICE,

ALBANY, *May* 10, 1910.

To the Honorable, the Commissioner of Agriculture, Albany, N. Y.:

Dear Sir.— I am in receipt of your recent favor requesting an opinion as to whether it would be permissible for you to apportion moneys to the agricultural fairs permitting the game known as " throwing rings at knives or canes " to be operated upon their grounds during their annual meetings or exhibitions. It further appears from your communication that section 310 of the Agricultural Law provides in general terms that these fairs shall not permit the use of any gambling device or the playing or carrying on of any game of chance upon the ground used by it, and if the authorities permit any of the above they shall forfeit their right to any moneys that they might be entitled to receive under the provisions of the section. The said section also says after the above that: " This shall not be construed to prohibit horse racing or tests or trials of skill."

In regard to your question as to what constitutes gambling within the prohibition of this section, I respectfully call your attention to the opinion of former Attorney-General William S. Jackson under date of August 5th, 1908, which sets forth at length his interpretation of this section.

Your letter of February 23d seems to contemplate more particularly an interpretation as to whether or not the game known as " throwing rings at knives or canes " comes within the prohibition of this section. This is a game where the player gives a certain amount of money and receives a number of rings which he may throw at a knife or cane, as the case may be, with the understanding that if he throws the ring over the knife or cane it belongs to him, and if he does not succeed in getting it over such knife or cane, he gets nothing. The board or arrangement holding the knives or canes is stationery and immovable as far as this contest is concerned, and therefore for all the purposes, everything connected with this game is under the control of the player.

For that reason it seems to me that this is entirely a test of skill and does not come within the prohibition of this section.

Yours very truly,
EDWARD R. O'MALLEY,
Attorney-General.

Agricultural Law — Article V — Section 106.

Shipping of calves under age. Commissioner of Agriculture has the right to authorize agents to seize all calves under four weeks of age on shipment from New York State to points in Massachusetts.

(See opinion April 1, 1907, p. 456, Report; opinion February 16, 1911.)

STATE OF NEW YORK.

ATTORNEY-GENERAL'S OFFICE,

ALBANY, June 4, 1910.

To the Honorable, the Commissioner of Agriculture, Albany, N. Y.:

Dear Sir.— I am in receipt of your favor of May 10, 1910, requesting an opinion as to whether calves under four weeks old that are being shipped in New York State to points in Massachusetts, where they are sold in many instances for food purposes, should be seized under the provisions of article 5 of the Agricultural Law, more particularly the provisions of section 106. This section provides as follows:

"Section 106. SHIPPING, SLAUGHTERING AND SELLING VEAL FOR FOOD.— No person shall slaughter or expose for sale, or sell any calf or carcass of the same or any part thereof, unless it is in good healthy condition. No person shall sell or expose for sale any such calf or carcass of the same or any part thereof, except the hide, unless it was, if killed, at least four weeks of age at the time of killing. No person or persons shall bring or cause to be brought into any city, town or village any calf or carcass of the same or any part thereof for the purpose of selling, offering or exposing the same for sale, unless it is in a good healthy condition, and no person or persons shall bring any such calf or carcass of the same or any part thereof except the hide into any city, town or village for the purpose of selling, offering or exposing the same for sale, unless the calf is four weeks of age, or, if killed, was four weeks of age at the time of killing, provided, however, that the provisions of this section shall not apply to any calf or carcass of the same or any part thereof, which is slaughtered, sold, offered or exposed for sale, for any other purpose than for food. Any person or persons exposing for sale, selling or shipping any calf or carcass of the same will be presumed to be so exposing, selling or shipping the said calf or carcass of the same for food. Any person or persons shipping any calf for the purpose of being raised, if the said calf is under four weeks of age, shall ship it in a crate, unless said calf is accompanied by its dam. Any person shipping calves under four weeks of age for fertilizer purposes must slaughter the said calves before so shipping. Any person or persons duly authorized by the commissioner of agriculture may examine any calf or veal offered or exposed for sale or kept with any stock of goods apparently exposed for sale and if such calf is under four weeks of age, or the veal is from a calf killed under four weeks of age, or from a calf in an unhealthy condition when killed, he may seize the same and cause it to be destroyed and disposed of in such manner as to make it impossible to be thereafter used for food."

The section above quoted forbids the selling or exposing for sale of any calf under four weeks of age, and it further provides that any person or persons exposing for sale, selling or shipping any calf or carcass of the same will be presumed to be so exposing, selling or shipping the said calf or carcass of the same for food. Therefore, under the provisions of this section you have a right to assume that all calves which are under four weeks of age, and not accompanied by their dams, are being shipped for food purposes.

Section 3 of the Agricultural Law grants to the Commissioner of Agriculture, his clerks, assistants, experts, chemists, agents and counsel employed by the Commissioner, full access to cars and vessels used for the sale or transportation of any article or product with respect to which any authority is conferred by the Agricultural Law on said Commissioner.

In the case of the People v. Burdette Bishopp, reported in 106 A. D. at pages 266 to 269, Parker, P. J., for the court, in considering the same section under its former number, said that:

> "There can be no doubt but that the Legislature was authorized to enact the provisions of section 70-e (now section 106) of the Agricultural Law. It is an exercise of the police power in the interest of the public health, and that right has long been recognized by our own and by the Federal courts. Veal, as an article of food, is deemed by the Legislature to be injurious and unsafe when eaten within four weeks of its birth, and, for such reason, it is assumed by that section to regulate the use and sale of such veal as an article of food."

In the same case, in considering section 70-f (now section 107), which requires that all veal that is shipped shall have annexed thereto a tag stating the name of the person who raised the calf, the name of the shipper, the points of shipping and the destination and the age of the calf, the court said:

> "Neither does the section (70-f) violate subdivision 3 of section 8 of article 1 of the Federal Constitution, which gives to Congress power to regulate commerce. True, the prohibition against shipping without a tag is broad enough to apply

to veal intended to be shipped to another State, but that does not interfere with the regulation of commerce between the States. (Railroad Company v. Husen, 95 U. S. 465; Kidd v. Pearson, 128 U. S. 1, 23, 24; People v. Niagara Fruit Co., 75 A. D. 11; affirmed 173 N. Y. 629.) Within the authority of those cases the exclusive right to regulate commerce, etc., secured to Congress by the Federal Constitution is not invaded."

If the prohibition against shipping without a tag (section 107) is broad enough to apply to veal intended to be shipped to another State, certainly the language in section 106 against the shipping, slaughtering and selling veal for food is no less broad.

I therefore advise you that you have the right to seize calves under four weeks old which are being shipped in New York State to points in Massachusetts.

Yours very truly,

EDWARD R. O'MALLEY,

Attorney-General.

OPINIONS RENDERED THE STATE COMMISSIONER OF EXCISE.

State Finance Law — Section 2-a — State Employees, Excise Department.

Semi-monthly payment of salaries. Application of law to payment of special agents appointed under section 7, Liquor Tax Law.

STATE OF NEW YORK.

ATTORNEY-GENERAL'S OFFICE,

ALBANY, *July* 7, 1910.

Hon. MAYNARD N. CLEMENT, *Commissioner of Excise, Albany, N. Y.:*

Dear Sir.— Replying to your favor of the 4th inst. in which you ask for my opinion as to whether the provisions of **chapter 317** of the Laws of 1910, providing for the semi-monthly payment of the salaries of all officers of the State and the wages of all employees thereof, are applicable to the salary of special agents in your department under section 7 of the Liquor Tax Law, I beg to render you the following opinion:

Chapter 317 of the Laws of 1910, which adds a new section (2-a) to the State Finance Law, after directing the payment of salaries and wages of State officers and employees twice each month, contains the following sentence:

> "The provisions of this section shall be deemed to supersede any other provision of this chapter or of any general or special law inconsistent therewith."

Since the special agents appointed by you pursuant to section 7 of the Liquor Tax Law must be deemed employees of the State, I am clearly of the opinion that the new law is applicable to the payment of their salaries.

I have examined the case of People v. Stock, 26 A. D. 564, referred to in your letter. This case held that the provisions of sections 484 and 718 of the Code of Criminal Procedure, providing for an imprisonment of one day for every dollar of a fine imposed pursuant to judgment, were not applicable to a penalty imposed under section 34 of the Liquor Tax Law. This is not controlling in determining whether the above semi-monthly salary act applies to your special agents. The court found nothing inconsistent in having the two provisions stand together and because of the fact that the liberty of a citizen was in question construed the statutes strictly. In the question under consideration the Legislature by the incorporation of the sentence above quoted made certain the application of the act to all provisions of law inconsistent therewith.

Yours very truly,

EDWARD R. O'MALLEY,

Attorney-General.

Liquor Tax Law — (*Amended chapter* 484, *Laws* 1910).

Liquor tax bonds. When actions may be brought upon, under chapter 484.

STATE OF NEW YORK.

ATTORNEY-GENERAL'S OFFICE,

ALBANY, *August* 4, 1910.

Hon. MAYNARD N. CLEMENT, *Commissioner of Excise, Albany, N. Y.:*

Dear Sir. — Recurring to your letter of July 8th, 1910, in which attention is called to chapter 484 of the Laws of 1910, changing the time within which actions may be brought upon liquor tax bonds, I beg to say:

The only restriction upon the Legislature in the enactment of statutes of limitation is that a reasonable time be allowed for suits upon causes of action theretofore existing. When the question is brought before the court, the surrounding circumstances are regarded in determining whether the Legislature, in prescribing a period of limitation, has erred to the prejudice of substantial rights. The right of a person to enforce a claim against another is property, and if a statute of limitations acting upon that right deprives the claimant of a reasonable time within which suit may be brought, it violates the constitutional provision that no person shall be deprived of property without due process of law.

It would seem under the ruling of the case holding substantially as above that when a cause of action on a bond accrued two years prior to June 14th, 1910, or so nearly two years prior thereto that reasonable time would not be given to begin an action under the act prescribing the new limitation, the unconstitutionality of the law might be invoked by your department.

With this exception, the new statute would seem to apply to all liquor tax bonds that were issued before or after June 14th, 1910.

Respectfully yours,

EDWARD R. O'MALLEY,

Attorney-General.

OPINIONS RENDERED THE STATE COMMISSIONER OF FOREST, FISH AND GAME.

Forest, Fish and Game Law.

Authority of Commission to furnish trees free of charge to State institutions, agricultural societies and individuals, not found in statute.   (Chap. 466, Laws 1908.)

STATE OF NEW YORK.

ATTORNEY-GENERAL'S OFFICE,

ALBANY, *April* 7, 1910.

Hon. JAMES S. WHIPPLE, *Commissioner, Forest, Fish and Game Commission, Albany, N. Y.:*

Dear Sir.— I acknowledge your letter of the 3d inst., in which you enclose copy of a communication addressed by you to the Governor, and ask my opinion as to your power to furnish trees free of cost to State institutions, to county agricultural societies, and for the protection of highways to private individuals.   You state that you wish to know whether there is any authority by which you may furnish trees under these three different sets of circumstances, free of charge.

1 have carefully examined the statutes defining your powers and am unable to find any authorization for such action on your part. Section 40 of the Forest, Fish and Game Law, defining your general powers, is not broad enough to include any such right, so far as I am able to discover.   By chapter 466, Laws of 1908, which is the supply bill, an appropriation is made " for establishing additional nurseries for the propagation of forest trees to be furnished to citizens of the State at cost and planted under direction and regulation of the Forest, Fish and Game Commission, and to be used in reforesting denuded and burned lands in the forest preserve."

Nothing therein contained would authorize the procedure about which you request my opinion. I must therefore advise you that the power required for carrying out the above purposes does not seem to be granted to you under any statute which has been called to my attention or which I have been able to discover.

Very truly yours,

EDWARD R. O'MALLEY,

Attorney-General.

Forest, Fish and Game Commission — Forest Fires.

Audit and payment for services of laborers at forest fires, performed prior to the enactment of 1909, providing for fire patrols, should be made by the State under the provisions of the old statute.

(See letter June 19, 1909, L. B. 105, p. 917.)

STATE OF NEW YORK.

ATTORNEY-GENERAL'S OFFICE,

ALBANY, *May* 5, 1910.

Hon. J. S. WHIPPLE, *Commissioner, Forest, Fish and Game Commission, Albany, N. Y.:*

Dear Sir.— By your favor of April 19th, I am asked for an opinion " as to whether or not an expenditure caused for fighting fire prior to the enactment of the law of 1909, under the old system, could be paid and audited by the State under the new system and a legal charge for one-half thereof made against the town."

By section 71 of the Consolidated Forest, Fish and Game Law it was made the duty of the town board of audit to fix the price to be paid per day, not exceeding two dollars, for services of laborers at forest fires in their respective towns, and serve notice thereof on their town fire wardens and on the Forest, Fish and Game Commissioner, and if necessary to protect land in the forest preserve, the Commissioner was authorized to employ laborers not exceeding two dollars per day, and provided that all services rendered at forest fires, or in the prevention thereof should be town charges. It further provided that in towns where fire wardens were appointed by the Commissioner, the bills for services at fires must be approved by the fire warden and a duplicate bill, with his approval and a certificate of the town board of auditors showing the bill had been paid, should be filed with the Commissioner and on his (Commissioner's) approval, the Comptroller was required to pay one-half the amount so expended in such town to the town.

By chapter 474, Laws of 1909, the above section 71 was amended providing among other things as follows:

> " The wages and expense and keeping of supervisors and men summoned or employed to fight forest fires actually burning shall be fixed and paid for by the commissioner, and the labor reckoned and paid for by the hours of labor performed, which shall not exceed the rate of fifteen cents for each hour employed. The commissioner shall keep, or cause to be kept, an accurate account of the wages of men so employed and the expenses and the keeping of the men *and pay the same;* one-half the expense thereof shall be a charge upon and shall be paid by the state, and one-half thereof a charge upon and shall be paid by the town in which the men so employed were actually engaged in fighting fires."

Further provision is then made requiring the Commissioner to transmit a summary statement of the amount due to the State to the county clerk of each county wherein fires have occurred, and the county clerk is to deliver it to the board of supervisors of the county, and they in turn are required to levy and collect from the towns liable and pay it over to the Commissioner.

It will be noticed by the above that the compensation to be paid for the above work was fixed by the town board, not exceeding two dollars per day under the old system, and is now fixed by the Commissioner not exceeding fifteen cents per hour, so a new rate is established, and a different auditor is empowered to pass upon the bills.

It is a well established principle by both statutory construction and adjudication that an amendment, repeal or change of a statute shall not be given retroactive effect unless an intent is clearly expressed therein that it shall have such effect.

> N. Y. & O. M. R. R. Co. v. Van Horn, 57 N. Y. 473.
> G. & W. Ry. Co. v. N. Y. C. & H. R. R. R. Co., 163
>   N. Y. 232.
> Matter of Miller, 110 N. Y. 216.
> Article 5 of General Construction Law.

There is nothing in the amendment indicating an intention on the part of the Legislature that it should have retroactive effect. All employees who had rendered services prior to May 24, 1909, under the law as it existed at that time were entitled to compensation to be fixed by their town board, not exceeding two dollars per day. This right had accrued before the new law took effect and had become a vested right. It could not be divested by the passage of a new law which changed both the rate of compensation and the auditor for future work of that character.

> Cameron et al. v. N. Y. & M. V. W. Co. et al., 133
>   N. Y. 336.
> People ex rel. Standard Gas Co. v. Gilroy, 67 Hun, 323.

It cannot be said that the new law only changed the method of procedure for it goes much farther; it substitutes a different rate of compensation, a different auditor and provides an entirely different method by which the amount and value of the services are fixed and the amount paid. If it were only a question of procedure of auditing by the same board or authority and paying the same wages at the same rate, the new statute could be followed. but when a different rate is provided, and the judgment of the Commissioner is to be substituted for that of the town boards as to the rate of wages, it cannot be called simply a matter of procedure.

Again, it will be observed that the Commissioner is required by the new law to keep, or cause to be kept, an account of the wages of the men so employed, but he had no such authority under the old, and the only wages that he is authorized to pay are such as he has kept an account of.

. I am, therefore, of the opinion that all wages earned prior to May 25, 1909, should be fixed, audited and paid according to the statute as it existed prior to the amendment.

Yours truly,

EDWARD R. O'MALLEY,

Attorney-General.

Forest, Fish and Game Commission — Marine Fisheries.

Application to Superintendent of Marine Fisheries to lease shell fish lands under waters of Manhasset bay and Hempstead harbor; title to such land vests in State and not the town of North Hempstead.

(See opinion of March 4, 1901, p. 161, Report; see opinion of April 10, 1901, p. 329, Report.)

STATE OF NEW YORK.

ATTORNEY-GENERAL'S OFFICE,

ALBANY, *May* 20, 1910.

Hon. J. S. WHIPPLE, *Forest, Fish and Game Commissioner, Albany, N. Y.:*

Dear Sir.— I acknowledge your letter of the 13th inst., enclosing letter from Mr. B. Frank Wood, Superintendent of Marine Fisheries, under date of May 11, asking my opinion as to the powers of his department in reference to certain applications for shell fish lands under the waters of Hempstead harbor and Manhasset bay in the town of North Hempstead, county of Nassau. It appears from his communication that the town has filed with his bureau a formal remonstrance in the case of such applications, claiming that the jurisdiction over the lands under such waters is in the town and not in the State, and alleging that the town is the owner of said lands in fee.

On examination of the files of this office I find that the question of the ownership of these lands has been passed upon by former Attorneys-General. In the report of the Attorney-General for 1901, pages 161 and 329, former Attorney-General Davies ad-

vised that the State and not the town held title to the lands under
the water of Manhasset bay and Hempstead harbor respectively.
I also find from the files of the Land Board that there have been
repeated grants of land made by the Commissioners of the Land
Office, under these two bodies of water.

I see no reason for differing with the conclusions reached by my
predecessor after the careful examination which he made, in the
two opinions already mentioned, especially in view of the long
practice by the State based upon the assumption that title to these
lands was in the State. The town of North Hempstead uniformly
protests before the Commissioners of the Land Office to the granting of any application for such lands, but such protest has been
always overruled. I therefore advise you that under the foregoing
decisions and precedents, it is my opinion that the State of New
York has title to the lands under the waters of Hempstead harbor
and Manhasset bay.

Very truly yours,

EDWARD R. O'MALLEY,

Attorney-General.

---

*State Constitution — Section 7 — Article 7 — State Forest
Preserve.*

Construction of Forest Home Road, Harrietstown, Saranac Lake
  to Saranac Inn. County Superintendent of Highways may
  not use stone from ledge on State lands to macadamize road.
  (See Forest, Fish and Game Law, section 5, chapter 24).

(See opinions February 18, 1895, p. 89, Report; June 22, 1903,
  p. 364, Report).

STATE OF NEW YORK.

ATTORNEY-GENERAL'S OFFICE,

ALBANY, *June* 14, 1910.

Hon. JAMES S. WHIPPLE, *Forest, Fish and Game Commissioner,*
  Albany, N. Y.:

Dear Sir.— I am in receipt of your letter of the 2nd inst.,
wherein you state that you are in receipt of a letter from Mr.

S. A. Howard, county superintendent of roads of Franklin county, under date of May 31st as follows:

> "It is our intention to macadamize the Forest Home Road in the town of Harrietstown reaching from Saranac Lake to Saranac Inn. In order to do so we must obtain our stone from the ledge situated at the roadside near .Fish Creek. This ledge is on State lands but there are no trees to be cut or damage to be done. Have you any objections to us using stone?"

You ask me to give the department my opinion in view of section 7, article 7 of the Constitution, as to whether you have any authority to allow county authorities to use the stone in said ledge referred to, there being no trees to cut and no damage to be done, except the taking away for this purpose of the stone which belongs to the State.

In reply thereto would say, article 7, section 7 of the State Constitution provides as follows:

> "The lands of the State, now owned or hereafter acquired, constituting the forest preserve as now fixed by law, shall be forever kept as wild forest lands. They shall not be leased, sold or exchanged, or be taken by any corporation, public or private, nor shall the timber thereon be sold, removed or destroyed."

Attorney-General Hancock in an opinion to the secretary of the New York State Forest Commission (Attorney-General's report 1895, page 89) in construing the above section of the Constitution says:

> "The object of this provision of the fundamental law, which took effect on January 1, 1895, is that thenceforth the Forest Preserve of the State shall forever be securely fixed beyond the cupidity of man — they 'shall be forever kept as wild forest lands.' "

Attorney-General Cunneen in an opinion to the Governor (Attorney-General's report 1903, page 365) in construing the above section of the Constitution says:

" The expression ' wild forest lands ' in the Constitution indicated that it was intended to preserve these lands as a wilderness, in which the work of man should not appear."

Further at page 366, he says:

" I concur in the opinion of Attorney-General Hancock, and think that it was contemplated that these lands should remain subject to natural conditions and results, without the intervention of man, in cutting, pruning or otherwise cultivating the woods or the lands."

It must be borne in mind that each of the opinions above referred to were rendered upon the question as to the right to cut timber in the Adirondack preserve, while the question here is whether stone can be taken from the preserve where " there are no trees to be cut or damage to be done."

Section 5 of the Forest, Fish and Game Law (chapter 24, Laws of 1909) defines the duties of the commissioner as follows:

" The commissioner shall have charge, control and management of the State lands and forests in the State forest preserve, parks and reservations; of the propagation and distribution of food and game fish and shell fish to supply the waters of the State; of hatching stations owned or operated by the State; of the enforcement of laws for the protection of fish and game and the forests; * * * and such other powers and duties as are or may be imposed upon him by law."

It will be seen that no power is vested in the commissioner to dispose of the mineral products in or upon the forest preserve.

I am therefore of the opinion that it was clearly the intent of the framers of the Constitution to preserve the lands constituting the forest preserve in their natural state and that you have no authority to allow county authorities to use the stone in the ledge referred to.

Yours very truly,

EDWARD R. O'MALLEY,

Attorney-General.

Forest, Fish and Game Law — Section 72.

Lumber company operating a wood railway as a railroad company, may not be directed by the Forest, Fish and Game Commission to cut or remove inflammable material from its right of way, without an order from the Public Service Commission.

STATE OF NEW YORK.

Attorney-General's Office,

Albany, *October* 10, 1910.

Hon. H. LeRoy Austin, *Forest, Fish and Game Commission, Albany, N. Y.:*

Dear Sir.— I have your letter of the 7th inst., in which you ask me for my opinion as to whether a lumber company operating a wood railroad is a railroad company within the meaning of section 72 of the Forest, Fish and Game Law, and may be required by you to clear its right of way of inflammable material, as therein provided.

Section 72 of the Forest, Fish and Game Law provides in part as follows:

"Every railroad company shall, on such part of its road as passes through forest lands or lands subject to fires from any cause, cut and remove from its right of way along such lands, at least twice a year, all grass, brush or other inflammable materials. Where the railroad runs through forest lands in counties containing part of the forest preserve, it shall so cut and remove the same from its right of way whenever required by the commissioner; * * *. The Public Service Commission must upon the request of the Forest, Fish and Game Commissioner, and on notice to the person or companies affected, require any person, railroad or other company having a railroad running through forest lands in counties containing parts of the forest preserve, to adopt such devices and precautions against setting fire upon its line in such forest lands as the public interest requires."

This same section further provides a penalty for violating its provisions.

25

You state that there are in certain of the forest preserve counties, lumber companies which operate wood railroads, the motive power being furnished by steam locomotives. These railroads, you say, are not regularly in the transportation business except as they draw logs, supplies, etc., for the companies owning them. You also state that they have no well defined right of way in the ordinary acceptance of the term, but are usually located upon a large tract of land owned by the company which operates them.

It is my opinion that the language of section 72, above quoted, clearly has reference to two classes of railroads — one operated by a railroad company, and the other operated by any person, railroad or other company. The first class is not large enough to include the sort of railroad which you define, but such road is clearly included in the second class. It follows from this that it is necessary for you in every case where such a railroad is concerned to apply to the Public Service Commission for an order requiring the adoption of the devices and protections which the public interest may require, and that you have no right to direct such company to cut and remove inflammable materials from its right of way without such an order under the second sentence of the section.

Very truly yours,
EDWARD R. O'MALLEY,
Attorney-General.

State Forest Preserve.

Buildings standing thereon may not be sold or removed by the Commissioner of Forest, Fish and Game.

STATE OF NEW YORK.

ATTORNEY-GENERAL'S OFFICE,

ALBANY, *October* 10, 1910.

Hon. H. LeRoy Austin, *Forest, Fish and Game Commissioner,*
Albany, N. Y.:

Dear Sir.— I have your letter of the 6th inst., in which you ask my opinion as to whether an occupant of buildings upon State lands in the forest preserve, who has been occupying the same in violation of the constitutional provision, and is about to remove therefrom, may purchase such buildings and remove them from the State land.

Section 42 of the Forest, Fish and Game Law provides in part as follows:

> " A person who cuts or causes to be cut or carries away or causes to be carried away any tree, timber, wood or bark from State lands in the forest preserve is guilty of a misdemeanor   *   *   *."

Section 7 of article 7 of the Constitution of the State of New York provides as follows:

> " The lands of the State, now owned or hereafter acquired, constituting the forest preserve as now fixed by law, shall be forever kept as wild forest lands.   They shall not be leased, sold or exchanged, or be taken by any corporation, public or private, nor shall the timber thereon be sold, removed or destroyed."

It is my opinion that under the above provisions you have no power to sell buildings standing on the forest preserve nor to allow them to be removed.

Very truly yours,

EDWARD R. O'MALLEY,

Attorney-General.

Forest, Fish and Game Law — Section 42.

Right of Forest, Fish and Game Commissioner to settle claim for penalty for trees taken away or destroyed, at less than $10. (Sections 5, 19, 21).

STATE OF NEW YORK.

Attorney-General's Office,

Albany, *November* 16, 1910.

Hon. H. LeRoy Austin, *Forest, Fish and Game Commissioner, Albany, N. Y.:*

Dear Sir.— Your favor of October 21, 1910, requesting my opinion as to whether or not the Forest, Fish and Game Commissioner has power to settle a claim for penalties for less than the total amount thereof, is received. You put the following specific question:

"Has the Forest, Fish and Game Commissioner any right to compromise and settle a claim for penalties under this section (the section referred to being section 42 of the Forest, Fish and Game Law) for an amount less than $10 for each tree cut, taken away or destroyed?"

Section 5 of the Forest, Fish and Game Law provides:

"The commissioner shall have charge, control and management of the State lands and forests in the State forest preserve, parks and reservations; * * * of the enforcement of laws for the protection of fish and game and the forest; * * *."

This provision apparently contemplates the exercise of considerable discretion on the part of the commissioner, and would seem to authorize him to settle a claim for penalties for less than the total amount thereof where the facts and conditions warrant. Sections 19 and 21, however, provide, relative to actions for penalties:

"§ 19. Except as otherwise provided in this chapter, actions for penalties for violations of the forest, fish and game provisions of this chapter shall be in the name of the people of the State of New York; and must be brought on the order of the commissioner. * * * Such actions may be discontinued by order of the court on the application of the commissioner upon such terms as the court may direct."

"§ 21. Moneys recovered in an action for penalties or upon the settlement or compromise thereof, and fines for violation of this chapter shall be paid to the commissioner * * *."

These provisions would clearly require an order from the court in case an action was discontinued without any recovery, and it would, I think, be wise in all cases to get an order of the court authorizing the settlement of an action that has been brought.

The remaining question is as to whether the commissioner would have the right to settle a claim for penalties for less than the total amount, without bringing an action. Your supplementary letter of November 12, 1910, states that this has been the practice, so far as you are able to ascertain, since the formation of the Forest, Fish and Game Commission.

While the matter is not free from doubt, in view of the continued practical interpretation by your department that it has this power of settlement, I am of opinion that you are authorized in continuing to settle claims for penalties for less than the total amounts of such penalties, before an action is instituted. The practical construction of the Forest, Fish and Game Law by the commission is entitled to great weight — in fact, almost controlling weight — in its interpretation.

People v. Adelphi Club, 149 N. Y. 5; page 11.
People v. Dayton, 55 N. Y. 367; page 378.

In 1909, section 14 of the Forest, Fish and Game Law, relating to the powers of game protectors, was amended by chapter 574 of the laws of that year, by the addition of the following sentence:

" Any regular or special game protector, fire superintendent or fire patrolman or inspector who shall compromise or settle any violation of the Forest, Fish and Game Law out of court, or without the order of the Forest, Fish and Game Commissioner, shall be guilty of a misdemeanor."

If it had been the intention of the Legislature that the commission also should not have power to settle any violation of the

Forest, Fish and Game Law out of court, it would seem that appropriate language would have been used, especially in view of the fact that this power had been exercised by the commissioner for a great many years. I should suggest, however, that if you desire this question settled beyond a doubt, you might bring the matter before the next Legislature so that this power of the commissioner might be expressed in unequivocal language.

Very truly yours,
EDWARD R. O'MALLEY,
Attorney-General.

Forest, Fish and Game Law — Sections 126, 127.

Removal of carp by nets from public waters not allowable, and license may not be granted by the Forest, Fish and Game Commissioner under section 165.

STATE OF NEW YORK.

ATTORNEY-GENERAL'S OFFICE,

ALBANY, November 16, 1910.

Hon. H. LeRoy AUSTIN, Forest, Fish and Game Commissioner, Albany, N. Y.:

Dear Sir.— I beg to acknowledge receipt of your communication of November 3, 1910, wherein you ask my opinion whether the commissioner may, under the provisions of section 165 of the Forest, Fish and Game Law, grant a license to one or more individuals to catch and remove carp from public waters of the State under an arrangement whereby the netting is to be inspected by the department and a fee is to be paid to the State based upon the pounds of fish so taken.

Section 165 to which my attention is directed provides:

> " The commissioner may take fish with nets at such times and in such manner as he may deem proper for the artificial propagation of fish. The commission may also remove or cause to be removed from public waters fish which hinder or prevent the propagation of game or food fish. Such removal

shall be effected by such means and under such regulations as the commissioner may provide. Moneys realized from fish so removed may be used by the commissioner in continuing the work of removal. Any person not in charge of a State net who shall handle or take fish while confined therein, or shall fish within one hundred feet of any leader or net in use by the State shall be guilty of a misdemeanor."

Under this section it seems clear that the *commission*, if it is satisfied that the carp is a fish which hinders or prevents the propagation of game or food fish, may remove or cause the same to be removed from public waters by such means or under such regulations as the commissioner provides. It would apparently mean that the work of removal is to be done by the commission acting through its officers or agents in charge of the removal, as the act of the *commission* for the general good of the public in the removal and destruction of such fish; but to my notion, this does not contemplate such removal by means of a *license* granted to any individual along the lines suggested by you.

The provision with regard to licenses to any persons to take fish with nets is found in section 126 and section 127 of the Forest, Fish and Game Law and the rules and regulations of the commission with regard to net licenses. The fish which may be taken are specifically named in section 126 and the carp is not one of the fish specified in that section, for the taking of which by nets a license may be granted.

I, therefore, give it as my opinion that you may not grant a license under the provisions of section 165 for the catching and removal of carp in the manner suggested in your communication.

Respectfully yours,

EDWARD R. O'MALLEY,

Attorney-General.

Forest, Fish and Game Law — Section 22.

Right of Forest, Fish and Game Commissioner to pay moities to peace officers and private citizens prosecuting violations of the Game Law.

STATE OF NEW YORK.

ATTORNEY-GENERAL'S OFFICE,

ALBANY, *November* 16, 1910.

Hon. H. LeRoy AUSTIN, *Forest, Fish and Game Commissioner, Albany, N. Y.:*

Dear Sir.— I have been requested by your chief game protector under date of November 4, 1910, to render an opinion regarding the right of the Forest, Fish and Game Commission to pay moities to peace officers and private citizens where they have prosecuted violations of the Game Law and recovery has been had.

Section 22 of the Forest, Fish and Game Law provides that

" A private person, on giving security for costs to be approved by a judge of the court in which the action is brought * * * may recover in his * * * name any penalty imposed by this chapter for a violation of the fish and game provisions thereof, and shall be entitled in case of collection, to one-half of the recovery; the balance shall be paid to the commissioner."

Section 218 of the same law provides for the bringing of a similar action upon like security for costs and with like right to one-half of the recovery by a private person, other than the owner or lessee of the premises upon which the penalty is incurred, for the recovery of penalty under article 12 of the laws with regard to marine fisheries.

Section 104 of the same law regarding hunting licenses provides that

" All prosecutions for a violation of the provisions of this chapter relating to licenses may be brought by any person in the name of the people of the State of New York against any person or persons violating any of the provisions of this chapter so far as it relates to licenses before any court of competent jurisdiction; * * * one-half of the amount recovered in a penal action under this section, in so far as it relates to licenses * * * shall be paid to the person filing the complaint in such action by the State treasurer on approval of the commissioner, unless such person is a regular game protector."

Section 17 of the Forest, Fish and Game Law provides for the appointment by the commission of special game protectors and provides for the payment to them of one-half of the fines and penalties.

Outside of the first three sections above referred to, the provisions of the Forest, Fish and Game Law, with regard to the payment of moieties, seem to restrict such payment to special protectors duly appointed as such by the commission. In so far as moieties may be paid to any other person, whether peace officers or private citizens, it seems that such payment may be made only in cases where such persons, after having given security against costs as required by sections 22 and 218, prosecute actions to recovery, or where a complaint by such person of a violation of the provisions of section 104 above referred to results in a recovery.

Respectfully yours,

EDWARD R. O'MALLEY,.

Attorney-General.

OPINIONS RENDERED THE STATE COMMISSIONER OF HEALTH.

Public Health Law — Sections 20, 21 — Village Law — (Consolidated) — Sections 42, 43.

Office of president of village and of health officer not incompatible. Position of health officer not a village office. He acts as executive officer of the board of health, by whom he is appointed.

(See opinions May 7, 1903, p. 345, Rep.; November 16, 1905, p. 368, Rep.; letter April 8, 1909, L. B. 102, p. 931).

STATE OF NEW YORK.

ATTORNEY-GENERAL'S OFFICE,

ALBANY, *January* 12, 1910.

Hon. EUGENE H. PORTER, *Commissioner of Health, Albany, N. Y.:*

Dear Sir.— In reply to your favor of April 17 and supplemental letter from your chief clerk Mr. Beagle under date of August 13, with which you forwarded me a copy of the opinion of former Attorney-General Cunneen, in which I am asked for an opinion as to the right of a person to hold the office of president of a village and health officer thereof at the same time, I beg to state that on or about April 6 a letter was received from one Joseph L. Glover of Ardsley, making a similar inquiry and was placed upon the desk of Deputy Fisher who made reply thereto under date of April 8, in which he arrived at the conclusion that the two offices are not incompatible and that the prohibition contained in section 42 of the Village Law did not apply to a health officer, for reasons therein stated.

Section 42 of the Consolidated Village Law reads as follows:

"§ 42. ELIGIBILITY TO OFFICE.— A president or trustee, or a fire, water, light, sewer or cemetery commissioner must, at the time of his election, be owner of property assessed to him on the last preceding assessment-roll, and must also be the owner during the term of his office of property assessed to him on the assessment-roll of said village; except that a president or trustee elected at the first village election must be the owner of property assessed upon the last preceding town assessment-roll. Any resident elector is eligible to any other village office. A resident woman, who is a citizen of the United States, and of the age of twenty-one years, is eligible to the office of village clerk or deputy clerk. A person shall not hold two village offices at the same time, except the offices of collector and police constable or water and light commissioner; and except that village trustees may also be water commissioners."

Section 43 of the same law, which is entitled " List of village officers; mode of choosing; official year; terms of office," reads in part as follows:

" Every village shall have a president, not less than two trustees, a treasurer, a clerk and a street commissioner. Except as herein provided, every village shall also have a collector, but a village of the first class may, upon the adoption of a proposition therefor at a special election, determine that no collector shall thereafter be elected therein. A village of the first or second class may also have a deputy clerk, and any village may have a village engineer.

" There shall be a board of health in each village, consisting of not less than three nor more than seven persons, appointed by the board of trustees of such village, in the manner provided by article three of the Public Health Law. The president, trustees, treasurer, collector, police justice and assessors shall be elective officers, except that in a village of the first or second class the treasurer may be appointed, upon the adoption of a proposition therefor at a village election. All other village officers shall be appointed by the board of trustees, except as otherwise provided herein."

The position of health officer is not listed as a village office and nowhere referred to in either section, and no provision is made in the Village Law for his election or appointment. This section specifies what village officers shall be elected, and the second paragraph above quoted closes with this significant sentence: " *All other village officers shall be appointed by the board of trustees, except as otherwise provided,*" and inasmuch as it is not otherwise provided in such act for the election or appointment of a health officer, and as such health officer is to be appointed by the board of health, and not by the board of trustees, it is very apparent that he is not an officer of the village within the meaning of section 42, and would not be holding two village offices if he should be president of the village and health officer at the same time.

By section 20 of the Public Health Law, as amended by chapter 165 of the Laws of 1909, the board of trustees of a village are authorized to appoint not less than three nor more than seven persons " *not trustees of the village* " as a local board of health, and they are given authority to appoint a competent physician " not a member of the local board of health, to be health officer for the municipality. The term of office of the health officer shall be four years, and he shall hold office until the appointment of his successor. * * * The health officer need not reside within the village or town for which he shall be chosen, but unless he shall, he must reside in an adjoining town." It will be observed by the above quotations that a trustee cannot be selected as a member of the board of health, but there is no prohibition against the appointment of the president or a member of the board of trustees to the position of health officer.

If the position of a health officer for a village or town is an office of such municipality, he would be ineligible under section 3 of the Public Officers Law to hold such office unless he resided within the village or town within which his official functions are required to be exercised, but the health officer may either reside in the municipality for which he shall be chosen or in an adjoining town.

Section 21 of the Public Health Law, which is entitled " general powers and duties of local boards of health," reads in part as follows:

"Every such local board shall prescribe the duties and powers of the local health officer, who shall be its chief executive officer, and direct him in the performance of his duties and fix his compensation."

His legal status is thus established by statute as "the chief executive officer" of the board of health, not of the village. He is to carry out the direction of the board of health — in other words, to act as the agent or executive officer of the board of health. He is appointed by the board of health and his compensation is fixed by such board; he may reside in the village or in some adjoining town; he is not amenable to the board of trustees of the village; neither is he elected by the voters of the village or appointed by the board of trustees, and it cannot be said that his occupancy of such a position makes him a village officer within the meaning of section 42 of the Village Law.

It is distinctly held in Bamber v. City of Rochester, 63 Howard, 103, Judge Haight writing the opinion of the General Term, that boards of health of municipalities are not officers or agents of the same, and at page 109 he says:

"In the first place, the council has not power to control them in the discharge of their duties, for a portion of those duties, at least, are prescribed by the general statute of the State. In the second place, the duties devolving upon the board of health do not relate to the exercise of corporate powers; neither are their duties for the benefit of the corporation in its local or special interest. The duties relate to the preservation of the health of the public; the individuals residing in the city may be benefited by the faithful discharge of the duties of such officers; so may the public at large. The duties of such officers are, therefore, public in their nature, and they should be regarded as servants and agents of the public instead of the corporation."

(See also other cases cited by Judge Haight).

In the light of this decision and in the absence of any statute making a health officer a village officer, I do not think it can be said that appointees of a health board are officers of the corporation

and therefore ineligible to hold any other village office. As the
duties of a president or trustee are not incompatible with the
duties of a health officer, I am of the opinion that a president or
trustee of a village is not prohibited by section 42 of the Village
Law from holding the position of health officer at the same time.

Yours truly,

EDWARD R. O'MALLEY,

Attorney-General.

Public Health Law — Sections 76–86 — Sewers — Municipalities.
Discharge of sewers into waters of the State forbidden without a
   permit from the Commissioner of Health. Term " waters of
   the State." Whether sections 76–86 apply to all cities and
   villages including Greater New York. Enforcement penalty
   for violation law. Prevention by State of construction of
   sewers without approved plans, etc.

STATE OF NEW YORK.

ATTORNEY-GENERAL'S OFFICE,

ALBANY, *January* 18, 1910.

Hon. EUGENE H. PORTER, *Commissioner of Health, Albany,*
   N. Y.:

Dear Sir.— I have the honor to acknowledge the receipt of your
communication asking my opinion upon several questions concerning the interpretation of the Public Health Law. My attention
is called to section 76 to 86, inclusive, of the Public Health Law.
Without quoting these sections at length it is sufficient to say, so
far as the subjects under consideration are concerned, that they
contain the following provisions:

That no municipality shall maintain sewers which have been
constructed, extended or enlarged since May 7, 1903, which discharge into any of the waters of this State without a permit from
the State Commissioner of Health. These permits are operative
when recorded in office of clerk of the county where the outlet of
the sewer system is located and a copy transmitted to the board of

health of the municipality. Section 84 prescribes the manner in which violations of the provisions of these sections shall be dealt with, and is as follows:

"§ 84. VIOLATIONS; SERVICE OF NOTICE; ACTIONS BY LOCAL BOARDS.— The local board of health of each municipality shall promptly ascertain every violation of, or noncompliance with, any of the provisions of section 76 of this article or of the permits for the discharge of sewage or refuse or waste material into any of the waters of the State herein provided, which may occur within that municipality. The board of health shall on the discovery of every violation of or noncompliance with any of the provisions of said section or of any permit duly issued, serve a written notice on the person or corporation responsible for the violation or noncompliance, together with a copy of sections 76 to 86, inclusive, of this article, and of the permit, if any, violated or noncomplied with, specifying the particular provision being violated or noncomplied with, and stipulating the length of time within which the violation or noncompliance must cease. If at the expiration of the stipulated length of time, the violation or noncompliance shall still continue, the board of health shall at once report the violation or noncompliance to the State Commissioner of Health who shall at once give a hearing to and take the proof of the persons charged with such violation or noncompliance and investigate the matter and if he finds a violation or noncompliance to exist he shall at once certify that fact to the board of health of the municipality, which shall immediately bring an action in a court of record, which action shall be tried in the county wherein the cause of action arose against the person or corporation responsible for the violation or noncompliance, for the recovery of the penalties incurred and for an injunction against the continuation of the violation or the noncompliance."

The questions which you ask concerning this law are set out below:

"1. What is the legal definition of the term used in said act 'the waters of the State?'"

In general, waters may be divided into four classes: First, those in which the tide ebbs and flows; second, those tideless waters of greater magnitude which are actually navigable and whose use for purposes of navigation and commerce is open and notorious and a matter of common knowledge. Among the second group may be classified the upper part of the Hudson river, Lake Champlain, the Niagara river, the St. Lawrence river, and Lake Ontario; third, waters of less magnitude which may be in fact navigable or dedicated to public use for navigation or as a highway. In many cases the public nature of such waters is doubtful and often is a question requiring proof. Among waters of this group may be classed the Chenango and Susquehanna rivers and many of the lakes and streams in the Adirondack section; fourth, those waters which have no navigable capacity whatever and are the subject of private ownership. So far as I am able to ascertain there has been no judicial determination of the term "the waters of the State" as used in this act. There is no question, in my opinion, but that the Legislature intended this statute to apply to all such waters as may be included within the first two classes mentioned above. It is highly probable also that it intended to include the third class and in my judgment the courts would so interpret this statute. The fourth class is, of course, not included.

"2. Do sections 76 to 85, above cited, apply to all the cities and villages of the State, including Greater New York?"

There is no exception made in the statute of any city, village or municipality. There is nothing to indicate that in using the word "municipality" Greater New York or any other city is excepted. The statute is drawn broadly and evidently applies to every city and village in the State. In 1903 the Legislature enacted a law providing for a commission to investigate certain matters pertaining to sewers draining into New York harbor. Pursuant to chapter 639 of the Laws of 1906 this commission was succeeded in that year by a new commission vested with authority to investigate the sewage question generally so far as it related to Greater New York. This commission, however, only had authority to investigate and report, and none of the provisions of the law creating it have any effect upon the sections of the Public Health Law under consideration.

"3. Can the State enforce the penalties against the municipalities provided in section 85?"

The method of prosecuting actions for the penalties which are prescribed in section 85 is set out in section 84, which is quoted in full above. An examination of this section shows that if, after an investigation, the State Commissioner of Health shall certify to the local board of health that there is a violation of or noncompliance with the statute, the local board shall immediately bring an action in a court of record. The action may be brought by the local board of health for the recovery of the penalties incurred and also for an injunction against the continuation of the violation or the noncompliance. The section is silent as to any action being brought by the State Commissioner of Health. The action is, of course, a purely statutory one and can be brought only by such parties as are named in the statute. If the Legislature had intended that this cause of action should exist in favor of the State Commissioner of Health it certainly would have so stated. It follows, therefore, that this question should be answered in the negative and that actions to recover penalties and for injunction against continued violations of these sections can only be maintained by the local boards of health.

"4. Can the State prevent further construction of sewers by municipalities when plans have not been approved as provided by this act?"

The only practical method of preventing further construction of sewers which constitutes violations of these sections is by a suit for an injunction as is provided in section 84 above quoted and referred to. The duty of bringing and the right to maintain these actions belong to the local boards of health in the same manner as in actions for penalties. The answer to this question would, therefore, be in the negative, the same as to the preceding question.

I beg leave to call your attention to section 86, which states in substance that none of the provisions of the preceding sections diminish or modify common law rights of action in reference to pollution of waters. The common law right of action exists in favor of the people as against every person, corporation and municipality maintaining any kind of a sewer which is in fact a nuisance or a menace to public health. Such an action can be maintained for an injunction restraining the continuance of the nuisance. In such cases, however, the mere fact that the sewer discharged into waters of the State without the permission of the State Commissioner of Health would not alone be sufficient upon which to base an action. The right of action would depend upon whether or not the sewer actually created a nuisance or a menace to health.

Yours very truly,

EDWARD R. O'MALLEY,

Attorney-General.

Public Health Law — Sections 4, 5, 21, 22 — Vital Statistics.

Commissioner of Health is empowered to make such rules in the performance of his duties relative to vital statistics, as will best secure a proper record. Case of Smith v. U. S. Casualty Company, 179 N. Y. 420, gives an individual a right to change his name without application to the court, but does not prevent the Commissioner of Health from prescribing necessary rules.

STATE OF NEW YORK.

ATTORNEY-GENERAL'S OFFICE,

ALBANY, *April* 13, 1910.

Hon. EUGENE H. PORTER, *Commissioner of Health, Albany. N. Y.:*

Dear Sir.— Your favor of April 11, 1910, is received. You ask whether the case of Smith v. U. S. Casualty Co., 197 N. Y. 420, requires any change in the rules relative to vital statistics.

The Public Health Law provides in section 4, relative to the duties of the commissioner, that:

" The commissioner of health shall take cognizance of the interests of health and life of the people of the state, and of all matters pertaining thereto. * * * He shall obtain, collect and preserve such information relating to mortality, disease, and health as may be useful in the discharge of his duties or may contribute to the promotion of health or the security of life in the state."

Section 5 provides:

" There shall be in the state department of health a bureau of vital statistics for the registration of births, marriages, deaths and prevalent diseases, which shall be under the general charge and supervision of the commissioner of health. He shall prescribe and prepare the necessary methods and forms for obtaining and preserving such statistics, and to insure the prompt and faithful registration of the same in the several municipalities and in the state bureau."

Sections 21 and 22 of the Public Health Law contain provisions relating to the duties of local boards of health in obtaining the necessary information to enable the commissioner to properly perform his duties with regard to vital statistics.

The decision in the case of Smith v. U. S. Casualty Company, holding that a person may change his name without application to the court by the adoption and use of another name, merely passes upon the right of an individual in regard to changing his name. This does not involve the right of the Commissioner of Health to make such rules and regulations as he deems will best subserve the purpose of procuring a proper record of vital statistics.

The obtaining of vital statistics is a matter of public concern and the Health Commissioner has the power to prescribe such rules as in his opinion will best accomplish this purpose.

Yours truly,

EDWARD R. O'MALLEY,

Attorney-General.

Public Health Law — Section 20 — Municipalities.

Removal of Commissioner of Public Health, city of Binghamton, must be approved by State Commissioner of Health. (Binghamton charter, chapter 751, Laws 1907.)

(See opinion October 26, 1910).

STATE OF NEW YORK.

Attorney-General's Office,

Albany, *May* 16, 1910.

Hon. Eugene H. Porter, M. D., *State Commissioner of Health, Capitol, Albany, N. Y.:*

Dear Sir.— I have the honor to acknowledge the receipt of your request for my opinion as to whether or not the removal of the health officer of the city of Binghamton is required by law to be approved by you before such removal can take place.

The Binghamton charter (chapter 751, Laws of 1907) provides for a Commissioner of Public Health in that city who is vested with substantially the same powers and charged with the same duties as local boards of health in other cities. The act (section 304) says:

"So much of the general health law of the state as relates to the creation of local boards of health shall not apply to the city of Binghamton after this act takes effect."

Section 305 provides that

"The Commissioner of Public Health shall exercise all the powers, and be charged with all the duties conferred upon or required of local boards of health by the general laws of this state, so far as the same pertain to cities, with the exceptions, limitations and additions contained in this act."

In the Binghamton charter, I find no provisions which can be considered as exceptions, limitations or additions to the General Law so far as it relates to the removal of the health officer. The provisions above quoted indicate that it was intended to have the law the same in Binghamton as in other municipalities with the one essential difference; namely, that instead of a board of health, there is one commissioner vested with the same powers as a board of health in other places. Section 20 of the Public Health Law says that the health officer,

"may be removed for just cause by the local board of health or the state commissioner of health after a hearing; such removal by the local board of health must be approved by the state commissioner of health."

Inasmuch as there is nothing in the city charter to except or limit this provision of the General Law making the removal subject to the State commissioner's approbation, but, on the other hand, as the charter seems to clearly intend that the General Law shall apply in practically all respects except the substitution of one commissioner for the usual board of health, it therefore follows that the removal of the health officer must be approved by the State Commissioner of Health, in accordance with the General Law.

Yours respectfully,

EDWARD R. O'MALLEY,

Attorney-General.

Public Health Law — Sections 20, 21 — *Tuberculosis Hospitals.* Charges preferred against and subsequent removal of Dr. William B. Cochrane, health officer, town of Brighton, Monroe county, by local health board, for acting contrary to wishes of citizens in not sufficiently opposing the establishment of a tuberculosis hospital, not a " just cause " for removal.

(Public Health Law, section 319).

STATE OF NEW YORK.

Attorney-General's Office,

Albany, *June* 24, 1910.

Hon. Eugene H. Porter, *Commissioner of Health, Albany, N. Y.:*

Dear Sir.— Replying to your favors of the 9th ult., and the 15th inst., I beg to render you the following opinion:

From your letters and the inclosures the following facts appear: On the 10th of November, 1909, an application was filed with you by the board of supervisors of the county of Monroe pursuant to section 319 of the Public Health Law for permission to establish a hospital for the treatment of tuberculosis in the town of Brighton in the county of Monroe. Upon that petition you, with Dr. William B. Cochrane, health officer of the town of Brighton, duly held a hearing in the court house in the city of Rochester on the 11th of December, 1909, at which time evidence in opposition to the prayer of the petition was taken and the site of the property was inspected. After consideration the board, composed of yourself and Dr. Cochrane, granted the application of the board of supervisors.

It seems that prior to the date of that hearing the health board of the town of Brighton directed its health officer, Dr. Cochrane, to oppose the erection of the hospital at the site in question, and that Dr. Cochrane at various times objected to the selection of the site on various grounds.

On the 6th of April, 1910, copy of charges preferred against Dr. Cochrane was filed with you charging him with disobedience of the directions of the local board of health, with acting contrary to the wishes of the citizens of Brighton, with being of vacillating mind and unreliable in statement, and, after having made the decision above referred to in conjunction with yourself, with having subsequently stated that he was sorry he had given his consent and would cause his name to be withdrawn therefrom, which he did not do. Hearings on these charges were had beginning on the 23d day of February, 1910, and on the 28th day of February, 1910, a resolution was adopted by the health board of the town of Brighton sustaining the charges and removing Dr. Cochrane from his office as health officer of the town of Brighton. Certified copy of that resolution was forwarded to you for your approval pursuant to section 20 of the Public Health Law.

You ask to be advised as to whether chapter 171 of the Laws of 1909, amending section 319 of the Public Health Law, imposes a duty upon the local health officer separate and distinct from his connection with his local board of health, so that, if he decided a case presented to him under said statute contrary to the wishes, knowledge and consent of the members of the board of health, it would be "just cause" for removal by the local board of health as provided by section 20 of the Public Health Law. And you further ask to be advised whether if these charges constitute "just cause" for removal by the board of health, the procedure of the board in so removing him was legal, it appearing that five members thereof sat and took the evidence of witnesses some of whom though not sitting were members of the board and others were members actually voting on the resolution of removal.

Section 20 of the Public Health Law provides as follows:

"   *   *   * The local board of health shall appoint a competent physician, not a member of the local board of health, to be the health officer of the municipality. * * * He may be removed for just cause by the local board of health or the state commissioner of health after a hearing; such removal by the local board of health must be approved by the state commissioner of health. * * *."

Section 21 of the Public Health Law contains the following provision:

"   *   *   * Every such local board of health shall prescribe the duties and powers of the local health officer, who shall be its chief executive officer, and direct him in the performance of his duties, and fix his compensation."

Section 319 of the Public Health Law provides as follows:

"CONSENTS REQUISITE TO THE ESTABLISHMENT OF HOSPITALS OR CAMPS FOR THE TREATMENT OF PULMONARY TUBERCULOSIS.— A hospital, camp or other establishment for the treatment of patients suffering from the disease known as pulmonary tuberculosis, shall not be established in any town by any person, association, corporation or municipality except when authorized as provided by this section. The person, association, corporation or municipality proposing to establish such a hospital, camp or other establishment shall file with the state commissioner of health a petition describing the character thereof, stating the county and town in which it is to be located and describing the site in such town for

such proposed hospital, camp or other establishment, and requesting the commissioner to fix a date and place for a hearing on such petition before the state commissioner of health
and the local health officer, *who shall constitute a board to
approve or disapprove the establishment of such hospital,
camp or other establishment in accordance with such petition.*
The state commissioner of health shall fix a date and place
for a hearing on such petition, which date shall be not less
than thirty nor more than forty days after the receipt thereof.
A notice of such hearing specifying the date and place thereof
and briefly describing the proposed site for such hospital,
camp or other establishment shall be mailed to the person,
association, corporation or municipality proposing to establish the same and to the *health officer* and *each member* of
the board of health of the town in which it is proposed to
establish such hospital, camp or other establishment at least
twenty days before the hearing, and also publish twice in a
local newspaper of the town, or if there is no such paper published therein, then in the newspapers of the county designated in pursuance of law to publish the session laws. At
the time and place fixed for such hearing the state commissioner of health and the local health officer shall hear the
petitioner and any person who desires to be heard in reference to the location of such hospital, camp or other establishment, and they shall within thirty days after the hearing, if
they are able to agree, approve or disapprove of the location
thereof and shall notify the person, association, corporation or
municipality of their determination. The determination of
the state commissioner of health and local health officer shall
be final and conclusive; * * *."

The statute then provides for further proceedings in case the
health officer and the commissioner of health cannot agree as to
the granting of the petition.

A careful examination of the foregoing provisions of the statute
convinces me that the health officer while sitting with yourself as
a board under the provisions of section 319 of the Public Health
Law, taking evidence for and against the prayer of the petition
and taking part in the rendering of a determination thereon acts

in a judicial capacity separate and distinct from the executive duties which are provided for by sections 20 and 21 of the Public Health Law, and that when so acting, it must necessarily follow, he is not subject to the directions or control of the local board of health. I assume that the notice to the local board of health of the date of the hearing upon the petition of the board of supervisors was given as required by the statute. This provision of law is an additional evidence of the intent of the statute to separate the powers and duties of the local health officer while acting on the board in question from those executive duties provided in sections 20 and 21.

Since, therefore, Dr. Cochrane while acting with yourself on that board was not subject to the directions of the local board of health and was performing a judicial function, any direction to him by the local board of health purporting to control the exercise of his judgment in that capacity was a nullity, the disobedience of which cannot constitute " just cause " for his removal, nor in my opinion do statements made by him at other times indicating an opposition to the prayer of the petition, contradictory though they may have been to his determination upon the question, constitute " just cause " for his removal within the meaning of the statute.

In view of the foregoing conclusion it is unnecessary to pass upon the second question involved in your communication.

Very truly yours,
EDWARD R. O'MALLEY,
Attorney-General.

*Public Health Law — Sections 70, 71 — Public Water Supply.
City of New York.*

Rules and regulations for protection of watersheds of public water
supplies. Abatement nuisances, condemnation of property
affected, payment, damages, etc. Enforcement of rules lies
within authority of local board of health.

STATE OF NEW YORK.

ATTORNEY-GENERAL'S OFFICE,

ALBANY, *June* 29, 1910.

Hon. EUGENE H. PORTER, *State Health Commissioner, Albany,
N. Y.*:

Dear Sir.— I have carefully examined the questions laid before
me in your communication of May 28, 1910, and have the honor
to reply herewith.

You state that the enforcement of sections 70 and 71 of the
Public Health Law in respect to the public water supply of the
city of New York is ineffective. Those sections provide a means
for protecting the watershed of any public water supply and, so
far as they relate to the questions you raise, are as follows:

"§ 70. RULES AND REGULATIONS OF DEPARTMENT.— The
state department of health may make rules and regulations
for the protection from contamination of any or all public
supplies of potable waters and their sources within the state.
If any such rule or regulation relates to a temporary source
or act of contamination, any person violating such rule or
regulation shall be liable to prosecution for misdemeanor for
every such violation, and on conviction shall be punished by a
fine not exceeding two hundred dollars, or imprisonment not
exceeding one year, or both. If any such rule or regulation
relates to a permanent source or act of contamination, said
department may impose penalties for the violation thereof or
the noncompliance therewith, not exceeding two hundred dollars for every such violation or noncompliance. * * *."

"§ 71. INSPECTION OF WATER SUPPLY.— The officer or

board having by law the management and control of the
potable water supply of any municipality, or the corporation
furnishing such supply, may make such inspection of the
sources of such water supply, as such officer, board or corporation deems advisable, and to ascertain whether the rules
or regulations of the state department are complied with, and
shall make such regular or special inspections as the state
commissioner of health may prescribe. If any such inspection
discloses a violation of any such rule or regulation relating
to a permanent source or act of contamination, such officer,
board or corporation shall cause a copy of the rule or regulation violated to be served upon the person violating the same,
with a notice of such violation. If the person served does
not immediately comply with the rule or regulation violated,
such officer, board or corporation shall notify the state department of the violation, which shall immediately examine into
such violation; and if such person is found by the state
department to have actually violated such rule or regulation,
the commissioner of health shall order the local board of
health of such municipality wherein the violation or the noncompliance occurs to convene and enforce obedience to such
rule or regulation. If the local board fails to enforce such
order within ten days after its receipt, the corporation furnishing such water supply, or the municipality deriving its water
supply from the waters to which said rule or regulation relates,
or the state commissioner of health or the local board of
health of the municipality wherein the water supply protected by these rules is used, or any person interested in the
protection of the purity of the water supply, may maintain
an action in a court of record, which shall be tried in the
county where the cause of action arose against such person,
for the recovery of the penalties incurred by such violation,
and for an injunction restraining him from the continued
violation of such rule or regulation."

You state that the procedure under these statutes has been very
unsatisfactory owing to the fact that the New York city authorities
cannot secure a verdict in local courts for violations of the rules
and that property owners insist that the city of New York must

compensate them for any damages occasioned by enforcing the rules. My attention is directed by you to an opinion of a former Attorney-General which holds that before penalties can be inflicted as provided in the statute above quoted, the corporation for whose benefit the rules are made must pay or tender to the owner of the property affected by the enforcement of such rules the amount of the damages for making the required changes.

The first question is whether conditions which are in and of themselves nuisances can be abated by any action that may be taken either by yourself or by the municipal authorities.

As a general rule an action to abate a condition which is a nuisance, *per se,* can be maintained by any person or corporation affected by it. If conditions exist which are in and of themselves public nuisances to the city of New York and its inhabitants, actions can be maintained by that municipality to abate those conditions.

Your second question is in respect to rules and regulations, the enforcement of which necessitates the payment or tender to the owner of the property affected of the amount of the damages occasioned by the necessary changes, and whether there is any method by which the city can proceed other than to ascertain and pay the damages, which procedure, you state, amounts virtually to a condemnation of the property affected.

The opinion of the former Attorney-General, a part of which you quote, substantially answers this question. It points out that, under our Constitution, private property cannot be taken for public use without compensation.

Under statutes authorizing the exercise of eminent domain and the taking of private property for public use, which provide for compensation, and where a fund is provided from which payment is to be made for the property taken, it is not necessary to pay or tender damages prior to the exercise of eminent domain. It has been held by eminent authority that before property can be taken without first ascertaining and paying the damages, certain and ample provision must be first made by law, so that the owner may coerce payment without any unreasonable or unnecessary delay (People v. Hayden, 6 Hill, 359.) These sections, 70 and 71, of the Public Health Law, provide methods for establishing and enforcing certain rules and regulations, but do not provide any means of compensation where the enforcement of the rules would amount to a taking of private property.

It is difficult to conceive how, for instance, a farmer could be forbidden to use his pasture lest it contaminate a city water supply, unless he receives just compensation for prohibiting such use. I find no power given in the statute by which the city could proceed to enforce regulations amounting to the taking of property without first paying or tendering the damages.

As to an expression of opinion concerning the conditions in general which are obstacles to the enforcement of these regulations, permit me to point out that the statute imposes the duty of enforcing these rules and regulations regarding watersheds primarily upon the local authorities. It states that, if a violation has occurred, the Commissioner of Health shall order the local board of health to enforce obedience to the rules and regulations. This duty is first placed upon the local board. In case it fails to enforce the orders of the Commissioner of Health, then an action can be maintained by the corporation furnishing the water supply, or the municipality, or the Commissioner of Health.

You state that the prosecution of these actions by the commissioner of water supply of the city of New York has not been altogether successful. Undoubtedly the counsel acting in these cases is more conversant with the reasons why it is difficult to maintain these actions and is in a much better position to advise concerning the situation than I. Therefore, your suggestion that I may be able to point out some effective means of improving the conditions is one on which it is difficult to advise.

Very respectfully yours,

EDWARD R. O'MALLEY,

Attorney-General.

Public Health Law — General Municipal Law.

Local boards of health operating under city ordinance may not compel farmers peddling milk which they produce on their own farms, to take out license to so peddle. Producer of farm produce may peddle without city license.

STATE OF NEW YORK.

Attorney-General's Office,

Albany, *August* 11, 1910.

Dr. Eugene H. Porter, *Commissioner of Health, Albany, N. Y.:*

Dear Sir.— I beg to acknowledge the receipt of your communication of August 9th, 1910, in which you request an opinion as to the right of a local board of health, operating under city ordinances, to compel farmers, peddling milk which they produce upon their own farms, to take out a license to so peddle, and, if it has a right to compel them so to do, as to whether such board of health has a right to collect from such milk producers a fee as a license fee.

The provisions of chapter 389 of the Laws of 1901, to which you call my attention, are now found in section 81 of the General Municipal Law, which provides:

" The governing board of a municipal corporation shall not by ordinance or otherwise regulate or prohibit the pursuit or exercise of hawking and peddling farm produce, except hay and straw, within the limits of any such municipal corporation, if such farm produce is hawked or peddled by the producer thereof, or his servants or employees; nor shall the governing board of any such municipal corporation pass an ordinance requiring such producer to secure a license for peddling and hawking such farm produce within the limits of such municipal corporation. * * * This section shall not apply to cities of the first class."

Under reported cases, and as generally defined, milk is included in the term " farm produce " used in the above act.

The Legislature may authorize a municipal corporation to regulate hawking and peddling in its streets, but such a statute, being in restriction of the common law, must receive a strict construction, and it must appear that the act sought to be interfered with is clearly within its inhibition.

The act in question expressly provides that a municipal corporation may not, by ordinance or otherwise regulate or prohibit the pursuit or exercise of hawking and peddling farm produce by the producer thereof or pass any ordinance requiring him to secure a license so to do.

I conclude, therefore, that in municipal corporations, other than cities of the first class, a local board of health, operating under city ordinances, has no right to compel farmers to take out a license to peddle milk which they produce upon their own farms, and no right to collect from such milk producers a fee as a license fee.

Very respectfully,

EDWARD R. O'MALLEY,

Attorney-General.

Public Health Law — Section 20 — Public Officers Law — Sections 30, 10.

Action of board of health, village of Fort Edward, in displacing Dr. Mott as health officer, because of his failure to take the oath of office, and appointing Dr. Holliday to succeed him, legal.

STATE OF NEW YORK.

ATTORNEY-GENERAL'S OFFICE,

ALBANY, *September 9, 1910.*

Hon. EUGENE H. PORTER, *Commissioner of Health, Albany, N. Y.:*

Dear Sir.— I beg to acknowledge receipt of yours in which you state that Dr. O. H. Mott was appointed health officer of the village of Fort Edward on December 13, 1907, for a term of four years; that on the second day of May you were notified by H. P. Turney, secretary of the board of health of the village of Fort Edward; that at a meeting of the board of health on April 29, 1910, a resolution was adopted by the board appointing Dr. Hamilton Holliday to succeed Dr. Mott; that you were advised that the appointment of Dr. Holliday was made owing to the failure of Dr. Mott to file an oath of office after being appointed to the office, and asking me to advise whether there is any provision of law requiring a local health officer to file an oath of office, and whether I considered the action taken by the board of health of the village of Fort Edward legal in displacing Dr. Mott without having conformed with the provisions of section 20 of the Public Health Law in preferring charges and holding a hearing before declaring the office vacant.

Article 13, section 1, of the State Constitution provides:

> " Members of the Legislature, and all officers executive and judicial, except such inferior officers as shall be by law exempted shall, before they enter on the duties of their respective offices, take and subscribe the following oath or affirmation: * * * ."

Section 20 of the Public Health Law provides among other things as follows:

> " The local board of health shall appoint a competent physician, not a member of the local board of health, to be the health officer of the municipality. The term of office of the health officer shall be four years and he shall hold office until the appointment of his successor. He may be removed for just cause by the local board of health or the state commissioner of health after a hearing; such removal by the local board of health must be approved by the state commissioner of health."

Section 10 of the Public Officers Law provides:

> " Every officer shall take and file the oath of office required by law before he shall be entitled to enter upon the discharge of any of his official duties. * * * "

Section 30 of the Public Officers Law provides as follows:

> " Every office shall be vacant upon the happening of either of the following events before the expiration of the term thereof:
>
> 1. * * * *

7. His refusal or neglect to file his official oath or under-taking, if one is required, before or within fifteen days after the commencement of the term of office for which he is chosen, if an elective office, or if an appointive office, within fifteen days after notice of his appointment, or within fifteen days after the commencement of such term;   *   *   *."

It would seem that the health officer of a village is a public officer and I find no provision of law which exempts such health officer from taking the constitutional oath of office.

I am therefore of the opinion that the action taken by the board of health of the village of Fort Edward in displacing Dr. Mott is legal and that the provisions of section 20 of the Public Health Law above quoted, requiring the preferring of charges and holding a hearing before declaring the office vacant did not apply inasmuch as a vacancy existed in the office by failure of Dr. O. H. Mott to take and file the oath of office required by statute.

Yours very truly,

EDWARD R. O'MALLEY,

Attorney-General.

Public Health Law — Section 20.

Charges filed for removal of health officer, city of Binghamton.

(See opinion May 16, 1910.)

STATE OF NEW YORK.

Attorney-General's Office,

Albany, *October 26*, 1910.

Hon. Eugene H. Porter, *Commissioner of Health, Albany, N. Y.:*

Dear Sir.— I beg to acknowledge receipt of your communication of September 12, 1910, in reference to a hearing noticed by and before you, on charges filed with you against the health officer of the city of Binghamton, together with the accompanying copy of objections, filed on behalf of said health officer, to his being required to answer or to be tried upon charges, on the ground that on February 11, 1910, the same complainant filed charges, substantially identical to those preferred before you, with the commissioner of health of Binghamton who had jurisdiction to hear and determine the same, and that the objections were brought to trial before said commissioner and that he found and determined that the facts shown in the evidence were insufficient to warrant the removal of the health officer.

The attorney for the objector contends that jurisdiction to remove a health officer is concurrent in the State Commissioner and in the city commissioner (standing in the place of the local board of health) ; that the city commissioner before whom proceedings were first brought should be deemed to have acquired thereby exclusive jurisdiction and that a person tried and acquitted before one authority having jurisdiction should not be required to meet the same charges before the other authority having concurrent jurisdiction therewith; and that, when a proceeding has been brought before the local authority and a determination made on the merits, the statute gives the State Commissioner of Health the right to review only when the judgment and decision are of removal.

My opinion is asked upon the following questions:

1. Whether or not you have authority to hear charges, in view of the fact that the health officer has already been tried on charges before the city commissioner, and whether or not the latter acquired exclusive jurisdiction.

2. Whether or not you have jurisdiction to hear charges identical with those that have been already presented to the city commissioner, or whether such hearing, if any, must be confined to matters outside of those already brought before the city commissioner.

Section 20 of the Public Health Law provides as follows:

"He (the health officer) may be removed for just cause by the local board of health or the state commissioner of health after a hearing; such removal by the local board of health must be approved by the state commissioner of health."

Thus it would seem that proceedings may be instituted, either before the local board of health or the State Commissioner, and may be prosecuted to a determination. The State Commissioner may remove a health officer upon findings of charges proven, if the proceeding is brought before him. Where the local board entertains a hearing upon charges brought before it, its judgment of removal (if one follows) may not be carried into effect without the approval of the State Commissioner. Otherwise, there seems to be no limitation imposed by statute upon the determination of the local board.

It is, perhaps, too broad to .say that jurisdiction to remove is concurrent. But jurisdiction to entertain charges, in the first instance, is concurrent. A complainant has his choice of the forum in which he may lodge and try his charges. There is no provision in the statute for any approval by the State Commissioner when the judgment of the local board dismisses the charges; nor is there any provision for a review of such judgment by appeal to the State Commissioner. Subject only to the provision as to approval, above noted, the local board is apparently given concurrent power with the State Commissioner to hear and decide.

It would appear in this case that the complainant made his choice of one of the tribunals having concurrent jurisdiction; he lodged his charges before it; he prosecuted his case to a final determination and he failed to sustain his charges on the merits. I do not believe that it was intended that he might thereafter institute another proceeding, on the same charges, before the other authority.

It is my opinion that the hearing and determination of the charges by and before the city commissioner were a final adjudication of the same; that they operated as a bar to a hearing by you upon charges identical with those already presented; and that, so far as you may have jurisdiction to entertain charges against the health officer, such hearing, if any, must be confined to matters outside of those already brought and tried out before the city commissioner.

Respectfully yours,

EDWARD R. O'MALLEY,

Attorney-General.

OPINIONS RENDERED THE STATE COMMISSIONER
OF LABOR.

___

Labor Law — Section 3 — Eight Hour Law — State Institutions.
State reservation at Niagara not a State institution, and persons
employed upon do not come within provisions of above
section.

(See opinion July 26, 1910.)

STATE OF NEW YORK.

ATTORNEY-GENERAL'S OFFICE,

ALBANY, *June* 16, 1910.

Hon. JOHN WILLIAMS, *Commissioner of Labor. Albany. N. Y.:*

Dear Sir.— I acknowledge your letter of the 15th inst., in which
you ask my opinion as to whether the State Reservation at Niagara
is a "State institution" within the meaning of the term as used
in section 3 of the Labor Law, where it provides that "nothing in
this section shall be construed to apply to persons regularly employed in state institutions."

It is my opinion that the State Reservation at Niagara is not a
State institution within the meaning of this language. The board
known as the Commissioners of the State Reservation at Niagara
is given the control and management of the property constituting
such reservation. The purpose of the reservation is to restore the
scenery of Niagara Falls and preserve it in its natural condition
free of access to all. (Public Lands Law, article IX.) The
reservation itself is not an institution in any sense but simply a
certain parcel of land described in the statute. (Public Lands
Law, § 108.)

The mere fact that the persons employed on the reservation are
employed by a State commission is not sufficient, in my judgment,
to bring them within the language above quoted. This is shown
by the amendment to this very section of the Labor Law made by

the Legislature in 1900 in adding to the above quoted exception in section 3, the following:

" * * * or to engineers, electricians and elevator men in the department of public buildings during the annual session of the legislature." (Chapter 298, Laws of 1900, amending chapter 415, Laws of 1897, as amended by chapter 567, Laws of 1899.)

At the time of this last amendment the employees so specifically excepted from the operation of section 3 were under the Trustees of Public Buildings, which Trustees had control of the department of public buildings. It is evident from this amendment that the words "State institutions" were not deemed broad enough by the Legislature to include the capitol and other public buildings under the control of the Trustees of Public Buildings. The amendment, therefore, is a legislative interpretation of the meaning of these words in accordance with the opinion herein rendered.

Very truly yours,

EDWARD R. O'MALLEY,

Attorney-General.

Labor Law — Sections 2, 3 — Eight Hour Law.

Employees of State Reservation at Niagara acting as police, and wearing uniforms and badges, not subject to provisions of.

(See opinion June 16, 1910.)

STATE OF NEW YORK.

ATTORNEY-GENERAL'S OFFICE,

ALBANY, *July* 26, 1910.

Hon. JOHN WILLIAMS, *Commissioner of Labor. Albany. N. Y.:*

Dear Sir.— I am in receipt of a letter from Acting Commissioner William W. Walling asking for my opinion as to the applicability of the Eight Hour Law to certain employees of the State of New York at the State Reservation at Niagara Falls, who have police power and wear uniforms with badges. The enclosure accompanying the letter contains a list of employees, among which are those described as police constables, night watchmen, ticket men and caretakers, all of whom possess police powers and are required to work more than eight hours per day.

The provisions of the Labor Law under which this question arises are sections 2 and 3, which read as follows:

> "Section 2. DEFINITIONS — EMPLOYEE.— The term 'employee,' when used in this section, means a mechanic, workingman or laborer who works for another for hire. * * *"
>
> "§ 3. HOURS TO CONSTITUTE A DAY'S WORK.— Eight hours shall constitute a legal day's work for all classes of employees in this state except those engaged in farm and domestic service unless otherwise provided by law. * * *"

Under the above provisions, the answer to your proposition involves the determination of whether the employees above referred to are employees within the meaning of the Labor Law. It has been held that this provision of the Labor Law does not apply to uniformed members of the fire department in the city of New York. Under the decisions construing the definition of "employee" as used in the above statute, I am clearly of the opinion that the Eight Hour Law does not apply to employees of the State at the Niagara Reservation who are performing the duties and have the powers of policemen.

Yours very truly,

EDWARD R. O'MALLEY,

Attorney-General.

Labor Law — Section 3 — Eight Hour Law — State Institutions.

Men "regularly employed" in State institutions may be placed on "construction, additions and improvements" without coming under the general provisions of the Eight Hour Law.

STATE OF NEW YORK.

ATTORNEY-GENERAL'S OFFICE,

ALBANY, *August* 17, 1910.

HON. JOHN WILLIAMS, *Commissioner of Labor, Albany, N. Y.:*

Dear Sir.— I have your letter of recent date in which you call my attention to the fact that the Labor Law in section 3 provides that eight hours shall constitute a day's work for all classes of employees in this State, but that this contains a proviso to the effect that persons regularly employed in such institutions are not affected thereby. You also call my attention to the fact that the Legislature in the annual appropriation bill provides a lump sum for the "maintenance" of such institutions and that out of this appropriation are paid the salaries of all persons "regularly employed" therein. In addition to this, in special appropriations sums of money are provided for "construction, additions and improvements" at such institutions. In view of these facts, you ask me whether laborers, workmen or mechanics who are "regularly employed" in such institutions and whose salaries are paid out of the maintenance funds may be employed by the management upon "construction, additions and improvements" which are paid for out of special appropriations, without coming under the general provisions of said section 3.

This question must be answered in the affirmative as it assumes the fact that these men are "regularly employed" in these institutions. Whether or not they come under the provisions of this section depends on the question of fact in each instance as to whether or not they are regularly employed at the institution. Neither the nature of the work nor the appropriation from which they are to be paid has any connection with this determination.

Very truly yours,

EDWARD R. O'MALLEY,

Attorney-General.

OPINIONS RENDERED THE STATE FISCAL
SUPERVISOR.

_State Institutions — New York State Soldiers' and Sailors' Home,
Bath._

Reappointment " master mechanic " not within contemplation of
statute. Section 8 of the Public Buildings Law clothes the
State Architect with the duty of preparing drawings, specifications, etc., and board of trustees may not delegate power to
others.

STATE OF NEW YORK.

ATTORNEY-GENERAL'S OFFICE,

ALBANY, _March_ 29, 1910.

Hon. DENNIS McCARTHY, _Fiscal Supervisor, Albany, N. Y._:

Dear Sir.— I acknowledge your letters of the 22d and 23d
insts. enclosing letter from the commandant of the New York
State Soldiers' and Sailors' Home at Bath, and asking my opinion
upon the question therein presented.

It appears that the board of trustees of this institution has
unanimously passed a resolution favoring the reappointment of
one of the employees of the institution to the position of master
mechanic. It appears that this same employee was appointed to
such position in 1905 and that the then Fiscal Supervisor dis-
allowed his salary on the ground that the Public Buildings Law,
under section 8, provided that the same work which he was appointed to perform should be done by the State Architect and that
therefore his appointment to the position was illegal.

The duties of the position of master mechanic as created by the
board of trustees are stated as follows: '

First. To perform ordinary carpenter work.

Second. To have charge of the carpenter repair work of the
institution and of the force of carpenters, painters and some other
employees.

Third. To inspect all carpenter construction work being done under contract and to prepare plans for new buildings and carpenter construction work and to estimate the cost.

Section 8 of the Public Buildings Law provides as follows:

" Section 8. Duties.— The state architect shall prepare the drawings and specifications and supervise and control, as architect, the construction of all new buildings erected at the expense of the state. He shall also prepare the drawings and specifications for additions to existing buildings, and for the alteration or improvement thereof. He shall see that the materials furnished and the work performed in constructing, altering or improving any such building are in accordance, with such drawings and specifications, and that the interests of the state are fully protected, * * *."

It is claimed in the letter from the commandant that plans and estimates have always been called for by your department, and stress is laid in his letter on the fact that there are 76 buildings belonging to the institution which cost in the aggregate more than half a million dollars, so that there is a large amount of repairs and improvements being done at the institution.

On the other hand, in your letter it is stated that you fail to find any instance in which your department has requested the commandant to have prepared at his institution any plans or specifications, with the exception of a request to show new farm fences required, in response to which a crude sketch was received, and that, on the contrary, there is correspondence which recites specifically that your department does not expect any plans for buildings to be made by any employee of the Home. It is also pointed out in your letter that this institution is the only one reporting to your department which has asked for a master mechanic, although the New York State Reformatory at Elmira, the Eastern New York Reformatory at Napanoch, the New York House of Refuge at Randall's Island, the Rome State Custodial Asylum, and the Craig Colony for Epileptics at Sonyea each have property valued at considerably more than the property of this institution.

It would seem from an examination of section 8 of the Public Buildings Law, quoted above, that the State Architect is required by statute to perform all of the more important duties assigned by the board of trustees of this institution to the position of master mechanic. It is therefore my opinion that the statutes do not contemplate conferring upon such board the power to appoint any other person to perform the same functions. It is certainly contrary to public policy to have an unnecessary duplication of offices, and no statute will be interpreted as permitting such duplication unless compelled by the clearest language. There is nothing in the act defining the powers of the board of trustees of this institution which specifically gives it the power to appoint any such employee, and I am therefore of the opinion that the ruling made by your department is correct and that the board of trustees has no power to delegate to any employee appointed by it the duties which by the statute devolve upon the State Architect and must be performed by him.

Very truly yours,

EDWARD R. O'MALLEY,

Attorney-General.

———·

State Charities Law — Section 48 — State Institutions — Contracts.

State Fiscal Supervisor may disapprove contract made between the purchasing committee of superintendents, and the Van Wyck Thorpe Company, of Hudson, for delivery of coal.

STATE OF NEW YORK.

ATTORNEY-GENERAL'S OFFICE,

ALBANY, *April* 25, 1910.

Hon. DENNIS McCARTHY, *Fiscal Supervisor, Albany, N. Y.:*

Dear Sir.— I have your letter of the 23d inst., in which you ask my opinion as to your right to disapprove a contract which you state was made on March 28, 1910, between the purchasing committee of superintendents for institutions reporting to your department and the Van Wyck Thorpe Company, of Hudson, for coal. I note that this contract has not yet been delivered to you for approval but that you are just in receipt of an analysis of coal delivered which indicates to you that a delivery has been made under it.

Section 48 of the State Charities Law provides the method by which a purchasing committee of superintendents and managers or trustees of institutions reporting to you may be created and defines the powers of such committee. It provides in part:

"Such purchasing committee may appoint a secretary who is also a stenographer and may also consider proposals and make awards under joint contracts for the purchase of staple articles of supplies for any or all of the state institutions reporting to the fiscal supervisor and shall appoint a committee of two to execute joint contracts in accordance with such awards, *subject to the approval of the fiscal supervisor.*"

It is further provided that all powers conferred by this section upon the purchasing committee shall be exercised subject to the powers possessed or hereafter conferred upon you.

It is my opinion that under the foregoing provisions of the statute you may disapprove the contract entered into by the purchasing committee for the supply of coal referred to in your letter. Such action on your part, however, should be taken promptly as soon as the terms of the contract are called to your attention. From the statement contained in your letter it appears that you are only just aware of the fact that the contract is being acted upon, and I therefore infer that there has not been any delay on your part which could possibly be claimed to estop you from exercising your rights.

I therefore advise you that, if you so desire, you may notify the contractor and the purchasing committee at once that you disapprove the contract or that you withhold approval until its specifications are made satisfactory to you.

Yours respectfully,

EDWARD R. O'MALLEY,

Attorney-General.

State Finance Law - - Sections 16, 37 — State Institutions.

Soldiers' Home at Bath may not furnish tallow to Troy firm and receive in exchange laundry and toilet soap. State Finance Law clearly provides that all supplies shall be purchased for cash, and products sold for cash, and prohibits such exchanges by State institutions.

(See opinion June 22, 1899, p. 273, Report.)

STATE OF NEW YORK.

ATTORNEY-GENERAL'S OFFICE,

ALBANY, *May* 3, 1910.

Hon. DENNIS McCARTHY, *Fiscal Supervisor. Albany, N. Y.:*

Dear Sir.-- I have your letter of the 20th ultimo in which you ask my opinion upon the legality of the following transaction:

You state that one of your inspectors has reported that as a result of his inspection of the New York State Soldiers' and Sailors' Home at Bath, he has discovered that "the laundry and toilet soap supplied is furnished by a Troy firm in exchange for tallow which the institution saves and sends to them." You state that it was formerly the custom of this institution to sell the tallow obtained by rendering the grease from meat and to turn the proceeds over to the State Treasurer. You also state that there is no information on file in your department to show the price allowed for this tallow nor the price at which the soap is supplied. You also call my attention to a similar case which was discovered at the Rome State Custodial Asylum some years ago and was directed by one of your predecessors to be discontinued although, as also appears from your letter, in a number of individual instances, with the concurrence of the Comptroller, certain other institutions have been permitted to make exchanges such as the exchange of bones for fertilizer, the exchange of wheat for flour or feed, and the exchange of vegetables for canned goods.

I have carefully examined this question and it is my opinion that under the law such a practice is illegal. The provisions of the State Finance Law seem clearly to contemplate that the business of all State institutions must be conducted on a cash basis; that all supplies shall be purchased for cash; and that all produce shall be sold for cash which shall be turned over to the State Treasurer. Section 16 of the State Finance Law provides in part as follows:

"All purchases for the use of any department, office or work of the State government shall be for cash."

Section 37 of the same law provides in part as follows:

" Every state officer, employee, board, department or commission receiving money for or on behalf of the state from fees, penalties, costs, fines, *sales of property* or otherwise * * *,"

shall pay monthly to the State Treasurer all such money.

In considering the effect of this section, former Attorney-General Davies held that it prevented the payment for supplies and labor with farm produce by the New York Agricultural Experiment Station. In the course of this opinion he says (Report of Attorney-General, 1899, page 273):

" It is evident to me that among the purposes sought by the Legislature in enacting that statute was that of prohibiting State officers or boards from indiscriminately paying out moneys without first having the transaction approved as required by law. This will undoubtedly cause some inconvenience and extra labor but it causes a uniformity of action on the part of all departments and institutions of the State. * * * The products should be sold for cash and payment for supplies, labor, etc., received or enjoyed by the Experiment Station should be paid for in cash in the manner prescribed by law."

I fully concur in the above reasoning and in my judgment it is equally applicable to the cases mentioned in your letter. I must therefore advise you that under the law, all exchanges by State institutions of their products for other products is prohibited.

Very truly yours,

EDWARD R. O'MALLEY,

Attorney-General.

State Charities Law — Section 45 — State Institutions.

1. Fiscal Supervisor may cause estimates to be revised by officers of State institutions so as to cause a reduction of amount.
2. Power of Fiscal Supervisor to enforce compliance by subordinate officers with requests for economy, only in such manner as is prescribed in section 45.
3. Fiscal Supervisor not liable for expenditure of State institutions on excess of amount appropriated, as board or officer making such contract would be held responsible.

STATE OF NEW YORK.

ATTORNEY-GENERAL'S OFFICE,

ALBANY, *May* 6, 1910.

Hon. DENNIS McCARTHY, *Fiscal Supervisor, Albany, N. Y.:*

Dear Sir.— Referring to your letters of the 18th ultimo and 4th instant, in which you ask my opinion upon various questions, I beg to advise you as follows:

The first question which you ask is whether, under section 45 of the State Charities Law, you have the power to return estimates submitted to you by State institutions, with the direction that they be revised by the officers of such institutions so as to bring about a certain definite reduction which you deem necessary.

Section 45 of this law provides in part as follows:

> "The fiscal supervisor may cause such estimates to be revised either as to quantity or quality of supplies and the estimated cost thereof, and shall certify that he has carefully examined the same and that the articles contained in such estimate, as approved or revised by him, are actually required for the use of the institution, and shall thereupon present such estimate and certificate to the comptroller."

As you point out, there is no specific provision in this section as to how or by whom these estimates shall be revised. There is much force in your contention that persons located at the institution and familiar with its more pressing needs, are in better position to make such revision in some respects, than are you. It is

therefore my opinion that you have the right to " cause such estimates to be revised " by the several institutions submitting them,
and that such practice on your part is legal.

The second question which you ask is for my opinion " as to the
powers of the Fiscal Supervisor in the matter of enforcing compliance, by the subordinate officers of the institutions reporting to
him, with recommendations made by the Fiscal Supervisor for
securing greater economy in the administration of the institutions."

This is a general question which it is difficult to answer
specifically. Your powers over such institutions are clearly defined
by the statute; in so far as you may enforce compliance with your
suggestions by revising the estimates in the manner authorized by
section 45 of the State Charities Law, your right to do so is clear.
Beyond this, I find nothing in the statute which will give you more
than advisory powers.

Your third question is for my opinion " as to the financial
responsibility of the Fiscal Supervisor for the expenditures of the
institutions reporting to him, in excess of the amounts appropriated therefor."

This is another general question and the answer to it might
possibly be varied by particular circumstances. However, I
assume it to mean whether or not you are liable personally for a
State institution exceeding in its expenditures the amount of the
appropriation made for such expenditures. Under section 45 of
the State Charities Law it is provided that after revising the estimates you shall certify that you have " carefully examined the
same and that the articles contained in such estimate, as approved
or revised by " you, " are actually required for the use of the institution, and shall thereupon present such estimate and certificate
to the Comptroller." The statute further provides:

" Upon the revision and approval of such estimate, the
comptroller shall authorize the boards of managers, trustees
or other managing officers of such institutions to make drafts
on him, as the money may be required for the purposes mentioned in such estimates, which draft shall be paid on his
warrant, out of the funds in the treasury of the state appropriated for the support of such institutions."

It is obvious, from an examination of these provisions, together with the provision that these estimates shall be given monthly in advance, that your approval is contemplated as a condition precedent to the actual incurring of liability. In any view, however, such liability is not actually incurred by you but by the board or officer entering into the contract, so that there would seem to be no possibility of a violation by you of section 35 of the State Finance Law. It is therefore my opinion that in the ordinary case you would be under no personal liability for an expenditure by an institution reporting to you in excess of the amount appropriated to it. The question would seem to be largely academic because unless the Comptroller and the Treasurer are both negligent, no such expenditure could be made.

Very truly yours,

EDWARD R. O'MALLEY,

Attorney-General.

State Charities Law — Section 45 — State Institutions.

Purchasing of supplies necessary for the entertainment of managers or trustees of the institution to be included in supplemental estimates. Fiscal Supervisor should authorize all supplies for officers or employees of such institutions to be added to the usual supplies for the general use of the institutions, and should not permit any extra supplies to be delivered without going into the storehouse of the institutions.

STATE OF NEW YORK.

ATTORNEY-GENERAL'S OFFICE,

ALBANY, *June* 13, 1910.

Hon. DENNIS McCARTHY, *Fiscal Supervisor, Albany, N. Y.:*

Dear Sir.— I acknowledge your letter of the 6th inst. in which you enclose copy of letter written by you to the superintendents of the institutions reporting to you, and request my opinion upon the legality of the expenditure therein authorized. Said letter states that your department will approve items for food supplies necessary and proper for the entertainment of managers or trustees of the institution and other official guests, which may be included in supplemental estimates at the close of the months in which the purchases are made, to an amount not exceeding $75 a year for each institution.

Section 45 of the State Charities Law provides in part as follows in reference to institutions reporting to you:

"* * * Nor shall the treasurer of any institution named or referred to in this section pay accounts for supplies furnished to officers and employees unless the same be drawn from the ordinary supplies provided for the general use of the institution."

You ask whether this provision renders the expenditures above mentioned in any manner unlawful.

The meaning of this language is not as clear as could be desired. Its general purpose, however, is apparent. It is evidently intended to prevent officers or employees from purchasing supplies for themselves and charging them to the institutions. To avoid this, it is provided that the treasurer shall not pay any accounts for supplies so furnished. All supplies for officers and employees must be drawn from the ordinary supplies provided for the general use of the institution.

In my judgment, this does not mean that officers and employees shall not receive any different diet from that given the inmates of the institution. As you stated to me verbally, such a construction would make it extremely difficult to secure the class of persons desired for officers and employees. In my opinion, all that is required is that the supplies used shall first go into the general storehouse of the institution, and that officers and employees alike shall receive supplies only from this source. It does not mean that they can receive only supplies which are given likewise to inmates.

From this it would follow that there would be no objection to the course outlined in your letter on the ground that it contemplated allowing certain officers different food supplies than are ordinarily furnished the inmates of the institution. Accordingly, if under your authorization supplies for the entertainment of managers and official visitors are added to the ordinary supplies for the general use of the institution and used only from such supplies, there would seem to be no violation of the law. If, on the other hand, your authorization should be taken as permitting officers to order unusual supplies to be delivered directly to themselves without going into the storehouse of the institution, there would seem to be a clear violation of the law.

Very truly yours,

EDWARD R. O'MALLEY,

Attorney-General.

State Institutions.

Traveling expenses of managers or trustees of State charitable institutions may be paid either by authorization of the board of trustees, or by the approval of the Fiscal Supervisor.

STATE OF NEW YORK.

ATTORNEY-GENERAL'S OFFICE,

ALBANY, *September* 3, 1910.

HON. DENNIS MCCARTHY, *Fiscal Supervisor, Albany, N. Y.:*

Dear Sir.— In reply to your favor of August 30th asking for my opinion as to the construction of the last sentence of the Appropriation Law, chapter 512, Laws of 1910, I would say that I am of opinion that a manager, trustee or officer of any State charitable institution may be reimbursed for his actual traveling expenses while in the performance of official duties, other than attending meetings of the board at the office of the institution, in either of two cases; first, when authorized by resolution of the board of managers of the institution of which he is a member; second, when he has the approval of the Fiscal Supervisor of State Charities, and that it is no longer required that the resolution of the board of managers be approved by the Fiscal Supervisor.

Yours very truly,

EDWARD R. O'MALLEY,

Attorney-General.

State Charities Law — Section 51 *— State Institutions.*

Traveling expenses managers State School for the Blind. Actual and necessary expenses to be paid under provisions of section 51 and not under provisions of Education Law, section 947.

STATE OF NEW YORK.

ATTORNEY-GENERAL'S OFFICE,

ALBANY, *December* 3, 1910.

Hon. DENNIS McCARTHY, *Fiscal Supervisor. Albany, N. Y.:*

Dear Sir.— I beg to acknowledge receipt of your letter of August 31st in which you ask for my opinion as to whether the managers of the State School for the Blind should be allowed mileage at the same rate as that paid to the members of the Legislature for distances actually traveled, as provided in section 7 of chapter 744 of the Laws of 1867 (now section 947 of the Education Law) or should be allowed their actual and necessary expenses as set forth in section 51 of the State Charities Law.

I would say in reply that I am of opinion that the provisions of section 51 of the State Charities Law are controlling and that the managers of this institution should be paid their actual traveling expenses and not be allowed mileage.

Yours very truly,

EDWARD R. O'MALLEY,

Attorney-General.

OPINION RENDERED THE STATE PRINTING BOARD.

State Printing Law.

In absence of provision for rebinding old books, State departments may have such work performed outside of State printing plant.

STATE OF NEW YORK.

Attorney-General's Office,

Albany, *January* 11, 1910.

State Printing Board, Albany, N. Y.:

Gentlemen.— Your communication of the 6th inst., received in which you ask an opinion from this office as to whether State departments are obliged, under the State Printing Law, to have old books rebound by the State printing plant.

An examination of the statute fails to reveal any provision for the rebinding of old books. I have also examined the printing contract for the year 1910 and find no terms provided for the rebinding of old books where there is no printing to be done. I am of the opinion, therefore, that such work may be performed outside of the State printing plant.

Yours respectfully,

EDWARD R. O'MALLEY,

Attorney-General.

OPINION RENDERED THE STATE RESERVATION AT NIAGARA.

State Reservation at Niagara.

Permit given by commissioners to guide for term of five years, and construction of building by him upon the State Reservation to be used as a rest house in return for grant of such permit, not in conflict with statute. (Public Lands Law, sections 102, 105.)

STATE OF NEW YORK.

ATTORNEY-GENERAL'S OFFICE,

ALBANY, *January* 19, 1910.

Hon. CHARLES M. DOW, *President, Commissioners of the State Reservation at Niagara, Niagara Falls, N. Y.:*

Dear Sir.— I have your letter of the 19th inst., in which you ask my opinion upon the following question:

You state that your commission has for many years given a permit to one or two persons to conduct visitors behind the Falls, furnishing a guide and proper clothing for the trip. For the clothing and guide's service a reasonable charge is made. The person receiving this permit has paid an annual compensation to your commission for the State for the privilege thus given, which amount, until recently, has been $1,500 a year. Your commission now desires to grant this privilege to the same person who has held it for many years, for a term of five years, in return for which he is willing to construct upon the reservation a building to be used by the public as a rest house and public comfort station and of the value of at least $20,000. No charge will be made to any one for the use of this building or any of its accommodations, and the use of a part of it will be given the licensee for the transaction of his business.

You state that the power to grant a permit of this character and receive therefore an annual compensation has never been doubted in the past, and that your commission now desires to know if there is any legal objection to granting this permit and receiving compensation therefor in the construction of the building instead of in money. You also state that this building is a desirable addition to the State property, much needed for public convenience, and that this method of erecting it will save an appropriation by the Legislature for that purpose.

I have carefully examined the law upon this question, and it is my opinion that there is no legal objection to the course proposed.

Section 102 of the Public Lands Law, defining the power of your commission, states that it shall

> " Have the control and management of the state reservation at Niagara."   .   .   -
>
> " Lay out, manage and maintain such reservation and make and enforce ordinances, by-laws, rules and regulation necessary to effect the purpose thereof, and for the orderly transaction of business, not inconsistent with law,   *   *   *."

It is also provided in the same section that the commissioners shall

> " Pay into the treasury of the state on the first day of each month all receipts and earnings of whatever nature other than receipts from the state treasurer."

Section 105 provides as follows:

> " GIFTS OF PROPERTY FOR PURPOSES OF THE RESERVATION. — Real and personal property may be granted, conveyed, bequeathed or devised to and taken by the state in aid of the purposes of such reservation, or to increase the same, or on such trusts or conditions as may be prescribed by the grantors or devisors thereof, provided the same be accepted or agreed to in writing by such commissioners. All such property shall be managed and controlled by the commissioners, and the rents, issues and profits thereof shall be turned into the state treasury, except where such rents, issues and profits were specifically devised or bequeathed to be used for a specific and definite purpose."

Under the authority conferred upon your commissioners by the foregoing law, it seems to me within your power that to secure the safety of the public you should grant an exclusive permit to some one known to be reliable for acting as guide under the Falls, and that you are also authorized to charge a reasonable fee for such privilege.

If in the judgment of your commission it is desirable to have this building erected upon land of the State, to become the property of the State, I see no legal objection to your receiving it instead of money in return for the grant of the permit.

Yours respectfully,

EDWARD R. O'MALLEY,

Attorney-General.

OPINIONS RENDERED THE STATE SUPERINTEND-
ENT OF BANKS.

Banking Law — Section 69 — Stock Corporations Law — Section 25.

Annual meeting Bank of Lake Placid for election of directors. Where requirement regarding publication of notice was disregarded, but said notice was served on all stockholders personally or by mail, and such meeting held and directors elected in every other respect in a legal manner, a waiver signed by each stockholder approving such vote under section 42 of the General Corporations Law, renders such election legal and valid.

STATE OF NEW YORK.

ATTORNEY-GENERAL'S OFFICE,

ALBANY, *February* 2, 1910.

Hon. GEORGE I. SKINNER, *First Deputy Superintendent, Banking Department, Albany:*

Dear Sir.— I beg to acknowledge receipt of your letter of January 21st, requesting my advice concerning the annual meeting of the Bank of Lake Placid. The following facts appear:

The annual meeting of the stockholders of the bank was held within ten days of the second Tuesday in January last, in accordance with the provision of section 69 of the Banking Law. This section also provides: " Notice of such meeting shall be given as required by the Stock Corporation Law." Section 25 of the last mentioned law states: " Notice of the time and place of holding any election of directors shall be given by publication thereof, at least once in each week for two successive weeks immediately preceding such election, in a newspaper published in the county * * *." This requirement of publication of the notice was not fulfilled, but the meeting was held as above stated, actual notice having been served upon all of the stockholders either personally or by mail on or before the first day of January.

In view of the above facts you ask my advice as to what course should be pursued by the bank to elect new directors or whether the old directors hold office until the next annual meeting.

Upon the facts as stated it appears that an election of directors was held, which was legal, both as to time and otherwise, in every respect except that the notice of the annual meeting was not published in the newspapers as required by section 69 of the Banking Law.

I am of the opinion that section 42 of the General Corporation Law is applicable to this question. The section provides that " Whenever, under the provisions of any corporation law, a corporation is authorized to take any action after notice to its members or after the lapse of a prescribed period of time, such action may be taken without notice and without the lapse of any period of time, if such action be authorized or approved, and such requirements be waived in writing by every member of such corporation or by his attorney thereunto authorized." In my judgment the purpose of this statute is to govern exactly such a situation as is here presented.

I therefore respectfully advise that upon the signing of a waiver by each stockholder of record entitled to vote at a meeting, authorizing and approving the election of the directors which was held at the required time, and waiving the statutory requirement of publication of the notice, the election of the directors, if otherwise according to law, would become legal and valid.

Respectfully yours,

EDWARD R. O'MALLEY,

Attorney-General.

Banking Law — Sections 310, 311 *— General Corporations Law — Section* 35.

Loan associations organized under article 10. Where Superintendent of Banks refuses to renew license and action to dissolve corporation is begun, the association may collect claims due it previous to appointment of receiver.

STATE OF NEW YORK.

ATTORNEY-GENERAL'S OFFICE,

ALBANY, *March* 22, 1910.

Hon. O. H. CHENEY, *Superintendent of Banks, Albany, N. Y.:*

Dear Sir.— I have your favor of March 17th, in which you ask whether a personal loan association organized pursuant to article 10 of the Banking Law is allowed to collect claims due it after the Superintendent of Banks has refused to renew its annual license.

Section 310 of the Banking Law provides that a company of this character shall file a bond with the Superintendent of Banks and obtain a license from him authorizing it to do business.

Section 311 provides in part:

" Said bond shall be renewed and refiled annually in January of each year and shall be approved by the superintendent of banks and a new license issued on or before the first day of March, or the corporation shall within thirty days thereafter cease doing business and proceedings for dissolution shall be instituted by the attorney-general at the request of said superintendent."

This provision gives the Superintendent of Banks the power to bring an action to dissolve such a corporation and in that action a receiver may be appointed.

Section 35 of the General Corporation Law provides:

" Upon the dissolution of any corporation its directors, unless other persons shall be appointed by the legislature or by some court of competent jurisdiction, shall be the trustees of its creditors, stockholders or members and shall have full power to settle its affairs, collect and pay outstanding debts, and divide among the persons entitled thereto the money and other property remaining after payment of the debts and necessary expenses."

While the corporation can do no new business by reason of the refusal of the Superintendent of Banks to renew its license, I am of the opinion that the corporation has the same right, previous to the appointment of a receiver, to collect any legal claims due it as the trustees of a dissolved corporation would have to collect its assets until a receiver had been appointed.

Yours very truly,

EDWARD R. O'MALLEY,

Attorney-General.

Banking Law - - Section 193 - - Trust Companies.

Stocks and bonds constituting capital investment may be entered on reports of trust companies under the supervision of the Superintendent of Banks, at amortized value, if market value is higher than amortized value.

STATE OF NEW YORK.

ATTORNEY-GENERAL'S OFFICE,

ALBANY, *April* 28, 1910.

Hon. O. H. CHENEY, *Superintendent of Banks, Albany, N. Y.:*

Dear Sir.— I have your letter of the 13th inst., in which you request my opinion upon the question submitted to you by the vice-president of the Guardian Trust Company, asking whether or not you have the power to require that bonds constituting capital investment of trust companies shall be entered in their reports to you at their market value.

I have carefully examined the statute and beg to advise as follows: Section 193 of the Banking Law provides in part:

"Stocks or bonds constituting a part of the lawful investment of capital of any such corporation shall not be valued upon its books or entered in its reports to the superintendent of banks at a higher price or value than their investment value as determined by amortization, * * *."

This provision is mandatory to the effect that no *higher* value shall be given to stocks or bonds than the amortized value. It does not, however, limit any further than this the general power conferred upon you by section 21 of the Banking Law to prescribe the form and material contained in the reports submitted by corporations subject to your supervision. It is therefore my opinion that with this one limitation you have the power to prescribe that the market value of stocks and bonds rather than the amortized value shall be entered in the reports to you. In other words, your instructions could read substantially as follows:

" Extend market value, except that bonds constituting capital investment should be carried at amortized value if market value is higher than amortized value."

Very truly yours,

EDWARD R. O'MALLEY,

Attorney-General.

Banking Law — Section 146 — Savings Banks Investments.

Bonds of Kansas City comply with section 146 and are legal investments for savings banks of New York State.

(See opinion May 21, 1910).

STATE OF NEW YORK.

ATTORNEY-GENERAL'S OFFICE,

ALBANY, *May* 19, 1910.

Hon. O. H. CHENEY, *Superintendent of Banks, Albany. N. Y.:*

Dear Sir.— I acknowledge the letter from your first deputy, Mr. Skinner, under date of May 6, in which my opinion is asked as to whether or not the bonds of Kansas City, Kansas, are legal investments for savings banks of this State, and inclosing certain data upon which to base such opinion.

I have carefully examined this question, and from the data so submitted and from the statement published in White & Kemble to the effect that the State of Kansas has not repudiated or defaulted in the payment of any part of the principal or interest of any debt authorized by its Legislature to be contracted, I am of opinion that such bonds are legal investments for savings banks of this State. From the evidence before me I am satisfied that such bonds comply with the requirements of section 146 of the Banking Law.

Very truly yours,
EDWARD R. O'MALLEY,
Attorney-General.

Banking Law — Sections 214, 216, 217 *— Savings Banks.*

Home Cooperative Savings and Loan Association, Poughkeepsie. Where matured value of shares reaches excess of $200 the fixed sum in by-laws; the entire earnings should be paid to stockholders.

STATE OF NEW YORK.

ATTORNEY-GENERAL'S OFFICE,

ALBANY, <i>May</i> 20, 1910.</div>

Hon. O. H. CHENEY, *Superintendent, Banking Department, Albany, N. Y.:*

Dear Sir.— Replying to your favor of April 5th, asking for an opinion with regard to the interpretation to be placed upon section 217 of the Banking Law, and in which you inclose a copy of a letter dated April 4, 1910, from John B. Robinson, secretary of the Home Cooperative Savings and Loan Association, Poughkeepsie, N. Y., I beg to advise as follows:

The section in question is as follows:

> "When each free share reaches its matured value all payments of dues thereon shall cease and the holder thereof shall be paid out of the funds of the association, *the matured value thereof* with such rate of interest as shall be determined by

the by-laws from the time the board of directors shall declare such shares to have matured until paid."

Mr. Robinson asks:

" I would like to know if the law means to give the holders of maturing shares, just the maturing value as called for in our by-laws, (which in our case is $200) or if it would be *legal* to give them the full amount that the shares might run in excess of the two hundred, which in our case will be somewhere between three to five dollars more on each share."

The section in question must be construed in the light of what the law evidently seeks to accomplish. The fact that the by-laws of the association name the fixed sum of two hundred dollars as the " matured value " is not controlling.

Section 214 of the Banking Law provides:

" The capital of said association shall consist of the accumulated savings of its members which it holds, and shall be divided into shares of a matured value of not less than fifty dollars nor more than two hundred and fifty dollars."

Endlich on Loan Associations, section 26, says:

" Each series constitutes in effect an association by itself."
" § 118. The members of one series can not have any other or greater rights than those of all the others."

People v. Lowe, 117 N. Y., page 175, holds:

" Each member for each share held by him is entitled to the same amount."

Vierling v. Mechanics, etc. Association, 117 Ill. 524, holds:

" Each series of stock should be treated as distinct and financially independent of other series.

Christians Appeal, 102 Pa., page 189, holds:

" If the association has been prosperous they (the stockholders) have a right * * * to demand and receive their proportionate share of the accumulated fund."

Section 216 of the Banking Law, provides:

"The boards of directors may at their discretion under rules made by them retire the free shares and prepaid shares * * * and *they shall be paid the full value of their shares less all fines.*"

The converse of the proposition here presented has several times been held, viz: Where the stock has accumulated less than the face value of the certificate, in which case only the amount that such certificate has earned, may be recovered. The leading case is O'Malley v. People B. & L. S. Association, 92 Hun 572, which is supported by Heslin v. Eastern B. & L. Association, 61 App. Div. 456.

In view of the above, I advise that it is legal for Mr. Robinson's association to pay the entire earnings to the shareholders of any maturing series.

Yours respectfully,
EDWARD R. O'MALLEY,
Attorney-General.

———

Banking Law - Section 146 - - Savings Banks — Investments.

Bonds of the city of Seattle are legal investments for the saving-banks of New York State. (See letter January 18, 1910. L. B. 117, p. 23.)

(See opinion May 19, 1910).

STATE OF NEW YORK.

ATTORNEY-GENERAL'S OFFICE,

ALBANY, *May* 21, 1910.

Hon. O. H. CHENEY, *Superintendent of Banks, Albany, N. Y.:*

Dear Sir.— Some time ago I received from you a request for my opinion as to whether bonds of the city of Seattle are legal investments for savings banks in this State. I have not answered that request sooner because, as I informed you, I did not have the necessary information upon which to base an opinion. I have

just been supplied with the data which was missing, and from a
careful examination of the same it is my opinion that bonds of
the city of Seattle are legal investments for savings banks of this
State.

The only question of law entering into this determination was
whether certain local improvement bonds and warrants issued by
the city should be included as part of the city indebtedness under
the provisions of subdivision 5, section 146 of the Banking Law,
which is in part as follows:

"If at any time the indebtedness of any such city, together
with the indebtedness of any district, or other municipal corporation or subdivision except a county, which is wholly or
in part included within the bounds or limits of said city, less
its water debt and sinking fund, shall exceed seven per centum
of the valuation of said city for purposes of taxation, its bonds
and stocks shall thereafter, and until such indebtedness shall
be reduced   *   *   *   cease to be an authorized investment
*   *   *."

From a careful examination of the local improvement bonds and
warrants issued by the city of Seattle, and of the provisions of the
charter and the statutes together with the court decisions interpreting the same, it is my opinion that they do not constitute
" indebtedness of any such city " or " indebtedness of any district   *   *   *   which is wholly or in part included within the
bounds or limits of said city " within the meaning of this statute.
They are not the indebtedness of the city, it being expressly stated
on their face that they are charges only against certain specified
assessments.   They are likewise not the indebtedness of any district.   The local improvement districts are organized under the
provisions of the charter of the city of Seattle and do not constitute corporations.   The local improvement districts are merely
the areas determined to be benefited by the improvement upon
which the assessments are imposed.   There is no indebtedness of
the district, therefore, particularly in view of the fact that the
only security of the holders of the bonds is the enforcement of the
special assessments.   It is my opinion that the statute clearly
refers only to indebtedness of some *corporate* district, the language

being " any district or other municipal corporation," and that it
has no application to mere charges against a local assessment fund.
I have therefore not included these local improvement bonds and
warrants in estimating the total amount of the indebtedness,
although I have included indebtedness of school districts and other
corporate districts.

Very truly yours,

EDWARD R. O'MALLEY,

Attorney-General.

Banking Law — Sections 17, 18, 19 and 197 — Trust Companies.
Carnegie Trust Company doing business under a special charter
is subject to provisions of sections 17, 18 and 19 of the Banking Law which safeguard rather than take away power conferred by such charter of trust company.

STATE OF NEW YORK.

ATTORNEY-GENERAL'S OFFICE,

ALBANY, *May* 25, 1910.

Hon. GEO. I. SKINNER, *First Deputy Superintendent, Banking
Department, Albany, N. Y.:*

Dear Sir.— Your communication of the 24th inst., received,
requesting my opinion as to whether the Carnegie Trust Company
is subject to the provisions of sections 17, 18 and 19 of the Banking Law.

The Carnegie Trust Company is doing business under a special
charter granted by chapter 599 of the Laws of 1898 to the incorporators of the Security Assurance Company. This act was
amended in some particulars not pertinent to the question here
involved by chapter 147 of the Laws of 1906, and subsequently
the name " Security Assurance Company " was changed to the
now name " Carnegie Trust Company " by order of court.

By the special act of 1898 varied powers were conferred on the
trust company, being substantially the power of a trust company
organized under the Banking Law. By section 6 of this special act

the company is required to report to the Banking Department and
the Supreme Court is authorized to order an examination of the
books and accounts of the company. Section 7 of the act provides
as follows:

> "The rights, powers and privileges herein granted to said
> corporation shall not be controlled, limited or restricted by
> any existing statute or law of this state; but so far as such
> statute or statutes of law are or might otherwise be incon-
> sistent with the provisions of this act or any of them they are
> and shall be deemed to be altered and amended so far as they
> are or might be applicable to said corporation, so as to con-
> form to the provisions of this act which provisions shall be in
> lieu of all provisions in said statutes relating to the same sub-
> ject matter. *Except as last above provided and except upon
> subjects or matters relating to which special provision is made
> in this act, the said corporation shall be subject to and en-
> titled to the benefits of all general laws of this state relating
> to corporations and applicable to such corporations.* The
> amendment of any such general laws shall not be deemed to
> be intended to amend any of the express provisions of this
> act unless such intention is clearly expressed in the act or acts
> making such amendment of such general laws."

Section 17 of the Banking Law (chapter 10, Laws of 1909)
empowers the superintendent to require the institution to make
good in various ways any impairment of the capital of any corporation which is subject to the Banking Law; it further empowers
the superintendent to require the discontinuance of any "unsafe
or unauthorized practices" by such corporation. Section 18 provides for an action of dissolution against any such corporation for
reasons set forth in the section, among which are impairment of
capital or for an "unsound or unsafe condition" of the company.
Section 19 provides for proceedings against and liquidation of
delinquent corporations subject to the Banking Law.

In connection with this should be considered section 197 of the
Banking Law, which provides:

> "Every trust company incorporated by a special law shall
> possess the powers of trust companies incorporated under this

27

chapter and shall be subject to such provisions of this chapter as are not inconsistent with the special laws relating to such specially chartered company."

In my judgment, section 197 above quoted and section 7 of the special charter of the Carnegie Trust Company are substantially equivalent to each other. By the terms of both these sections, the company is made subject to the provisions of the Banking Law, and the only question is whether sections 17, 18 and 19 of such law are inconsistent with the provisions of the special charter under which the company is doing business.

Section 197 has been interpreted in the case of Venner v. Farmers' Loan and Trust Co., 54 A. D. 271, affd. 176 N. Y. 549. In that case, the defendant trust company was doing business under a special charter, and the court in deciding that it had all the powers conferred on a trust company by the Banking Law in addition to those conferred in its special charter, said in relation to section 197 (then section 163) at page 274:

" The intent and scope of the Banking Law are quite apparent, the purpose being to bring all companies doing a trust company business, as well as banks, under the State Banking Department, and, by requiring them to make and file reports of their condition at stated times, to subject them to the same supervision, direction and control as that department had a right to exert over banks and other moneyed institutions. Whilst, therefore, *the purpose was to impose upon all companies which through special charters had obtained the right to do a trust company business the same burdens and obligations as trust companies formed under the general act,* at the same time there were conferred upon such specially chartered corporations the same rights and privileges as were given to trust companies formed under the general act.

" This, we take it, is the scope of section 163 of the Banking Law already quoted; and the concluding language of the section that they — meaning trust companies — ' shall be subject to such provisions of this chapter as are not inconsistent with the special laws relating to such specially chartered company,' was not intended to deprive specially chartered companies of the privilege of doing a general trust company business, but was intended to save rights conferred by special charters. In other words, *in making them subject to the provisions of the Banking Law, it imposed all the burdens and obligations which rested upon companies formed under the general act,* while at the same time conferring upon them the same rights and privileges which such companies possessed and saving such specially granted powers as were given by special charters and which were not inconsistent with the provisions of the Banking Law."

In other words, the Banking Law provides for a central administration of all the trust companies of the State, whether incorporated by special act or under the general law. In order that that administration be efficient in safe-guarding the public interest, certain necessary powers have been conferred in said law. In sections 17, 18 and 19 are contained some of the most important of these powers. They neither take away nor restrict nor modify in any way the powers conferred by the special charter of the trust company under consideration. They simply regulate and safeguard the exercise of such powers by the company. They are in no wise inconsistent with such powers, nor can it be said that special provision is made in such charter in relation to the matters contained in the said sections. They are simply regulatory measures of administration.

It is my opinion, therefore, that the Carnegie Trust Co. is subject to the provisions of sections 17, 18 and 19 of the Banking Law.

Very truly yours,

EDWARD R. O'MALLEY,

Attorney-General.

Banking Law — Section 300 — Safe Deposit Companies.

Corporation desiring to organize for the purpose of storing " Old records, documents and papers," is such a corporation in part as a safe deposit company, and may not be organized under the Business Corporations Law.

STATE OF NEW YORK.

ATTORNEY-GENERAL'S OFFICE,

ALBANY, *June* 3, 1910.

Hon. O. H. CHENEY, *Superintendent of Banks, Albany, N. Y.:*

Dear Sir.— I acknowledge the letter of your first deputy under date of the 28th ult., in which a copy of letter from Morton Stein is enclosed, asking whether a corporation which he proposes to organize must be formed under the provisions of section 300 of the Banking Law.

It appears from Mr. Stein's letter that he proposes to acquire real estate and erect a twelve-story fire proof building in which old papers and records may be stored, fire proof rooms and sections may be rented and fire proof lock boxes maintained, all for the storage of old papers and documents. It is stated that the com-pany will not receive upon deposit for safe keeping or storage " jewelry, plate, money, specie, bullion, stock, bonds, securities and valuable papers of any kind and other valuable personal prop-erty and will not let out vaults, safe and other receptacles for such use and purposes, *except as to old records, documents and papers.*" This is the statement of the purposes of the corporation as set forth in Mr. Stein's letter.

Section 300 of the Banking Law provides in almost the identi-cal language that safe deposit companies may be formed for the purpose of taking and receiving upon deposit as bailee, for safe keeping and storage, the items above enumerated in quotation marks. It is clear, therefore, that the proposed corporation is to be formed for the purpose of doing with old records, documents and papers what a safe deposit company organized under this sec-tion may do with those things and many others. In other words, only a part of the powers which might be obtained by a safe deposit company are to be taken by the proposed corporation. This fact, however, does not alter the fact that the power which is to be taken is one included in the general provisions of this section. It would follow from this that such a corporation could be formed under the provisions of this section of the Banking Law. No corporation need assume all the powers or be formed for all the purposes herein enumerated, and the mere fact that it wished to discard one or more would not prevent its incorporating under this provision.

From this it follows that the corporation in question could not be organized under the Business Corporation Law which expressly excludes from its operation a corporation provided for by the Banking Law.

Very truly yours,

EDWARD R. O'MALLEY,

Attorney-General.

Banking Law — Sections 13, 197 *— Trust Companies — Revision of Charter.*

Organization of under special charter of the United States and Mexican Trust Company under the laws of the State of Alabama. Said company may not revive the charter of the Metropolis Finance Company, its corporate powers having ceased by non-compliance with section 36 of the General Corporation Law, and no business having been done by said corporation.

STATE OF NEW YORK.

ATTORNEY-GENERAL'S OFFICE,

ALBANY, *June* 8, 1910.

Hon. O. H. CHENEY, *Superintendent of Banking Department, Albany, N. Y.:*

Dear Sir.— I am in receipt of your communication, requesting my opinion as to the right of the United States & Mexican Trust Co., a foreign corporation, to revive the charter of the Metropolis

Finance Co. and to do business within this State under its provisions; also enclosed correspondence and memorandum of H. D. Estabrook, Esq., counsel for the said companies.

From the papers submitted by you in regard to the questions involved, it appears that the Metropolis Finance Co. was incorporated under a special charter granted by chapter 1033 of the Laws of 1895. Sections 4 and 5 of this charter give the Finance Company all the powers of a trust company, organized under the Banking Law.

It appears from your letter that the incorporators of the Metropolis Finance Co. have never done any business in this State under the charter thus granted; also counsel for the company in his memorandum states that although this charter was granted fourteen years ago, " no real organization has ever been effected under it and no real business done by the corporation." The United States & Mexican Trust Co., organized under a special charter of the State of Alabama, it appears, now desires to use the charter of the Finance Company to do business in this State.

Section 36 of the General Corporation Law provides,

"If any corporation, except a railroad, turnpike, plank road or bridge corporation, shall not organize and commence the transaction of its business or undertake the discharge of its corporate duties within two years from the date of its incorporation, *its corporate powers shall cease.*"

This section is applicable to corporations of the character of the Finance Company.

It would seem to be conceded that the Finance Company has not complied with the terms of the above section and, therefore, its corporate powers have ceased, if the forfeiture provided for in that section is self-executing. The case of Matter of the New York & Long Island Bridge Co. vs. Smith, 148 N. Y. 540, lays down the principle at page 547 that " the question as to whether a forfeiture is or is not self-executing, depends wholly upon the language employed by the Legislature." In the case of In Re Brooklyn, Winfield & Newton Railway Co., 72 N. Y. 245, where the words of forfeiture were, " Its corporate existence and powers shall cease," it was held that upon default the corporation's existence and powers ceased, without judicial proceedings. The authority of this case has not since its adjudication been disturbed, but was expressly approved in the Matter of the New York & Long Island Bridge Co., supra, and in the very recent case of Matter of Brooklyn Q. C. & S. R. R. Co., 185 N. Y. 171.

The language of forfeiture in section 36 is " its corporate powers shall cease." This must be considered equivalent to the language of forfeiture in the case of In Re Brooklyn, Winfield & Newton Railway Co., supra, and therefore such case must be considered controlling on the question here involved.

I also call your attention to section 13 of the Banking Law, to which the Finance Company is undoubtedly subject under section 197 of the Banking Law. Section 13 provides for an affidavit to be made before commencing business, which shall state,

" That the whole of its capital stock or such portion thereof as shall by law be required to be paid or secured before the commencement of its operations, has been actually paid or secured to be paid according to law."

And it further provides that,

" Every such corporation *shall cease to be a corporation* if the affidavit above required shall not be made and filed within one year from the time its charter shall be granted."

It is, therefore, my opinion that the corporate powers and existence of the Metropolis Finance Co. have been forfeited under the self-executing language of the above sections of the General Corporation Law and Banking Law, and no judicial proceedings to determine such forfeiture are necessary.

Very truly yours,

EDWARD R. O'MALLEY,

Attorney-General.

Banking Law — Section 155.

Dime Savings Bank of Williamsburg. Payment to trustee for services of keeping the minutes of monthly meetings, even though the said trustee be an attorney, is not within the meaning of the above section:

STATE OF NEW YORK.

ATTORNEY-GENERAL'S OFFICE,

ALBANY, *June* 8, 1910.

Hon. O. H. CHENEY, *Superintendent Banking Department, Capitol, Albany, New York:*

Dear Sir.— Replying to your letter of May 12th in which you ask whether the Dime Savings Bank of Williamsburg could properly pay for the services of one of its trustees who acts as secretary to the Board of Trustees and keeps the minutes of the monthly meetings, the trustee so acting as secretary being a lawyer and without whose legal advice it would probably be necessary to occasionally employ an attorney, I beg to advise as follows:

Compensation of officers is regulated by section 155 of the Banking Law, viz.:

" The trustees of any such corporation acting as officers of the same, *whose duties require and receive their regular and faithful attendance at the institution,* and the trustees appointed as a committee to examine the vouchers and assets pursuant to section one hundred and fifty-seven of this chapter, or to perform the duties required by subdivision six of section one hundred and forty-six of this chapter, may receive such compensation as in the opinion of a majority of the board of trustees shall be just and reasonable; but such majority shall be exclusive of any trustee to whom such compensation shall be voted. Trustees, as such, shall not be paid for their attendance at meetings of the board."

The statute provides for compensation to trustees only when their duties *require and receive their regular and faithful attendance at the institution,* with the two exceptions noted therein. Any person accepting the position of trustee of a savings bank must expect to give, without pay, a reasonable amount of time to the performance of his duties.

Attendance at the monthly meetings of the trustees and keeping the minutes of the meetings would not, in my opinion, entitle a trustee to compensation within the meaning of the section.

Respectfully yours,

EDWARD R. O'MALLEY,

Attorney-General.

Banking Law — Section 19 — *Loan Associations.*

Superintendent of Banks must require liquidation of the Union Dime Permanent Association to continue until remaining assets are distributed among the members.

STATE OF NEW YORK.

ATTORNEY-GENERAL's OFFICE,

ALBANY, *June* 28, 1910.

Hon. O. H. CHENEY, *Superintendent, Banking Department, Albany, N. Y.:*

Dear Sir.— I beg to reply to your communication of June 16th, 1910. You state that your department, in liquidating the business of the Union Dime Permanent Loan Association of Rochester, has provided for the payment of all general creditors and there now remains approximately $100,000 to be distributed among the shareholders or members of the association.

You call my attention to section 19 of the Banking Law, which refers to the liquidation of money corporations and which states:

" Whenever the superintendent shall have paid to each and every depositor and creditor of such corporation (not including stockholders) * * * the full amount of such claims, and shall have made proper provision for unclaimed and unpaid deposits or dividends, and shall have paid all the expenses of liquidation, the superintendent shall call a meeting of the stockholders of such corporation. * * * At such meeting the

stockholders shall determine whether the superintendent shall
continue a liquidator and shall wind up the affairs of such
corporation, or whether an agent or agents shall be elected for
that purpose * * * ."

The question presented for my consideration is whether under
conditions above recited, the superintendent can still continue the
liquidation and distribute the assets among the members, or
whether they are entitled to be called together and to determine
whether the superintendent or their elected agent or agents shall
make the distribution.

The statute above quoted refers to a condition where the superintendent has provided for the payments of all claims against
a corporation except those of the stockholders.   After he has
done that he must allow the stockholders to say whether they
want him to proceed to distribute the remaining assets, or whether
they desire to do it themselves.   Such a condition does not exist
in connection with the Union Dime Permanent Loan Association.
While the members are called shareholders, they do not own shares
of stock in the true sense of the word.   Their claims against the
association arise out of moneys they have deposited with or placed
in the custody of the Association.   These transactions are very
much in the nature of deposits in savings banks.   The relations of
the members to the association are more nearly analagous to those
of depositors than of stockholders.   You will notice that the statute requires the superintendent, before he shall call the stockholders together, to make provision for all unclaimed and unpaid
deposits or dividends.   In this case, in order to do this, he will
first have to proceed to pay these shareholders their respective
shares of the remaining assets to satisfy, as far as possible, their
claims for the moneys they have deposited to their respective
credits in this association.

This is not so much a question as to whether these shareholders
are " stockholders " as it is a question whether they are " depositors."   In my judgment the statute clearly intends to require the
superintendent to liquidate such institutions as this to the extent
of distributing to the members or shareholders.   These persons are
often quite as numerous as the depositors in a bank and often
scattered over a wide territory, so that it is impossible for them to

take wise and concerted action in reference to the further liquidation of their association, as stockholders may do. The term
"stockholders," as used in the statute, is not properly a designation of the members of such an association. They are called
"stockholders" or "shareholders" for want of a better term.
They are actually members, and not stockholders. It is the clear
intent of the law that such persons should have the benefit of a
liquidation by the superintendent as much as have depositors of a
bank.

Therefore, in my opinion, it follows that section 19 of the Banking Law not only authorizes, but requires the liquidation of the
Union Dime Permanent Loan Association to be continued by the
superintendent until the remaining assets are distributed as far as
possible to settle the claims of the members.

Yours respectfully,

EDWARD R. O'MALLEY,

Attorney-General.

• *Banking Law — Section 186, Subdivision 11 — Trust Companies
— Branch Banks.*

Establishment of branch offices in foreign cities not lawful except
by written approval of the Superintendent of Banks.

STATE OF NEW YORK.

ATTORNEY-GENERAL'S OFFICE,

ALBANY, *July 27,* 1910.

Hon. O. H. CHENEY, *Superintendent of Banks, Albany, N. Y.:*

Dear Sir.— I beg to reply herewith to your request for my
opinion concerning the rights of trust companies organized under
the laws of this State, to open and maintain branch offices for the
purpose of carrying on the ordinary business of such institutions
in foreign cities.

Your communication has reference to two classes of trust companies — one class comprising those organized under the general
Banking Law in accordance with the general statutes, and the other

class comprising a number of trust companies organized and doing business under special acts of the Legislature. You state that you desire to be advised whether or not such corporations can transact any business through branch offices located in foreign countries, and if so, to what extent.

As to those institutions established under the general Banking Law, the provisions and restrictions in reference to branches contained in the general statutes are clearly applicable. These are found in subdivision 11 of section 186 of the Banking Law and are as follows:

"No such corporation shall transact its ordinary business by branch office in any city not named in its certificate of incorporation or charter as the place where its business is to be transacted. No trust company shall open a branch office without first having obtained the written approval of the superintendent of banks to the opening of such branch office, which written approval may be given or withheld in his discretion, and shall not be given by him until he has ascertained to his satisfaction that the public convenience and advantage will be promoted by the opening of such branch office; and, provided further, that no trust company in this state, or any officer thereof, shall open or maintain a branch office, unless the capital of such trust company actually paid in cash shall exceed the amount required by the law under which it was incorporated by the sum of one hundred thousand dollars for each branch office so opened or maintained. Every trust company and every such officer or director opening a branch office without such written approval shall forfeit to the people of the state the sum of one thousand dollars for every week during which any branch office shall be maintained without such written approval."

Briefly, the meaning of the statute is that, first, there shall be no branch except in a city named in the certificate of incorporation; second, there shall be no branch without the approval of the superintendent, which approval shall not be given except for the public convenience and advantage and except when the trust company's capital actually paid in cash shall exceed by one hundred thousand dollars the amount required by law.

The statute quoted above seems to refer to branches at which the ordinary business of the trust company is conducted. The restrictions in the statute evidently do not apply to branches or offices at which ordinary banking business is not conducted but at which transactions occur that are controlled and directed through the principal place of business of the institution. Such transactions are not of the nature of ordinary banking business, all the business that is done being passed on by those in charge of the principal office. My conclusion, therefore, as to trust companies organized under the Banking Law, is that they are prohibited from establishing branches for the transaction of regular banking business except in cases specifically described in the statute above quoted; that is to say, no such corporation shall in any event transact its ordinary business by branch office in any city not named in its certificate of incorporation as the place where its business is to be transacted, and even in such cities, only upon the written approval of the Superintendent and upon the conditions specified in respect to the capital.

Among the institutions referred to in your communication as being organized by special legislative enactment you name the Farmers' Loan and Trust Company, the Trust Company of America, the Guaranty Trust Company of New York, and the Equitable Trust Company. As to these trust companies, the question is more complex and can only be answered after an examination of their respective charters.

The Farmers' Loan and Trust Company was incorporated under the name of the Farmers' Fire Insurance and Loan Company, by chapter 50, Laws of 1822. Its name was changed by legislative act in 1850 and various acts have amended its original charter. The only city mentioned either in the original act or in any of the amendments is the city of New York. The charter, together with all amendments thereof, is silent as to branches. There is nothing in the charter to indicate that this company is exempt from the general statutes in reference to branches. Therefore, under its charter, this company can only establish branches in accordance with section 186 of the Banking Law.

The same conclusion is reached concerning the Trust Company of America, which was organized under the general law and by a merger absorbed the North American Trust Company which was in turn a merger of that company and the International Banking and Trust Company, both companies having been chartered by special acts. The Trust Company of America also absorbed by merger the Colonial Trust Company and the City Trust Company of New York. I have examined all the charters of these constituent companies which by the various mergers have become and now constitute The Trust Company of America. None of them make any reference to any cities other than New York and all of them are silent as to branches except the charter of the American Bond and Mortgage Company, the name of which was changed to the International Banking and Trust Company prior to its merger into the North American Trust Company. The charter (chapter 555, Laws of 1899) recites that

" The principal offices of the company shall be in the city of New York, but it may by and with the consent of the superintendent of banks establish branches and agencies throughout the United States or elsewhere."

Inasmuch as the only power of the Superintendent to grant such consent is limited by the provisions of the Banking Law, and in view of the fact that the several special charters confer no special powers in relation to the establishment of branches, other than that above quoted, The Trust Company of America is also, in my judgment, limited as to its branches by the restrictions of section 186.

The original charter of the Guaranty Trust Company of New York, which was chartered (chapter 179, Laws of 1864) as the New York Guaranty and Indemnity Company, the name having been changed by order of the Supreme Court, recites that the company is " to be located in the city of New York." This charter was, however, amended in 1896 by filing an amended certificate of incorporation as provided in section 32 of the Stock Corporation Law which allows any corporation organized by general or special act to extend its powers so as to include any power which may have been conferred by law upon corporations engaged in a business of the same general character.

The amended certificate contains the following:

"That the extension of business and powers and rights proposed and intended to be effected by the execution and filing of this amended certificate, is the transaction by said corporation of its ordinary business by branch office in London, England."

This extension of power to establish a branch in London was · approved in writing by the then Superintendent. It appears, therefore, that the requirements of section 186 have been complied with, and that this company, under its charter as now amended, can only maintain branches in New York and London.

The remaining company, the Equitable Trust Company, was chartered by special act (chapter 604, Laws of 1871) as the Traders' Deposit Company. The name was later changed to the one now used. The charter makes no mention of any city in which business is to be conducted, and my conclusion is the same as in the other cases — namely, that the provisions of the general law are applicable.

In addition to the foregoing considerations in reference to these four companies which are doing business under special charters, attention should be directed to section 197 of the Banking Law, which is as follows:

"Section 197. POWERS OF SPECIALLY CHARTERED TRUST COMPANIES.— Every trust company incorporated by a special law shall possess the powers of trust companies incorporated under this chapter and shall be subject to such provisions of this chapter as are not inconsistent with special laws relating to such specially chartered company."

I do not find any provisions in the special charters above referred to which are in any way inconsistent with the requirements of section 186. No powers are conferred exempting these companies from the restrictions of the general law concerning branches. Analogously to the opinion which I rendered on May 25, 1910, to your department concerning this section of the law, I think the general act in reference to branches does not take away or restrict or modify in any way the powers conferred by the special charters, and the provisions of the statute are in no way inconsistent with the special rights conferred by such charters.

My opinion, therefore, is that the trust companies above mentioned, having special charters, are subject to the provisions of section 186; that they may not establish branches for the purpose of conducting the ordinary business of a trust company in any cities not named in their charters, and that even in such cities, branches may not be established except on the written approval of the Superintendent and after complying with the requirements in respect to the capital.

Yours very truly,

EDWARD R. O'MALLEY,

Attorney-General.

Banking Law — Section 2 (Chapter 127, Laws 1910) — Personal Loan Associations.

Must have capital of at least $10,000 in order to procure a license from the Superintendent of Banks.

STATE OF NEW YORK.

ATTORNEY-GENERAL'S OFFICE,

ALBANY, *September 29, 1910.*

Hon. O. H. CHENEY, *Superintendent of Banks, Albany, N. Y.:*

Dear Sir.— I beg to acknowledge the receipt of your favor of September 19th, in which you ask " whether under the provisions of chapter 127 of the Laws of 1910, the so-called ' personal loan associations ' that were organized prior to the passage of the act and which have a capital of less than $10,000, must increase their capital to $10,000 or more each in order that the Superintendent of Banks may have power to issue licenses hereafter."

Prior to the enactment of this chapter of the laws of 1910, there was no provision of the Banking Law requiring that corporations of this character should have a capital of at least $10,000, or any required amount.

Under the terms of section 2 of chapter 127 of the Laws of 1910 (section 310 of the Banking Law as amended) every corporation hereafter formed must have a paid-in capital of at least $10,000 before the Superintendent of Banks shall issue a license authorizing it to do business. This section further provides that such license shall expire on the 31st day of March in each year and is similar in this respect to the provisions of this section of the Banking Law as it existed prior to the amendment.

Section 311 of the Banking Law, as amended by section 3 of chapter 127 of the Laws of 1910, contains the following sentence:

" No license shall hereafter be issued to any such corporation unless it has unimpaired capital of at least ten thousand dollars."

This sentence is new and requires that every corporation of this character must have a capital of at least $10,000 in order to do business after the 31st day of March, 1911.

I am, therefore, of opinion that the Superintendent of Banks would not have the power to issue a license to any corporation coming under the provisions of article X of the Banking Law unless such corporation has a capital of at least $10,000.

Yours very truly,

EDWARD R. O'MALLEY,

Attorney-General.

Banking Law — Section 211, 233 *(Amended by Chapter* 126, *Laws* 1910) — *Savings and Loan Associations.*

Not the duty of the Superintendent of Banks to require associations to amend by-laws. Where by-laws are, in violation of the statute they become void. Amendment or alteration of by-laws must be made with consent of stockholders.

STATE OF NEW YORK.

ATTORNEY-GENERAL'S OFFICE,

ALBANY, *October* 3, 1910.

Hon. O. H. CHENEY, *Superintendent of Banks, Albany, N. Y.:*

Dear Sir.— Referring to communication from your second deputy under date of September 29 in reference to the proper inter-

pretation of section 211 and section 233 of the Banking Law, as
amended by chapter 126, Laws of 1910, taking effect January 1.
1911, I beg to advise you as follows:

Section 211 of this act provides what the by-laws of a savings
and loan association shall contain. Some of these provisions,
however, are optional, and none of them are in the actual form of
by-laws. The intent of the section is merely to prescribe rules
governing the adoption or amendment of by-laws. It is also provided, however, that by-laws may be amended or altered only after
the change or amendment has first been submitted to the Superintendent of Banks and received his written approval, and thereafter
also has been duly adopted at a meeting of the stockholders, of
which meeting thirty days notice by mail shall be given.

Section 233 of this law provides that the articles of association,
certificate of incorporation, " by-laws or rules of every such association heretofore made or existing, are hereby modified, altered
and amended to conform to the provisions of this chapter, and the
same are declared void where such articles of association, certificate
of incorporation, by-laws or rules are inconsistent with the provisions of this chapter."

The questions which you ask are as follows:

" 1. Is the Superintendent of Banks charged with any
official obligation to require associations to amend their by-
laws so that they shall comply with the provisions contained
in chapter 126 of the Laws of 1910, provided that the practices of the associations are not permitted to be in violation of
the statute ?."

" 2. Is it a reasonable and correct construction of sections
211 and 233 of chapter 126 of the Laws of 1910, that by-laws
of associations of the character under consideration, prepared
prior to December 31, 1909, and approved by the Superintendent of Banks, will become effective simply by operation
of the statute, and need not be voted upon by shareholders?"

It is my judgment that the first question must be answered in
the negative. The statute does not impose upon the Superintendent
any obligation to require associations to amend their by-laws. It
merely provides that any by-laws in violation of the provisions of
the article, as so amended, shall become void.

The second question, it seems to me, must be answered in the negative. There is no provision by which by-laws may be amended or altered without the consent of the stockholders. The operation of the statute is only to void such by-laws as are in conflict with its provisions, and the expression that they are " hereby modified, altered and amended to conform to the provisions of this chapter " cannot be self-executing because there is no definite set of by-laws prescribed by such chapter. The amendment, therefore, must be carried out in the form prescribed by section 211 already referred to.

Very truly yours,

EDWARD R. O'MALLEY,

Attorney-General.

· · Banking Law — Article VIII.

Corporations organized under the General Corporation Law or the Stock Corporation Law, may not engage in the business of mortgage, loan and investment companies, without the approval of the Superintendent of Banks, and said Superintendent may at his discretion decline an authorization certificate.

(See opinion September 6, 1906, p. 513, Report.)

STATE OF NEW YORK.

ATTORNEY-GENERAL'S OFFICE,

ALBANY, *October* 28, 1910.

Hon. O. H. CHENEY, *Superintendent of Banks, Albany, N. Y.:*

Dear Sir.— I am in receipt of your communication of the 22d instant.

In such communication you first request my opinion whether a corporation organized and conducted under the General or Stock Corporation Law can exercise the powers of a mortgage, loan and investment company organized under article VIII of the Banking Law, " without regard to the provisions of the Banking Law, or the supervision of the banking department." It is my opinion that they cannot. In order to exercise the powers of a mortgage loan and investment company a corporation must be organized pursuant to article VIII of the Banking Law and be subject to all the provisions of such law. Your attention is called to the opinion of this office rendered to your department under date of September 6, 1906, and to be found in the report of the Attorney-General for that year, at page 513. With his opinion on this question I am in hearty concurrence.

Your second question relates to mortgage companies operating in this State without regard to the provisions of the Banking Law. How such companies may be dealt with is well set forth in the opinion above referred to at pages 513 and 515:

> "If it shall appear to you that a business corporation is, within the principles as above stated, engaged in the business of a corporation provided for by the banking laws, and you should have the evidence upon that subject, it would be competent under subdivision 5, of section 1797 of the Code of Civil Procedure, for the Attorney-General to bring an action upon leave of the court, against the corporation to procure a judgment vacating the charter or annulling the existence of the corporation upon the ground that it was exercising a privilege or franchise not conferred upon it by law. Of course, upon such an application notice under section 1799 of the Code would be given to the corporation, and it would have an opportunity to be heard in opposition thereto. But I think good practice would require that the corporation have a hearing before the Attorney-General before any application to annul its charter was made to the court."

Your third question is whether the Superintendent of Banks is justified in declining to issue an authorization certificate permitting the organization of a mortgage loan and investment company under the provisions of article VIII where there is an avowed purpose upon the part of the corporation to do a second mortgage business. The Superintendent of Banks has discretion under section 32 of the Banking Law to decline to approve the incorporation of such a company and may decline to issue his authorization certificate. See opinion of Attorney-General on this very point ren-

dered to your office under date of November 11, 1904, and to be
found in Attorney-General's report of that year, at page 403.
Whether the Superintendent is justified in declining because of its
purpose to do a second mortgage business is a question to be determined by him in the exercise of his sound administrative discretion.

Very truly yours,

EDWARD R. O'MALLEY,

Attorney-General.

Banking Law — Section 146 — Savings Banks — Investments.
Not lawful for savings bank to enter into agreement to loan on
bond and mortgage to amount of $65,000 where property is
encumbered in sum of $74,000, said bank acting as a trustee
in accounting for moneys, etc.

STATE OF NEW YORK.

ATTORNEY-GENERAL'S OFFICE,

ALBANY, *November 23*, 1910.

Hon. O. H. CHENEY, *Superintendent of Banks, Albany, N. Y.:*

Dear Sir.— I beg to acknowledge the receipt of your favor of
November 10th enclosing a form of a so-called participating agreement, together with a copy of a letter from Cyril H. Burdette to
George W. Dayton, Jr. The facts upon which you desire an opinion, as I understand them, are briefly as follows:

A piece of real property upon which a savings bank would be
authorized to loan on bond and mortgage to the amount of $65,000
is encumbered in the sum of $74,000. It is desired that the fol-
lowing arrangement be made: The owner of the present mortgage
of $74,000 is to assign the same to the savings bank which is to
become the absolute owner thereof to the amount of $65,000 and
to have the right to collect the sum of $65,000 and interest before
anything is payable to the present mortgagee with the agreement
that if more than $65,000 and interest is collected it will be turned
over by the savings bank to the said mortgagee who shall have a
right to an accounting for all moneys received by the savings bank

in excess of the amount to which it is entitled under this agreement. You ask whether this can be done. Savings banks are
strictly confined in their investments to those set forth in section
140 of the Banking Law. While the above arrangement does not
violate the provisions that a savings bank shall not loan in excess
of sixty per centum of the value of real estate as certified by a committee of its trustees, the banking act does not give a savings bank
the right to act as trustee. As to the balance of the mortgage
assigned over and above the sum of $65,000, the savings bank, in
my judgment, stands in the position of a trustee, or at least in an
analogous position, and while it may have no active duty to collect
this amount it is under the obligation of accounting for any money
that may come into its hands over and above the amount to which
it is legally entitled. The Legislature in enacting the provisions
relative to savings banks did not contemplate or intend that savings
banks should enter into transactions of this character. I am therefore of opinion that a savings bank cannot legally enter into an
agreement of the kind above set forth.

Very truly yours,
EDWARD R. O'MALLEY,
Attorney-General.

Banking Law — Sections 17, 19.

Sale of stock of Maiden Lane Safe Deposit Company for non-pay-
ment of assessments. Duty of Superintendent of Banks as to
disposition of proceeds of sale and issuance of new stock certificates.

(See opinion February 19, 1903, p. 266, Report.)

STATE OF NEW YORK.

ATTORNEY-GENERAL'S OFFICE,

ALBANY, *December* 16, 1910.

Hon. O. H. CHENEY, *Superintendent of Banking Department,*
Albany, N. Y.:

Dear Sir.— I have your letter of December 14th, with reference
to the sale of stock of the Maiden Lane Safe Deposit Co., pursuant

to section 17 of the Banking Law, for the purpose of collecting assessments from certain delinquent stockholders. I understand that your department has taken possession of the company under section 19 of the Banking Law, by reason of the impairment of the capital, and that the directors have advertised the sale of stock of certain delinquent stockholders at a price not less than $56 per share and the costs of sale, and that $56 per share is the amount of assessment, and $56 plus the costs of sale is the amount of the valuation placed upon the stock by the Superintendent.

You ask to be advised as to the disposition of the proceeds of the sale and whether upon receiving payment of the amount of the assessment with the costs of sale, the directors may issue new certificates of stock to the purchasers upon such sale.

This question was presented to the Attorney-General in 1903 and in an opinion contained in letters dated February 19 and 26, 1903, the Attorney-General then stated that "the purchaser is required to pay the corporation in trust for the former owner of the stock which he purchased, the amount of his bid, and then to pay to the corporation the par value of his stock, less the value of the stock as fixed and determined by the Superintendent of Banks; and upon making such payment and only then is he entitled to the new certificate." This opinion was given under the statute as it then stood, which provided that "such stock shall not be sold for a smaller sum than the valuation put on it by the superintendent in his determination and certificate; and the necessary costs of sale shall be paid out of the avails of the stock sold." The statute has been materially amended and section 17 of the Banking Law now reads as follows:

"But such stock shall in no event be sold for a smaller sum than the valuation put on it by the superintendent in his determination and certificate, which valuation shall not be less than the amount of the assessment called for and the necessary costs of sale. Out of the avails of the stock sold the directors shall pay the necessary costs of sale, and the amount of the assessment called for thereon. The balance, if any, shall be paid to the person or persons whose stock has been thus sold. A sale of stock as herein provided shall effect an absolute cancellation of the outstanding certificate or certificates evidencing the stock so sold, and shall make the same null and void, and a new certificate or new certificates shall be issued to the purchaser or purchasers of said stock."

The change in the law was made to meet the situation arising as a result of the Attorney-General's opinion, which made it often impossible to dispose of stock upon assessment sale by reason of the fact that the purchaser had to pay not only the amount of the assessment and costs, but also the par value of the stock, less the Superintendent's valuation. This ruling frequently prevented stock being sold at all. The statute now provides that the stock shall not be sold for less than the valuation, but it permits the Superintendent to make a valuation for the exact amount of the assessment plus the costs of sale, and I understand it is the regular practice of the Superintendent to make his valuation at that figure.

Under the present section, I am of the opinion that the law contemplates the sale of stock for the amount of the assessment and costs without any further payment, for it expressly states that "the balance, if any, shall be paid to the person or persons whose stock has been thus sold." It clearly indicates that the purchaser of it may obtain the stock upon payment of those sums without paying the par value to the corporation. After the sale has been made, the avails shall be used, first, to pay the costs of sale, and second, the amount of the assessment. Upon the payment being made, the outstanding certificate becomes null and void and the new certificate shall be issued to the purchaser of the stock.

Yours very truly,

EDWARD R. O'MALLEY,

Attorney-General.

OPINIONS RENDERED THE STATE SUPERINTEND-
ENT OF INSURANCE.

Insurance Law.

Investigation of incendiary fires. Duties of coroners and sheriffs. Whether coroner may act with jury. (Chapter 66, Laws 1909, §§ 952h, 952o; Code of Civil Procedure, §§ 773, 774, 775, 776.)

STATE OF NEW YORK.

ATTORNEY-GENERAL'S OFFICE,

ALBANY, *February* 3, 1910.

Hon. WILLIAM H. HOTCHKISS, *Superintendent of Insurance. Albany, N. Y.:*

Dear Sir.— By your favor of the 2d instant, with which you forward me a copy of a letter addressed to you by George T. Peck, S. A., Pennsylvania Fire Insurance Company, of same date, I am asked for an opinion as to the power of a coroner to act with a jury in the investigation of fires, where there is ground to believe that a building has been maliciously set on fire; and in reply I beg to state that it appears by chapter 66 of the Laws of 1909 (vol. 1, page 96), sections 952h to 952o, inclusive, that it is made the duty of a coroner, sheriff or deputy sheriff of a county in which a crime is supposed to have been committed, whenever it is made to appear that there is ground to believe that any building has been maliciously set on fire or attempted to be set on fire, as required by section 952h, to proceed with an investigation as provided by the above-mentioned act.

Section 952i reads as follows:

" Section 952i. POWERS OF SHERIFFS AND CORONERS.— For this purpose he shall possess all the powers conferred upon coroners for the purpose of holding inquests by the first four sections of article first of title seventh of chapter second of part fourth of the revised statutes."

It will be observed that this section gives the officer acting, whether he be a coroner, sheriff or deputy sheriff, all of the powers

conferred upon coroners by the first four sections of article first
of title seventh, chapter 2, part 4, of the Revised Statutes, and
upon examination it is found that the above four sections of the
Revised Statutes have been re-enacted into sections 773, 774, 775
and 776 of the present Code of Criminal Procedure, and relate to
the powers of coroners in summoning juries, subpœnaing of witnesses, compelling their attendance and their punishment in the
event of their disobedience of the subpoena.

It will also be observed that, by section 773, id., coroners cannot
summon a jury for the investigation of a killing or dangerous
wounding, except where it occurred in a county in which is situated in whole or in part a city having a population of more than
500,000, as appears by the last state enumeration, but no such
limitation applies to an investigation provided for by section 952h
as to the origin of a fire, and it appears to be mandatory upon either
a coroner, sheriff or deputy sheriff to proceed with an investigation
as provided by section 952h upon the presentation to him of the
affidavit and request therein specified.

Yours respectfully,

EDWARD R. O'MALLEY,

Attorney-General.

---

*Insurance Law — Article VII — Sections 230, 232, 233, 237 —
Fraternal Beneficiary Societies.*

Royal League of America not legally organized under requirements
of section 54, and cannot transact the business of insurance in
New York State, without certificate of authority from the
Superintendent of Insurance.

STATE OF NEW YORK.

ATTORNEY-GENERAL'S OFFICE,

ALBANY, June 8, 1910.

Hon. WILLIAM H. HOTCHKISS, *Superintendent of Insurance,
Albany, N. Y.:*

Dear Sir.— I have your letter of the 25th ult., in which you
transmit to me certain papers in reference to the Royal League of

America, with a request for my opinion as to the right of this association to transact the business of insurance in this State. It appears from these papers that the Royal League of America is an association of individuals engaged in the business of fraternal insurance as defined in article VII of the Insurance Law. This association has never been incorporated nor has it received any certificate of authority from your department to transact business. The claim of the association is that such certificate of authority is unnecessary, and that individuals may associate themselves together in this State for the purpose of transacting fraternal insurance business without being required to obtain the consent of the Superintendent of Insurance.

I have read with great care the brief submitted on behalf of the association, and the somewhat voluminous correspondence between your department and their counsel both before and after the admission of such memorandum. I am unable, however, to agree with the position of the association, for in my judgment it is illegal under the laws of this State for such individuals to associate themselves together for this purpose without first obtaining your certificate of approval.

Without attempting to consider in detail the various statutes involved and the various arguments made both for and against this proposition, I will endeavor to state concisely the reasons which induce me to reach this conclusion:

An analysis of the provisions of section 54 shows that it requires all individuals and associations engaging in the business of insurance in this State to possess the same capital as required of a corporation doing a similar business, to make a deposit with the Superintendent of securities to the same amount required of such corporations, and to procure a certificate from the Superintendent that they have complied with all the provisions of law which an insurance corporation doing business in this State is bound to observe, and that the business of insurance specified in such certificate may safely be entrusted to them. Every such person or association is expressly made subject to the insurance laws of the State and to the jurisdiction and supervision of the Superintendent, in the same manner as if an insurance corporation, and no such person or association is permitted to transact business under a corporate or fictitious name nor under any name other than the true name of the person or persons comprising the association.

Section 57 provides that the provisions of article I (which includes section 54) shall not apply to *corporations* specified in article VII. This exemption applies only to fraternal corporations and does not apply to this unincorporated association.

Section 233 is the section upon which the association relies as exempting it from the requirements of section 54 above set forth. This latter section provides that all fraternal beneficiary societies or associations, voluntary or incorporated, shall be " exempt from the provisions of the other insurance laws of the State, and shall be subject only to the provisions of this article, and such provisions in article one of this chapter as may be specially applicable thereto."

It is my opinion that this section is not broad enough to exempt the present association from the requirement of the certificate contained in section 54. In the first place, section 233 applies only to " all beneficiary societies, orders or associations whether voluntary or incorporated." It does not apply to individuals. Individuals cannot associate themselves together in a fraternal beneficiary association without engaging in the business of fraternal insurance by the very act of forming such association. It therefore follows that if individuals organize such an association without the consent of the Superintendent of Insurance, they, as individuals, are violating the provisions of section 54, and such violation is coincident with the formation of the association. Therefore the association is not lawfully organized, because its organization is the result of unlawful acts of the individuals attempting to form it. It follows that the exemption given by section 233 can never be claimed, since such exemption extends only to lawfully organized associations.

In the second place, section 233 by its very terms provides that mutual benefit fraternities shall be subject " to such provisions of article one of this chapter as may be specially applicable thereto." It is evident from this that the Legislature intended such fraternities to be subject to some of the provisions of article I. Examination of the various sections contained in article I shows, first, that by section 57 above mentioned, none of its provisions are applicable to *incorporated* fraternities. It follows that the only sections which could have been specially applicable to fraternities are those applying to voluntary associations. The only section in article I specifically applying to voluntary associations is this very section 54. It would seem to follow, therefore, that by the very terms of the exemption contained in section 233, section 54 is not intended to be excluded.

It is doubtless true that certain of the requirements of section 54 have no force when applied to a fraternal association since fraternal corporations are not required to possess any particular capital or to deposit securities with the Superintendent. This, however, does not prevent the other parts of the section, which clearly can apply, from being given effect. There is nothing in section 239 exempting fraternal beneficiary societies, orders or associations from the provisions of sections 230–232, which prevents the above application of section 54.

For these various reasons, it is my opinion that the association of individuals known as the Royal League of America was illegally formed, since its very organization was not made in accordance with the requirements of section 54 of the Insurance Law.

In addition to the foregoing provisions, it is also my opinion that section 237 clearly declares the intent of the Legislature to require such voluntary associations to procure such certificate from the Superintendent of Insurance before engaging in business. This section, which provides for the filing with your department of an annual report by every fraternal society, order or association, applies equally to voluntary associations and to corporations, and provides in part as follows:

"Any person who shall act within this State as supreme, grand or subordinate officer, trustee, agent, solicitor or collector for any such fraternal beneficiary society, order or association, which shall have * * * failed or neglected to procure from the superintendent, the certificate of authority to transact business in this state required by law, shall forfeit to the people of the state the sum of one hundred dollars for every such offense."

This same section also makes it a similar offense for any such officer to refuse to permit the Superintendent or any examiner

appointed by him to make an examination of the condition and
business of such fraternity, and provides in the last sentence that
if any such refusal prevents such examination, the Superintendent
" shall revoke the certificate of authority issued to such fraternal
beneficiary society, order or association." The provisions of this
section, therefore, clearly indicate to my mind the legislative
intent to require of all mutual benefit fraternities the procuring of
a certificate from the Superintendent of Insurance.

I return herewith the exhibits handed me with your letter which
you requested me to return.

Very truly yours,

EDWARD R. O'MALLEY,

Attorney-General.

---

*Insurance Law — Article IX, Section 260 (Amended Chapter
328, Laws 1910) — Co-operative Fire Insurance Companies. .*

Continuance of existing corporations. Papers necessary for filing
with the Superintendent of Insurance.

(See opinion November 15, 1910.)

STATE OF NEW YORK.

ATTORNEY-GENERAL'S OFFICE,

ALBANY, *August* 19, 1910.

Hon. WILLIAM H. HOTCHKISS, *Superintendent of Insurance.*
Albany, N. Y.:

Dear Sir.— I beg to acknowledge receipt of your communication
of August 17, 1910, asking for my opinion as to what paper or
papers your department is authorized, under article IX, section
260, of the Insurance Law, as amended by chapter 328 of the Laws
of 1910, to accept from companies organized under chapter 287,
Laws 1878, chapter 326, Laws 1880, and chapter 573, Laws 1886,
as their certificates of incorporation.

Chapter 573 of the Laws of 1886 was a revision and consolidation of chapter 287, Laws of 1879, and chapter 362, Laws of 1880.
and provides, as did each of the acts therein consolidated, that it

should be lawful for "persons to form themselves into an incorporated company * * * by making, signing and acknowledging * * * a certificate of their intention to form said corporation * *. *." None of the acts in question seem to make any provision as to filing or recording in any public office such original certificate and it may be, with force, claimed that the corporation was formed by the making, signing and acknowledging of the certificate and that production thereof, or of a duly authenticated copy thereof, would be sufficient proof of the incorporation. This claim of the effect of the making, signing and acknowledging of the certificate, irrespective of any filing seems to be supported by the first sentence of the next section, section 2, that every corporation *formed* under the provisions of this act shall proceed to choose directors and officers.

In this view of the act, the certificate above referred to would be the certificate of incorporation, and a duly verified copy thereof would be sufficient for the purposes of your department.

In each of the laws above referred to, section 3 thereof provides for the making, by the directors, of a statement containing, among other things, " a copy of the articles and by-laws of the company " and provides for filing such statement in the office of the county clerk, the town clerk or the Secretary of State, or some or all of those officers, according to the various requirements of the acts.

The term " articles," as used with reference to incorporated companies, has the usual significance of, and has in some reported cases been decided to mean, " articles of incorporation," so that a copy of the certificate of intention (considered as the " articles " or certificate of incorporation) would necessarily be found in the statement above referred to.

It is true that the making and filing of this statement must be done " before doing business " under the old law, and it is difficult to see how any such company could lawfully engage in the business of insurance without having made and filed the same, in which event, a copy of it ought to be obtainable, but irrespective of this question, the provision of section 260, as amended, is that on filing of the requisite copies of the certificate of incorporation and by-laws, duly verified, " the superintendent of insurance shall, if in his judgment such corporation *will* safely conduct the business of insurance in this state, issue to such corporation a certificate, authorizing it to continue in the business of insurance in this state, of the kind specified in such by-laws and within the territory in which it does business at the time of such filing, etc."

I note also that the directors, whose duty it is to make and file such statement, are referred to in the acts in question as the directors of such *corporation,* as though the incorporation had been completed by the making of the certificate of intention.

The main thought seems to be to get before your department verified copies of the certificate of incorporation and by-laws. I am of the opinion that the filing of copies of both the certificate and statement referred to is the best practice, as showing not only full compliance with the statutes in force at the time of incorporation, but as showing also authority to transact business under the certificate. I believe, however, that it would be a substantial compliance with the provisions of section 260 of the Insurance Law, as amended, if the corporation should file with you either (1) copies of the certificate of intention, or, (2) a copy, duly verified, of the statement above referred to, which contains copies of such articles and by-laws.

If a company is unable to establish by either of these methods its corporate existence, it would be able to obtain a certificate under section 261 only by satisfying you that it is one of the " voluntary associations which at the time this act takes effect are doing business, etc.," and furnishing you copies of the original articles of association and of the by-laws in force at the date of such application, duly verified.

Respectfully yours,

EDWARD R. O'MALLEY,

Attorney-General.

Insurance Law — Sections 232, 233, 239 — Fraternal Beneficiary Societies.

Knights of Joseph, of Ohio, required to secure certificate from Superintendent of Insurance before transacting business in State of New York.

STATE OF NEW YORK.

ATTORNEY-GENERAL'S OFFICE,

ALBANY, *August 22*, 1910.

Hon. WILLIAM H. HOTCHKISS, *Superintendent of Insurance, Albany, N. Y.:*

Dear Sir.— Replying to your letter of the 5th inst., in which you ask me for my opinion as to whether the order of Knights of Joseph, a fraternal beneficiary society incorporated under the laws of Ohio, is required to secure a certificate from you before being permitted to transact business in this State, I beg to advise you as follows:

As requested by the representative of this society, I granted a hearing to its counsel and officers, and have received in addition a carefully prepared memorandum setting forth clearly the contention of the society. It appears from this that this is a mutual benefit fraternity in that it is composed of members who are proposed, elected and initiated in subordinate lodges, councils or other bodies according to the constitution, laws, rules, regulations, rites and ceremonies of such society. It has been doing business in this state for some time without receiving permission from your department and at the present time has approximately fifteen hundred members in this State. It is, however, an Ohio corporation, the total membership of which is above eleven thousand.

The claim of the society is, in brief, as follows: Section 233 of the Insurance Law defines certain mutual benefit fraternities, and provides that they shall be subject only to the provisions of article VII and such provisions of article I as may be specially applicable thereto. Section 232 provides that no fraternal beneficiary society organized under the laws of any other State shall transact business

28

here until it has received from the Superintendent a certificate of authority to transact such business. Section 239 provides in part as follows:

"All fraternal beneficiary societies, orders or associations, as defined by section two hundred and thirty-three of this chapter, shall be subject to all the provisions of this article, except sections two hundred and thirty to two hundred and thirty-two, both inclusive, together with their members and beneficiaries, and entitled to all the rights, privileges and benefits of this article."

It is strenuously contended on behalf of this society that it falls within the last quoted exemption so that the provisions of section 232 have no relation to it. There is much force in this contention provided the society falls within the definition of mutual benefit fraternities made by section 233. After careful consideration, however, I am unable to agree with the view that this society is included in that definition.

The exact language of section 233 upon which it must be answered is as follows:

"All beneficiary societies, orders or associations, whether voluntary or incorporated under the laws of this state or any other state or territory of the United States or of the District of Columbia, doing any business in this state authorized by this article, and the members of which are proposed, elected and initiated in subordinate lodges or councils or other bodies, by whatever other name known, according to the constitution, laws, rules, regulations, rites and ceremonies of such societies, orders or associations, respectively, now existing in this state. or which may be hereafter instituted, organized or authorized to do business, in this state, are declared to be mutual benefit fraternities and exempt from the provisions of the other insurance laws of the state, and shall be subject only to the provisions of this article, and such provisions of article one of this chapter as may be specially applicable thereto."

This section is substantially section 6 of chapter 520, Laws of 1889. It must be interpreted in connection with section 232.

which is substantially section 5 of chapter 520, Laws of 1889, which provides in part as follows:

"No fraternal beneficiary society, order or association organized under the laws of any other state * * * and not now doing business in this state, shall transact business herein * * * until such society, order or association has received from the superintendent a certificate of authority to transact business in this state * * *."

Reading these two sections together, it is my opinion that they contemplate that all foreign fraternities not then doing business in the State should require such certificate of approval as a prerequisite to receiving the right to transact business here. In other words, the expression "instituted, organized or authorized to do business, in this state" must be strictly construed, and requires a corporation or society to be either instituted in this state, organized in this state, or authorized to do business in this state.

Very truly yours,

EDWARD R. O'MALLEY,
Attorney-General.

Insurance Law — Article IX — Sections 260, 261 — Co-operative Fire Insurance Corporations — Voluntary Associations.

Questions arising under amendment of above law by chapter 328, Laws 1910, as to issuing certificates of authority, etc.

STATE OF NEW YORK.

ATTORNEY-GENERAL'S OFFICE,

ALBANY, *August* 25, 1910.

Hon. WILLIAM H. HOTCHKISS, *Superintendent of Insurance,* Albany, N. Y.:

Dear Sir.— I beg to acknowledge receipt of your communication of August 3, 1910, asking for an opinion in answer to several questions arising under article IX of the Insurance Law as amended by chapter 328 of the Laws of 1910, in sections 260 and

261 thereof relative to the issuing of certificates of authority to co-operative fire insurance corporations and voluntary associations doing business in this State.

I. Section 260 provides that all corporations formed pursuant to the laws therein referred to are thereby continued in existence and made subject to the provisions of the article in question and it provides that such corporation *shall file* copies of its *certificate of incorporation and by-laws* in force at the time of such filing, duly verified by affidavit to the effect that they are true copies. Upon the filing of such copies the Superintendent shall issue the certificate provided for by the act.

I note that you advise that it will be impossible for some companies, which are desirous of complying with this law, to file copies of their certificates of incorporation as they are unable to find any in existence, although all have by-laws under which they transact business.

I am of the opinion that the mere filing of copies of the by-laws, claimed to be in force at the date of applying for a certificate, will not be sufficient and that there is no escape from the mandatory provision requiring the filing of a copy of the certificate of incorporation, duly verified; and that, in case such copy of certificate of incorporation is not so filed with you, whatever the reason for the failure, you are not authorized to issue the certificate provided for by the act.

II. With regard to voluntary associations which at the time the act took effect, to wit, on July 1, 1910, were doing, in this State, insurance business of the kind and on the plan similar to those of the corporations specified, section 261 provides *that they shall file with you,* in addition to their application for a certificate therein mentioned, copies of the *original articles of association and of the by-laws in force on the date of such application,* duly verified and thereupon such voluntary association *shall become a corporation* subject to the same articles of association and by-laws.

I note that many associations have been unable to find any articles of association under which they have been doing business. I am of the same opinion in regard to such associations as stated above in respect to corporations, that the filing of copies of their by-laws alone is not sufficient and that there must be filed with you copies of their original articles of association, duly verified, and that in default thereof no certificate of authority may be issued by you.

This may work a hardship in many cases where it may prove impossible to file copies of the certificates of incorporation or articles of association, as the case may be. It is unfortunate that the Legislature did not, by some saving clause, make provision to cover such cases. But I do not see any escape from the conclusion I have reached, under the terms of the sections in question.

The issuing of the certificate provided by the act serves as authority, not only to existing corporations but to voluntary associations, to conduct the business of insurance as *corporations*, but may serve, under section 269 of the act, to extend their corporate existence for twenty-five years. Any other than a strict insistence upon the observance of the terms of the act would permit the Superintendent of Insurance to assume, without the evidence before him which the section requires, that the applicant *is* in fact a corporation or association such as the statute contemplates and, by his certificate, to confer corporate authority, with the extended term, upon those who are unable to produce proof that they are or ever were legally organized or constituted or to furnish information of the terms of their certificates of incorporation or articles of association. I can find no warrant either in reason or authority for indulging in such an assumption.

III. As to the classes of co-operative companies which are unable to obtain copies of their certificates of incorporation, which you subdivide as

(a) Companies which were regularly organized pursuant to some statute of this State;

(b) Companies whose officers believe that they were duly incorporated but are unable to prove that they are existing corporations;

Concerning which you ask whether they may proceed under section 52 of the Insurance Law, I beg to say:

Section 52, entitled " Reorganization of existing corporations and amendment of certificates " provides that *any domestic corporation* existing or doing business on October 1, 1892, may accept

the provisions of the chapter and amend its charter to conform
with the same; that thereafter it shall be deemed to have been
incorporated under that chapter; and that every such corporation,
in reincorporating, may so adopt in whole or any part a new charter, in conformity therewith and include therein any or all provisions of its existing charter and any or all changes from its
existing charter, etc. It also provides that *every domestic insurance corporation* may amend its charter or certificate of incorporation by inserting therein any statement or matter which might
have been originally inserted or by inserting therein any powers
which at the time of such amendment may have been conferred
by law upon domestic insurance corporations engaged in a business of the same general character, or which might be included
in the certificate of a domestic insurance company organized
under any general law of this State for a business of the same
general character.

The repeal, by chapter 328 of the Laws of 1910 of former
articles 9 and 10, repeals former section 277 of the Insurance
Law which provided for the reorganization of existing co-operative
fire insurance companies; by section 260 of the new law such
corporations are made subject to the provisions of the new article
IX; and section 268 of said new article makes section 52, above
referred.to, to apply to " any corporation to which a certificate *shall
be issued, pursuant to the terms of this article."*

(a)   This would seem to mean, not that a company of the kind
specified in section 260, such as you include in (a), could reorgan-
ize under section 52 for the purpose of furnishing itself with a
charter or certificate of incorporation, of which it could make
proof to entitled it to a certificate of authority under section 260,
but rather that an existing company to which a certificate of
authority under section 260 *shall be issued pursuant to the terms
of this article,* might thereafter be subject to the provisions of
section 52.

(b)   It would follow that corporations that believe that they
are incorporated, but are unable to prove that they are existing
corporations, could not bring themselves under section 52; and
that, to treat them as voluntary associations, they must have been
such when the act in question took effect and must furnish you a

verified copy of their original articles of association, which manifestly they probably could not do.

As to the steps to be taken or the procedure to be followed by the companies affected and referred to in your letter, I beg to say that in my judgment no general opinion can be given, as each case must, almost of necessity, depend for decision upon the precise facts applicable thereto.

Respectfully yours,

EDWARD R. O'MALLEY,
Attorney-General.

Insurance Law — Section 137.

Residents of New York who have received certificates under above section authorizing them to write surplus lines, may place such insurance in foreign or unauthorized Lloyds without becoming liable for criminal misdemeanor under section 300, article X (Chapter 638, Laws 1910.)

STATE OF NEW YORK.

ATTORNEY-GENERAL'S OFFICE,

ALBANY, *August* 26, 1910.

Hon. WILLIAM H. HOTCHKISS, *Superintendent of Insurance, Albany, N. Y.:*

Dear Sir.— I beg to acknowledge receipt of your communication of August 17th, 1910, in which you ask for an opinion whether residents of New York who have received or shall hereafter receive certificates under section 137 of the Insurance Law, authorizing them to write surplus lines, can place insurance in foreign or unauthorized Lloyds without becoming liable to criminal prosecution as for a misdemeanor in view of section 300 of the Insurance Law, added thereto by chapter 638 of the Laws of 1910.

Section 300 of article X of the Insurance Law, added by chapter 638 of the Laws of 1910, provides:

"No persons, partnerships or associations other than those specified in this section, and which shall receive the certificate

of the superintendent of insurance specified in section three
hundred and one of this chapter, shall, after January first,
nineteen hundred and eleven, engage in the business of insurance in this state as Lloyds or inter-insurers. Any persons,
partnerships or associations which, after January first, nineteen hundred and eleven, shall in this state engage in the business of insurance as Lloyds or inter-insurers, or represent or
advertise that they are so engaged, without having been authorized so to do in accordance with the provisions of this article,
and any agent, subagent, or representative of any such persons, partnerships, or associations not so authorized to do
such business in this state, who shall after January first, nineteen hundred and eleven, in any way represent any such unauthorized persons, partnerships or associations, directly or
indirectly, in engaging or attempting to engage in the business of insurance in this state, shall be guilty of a misdemeanor."

By section 137 of the Insurance Law, in force and effect in its
present form since 1894, it is provided that the Superintendent of
Insurance may issue to citizens of this State revocable licenses " to
act as agent to procure policies of fire insurance from corporations,
persons, partnerships and associations which are not authorized to
do business in this state." Section 137 is made to apply specifically to the procurement of surplus lines (as to which your inquiry
is directed) when " the party desiring insurance is, after diligent
effort, unable to procure the amount required to protect the property owned or controlled by him from the insurance corporations
duly authorized to transact business in this state."

The license provided for by section 137 permits the party named
in such license to act as agent to procure policies (i. e., policies for
surplus lines) in the manner and subject to the conditions specified in the section, from corporations, etc., not authorized. It
does not seem to me that this is such " engaging in this state in
the business of insurance or such representing unauthorized persons, etc., in engaging or attempting to engage in the business of
insurance," as is intended to be made a misdemeanor by section
300.

The statute recognizes the necessity of the placing of surplus lines with unauthorized companies and permits it under the conditions and restrictions contained in section 137, which is still a substantial part of the entire scheme of the Insurance Law. Article X seems to have made provision for authority to hitherto unauthorized Lloyds to engage in business in this State and is designed to do away with a business which has militated against authorized companies, duly admitted, and which pay taxes to the State; but section 300 is penal in its nature and should not be strained to make that a misdemeanor which is apparently permissible under another section of the chapter, relative to surplus lines.

I am of the opinion, therefore, that residents of New York who have received or shall hereafter receive certificates under section 137, authorizing them to write surplus lines, may place such insurance in foreign or unauthorized Lloyds without becoming liable to criminal prosecution as for a misdemeanor.

Very respectfully yours,

EDWARD R. O'MALLEY,

Attorney-General.

Insurance Law — Section 107 — Accident and Health Policies. Standard provisions. Whether " beneficiary clause " gives such beneficiary the right to become an "insured" under section 55.

STATE OF NEW YORK.

ATTORNEY-GENERAL'S OFFICE,

ALBANY, *September* 19, 1910.

Hon. WILLIAM H. HOTCHKISS. *Superintendent of Insurance,* Albany, N. Y.:

Dear Sir.— I beg to acknowledge receipt of your communication of September 9, 1910, asking for an opinion in connection with the putting into effect of chapter 636 of the Laws of 1910, being section 107 of the Insurance Law.

Your letter calls attention to the fact that many accident companies have filed with you for approval policies containing what is known as a "beneficiary clause," by which it is provided that a beneficiary named in the policy, as well as the person insured by the policy, is also covered in case such beneficiary is injured by accident.

The question submitted is, whether such a beneficiary, having from such a policy the right to recover indemnity in case of an accident to him, becomes by reason of that fact an insured within the meaning of section 55 of the Insurance Law, so that such beneficiary must also make application for the insurance and sign the application required therefor.

Section 55 of the Insurance Law provides:

    * * * "No policy or agreement for insurance shall be issued upon the life or health of another or against loss by disablement by accident except upon the application of the person insured; but a wife may take a policy of insurance upon the life or health of her husband or against loss by his disablement by accident; an employer may take out a policy of accident insurance covering his employes collectively for the benefit of such as may be injured, and a person liable for the support of a child of the age of one year and upward may take a yearly renewable term policy of insurance thereon. * * * ."

By the section in question, policies against loss by disablement by accident are included in the policies or agreements for insurance that may not be issued "except upon the application of the person insured." There is a distinction, well recognized but not always critically applied, in the use of the terms "insured," meaning the life, property, etc., upon the loss of which the insurance becomes payable, and the "assured," meaning the beneficiary or person to whom the insurance under such loss is payable. By the proposed form of insurance referred to by you, the beneficiary also becomes, in certain contingencies, an "insured." Under the prohibitive terms of the statute (with the exceptions which the statute itself points out) it seems that such policy or agreement of insurance may not be issued except upon the application of the beneficiary who thereby becomes a "person insured" under the policy.

It would follow that where written applications, with the signature of the proposed insured, are required, such application should be signed by the beneficiary who may come within the class to which this opinion is directed, subject to the exceptions specified in section 55.

Very truly yours,

EDWARD R. O'MALLEY,

Attorney-General.

Insurance Law — Fraternal Beneficiary Societies.

Whether Mutual Savings Life Insurance Society may at some future time extend its corporate existence, even though its risks have been reinsured and it is practically dissolved.

STATE OF NEW YORK.

Attorney-General's Office,

Albany, *November* 4, 1910.

Hon. William H. Hotchkiss, *Superintendent of Insurance, Albany, N. Y.:*

Dear Sir.—By your letter of October 5, 1910, referring to the proposed dissolution of the Mutual Savings Life Insurance Society, a fraternal beneficiary society, it appears that the question has arisen whether such a society, upon the reinsurance of its risks and loss of all its members, is dissolved and its corporate existence terminated so as to make it impossible for its former owners to apply for permission to do business again or to dispose of the franchise to others who may wish to use it.

Assuming that the society now has, or upon taking the steps suggested, will have, no members; that there are no assets or liabilities; that all of its risks have been reinsured and the society has done no business for more than a year, I am of the opinion that the corporate existence still continues. The question is not free from doubt, however, in the case of a non-stock corporation of this kind.

The early common law recognized the loss of all the members as one of the means whereby a corporation was dissolved and its existence terminated. (1 Bl. Com. 485.) This rule has unquestionably been changed so far as stock corporations are concerned, and many cases have held that the corporation continues to exist until it is judicially dissolved or the term of its existence, mentioned in its charter, expires.

> People v. Ballard, 134 N. Y. 269.
> Hitch v. Hawley, 132 N. Y. 212.
> Geneva Min. Spring Co. v. Coussey, 45 A. D. 268.
> People v. Twaddell, 18 Hun, 427.
> L. D. Garrett Co. v. Morton, 35 Misc. 10; reversed on
> other grounds in 65 A. D. 366.

The theory of these cases seems to be that the corporation is an artificial person created by the State and only the State can destroy it. In this State the Legislature has prescribed the means of terminating the franchise by judicial decree, and the courts have held that this method is exclusive.

I am inclined to think that the courts would apply the same doctrine to a non-stock corporation situated like the Mutual Savings Life Insurance Society, though I am unable to find any authority in this State, which is exactly in point. The fact that all the members of the society have consented to the reinsurance and released the society from all obligation on their policies no doubt prevents their claiming any insurance from the society. And I assume it is true that there are no tangible assets. But the franchise itself may be considered an asset, and experience has shown that dormant franchises have been transferred. In case this franchise should be sold, it would seem that the members who were such at the date of reinsurance would be entitled to the proceeds, nor is it apparent that the mere consent to the reinsurance destroys their membership or interest in any other rights they may have in the corporation. In view of the fact that the society's constitution provides that " the term of office of the officers of the society shall expire at the annual session in June of each year, but each officer shall continue in office until his successor shall have been elected and qualified " (article VIII, section 3), it would appear that there are persons still in being who may execute a transfer, whether such transfer would be valid unless authorized by the members is doubtful, but it might be made *pro forma*.

It appears by the constitution that there are two classes of members in the society, who are distinguished as "beneficial" and "social" members. The difference seems to be that beneficial members are those participating in the insurance element of the organization and the social members are such as do not participate therein (article II, section 1). There is nothing to indicate any distinction between the two classes with regard to the right to vote, and even if the consent to reinsurance has reduced the beneficial membership to the rank of social membership, or merely destroyed its insurance rights as against the society, it appears probable that, as a matter of fact, there is still a membership, composed of social members and beneficial members with modified rights, capable of voting and authorizing a transfer of the franchise by the existing officers. I do not wish to be understood as expressing an opinion that either the revived society or its transferees could lawfully renew the business of the society without the permission of the Department of Insurance, but merely as expressing my opinion, from the information contained in your letter and in the constitution and laws of the society, that the society may either apply for leave to renew its business or transfer its franchise to others, or at least may readily put itself in such a position.

Very respectfully yours,

EDWARD R. O'MALLEY,

Attorney-General.

Insurance Law — Sections 260, 262 — Co-operative Fire Insurance Corporations.

Extension of business possible only when statement filed under section 260 precedes one filed under section 262.

(See opinion, August 19, 1910.)

STATE OF NEW YORK.

ATTORNEY-GENERAL'S OFFICE,

ALBANY, *November* 15, 1910.

Hon. WILLIAM H. HOTCHKISS, *Superintendent of Insurance, Albany, N. Y.:*

Dear Sir.— In reply to your letter of September 29, 1910, in reference to the right of a co-operative fire insurance company to extend its business immediately upon filing the statement mentioned in section 262 of article IX of the Insurance Law, as amended by chapter 328 of the Laws of 1910, and prior to the issue of the certificate mentioned in section 260 of the same chapter, I beg to give my opinion as follows:

Section 262 of the Insurance Law, as amended by chapter 328, provides among other things as follows:

> " Advance premium corporations shall do business in not more than five adjoining counties until the amount of insurance in force exceeds one million dollars, whereupon any such corporation may do business in any number of counties, on filing with the superintendent of insurance a verified statement showing such amount of insurance in force and the counties in which such corporation intends to do business; but such a corporation shall not be authorized or permitted to begin or to do business until or unless it shall have bona fide applications for insurance in force in the county in which its principal office is located amounting to two hundred thousand dollars."

Section 260, as amended by chapter 328, provides that all corporations formed pursuant to certain laws specified therein (being co-operative insurance corporations) are continued in existence and made subject to the provisions of article IX. It then provides:

* * * " Each such corporation shall file with the superintendent of insurance, not later than September first, nineteen hundred and ten, copies of its certificate of incorporation and by-laws in force at the time of such filing, duly verified by its president and secretary by affidavits to the effect that the same are true copies. On the filing of such copies, so verified, the superintendent of insurance, if in his judgment such corporation will safely conduct the business of insurance in this state, shall issue to such corporation a certificate authorizing it to continue in the business of insurance in this state of the kind specified in such by-laws and within the territory in which it does business at the time of such filing. * * * "

Section 262, a portion of which is quoted above, first defines co-operative fire insurance corporations and then goes on to specify the risks which these corporations may insure, and classifies the corporations according as they do business on the advance premium plan or on the assessment plan. Then follows the provision, quoted in your letter, limiting the territory in which such corporations may do business, and providing for the extension of the territory on filing the statement showing that the corporation has insurance in force amounting to more than one million dollars.

From a careful reading of this section it seems clear that its provisions, limitations and sanctions apply only to the corporations mentioned at the beginning of the section, viz.: "All corporations to which certificates of authority shall be issued, pursuant to sections two hundred and sixty and two hundred and sixty-one." I am of the opinion that no corporation can take advantage of the provisions of section 262, except such as have received certificates pursuant to sections 260 or 261, or upon due incorporation. The wording of section 260 confirms this view. It provides, among other things, that " each such corporation shall file with the superintendent of insurance, not later than September first, nineteen hundred and ten, copies of its certificate of incorporation and by-

laws," and also that "no such corporation shall continue such
business without such certificate after December thirty-first."
Therefore, in view of the provisions of section 260 applying to all
co-operative insurance corporations, and in the absence of any express provision to the contrary in 262, I think that the issue of a
certificate under 260 must precede any extension of business on
filing the statement under 262.

I appreciate that a corporation, by duly filing a proper certificate of incorporation and by-laws, and also a proper statement
under 262, may have done all that is required of it by law in order
to extend its business. But I cannot assume the responsibility of
giving an opinion that the certificate of the superintendent need
not be issued before business is extended. Such certificate seems to
be a condition precedent. No doubt the Legislature might have
provided for the temporary extension of business during the in-
terim between the filing of the papers by the insurance company
and the issue of the certificate by the department, but it has not
done so.

Respectfully yours,

EDWARD R. O'MALLEY,

Attorney-General.

Insurance Law — Section 137 — Foreign Insurance Companies.

Licensed agents effecting insurance with unauthorized companies
where policy is afterward canceled by the assured. Whether
agents should pay three per cent. tax upon gross premium, etc.

(See opinion, Nov. 29, 1893, p. 388, Rep.)

STATE OF NEW YORK.

ATTORNEY-GENERAL'S OFFICE,

ALBANY, *November 23*, 1910.

Hon. WILLIAM H. HOTCHKISS, *Superintendent of Insurance.*
Albany, N. Y.:

Dear Sir. — Your favor of October 28, 1910, is received. You
state that a person duly licensed under the provisions of section

137 of the Insurance Law procured insurance for a client in a company not authorized to do business in this State; that the policy was issued in good faith but was afterwards canceled by the assured.

Section 137 provides that a person authorized to procure insurance in companies not authorized to transact business in this State shall pay " a sum equal to three per centum upon the amount of the gross premiums charged to policyholders upon all policies procured by him."

You further state that the licensed agent, by reason of the cancellation of the policy, will receive no premium from the assured, and ask my opinion as to whether or not he should pay a tax at the rate of three per cent. upon the gross premium charged on this policy. It has been held by this office that agents authorized under this section to procure insurance are the agents of the insured and not of the insurers. (Report of Attorney-General, 1893, 388.) Inasmuch as this insurance was actually procured, though afterwards cancelled, I can see no reason why the agent should not pay the tax of three per cent., especially as he was the agent of the assured and could make such arrangement with him as he saw fit to protect himself as to the payment of this tax in case the policy was cancelled by the assured.

Very truly yours,

EDWARD R. O'MALLEY,

Attorney-General.

Insurance Law — Section 170 — Title Companies.

Home Title Insurance Company. Powers of this or any other title company organized under the provisions of section 170 to accept deposits from individuals, giving in exchange certificates of indebtedness providing as to investment in mortgage loans, etc., or to borrow moneys for the purpose of carrying on a mortgage investment business.

STATE OF NEW YORK.

ATTORNEY-GENERAL'S OFFICE,

ALBANY, *December* 5, 1910.

Hon. WILLIAM H. HOTCHKISS, *Superintendent of Insurance, Albany, N. Y.:*

Dear Sir. — I am in receipt of your letter of the 18th ultimo in which you ask me to answer two questions, as follows:

1. "Can the Home Title Insurance Company, or any other title company, organized to do the business specified in subdivision one of section 170 of the Insurance Law, accept deposits of money from individuals and issue in exchange therefor certificates of indebtedness which will provide that the moneys received shall be merged with the general funds of the company and invested in mortgage loans, the holder of the certificate to receive four per cent. interest, and the company to have the option to give the holder at any time a guaranteed mortgage at five and one-half per cent. equal to the amount of such deposit, or a certificate giving the holder an interest in a larger guaranteed mortgage at the same rate, which interest shall be equal to the amount of such deposit?"

2. "Can the Home Title Insurance Company of New York, or any company organized under subdivision one of section 170, borrow moneys from financial institutions for the purpose of re-investing the same in mortgages with the intention of selling the mortgages thus created to private individuals — in other words, borrow money that it may do a mortgage investment business?"

The Home Title Insurance Company claims the right to exercise these functions and has submitted a brief in support of its contention.

This company is a corporation organized under subdivision one of section 170 of the Insurance Law, and its charter provides that the purpose for which it is founded are as therein provided. The powers conferred by this subdivision are as follows:

1. To examine titles to real property and chattels real.

2. To procure and furnish information in relation thereto.

3. To make and guarantee the correctness of searches for all instruments, liens or charges affecting the same.

4. Guarantee or insure the payment of bonds and mortgages.

5. Guarantee and insure the owners of real property and chattels real and others interested therein against loss by reason of defective title thereto and other incumbrances thereon.

It is manifest and admitted by the company that the power to do the business described in the above questions submitted to me is not directly conferred upon it by statute or its charter.

Section 10 of the General Corporation Law provides:

"No corporation shall possess or exercise any corporate powers not given by law or not necessary to the exercise of the power so given."

The points contended for in the company's brief are:

First. That the company has the right to borrow money.

Second. That it has the right to borrow it for the purpose of transacting the business of buying and selling bonds and mortgages.

Third. That having the power to borrow there is nothing improper in the use of the certificate of indebtedness mentioned in question No. 1.

The argument in support of the second point is that corporations engaged in business have the right to use all reasonable and proper means to make their business profitable. It admits that corporations can only exercise such incidental powers as are necessary to carry into effect the express objects for which they were organized as provided in their charters, but contends in effect that the word "necessary" as employed in section 10 of the General Cor-

poration Law embraces the exercise of any power that is convenient to the company to use in aid of its lawful purposes. It is further argued that the borrowing of money is convenient and in the
reasonable use of the term essential for the purchase and sale of
mortgages, and that the borrower has the right to issue therefor
any evidence of indebtedness not specifically prohibited by statute,
and that such being the case the borrowing of money from banks
for such purposes or the receiving of deposits from individuals for
which there is issued the certificate or evidence of indebtedness
above set forth, is incidental and necessary to the exercise of the
powers conferred by its charter.

It is undoubtedly true that such a company may invest its surplus funds in mortgages and that it later has the power to sell such
mortgages. This is equaly true of any company organized under
the Insurance Law, yet it can hardly be contended that the purchase and sale of bonds and mortgages is a part of the business
that an ordinary insurance company is incorporated to engage in
and it could scarcely be claimed that an ordinary life or fire insurance corporation would be authorized to borrow money with which
to buy and sell mortgages.

I am unable to find any express power conferred upon a company incorporated under and the business of which is defined by
subdivision one of section 170 of the Insurance Law to engage in
the business of buying and selling mortgages. The transaction of
such business is not among the purposes mentioned for which the
company was organized and is not a business that the charter auth-
izes the company to engage in. While it doubtless might add to the
profits of a company organized for the purpose of guaranteeing
searches and guaranteeing the payment of bonds, it can hardly be
maintained that the purchase and sale of a mortgage is necessary
to the business of guaranteeing its payment.

In the case of People ex rel. Tiffany & Co. v. Frank Campbell
et al., 144 N. Y. 166, the principle was recognized that a corporation possesses not only the power specifically granted by its charter,
but also such powers as may be necessary to the exercise of the
powers conferred. But it was, however, set forth that implied
powers which are merely convenient or useful and not essential to
its business cannot be exercised by it.

The case just referred to was one where a manufacturing corporation, engaged in the business of supplying from other sources certain manufactured goods to complete its stock for sale. The company claimed that the exercise of this power was subsidiary and incidental to its business as a manufacturing corporation and, therefore, within its powers. Chief Judge Andrews, in his opinion, concurred in by all of the court, said:

"Whatever incidental powers are reasonably necessary to enable it to perform its corporate functions are implied from the powers affirmatively granted. (Citing Curtis v. Leavitt, 15 N. Y. 64.) But powers merely convenient or useful are not implied if they are not essential, having in view the nature and object of the incorporation. The power assumed by the relator in this case to supply from other sources goods which it could not itself profitably manufacture, was a convenient and useful one, and doubtless contributed to the success of its general business, but it cannot, we think, be said to be essential to its business as a manufacturing corporation. * * * This part of the relator's business was not, we think, within its chartered powers."

While it may be profitable or desirable for the Home Title Insurance Company, and for other companies incorporated under the section under which this company was organized, to borrow money from banks and invest the same in bonds and mortgages and to receive deposits and issue interest-bearing certificates therefor and later at its option take up these certificates in the manner above mentioned, yet I am unable to see by what mental process the conclusion is reached that the transaction of such business is necessary to the exercise of the powers of examining titles or procuring information relative to real property, to guarantee the correctness of searches, to guarantee the payment of bonds and mortgages or to insure owners of real property against loss by defective title.

In my opinion it is no more essential to the transaction of the business for which the company was organized than was the purchase of goods that it could not profitably make by a manufacturing corporation for the purposes of supplementing its own product and completing its stock of goods; and in my opinion the line of reason ing of the court in Tiffany & Co. v. Campbell, above cited, is applicable to this case.

A question also arises as to whether the transaction of the business described in question No. 1 would not be a violation of section 22 of the General Corporation Law prohibiting a corporation not organized under the Banking Law to exercise certain powers therein specified.

In view of the conclusion above set forth it does not seem necessary, however, to express any opinion upon this phase of the case.

Yours very truly,

EDWARD R. O'MALLEY,

Attorney-General.

OPINIONS RENDERED THE STATE SUPERINTENDENT OF PRISONS.

Prison Law — Sections 214, 215, 216, 217 —- *Prisoners —
Paroles.*

Violation of parole by prisoner John Burns. If in the actual custody of the agent and warden of Sing Sing, such officer or the Board of Parole may not surrender said prisoner to the authorities of the United States or other states for crime committed in another State. Parole Board may retake and imprison him in accordance with section 217.

(See opinions November 29, 1909, p. 819, Rep., January 24, 1910.)

STATE OF NEW YORK.

ATTORNEY-GENERAL'S OFFICE,

ALBANY, *February* 10, 1910.

Hon. C. V. COLLINS, *Superintendent of State Prisons, Albany.
N. Y.:*

Dear Sir.— I am informed by your favor of the 1st inst., that one John Burns was, on July 27, 1909, paroled, and that while

out upon parole, he had stolen property and had left his home
without permission of the Superintendent of State Prisons and thus
violated the conditions of his parole; that on or about December
20, 1909, the prisoner was located in New Jersey and was then
under arrest for some charge, not stated, and that, on January 27,
1910, the warden at Sing Sing prison was notified that Burns
would be taken to Brooklyn by a United States deputy marshal to
answer to a charge of counterfeiting, and I am asked for an opinion
" as to the propriety or legality of a prisoner on parole in the
custody of the agent and warden, being taken from such custody
by either the authorities of the United States or any State, without
notice to the authorities of the State of New York, in whose custody
a prisoner on parole is and remains until finally discharged."

It is provided by section 214 of the Prison Law that a paroled
prisoner shall remain in the legal custody and under the control
of the agent and warden of the State prison from which he is so
paroled until the expiration of the maximum term of his sentence;
by section 215 that if the agent and warden or any member of the
board of parole have any reasonable cause to believe that the
prisoner has violated the parole or lapsed or is about to lapse into
criminal ways or company, then a warrant is to be issued for his
retaking, and by section 217, the board of parole, after a hearing,
or if the prisoner has not been returned, declare him to be delinquent and thereafter imprisoned for a period equal to the unexpired
maximum term of the sentence of such prisoner, and while a
prisoner upon parole is constantly subject to rearrest in the event
of his lapsing into evil ways, he is not otherwise immune from
arrest for crimes committed while so on parole, and if he leaves
the State and commits a crime in some other State, or against
the laws of the United States, he would be subject to arrest, prosecution, conviction, and confinement therefor, notwithstanding the
parole custody, but if he was in the immediate and actual custody
of a parole officer, or other officer authorized to make the arrest,
as provided by section 216 of the Prison Law, I do not know of
any law that would compel a surrender of the prisoner to the
United States authorities or to the authorities of another State for
some other crime, neither do I find any provision by which the
board of parole could demand or compel the surrender of such a

prisoner, arrested for a crime committed by him while on parole, until he had been tried, and if convicted, until he had served the sentence imposed upon him for such subsequent offense.

After he has been discharged, either upon acquittal after trial, or upon expiration of sentence, it would be not only the right, but the duty, of the parole board to retake and imprison him as provided by section 217 of the Prison Law, and deal with him as the facts and circumstances would seem to justify.

If the board of parole could in all instances compel the surrender of a prisoner who has committed a crime while upon parole, and reimprison him until he has served out his unexpired maximum term, which might be several years, much or all of the evidence of such subsequent crime might disappear in the interval and conviction be thus rendered impossible, and the prisoner escape just punishment.

As to the propriety of the federal authorities or those of some other State, in taking into and holding in custody a paroled prisoner, particularly if the fact of his being a paroled prisoner is known at the time of his arrest, is more a matter of comity than otherwise, but certainly an officer, federal or otherwise, knowing that a party is under parole, should not withhold arrest for a subsequent offense if it was of a serious character and allow an escape while waiting for the retaking of the prisoner by a parole officer.

Yours very truly,

EDWARD R. O'MALLEY,

Attorney-General.

Prisoners.

Erroneous spelling of name of prisoner Luigi Gambacorta, in death warrant, should not delay its execution, and warden should proceed to carry it out.

(See opinion February 16, 1910).

STATE OF NEW YORK.

ATTORNEY-GENERAL'S OFFICE,

ALBANY, *February* 15, 1910.

Hon. C. V. COLLINS, *Superintendent of State Prisons, Albany, N. Y.:*

Dear Sir.— I have your favor of February 10 relating to the discrepancy in the name of Luigi Gambacorta, as appears upon his death warrant and the order of affirmance of his conviction by the Court of Appeals, and I am informed by the papers and copies forwarded to me that the prisoner in question was indicted under the name of "Louigi Giambacurta;" that upon the trial, upon motion of the district attorney, the name was amended to read "Luigi Gambacorta;" that the death warrant was made out against "Louigi Giambacurta;" that in the notice of appeal made by the defendant's attorney, the name was spelled "Luigi Gambacorta;" and that in the order of affirmance of the judgment by the Court of Appeals, directing his execution during the week beginning Monday, the 21st day of February, 1910, his name is spelled as the same was amended upon the trial, viz: "Luigi Gambacorta," and inquiry is made by Mr. Benham, the warden, if an amendment should not be made in the name of the defendant appearing in the death warrant before the execution of the prisoner.

Section 277 of the Code of Criminal Procedure reads as follows:

"If a defendant is indicted by a fictitious or erroneous name, and in any stage of the proceedings his true name is discovered, it may be inserted in the subsequent proceedings, referring to the fact of his being indicted by the name mentioned in the indictment."

It appears that the provisions of this section were carried out and the true name of the defendant seems to have been used in all subsequent proceedings except in the death warrant, and the insertion therein of the name under which he was originally indicted was evidently a clerical mistake. There is no question raised as to the identity of the prisoner, or that the person whose name is spelled " Louigi Giambacurta " in the original death warrant is the same person whose true name is " Luigi Gambacorta." It does not appear that any question is now being made by the defendant or his counsel to the effect that he is not the person named in the original death warrant, or otherwise.

Both the given and surname of the defendant, whichever way it is spelled, would sound alike when it is spoken or pronounced and the doctrine of *idem sonans* therefore applies.

" The absence of a definite set of rules for the spelling and pronunciation of the names of persons, and more especially of surnames, has led the court to the adoption of a principle known as the rule of *idem sonans*. This rule may be stated to be that absolute accuracy in spelling names is not required in legal documents or proceedings, either civil or criminal; that if the name as spelled in the document, though different from the correct spelling thereof, conveys to the ear, when pronounced according to the commonly accepted methods, a sound practically identical with the correct name as commonly pronounced, the name as thus given is a sufficient designation of the individual referred to, and no advantage can be taken of the clerical error."

16 Am. & Eng. Enc. Law, 122.
Hubner v. Reickhoff, 103 Iowa, 370.

" Many of the cases are criminal and the question is one of identity of the person charged with the person on trial, and many others present the question of the identity of the person in court, sought to be charged with an obligation or . duty, with the one named in an instrument or document."

Id., 103 Iowa, 370.

In State v. White, 27 American State Reports, at page 784, the court quotes with approval from Bishop's Crim. Proc., section 126, the following:

" The law does not take notice of orthography; therefore, if a name is misspelled, no harm to the prosecution can come from this, provided the name as written in the indictment is *idem sonans*, as the books express it, with the true name."

At page 785, *supra*, the court says:

" It seems to us, therefore, that without referring to the numerous cases in the books where slight variations in orthography have sometimes been held fatal and sometimes not, without reference to any definite rule, it would be better to follow the rule which may be deduced from the more modern decisions, to this effect, that where the name as written in the indictment may be pronounced (although such may not be the strictly correct pronunciation) in the same way as the name given in the evidence, the variance will not be regarded as fatal unless the varient orthography be such as would be likely to mislead the defendant in preparing his defense."

In Schooler v. Asherst, 13 Am. Doc. 233, it is said:

" The doctrine of *idem sonans* has been much enlarged by modern decisions to conform to the governing rule that a variance, to be material, must be such a one as has misled the opposite party to his prejudice."

Adopting the suggestions and rulings of the courts so far as they apply to the matter under consideration, and upon principle. I am very clearly of the opinion that the difference in the spelling of the name of the defendant should be disregarded by the warden and he should proceed to carry out and execute the death warrant upon the person of Luigi Gambacorta, whose name is inaccurately spelled therein as " Louigi Giambacurta."

Yours truly,

EDWARD R. O'MALLEY,
Attorney-General.

Prisoners -- Code of Criminal Procedure — Sections 277, 542.
Change of name of prisoner " Frank Schleimann," alias " John
Smith," etc., convicted of murder, as it appears in order of
the court directing execution, to " Frederick Schleimann " in
death warrant. Warden of prison should carry out execution
upon the order of the Court of Appeals.

(See opinion February 15, 1910).

STATE OF NEW YORK.

ATTORNEY-GENERAL'S OFFICE,

ALBANY, *February* 16, 1910.

Hon. C. V. COLLINS, *Superintendent of State Prisons, Albany,
N. Y.:*

Dear Sir.- By your favor of the 10th inst., with the inclosure
accompanying it, I am informed that one Frank Schleimann, alias
John Smith (or Smyth) was convicted in October, 1909, under
the title of " John Smyth alias Frank Schleimann," of murder in
the first degree, and ordered executed in the week beginning November 15, 1909, and that it is stated in the death warrant that his
true name is " Frederick Schleimann;" that an appeal was taken
by said defendant by Edward J. Reilly, his attorney, in the name
of " Frank Schleimann alias John Smith;" that a notice pursuant
to section 523 of the Code of Criminal Procedure was served by
the district attorney upon you, entitled " Frank Schleimann alias
John Smith;" that an order was made by the Court of Appeals
on January 28, 1910, affirming the original judgment and directing the execution of said defendant during the week beginning
March 14, 1910, and that said order is entitled " The People of
the State of New York against Frank Schleimann alias John
Smith," and the defendant is designated in the body of the order
as " Frank Schleimann alias John Smith," and it appears by copy
of a letter from the district attorney of the county, who was charged
with the management of such case in behalf of the people, that
the change in the name " John Smyth alias Frank Schleimann,"
as stated in the original death warrant, to " Frank Schleimann
alias John Smith " was brought about by and through the defend-

ant's notice of appeal, which changed name appears to have been followed in all subsequent papers, and now you ask for my opinion " as to whether this order of the Court of Appeals against Frank Schleimann should be carried out against the person who is known to me as John Smyth, alias John Schleimann."

Section 277 of the Code of Criminal Procedure provides as follows:

> " If a defendant is indicted by a fictitious or erroneous name, and in any stage of the proceedings his true name is discovered, it may be inserted in the subsequent proceedings, referring to the fact of his being indicted by the name mentioned in the indictment."

I assume from the fact that it is stated in the original order of execution that the prisoner's true name is " Frank Schleimann," that it developed upon the trial that that was his true name, and that thereafter his true name was very properly inserted in all subsequent proceedings, and it is more than probable that the addition of the words " alias John Smith," was inserted to conform the papers to the requirements of the last portion of section 277, but in any event the defendant has not been prejudiced by the change, as there seems to be no question raised by anybody but that the warrant, notice of appeal and order of the Court of Appeals, all relate and apply to the man against whom the sentence is entered.

It was held in People v. Everhardt, 104 N. Y. 591, that, " while the fictitious names might have been omitted after the true name was discovered, no material error was committed by the repetition of them."

The variance has worked no prejudice against the defendant.

Walter v. People, 32 N. Y. 147, 164.

Section 542 of the Code of Criminal Procedure provides that the appellate court, " after hearing the appeal, must give judgment without regard to technical errors or defects or to exceptions which do not affect the substantial rights of the parties."

It has been held in numerous cases that, " the power conferred on the court (appellate) by sections 528 and 542 is not to be exercised upon the mere appearance of some error to which no exception was taken unless the substantial rights of the accused can be seen to have been affected by it and hence justice demands a new trial."

(See cases cited under section 542, Code of Criminal Procedure).

I think it is the duty of the warden under section 543 of the Code of Criminal Procedure, to execute the warrant according to its direction upon the prisoner held thereunder, without regard to the changes that have been made in his name.

If there was some doubt about the person that is intended to be named, or against whom the warrant runs, a different question would be involved, but under the facts and circumstances, as disclosed by the copies of documents forwarded to me, I advise you that it is the duty of the warden to carry out the death warrant and the order of the Court of Appeals upon the person against whom it is directed.

Yours very truly,

EDWARD R. O'MALLEY,

Attorney-General.

Prisoners — State Hospitals — Paroles.

Case of Jacob Goetz, sentenced to Elmira Reformatory and upon development of insanity committed to Dannemora State Hospital. Eligibility of to parole in custody of his father under section 150, Insanity Law.

STATE OF NEW YORK.

ATTORNEY-GENERAL'S OFFICE,

ALBANY, *March* 25, 1910.

Hon. C. V. COLLINS, *Superintendent of Prisons, Albany. N. Y.:*

Dear Sir.— I beg to acknowledge receipt of your favor of February 21, with which you forward to me a letter from Charles H. North, medical superintendent at Dannemora State Hospital, asking for my opinion as to the eligibility to parole of one Jacob Goetz, who was originally sentenced to Elmira Reformatory and whose maximum term of two years and six months expired January 19, 1910. It also appears that the patient, Goetz, developed insanity while at the reformatory and on May 5, 1909, was committed to the Dannemora State Hospital as provided by section 148 of the Insanity Law, and at the expiration of the maximum term of his criminal sentence, being still insane, he was retained at the hospital under a new commitment issued by Hon. John B. Riley, county judge of Clinton county, as provided by section 149 of the Insanity Law, and it is now recommended by the State Lunacy Commission that he be paroled to the custody of his father, who is desirous of placing the patient in an institution in Europe, and that the father is able and willing to comfortably maintain him.

I am also informed by the correspondence " that the patient is one who, so far as his mental condition is concerned, could be paroled under these circumstances but who otherwise would not be considered a proper case for home care."

The only provision I can find for the paroling of patients in State hospitals is contained in section 94 of the Insanity Law, and the portion referred to reads as follows:

" The superintendent may grant a parole to a patient not exceeding six months, under general conditions prescribed by the commission."

It is, however, very doubtful about the above quoted provision applying to inmates of the Dannemora State Hospital as article 4 of the Insanity Law (wherein the above quoted sentence is found) makes general provisions for the commitment, confinement and discharge of patients committed to insane institutions, not in confinement on a criminal charge.

Article 6 relates specifically to the Dannemora State Hospital, and prescribes the method of transfer of prisoners from the State prisons, reformatories and penitentiaries thereto, the custody of prisoners therein and discharges therefrom, and in section 150, which is entitled " Discharge of Insane Convicts after expiration of terms " provides in part as follows:

" The medical superintendent of the Dannemora hospital may discharge and deliver any patient whose sentence has expired, and who is still insane, but who, in the opinion of the superintendent, is reasonably safe to be at large, to his relatives or friends who are able and willing to comfortably maintain him without further public charge * * *."

This provision appears to just fit the condition of the patient Goetz. His sentence has expired, he is still insane, his father is able and willing to comfortably maintain him, and the medical superintendent has stated in his letter that he could be paroled "so far as his mental condition is concerned." The parole referred to by Dr. North and which was contemplated by the Lunacy Commission reads as follows:

"Upon the condition that his father agrees in writing to return him forthwith to Dannemora upon the occurrence of any outbreak or the performance of any assaultive act, and upon the further condition that the father agrees in writing to take or send the patient to Europe within two weeks after his discharge from Dannemora on this parole, unless already returned to Dannemora."

It is very evident from the above that Dr. North regards the patient's condition to be such that he is reasonably safe to be at large, in the care of his father, and that being his condition it would seem to be the better practice to discharge him as provided by section 150 of the Insanity Law rather than to resort to a parole, the validity of which would be questionable.

It has been repeatedly held that where there is a conflict or inconsistency between the provisions of a special and general statute, that the special law will control as to all matters embraced within its provisions, and as special provision is made by article 6 of the Insanity Law for the commitment to, custody in, and discharge from the Dannemora State Hospital, such provisions must be followed, inasmuch as there does not appear to be any provision for the parole of patients in article 6; but if it is deemed desirable by the Lunacy Commission that it should have direct authority to parole Dannemora inmates whose terms of imprisonment have expired but who continue to be insane, it would be advisable to secure an amendment of article 6, giving such power to the commission.

Yours truly,

EDWARD R. O'MALLEY,

Attorney-General.

Prisoners — Indeterminate Sentence — Commutation — Paroles.

Prisoner held under indeterminate sentence prior to April 6, 1903, entitled to commutation which he may earn even though he may violate his parole. For violation of such parole he must serve out his unexpired term, but is not deprived of commutation.

(See opinions February 2, p. 791, Rep.; June 11, p. 802, Rep; July 7, p. 808, Rep.; July 19, p. 811, Rep.; October 18, p. 282, Rep.; November 11, 1909, p. 813, Rep.).

STATE OF NEW YORK.

ATTORNEY-GENERAL'S OFFICE,

ALBANY, *April* 2, 1910.

Hon. C. V. COLLINS, *Superintendent of State Prisons, Albany, N. Y.:*

Dear Sir.— In reply to your favor of March 15, I beg to state that I think a prisoner sentenced by an indeterminate sentence for an offense committed prior to April 6, 1903, is entitled to a commutation.

People ex rel. Adams v. Johnson, 44 Misc. 550.

I note the apparent conflict in the provisions of sections 217 and 230 of the Prison Law, but section 217 is found in article 8 which relates to the subject of parole, and while it provides that a delinquent prisoner after arrest " shall be imprisoned in said prison for a period equal to the unexpired maximum term of sentence of such prisoner," I do not think it was the intention of the Legislature that the language of such section should be construed any stronger against the prisoner than an original sentence which, in the language of section 2183 of the Penal Law, must be inflicted " by confinement at hard labor in a State prison," and it might be argued with the same consistency that there is a conflict between the above section of the Penal Law and section 230 of the Prison Law.

It is provided by section 230 that

" Every convict confined under a definite sentence in any state prison or penitentiary in this state * * * may earn

29

for himself or herself a commutation or diminution of his or
her sentence or sentences, as follows: * * *."

The sentence of the prisoner under consideration, as above
stated, is entitled to the benefit of the commutation law, as the
offense was committed prior to April 6, 1903, notwithstanding it
was an indeterminate sentence, unless he is excluded by section
217 of the Prison Law on account of his delinquency.

If the term " every " used in section 230 is construed in its
ordinary sense, it certainly covers all prisoners in a class with the
prisoner under consideration and he would be entitled to earn
commutation.

Again, commutation is allowed for " good conduct in prison or
penitentiary," by section 235 of the Prison Law, and if a prisoner's
conduct in confinement is uniformly good, it would appear that
he has met the requirement of the statute and is entitled to the
reward given him thereby.

The provisions of section 217, requiring a delinquent prisoner
to serve out his unexpired maximum term, applies to paroled
prisoners, and while its provisions are apparently in conflict with
section 230, yet if both are given their proper construction, in
the light of their respective positions in the Prison Law, the inconsistency largely disappears, as it appears more reasonable that
section 217 was adopted to punish the delinquent for his violation
of his parole while at large, than that he should be doubly punished
by being not only deprived of further parole but must also forfeit
all rights to commutation.

After all reasoning and arguments are exhausted some doubt
must continue to exist as to the true construction of these conflicting provisions of the statute, and it will be better to adopt the one
which will lead to encouragement to good conduct rather than
one which will close all hope of reward and create within the
mind of the convict a wanton, reckless disregard of prison
discipline.

It is therefore my opinion that the prisoner referred to in your
letter, and all others held under similar sentences and conditions
should be allowed such commutation as he or they may earn.

Yours truly,
EDWARD R. O'MALLEY,
Attorney-General.

Prisoners — Indeterminate Sentence.

The Board of Parole may not under section 218 of the Prison Law grant a discharge to prisoner serving on September 7, 1907, an original sentence for murder, second degree. The amendment of 1907 does not make such sentence an *original* indeterminate sentence. Such case should be reported by said board to the Governor.

STATE OF NEW YORK.

ATTORNEY-GENERAL'S OFFICE,

ALBANY, *April* 8, 1910.

Hon. C. V. COLLINS, *Superintendent of State Prisons, Albany, N. Y.:*

Dear Sir.— I have your letter of the 8th inst., in which you request my opinion upon the following proposition:

Section 1048 of the Penal Law makes the penalty for murder in the second degree an indeterminate sentence, the minimum of which is twenty years and the maximum the offender's natural life. It is also provided:

" Any person serving a term of imprisonment for life under an original sentence for murder in the second degree on the first day of September, nineteen hundred and seven, shall be deemed to be thereafter serving under such an indeterminate sentence."

This section of the Penal Law is derived from section 187 of the Penal Code, as amended by Laws of 1907, chapter 738. Prior to this amendment, section 187 of the penal Code provided:

" Murder in the second degree is punishable by imprisonment for the offender's natural life."

Section 218 of the Prison Law provides in part as follows:

" If it shall appear to said board of parole that there is reasonable probability that any prisoner so on parole will live and remain at liberty without violating the law, and that his absolute discharge from imprisonment is not incompatible

with the welfare of society, then said board shall, if such
prisoner was *originally* sentenced to an indeterminate term.
issue to said prisoner an absolute discharge from imprisonment upon such sentence, which shall be effective therefor,
and if such prisoner was *originally* sentenced to a definite
term, the said board shall report his case to the governor with
such information and recommendations as they may deem
proper, for his discretionary action."

You ask my opinion as to whether, in the case of men who were
serving an original sentence for murder in the second degree on
September 1, 1907, the Board of Parole has authority to grant an
absolute discharge under this section.

It is my opinion, from an examination of these various provisions, that no such power exists. The amendment of 1907, referred to above, does not purport to say that men serving a de-
terminate sentence for murder in the second degree when that act
took effect shall thereafter be deemed to have been *originally* sentenced to an indeterminate sentence. It merely provides that they
shall *thereafter* be deemed to be serving under such indeterminate
sentence. Section 218 of the Prison Law was in force at the time
the 1907 amendment was enacted, and the language of that amendment must therefore be read in the light of the existence of such
section. It is clear, in my judgment, that the amendment is not
broad enough to give the Board power to discharge prisoners who
were originally sentenced to a definite term even though after such
amendment the term became indefinite. It follows from this that
the proper course for the Board of Parole, under this section, would
be to report the case to the Governor with such information and
recommendations as they may deem proper, for his discretionary
action.

Very truly yours,

EDWARD R. O'MALLEY,

Attorney-General.

Prisoners — Definite Sentences — Paroles.

Prisoners who were committed to houses of refuge when children, and now serving definite sentences for felonies, are not entitled to the benefits under chapter 489, Laws of 1909. Section 211 makes no discrimination as to age of person convicted.   (See opinion, June 16, 1910.)

STATE OF NEW YORK.

ATTORNEY-GENERAL'S OFFICE,

ALBANY, *June* 2, 1910.

Hon. CORNELIUS V. COLLINS, *Superintendent of State Prisons, Albany, N. Y.:*

Dear Sir. — I am in receipt of your letter of May 24, 1910, in which you state that you have some prisoners serving definite sentences who were as children committed to houses of refuge, etc., for felonies, and you ask if they are barred from the benefits of chapter 489 of the Laws of 1909, and if not, how young a boy must have been at the time of the first sentence in order that such sentence shall not count against him.

This act extending to prisoners serving definite terms for felonies, the benefit of parole and changing and shortening such terms by making them indeterminate is extended by the statute to a prisoner " who has never before been convicted of a crime punishable by imprisonment in a state prison."

It will be noted that the statute does not include all persons who have not previously served a sentence in a State prison but only those who have not before been convicted of a crime so punishable. By the statutory definition every felony is punishable by imprisonment in a State prison. Section 211 makes no discrimination with respect to the age of the person so convicted and I know of no rule of law that would permit the Board of Parole to so discriminate.

I am, therefore, of the opinion that any person who has been convicted of a crime punishable by imprisonment in a State prison previous to his conviction of the crime for which he is serving sentence is not entitled to the benefit of chapter 489.

Yours very truly,

EDWARD R. O'MALLEY,

Attorney-General.

Prisoners — Paroles.

Under provisions of the Penal Code, sections 699, 2186, offenses committed by minors are misdemeanors, not felonies, and prisoners under sixteen years of age not under the law guilty of felony, are entitled to the benefits of chapter 489, Laws of 1909.

(See opinion June 2, 1910.)

STATE OF NEW YORK.

ATTORNEY-GENERAL'S OFFICE,

ALBANY, *June* 16, 1910.

Hon. CORNELIUS V. COLLINS, *Superintendent of State Prisons. Albany, N. Y.:*

Dear Sir.— Supplemental to the opinion sent you under date of the 2d instant in reply to your letter to me of the 24th ultimo, relative to the rights of prisoners to the benefits of chapter 489 of the Laws of 1909, who, as minors, have been previously convicted of felony, I wish to call attention to the fact that in 1909 it was provided by section 2186 of the Penal Law that

"A child of more than seven and less than sixteen years of age, who shall commit any act or omission which, if committed by an adult, would be a crime not punishable by death or life imprisonment, shall not be deemed guilty of any crime but of juvenile delinquency only."

For several years previous thereto section 699 of the Penal Code provided:

" The commission by a child under the age of sixteen years, of a crime, not capital or punishable by life imprisonment, which, if committed by an adult, would be a felony, renders such child guilty of a misdemeanor only."

Hence, under such enactments no offense committed by a child under sixteen years of age is a felony or a crime punishable by imprisonment in a State prison unless it be a capital crime or one punishable by life imprisonment.

In acting under the opinion referred to, these provisions should be kept in mind, and such persons under sixteen years of age, not convicted of a capital crime or a crime punishable by life imprisonment, are not, under the law, guilty of a felony and hence are entitled to the benefits of chapter 489 above referred to.

Yours very truly,

EDWARD R. O'MALLEY,

Attorney-General.

Penal Code — Section 2193 *— Prisoners — Illegal Sentence.*

Authority of court to issue order directing agent or warden to deliver prisoner to sheriff for pupose of re-sentence.

STATE OF NEW YORK.

ATTORNEY-GENERAL'S OFFICE,

ALBANY, *June* 20, 1910.

Hon. C. V. COLLINS, *Superintendent of State Prisons, Albany, N. Y.:*

Dear Sir.— By your favor of March 21, 1910, I am asked for my opinion as to the authority of a court to issue an order upon its own motion directing the agent and warden to deliver a prisoner, illegally sentenced, to the sheriff of the county where sentenced for the purpose of having said prisoner returned to the court for re-sentence.

Authority for the return of prisoners illegally sentenced in respect to the time of year when sentence shall expire, is found in the latter part of section 2193 of the Penal Law and reads as follows:

" The officers of every prison or penitentiary are hereby expressly prohibited from taking into their custody any convict sentenced in violation of the provisions of this section, and any convict so illegally sentenced shall be returned by the sheriff of the county where the conviction was had to the court to be re-sentenced in conformity to the provisions of this section. Provided that if it shall appear to the officers of any prison or penitentiary at the time it is sought to incarcerate a convict therein that the court which imposed the sentence has adjourned, then it shall be lawful for said officers to receive said convict and hold him in their custody until he can be re-sentenced as herein provided, and the second re-sentence shall be deemed to have begun on the date of the convict's reception under his first sentence. The officers of any prison or penitentiary shall, in the case of a convict so illegally sentenced to imprisonment therein, immediately notify the court of their action."

Beginning with a line of English cases, it has been held generally that criminal courts have power over their own records and judgments which may be exercised in certain cases and to a certain extent. In People v. Trimble, 60 Hun, 364, it is held that

"A court which has pronounced a sentence which violates section 697 of the Penal Code, has power to correct the sentence on its own motion and at the same term."

In Miller v. Finkle, 1 Park. Cr. Rep., at page 376, it is said.

" The courts cannot forgive or remit or absolve, from the consequences of a criminal judgment, but they may see that the judgment itself is in conformity to law. * * *

" If by inadvertence in pronouncing a sentence, a requirement of the statute has been overlooked, it may be corrected by the same tribunal before further action is taken.

" I think it is a safe rule to lay down that the court of criminal jurisdiction may vacate or modify a judgment at the same term at which it is pronounced."

It would seem that a portion of section 2193 of the Penal Code quoted above goes a step farther than this in providing that

" If it shall appear to the officers of any prison or penitentiary at the time it is sought to incarcerate a convict therein that the court which imposed the sentence has adjourned, then it shall be lawful for said officers to receive said convict and hold him in their custody until he can be re-sentenced as herein provided."

In my judgment, section 2193 is ample authority for the court to issue an order upon its own motion directing the agent and warden to deliver a prisoner illegally sentenced to the sheriff of the county where sentenced for the purpose of having said prisoner returned to the court for re-sentence.

Yours respectfully,

EDWARD R. O'MALLEY,

Attorney-General.

Prisoners — Paroles.

Case of one Charles E. Leavitt, punishable by imprisonment in State's prison, ineligible to parole.

(See opinion July 7, 1909.)

STATE OF NEW YORK.

ATTORNEY-GENERAL'S OFFICE,

ALBANY, *June* 30, 1910.

Hon. C. V. COLLINS, *Superintendent of State Prisons, Albany, N. Y.:*

Dear Sir.— I have your favor of June 27, 1910, in which you ask for my opinion as to whether Charles E. Leavitt is entitled to the benefits of chapter 49 of the Laws of 1909.

In reply I would beg to refer you to the opinion rendered to you on July 7, 1909, in the case of James B. Kellogg. Inasmuch as the offense for which Leavitt was sentenced in the United States Court was punishable by imprisonment in a state prison (see sections 5480, 5541 and 5542 of the Revised Statutes of the United States), I am of the opinion that he is ineligible for parole.

Yours very truly,

EDWARD R. O'MALLEY,

Attorney-General.

Penal Law — Sections 1897, 1935 — Felonies.

Penalty for carrying dangerous weapons.

STATE OF NEW YORK.

ATTORNEY-GENERAL'S OFFICE,

ALBANY, *August* 11, 1910.

Hon. C. V. COLLINS, *Superintendent State Prisons Department.
Albany, N. Y.:*

Dear Sir.— Your favor of August 10th received, in which you ask for an opinion " as to what is the maximum penalty for criminally carrying a weapon."

I assume you have reference to the offense of carrying and use of dangerous weapons as provided by the first paragraph of section 1897 of the Penal Law, which reads:

> "A person who attempts to use against another, or who carries, or possesses any instrument or weapon of the kind commonly known as a slung-shot, billy, sandclub or metal knuckles, or who with intent to use the same against another, carries or possesses a dagger, dirk or dangerous knife is guilty of a felony."

Your attention is also called to section 1935 of the same law. which provides the punishment of felonies when not otherwise fixed by statute and reads:

> "A person convicted of a crime declared to be a felony for which no other punishment is specially prescribed by this chapter, or by any other statutory provision in force at the time of the conviction and sentence, is punishable by imprisonment for not more than seven years, or by a fine of not more than one thousand dollars, or by both."

There does not seem to be any specially prescribed statutory punishment of the felony mentioned in section 1897, referred to, other than that prescribed by section 1935; therefore, the maximum punishment of such offenses would be imprisonment for not more than seven years, or by a fine of not more than one thousand dollars, or by both.

Yours very truly,

EDWARD R. O'MALLEY,

Attorney-General.

Prisoners — Paroles — Indeterminate Sentence.

Case of Alfred J. Walker. Term "maximum penalty" does not include fine. Prisoner subject to parole.

STATE OF NEW YORK.

ATTORNEY-GENERAL'S OFFICE,

ALBANY, *September 9,* 1910.

Hon. C. V. COLLINS, *Superintendent of State Prisons, Albany, N. Y.:*

Dear Sir.— Your favors of August 24 and September 10, 1910, were duly received.

You ask for a construction of the provisions of chapter 669 of the Laws of 1900 and state the following facts: Alfred J. Walker was sentenced March 3, 1908, for the crime of criminally receiving stolen property, under an indeterminate sentence, the minimum term of which was three years and four months and the maximum four years and four months. He was never before convicted.

Chapter 669 of the Laws of 1910 and section 211-a of the present law provide:

" Section 211-a. PAROLE OF CERTAIN INDETERMINATES.— Each person confined in a state prison who has never before been convicted of a crime punishable by imprisonment in a state prison, having an indeterminate sentence whose minimum, unless fixed by law, is more than one-half of the maximum penalty prescribed by law for the crime of which he was convicted, or who may hereafter receive such sentence, shall, when he has served a period of time equal to one-half the maximum penalty prescribed by law for the crime of which

he was convicted, be subject to the jurisdiction of the board
of parole for state prisons and said board shall have the same
authority as to the parole and discharge of such prisoner that
it would have had if the minimum sentence imposed by the
court had been for a period equal to one-half the maximum
penalty prescribed by law for the offense of which he was convicted, but no person shall be paroled who has served less
than one year."

Section 1308 of the Penal Law fixes the penalty for receiving
stolen property by imprisonment in the state prison for not more
than five years, or in a county jail for not more than six months
or by a fine of not more than two hundred dollars, or by both
such fine and imprisonment.

Section 484 of the Code of Criminal Procedure provides that
" A judgment that the defendant pay a fine may also direct that
he be imprisoned until the fine be satisfied, specifying the extent
of the imprisonment, which cannot exceed one day for every dollar
of the fine."

The question asked by you is whether the maximum penalty as
used in this section includes both imprisonment and fine. I am
of opinion that the use of this term " maximum penalty " in the
above section was intended to apply to the maximum term of imprisonment in state's prison and not to include the fine, and that
the prisoner would be subject to parole after having served two
years and six months.

This opinion is confined to the particular facts in this case, a-
a different situation might arise where a fine was actually imposed.

Very truly yours,
EDWARD R. O'MALLEY,
Attorney-General.

Prisoners — Sentences.

Commitment of Antonio Craranino, whether sentence is illegal.

STATE OF NEW YORK.

ATTORNEY-GENERAL'S OFFICE,

ALBANY, *September* 10, 1910.

Hon. C. V. COLLINS, *Superintendent New York State Prison Department, Albany, N. Y.:*

Dear Sir.— I acknowledge the receipt of your favor of July 11th with inclosures, viz: Communication from **Frank V.** Cole, agent and warden of Clinton prison, addressed to you, and a copy of the commitment of Antonio Craranino to that prison.

Mr. Cole in his letter says:

"I am sending you copy of commitment in the case of No. 8457 Antonio Craranino. The question with me is whether this man has not received an illegal sentence. If he was tried he could be tried on only one charge and sentenced to five years the maximum either for burglary, third, or grand larceny, second. At least this is my opinion of the case. Will you please submit the matter for decision by the Attorney-General?"

You ask in your letter for an opinion in relation to the matter referred to by Mr. Cole.

I assume from the commitment that the conviction of Craranino was obtained under an indictment containing two counts — one for burglary, third degree, the other for grand larceny, second degree— both arising out of the same transaction, the jury returning a general verdict of guilty upon the whole indictment, and thereupon the court imposed a sentence of not less than five years and six months or not more than seven years and six months.

The conviction occurred while the Penal Code was in effect.

Section 506 of the Penal Code provides:

"A person, who, having entered a building under such circumstances as to constitute a burglary in any degree, commits any crime therein, is punishable therefor, as well as for the burglary; and may be prosecuted for each crime, separately, or in the same indictment."

I think that under this section, Craranino was properly indicted, tried and convicted for both offenses and can be punished for each.

This section was under consideration in People ex rel. Dawkins v. Frost, 58 Misc. 618, in which Crane, J., having it in mind, said:

"But yet the whole matter of procedure is within the power of the legislature to regulate, so long as the defendant is not deprived of any of his constitutional privileges; and the procedure upon the charges of larceny and burglary has been specially provided for, so that these may be united in the one indictment, tried together, and the defendant, if he be found guilty of both, punished for each separately."

The maximum punishment for each of these offenses is imprisonment in the state's prison not exceeding five years (sections 507–534 of the Penal Code); therefore, if the judgment was intended as punishment for both offenses, which I think must be presumed from the circumstances and the commitment, it did not exceed the punishment prescribed by law for both offenses when combined in one judgment or sentence.

It may be that a separate judgment should have been entered and a separate sentence imposed for each offense; the second sentence to commence at the expiration of the first, in pursuance of section 694 of the Penal Code. Notwithstanding, however, the judgment as entered is still valid and he would not be entitled to be discharged.

Yours very truly,

EDWARD R. O'MALLEY,

Attorney-General.

State Institutions — Matteawàn State Hospital.

Authority of justice of the peace to visit and investigate treatment of insane patients with a view to criminal prosecution of the attendants.

(See section 608, Code of Criminal Procedure; rule 27 Lunacy Commission).

STATE OF NEW YORK.

Attorney-General's Office,

Albany, *October* 23, 1910.

Hon. C. V. Collins, *Superintendent of Prisons, Albany, N. Y.:*

Dear Sir.— I am in receipt of your communication of October 20, 1910, requesting my opinion relating to certain matters set forth in a letter of Dr. Lamb, superintendent of Matteawan State Hospital, and of date October 17, 1910, which you inclosed.

It appears from Dr. Lamb's letter that a justice of the peace, one Sherwood Phillips, accompanied by counsel, appeared at his institution and asked to interview patients in regard to the treatment of certain patients by an attendant named McDonald. The purpose of the magistrate and his counsel according to a letter of his counsel to Dr. Lamb was "not to investigate treatment of patients but to prosecute criminally McDonald." It is further stated in the counsel's letter that " he (the magistrate) is compelled on the information laid before him to make this examination of witnesses and make a determination as to whether a crime has been committed or not." It appears that Dr. Lamb refused such interviews, holding, as he states in his letter, " that inasmuch as the original charge was made by a lunatic, without substantiation, and that all these lunatics are under my especial care and treatment, that a local peace officer has no jurisdiction over them at all and that he cannot make any inquiry therein."

In my judgment this position of Dr. Lamb is not tenable. It is true that a justice of the peace has no visitorial power over a State institution, but on the other hand he has undoubted power to inquire into crimes committed within his criminal jurisdiction whether within a State institution or whether committed by an employee or inmate of such institution. However, he cannot exercise under the guise of his criminal jurisdiction visitorial powers but must follow, inasmuch as his jurisdiction is statutory, the due procedure laid down in our Code of Criminal Procedure.

The proceeding of the justice under consideration is to determine whether a crime has been committed. Such a proceeding in order to be valid must comply with certain well defined requirements. These requirements are well summarized in the head note of the case of People ex rel. Livingston v. Wyatt, 186 N. Y. 383, as follows:

" An information sufficient to authorize a magistrate to
. issue a subpoena for the purpose of investigating whether a
crime has been committed must be sworn to and cannot rest
wholly on information and belief. Facts enough must be
stated to show that the complainant is acting in good faith,
and that he has reasonable grounds to believe that a crime
has been committed by some person named or described. The
law does not permit an inquiry based upon hearsay and the
mere chance that some crime may be discovered, and a magistrate acts without jurisdiction upon an information of that
character."

Assuming that the proceeding under consideration is valid and complies with the above requirements, yet the justice of the peace has no more power or privilege to see patients or inmates of Matteawan than any other visitor. However, under section 608 of the Code of Criminal Procedure he may issue subpoenas in such proceeding for witnesses within the State either on behalf of the people or of the defendant. The fact that such witnesses may be inmates of Matteawan does not deprive the magistrate of this power of subpoenaing them, except that such subpoenas must be served in accordance with rule 27 of the Commission of Lunacy in relation to the service of legal process on patients of State institutions. This rule provides that the superintendent in charge of an institution for the care and treatment of the insane " is not to permit the service of any legal process * * * except upon the order of a judge of a court of record, which shows that the judge had notice of the fact that the person sought to be served was at the date of the order an inmate of such institution." The commission has jurisdiction over Matteawan and their rule was adopted by virtue of the powers lodged in them by the Insanity Law, and in my judgment is a vital exercise of their rule-making power required by the welfare of the institutions under their jurisdiction. Where, therefore, a proper order accompanies a subpoena such inmate would have to be produced in court, unless, of course, the condition of the patient were such that the subpoena could not be complied with.

Very truly,

EDWARD R. O'MALLEY,

Attorney-General.

Prisoners — Indeterminate Sentence — Paroles.

Case of Louis de Beauval under two indeterminate sentences, parolable ,when he has served two minimum sentences.

STATE OF NEW YORK.

ATTORNEY-GENERAL'S OFFICE,

ALBANY, *November* 19, 1910.

Hon. C. V. COLLINS, *Superintendent of State Prisons, Albany. N. Y.:*

Dear Sir.— By your favor of September 6th, I am informed that one Louis de Beauval is confined under two indeterminate sentences, the first for not less than three years and six months, nor more than four years and nine months and the second for not less than three years nor over five years, and you ask for my opinion as to when he will be parolable.

It is provided by section 2189 of the Penal Law (formerly Penal Code, 687-a) that a person *never before convicted of a crime punishable by imprisonment in a state prison,* can be sentenced to prison under an indeterminate sentence, and by article 8 of the Prison Law it is provided that every person who has never before been convicted of a crime punishable by imprisonment in a state prison can be paroled, and by chapter 669, Laws 1910, a new section has been added to the Penal Law and numbered 211-a, providing that in all cases of first conviction, unless the minimum sentence is fixed by law, the prisoner shall be subject to the jurisdiction of the Board of Parole after he has served one-half of the maximum sentence imposed by the court, whether the minimum sentence exceeds one-half of the maximum sentence or not.

It is very evident that the Legislature intended that no prisoners should be entitled to parole except those serving a first sentence in a state prison, and that indeterminate sentences should only be made in such cases. It was held, however, in People ex rel. Dawkins v. Frost, 129 App. Div. 498, that indeterminate sentences could be imposed against a prisoner convicted of the two offenses of burglary and grand larceny charged in the same indictment, and growing out of the same transaction, and following this decision and assuming that the prisoner de Beuval was sentenced at the same time for two offenses growing out of the same transaction, I must advise you that he will be parolable when he has served the two minimum sentences.

Yours truly,

EDWARD R. O'MALLEY,

Attorney-General.

Prison Law — Section 243 — Prisoners — Commutation of Sentence.

Person convicted of crime after discharge from prison because of commutation earned by him, shall serve out such forfeited commutation upon his return to prison after a subsequent sentence.

STATE OF NEW YORK.

ATTORNEY-GENERAL'S OFFICE,

ALBANY, *December 5, 1910.*

Hon. C. V. COLLINS, *Superintendent of State Prisons, Albany, N. Y.:*

Dear Sir.— By your favor of April 25, 1910, I am informed that a prisoner sentenced to a four years imprisonment, earned and received commutation of one year, and was released at the expiration of three years of imprisonment; that the same prisoner was convicted of another crime within a year after his first discharge, and was again sentenced to imprisonment for four years; that he again earned a year's commutation, and after he had served three years of his second sentence, he was continued in prison for another year in addition for the year's commutation upon his first sentence which he had forfeited by being convicted of the second offense, and thus serves four years during his second imprisonment; that within one year after his second discharge he is again convicted and sentenced to state prison; and the question is now asked " must he serve the one year commutation allowed on his second sentence, or will the fact that his third sentence was not imposed until after the date of the expiration of the full term for which he was sentenced (the second time) relieve him from that penalty."

It is very clear that the Legislature intended by the provisions of section 243 of the Prison Law, that if a person was convicted of a crime within the period in which he is relieved from imprisonment on account of commutation earned by him, that he shall be required to serve out such forfeited commutation upon his return under a subsequent sentence, in addition to the term of such subsequent sentence, and inasmuch as the prisoner referred to in the above proposition committed a third offense within the time allowed him for commutation on his second term he is squarely within spirit of the act if not within the letter thereof, and that he should be required to serve out the commutation which he was accorded at the expiration of his second term, and which he forfeited by the commission of a crime while he was still within his commutation period.

It is more than probable that the Legislature did not have in mind a case exactly like the one instanced by you, and the language used in the statute is somewhat ambiguous when applied to the conditions named in your letter, but to adopt a construction that he is not liable to serve out the forfeited commutation at the expiration of his third term simply because he had served the full four years, one year of which was served as forfeited commutation, would be doing violence to the very purposes of the act, and relieve the prisoner of a portion of his punishment through a technicality,

that it was the plain intent of the Legislature that he should endure
on account of his commission of another offense while he is receiving the benefit of the law's favor.

The changes made by chapter 403 of the Laws of 1910 provide
that such forfeited commutation shall be worked out before the
beginning of the service of such new sentence, which will do away
with all doubt in the future, and seems to be along the line of this
opinion.

I therefore advise you that the prisoner referred to in your
letter should be required to serve the one year's commutation
allowed on his second sentence, in addition to the sentence imposed
for the third offense.

Yours truly,
EDWARD R. O'MALLEY,
Attorney-General.

Prison Law — State Prisons.

Scale of wages of guards at Dannemora and Matteawan. Previous
service as attendant not to count, the latter being in the noncompetitive class, and under provisions of the Insanity Law,
while the position of guard is in the competitive class and
comes under the provisions of the Prison Law.

STATE OF NEW YORK.

ATTORNEY-GENERAL'S OFFICE,

ALBANY, December 16, 1910.

Hon. C. V. COLLINS, Superintendent of State Prisons, Albany,
N. Y.:

Dear Sir.— I am in receipt of your favor of November 26th, in
which you say:

> " Referring to section 114 of the Prison Law (chapter 47,
> Laws of 1909), Warden Cole of Clinton prison asks for an
> opinion as to whether or not in fixing the graduated scale of
> guards' wages, he should take into account time served by
> such guards as attendants at Dannemora or Matteawan State
> Hospitals. Several men who have been attendants at Dan-
> nemora State Hospital for a longer or shorter period have

from time to time taken the civil service examination for prison guards and have been appointed at Clinton prison, and the warden is in doubt as to what action to take relative to fixing their salaries."

Section 114 referred to, in so far as is material to your question, reads as follows:

"Officers designated as keepers prior to June 1, 1904, shall be classified as guards. The several guards shall be paid only for services actually rendered, and their annual compensation shall be subject to pro rata deduction for time not served. The compensation of guards appointed after said date, shall be as follows: For the first year's service, six hundred sixty dollars; for the second year's service, seven hundred forty dollars; for the third year's service, eight hundred twenty dollars; for the fourth year's service, and thereafter, nine hundred dollars. The annual compensation of guards in service on said date shall be for services thereafter rendered, as follows: To those serving their first year as prison officers, seven hundred eighty dollars; to those serving their second year as prison officers, eight hundred twenty dollars; to those serving their third year as prison officers, eight hundred sixty dollars; to those who have served three or more years as prison officers, nine hundred dollars."

The attendants at Matteawan and Dannemora State Hospitals are appointed by the medical superintendents thereof, each making the appointments for his respective hospital and fixing the compensation that such attendant shall receive with the approval of the Superintendent of State Prisons.

Guards, pursuant to the Civil Service Law, are in the competitive class and attendants are in the noncompetitive class. The services of a guard and those of an attendant are methodically different and performed under different circumstances and in different institutions which are governed by separate statutes, one by the Prison Law and the other by the Insanity Law. The compensation of a guard is made dependent upon the length of time of service, and that of an attendant is not; therefore, by reason of these unrelated conditions and circumstances, under which the services of a guard and those of an attendant are rendered, there would seem to be no analogy between the two positions in so far as the application of the statute in question might be concerned.

By the language of the statute it is confined to the services of a guard as such, and it would require a strained construction to make it applicable to the previous service of a person while an attendant fixing his compensation as a guard.

I am, therefore, of the opinion that in fixing the compensation of a guard, pursuant to section 114 of the Prison Law, his previous services while an attendant at Matteawan or Dannemora State Hospitals should not be taken into consideration.

Yours very truly,

EDWARD R. O'MALLEY,

Attorney-General.

OPINIONS RENDERED THE STATE SUPERINTENDENT OF PUBLIC WORKS.

Highway Law — Section 15 — Consolidated Canal Law — Chapter 5 --- Article 8 — State Indian Reservations.

Supervision and control of highways and bridges constructed by State on Indian Reservations, is vested in the Highway Commission, the Superintendent of Public Works having supervision only where such highways and bridges cross canals. Provisions of article 8, chapter 5, Consolidated Canal Law, not abrogated by the Highway Law.

STATE OF NEW YORK.

ATTORNEY-GENERAL'S OFFICE,

ALBANY, *June* 20, 1910.

Hon. FREDERICK C. STEVENS, *Superintendent of Public Works, Albany, N. Y.:*

Dear Sir.— I acknowledge the receipt of your favor of April 12, 1910, in which you state:

"The enactment of the Highway Law and the creation of the Highway Commission, resulted in taking from the Depart-

ment of Public Works certain duties which the Legislature
by special appropriation had formerly committed to this department, such as the repair and maintenance of roads and
bridges on Indian highways. My understanding is that this
change was by inference rather than by specific provision, the
inference being based on the fact that the Highway Law gives
the Highway Commission supreme power in the matter of
the care and maintenance of all roads and bridges.

" In view of the construction which has been placed upon
this matter, I would be glad to be advised by you what in
your judgment is the duty, responsibility and authority of
the Superintendent of Public Works so far as relates to the
maintenance and repair of bridges on highways leading over
the canals and various feeders of the State; that is to say,
whether the responsibility for the repair, reconstruction and
maintenance of such structures is still in the hands of the
Superintendent of Public Works, or if this, too, has been
transferred to the hands of the Highway Commission."

The supervision and control of bridges constructed or to be constructed by the State on Indian reservations was changed from
the Superintendent of Public Works to the Highway Commission
by the last sentence of section 157 of the Highway Law, which
provides:

" The Commission shall have exclusive supervision and
control of all bridges constructed or to be constructed by the
State on any Indian reservation and may make and enforce
such reasonable rules and regulations concerning their use
as it shall deem necessary."

Also see chapter 46 of the Laws of 1910, which amends the
Highway Law by adding two new sections, 158 and 159, which
authorize the Highway Commission to appoint a superintendent of
highways in each Indian reservation, who is to exercise the powers
and perform the duties imposed upon town superintendents, and
also provides for the custody and expenditure of highway money
used in connection therewith.

Article 8 of chapter 5 of the Consolidated Laws (Canal Laws),
formerly article 7 of chapter 338 of the Laws of 1894, prescribes

the powers and duties of the Superintendent of Public Works regarding the control, construction and maintenance of bridges and highways connected with the operation of the canals of the State. In my opinion the provisions of this article have not been abrogated by the Highway Law.

Respectfully yours,

EDWARD R. O'MALLEY,

Attorney-General.

Lien Law -- Section 82 — Liens and Mortgages on Vessels.

Interpretation of recent amendments as contained in chapter 182 Laws of 1910, regarding liens and mortgages on vessels used for navigation on the canals and waterways of the State. Filing of in county clerk's office and office of Superintendent of Public Works.

STATE OF NEW YORK.

ATTORNEY-GENERAL'S OFFICE,

ALBANY, *July* 12, 1910.

HON. FREDERICK C. STEVENS, *Superintendent of Public Works, Albany, N. Y.:*

Dear Sir. — I beg to acknowledge the receipt of your communication asking my advice in reference to the recent amendments of the Lien Law, contained in chapter 182 of the Laws of 1910.

Heretofore notices of liens and mortgages on certain vessels operating on State canals and other waters were filed with the Comptroller. The amendment to the law provides that these instruments hereafter be filed, not with the Comptroller, but in the office of the Superintendent of Public Works.

You ask whether a copy of a notice of lien or chattel mortgage should be accepted for filing, or whether you should require a duplicate original or certified copy of the instrument to be filed.

Section 82, as amended, provides that in the case of a lien upon a vessel built, used or fitted for navigation of any of the canals or lakes of the State, the lienor shall immediately after filing the notice (of lien) in the county clerk's office, file *a copy thereof* in the office of the Superintendent of Public Works of the State, *duly certified* by the county clerk in whose office the original notice is filed.

It is clear from the foregoing that in the case of a notice of a lien, a copy certified by the county clerk in whose office the original is filed must be presented to your office for filing. In the case of a chattel mortgage, however, as is provided in section 232 of the Lien Law, it is sufficient to file the mortgage or a true copy thereof. The usual practice is for the mortgagee to retain in his possession the original mortgage and file a copy which is, of course, not certified. · In the case of a chattel mortgage, it is sufficient if the instrument is denoted as a true copy but in the case of a notice of lien the copy must be certified by the county clerk.

You also state that section 82 provides that the lien must be verified by the lienor and you ask whether this provision as to verification applies as well to instruments operating 'as chattel mortgages. A lien is in the nature of a claim and naturally should be verified. A chattel mortgage, however, is executed by the owner of the property and consequently does not need to be verified, and in fact, is valid without the usual acknowledgment necessary on mortgages affecting real estate.

You also ask whether or not the Superintendent of Public Works must accept for filing any instrument tending to operate as a notice of lien or chattel mortgage, if in proper form and accompanied by the legal fee for filing, which does not show on its face that the vessel covered by such lien or mortgage is one to be used on the canals or lakes of the State, or is a canal boat, steam tug, scow or other craft navigating the canals of this State. In my judgment, if a lienor offers such an instrument for filing in your office, it is proper for you to assume that the vessel affected is of the kind specified in the statutes. If it is not, that is a matter for the owner to prove and any objections to your filing the instrument can be raised by him at such time as he sees fit. If you should refuse to accept for filing a mortgage affecting a canal boat on the ground that the instrument did not show on its face that it was such a lien as the statute requires to be filed in your office, the mortgagee would be entitled to a writ of mandamus to compel you to file it. Hence, the wisest course and undoubtedly the one which would involve the least difficulty, would be for you to accept for filing such instruments as are presented in proper form with the required fee.

Yours respectfully,

EDWARD R. O'MALLEY,

Attorney-General.

———

Barge Canal -- Leases — Surplus Waters.

Lease by State of Troy dam to Lansingburgh Dry Dock and Hydraulic Company, in 1832, and to George Tibbits in 1835. Right of Superintendent of Public Works to terminate said lease on account of deepening of Hudson river near Troy, calling for abandonment of dam.

(See opinion August 23, 1910.)

STATE OF NEW YORK.

Attorney-General's Office,

Albany, *July* 14, 1910.

Hon. Frederick C. Stevens, *Superintendent of Public Works, Albany, N. Y.:*

Dear Sir.—-I have the honor to acknowledge the receipt of your favor of the 30th ultimo, in which you ask for my opinion with reference to certain water leases at the Troy dam. From your letter and from an examination of the leases and from discussions with your department and the members of the Advisory Board of Consulting Engineers, the following facts appear:

On the 2d day of January, 1832, the State leased certain surplus waters at the east end of the Troy dam to the Lansingburgh Dry Dock and Hydraulic Company pursuant to section 106, title 9, chapter 9 of the Revised Statutes, and on the 26th day of November, 1835, the surplus waters at the west end of the same dam were leased to one George Tibbits pursuant to the same law.

The first of these leases was recorded in the Rensselaer county clrk's office in volume 25 of deeds at pages 280, 281, and the second in the Albany county clerk's office in book LL of deeds at page 402. Both of these instruments provided for the payment of annual rentals and for terms of nine hundred and ninety-nine years. These rents have been paid to date. I assume that both of these leases are now owned by the International Paper Company.

The instruments contain the following provisions:

" * * * the use of the surplus water which may be taken at the east (west) end of the aforesaid dam, and not ˙exceeding one-half of the quantity which may be taken at both ends of said dam, such surplus water to be taken and drawn from the said dam at such place and in such manner, and be discharged at such place and in such manner, as the acting canal. commissioner or the canal commissioners shall from time to time direct; saving and reserving to the said parties of the first part the right wholly to resume the waters hereby conveyed and the privilege hereby granted, and to control and limit the use of said water and privileges whenever, in the opinion of the Canal Board or of the Legislature the necessary supply of water for *use of any State canal*, or the safety of such canal, or works connected therewith, shall render such resumption, control or limitation necessary. And in case any such resumption shall be made, or control or limitation imposed, no compensation or damages shall be allowed for any improvements or erections made, or which may be made under or in consequence of this grant or lease. And also saving and reserving to the said parties of the first part the right, without making any compensation to the said parties of the second part, or any other person claiming under them, wholly to abandon or destroy the work, by the construction of which the said surplus water has been created, whenever, in the opinion of the canal commissioners, the occupation and use of said work shall cease to be advantageous to the State."

At the present time the canal system of the State uses a portion of the Hudson river from Waterford to and through this dam for navigation purposes. The river and harbor bill, passed by the last Congress, contains an item for the improvement of the Hudson river in the vicinity of Troy in such a manner as to result in a channel of at least twelve feet in depth and two hundred feet in width to connect with the Barge canal at Waterford. This action of the Federal government was taken at the request of the State of New York as expressed by its canal officials and citizens. The tentative plan of Colonel Black of the corps of engineers, U. S. A., calls for the construction of a dam in the Hudson river at a point about eight hundred feet up stream from, and for the abandonment of the present Troy dam.

Under the above facts the question arises as to what are the rights and duties of the Superintendent of Public Works and all other officials of the State charged with the construction of the Barge canal with reference to the cancellation or termination of these water leases.

It is, of course, indisputable that no portion of the Erie or Champlain canals can be abandoned so as to result in the destruction of a navigable communication with the Hudson river. If in the prosecution of the work directed by chapter 147 of the Laws of 1903 and the acts amendatory thereof and supplemental thereto, the State should construct a new dam at the site above mentioned and should thereby as a necessary result of the improvement abandon the Troy dam, it is my opinion that under the last sentence of the above quotation the Superintendent of Public Works, in whom are vested the powers of the Canal Commissioners, with the approval of the Canal Board, would have the power to wholly abandon or destroy the Troy dam without the payment of compensation to the present owners of the water leases, whenever the new dam should be in a condition to continue navigation past the point of the present Troy dam; and if canal navigation in both canals could be maintained to the Hudson by means of the canal now entering the river at Albany and without the use of the Troy dam, that dam might in like manner be abandoned and destroyed when to do so would be advantageous to the State. What the State through the proper officials can do performing the work itself, it is my opinion it can likewise do when the work is being performed for it by the Federal government.

This abandonment and destruction of the Troy dam should be accomplished after giving notice to the present owners of those water leases of the proposed action of the State, and of the time when by virtue of the completion of the new dam or by the divert-'ing of all canal navigation through the Albany terminal the old dam ceases to become a necessary part of canal works.

Yours very truly,

EDWARD R. O'MALLEY.

Attorney-General.

Barge Canal — Contracts.

Contract No. 46. Aqueduct at Montezuma. Contractor's liability regarding endangering structure by cutting through Erie canal. Surety company should consent to and approve permit issued for such work.

STATE OF NEW YORK.

ATTORNEY-GENERAL'S OFFICE,

ALBANY, *November* 11, 1910.

Hon. FREDERICK C. STEVENS, *Superintendent of Public Works, Albany, N. Y.:*

Dear Sir.— Replying to your favor of the 10th inst., in which you ask my opinion as to whether in allowing the contractor on contract No. 46 to pass his plant from one portion of his contract to the other by cutting through the Erie canal near the Montezuma aqueduct by a permit, a copy of which you have submitted to me, the surety company on the contractor's bond would be held liable for any damage that might result to the aqueduct and the canal, I beg to advise you as follows:

Under special specification 4-s of the contract it is provided that the removal of the Montezuma aqueduct, which divides this contract into two portions, and the excavation of the canal beneath the same, are not included in the contract and in this part of the contract it is further provided that " the contractor must make his own arrangements to pass the aqueduct without interfering with or endangering that structure."

The contract also contains the usual clauses Nos. 17 and 22 with reference to the conducting of the work so as not to interfere with the navigation of the present canal, and an agreement on the part of the contractor to indemnify the State and save it harmless from all damages resulting from any wrong or negligence in the execution of the contract or anything incidental thereto or connected therewith. For the faithful performance of this contract and the discharge of the obligations thereof, the surety company which executed the faithful performance bond, is responsible. However, the surety company has the right to insist that the State not only shall not waive any of the provisions of the contract which tend to make the safety of the canal structures more certain, but also that the State shall not do any act or permit the doing of any act which might result in damage. In other words, the surety company has, in my opinion, the right to have the State require the contractor to live up to the exact and precise terms of his contract and in particular as to the question involved in this opinion, to require the contractor to use even the most expensive method in passing the aqueduct at Montezuma, if such method is the safest for the stability of those canal structures.

I am therefore of the opinion that in order to hold the surety company responsible for any defect and any damage which might result from that defect in the proposed plan to pass the aqueduct, it is necessary to have the surety company on the bond of contract 46, consent to and approve of the issuance of the permit, dated September 9, 1910, and that there should be included in the form of such approval and acceptance a clause to the effect that the obligations as to safety of canal structures embodied in that permit should be deemed a part of the general obligations of the contractor as defined by the general contract.

I return herewith copy of permit referred to.

Yours very truly,

EDWARD R. O'MALLEY,

Attorney-General.

OPINIONS RENDERED THE STATE SUPERINTEND-
ENT OF WEIGHTS AND MEASURES.

Domestic Commerce Law — Sealers of Weights and Measures.
Testing of accuracy of money value on computing scales by county
sealer.
(See opinion November 15, 1909).

STATE OF NEW YORK.

ATTORNEY-GENERAL'S OFFICE,

ALBANY, *May* 19, 1910.

Hon. FRITZ REICHMANN, PH.D., *Superintendent of Weights and
Measures, Room* 427, *Capitol, Albany, N. Y.:*

Dear Sir.— I acknowledge your letter of the 17th inst., in which
you ask whether under section 13, chapter 187, Laws of 1910, a
scaler of weights and measures has authority to test the correctness of the indicated money values on so-called computing scales.
The section in question reads in part as follows:

" Where not otherwise provided by law, the county sealer
shall have the power within his county to inspect, test, try
and ascertain if they are correct, all weights, scales, beams,
measures of every kind, instruments or mechanical devices
for measurement and the tools, appliances or accessories connected with any or all such instruments or measurements used
or employed within the county by any proprietor, agent, lessee
or employee in determining the size, quantity, extent, area or
measurement of quantities, things, produce, articles for distribution or consumption offered or submitted by such person
or persons for sale, for hire or award. He shall at least twice
in each year and as much oftener as he may deem necessary
see that the weights, measures and all apparatus used in the
county are correct."

It is my opinion that the foregoing language is broad enough to
empower a county sealer to test the correctness of the indicated

money values on so-called computing scales. Such indication of money value is merely another form in which the weight of the articles is expressed, and in order to adequately test the correctness of the scales, the correctness of such indication as well as the correctness of the weight indication may properly be checked.

Very truly yours,

EDWARD R. O'MALLEY,

Attorney-General.

Domestic Commerce Law — County Sealer of Weights and Measures.

Creation of office of county sealer under the provisions of chapter 187, Laws of 1910, section 13. Duty of supervisors if necessary, to call special meeting to appoint.

STATE OF NEW YORK.

ATTORNEY-GENERAL'S OFFICE,

ALBANY, *July* 12, 1910.

Hon. FRITZ REICHMANN, *Superintendent of Weights and Measures. Albany. N. Y.:*

Dear Sir.— Replying to yours of the 9th inst., wherein you ask for my opinion on the following question, namely, " In order to comply with the provisions of Sealer of Weights and Measures and supplying him with a salary in accordance with section 13, chapter 187 of the Laws of 1910, should the board of supervisors call a special session for the purpose of making such appointment and providing such salary if there is no other meeting of the board of supervisors scheduled before their regular meeting in November ? " In reply, I would say section 13, chapter 187 of the Laws of 1910, above referred to, provides as follows:

" § 13. COUNTY SEALER; DUTIES OF COUNTY SEALER; DUTY OF SUPERVISORS.— There shall be a county sealer of weights and measures in each county, who shall be appointed by the board of supervisors and hold office during the pleasure of such board. He shall be paid a salary determined by the board of supervisors and shall be provided by them with the necessary working equipment of standard weights and measures. * * * "

This statute creates the office of county sealer of weights and measures and makes it the duty of boards of supervisors to appoint such an officer and fix his salary.

I am therefore of the opinion that the board of supervisors should make such appointment, and if in their discretion it is advisable to call a special meeting for such purpose, such appointment can be made at such special meeting.

Yours very truly,

EDWARD R. O'MALLEY,

Attorney-General.

Sealer of Weights and Measures.

Jurisdiction of county sealers does not extend to cities within county.

STATE OF NEW YORK.

ATTORNEY-GENERAL'S OFFICE,

ALBANY, *October* 19, 1910.

Hon. FRITZ REICHMANN, *Superintendent of Weights and Measures, Albany, N. Y.:*

Dear Sir.— I am in receipt of your favor of September 15th, in which you ask me in substance for an opinion whether a county sealer of weights and measures, appointed pursuant to section 13 of chapter 25 of the Laws of 1909, as amended by chapter 187 of the Laws of 1910, has jurisdiction in the cities within his county.

Section 13 aforesaid in part provides:

" There shall be a county sealer of weights and measures in each county, who shall be appointed by the board of supervisors and hold office during the pleasure of such board. He shall be paid a salary determined by the board of supervisors and shall be provided by them with the necessary working

30

equipment of standard weights and measures. He shall take
charge of and safely keep the county standards. Where not
otherwise provided by law, the county sealer shall have the
power within his county to inspect, test, try and ascertain if
they are correct, all weights, scales, beams, measures of every
kind, instruments or mechanical devices for measurement and
the tools, appliances or accessories connected with any or all
such instruments or measurements used or employed within
the county by any proprietor, agent, lessee or employee in
determining the size, quantity, extent or area or measurement
of quantities, things, produce, articles for distribution or
consumption offered or submitted by such person or persons
for sale, for hire or award. He shall at least twice in each
year and as much oftener as he may deem necessary see that
the weights, measures and all apparatus used in the county
are correct."

Section 14 of the same chapter provides:

" There shall be a city sealer of weights and measures to
be appointed by the mayor with the approval of the common
council of each city. He shall be paid a salary to be fixed
and determined by the board or body authorized to determine salaries of city officials, and no fees shall be charged or
received by him or by the city for the inspecting or testing
of weights, measures or weighing or measuring devices. He
shall perform in his city the duties of and have like powers
as a county sealer in a county. This section shall not apply
to the city of New York."

This section is applicable to all cities except the city of New
York, as is apparent by its language.

It will be observed from the foregoing quoted laws prescribing
the duties and powers of a county and city sealer of weights and
measures that if it were intended that a county sealer of weights
and measures should have jurisdiction in cities within his county,
such cities would have two officers whose prescribed duties and
powers are the same, and each duplicating the work of the other.
Such a condition I think could not have been intended. I think
the language, " where not otherwise provided by law, the county

sealer shall have the power within his county, * * *," above quoted, intends to exclude from the jurisdiction of the county sealer of weights and measures cities within his county which are provided with a sealer of weights and measures, pursuant to section 14.

In view of the foregoing conclusions and the laws above quoted, I am of the opinion that the jurisdiction of a county sealer of weights and measures does not extend to the cities within his county.

Answering the proposition that a city should not be required to pay a city sealer and also its proportionate share of the salary of a county sealer, I beg leave to suggest that this requirement appears to be in accord with the laws creating the offices of county attorneys and county engineers, both of the last named officers being paid by the county at large, although they have no duties to perform in any city situate within their county.

Yours truly,

EDWARD R. O'MALLEY,

Attorney-General.

OPINION RENDERED THE STATE TRUSTEES OF PUBLIC BUILDINGS.

Trustees of Public Buildings — Education Building. Claim of R. T. Ford Company regarding increased cost of liability . insurance, not allowable.

STATE OF NEW YORK.

ATTORNEY-GENERAL'S OFFICE,

ALBANY, *November* 15, 1910.

To the Honorable, The Trustees of Public Buildings, Albany, N. Y.:

Gentlemen.— On the 30th of September, 1910, you requested my opinion as to your authority to permit extra compensation for

increased cost of liability insurance in pursuance of a claim made
to you by the R. T. Ford Company, a contractor engaged in the
construction of the new Education Building. In reply to your
request I have the honor to render you the following opinion:

The contract entered into by the State with the R. T. Ford
Company contains in paragraph 37 the following clause:

> " The contractor shall keep his employees insured against
> accident and shall secure and protect the State from any lia-
> bilities or damages in this connection."

By chapter 674 of the Laws of 1910, the Legislature passed the
so-called Compulsory Workmen's Compensation Law relating to
certain employments, including the erection or demolition of
buildings in which there is required iron or steel frame work, in
which class of construction the work provided for in the Ford
contract falls. There was also passed at the last session of the
Legislature chapter 352, which made certain amendments to the
Labor Law in relation to employers' liability, by virtue of which
it was provided, among other things, that the burden of proving
absence of contributory negligence, which formerly rested on the
plaintiff, was abolished and that burden as a defense to a plaintiff's
claim was placed upon the defendant in such actions.

As a result of the passage of these laws, which went into effect
on the first day of September, 1910, it is alleged by the contractor
that the cost of carrying liability insurance on its contract has
increased two per cent. That by these enactments there has been
placed a greater burden of responsibility upon employers of labor
in the specified classes than formerly existed is conceded. Because
the State has so increased its burden of responsibility and with it
the cost of obtaining liability insurance, the contractor urges that
it properly has a claim for extra compensation equal to the amount
of such increased cost.

Referring to the clause quoted from the contract it will be
observed that the obligation imposed thereby upon the contractor
is that it shall keep its " employees insured against accident and
shall secure and protect the State from any liabilities and damages
in this connection." Broadly interpreted this clause means not
merely that the contractor shall insure against claims made against

it by its employees for damages arising out of negligence of any description but that it should insure those employees against damages arising out of any accident, whether due to negligence or not. In this light it is apparent that the State was seeking by the incorporation of these words in the contract to secure the laborers engaged upon the new Education Building from loss or damage, which might result during their employment upon the State's property. In this view of the contract it must follow that the passage of the above laws has placed upon this contractor a responsibility no greater or even as great as that assumed by it in the execution of the agreement. In this view of the case it cannot have any claim for extra compensation based on the increased cost of liability insurance.

It is urged, however, that the meaning of the clause quoted is that the contractor should merely provide the usual employer's liability insurance. This seems to have been the interpretation placed thereon by the contractor itself and accepted by the State for it appears that only employers' liability insurance was provided and that in the progress payments and progress certificates an estimate of the pro rata share of such insurance was included as a basis for payment by the State.

If this interpretation is accepted it must follow that because an increased burden of responsibility has been placed upon the employer by the passage of the above mentioned laws, reasonably resulting in an increased cost of insurance, it has been sought to place upon the contractor a greater obligation than existed at the time of the execution of the contract.

Section 10 of article 1 of the United States Constitution forbids any State to pass any law impairing the obligation of contract, and it has been held that this inhibition applies as well to contracts of the State itself as to the contracts of private individuals or corporations. The increasing of the burdens of the contractor in this case would be an impairment of the obligation of its contract and invalid as to that contract. The State can require no greater responsibility on the part of the contractor than was imposed by the contract at the time of its execution. It must follow that the contractor is not required to furnish any further or more expensive insurance than it was required to furnish prior

to the passage of the above laws, and that it has no claim for compensation for the cost of such increased insurance if it sees fit
to carry such policies for its own benefit.

In either interpretation of this contract, it is my opinion that
the claim of the R. T. Ford Company cannot be allowed.

Respectfully yours, .

EDWARD R. O'MALLEY,

Attorney-General.

OPINIONS RENDERED STATE INSTITUTIONS.

State Institutions — Craig Colony.

Law authorizing detention of epileptics in Craig Colony against
their will, not within the power of the Legislature to enact.
The act of 1909 permitting Rome Custodial Asylum to detain
feeble-minded persons and idiots, would not apply to epileptics unless some cause were shown rendering them unsafe to
be at large.

(See letter February 28, 1905, L. B. 85, p. 196).

STATE OF NEW YORK.

ATTORNEY-GENERAL'S OFFICE,

ALBANY, *February* 1, 1910.

WILLIAM T. SHANAHAN, M. D., *Medical Superintendent, Craig
Colony for Epileptics, Sonyea, N. Y.:*

Dear Sir.-- I am in receipt of your letter of January 26th last
in which you call my attention to an act of the Legislature of 1909,
permitting the Rome State Custodial Asylum for feeble-minded
persons and idiots to detain inmates until discharged by its board
of managers, and to arrest and return inmates who have escaped
therefrom, and in which you ask if a similar law could not be
enacted to apply to the Craig Colony for Epileptics.

I note also what you state with reference to an opinion rendered by Attorney-General Mayer in 1905 to the effect that a law giving to the managers of your institution the right to detain a patient against his will, whose only infirmity is epilepsy, and to arrest and return him to said institution should he escape, would be unconstitutional.

As stated in substance in the opinion of Attorney-General Mayer, the test seems to be whether the liberty of the person confined is dangerous to the public welfare, or whether such person is incapable of caring for himself.

The inherent and constitutional right of liberty guaranteed to every citizen is safeguarded by the authority lodged in the State to detain criminals, persons suffering from contagious or infectious diseases, persons incompetent to direct and control their own acts because of insanity, idiocy and the like, and persons whose detention is required for some purpose involving the public welfare. Beyond this the Legislature may not go.

I am of the opinion that the fact that a person is an epileptic is not alone a sufficient cause to deprive him of his liberty. Epilepsy *ipso facto* does not render its subject a menace to the public welfare, nor does it follow that a person so afflicted is an incompetent. It is not a contagious or infectious disease. I know of no policy of public welfare that would justify the involuntary confinement of an epileptic unless some further cause were shown.

Yours very truly,

EDWARD R. O'MALLEY,

Attorney-General.

State Institutions — State Agricultural and Industrial School at East Rochester.

Transfer of State land to the Erie Railroad Company for a driveway, can only be made through the Commissioners of the Land Office under section 8 of the Railroad Law. (See also section 110, Public Lands Law.)

(See opinion February 16, 1910.)

STATE OF NEW YORK.

ATTORNEY-GENERAL'S OFFICE.

ALBANY, *March* 9, 1910.

Hon. ANDREW H. BOWN, *Secretary of the Board of Managers of the State Agricultural and Industrial School, East Rochester, N. Y.:*

Dear Sir.— I have your valued favor of the 9th instant requesting advice as to the power of the board of managers of the State Agricultural and Industrial School to grant the application of the Erie Railroad Company made to said board for permission to extend its driveway on a portion of the State lands, and the proper procedure to bring about the transfer of State lands to said railroad company for such purpose.

The statute governing this institution and defining the power of the board of managers thereof makes no provision for the granting by said board of managers of lands used for reformatory purposes, belonging to the State of New York. (State Charities Law, §§ 180 and 182.)

Application for the transfer of land to this railroad company should be made under the provisions of section 8 of the Railroad Law. That section reads in part as follows:

"The commissioners of the land office may grant to any domestic railroad corporation land belonging to the people of the state, except the reservation at Niagara and the Concourse lands on Coney Island, which may be required for the purposes of its road on such terms as may be agreed upon by them; or such corporation may acquire title thereto by condemnation;

and the county or town officers having charge of any land belonging to any county or town, required for such corporation for the purposes of its road, may grant such land to the the corporation for such compensation as may be agreed upon." * * *

This section of the Railroad Law is fortified by section 110 of the Public Lands Law, as follows:

" This chapter shall not limit or modify the provisions of the railroad law relating to the grant or acquisition, for railroad purposes, of any lands belonging to the people of the state."

I, therefore, advise that application for the transfer of a portion of said State lands to the Erie Railroad Company for the purposes first mentioned be made pursuant to the provisions of the Railroad Law above quoted.

> Yours very truly,
> EDWARD R. O'MALLEY,
> *Attorney-General.*

State Charities Law (Cons.)— Section 45, Article 4 — State Finance Law — Section 17, Article 2 — State Institutions.

State Custodial Asylum, Newark, families of superintendent and steward, maintenance of, can only be legally granted by the Salary Classification Commission.

(See opinion August 26, 1909, p. 915, Report.)

STATE OF NEW YORK.

ATTORNEY-GENERAL'S OFFICE,

ALBANY, *March* 26, 1910.

ETHAN A. NEVIN, M. D., *Superintendent. New York State Custodial Asylum, Newark, N. Y.:*

Dear Sir.— Your letter of February 19 received, with reference to an opinion from this office as to whether the families of the superintendent and steward of your institution should be allowed maintenance, under section 45, article 4, of the Consolidated State Charities Law, the latter part of which reads as follows:

" No persons, other than the officers and employees of such institutions, and the families of the superintendents, medical officers, adjutants, quartermasters or stewards, necessarily residing therein, shall be allowed rooms and maintenance, except at a rate fixed by the state comptroller and the fiscal supervisor with the approval of the governor."

The last part of section 17 of article 2 of the State Finance Law provides:

" The state comptroller and the president of the state board of charities shall from time to time classify into grades the officers and employees of the various charitable and reformatory institutions required by law to report to the fiscal supervisor and in the month of September of each year recommend to the governor such changes in the salaries or wages of such officers and employees for the ensuing fiscal year as may seem proper, but such changes shall not be made unless the governor shall approve the same in writing. Differences in the expense of living and rates of wages in the localities in which such institutions are situate may be considered. The comptroller shall have the power of audit subject to such classification."

This section creates the Salary Classification Commission, composed of the State Comptroller and president of the State Board of Charities, with power to fix the salaries of the superintendent and steward of your institution. Such maintenance and other privileges could not be legally granted except as a part of the salaries or wages of such officers, and therefore can be granted only by the Commission.

Section 45 of the State Charities Law does not direct that maintenance must be furnished the officers and employees or the families of the superintendent and steward of charitable institutions, but merely that such maintenance shall not be granted to any one except the officers or employees named therein.

I am of the opinion, therefore, that the Salary Classification Commission has the power to allow or withhold such maintenance, and that unless they have acted in the case you suggest, the families in question are not entitled to maintenance.

Very truly yours,

EDWARD R. O'MALLEY,

Attorney-General.

State Charities Law — Section 205 — State Institutions.

Expenses incurred by board of managers of the New York Training School for Girls, Hudson, for return of females improperly committed to such institution from the counties of New York and Kings, are a charge upon such counties, and the bills therefor should be presented to the comptroller of the city of New York.

STATE OF NEW YORK.

ATTORNEY-GENERAL'S OFFICE,

ALBANY, *April* 21, 1910.

HORTENSE V. BRUCE, M. D., *Superintendent, New York State Training School for Girls, Hudson, N. Y.:*

Dear Madam.— I beg to acknowledge receipt of your letter of March 26th, requesting my opinion as to what officials in New York and Kings counties it is proper to send bills for expenses incurred by the board of managers of your institution for the return of females improperly committed to it. You state in your letter that section 205 of the State Charities Law provides that the cost and expense of the return of such females necessarily incurred and paid by such board of managers shall be a charge against the county from which said female was committed, to be paid by such county to such board of managers in the same manner as other county charges are collected.

County charges are paid by submitting them to the board of supervisors of the county, which has authority to "audit all accounts and charges against the county, and direct annually the raising of sums necessary to defray them in full" (section 12, subdivision 2, County Law). In New York and Kings counties, however, that are no boards of supervisors, the duties and powers

of such boards being vested in the board of aldermen of the city
of New York, in accordance with section 26 of article 3 of the
Constitution, which is as follows:

"There shall be in each county, except in a county wholly
included in a city, a board of supervisors, to be composed of
such members and elected in such manner and for such period
as is or may be provided by law. In a city which includes an
entire county, or two or more entire counties, the powers and
duties of a board of supervisors may be devolved upon the
municipal assembly, common council, board of aldermen, or
other legislative body of the city."

Sections 1, 3 and 4 of the Greater New York charter vest all of
the duties and powers of the several municipal and public corporations united and consolidated within the city of New York in the
board of aldermen of that city and provide that such board shall
exercise all the powers vested in the corporation of the city of New
York, and further provide that all valid and lawful charges and
liabilities which may accrue against any of the municipal or public
corporations (which would include the counties of New York and
Kings) shall be deemed and taken to be a like charge against or·
responsibility of the city of New York.

Section 900 of the city charter provides that the comptroller shall
prepare and submit to the board of aldermen, at least four weeks
before its annual meeting, for the purpose of imposing the annual
taxes, a statement setting forth the amounts by law authorized to
be raised by taxes on account of the counties of New York, Kings,
Queens and Richmond. Section 902 stated that in the statement
submitted to the comptroller, as above mentioned, he shall state
specifically the sums necessary to be raised to pay county charges.
It therefore appears that the charges for the return of females improperly committed from New York and Kings counties, which
are lawful charges against those counties, should be presented to
the comptroller of the city of New York, so that he may include
them in his statement to the board of aldermen, as specified in the
sections of the charter referred to above.

Yours respectfully,

EDWARD R. O'MALLEY,

Attorney-General.

State Institutions — Rome State Custodial Asylum.

Superintendent no right to open mail of inmates under ruling of Assistant Attorney-General for the Post Office Department, but may make rules subject to approval of State Board of Charities, to prevent letters being sent or their delivery to such inmates where necessary for the safe administration of such institution.

STATE OF NEW YORK.

ATTORNEY-GENERAL'S OFFICE,

ALBANY, *May* 3, 1910.

CHARLES BERNSTEIN, M. D., *Superintendent, Rome State Custodial Asylum, Rome, N. Y.:*

Dear Sir.— I have your favor of the 12th of February, 1910, asking my opinion as to your right, as superintendent of the Rome State Custodial Asylum, to open mail of its inmates.

Section 1431 of the Postal Laws and Regulations (1893) provides:

"Any person who shall take any letter, postal card or packet, although it does not contain any article of value or evidence thereof, out of a post office or branch post office, or from a letter or mail carrier, or which has been in any post office or branch post office, or in the custody of any letter or mail carrier, before it has been delivered to the person to whom it was directed, with a design to obstruct the correspondence, or pry into the business or secrets of another, or shall secrete, embezzle, or destroy the same, shall for every such offense be punishable by a fine of not more than five thousand dollars, or by imprisonment at hard labor for not more than one year, or by both."

Based on this section is the following regulation, No. 382, which may be found at page 91 of the Postal Laws and Regulations (§ 451, P. L. & R., 1893):

"A letter once placed in the post office is in the custody of the department for transmission and delivery to the party addressed. Neither postmasters nor officers of the law have any authority to open it under the pretext that there might be something improper or even criminal in it, or that would aid in the detection, or furnish evidence for the conviction of offenders against the law."

Hon. John L. Thomas, Assistant Attorney-General for the Post Office Department, in a communication dated December 20, 1893, made the following decision:

"The authorities in control of the asylum have no right to open and inspect letters addressed to or sent by the inmates under their care and in their custody without their consent. This ruling does not preclude such authorities, however, from preventing the delivery of letters to such inmates or to prevent letters from being sent by them to outside parties, when it might, in their judgment, probably interfere with the safe and due administration of the affairs of such institution. Of course, here as elsewhere, a sound discretion should be exercised in this respect, and with that the Post Office Department would be content."

I understand this decision is still in full force and effect. The State Charities Law, section 92, provides:

"The board of managers shall * * * 2. Establish by-laws, rules and regulations subject to the approval of the state Board of Charities for the internal government, discipline and management of the asylum."

The official orders and regulations of the State Lunacy Commission, Form 40, subdivision 2, provide:

"When a lawfully adjudged and committed lunatic, who is an inmate of a hospital or asylum, has no guardian or committee, lawfully appointed, mail matter addressed to such inmate and delivered, in pursuance of the foregoing direction of the post office department, to the keeper or superintendent of the hospital or asylum, may, in the discretion of such keeper or superintendent, be delivered to such inmate unopened, if, in his judgment, it is safe to do so; or, if he has a well-grounded reason to believe that to deliver such mail matter to such patient would be unsafe or unwise and prejudicial to the interests of such patient or of the institution, *such keeper or superintendent may withhold such mail matter for examination and detention or destruction, if deemed advisable, always having due regard to the prevailing rule as to the inviolability of mail matter and seeking to maintain it whenever it is practicable or proper to do so.*"

Therefore, under the ruling of the Post Office Department and the statute governing charitable institutions, which I have already quoted, you have no right to open mail addressed to inmates, but you have the right and authority to make rules and regulations subject to the approval of the State Board of Charities preventing the delivery of letters to such inmates or to prevent letters from being sent by them to outside parties when it might, in your judgment, probably interfere with the safe and due administration of the affairs of such institution.

Yours very truly,

EDWARD R. O'MALLEY,

Attorney-General.

State Institutions — New York State Soldiers' and Sailors' Home, Bath.

Section 60 of article V of the Public Buildings Law, requiring the Governor, Attorney-General and the Department Commander of the G. A. R. to act as *ex-officio* trustees, repealed by chapter 149, Laws of 1909, amending State Charities Law and bringing said institution under the supervision of the Fiscal Supervisor.

STATE OF NEW YORK.

ATTORNEY-GENERAL'S OFFICE,

ALBANY, *May* 7, 1910.

Hon. WILLIAM H. NICHOLS, *Secretary, New York State Soldiers' and Sailors' Home, Bath, N. Y.:*

Dear Sir.— I am in receipt of a letter forwarded by you signed by J. E. Ewell, commandant of the New York State Soldiers' and

Sailors' Home, asking whether the Governor, the Attorney-General and the Department Commander of the G. A. R. under the present law are *ex-officio* trustees of such institution.

Section 60 of article V of the Public Buildings Law provides in part that the New York State Soldiers' and Sailors' Home " shall continue to be under the management and control of a board of trustees consisting of twelve members of which the governor, the attorney-general and the commander of the department of New York, Grand Army of the Republic, shall be *ex-officio* members."

While the act of which this is a part was one of the consolidated laws passed in 1909, this section was simply a restatement of chapter 108 of the Laws of 1903 and under the Construction Act it cannot be held that its inclusion in the consolidated laws gave force or effect to any statutes theretofore either expressly or impliedly repealed.

Chapter 433 of the Laws of 1908 in part provided:

" Each of the charitable and reformatory institutions * * * shall be under the control and management of boards of seven managers to be appointed for the institution by the governor by and with the advice and consent of the Senate."

This section was restated in the consolidation of the State Charities Law in 1909 and was afterwards amended by chapter 149 of the Laws of 1909 by striking out the words " each of the charitable and reformatory institutions " and inserting in place thereof the words " each of the state institutions reporting to the fiscal supervisor." The New York State Soldiers' and Sailors' Home is such an institution. It would therefore seem that the section of the Public Buildings Law providing for twelve trustees for this institution, three of whom should consist of the Governor, the Attorney-General and the Department Commander of the G. A. R., was repealed by the section above quoted, and that such persons are no longer *ex-officio* trustees of the institution.

Yours very truly,
EDWARD R. O'MALLEY,
Attorney-General.

State Institutions — New York State Training School for Girls. Superintendent's leave of absence for one year without pay. Board of managers no authority to pay the assistant superintendent the salary of the superintendent, no vacancy in office having been declared.

STATE OF NEW YORK.

ATTORNEY-GENERAL'S OFFICE,

ALBANY, *June* 9, 1910.

THOMAS WILSON, M. D., *Executive Committee, Board of Managers, New York State Training School for Girls, Hudson, N. Y.:*

My Dear Sir.— I have your letter of the 30th inst., in which you ask my advice as to the right of the board of managers of your institution to pay the assistant superintendent the salary of the superintendent while the latter is away from the institution on a leave of absence without pay and the former is acting superintendent. It appears from your letter that the salary of the superintendent of the school as established by the Salary Classification Commission is from $1,500 to $1,800 per year with maintenance, increasing from minimum to maximum at the rate of $100 per year. The superintendent's salary for the present fiscal year is stated to be $1,700. You state that your board has granted a leave of absence of one year to the superintendent — eleven months without pay and one month with pay as representing her vacation. Under these conditions your board believes it proper to continue to pay the present salary to the assistant superintendent who will act in place of the superintendent, and asks whether this may regularly be done. You also enclose a copy of a letter from the Fiscal Supervisor to your board in reference to this matter, in which it is suggested that your board declare the position of superintendent vacant and appoint the assistant superintendent to the position of superintendent. You state, however, that your board does not consider the position vacant in this sense.

Although it would seem proper that the acting superintendent should receive the salary of the superintendent for the time in which she is acting in that position, nevertheless, if there is no vacancy in the position of superintendent I cannot see how this can be accomplished. It is the duty of the assistant superintendent to perform the work of the superintendent in the absence of the latter, whether such absence be only for one day or for one year. It is therefore my opinion that if your board does not desire to declare the position of superintendent vacant, the salary of the superintendent cannot be paid to the assistant superintendent. The only way in which the salary of the latter can be increased is by such action as would be necessary to increase it if the superintendent were present.

Very truly yours,

EDWARD R. O'MALLEY,

Attorney-General.

State Institutions — State Finance Law - Section 2a.

State officers and employees; amendment to law providing for semi-monthly payment of salaries, applies to the employees of State institutions.

(See opinion June 7, 1910.)

STATE OF NEW YORK.

ATTORNEY-GENERAL'S OFFICE,

ALBANY, *June* 13, 1910.

BENTON McCONNELL, ESQ., *Treasurer, New York State Soldiers' and Sailors' Home, Hornell, N. Y.:*

Dear Sir.— I have your favor of the 11th inst., in which you ask my opinion as to whether chapter 58, Laws of 1910, requiring the semi-monthly payment of all State officers and employees on the first and sixteenth of each month applies to your institution.

In reply to this I will say that the law plainly applies to all State officers and employees, and that, as the employees of your institution are paid directly by the State, they clearly come within its provisions. I have rendered an opinion upon this matter to the State Comptroller and enclose you herewith a copy of the same for your information.

Very truly yours,

EDWARD R. O'MALLEY,

Attorney-General.

State Charities Law — Sections 199, 202, 204, 208 — *State Institutions.*

New York State Training School for Girls, Hudson. Board of managers have no right to disregard the commitment of the court, and refuse to admit new pupils and inmates on the ground that proper accommodations cannot be had. They should confer with the State Board of Charities regarding such matters.

STATE OF NEW YORK.

ATTORNEY-GENERAL'S OFFICE,

ALBANY, *August* 23, 1910.

CHARLES H. STRONG, ESQ., *President, Board of Managers, New York State Training School for Girls, Hudson, N. Y.:*

Dear Sir.— Referring to my letter of the 21st ultimo to your superintendent in reference to the right of your institution to refuse to accept new pupils and inmates on the ground that you had no proper accommodations for them, and to your letter to me of the 12th inst., in which you set forth your views of the statute, permit me to advise you as follows:

The question presented is whether your board of managers has the right to instruct your superintendent to refuse to accept girls regularly committed to your institution by a court of competent jurisdiction, on the ground that in the judgment of the board there are no proper accommodations for such additional inmates. You point out in your letter that the total possible capacity of the institution is 379, which includes nine rooms in the main building which is designed for officers only and which, under the policy of your board, has not been used for housing any girls. This estimate also includes 93 rooms in " Stuyvesant," the so-called prison building, which has been condemned. I note that it is your fixed policy to transfer all inmates from this building to other cottages and that you do not care to be responsible for placing girls in this building. Your actual population is 324, not counting 10 babies. The capacity under the above exceptions is 277. The only actual vacant rooms in the institution are in " Lowell," in which the most vicious

and unmanageable of the girls are housed, and in this condemned
building.

The Superintendent of Prisons has recently complained that
various sheriffs had reported your refusal to receive girls committed to your institution. After the receipt of this communication I had a conference with your superintendent and with the
secretary of the State Board of Charities, to which your institution
is subject. As a result of this conference it would seem that it is
the opinion of the secretary of the State Board of Charities that it
would be physically possible for your institution, by making certain
rearrangements, to care for more inmates than you now have, and
the secretary himself stated that there was, in his opinion, no sufficient reason for refusal in case you should be cited by the court
to explain your disobedience of the commitment.

Section 199 of the State Charities Law, continuing your institution, provides that it is continued " as a reformatory institution
* * * for the reception of all girls not over the age of sixteen
years, who shall be regularly committed thereto * * * by any
court having authority to make such commitments * * *."
Section 202, defining the duties of the superintendent, provides
that " under the direction of such managers she *shall receive and
take* into such institution all females regularly committed thereto
by any court or magistrate having authority to make such commitment." Section 204, subdivision 4, seems to disclose that magistrates shall have power to commit females to this institution, and
taken in connection with section 208, this intention seems clear.
The latter section provides that your managers shall employ female
marshals to convey from the place of conviction to the place of the
institution " all females regularly committed thereto."

In view of these facts, it is my opinion that under the foregoing
provisions of the statutes your institution is required to receive all
persons committed by competent tribunals, State or otherwise. Of
course, if it were physically impossible for you to comply with the
mandate of the court, such impossibility would constitute a defense
and would prevent your punishment for contempt for refusing to
obey the order of commitment.

Section 9 of the State Charities Law gives the State Board of
Charities power to establish rules for the reception and retention
of inmates in all institutions subject to its jurisdiction, and section

18 of the same law gives this same board the power to make transfers of inmates from one institution to another. It is my opinion that it is the duty of your board to communicate the facts to the State Board of Charities in order that that board may take such action in the premises as it deems necessary. The question as to whether or not you must receive any particular person committed is one of fact in each instance to be determined by the conditions existing and the peculiar circumstances surrounding each case. It is impossible for me to lay down any definite line of demarkation in view of the general supervisory power conferred upon the State Board of Charities over your institution both in respect to the reception, retention and management of inmates. I therefore advise that this matter should be taken up with that board as a question of policy. Unless, however, it is actually impossible for you to receive girls regularly committed, I must advise you that you are not justified, in my opinion, in disregarding the commitment of the court.

Very truly yours,

EDWARD R. O'MALLEY,

Attorney-General.

State Institutions — New York State Training School for Boys.

Contract with New York Central Railroad for constructing spur track, should not omit the provisions required by section 14 of the Labor Law, that only citizens of the United States shall be employed. Contract should also be approved by the Fiscal Supervisor in accordance with the provisions of subdivision 6, chapter 526, Laws 1910.

STATE OF NEW YORK.

ATTORNEY-GENERAL'S OFFICE,

ALBANY, *December* 20, 1910.

Hon. ROBERT W. HILL, *Secretary, Commission to Select a Site for the New York State Training School for Boys, Capitol, Albany, N. Y.:*

Dear Sir.— Pursuant to your oral request asking me to examine the contract dated December 10, 1910, between the New York

Central & Hudson River Railroad Company and the New York
State Training School for Boys Site Commission, for the construction of a spur track, which contract already executed has been submitted to me by the State Architect, and if I find it to be in proper
form, to approve it, I have examined the contract and I find that I
cannot approve it for the following reasons:

1. There has been omitted from it the provision required by
section 14 of the Labor Law, which provides, among other things,
that only citizens of the United States shall be employed and
preference given citizens of the State of New York.

On November 3, 1910, you wrote this department a letter in
reference to this contract, wherein you asked whether the provision of the Labor Law, requiring that only citizens of the United
States shall be employed on work under contract with the State of
New York, is valid, and a deputy replied to your favor by letter,
dated November 10, 1910, in which it was stated that the only case
where this question has ever been passed upon was in People vs.
Warren, 13 Misc. 615, and that it was there held that such a provision is unconstitutional and void, and the letter concluded that in
the absence of any appeal from the decision in that case, or any
conflicting decision, you were authorized to execute a contract
omitting such provision.

The case cited is an isolated one which arose in the Superior
Court of Buffalo in July, 1895, and the only question passed upon
by the court was whether it was a crime for a contractor with a
municipal corporation for the construction of public works to
employ alien labor upon such works. The statute there under consideration was chapter 622 of the Laws of 1894 and the language
of section 14 of the present Labor Law is not identical with the
language in that act.

Furthermore, since that decision and in 1905 the people of this
State adopted an amendment to the Constitution (article XII,
section 1), which provides,

> " * * * and the legislature may regulate and fix the wages
> or salaries, the hours of work or labor, and make provision for
> the protection, welfare and safety of persons employed by the
> State, * * * or other civil division of the State or by any

contractor or subcontractor performing work, labor or services for the state, * * *."

This gives to the Legislature very broad powers in dealing with labor. Under the above quoted constitutional provision most of the present Labor Law has been enacted. The section in question in its present form has not been passed upon by the courts. It therefore seems to me in view of the change in the statute and the amendment of the Constitution, that the decision of the Superior Court of Buffalo can hardly be considered the law at the present time. Whether the Legislature under the provisions of the Constitution quoted had the power to enact the provision of the Labor Law under discussion may be open to dispute, and it would be well, as I have heretofore suggested to the Labor Commissioner, that the question of the constitutionality of it be tested in the proper forum and in that way the matter set at rest.

More than that, it has heretofore been the custom to insert in all contracts wherein the State was a party, a provision in compliance with section 14 of the Labor Law. In view of these facts, I do not feel authorized under the law in advising you to omit said section from the contract.

I, therefore, withdraw the letter to you of November 10th and overrule the views therein expressed and advise you that I cannot approve this contract without compliance with said provision of the Labor Law.

2. As the contract directs the performance of the work without public advertisement and without a preliminary deposit, it should comply with subdivision 6 of chapter 526 of the Laws of 1910, viz., be approved by the Fiscal Supervisor of State Charities.

Yours very truly,

EDWARD R. O'MALLEY,

Attorney-General.

OPINIONS RENDERED OTHER THAN STATE DEPARTMENTS.

Public Officers Law — Section 15 — Justices of the Peace.

When constitutional oath of office has been taken and copies filed with town clerk, but duplicate copy not sent to county clerk until expiration of fifteen days, said county clerk should file such copy, the acts of said justice, having entered upon the discharge of his duties, being valid.

STATE OF NEW YORK.

Attorney-General's Office,

Albany, *February* 25, 1910.

B. H. Oberdorf, Esq., *County Clerk, Geneseo, N. Y.:*

Dear Sir.— I am pleased to acknowledge receipt of your favor under date of February 10, 1910, asking to be advised as to your course in reference to filing the oath of office of J. R. Taylor, who was elected a justice of the peace of the town of Portage, in your county, in March, 1909, term to commence on January 1, 1910.

I am informed by the correspondence and certified copy of oath that Mr. Taylor took his constitutional oath of office on the 14th day of January, 1910; that the same was taken in duplicate and both left with the town clerk on that day; that one of the duplicates was duly filed in the office of the town clerk on that day and he promised to forward the other to the county clerk and that through some inadvertence the town clerk failed to forward a certified copy of the oath in the county clerk's office until on or about January 26, 1910.

On February 5, 1910, I wrote Mr. Taylor that the county clerk should file the oath of office.

I desire to call your attention to section 15 of the Public Officers Law which provides that all of the official acts performed by a public officer who has entered upon the discharge of his duties without taking and filing an official oath or an official undertaking, shall be valid.

It has been repeatedly held that the failure of a person elected to a public office, to file an oath within the time required by statute does not *ipso facto* vacate the office. Such an officer holds his office by a defeasible title and he is placed in a position where the office could be declared vacant or forfeited by a proper tribunal for such failure, but this defect in his title can be cured at any time before it is declared forfeited by the filing of such oath in the county clerk's office.

> Matter of Kerr, 57 Misc. 324.
> Foote v. Stiles et al., 57 N. Y. 399.
> Cronin v. Stoddard, 97 N. Y. 271.
> People ex rel. Brooks v. Watts, 73 Hun, 404.
> People ex rel. Wilson v. Board, 59 Hun, 204–206.

I think it is your duty to file the oath of office of Mr. Taylor notwithstanding it did not reach your office until after the expiration of the fifteen days, and I do not think the official actions of Mr. Taylor are invalid on account of the failure of the town clerk to forward the duplicate to you within that time.

> Yours truly,
> EDWARD R. O'MALLEY,
> *Attorney-General.*

Election Law — Section 73.

Where city of the third class, or village has been made subject to the provisions of article III of the Election Law by vote of the people at a general election, such decision may only be changed by vote at another general election, but if made subject to provisions of article III by resolution of the committees entitled to representation on board of inspectors, change can only be made by a like resolution of such committees as provided under section 73.

STATE OF NEW YORK.

ATTORNEY-GENERAL'S OFFICE,

ALBANY, *March* 16, 1910.

Hon. HENRY G. PERKINS, *Assemblyman, Albany. N. Y.:*

Dear Sir.- In reply to your favor of the 12th instant, I beg to state that, by section 73 of the Election Law, it is provided that no city of the third class or village shall be subject to the provisions of article III of the Election Law, unless special action is taken by the committees of each political party entitled to representation upon the board of inspectors or the question has been settled by a submission of the same to the voters of the city or village, as provided by section 73 above referred to.

The last paragraph of such section reads as follows:

"A similar procedure shall take any such city or village which has so elected to come within the provisions of this article out of such provisions and make them thereafter no longer applicable to such city or village; but if the decision to come under this article was made at a general election, such decision can be changed only at a general election."

It is very clear from the above quoted paragraph that if any such city or village has been made subject to the provisions of article III of the Election Law, it can be taken out of said provisions by a similar procedure, but if it was made subject to such provisions by a vote of the people at a general election, it can only be changed back by vote at another general election; and it is equally plain that if a city or village was made subject to the provisions of article III by resolutions of the committees of the parties entitled to representation on the board of inspectors, it can be changed and the city or village relieved from the provisions of that article by like resolutions made and filed by the respective committees of the parties entitled to representation upon the election boards, in the office of the county clerk and Secretary of State, declaring that they desire that the city or village be taken out of the provisions of article III, and upon the filing of such resolutions, as provided by section 73 of the Election Law, the provisions of article III will no longer apply to such city or village.

Yours truly,

EDWARD R. O'MALLEY,

Attorney-General.

Consolidated School Law — Union Free Schools.

District within village of Pulaski. Annual election of trustees to be held pursuant to provisions of general act relating to public instruction. (Cons. School Law of 1894; Education Law of 1909.)

STATE OF NEW YORK.

ATTORNEY-GENERAL'S OFFICE,

ALBANY, *April* 8, 1910.

Board of Education of Union Free School District, Village of Pulaski, N. Y.:

Gentlemen.— By your favor (written by N. B. Smith) under date of March 4th, and subsequent letter under date of March 10th, I am asked for an opinion as to the time and manner of electing the members of your board.

By the correspondence before me it appears that by chapter 305, Laws of 1853, certain school districts and parts of districts within the village of Pulaski were consolidated into one district, the bounds of which were coterminous with the village, and by section 2 of such special act, nine persons were named and appointed .

trustees of said district, to be divided into three classes, and it was so arranged that the terms of three of such trustees should expire each year, and the first Tuesday of October was fixed as the date for holding the annual school meeting. A couple of amendments were made to such act in 1855 and 1864, but did not touch the question under consideration.

By chapter 254 of the Laws of 1892, several of the sections of the original act were amended, and it was organized into a union free school district, and section 2 was amended to read as follows:

" The present trustees of said school district number seven shall remain in office and act as trustees of said union free school district until the respective terms for which they have been elected and qualified shall expire, and at each annual school meeting held thereafter, pursuant to the provisions of the general act relating to public instruction, there shall be elected three trustees to supply the place of those whose terms of office shall then expire. If, at any meeting so annually held, there shall be a failure to elect said trustees, the class whose terms would then expire shall hold until others are duly elected in their stead. Notice of the annual or any special district meeting may hereafter be given by posting the same in three public places in said village and also publishing in the newspaper printed in said village, if any shall be published therein, and the same shall be deemed a valid and sufficient notice for all purposes."

This amendment changed the time and manner of electing the trustees in the Pulaski district from the first Tuesday of October to the time provided for holding annual school meetings pursuant to the provisions of the general act relating to public instruction.

At the time of the above amendment the general act provided for the election of trustees in a union free school district, whose limits corresponded with those of an incorporated village or city, in classes of three each year to hold three years, thus making a board composed of nine members, their regular terms of service to be computed from the date of the charter election in such village, " and thereafter there shall be annually elected in such villages and cities, at the charter elections, by separate ballots, to be endorsed 'school trustees,' in the same manner as the charter officers thereof, trustees of the said union free schools, to supply the places of those whose terms by the classification aforesaid are about to expire." This general provision was incorporated in the Consolidated School Law of 1894, and re-enacted without material change in the Education Law of 1909, and became section 222 of the last mentioned act, and still remains in force.

I think it was the intention of the Legislature that the annual election of trustees in the Pulaski school district should be held at the same time as the charter election in said village. The amendment made by chapter 254 of the Laws of 1892 superseded the provisions of section 2 of chapter 305 of the Laws of 1853, as to the *time and manner of holding* the annual school meetings in such district and to conform such election to the general act, but in all other respects the special provisions relating to such district remain intact, and are applicable thereto, as I am unable to find that they have been repealed. The provisions of chapter 254, Laws of 1892, in reference to giving notice of annual and special school meetings, as provided in section 2, and authorizing expenditures as indicated by section 7, are still in force, as well as all other provisions thereof, if there is any conflict between the same and the General Education Law, but there is no conflict between such special act and the Education Law as to the time when the annual school meeting in said Pulaski district shall be held, as section 2 provides that such annual meeting shall be held pursuant to the provisions of the general act relating to public instruction.

Yours truly,
EDWARD R. O'MALLEY,
Attorney-General.

Public Health Law — Sections 103, 144 as amended, and Section 130 — Health Officer, Port of New York.

Whether amendments in law regarding fees, etc., provide sufficiently for department expenses of port. Provisions regarding visitation of vessels under section 130. Right of health officer to sell steam vessels unfit for service.

(See opinion February 21, 1911.)

STATE OF NEW YORK.

ATTORNEY-GENERAL'S OFFICE,

ALBANY, *August* 16, 1910.

Dr. A. H. Doty, *Health Officer, Port of New York, Quarantine, L. I.:*

Dear Sir.— I beg to acknowledge the receipt of your communication of August 12, 1910, in which you ask for an opinion upon the following questions:

1. Whether the amendments to sections 103 and 144 of the Public Health Law will provide for the expenses of your department previous to October 1st, which cannot be cared for by the present income.

2. Whether, under section 130 of the same law, the visitation of certain vessels depends on the decision of the health officer.

3. Whether the health officer may sell certain steam vessels which are unfit for service, the amount secured thereby to become part of the income of your department.

In reply to the foregoing, I beg to advise:

1. The amendments to the Public Health Law by chapter 425 of the Laws of 1910 seem designed to do away with the present method of providing, from fees, etc., collected, the means and income for the maintenance of your department and to put that department upon the same basis as other departments by the appropriation of moneys by the Legislature to pay for such maintenance.

Section 144 of the Public Health Law, as amended by chapter 425, Laws of 1910, provides, among other things:

"The salary of the health officer and of all persons appointed or employed by him, and all the expenses necessarily incurred by him in the performance of the duties of his office, shall be paid by the state out of money appropriated therefor. There may be annually appropriated for the health officer a contingent fund which, notwithstanding any other provision of law, may be paid to him by the treasurer on the warrant of the comptroller. Such fund may be used by him to pay the current expenses of his office for which an immediate payment in cash is required, but he shall render to the state comptroller on or before the fifth day of each month a sworn itemized statement of all expenditures from such fund during the preceding calendar month."

The provision of the law with regard to the collection of fees is still retained. These fees, under section 37 of the State Finance Law, have heretofore been excepted from the requirement providing for payment thereof to the state treasurer and have been made applicable to the general maintenance of your department. Section 103 of the Public Health Law, as amended by chapter 425, Laws of 1910, provides that the health officer

" * * * in case of an emergency arising, shall use all means conducive to the protection of the public health, and if the balance in the contingent fund is insufficient therefor, may, with the approval of the governor and notwithstanding the provisions of section thirty-seven of the state finance law, expend such portion of the fees collected by him as may be needed. If such expenditure is made the health officer shall render to the state comptroller on or before the fifth day of the succeeding month a sworn itemized statement of all such expenditures made during the preceding calendar month."

Section 37 of the State Finance Law has also been amended by chapter 440 of the Laws of 1910, by which the words " except the health officer of the port of New York " have been omitted from said section.

The foregoing amendments are to take effect October 1, 1910, and chapter 512 of the Laws of 1910 (the appropriation bill) makes provision for the appropriation of the amounts named in that act, to be paid to the health officer for the several purposes specified, for the fiscal year beginning October 1, 1910.

It would thus appear that, from and after October 1, 1910, all salaries and expenses of your department are to be paid out of the moneys appropriated *therefor*. In so far as any contingent fund may be provided by appropriation, such fund may be used to pay " the current expenses " of your office for which an immediate payment in cash is required, by which I understand is meant the expenses of the current or ensuing year beginning October 1st. Should an emergency arise, requiring the use of means to protect the public health and should the balance in the contingent fund be insufficient therefor, then the health officer may, with the approval of the Governor, expend such portion of the fees collected by him as may be needed.

From the foregoing, I am of the opinion that the sections above noted will not provide for expenses of your department prior to October 1, 1910, which cannot be cared for by your present income.

2. Section 130 of the Public Health Law provides for the detention at quarantine, until permit for discharge is given, of every vessel from any place where a quarantinable disease existed, and further provides:

> " Every vessel arriving at the port of New York from any foreign port and every vessel from a domestic port shall, on their arrival at the quarantine ground, be subject to visitation by the health officer."

1 am of the opinion that, while all vessels are *subject* (*i. e.* liable) to visitation by the health officer, such visitation depends upon the decision of the health officer, and that he may dispense with such inspection if he regards it unnecessary for the protection of the public health.

3. I find no warrant in the law, other than by implication under section 37 of the State Finance Law as it now reads, which would authorize you to sell the boats in question. However that may be, the amendment to section 37 by chapter 440, Laws 1910, above noted, will require that, after October 1, 1910, all moneys derived from the sources therein specified shall be turned over to the State treasurer, except so far as, under section 103 of the Public Health Law, as amended by chapter 425, Laws of 1910, you may use such

portion of the *fees* collected as may be necessary, for the purposes and in the manner in said section set forth; therefore, no moneys resulting from any sales, even if made, can become a part of the income of your department.

Yours very respectfully,

EDWARD R. O'MALLEY,

Attorney-General.

Motor Vehicle Law — Section 289 — Subdivision 4 — Chauffeurs — Licenses.

Where chauffeur fails to pass examination, and seeking to evade the law, acquires a share in his employer's car, he still comes under the provisions of the statute if hired to operate the car, and must procure a license under section 289.

STATE OF NEW YORK.

ATTORNEY-GENERAL'S OFFICE,

ALBANY, *September 21, 1910.*

Automobile Club of America, Bureau of Tours, Fifty-fourth Street, New York City.

Gentlemen.— Replying to your letter of the 20th inst., in which you state that certain chauffeurs who have failed to pass the examinations have acquired shares in their employers' cars, in some cases to the extent of only one dollar, in order that they may drive the cars without a license and avoid the law, and asking my opinion upon the validity of this procedure, I beg to advise as follows:

Section 289, subdivision 4, of the Motor Vehicle Law, provides in part as follows:

"No person shall operate or drive a motor vehicle as a chauffeur upon a public highway of this state after the first day of August, nineteen hundred and ten, unless such person shall have complied in all respects with the requirements of this section * * *."

31

Section 281 defines the term " chauffeur " as meaning " any person operating or driving a motor vehicle as an employee or for hire." It is my opinion that if the person owning a part interest in a car is employed to operate the car by the owner of the other interest and actually does operate it for wages or for hire, he comes within the terms of this definition and is therefore not allowed to operate unless he first obtains the license provided by section 289.

Very truly yours,

EDWARD R. O'MALLEY,

Attorney-General.

Education Law — Section 382 — (Amended by Chapter 607, Laws 1910).

Manner of election of school directors at general election in towns.

STATE OF NEW YORK.

ATTORNEY-GENERAL'S OFFICE,

ALBANY, October 4, 1910.

Dear Sir.— By reason of the numerous inquiries made for information relative to the nomination and election of two school directors in each town at the ensuing election, I have prepared this letter, which I trust will answer all questions along those lines.

It is provided by subdivision 1 of section 382 of the Education Law, as amended by chapter 607 of the Laws of 1910, that

" Two school directors shall be elected for each town at the general election held in the year 1910; "

and the last sentence of the same subdivision provides:

" Such directors shall be elected in the same manner that town officers are elected at town meetings held at the time of a general election, and the provisions of the Election Law relating to the nomination and election of town officers shall apply to the nomination and election of such directors."

It is, therefore, necessary to elect two school directors in each town at the ensuing election whether the biennial town meeting in your town is held at the same time of the general election this year or next, and if your town election is held at any time between the 1st day of February and the 1st day of May, it will also be necessary for you to elect the two directors at the general election to be held November 8, 1910.

Section 341 of the Election Law prescribes the manner in which town officers shall be elected at town meetings held at the time of a general election, and, as far as material, reads as follows:

" In towns in which town meetings are held at the time of a general election, in an odd numbered year, the names of candidates for town offices shall be printed on the same ballots as the names of candidates for other offices voted for in such towns at such general election. In towns in which town meetings are held on general election day in an even numbered year, the names of candidates for town offices shall be printed on separate ballots; * * *."

This being an even numbered year, it is apparent from the above quoted portion of such section that the name of such candidates for school directors and all other town officers, if any are to be elected this year, should be placed upon a separate ballot from the one upon which the candidates for other offices to be elected this year will appear.

The same section of the Election Law from which the last above quotation is made provides that the ballots and sample ballots for town officers shall be provided by the town clerk, and consequently at the town's expense.

The nominations for school directors should be made in the same manner as nominations of candidates for other town office are made, and if a town is divided into two or more election districts, the same method should be followed in making nominations for school directors this year as has been heretofore established by rule or practice in such towns.

A committee appointed pursuant to section 135 of the Election Law has no authority to make the nominations for school directors, unless a town primary has been held and nominations made and some of the causes mentioned therein exist which require the action of such committee. A committee appointed by some prior primary to fill vacancies upon a ticket nominated thereat, would not have the power or authority to make original nominations for school directors to be elected on November 8th as the authority of all such committees terminated at the election following their appointment.

One of the directors should be for a short term and one for the long term, and the ballots should state which candidate is for short and which for long term.

The proposed constitutional amendment should be numbered one and the State proposition should also be numbered one, but both amendment and proposition can be upon one ballot.

A separate ballot box should be provided for the school directors and town officers when candidates as provided by the last paragraph of section 316 of the Election Law, and if a town proposition is also to be submitted to the electors in any town a separate box should be provided for the same.

Certificates of nomination for school directors should be made in duplicate, and one filed with the town clerk and one with the county clerk at least fifteen days before election. (See sections 127 and 128, Election Law.)

Certificates and returns should be made by the inspectors of the canvass of the school directors and delivered to the justices of the peace and town clerk as provided by section 65 of the Town Law.

Section 398 of the Election Law provides:

" The officers or board charged with the duty of providing ballots for any polling place shall provide therefor two sample ballots which shall be arranged in the form of a diagram showing the entire front of the voting machine as it will appear after the official ballots are arranged for voting on election day. * * * "

As both the county and town clerks will be required to participate in the furnishing of ballots this year, it will be necessary for those officers in towns in which voting machines will be used, to confer as to the form of ballots, sample ballots and numbering on machines so that no confusion may arise, and the process of voting with the machines will be made plain and easy to be understood by all the voters.

Yours truly,
EDWARD R. O'MALLEY,
Attorney-General.

OPINIONS RENDERED THE COMMISSIONERS OF THE LAND OFFICE.

STATE OF NEW YORK.

ATTORNEY-GENERAL'S OFFICE,
ALBANY, January 10, 1910.

BEFORE THE STANDING COMMITTEE ON THE HEARING OF REMON-STRANCES OF THE COMMISSIONERS OF THE LAND OFFICE.

In the Matter of the Application of EDGAR B. MULFORD for a grant of land under the waters of Gardiners Bay, town of Easthampton, Suffolk county.

To the Commissioners of the Land Office:

Gentlemen.— The above entitled application having been referred to the standing committee by your honorable board, we, the undersigned have the honor to report that the matter came on for hearing before your committee on January 4, 1910, at which time the applicant appeared by his attorney and the remonstrants, the town board of the town of Easthampton, and the board of trustees of the freeholders and commonalty of said town also appeared, and that at the hearing it was shown that the greater part of the lands under water applied for are natural clamming grounds which have been used from time immemorial by the inhabitants of said town, for the digging of soft shell clams, which industry has afforded means of livelihood for many of the

citizens of said town; the applicant disclaims any intention of
filling in any part of the land under water applied for and the
only purpose of the grant is to be to enable the applicant to erect
docks or piers; he applies for a strip of land 500 feet long in
front of the whole of his uplands, and extending 140 feet into the
waters of the bay, and offers to the State $25 for the grant applied
for.

Your committee does not think that it is for the best interests of
the State that this grant should be made and recommends that the
board, in its discretion, deny the application. The applicant has
a perfect right to erect a pier in front of his uplands without a
grant from the land board, under the decision in Trustees of
Brookhaven v. Smith, 188 N. Y. 74, and your committee thinks
that the applicant should be confined to that privilege at the
present time.

Respectfully submitted,

EDWARD R. O'MALLEY,

Attorney-General.

FRANK M. WILLIAMS,

State Engineer and Surveyor.

STATE OF NEW YORK.

ATTORNEY-GENERAL'S OFFICE,

ALBANY, *February* 8, 1910.

BEFORE THE COMMISSIONERS OF THE LAND OFFICE.

In the Matter of the Petition of HARRIET M.
SPRAKER and CAROLINE S. CARROLL, as
residuary devisees and surviving trustees
under the will of John H. Starin, deceased,
for a confirmatory grant of lands under water
in Long Island Sound adjoining Glen Island,
which were granted to John H. Starin on
November 29, 1891, by a defective description.

To the Commissioners of the Land Office:

Gentlemen.— This petition calls attention to an error made in
a grant of lands under water made to John H. Starin on November 29, 1891. The error consisted in the description of the course
of the southwesterly boundary of the lands thereby granted, and
in the patent that course was described as south 9° 38′ east 590
feet. It is now shown by an accurate survey that the description
of this course was erroneous as was also the distance. The course
should have been south 11° 37′ 35″ east 666.60 feet, in order to
join the southwest corner of a previous grant made in the year
1879 to Mr. Starin, as was the intention of the 1891 grant. A
confirmatory grant by changing the course above mentioned from
south 9° 38′ east 590 feet to south 11° 37′ 35″ east 666.60 feet
to the southwest corner of lands under water granted to John H.
Starin by the People of the State of New York, December 29,
1879, would include no additional land.

The Public Lands Law, by section 7, gives your honorable body
full power to cause to be issued a confirmatory grant where the
previous patent was manifestly erroneous in· description, as the

patent of 1891 undoubtedly was because the lines would not join, and your board has full power to make the confirmatory grant applied for, in accordance with amended petition.

Respectfully submitted,

EDWARD R. O'MALLEY,

Attorney-General.

STATE OF NEW YORK.

Attorney-General's Office,

Albany, *February* 24, 1910.

Before the Commissioners of the Land Office.

In the Matter of the Application of Lillian V. Rourke for the sale to her as owner of certain tax lands in Kings county.

To the Commissioners of the Land Office:

Gentlemen.— This application having been referred to me for the purpose of making inquiry as to whether the petitioner, Lillian V. Rourke, was, as she claims, the fee owner of lots Nos. 142 to 146 inclusive on map No. 5 of the village of Fort Hamilton, Kings county, which lands were bid in by the State and still belong to the State under the 1877 and 1890 tax sales, I have to report that Mr. Stephen M. Hoyt, the attorney for the petitioner, has submitted a chain of title showing that Lillian V. Rourke took a deed for these lots on May 29, 1899, from James G. McMurray and others as heirs at law of Joseph McMurray, deceased, and that in 1903 she also took a deed from George Baxter and wife of lot No. 143. The chain of title further shows that Joseph McMurray was the grantee of all of said lots by a deed dated August 24, 1855.

I have procured from the State Comptroller a tax search which shows that all of these lots were sold at the 1866 tax sale and subsequently conveyed to various purchasers, George Baxter being the purchaser of lot No. 145. The purchasers of the other lots were John A. Newbold and Hiram Buck.

From the incomplete evidence adduced before me I am of the opinion that Lillian V. Rourke was not, except possibly as to lot No. 143, the owner in fee of the lands applied for, all of which has been owned by the State under both the 1877·and 1890 tax sales.

Respectfully submitted,

EDWARD R. O'MALLEY,

Attorney-General.

STATE OF NEW YORK.

ATTORNEY-GENERAL'S OFFICE,

ALBANY, *March* 24, 1910.

BEFORE THE STANDING COMMITTEE ON THE HEARING OF REMONSTRANCES OF THE COMMISSIONERS OF THE LAND OFFICE.

In the Matter of the Application of the TOWN OF RYE for a grant of land under water, pursuant to the provisions of chapter 711 of the Laws of 1907.

To the Commissioners of the Land Office:

Gentlemen.— This application was referred to your committee together with a remonstrance on behalf of the Oakland Beach Realty Company. Under chapter 711 of the Laws of 1907, a public park for the inhabitants of the town of Rye, Westchester county, was provided for, to be known as Rye Park. The act provided for the acquisition of certain lands adjacent to Long Island Sound for park purposes, and commissioners appointed by the act were authorized to issue bonds to pay for the property. The last section of the act provides that the Commissioners of the Land Office are authorized to release to the town any right of the State in and to any land under water adjacent to and in front of any uplands included in the boundaries of the park. The park commissioners have acquired the fee of a large parcel of land bounded by Rye Beach avenue, Forest avenue, Dearborn avenue and Long Island Sound. Adjoining this park property are the lands of the remonstrants, the Oakland Park Realty Company.

The remonstrants object to the making of the grant, principally for the reason that the Realty Company has a small beach of its own lying immediately to the west of the lands under water applied for, and has been in the habit of using the land between high and low water mark for bathing purposes — in fact, they have a bathing pavilion upon their own land.

The act above referred to, chapter 711 of the Laws of 1907, authorizes the commissioners to let the privilege of maintaining bath houses and bathing facilities at said park and also the privilege of maintaining a public restaurant and of letting boats for hire.

A hearing was duly held before your committee on January 4, 1910, when it was contended by the attorneys for the remonstrants, that as adjoining littoral and riparian owners they have, together with the public, the legal right of passage along the foreshore of the entire beach of Long Island Sound and that this is a paramount right to any right of the park commissioners in the exercise of any authority vested in them by the act aforesaid. The applicant denies that the remonstrants have any private right to the foreshore of the park as appurtenant to the land owned by them, and maintains that the Legislature, in the exercise of its governmental functions, has authorized the land board to release to the applicant any right of the people in and to the land under water in front of said park.

If the upland of Rye Park was in private ownership there might be some merit to the argument that the right of the public or *jus publicam,* consisting of the right to use the waters of the State for the purposes of navigation, bathing and fishing, with right of access thereto, existed, but as Rye Park was acquired and is owned by the town of Rye, a municipal corporation, under legislative enactment, for public use in the pursuit of health and happiness, your committee believes the remonstrance should be overruled and that the grant should be made as applied for.

Respectfully submitted,

EDWARD R. O'MALLEY,
Attorney-General.

FRANK M. WILLIAMS,
State Engineer and Surveyor.

STATE OF NEW YORK.

ATTORNEY-GENERAL'S OFFICE,

ALBANY, March 28, 1910.

. BEFORE THE STANDING COMMITTEE OF THE COMMISSIONERS OF THE LAND OFFICE ON THE HEARING OF REMONSTRANCES.

In the Matter of the Application of HENRY A. TABB, WILLIAM J. BURLEE and AMERICAN LINSEED COMPANY, for a grant of land under the waters of the Kill-von-Kull, at Port Richmond, Richmond county, for beneficial enjoyment.

To the Commissioners of the Land Office:

Gentlemen.— The above entitled application having been referred to us, together with the remonstrance of the corporation counsel of the city of New York, we have the honor to report that the matter was fully heard before our committee and that on such hearing the applicants failed to satisfy us that they are the owners of uplands adjacent to the lands under water applied for. The applicants own a parcel of about one acre of land lying on the south side of Richmond terrace or Shore road. They claim also to own a narrow strip of land lying on the north side of Richmond terrace and between said road and mean high water mark.

The corporation counsel maintains that, inasmuch as the original patent to the applicant's grantor contained an exception of a highway eight rods in width by the water side, the fee of the roadway of Richmond terrace (now only fifty feet wide) which it seems was originally laid out along the water's edge of the Kill-von-Kull, including any accretions thereto from the river, does not belong to the applicants and that the Commissioners of the Land Office have no power to make the grant applied for.

The testimony on both sides was entirely documentary and presents very difficult questions, and the facts are not entirely clear. No witnesses were presented by the applicants. The corporation counsel insists that the land applied for will be required by the city of New York in the making of water front improvements and shows that there is very little land under water along the Kill-von-Kull left ungranted by this board.

Under all these circumstances we recommend that your honorable board, in the exercise of a discretion committed to you by the Legislature, deny this application.

Respectfully submitted,

EDWARD R. O'MALLEY,

Attorney-General.

FRANK M. WILLIAMS,

State Engineer and Surveyor.

STATE OF NEW YORK.

ATTORNEY-GENERAL'S OFFICE,

ALBANY, *March* 28, 1910.

BEFORE THE COMMISSIONERS OF THE LAND OFFICE.

In the Matter of the Request of EUGENE L. FALK for a resale of certain abandoned canal lands in the city of Buffalo which were sold on March 16, 1909, under the direction of the State Engineer and Surveyor.

To the Commissioners of the Land Office:

Gentlemen.— I return the papers in this application and have the honor to report that I can see no reason why the contract of sale entered into should not be carried out. The sale was held legally, under the provisions of the Public Lands Law, by the State Engineer and Surveyor.

Respectfully submitted,

EDWARD R. O'MALLEY,

Attorney-General.

STATE OF NEW YORK.

ATTORNEY-GENERAL'S OFFICE,

ALBANY, *May* 2, 1910.

To the Commissioners of the Land Office:

Gentlemen.— With reference to a proposed bill recently introduced in the Legislature authorizing the Commissioners of the Land Office to convey to the heirs of Barbara Schuster, deceased, or to their assigns, without further payment therefor, all the right, title and interest of the State to certain lands in the town of Hamburg, Erie county, containing 50 acres, which were sold to Barbara Schuster by the State Engineer and Surveyor in the year 1888 pursuant to resolution of the Commissioners of the Land Office, and which matter has been referred to me by your honorable body, I have the honor to report:

That the lands in question were lands which had been acquired by the State at a Comptroller's tax sale held in 1881. The lands were sold upon the application of Casper Schuster, the husband of Barbara Schuster. He applied twice to the land board for the advertisement and sale of these lands. His first application to purchase was denied at a meeting of the land board held May 5, 1887. He subsequently renewed his application and on the 17th of November, 1887, the land board directed the land, which had been appraised at $1,000, to be sold pursuant to statute and the regulations of the board relative to the sale of tax lands under which the purchaser would only be entitled to quit-claim letters patent to said lands. Mr. Schuster well knew that he was purchasing a law suit with other persons who claimed title to said premises, when he offered to purchase the State's title.

At the State Engineer's sale Mr. Schuster paid $508 on account and gave his bond for the balance, $500, and a certificate of sale was issued by the State Engineer to Barbara Schuster, the wife of Casper Schuster. Mrs. Schuster is in default on the bond which is held by the State but in view of the peculiar circumstances concerning this matter and the litigation which has ensued, in all of which the Schusters have been successful, the State

Comptroller has been very lenient and has not brought any proceedings upon the bond nor has he asked that the said bond be forfeited.

In the case of People ex rel. Hall v. Woodruff, 57 A. D. 342, it was held that where a quit-claim patent was issued by the State (and no other form of patent for tax lands has been issued for many years), the failure of the State's title to the land conveyed does not create a legal claim for compensation under the provisions of section 6 (formerly section 5) of the Public Lands Law, and that the purchaser under such a patent is not entitled to reimbursement of the purchase money paid.

In the case of the People ex rel. Suydam v. Morgan, 45 A. D. 19, it would seem that the claim against the State must have been presented within the time allowed by law, and the court referred to the constitutional provision that " neither the Legislature, canal board, nor any person or persons acting in behalf of the State shall audit, allow or pay any claim which as between citizens of the State would be barred by lapse of time."

It would therefore seem that the proposed legislation would not be constitutional.

Messrs. Morey, Bosley & Morey, Buffalo, N. Y., the attorneys for the Schusters, who have had this recent bill introduced in the Legislature, endeavored to have me intervene on behalf of the State in an action brought against the Schusters by the Hennepin Improvement Company to try out the question of the title to the lands which the State sold, and in view of the fact that there was no legal obligation upon the part of the State to defend its title, I declined to appear in said action.

For the reasons above stated I cannot recommend the approval of the proposed legislation.

Yours very truly,

EDWARD R. O'MALLEY,

Attorney-General.

STATE OF NEW YORK.

ATTORNEY-GENERAL'S OFFICE,

ALBANY, *July* 29, 1910.

To the Honorable, The Commissioners of the Land Office:

Gentlemen.— With reference to your request of the 13th inst., to be advised as to certain trespass committed on lot 60, Artillery patent, Washington county, I beg to report to you as follows:

The papers sent to me with your request for investigation and action were by me forwarded to the State Engineer and Surveyor with my request for a report upon the facts, since the alleged trespass was said to be committed by the Atlantic Gulf and Pacific Company, being contractors on Barge canal contract No. 25. A copy of this report, dated July 26, 1910, is enclosed herewith. From this report it appears that the contractor above named is operating entirely within the lines of lands appropriated by the State for the purposes of its work, save .69 of an acre which is a rock ledge, upon which has been placed a small quantity of quarry rock. This quarry rock will be entirely removed at an early date and placed in the wash wall in the new canal. This is the only act of encroachment committed by the contractor outside of the lines of appropriated land, and in view of the statement of the State Engineer it seems to me that any action against the contractor is inadvisable.

I return herewith papers in the matter received by me on the 14th inst., together with a blue print showing the limits of the appropriated land.

Respectfully yours,

EDWARD R. O'MALLEY,

Attorney-General.

STATE OF NEW YORK.

ATTORNEY-GENERAL'S OFFICE,

ALBANY, *July* 29, 1910.

To the Honorable, The Commissioners of the Land Office:

Gentlemen.— Pursuant to your request of the 13th inst., asking to be advised as to your power to appoint a caretaker over certain

lands at Crown Point in the county of Essex, I beg to render
you the following opinion:

By chapter 151 of the Laws of 1910, the State accepted title
from the corporation of Witherbee, Sherman & Company of
certain lands in the town of Crown Point in the said county of
Essex, embracing the sites of Fort St. Frederick and Fort Amherst,
upon the condition described in the conveyances of those lands,
that they should be forever dedicated to the purpose of a public
park or reservation, the people of the State of New York agree-
ing to protect the fort ruins on said lands from spoliation and
further disintegration to the end that they may be preserved for
all time, so far as may be. The conveyances contain certain
restrictions as to mines and minerals and easements, which are
not necessary to be considered in discussing the question involved
in this opinion. No provision is made in the act for the appointment of any special officer or commission to care for this property,
the protection of which the State by the enactment of the above
law assumed.

The Public Lands Law provides in section 3 under the head of
powers and duties of the Commissioners of the Land Office, as
follows:

"Such commissioners shall have the general care and
superintendence of all State lands, the superintendence
whereof is not vested in some officer or board."

Since, therefore, the superintendence of the lands above described is not vested in some officer or board, it must necessarily
follow that the Commissioners of the Land Office are charged
with the general care and superintendence of this property. As
a necessary incident to the exercise of this power of care is the
power of the appointment or employment of caretakers.

However, it must be noted that no appropriation has been made
by the Legislature for the use of the Commissioners of the Land
Office in compensating such caretakers for their services.

Section 35 of the State Finance Law provides that a State
officer, employee, board, department or commission shall not contract indebtedness on behalf of the State, nor assume to bind the
State in an amount in excess of the money appropriated or otherwise lawfully available. This provision would seem to forbid any

agreement for compensation for the services of a caretaker until an appropriation has been made therefor. However, I am informed that certain individuals or historical societies have offered to take charge of these lands and care for them without cost to the State.

I am therefore of the opinion that the Commissioners of the Land Office have the power to appoint as caretakers such persons as agree to perform services free of charge to the State.

Yours very truly,

EDWARD R. O'MALLEY,

Attorney-General.

STATE OF NEW YORK.

ATTORNEY-GENERAL'S OFFICE,

ALBANY, *September* 21, 1910.

BEFORE THE COMMISSIONERS OF THE LAND OFFICE.

In the Matter of the Application of BENJAMIN R. BISSON for a release of the State's interest in certain lands in the city of Brooklyn which were owned by Mary Smith at the time of her death without heirs.

To the Commissioners of the Land Office:

Gentlemen.— The above entitled application is one made under chapter 509 of the Laws of 1909, amending the Public Lands Law, which provides that an application may be made to your honorable board for the release of escheated lands by the purchaser at a judicial sale or sheriff's sale on execution, or the alleged grantee of any person who would have succeeded by devise or otherwise to the title of such person but for his alienage or legal incapacity to take or convey the property so escheated.

In this case Mary Smith died in the city of Brooklyn in or about the month of February, 1904, leaving no heirs, but leaving a lot of land in the village of West Flushing, town of Newtown, Queens county. Thereafter and on or about October 4, 1907, one

John T. Gallagher, a creditor of said decedent, was appointed her administrator, and subsequently the said administrator petitioned the surrogate of Kings county for permission to sell the real estate of said decedent for the payment of her debts, and by a decree of the surrogate's court, dated June 2, 1908, the said administrator was authorized and directed to sell the above described real estate, which he did on July 24, 1908, and the petitioner herein, Benjamin R. Bisson, became the purchaser at said administrator's sale for the sum of two hundred dollars ($200). Although a notice of the proceeding in the surrogate's court for leave to the administrator to sell said real estate for the payment of debts was duly served on the Attorney-General, it is claimed by the petitioner herein that the surrogate's court lacked jurisdiction to order the sale of property of the State for payment of debts of a decedent, as the State is not bound by a judgment or decree of any of its courts except in those matters where it has by statute conferred jurisdiction and consented to be bound. There is no provision of law for making the State a party to such a proceeding. (See Seitz v. Messerschmitt, 117 A. D. 401, affd. 188 N. Y. 587.)

Because the petitioner could not acquire the State's title by reason of the decree of the surrogate of Kings county to lands which absolutely vested in the State upon the failure of heirs, but subject, however, to the payment of decedent's debts, the petitioner now asks relief at the hands of your honorable board.

It is my opinion, however, that the amendment to the Public Lands Law by chapter 509 of the Laws of 1909, authorizing your honorable board to act upon the application of the purchaser at a judicial sale did not embrace an application like the present one for the reason that, in my opinion, the sale by the administrator on the unauthorized decree of the surrogate was not a judicial sale. It is a question that I think the court should pass upon before the Land Board acts in applications of this kind, and it is my opinion that this application should be denied, which will give the petitioner the opportunity of suing out a writ of certiorari when the whole question can be determined by the court.

Respectfully submitted,
EDWARD R. O'MALLEY,
Attorney-General.

STATE OF NEW YORK.

ATTORNEY-GENERAL'S OFFICE,

ALBANY, *September* 21, 1910.

BEFORE THE COMMISSIONERS OF THE LAND OFFICE.

In the Matter of the Application of JOHN
FRANCIS LARKIN for a release of lands
escheated to the State by reason of the failure
of heirs of his wife, Elizabeth Ann Larkin,
deceased.

To the Commissioners of the Land Office:

Gentlemen.— The above entitled matter, having been referred
to me for my examination and report, I beg to submit the
following:

That John Francis Larkin on August 1, 1910, filed a petition
with your honorable board, pursuant to the provisions of the
Public Lands Law, and that he therein petitioned for the release
to him of the State's interest in and to two lots of land lying upon
Chazy Lake, in the town of Dannemora, Clinton county, together
containing about one-half acre.

This application is made in accordance with all the requirements of the statutes, and also in accordance with the rules of the
Commissioners of the Land Office governing such applications.

An examination of the verified petition and of the affidavits of
disinterested persons, with affidavits of publication and of posting
of notices of the application shows the following facts:

I. That the petitioner resides at No. 52 Quinby place, West
Orange, New Jersey, and is the widower of Elizabeth Ann Larkin,
deceased, who died intestate in the city of West Orange, New
Jersey, on June 28, 1908, he having been married to her for
seventeen years prior to her death.

II. That the said decedent was the owner in fee at the time of
her death of the said premises, and that the value thereof at the
present time is about $750, and that said property is subject to the
right of curtesy therein of the petitioner by reason of the facts that

the petitioner and his said wife, Elizabeth Ann Larkin, had a living child who died in infancy.

III. That the said Elizabeth Ann Larkin left her surviving no heirs at law whatever, and there is no other person than the petitioner who would have succeeded to any interest in such real estate.

IV. That the real estate described in the petition embraces all the property of which the said Elizabeth Ann Larkin died seized.

V. That the said premises were purchased by the petitioner in the name of his wife and the purchase money thereof paid for by him, and that all improvements upon said lands were made by the petitioner.

VI. That notice of application was made in proper form and duly published in the Plattsburgh *Daily Press,* a newspaper printed in the city of Plattsburgh, Clinton county, for the required period, and a copy thereof was duly posted on the doors of the Clinton county court house at Plattsburgh.

VII. Searches made by the county clerk of Clinton county show that one of the said lots was purchased from Sullivan King and wife, in the name of Mrs. Frank Larkin on September 23, 1897, for the consideration of $25, and that the other lot was purchased from Oscar L. Southworth and wife, in the name of Elizabeth Annie Larkin, on August 21, 1903, and that the title still stands in the name of the petitioner's wife, free from any liens or incumbrances.

VIII. The property is described as follows:

" All that tract or parcel of land situate in the town of Dannemora, county of Clinton, and State of New York, and being part of lot No. 34 C. W. M. Johnson's survey in 1885 and 1886, and filed in the Comptroller's office, which is bounded and described as follows: Beginning at a stake on said lot No. 34 at the boathouse on the west side of Chazy Lake, running thence southwesterly on the shore of Chazy Lake one hundred feet; thence north or northerly 150 feet; thence east 100 feet to Miss Larkins's line to the place of beginning. And also the land adjoining said described land, commencing at a cedar post in the said line and leading to the public highway sufficient for a road to said lot. The above described property is intended to be the same premises conveyed by Emma A. Goodrich to Oscar L. Southworth by deed dated June 24, 1902, recorded July 5, 1902, in Book 102 of Deeds, at page 287, in Clinton county clerk's office, and by said Oscar L. Southworth and wife conveyed to Elizabeth Annie Larkin by deed dated August 21, 1903, and recorded September 15, 1903, in said county clerk's office in Book 104 of Deeds, at page 617. Also, all that other piece or parcel of land situate, lying and being in the town of Dannemora, county of Clinton, and State of New York, and described as follows: Being a part of land deeded to Sullivan King by the State Comptroller on the seventh day of September, 1886, and on the 26th day of May, 1887, and bounded as follows: Beginning at a cedar stump on the lake shore, running southwest 100 feet along lake shore; thence northwest 150 feet to a poplar tree blazed on three sides; thence east 100 feet; thence south 150 feet to place of beginning, and being a part of lots 36 and 41, and containing one-fourth of an acre of land, more or less, being the same premises conveyed by said Sullivan King and wife to Mrs. Frank Larkin, by deed dated September 23, 1897, and recorded in the said county clerk's office September 24, 1897, in Book 95 of Deeds, at page 451."

Section 62 of the Public Lands Law (chapter 50, Laws of 1909) provides that a conveyance which may be made in the discretion of the Commissioners of the Land Office, releasing the interests of the State in escheated real estate, to a petitioner who is a surviving husband of any owner of any interest therein immediately prior to the escheat, shall be without consideration where the value of the property sought to be released shall not exceed ten thousand dollars ($10,000).

I therefore advise that your honorable board has full legal power to grant the prayer of the petitioner herein.

Respectfully submitted,

EDWARD R. O'MALLEY,

Attorney-General.

STATE OF NEW YORK.

ATTORNEY-GENERAL'S OFFICE,

ALBANY, *September* 21, 1910.

REPORT OF THE SPECIAL COMMITTEE TO THE COMMISSIONERS OF
THE LAND OFFICE.

In the Matter of the Petition to remove obstructions from certain lands under water in
the city of Dunkirk.   •

To the Commissioners of the Land Office:

Gentlemen.— We beg to advise that we have carefully examined this application and that in our judgment it should be
granted.   The docks which are sought to be removed appear to
be the property of the Erie Railroad Company, and are in such a
condition of disrepair that they constitute a menace to navigation.
They do not appear to join any uplands owned by that company
or to be upon any land granted that company by the State.

In view of these facts and of the fact that their removal will
make possible the construction of the new Federal dock which will
greatly improve navigation, it is my opinion that an action will
lie in the name of the people by the Attorney-General to compel
their removal as purprestures or nuisances obstructing navigable
waters.

Respectfully submitted,

EDWARD R. O'MALLEY,
Attorney-General.

FRANK. M. WILLIAMS,
State Engineer and Surveyor.

STATE OF NEW YORK.

ᷫ ATTORNEY-GENERAL'S OFFICE,

ALBANY, *September* 21, 1910.

To the Commissioners of the Land Office:

Gentlemen.— At a meeting of your honorable board, held June 21st last, there was referred to me a communication from Messrs. Greene, Hurd & Stowell of New York city, attorneys for the Cypress Hills Cemetery, with the request that I advise you as to the power of the board upon the application of the cemetery association that it be appointed the custodian of the Mount of Victory plot in Cypress Hills Cemetery. An appropriation of $3,500 for the care of this plot, set aside for the burial of the survivors of the War of 1812 and for the parking of said plot, was made by chapter 433 of the Laws of 1909, upon the proviso that such plot should be deeded by the cemetery association to the State. The title to the plot has been conveyed to the State with my approval and the deed formally placed upon record.

The statute makes no provision in express terms for a custodian of the plot. The plot is about fifty feet square and contains the remains of a number of the veterans of the War of 1812.

I am informed that up to the present time the plot has been maintained and cared for at the expense of the cemetery association which has the records of all the burials in said plot.

In response to your request I would call your attention to the provisions of section 3 of the Public Lands Law (chapter 50 of the Laws of 1909), which provides that the Commissioners of the Land Office shall have the general care and superintendence of all State lands, the superintendence whereof is not vested in some officer or board.

It is, therefore, my opinion that your honorable board is vested with the general care and superintendence of this plot of ground and may appoint a custodian.

I am in receipt this morning of a letter from Messrs. Greene, Hurd & Stowell, urging that the matter be brought to the attention of your board to-day for your consideration, and enclosing copies of plans, specifications and estimates showing the character of the improvement recommended by the committee on improvement of said cemetery and approved by the directors of the cemetery association. I submit the same to you for your consideration.

Should your board see fit to appoint the cemetery association as the custodian of said plot and should approve the proposed plans for the care and parking of the plot, the specifications and contracts to be entered into by the cemetery association should comply in all respects with the provisions of chapter 36 of the Laws of 1909 (the Labor Law) regarding eight hours of labor and providing as to the prevailing rate of wages.

Respectfully submitted,

EDWARD R. O'MALLEY,

Attorney-General.

STATE OF NEW YORK.

ATTORNEY-GENERAL'S OFFICE,

ALBANY, *November* 30, 1910.

BEFORE THE STANDING COMMITTEE FOR THE HEARING OF REMONSTRANCES.

In the Matter of the Application of GILBERT T. RAFFERTY for a grant of land under the waters of the St. Lawrence at Alexandria Bay.

To the Commissioners of the Land Office:

Gentlemen.— The above entitled application having been referred to us we have the honor to report:

That this applicant, who is the owner of Imperial Island in the St. Lawrence river, applies for a grant of certain land under water which constitutes a shoal in said river and is separated from Imperial Island over three hundred feet by the deep water of the St. Lawrence river. Several remonstrances have been filed against this application upon the ground that the lands under water applied for do not adjoin the applicant's uplands. As section 75 of the Public Lands Law only empowers the Land Board to make grants to owners of lands adjacent to the lands under water applied for, and as the statute further provides that no grant shall be made to any other person than the proprietor of the adjacent lands and any such grant made to any other person shall be void, we do not consider that a hearing is necessary in this matter and herewith return the papers with the recommendation that the application be denied for want of jurisdiction.

Respectfully submitted,

EDWARD R. O'MALLEY,
Attorney-General.

T. B. DUNN,
State Treasurer.

FRANK M. WILLIAMS,
State Engineer and Surveyor.

STATE OF NEW YORK.

ATTORNEY-GENERAL'S OFFICE,

ALBANY, *December* 14, 1910.

To the Commissioners of the Land Office:

Gentlemen.— The standing committee on the hearing of remonstrances of the Commissioners of the Land Office, to whom were referred the following applications for grants of land under water, hereby report that, inasmuch as the said committee has recommended to your honorable board by a report dated December 1, 1910, and which report was unanimously approved by said Commissioners and a copy of the same ordered sent to the Legislature, that in their opinion no further grants of lands under water should be made except possibly to municipalities until after the Legislature shall have defined the policy to be pursued by the State with reference to the leasing or granting of its public lands under water, we cannot consistently make any recommendations in the following matters pending before us, viz.:

Margaret Dolan and Guaranty Trust Company of New York.— Application for grants of lands under the Hudson river at Peekskill.

These are applications as now modified for the surrender of commerce grants made to John J. and Margaret Dolan, December 31, 1906, and to the Guaranty Trust Company, March 1, 1907, and for the issuance in lieu thereof of beneficial enjoyment grants. There is some doubt as to the power of the board to grant the relief sought. In this connection we have to state that a bill to authorize the Land Board to do this passed both houses of the Legislature at its last session, but failed to become a law by reason of the Governor's veto.

Hastings Pavement Company and National Brass & Copper Tube Company.— Applications for grants of lands under the Hudson river at Hastings, N. Y.

These applications for beneficial grants are for adjoining lands under water. The National Brass & Copper Tube Company secured from the Land Board in the year 1906 a commerce grant and without authority and through mistake of law they erected a factory on such land. The lands applied for by the pavement company have also been wholly or partially filled in and buildings have been erected upon a part of the lands they apply for. There is a new public street lying to the north of and adjoining lands applied for by the pavement company, which was laid out by the village authorities when the village abandoned a street further south running to the river across other lands of the National Brass & Copper Tube Company. It is complained by citizens of Hastings that this new street, only fifty feet wide, which is bounded on the north by other lands formerly under water, granted to the National Brass & Copper Tube Company, will not afford reasonable dockage to the village citizens, and should any grant hereafter be made to the pavement company, it should reserve an additional strip of water front along the pier and bulkhead line from said grant running easterly a sufficient distance to afford dock privileges at the south side as well as at the front of said public street to subserve the public interest, and any grant made to the National Brass & Copper Tube Company should be only upon condition of a grant by that company to the village of

Hastings of overlapping privileges to the north of said public street, which overlapping privileges said company has consented to grant.

GILBERT M. PLYMPTON.— Application for grant of lands under water of Long Island Sound at Great Neck, North Hempstead. This application is for a strip of land about one hundred feet in width extending about three hundred feet along applicant's up-lands between high and low water mark, and for an additional parcel extending out one hundred and fifty feet below low water mark, and eighty feet long, for the location of a dock to navigable water. The trustees of North Hempstead claim that these lands under water are natural shellfish grounds, and that the rights of the public in the foreshore should be preserved, and that shore front property in this vicinity is very valuable.

FREE & MURRAY REALTY COMPANY and CORNELIA J. HERSEY, AS TRUSTEE, ETC.— Applications for grants of lands under water of Hudson river at Tarrytown.

These applications have not been brought on for hearing before your committee, but your committee has viewed the premises and regardless of any remonstrances believe that both applications embrace more lands under water than the applicants would be legally entitled to. In any event, unless these applications are modified by reducing the acreage applied for, they should be denied. The Free & Murray Realty Company filed a previous application for same lands, which was denied by the Land Board on December 15, 1908.

BROOKLYN & CANARSIE REALTY CO.— Application for a grant 1.44 acres under water of Jamaica Bay, borough of Brooklyn, New York city, filed December 16, 1908.

CHARLOTTE P. GARDNER.— Application for a grant of 4.916 acres under water of Jamaica Bay, borough of Brooklyn, New York city, filed February 18, 1909.

HENRY ADAMS, JR.— Application for a grant of 2.385 acres at Mott's Point under water of Jamaica Bay at Far Rockaway, Queens county, filed April 29, 1909.

The city of New York claims title to these lands under water by virtue of colonial grants. The dock commission of New York city protests against the Adams application upon the ground that a

grant would be injurious to the public interests of the city. By
an act of the Legislature, chapter 568, Laws of 1909, there was
granted to the city of New York, all the lands under water of
Jamaica Bay excepting lands embraced in any application by
riparian owners filed with the Land Board prior to May 29, 1909,
and which might be thereafter granted by your honorable board,
upon condition that the United States government or the city of
New York should make an appropriation for the creation of a
new harbor in Jamaica Bay, which appropriation by the United
States government, we understand, has been made.

The city also claims that part of the land applied for in the
application of Brooklyn & Canarsie Realty Company lies within
the beds of Rockaway Parkway and Skidmore avenue, proposed
city streets, which in any event should be excepted from any grant
which may be made. In the Gardner application the city claims
that parts of the land applied for lie within the prolongation lines
of several city streets intersecting high water mark and that under
the terms of the grant to the city by the charter of the city of New
York, this board cannot grant such lands.

APPLICATION OF THE NEW YORK CENTRAL & HUDSON RIVER
RAILROAD COMPANY for a grant of a strip of land under water
nearly two miles in length under the waters of Hudson river,
between Croton and Oscawana, in town of Cortlandt, Westchester
county, under section 8 of the Railroad Law.

This application, filed June 9, 1910, includes the same lands
applied for by Wm. H. and Wm. P. Forbes, riparian owners,
whose application was filed May 16, 1910, and to whom a grant
was ordered to issue by the Land Board on September, 1910; but
the grant has not yet been actually issued; also by John Bannon,
Eugene Frost and James H. Hardy, other riparian owners, and
also lands under water in front of the uplands of Guillaume
Reussens, all of which riparian owners protest against the making
of a grant to the railroad company. The town board of Cortlandt
also protests against a grant being made at the foot of Furnace
Dock road, a public highway in said town, leading to the Hudson
river.

APPLICATION OF VILLA PARK ASSOCIATION OF GREAT NECK
for grant of land under water of Little Neck Bay, in town of
North Hempstead, Nassau County, of 6.519 acres.

Remonstrances to this application were filed by the town of North Hempstead, which claims title to these lands under water under colonial grants and also calls attention to protest by numerous citizens of the town, protesting against a grant in front of town road and the only road by which the public can reach the waters of Little Neck Bay, and also by the Citizens' League of Great Neck upon the ground that the application covers an undue area and also closes the approach of the public on a public highway to the water. Since the remonstrances were filed and after a hearing of this matter, the Citizens' League has agreed to withdraw its remonstrance upon the applicant's excluding from his application a strip six rods in width extending from Cedar drive to the westerly line of grant as applied for and making certain improvements mentioned in its written agreement with applicants, dated December 15, 1910. The applicants have filed an amended map and description in conformance with said agreement.

APPLICATION OF JOHNSTON BROS. REALTY CO. for grant of land under water of Raritan and Prince's Bays, Staten Island. The lands involved in this application were included in two water grants — one for commercial purposes to Joseph H. Seguine, dated March 13, 1837, and one for beneficial enjoyment to Algernon K. Johnston and others, dated December 22, 1881. The applicants' uplands are a small parcel of 0.077 acres at the foot of Seguine avenue. The lands now applied for by amended map are a narrow strip about fifty feet wide and extending over four hundred feet out to the United States pierhead line and containing 0.484 acres. The corporation counsel of New York city states in his letter of May 26, 1910, that he is informed by the president of the borough of Richmond that while Seguine avenue was not laid out to high water mark, yet as a matter of fact the street is in actual use down to the dock and that materials for repairs to streets and other public purposes are unloaded there and transported along Seguine avenue, and he accordingly suggests that under these circumstances the provisions of section 83 of the city of New York charter, granting to the city the fee of all lands under water within the projected boundary lines of streets intersecting the shore line in public use or which may be hereafter opened for public use, apply, the street being in actual use to the docks, unless the premises now applied for are covered by grants previously made.

APPLICATION OF GEORGE WEINSCHENCK, MARY J. ROBERTSON, REBECCA and THEODORE C. PARKER, for grants of land under the waters of Byram river at Fort Chester, Westchester county.

The applications have been heard by your committee, and as a result of such hearing, amended maps and descriptions have been filed in the Robertson, Weinschenck and Parker cases, to conform to the views of the State Engineer and Surveyor as to the lands which might properly be granted, if grants should be decided to be made at any time hereafter by the Land Board.

APPLICATIONS OF GEORGE J. BAILEY and ROBERT N. CODD, JR., to purchase certain islands in the Niagara river in the town of Tonawanda, Erie county.

These are small islands and in each instance the applicants offered $50. Your committee is unprepared to report upon the advisability of making these grants.

APPLICATION OF ELMER HARP for a grant of land under the waters of Niagara river, Buffalo, Erie county.

Remonstrances to this application have been filed by Victoria Handel and others upon the grounds that the lands applied for have already been granted to said remonstrances by letters patent, dated December 6, 1906, and for the further reason that the applicant is not the owner of adjacent uplands. The matter has not been brought on for hearing.

APPLICATION OF THE MIDLAND RAILROAD TERMINAL COMPANY for a grant of land under the waters of lower New York Bay, Midland Beach, Staten Island.

This is an application for a beneficial enjoyment grant for two parcels of land containing in the aggregate sixteen acres which were granted to this applicant on April 2, 1902, but with a special condition that there should not be erected or maintained any obstruction upon the land under water between the lines of high and low water marks which would in any manner prevent any person crossing and recrossing the foreshore at low tide. The present application is made for the purpose of freeing the grant from said restriction. A remonstrance has been filed by Sarah H. Barnes and others, the owner of uplands adjoining the uplands of the applicant in which they refer to the case of Barnes v. Midland Terminal Company, 193 N. Y. 378, being an action brought by said remonstrants to restrain said company from obstructing said passage of the public between high and low water marks as reserved in the grant, in which the Court of Appeals held that the plaintiffs were entitled to an injunction. The remonstrants alleged that the suit is still pending and objected to the making of the new grant applied for pending the determination of that suit. This matter has not been brought on for hearing before your committee.

APPLICATION OF THE STATEN ISLAND RAPID TRANSIT RAILWAY COMPANY for a grant of lands under the waters of the Kill-von-Kull at West New Brighton, Staten Island.

This application was filed October 28, 1907. A remonstrance to this application was filed by the Independent League of Richmond county upon the ground that public policy demands that the water front of Staten Island should be preserved for public uses and not conveyed to private corporations. It appears that some years ago a strip across the land under water now applied for was awarded to the applicant in certain condemnation proceedings in the Supreme Court but the official water grant map does not show such lands so condemned. The applicant has agreed to furnish a blue print copy of the condemnation map but the same has not yet been furnished. Without a clearer understanding as to the title of the applicants to land taken in such condemnation proceedings, this application cannot intelligently be acted upon. The commissioner of docks of the city of New York also certifies that a grant to the applicant would conflict with the rights of the city under the New York charter unless provision is made in the grant that access be furnished to the docks erected on the lands under water by the means of a public highway.

APPLICATION OF FRANK E. MORGAN for a small island located near Echo Island at New Rochelle, New York.

The applicant offers $20 for this island which is said to comprise 750 square feet in area. This matter was referred to the standing committee at a meeting of the Land Board held January 7, 1909, but the applicant has not brought the matter on for a hearing, nor has the committee visited the island in question. The advisability of selling this small island is questioned.

APPLICATION OF JOHN H. STARIN for Goose Islands in Long Island Town, near New Rochelle.

These three islands are barren rocks in New Rochelle harbor, comprising in the aggregate considerably less than an acre. The applicant offered $50 for these islands. It is questioned whether these islands should be sold by the State. In any event they should not be sold until after a conference with the Federal authorities who might at some future time see fit to demolish these islands as a menace to navigation.

APPLICATIONS OF CAROLINE L. COWL for grant of land under water of Long Island Sound, in town of North Hempstead, Nassau county, and of SARAH L. MEYER for grant of lands under water at Little Neck Bay, Queens county.

Remonstrances have been filed with these applications in the Cowl case. The town of North Hempstead remonstrates upon the ground that the land under water is comprised within the colonial patent held by the town. In the Meyer case the State of New York remonstrates upon the ground that the lands under water are owned by the State of New York under colonial patents to the former town of Flushing, and numerous citizens of Bay Side and Little Neck protest against the Meyer application upon the ground that the lands between high and low water mark applied for have been used by the citizens of that locality for years for the purposes of pleasure and as a roadway, and that the grant of these lands would interfere with their business occupations. These applications have not been brought on for hearing before your committee.

Respectfully submitted,

EDWARD R. O'MALLEY,

Attorney-General.

T. B. DUNN,

State Treasurer.

FRANK M. WILLIAMS,

State Engineer and Surveyor.

STATE OF NEW YORK.

ATTORNEY-GENERAL'S OFFICE,

ALBANY, *December* 14, 1910.

BEFORE THE STANDING COMMITTEE ON THE HEARING OF REMONSTRANCES OF THE COMMISSIONERS OF THE LAND OFFICE.

In the Matter of the Application of HENRY A. TABB, WILLIAM J. BURLEE and AMERICAN LINSEED COMPANY for lands under waters of the Kill-von-Kull, Staten Island.

To the Commissiohers of the Land Office:

Gentlemen.— This is an application for 2.909 acres of land under water. The corporation counsel of the city of New York objects strenuously to this application upon the ground that the applicants are not upland owners. The applicants' map "A" shows that their uplands are a wedge-shaped piece extending 242 feet on the southeast side of Richmond terrace, west of and adjoining John street, Port Richmond, and also a strip of land on the northwest or river side of Richmond terrace about three feet wide increasing to nearly forty feet in width opposite the centre of John street. The corporation counsel shows that the original colonial letters patent in 1680 of eighty-one acres, including all of applicants' uplands, reserved or excepted eight rods or 132 feet in breadth by the water side for a highway. Richmond terrace as it now exists is only 50 feet in width. Apparently encroachments upon the road have been made from time to time since it was opened over two centuries ago. Evidence was offered tending to show that the original high water line was southeast of the northwest line of the road and that whatever accretion has been made attached to the road. The city of New York is required by law to improve the water front of the Richmond borough and a grant of the lands applied to an individual would interfere in their plans for such improvements.

32

A similar report to this was submitted by us in this matter at a meeting of your honorable board on March 30, 1910 (see p. 4S, 1910 minutes). Mr. Van Name, of counsel for the applicant, requested that the matter be referred back to us to give him an opportunity to submit further testimony. This was acceded to. No further evidence has been offered that would warrant us in recommending that a patent issue to the applicants and we again recommend the denial of the application.

Respectfully submitted,

EDWARD R. O'MALLEY,
Attorney-General.

T. B. DUNN,
State Treasurer.

FRANK M. WILLIAMS,
State Engineer and Surveyor.

STATE OF NEW YORK.

ATTORNEY-GENERAL'S OFFICE,

ALBANY, *December* 14, 1910.

BEFORE THE STANDING COMMITTEE ON THE HEARING OF REMONSTRANCES OF THE COMMISSIONERS OF THE LAND OFFICE.

In the Matter of the Application of JOHN C. BOUTON for a grant of land under water at Pelham Manor, Westchester county. }

To the Commissioners of the Land Office:

Gentlemen.— The greater part of the lands under water applied for were granted December 1, 1898, to Adele L. Allen, an adjacent upland owner. Even were we to concede that the grant made to Mrs. Allen included land under water adjacent to her neighbor Bouton, still the lines of the grant as applied for by him are also improperly drawn and certainly include land under water in front of Mrs. Allen's upland.

The application should be denied with privilege to Mr. Bouton to renew his application after new advertisement and map to be first submitted to the State Engineer and Surveyor and to be considered by him in connection with said water grant, made to Adele L. Allen, one to the town of Pelham on November 23, 1871, and another grant recently made to A. V. H. Ellis and H. M. Hunter.

.Respectfully submitted,

EDWARD R. O'MALLEY,
Attorney-General.
T. B. DUNN,
State Treasurer.
FRANK M. WILLIAMS,
State Engineer and Surveyor.

STATE OF NEW YORK.

ATTORNEY-GENERAL'S OFFICE,

ALBANY, *December* 14, 1910.

BEFORE THE STANDING COMMITTEE ON THE HEARING OF REMONSTRANCES OF THE COMMISSIONERS OF THE LAND OFFICE.

In the Matter of the Application of the HUDSON WIRE COMPANY for a grant of land under water of the Hudson river at Ossining.

To the Commissioners of the Land Office:

Gentlemen.— The applicant's uplands lie on the east side of Water street. Between Water street and the railroad opposite said uplands are lands occupied by Charles Washburn and others on which there are several old buildings. This application includes all the land on which said buildings of Washburn and others are situated and also the railroad right of way and a large tract of land still under water west of the railroad. The claim was made that the original high water line extended to Water street and that the lands whereon the houses occupied by Washburn and others west of the street are erected, were filled in and are still State lands to which the applicant is entitled to a grant. An exhaustive hearing was had on the premises and testimony was adduced tending to show that there was some original upland to the west of Water street at this point.

Applicant has failed to prove that it is the owner of upland adjacent to original lands under water, and the application should be denied.

Respectfully submitted,

EDWARD R. O'MALLEY,
Attorney-General.

T. B. DUNN,
State Treasurer.

FRANK M. WILLIAMS,
State Engineer and Surveyor.

STATE OF NEW YORK.

ATTORNEY-GENERAL'S OFFICE,

ALBANY, *December* 14, 1910.

BEFORE THE STANDING COMMITTEE ON THE HEARING OF REMONSTRANCES OF THE COMMISSIONERS OF THE LAND OFFICE.

In the Matter of the Application of CHARLES G. WASHBURN for a grant of land under water of Hudson river at Ossining.

In the Matter of the Application of JOHN KELLY for a grant of land under water of Hudson river at Ossining.

To the Commissioners of the Land Office:

Gentlemen.— The Washburn application covers with other lands all that part of the lands also applied for by the Hudson

Wire Company lying west of the New York Central & Hudson River Railroad Company right of way. The Kelly application covers a part of land applied for by Washburn. They are both defective as claiming for the applicants as uplands, lands lying east of the railroad which were filled in artificially and the title to which still belongs to the State. Should a grant be made at any time in the future to the riparian owners of lands in the vicinity lying west of Water street, they should only be made upon application maps submitted to the State Engineer and Surveyor of lands originally under water projected from the line of original high water to be determined by the State Engineer from the old maps and evidence given on the Hudson Wire Company and John Kelly applications.

The applications as now made should be denied.

Respectfully submitted,

EDWARD R. O'MALLEY,
Attorney-General.

T. B. DUNN,
State Treasurer.

FRANK M. WILLIAMS,
State Engineer and Surveyor.

STATE OF NEW YORK.

ATTORNEY-GENERAL'S OFFICE,

ALBANY, *December* 14, 1910.

BEFORE THE STANDING COMMITTEE ON THE HEARING OF REMON-
STRANCES OF THE COMMISSIONERS OF THE LAND OFFICE.

In the Matter of the Application of the SOUND
VIEW LAND AND IMPROVEMENT COMPANY
for a grant of land under water of East river
at Classon's Point, borough of Bronx, New
York city.

To the Commissioners of the Land Office:

Gentlemen.— This is an application for a grant of 14.08 acres of land under water. The corporation counsel of New York city remonstrates on the ground that the land under water applied for belongs to the city under colonial patents to the late town of Westchester, and upon the further ground that the city has prepared maps under authority of chapter 466, Laws of 1901 and amendatory acts, planning for filling in to the bulkhead line and the location of several streets upon the lands now under water applied for. Moreover it appears from a comparison of the application map "A" with the official water grant map and particularly thereon of beneficial enjoyment grants made January 7, 1877 to Dr. Wooster Beach and others, and on January 20, 1885 to Wm. W. Tompkins and Charles H. Leland, then owners of uplands adjoining those of these applicants, that the lands applied for overlap the lines of one or both of the said former grants and it does not appear that the adjoining owners have had knowledge of this present application. Therefore, in its present condition, the application cannot even be approved as to form and should be denied.

Respectfully submitted, .

EDWARD R. O'MALLEY,
Attorney-General.

T. B. DUNN,
State Treasurer.

FRANK M. WILLIAMS,
State Engineer and Surveyor.

STATE OF NEW YORK.

ATTORNEY-GENERAL'S OFFICE,

ALBANY, *December* 14, 1910.

BEFORE THE STANDING COMMITTEE FOR THE HEARING OF REMONSTRANCES OF THE COMMISSIONERS OF THE LAND OFFICE.

In the Matter of the Application of WILLIAM
A. BROWN for a grant of land under water of
Peconic Bay, Greenport, Long Island.

To the Commissioners of the Land Office:

Gentlemen.— This is an application for 5.085 acres of land under water. The town board of Southold objects to this grant upon the ground that applicant has sufficient land under water adjacent to his uplands under water grant made in 1874 to Henry Schoonmaker, a predecessor in title of 6.37 acres adjoining lands now applied for, and that these lands under water are natural shellfish grounds, affording a livelihood to a large number of the inhabitants of that locality, and furthermore that a grant of the lands applied for would interfere with the intended projection by the town, of a highway known as Cherry Lane to the water of this cove. A large number of affidavits of residents of this community objecting to the grant as interfering with their privileges of natural shell fishery, were filed with your committee.

Your committee recommends the denial of this application.

Respectfully submitted,

EDWARD R. O'MALLEY,
Attorney-General.

T. B. DUNN,
State Treasurer.

FRANK M. WILLIAMS,
State Engineer and Surveyor.

STATE OF NEW YORK.

ATTORNEY-GENERAL'S OFFICE,

ALBANY, *December* 14, 1910.

BEFORE THE COMMISSIONERS OF THE LAND OFFICE.

In the Matter of the Application of HARRY MINTZ for a release of certain lands in the borough of the Bronx, New York city, said to have escheated to the State upon the death of John Hall.

To the Commissioners of the Land Office:

Gentlemen.— The above entitled matter has been investigated by me and I herewith return the application and other papers in this matter, together with the report from my New York deputy adverse to the claim of the petitioner.

I, therefore, recommend that this application be denied and that the matter should be re-referred to the Attorney-General for the purpose of bringing an action of ejectment against the persons in possession of said premises, to establish the State's title by escheat.

Respectfully submitted,

EDWARD R. O'MALLEY,

Attorney-General.

STATE OF NEW YORK.

ATTORNEY-GENERAL'S OFFICE,

ALBANY, *December* 19, 1910.

BEFORE THE STANDING COMMITTEE FOR THE HEARING OF REMONSTRANCES OF THE COMMISSIONERS OF THE LAND OFFICE.

In the Matter of the Application of AUGUSTUS V. H. ELLIS and HENRY M. HUNTER for lands under water of Long Island Sound, in town of Pelham, Westchester county.

To the Commissioners of the Land Office:

Gentlemen.— Certain remonstrances have been filed to this application, which has not been formally filed by the applicants. The applicants now file their notice of discontinuance of this application with proof of service thereof on attorneys for all the remonstrants.

The applicant should be permitted to discontinue this application.

Respectfully submitted,

EDWARD R. O'MALLEY,

Attorney-General.

T. B. DUNN,

State Treasurer.

FRANK M. WILLIAMS,

State Engineer and Surveyor.

STATE OF NEW YORK.

ATTORNEY-GENERAL'S OFFICE,

ALBANY, *December* 24, 1910.

BEFORE THE COMMISSIONERS OF THE LAND OFFICE.

In the Matter of the Application of ALGER F. RUSSELL, claiming to be owner, for the sale of certain tax lands in the borough of Richmond, New York city.

To the Commissioners of the Land Office:

Gentlemen.— This application was referred to me at a meeting of your honorable board, held on November 17th for the purpose of reporting whether the applicant's title is sufficient to warrant his application to be considered as an owner, or whether it is by a non-owner.

I have to report that the applicant's counsel has furnished me with searches of the United States Title Guaranty and Indemnity Company, showing that the lands in question were conveyed in 1877 to one Thomas Foley, who died in the year 1905, leaving a will, appointing executors, to whom were given powers to sell real estate. In pursuance of such power Patrick Sinnott, sole surviving executor of the last will and testament of Thomas Foley, deceased, conveyed the premises in question to Alger F. Russell, the applicant, by deed dated June 3, 1910, and recorded in Richmond county clerk's office, June 23, 1910.

I have, therefore, the honor to report that Mr. Russell should be considered as owner.

Respectfully submitted,

EDWARD R. O'MALLEY,

Attorney-General.

GENERAL INDEX.

General Reference to Opinions Rendered State Officers, Boards, Commissions, Etc., During the Year 1910.

Names of Persons and Officials Who Received Opinions.

Index to Opinions.

Lightning Source UK Ltd.
Milton Keynes UK
UKHW022051170219
337363UK00005B/1002/P